For Evan, Gabriel, and Eve

Dedicated to God

THE OXFORD ORAL HISTORY SERIES

J. Todd Moye (University of North Texas)
Kathryn Nasstrom (University of San Francisco)
Robert Perks (The British Library), *Series Editors*

Donald A. Ritchie, *Senior Advisor*

Approaching an Auschwitz Survivor: Holocaust Testimony and Its Transformations
Edited by Jürgen Matthäus

Singing Out: An Oral History of America's Folk Music Revivals
David K. Dunaway and Molly Beer

Freedom Flyers: The Tuskegee Airmen of World War II
J. Todd Moye

Launching the War on Poverty: An Oral History, Second Edition
Michael L. Gillette

The Firm: The Inside Story of the Stasi
Gary Bruce

The Wonder of Their Voices: The 1946 Holocaust Interviews of David Boder
Alan Rosen

They Say in Harlan County: An Oral History
Alessandro Portelli

The Oxford Handbook of Oral History
Edited by Donald A. Ritchie

Habits of Change: An Oral History of American Nuns
Carole Garibaldi Rogers

Soviet Baby Boomers: An Oral History of Russia's Cold War Generation
Donald J. Raleigh

Bodies of Evidence: The Practice of Queer Oral History
Edited by Nan Alamilla Boyd and Horacio N. Roque Ramírez

Lady Bird Johnson: An Oral History
Michael L. Gillette

Listening on the Edge: Oral History in the Aftermath of Crisis
Edited by Mark Cave and Stephen M. Sloan

Chinese Comfort Women: Testimonies from Imperial Japan's Sex Slaves
Peipei Qiu, with Su Zhiliang and Chen Lifei

Doing Oral History, Third Edition
Donald A. Ritchie

A Guide to Oral History and the Law, Second Edition
John A. Neuenschwander

Velvet Revolutions: An Oral History of Czech Society
Miroslav Vaněk and Pavel Mücke

Escape to Miami: An Oral History of the Cuban Rafter Crisis
Elizabeth Campisi

Dedicated to God

An Oral History of Cloistered Nuns

ABBIE REESE

OXFORD
UNIVERSITY PRESS

Oxford University Press is a department of the University of Oxford.
It furthers the University's objective of excellence in research, scholarship,
and education by publishing worldwide.

Oxford   New York
Auckland   Cape Town   Dar es Salaam   Hong Kong   Karachi
Kuala Lumpur   Madrid   Melbourne   Mexico City   Nairobi
New Delhi   Shanghai   Taipei   Toronto

With offices in
Argentina   Austria   Brazil   Chile   Czech Republic   France   Greece
Guatemala   Hungary   Italy   Japan   Poland   Portugal   Singapore
South Korea   Switzerland   Thailand   Turkey   Ukraine   Vietnam

Oxford is a registered trademark of Oxford University Press
in the UK and certain other countries.

Published in the United States of America by
Oxford University Press
198 Madison Avenue, New York, NY 10016

Catalogue record is available from the Library of Congress.

ISBN 978-0-19-994793-5 (hardcover); 978-0-19-049059-1 (paperback)

Contents

Preface

*I really think the presence of God would be the sense that you have. I think that's
the sense that the people have when they come here; they can tell this is a place
of God. And that's a special and wonderful thing, to have a place that's dedicated
to God. If I'm meant to be dedicated to God as His spouse, I need to be in a place
like this. This is the certain monastery that He decided, in His wisdom, that
I belong here, and that this is the place that is the best for me.*

Sister Mary Monica of the Holy Eucharist

A South African friend once described the documentation of others' stories
by way of biblical tradition; he referred to God's instructions to the Israelites,
to set up memorial stones as visual memories that would call to mind oral
histories of the hardships, triumphs, and God's miraculous interventions.

Oral history still yields these markers. The stories can serve as pillars and
reminders for present and future generations. As I worked on this book
about the Poor Clare Colettine Order in Rockford, Illinois, the community's
newest and youngest member, Sister Maria Benedicta, said to me, "I'm sure
anyone who falls in love, they look back and say, 'Oh, remember how we
met? Or how he showed his love?' It's the same, how God has shown His
personal love. I think it's a joy to look back."

I was drawn to the cloistered monastery, something of a cultural time
capsule, in part because the nuns do not "need" to be seen. At the outset, I probably had the incomplete sense that cloistered monastic nuns
are not keen on public performance because they are hidden from public view. I assumed that the nuns perform their idealized selves, that they
marry their ideal spouse, that they inhabit a societal role that represents
an ideal. I expected more uniformity of belief than I encountered: It takes

years for members to be socialized into a cloistered subculture, where communication is abbreviated and silence is observed. One nun's great-niece, when she was four years old, described her visits to the monastery as trips to "the Jesus cage." The nuns, who find the description amusing, make this distinction: The enclosure, rather than restricting them, offers freedom; the grille keeps the world out. The nuns revealed themselves, in one-on-one interviews, as self-deprecating and humorous, with a diversity of beliefs—opinions they did not know they did not share with one another because they observed monastic silence and did not have occasion to discuss matters they shared with me. Removing themselves from a visible, wider audience still impacts the congruity of their performances; there are high stakes in becoming absent from the world in order to enact one's beliefs for God. The rest of the community bears witness within the highly ritualized space that oscillates between the concrete and physical (demanding manual labor), and the intangible and virtual (prayers).

When I have talked about this oral history and photography project (and more recently, my filmmaking work with the community of cloistered monastic nuns), the most consistent, often pressing question is as predictable as the Liturgy of the Hours: How did I gain access? The short answer might seem evasive. Like any practice built on social contracts and long-term relationships, access is a matter of trust and negotiation. The fuller answer to this question of access begins with the recognition that any form of ethnographic work is a complicated endeavor; representing others and representing otherness are problematic territories, following an imperialistic tradition of exploiting native resources. The truth is, too, that it is difficult to dissect the evolution of a relationship or to unravel a process that unfolds fluidly. This work has probably sustained my intense focus because I find it challenging and nuanced.

My engagement with this community was predicated by variables that I could not have fully understood at the outset: the peculiar insider-outsider dynamic; a subculture facing an uncertain future (their possible extinction due to dwindling numbers); questions of power relations within the monastic hierarchy; and the contradictory nature inherent in a project that asks members of an insulated community (who seek anonymity, have limited contact with their closest loved ones, and observe monastic silence) to talk about themselves.

I began this project with a question: What compels a woman in this era of overexposure—at a time with the technological means to reach a global audience—to make a drastic, lifelong, countercultural decision for her life, in favor of obscurity? My assumption was that it would be of value to learn about the motivations and the lives of women who make vows of poverty, chastity, obedience, and enclosure. Cloistered monastic nuns mediate on behalf of humanity, believing that their prayers and penances can change the course of history.

I am not Catholic. During my first visit to the Corpus Christi Monastery, I explained that to the Mother Abbess. I said that I wanted to undertake a project about the lives of cloistered monastic nuns ever since I read an article about a trend, in Italy, of young women joining religious orders and wanting, in my recollection, a return to the habit. The way I remember the article, some of the women were the daughters of fashion designers. I told Mother Miryam that I did not know yet what form the project would take but that I wanted to work long-term with the community.

I acknowledged in our first meeting my awareness that monasteries were closing and that the number of women seeking religious life in the States was dwindling. She agreed; with changes following Vatican II, she said that nuns wearing habits are not as prevalent in mainstream culture's visual vocabulary. She said that nuns had been "erased from the landscape." Mother Miryam told me she would take my request under advisement and consult with the Vicaress, the other members of the elected council, and the rest of the community. A few weeks later, the answer was "yes"; I know now that the answer was "yes," by increments.

I was new, then, to the practice of oral history. As a teenager studying toward an undergraduate degree in history, I was prejudiced to be wary of traditional historical accounts, which have often privileged stories told from the perspective of the powerful, the victors in war, rather than the individuals and subcultures living on the fringe of the mainstream—those who are not compelled to add to the historical record with their own narratives. Having worked as a journalist and questioned some of that field's premises and practices, particularly interrogating distinctions between private performances and public lives, I took to the discipline of oral history when I first encountered it; I appreciated the pioneering figure of Alessandro Portelli, who called attention to the fact that memory, including collective memory, is faulty. When I first heard an elder in the field of oral history, perhaps when I was a fellow at Columbia University's Oral History Research Office Summer Institute in 2008, summarize a philosophy of oral history as advocating coauthorship and shared authority, this resonated with me.[1] A few years later, when I presented this work-in-progress at the Oral History in the Mid-Atlantic Region's annual conference, I was struck by another speaker's comments; Patrick Hurley, a political ecologist, said that whereas history can collapse identity, oral history features a multiplicity of identities.[2] I believe that we create stories to lend meaning, to call attention to themes, to explain our experiences. These stories reveal emotional and transcendent truths. As the South African journalist and poet Antjie Krog wrote of her homeland's struggle to reconcile after the horrors of apartheid: "We tell stories not to die of life."[3]

In working with the nuns, I demonstrated my rigor, my sincerity, my earnestness. I demonstrated, too, that I did not know enough of the culture. I think now that it took too long to realize that the nuns stand up as a sign of respect when the Mother Abbess walks into the room. (The first half-dozen times I visited with the Mother Abbess, though, I had a private audience; it was only when another nun was sitting and talking to me and the Mother Abbess walked into the room that I saw the nun stand. I then learned of the practice.) Only after I had extended my hand through holes in the metal grille in greeting the nuns did I realize that they do not, as a rule, touch even their loved ones; however, they will not refuse a hand that is extended to them. I course-corrected. The interviews continued. I was invited into the enclosure to make photographs. I respected their values and I picked up, probably intuitively and subconsciously at first, and then echoed their indirect style of communication. In retrospect, I understand that patience underscored this process. I made various requests; I waited. The nuns were gracious as I learned their culture. At times, I inadvertently tested the limits and was met with none-too-subtle jesting. During one of my first visits, in 2005, I asked the Mother Abbess if I could be "a fly on the wall" during one young woman's upcoming visit, when the two would discuss her interest in becoming a Poor Clare nun. My request was granted. Maybe thirty minutes into their conversation, I asked a question. The Mother Abbess glanced at me. "A fly, eh?" she said. "I wish I had a swatter!" I laughed nervously. She looked at me sternly, then smiled.

In tracing the lineage of this project, it seems constructive to describe my methodology by way of analogy. One day, while interviewing Sister Mary

Monica, I asked if she could talk about her notions of or experiences with mysticism. She mentioned a movie about Saint Faustina—"a true mystic," Sister Mary Monica said, "in that she gave up everything to be united with Christ." She continued: "So there it is. A true mystic is someone who gives up everything to be united with Christ, and so in that way we all can be mystics." She told me that in the monastery I should not expect to hear a lot of stories about mystical "experiences," that if anyone did have those experiences, she probably would not want to advertise it. Referring to Saint Teresa of Avila, who is said to have searched for God in her daily routines (in the "pots and pans"), Sister Mary Monica said, "I have to say I'm really plain Jane. I think that God speaks to me in the pots and pans. I think God is training me through the everyday life. I just need to be faithful where I am."

In a similar way, I think that the practice of oral history can be described as tending to the everyday, the "pots and pans." Other practitioners in the field of oral history have advised: *Consider the silences, the voices seldom heard in popular culture.* Cloistered nuns pursue anonymity and hiddenness; their tombstones do not document their birth names or birth dates. To respect the nuns' value of hiddenness and their desire for anonymity, we agreed that each would choose a pseudonym; their actual religious names would not be used. (At the Corpus Christi Monastery, the Mother Abbess assigns each woman her religious name; a postulant can submit three suggestions, and she is renamed during the Clothing Ceremony, when she progresses from postulant to novice.) The Vicaress chose the name Sister Maria Deo Gratias, Latin for "thanks be to God," because, she said, "If you're asking me about my vocation, that name depicts it. It's 'thanks be to God,' because it's all God's doing." The nuns also selected pseudonyms for their childhood names, for their lives before they were given religious names. One chose a pseudonym that was her actual childhood nickname; another chose the name of her niece.

After Mother Miryam and the community agreed to this project, each member decided whether or not she wanted to participate. One of the nuns explained her hesitancy to be interviewed but how she was compelled to take part. "Mother Abbess asked me," Sister Sarah Marie said. "I was like, 'Oh!' Just from the depths of me, 'Oh, Mother, no. What does she want to talk to me for?'" Mother Miryam told Sister Sarah Marie that I had seen the vase of roses on the ledge of the grille and had learned that when Sister Sarah Marie's mother died, in that same town, her body had been brought into the parlor for one final goodbye. "I was moaning and groaning," Sister Sarah Marie said. "So I said, 'You pray about it, Mother Abbess, and whatever you want me to do, I'll do. If you want me to talk to Abbie, I'll do it. But if you don't want me to talk to Abbie, I won't. You know my gut feeling is I'd rather not. But the only way I'm going to know God's will on this is through you, so you let me know.' So she told me, 'I think you should talk to her. I think maybe she'll understand our life a little bit more.' See this is what's wonderful about these superiors." Sister Sarah Marie then said that she teased the Mother Abbess that "God's going to get you." "But it was up to her to decide," Sister Sarah Marie said. "She knew my feeling, my gut feeling; I'd prefer not to because we live a hidden life. This is so precious to us. But Mother Abbess can see an insight into this, sees something more than I can see. She has a bit more direct contact with God than I do. Fine."

If Mother Miryam convinced Sister Sarah Marie to participate, Sister Sarah Marie then encouraged others to take part in the oral history interviews. Often, by way of introduction, the nuns would greet me for the first time and say that they heard I was not what one expects of a journalist or reporter or interviewer. One nun described herself as "social" and told me, "I love to talk"; she seemed especially gratified by the connection afforded by this project and she arranged, within the constraints of her community, more visits (telling Mother Miryam and me that she would be happy to meet with me again, if I would like).

Once, Sister Mary Nicolette broached me with a dilemma. I knew by then that the nuns relied on a number of individuals for daily provisions, such as a weekly donation of milk, an occasional box of fish, and help driving to appointments. Sister Mary Nicolette had asked permission from the Mother Abbess to share with me that in the past the nuns hand-poured candles to sell in their gift shop; they needed a precise thickness of wick and had lost their old connection. I told Sister Mary Nicolette that I could research this on the Internet and bring her the results. She hesitated, not wanting to impose on my time. I assured her it was no trouble. I found a supplier, purchased the wick online for less than $20, and had it shipped to the monastery. When I visited again, I declined the nuns' offers for reimbursement. I did this without hesitation or much reflection at the time. I believe in retrospect that this gesture impacted the dynamics of trust. This may have been, in anthropological terms, my contribution toward a gift exchange.

The nuns refer to themselves as "mothers of souls." As counterintuitive as it might seem, at first blush, that cloistered nuns would choose to participate in a project that brings attention to themselves, they voiced many times the possibility that young women might learn about the cloistered monastic vocation, which could lead to prospective members of their community. Another factor influenced their involvement. Saint Clare, the founder of their order, is the Patron Saint of Television. The nuns express a feeling of responsibility for the world beyond their enclosure, the hope that sharing their own life stories might further their mission as hidden witnesses.

Dedicated to God

Introduction

Left to the human condition, we fail. But when we have a structure and we have God calling us, for instance to poverty, chastity, and obedience, then it's like a gift. It's a way of providing us to respond to God more fully. Those are all gifts that we give to God. And in giving those gifts, definitely we receive from Him. He's not God way out there and He doesn't care. There's a personal relationship. So then I say, "I take you Lord for my all," and I know that God is my enough. I don't need to give myself in marriage, beautiful as it is.

Sister Maria Deo Gratias of the Most Blessed Sacrament

Like a crack magician, she pulls a photograph from a pocket hidden within the folds of her uniform. She shows no irony and does not register my surprise. She is presenting me a gift, showing me what she looked like before she came here a quarter century ago. She holds up the photo, and then slides it under the metal bars for closer inspection. I see an attractive twentysomething with teased hair and a revealing top.

She places a few more photographs on the ledge in front of me. She is smiling in each, caught midlaugh. She appears to be the center of attention, comfortable in her assigned or assumed role of entertainer. She claims she played the part well: the extrovert who knew how to have a good time.

Sister Sarah Marie, whom I have come to know as direct and self-deprecating—"Italian" is the word she thinks best captures her personality—wants me to study one of the photos and note the difference between her small nose in the picture and the big nose before me now. The reality of her improved features in the photograph is an illusion, she says; she wore makeup back then and knew how to apply it.

Maybe I did not seem convinced before today when we talked about her life on the outside. If the photos do not make the point clear enough, she states it bluntly: Sister Sarah Marie was "normal" before she entered. This information—not the tangible object before me—is the gift. She wants me to know that she and the other women who joined this cloistered monastery, who made three vows that mark men and women who profess vows to religious life—vows of poverty, chastity, and obedience—along with a fourth vow of enclosure, were once quite average.

In her twenties, when she was known as Tiffany, she intended to get married. "I always got along with men," she says. "I never had a problem with them. I never had that feminist problem when they opened the door for me. I always enjoyed their company. I always had guys as just friends. It was just natural. There it is."

Before embracing anonymity, before surrendering her name and shoes and freedom of movement for a demanding life in one of the strictest orders, she and the other members of this community dressed up and went on dates. One wanted to be a "cowboy."

I have interacted with Sister Sarah Marie on occasion since 2005, as I have worked on an oral history and photography project with her community of cloistered monastic nuns at the Corpus Christi Monastery in Rockford, Illinois. Members of the eight-hundred-year-old Poor Clare Colettine Order seek anonymity and observe monastic silence. A metal grille separates the nuns' enclosure from the outside world. Family members are allowed a limited number of visits each year, always separated by the metal grille.

The calling to cloistered monastic life took many of the Rockford Poor Clares by surprise. It defied their God-given temperament. It violated dreams. It dashed plans for marriage and children. It meant their world would shrink, temporally, to a fourteen-acre campus, so that their minds could dwell on God.

Several nuns volunteered, in the course of the oral history interviews, that outsiders label their life as a form of escapism. They took pains to point out that religious life is not a rejection of the world or its inhabitants; the enclosure is instead a means for embracing humanity, a calling to, not a running from. This is not a place for the faint of heart or for women who could not survive elsewhere in the world. Mother Miryam says life in an enclosure is easier if a woman is functional, or "whole," and that members should strive for wholeness, as humans, and for holiness.

"You know what you expect?" Sister Sarah Marie asks. " 'Yes, Abbie, that's true, I am in this life and it is beautiful.' Quiet. Never says a word. Shy. Withdrawn. You expect most women that would come here are introverted, withdrawn; maybe somebody should interview us that is majoring in abnormal psychology. But you have to be normal to live this life, Abbie. You have to be real normal. You have to date, go to parties. Because I think when you enter an enclosure, if you're abnormal, it's going to come out—if there's something wrong. In the active world, you can keep it under for a little bit, if you've got a little psychological disorder. Not here, Abbie. Not here. That's why, I mean, when they think, 'They must be a little bit dingy to be back there', it's just the opposite."

According to the treatise *Verbi Sponsa: Instruction on the Contemplative Life and on the Enclosure of Nuns*, a publication that is given to all Poor Clare postulants when they enter the Corpus Christi Monastery as part of their formation, a cloistered contemplative yearns for "fulfillment in God, in an uninterrupted nostalgia of the heart," and with a "monastic recollection" that enables a constant focus on the presence of God, her "journey slows down and the final destination disappears from view."[1]

Pope John Paul II described the institutes whose members are completely devoted to contemplation as "for the Church a reason for pride and a source of heavenly graces. By their lives and mission, the members of these Institutes imitate Christ in His prayer on the mountain, bear witness to God's lordship over history and anticipate the glory which is to come."[2]

A daily schedule alternates prayer and manual labor. In the Corpus Christi Monastery, the Blessed Sacrament is not exposed perpetually, twenty-four hours a day, seven days a week; that would require constant shifts, one member of the community always absent to be with the Blessed Sacrament in prayer and adoration. The community values togetherness, and so the Rockford Poor Clares observe a prolonged exposition of the Blessed Sacrament, with one nun in the presence of the Blessed Sacrament during the day, and often through the night.

The nuns make altar breads that are shipped off to different churches. They tend their gardens, growing many of the vegetables they eat and solving bug troubles by slipping nylon stockings over the cabbage heads. They repair benches in their woodshop, fully equipped after one woman entered decades ago and had her tools delivered to the monastery. A small gift shop sits at the entrance of the monastery, where the Poor Clares sell Communion veils that a few of them sew, cards that others make with pressed flowers, and rosaries they bead using Job's Tears grown on their property. They pray, while working on these items, for the person who will come into possession of them. The nuns see the shop as a form more of outreach than of revenue; they depend on benefactors for food and monetary donations. Through the benefactors, their trust in God is realized.

Here, the cloistered nun becomes anonymous to the world. She is hidden from view. Each follows her convictions at incredible personal cost. A few describe that when they first felt called to religious life, it seemed "too radical." Some families were so adamantly against monastic life, which appeared so restrictive to them, that they ended all contact after their daughter or sister became a Poor Clare Colettine. For others, the decision to enter a contemplative order could not have been more natural.

Sister Maria Deo Gratias recalls the moment she was called. She was in her sixth-grade classroom when she heard a directive to go to the chapel after school. Before the Blessed Sacrament, she says, "I knew I would be His the moment I knelt down." Although she was not yet familiar with the terminology for giving her life totally to the unseen entity she believed spoke directly to her heart, she told God, "I will marry you."

"From the experience I had," she says, "I never doubted ever my vocation from that moment on. I was His." Since then, she has accepted each degree of commitment that has opened before her, from the aspirature (a boarding school for girls interested in pursuing religious life), to the active order of nuns where she worked first as a gym teacher and later on at a hospital psychiatric ward (having trained in pastoral care), to her life now at the Corpus Christi Monastery.

To her, the challenge is basic: Become a saint.

Others in her community are less stoical. They share their doubts and struggles. In pursuit of perfection, they list the practical challenges, chief among them, twenty women sharing a kitchen. Each sleeps on a carpet-stuffed mattress; the older generations remember stuffing their pillows and mattresses with straw. They rise at midnight, four hours after retiring for sleep, to pray at the first of seven scheduled prayers in the Divine Office.

Sister Joan Marie, who has lived here longer than any other member, is not sure if, in more than sixty years as a cloistered monastic nun, she has ever adapted. "When things got hard, I got sick," she says. "So I escaped that way."

Mother Miryam was the youngest of twelve siblings, born to parents who modeled a beautiful marriage. "It's hard to give up marriage," she says. "It's hard to give up that type of love. It's hard to give up children." She was moved by her parents' intimacy: "They just worked for each other. You could tell they were very close. Every evening for as long as I could remember, when we were doing the dishes, they would go and sit down. Dad would sit in the big chair and Mom would sit in his lap. Always. Always. Always. There was just always a lot of love and care there."

When she felt called to religious life, she was stymied, intellectually. She thought, "How can I deny life to all the children I could have had? How can I ever do that? It's not right." "Of course," she says now, "it's very simple. It took me a while until it dawned on me: 'Well, if God didn't want you to marry, He never wanted those children to exist.' So that was fine. But it really was a struggle until it finally hit me. 'Don't be so stupid! You could have maybe had ten, twelve children, but God never wanted them to exist if He wanted you to be a religious.'"

Poor Clare nuns devote their lives to prayer and penance and sacrifice; this is what they call their charism—the special spirit and focus of their community. Sister Mary Nicolette describes their charism as "living a life for others. We withdraw from the world into an environment that enables us to make those sacrifices, to call down graces and to obtain graces for people. So it's a willing penance and a loving sacrifice." A select few nuns are assigned the duty of answering phone calls from the outside to a prayer hotline at the monastery and they all pray, seven times a day during the Divine Office, for personal and catastrophic events around the globe. In one of the paradoxes of this life, they believe that in removing themselves from the world and embracing a life of anonymity, unseen and unknown to the world at large, by undertaking lives of self-sacrifice and prayer behind the scenes, they have a greater impact on mankind than if they maintained direct contact with strangers and loved ones. Each member of this community believes that there is power, along with challenges, in this life.

Poor Clare Colettine nuns give up their birth names, as well as all material possessions, as concrete, external signs of their vows. They walk barefoot indoors as a sign of the poverty they embrace. (An exception is that the nuns are permitted to wear shoes as they age.) Just as their lives are anonymous, they are not memorialized in death. Burial takes place in a small cemetery on the property, with a stone marker at the gravesite revealing only the woman's religious name and death date, not her birth name or birth date, to signify the start of her life in eternity.

The nuns operate, although they might not use this term, as agents of change. They intervene in the course of history, believing that their prayers and penances for strangers and family can alter outcomes. At the ceremony when a nun makes final, permanent vows, she hugs her family members for one final time. This sacrifice serves a purpose: The material world is not the end, and their sufferings and martyrdoms allow God's will to become manifest in the world.

Members of this unique subculture live as intermediaries to another realm, and for the afterlife. Cloistered contemplatives "embody the exodus from the world in order to encounter God in the solitude of the 'cloistered desert,' a desert that includes inner solitude, the trials of the spirit and the daily toil of life in community," according to *Verbi Sponsa*.[3]

Expatriates of mainstream culture, the cloistered nuns work to adapt to an ancient religious rule, an enclosed culture loaded with visual imagery and symbolic identifiers. They learn to tie the prayer cord, worn around their waists, with four knots, which represent their four vows. In this highly selective and self-selected subculture, the women choose to enter this place and the community decides whether to receive or reject them when they are eligible to become novices, make temporary vows, and make their final solemn vows, through voting and anonymous ballots.

The nuns observe monastic silence, a custom to preserve their spirit of recollection, speaking only what is necessary in order to complete a task. Even written communication is abbreviated;[4] each nun is assigned a mark when she enters the Corpus Christi Monastery as her identification. The mark—a chalice or crown of thorns or wild rose—is used when the nuns write notes to one another. This symbol is stitched or written with permanent ink on the items the woman is assigned for her use. (She does not own the items, since each gives up her worldly possessions when she joins the community.) The Mother Abbess might assign a mark that corresponds with the Feast Day a woman enters the monastery, or she might be inspired by what she gleans of the woman's spirituality. A former Mother Abbess often assigned new entrants a mark that was one letter from the name Jesus, Joseph, Mary, Francis, Clare, or Colette.

In a place imbued with ritual, where members do not explain every custom, the cloister can be a mystery to its residents. Sister Joan Marie, the community's eldest nun by what the nuns term her rank (of longevity), having joined the monastery before any of the other current members, says, "It seemed very mysterious to me when I first entered, I guess, because I just never knew what was going to happen next. Pretty soon I got onto the rhythm, to the schedule. And now it even seems tighter because I can't make it. I can't run fast enough. But then I was able to keep up."

The cloistered life is one of paradox. The nuns live in the tension of certainty and uncertainty, maintaining deep belief and embodying their convictions in total commitment, yet are aware that they will not experience resolution—or know the results in this lifetime—of their lives of dedication and sacrifice. They are comfortable with the uncertainty.

Six decades after joining the enclosure, Sister Joan Marie can still view monastic life (and convey it) through the eyes of an outsider. She follows the order's strict rules, not knowing the fruits of her life of penance. The nuns perceive that others, even family, even Catholics, do not understand their decision to enter the order. Loved ones have expressed their disdain for their vocation. Some deem their life as irrelevant. Or crazy. Or different, hard to decipher.

A metal grille makes tangible the signature vow—enclosure—of this otherworldly realm, a cultural time capsule. The concrete and symbolic demarcation sets the nuns apart from the world. Even during visits with family (they are allowed up to four visits a year), a nun sits on one side of the grille, inside the enclosure, and she visits with her relatives—out in the world—on the other side of the grille. While the nun and her family could reach through the five-inch square gaps in the seventy-inch-wide by forty-five-inch-high metal grille to holds hands, they are not supposed to touch.

One nun tells an anecdote of an outsider's impressions of the cloister. Sister Sarah Marie's four-year-old great-niece had visited the monastery several times before, when her mother announced another visit. The child had replied, " 'Oh, yes, Mommy, that's the one that's in the cage.' And her mom says, 'Caylee!' And she says, 'Yes, Mommy, a Jesus cage.' "

The girl's mother prodded, and the girl described the "bars" she had seen—a zoo-like association with the place where religious women are kept and sometimes seen. Sister Sarah Marie believes the childlike understanding of her life is both profound and humorous. Sister Sarah Marie says it is an apt description of their physical space and their spiritual lives. "A Jesus cage,"

Sister Sarah Marie says. "A little four-year-old. She knew this looked like a little cage at a zoo or something, but she knew it was much deeper than that. This connected Jesus. I thought that was pretty profound. I told the sisters and we all kind of laughed. We laughed and said, 'Yes, the cage.' We laughed and laughed."

The nuns are lighthearted. They laugh at themselves and each other. Sister Maria Deo Gratias commends the nuns charged with maintaining the gardens; if it were her job to tend to the plants, she says, the monastery would host "ever-browns." Their childlike amusement says more about them and their outlook than it reveals of the strict demands of their vows to their order—a religious order the cardinals in Rome were reluctant to approve eight hundred years ago because they said it seemed impossible to live out Saint Clare's high ideals. Sister Mary Nicolette, who is translating from Italian to English a compilation of Poor Clare writings throughout the ages, recently translated this poignant sentence, by the Venerable Mary of Jesus of Agreda (1602–1665): "One of the lofty purposes of Christ coming into the world was to raise up poverty and to teach it to mortals who are horrified by it."

While others struggle to understand the nuns, they consider themselves chosen. They are the brides of Christ. Sister Maria Deo Gratias says,

A person can be very prayerful, and live her life on her own and consecrate herself privately to God; that's a private consecration. But if you want a public consecration, there has to be that acceptance. And then the Church accepts that and then in that acceptance of the superior, you pronounce the three vows. In the very beginning of the Church, that was lived but it wasn't specified in the terms that we say it now.

There was always what we called the Consecration of Virgins; there were some women who would give themselves to God—very early, even in the very beginnings of the Church in the 100s. In the very, very beginning of the Church there were people who set themselves apart to give themselves to God. They lived in chastity, they practiced poverty, and they certainly had obedience, to a limited degree, in the very beginning. Those individuals who were separate formed a community, and they had a superior that they could obey. You still had those who chose to be hermits on their own, just like we have today. We have hermits and consecrated virgins in the world, and then we have those that choose—and it's really a choice because of a divine inspiration that that person feels—that they're called by God to live in a community, so they join a community. And in joining that community, they freely give themselves to God by following the rule and the superior of that community.

The founding of the Poor Clare Colettine Order harkens back to 1212, when Clare Offreduccio, a young woman of noble birth whose parents planned to marry her off to a rich man, slipped away from home on the night of Palm Sunday to follow Saint Francis of Assisi, the founder of three Roman Catholic Franciscan orders: the Friars Minor (the Grey Friars), the Poor Clares (which began when he handed Clare her new garb), and the Third Order (laity who live in the world as Franciscans and who can marry).

Saint Clare, like Saint Francis, was born an aristocrat. Both embraced high ideals to live in absolute poverty and abandon material possessions—to the extent that Saint Francis initially restricted his disciples to one woolen coat and forbade them from wearing shoes. Pope Benedict XVI, in a biographical sketch of Saint Clare of Assisi, refers to her as "one of the best loved saints" whose "testimony shows us how indebted the Church is to courageous women, full of faith like her, who can give a crucial impetus to the Church's renewal."[5]

Saint Francis turned over the Church of San Damiano to Saint Clare for her new order to use as a convent.[6] The first woman to write a rule for a monastic community, Saint Clare met with resistance to her "Privilege of Poverty" from church authorities. Based on Saint Francis's ideal of utter poverty, the rule established that members of the community would not own any possessions, even the building they inhabited; this was deemed too extreme and impractical, impossible to live by. But at last, in 1253 Saint Clare's rule was approved.

Saint Clare's biological sister Agnes, her mother, an aunt, and a niece joined her community of Poor Ladies. In the 1300s, when the Poor Clare Order became lax in enforcing its original rule of possessing nothing in order to depend solely on God's provisions, Pope Benedict XIII nominated Colette of Corbie (a French hermit) to reform the order. The existing monasteries and new foundations that followed the reformed Holy Rule became known as Poor Clare Colettines.

The Poor Clare Colettines arrived in the United States with Mother Mary von Elmendorff of Dusseldorf, Germany, to found a new community in

Cleveland, Ohio. In 1916, following repeated requests by the Rockford, Illinois, diocese, nuns from the Cleveland community arrived in Rockford to start a new foundation.[7] In 1966, Reverend Loras T. Lane, the bishop of Rockford, wrote to the Rockford Poor Clare Colettines, "It is truly significant that the Bishops of Rockford, whose duty is to sustain and strengthen the faith of those entrusted for their care, have always maintained special interest in, and concern for, the welfare and success of your Monastery, wherein a small number of God's beloved souls have been called to serve Him in the cloistered atmosphere of prayer and meditation, of penance and sacrifice."[8]

For four years, the cloistered nuns occupied a Victorian home as their temporary monastery. In 1920, the bishop purchased a former sanitarium for the growing community. The building provided ample space but needed extensive remodeling. When the 1934 improvements were finally paid for, another bishop "encouraged the sisters to begin saving for a new monastery, as he considered the old building a real firetrap," the nuns wrote in their own historical account. "Due to the great increase in the cost of labor and building supplies, many years passed before there was any hope of replacing the temporary buildings in use since 1920."[9] In 1962, the Poor Clare Colettines moved into the newly constructed Corpus Christi Monastery.

"Poor Clare nuns live in utter freedom and simplicity," reads their brochure, entitled *Come Follow Me*.[10] It refers to a 1996 address by Pope John Paul II, in which he stated, "We come to understand the identity of the consecrated person, beginning with his or her complete self-offering, as being comparable to a genuine holocaust." The brochure explains the four vows:

By her vow of poverty the Poor Clare frees herself of all temporal concerns and puts in check the innate desire of man to acquire and possess. She, instead, understands herself to be a steward rather than an owner of God's manifold gifts. By the vow of chastity the Poor Clare expresses the yearning of a heart unsatisfied by any finite love. She proclaims to the whole world that God is enough by freeing her heart of any single human attachment in order to love God alone and all His creatures in Him. By her vow of obedience the Poor Clare freely renounces her own will, which is the most thorough sacrifice the human heart can make. She makes a holocaust of the very center of her being in order to conform her whole heart and will to that of her Beloved Spouse. By the vow of enclosure the Poor Clare leaves behind life in the world and lives in imitation of Christ's hidden life at Nazareth. Within the enclosure she is free to listen to the voice of the Bridegroom and offer herself as a victim with Jesus for the salvation of the world.[11]

The Franciscan friar Benet Fonck of the Order of Friars Minor (OFM) has interacted with the Poor Clare Colettine Order since he joined the Franciscan Order in 1965. Author of *To Cling with All Her Heart to Him: The Spirituality of Saint Clare*, Friar Fonck writes that Poor Clares heed Christ's command to Saint Francis to rebuild the Church and through their "poverty and prayer and simple proclamation fulfill this mandate in an especially effective and fruitful way."[12] Many women find contemplative cloistered life attractive, Friar Fonck writes, "because many of the monasteries are more conservative with full habits and a strict life-style; a good number of contemporary women seem to find a need satisfied with this kind of order and stability. The generation before them were accustomed to a more free-flowing and unstructured way of being a member of the Church. As the pendulum swings, their children have a longing and a need for something more conservative, more structured, and more tradition to satisfy their spiritual needs."[13] The Corpus Christi Monastery in Rockford is the type of conservative monastery that Friar Fonck describes: The nuns wear the full habit and they adhere to a strict lifestyle.

In 2012, the Poor Clare Colettine Order celebrated the eight hundredth anniversary of its founding. But at the same time, the population of religious communities is declining. Over the past four decades, the number of religious sisters in the United States dropped significantly—69 percent; from 179,954 in 1965 to 54,018 in 2012—even as the Catholic population in the country rose. From 1970 to 2010, there was a drop worldwide in the total number of women religious, from 1,004,304 to 721,935, according to the Georgetown University affiliated Center for Applied Research in the Apostolate, which conducts social scientific studies about the Catholic Church.[14] As of 2010, there were twelve Poor Clare Colettine monasteries in the United States, with a total membership of fewer than two hundred cloistered nuns. Twenty nuns currently reside within the Corpus Christi Monastery in Rockford, Illinois.

Sister Maria Deo Gratias says that when young women inquire about joining the Corpus Christi Monastery, and ask if they can bring a computer or cell phone into the monastery, she teases them by saying they will have a cell, but it is not the technology they might be thinking of; they would retire at night to a spartan room.

Until recently, Sister Maria Benedicta was the community's youngest member, a thirtysomething former college softball pitcher who grew up in Kansas and did not see a religious sister in person or in a movie until the fourth grade. Sister Maria Benedicta has embraced the hidden life. She is "good," the older nuns say; she is suited to this life. Sister Maria Benedicta is in the midst of a series of transitions, a process of detoxification from the world and integration into community that takes six years before she commits herself to this space for the rest of her life by professing final, solemn vows of poverty, chastity, obedience, and enclosure.

One afternoon, Sister Maria Benedicta sits and sews with the Mother Abbess. She has completed one year as a postulant and two years as a novice. She hopes to make first vows, a temporary three-year term. The community is scheduled to vote the following day in a yes-no ballot to allow or deny her passage to the next phase. Each member of the community will receive a piece of paper with the word "yes" typed on one side and the word "no" typed on the other; they will circle one word. (In the past, the nuns voted with beans—a white bean indicating "yes" and a dark bean meaning "no"; the new system was put into place to make it easier for the older nuns.)

Sister Maria Benedicta and Mother Miryam spar, verbally. Sister Maria Benedicta mentions the Mother Abbess's recent message to the religious sisters that they are to be a "yes" community. Sister Maria Benedicta coyly seeks reassurance that she will be accepted by consensus. Mother Miryam demurs, saying something about the virtue of patience and not knowing for certain just yet. In truth, there is little doubt that Sister Maria Benedicta will be accepted by the community. She must know this, and so she turns and addresses me, a mostly silent but conspicuous presence. Sister Maria Benedicta counters the wait-and-see approach and jokingly provokes: Do I have extra space in my house?

I say that I do, indeed, have a spare room and could definitely arrange chores for someone with her carpentry skills. At this point, Mother Miryam tells Sister Maria Benedicta that making backup plans could be construed as less than the requisite seriousness needed to join the community. Both women are still teasing. Still, Sister Maria Benedicta blushes and her tone turns solemn. They discuss the demands and the joys of the cloistered monastic life. Sister Maria Benedicta makes clear she really does want this life, within these walls.

She, like the nineteen other women in the Corpus Christi Monastery, wants to become a Poor Clare to devote her life to prayer, to intercede on behalf of humanity. She has left the world because of her devotion to it.

Sister Maria Benedicta continues the detailed work of affixing beads to a veil for her biological sister's upcoming wedding, a ceremony that Sister Maria Benedicta will not attend because she cannot leave the monastery. She falls back on what seems to be second nature; her cheeky analysis amuses Mother Miryam, who is sewing a baptismal gown and bonnet to sell in the gift shop. Sister Maria Benedicta tells Mother Miryam about a conversation that also took place in my presence with her Novice Mistress, Sister Mary Nicolette, earlier that same day in the woodshop. Sister Mary Nicolette, elected by the community to the post, oversees Sister Maria Benedicta's instruction and guides her toward the Poor Clare ideals. While the two stood near a window, sending a plank through the teeth of a table saw, the afternoon sunlight refracted particles of sawdust, which appeared to glow around Sister Mary Nicolette. I photographed the pair and commented on the beautiful imagery. Then I opened myself up to their teasing by saying, earnestly, that the scene looked almost "mystical" or "magical." Both Sister Maria Benedicta and Sister Mary Nicolette laughed. They joked that it was "holy dust," or "mystical dust."

Sister Maria Benedicta suggested that Sister Mary Nicolette should be canonized because the glow proved she is a saint. At this point in Sister Maria Benedicta's retelling, Mother Miryam quips that it is a good thing a photograph documented the event, as that might be the closest Sister Mary Nicolette gets to becoming a saint. Sister Maria Benedicta laughs.

Cloistered monastic nuns submit to a radical life, a hard life, but they rarely allow themselves—or anyone else who enters these walls—to be too pleased with herself or her own progress.

Here, Sister Maria Benedicta is striving for perfection. Here, women who have departed contemporary American culture at various stages over the last century move together in a routine yet timeless space, focused on eternity as they synchronize to the cycle of prayers, manual labor, prayers, sleep, prayers.

They pull weeds and sew veils. This work frees their minds to contemplate God and pray for others.

One day after sewing with Mother Miryam, Sister Maria Benedicta learns that she has, indeed, been accepted by the community and can thus advance and make temporary vows as a Poor Clare Colettine nun. She and her community will continue to discern for the next three years until she can make final vows whether she truly is called to this vocation, in this place.

In a somber, reflective moment, during a one-on-one interview, Sister Maria Benedicta shares her most basic desire. "It's not just that I want to get to heaven," she says. "I want everyone else to get there, too. And it is very urgent. It's life or death, for eternity."

In this pursuit, she wants nothing less than to change the world, anonymously, by living virtue.

Sister Mary Monica
of the Holy Eucharist

I started when I entered: I was counting the first week and I was making percentages. My nickname was Sister Calculata because I was counting and counting and counting. I didn't do this out in the world; I never had something to look forward to as much as this, or something that I thought was really important.

It has been a drain for me, for fifteen years to desire to be our Lord's spouse and to not be able to do so, to long so much for this and to have the longing unfulfilled. Finally, by the Church, I am His spouse and that's a wonderful thing.

When I was real little, I thought about having the call to be a nun. And I decided against it because I really was more interested in the things of the world. I really think it was a call inside from God. I had this feeling that I was never meant to marry—a man anyway. I had this conviction that I was not meant to marry. And it was very strong. I think God was trying to tell me, but I did shut the door. I shut the door. I will admit I really deeply regret that. I really do because I really feel like I said "no" to God. I trust that He makes good out of that, but I will admit that I admire the sisters here that were courageous enough, and self-giving and selfless enough, to give themselves to Jesus right away and not get caught up in what they wanted and the things of the world. I very much admire the sisters here who did that and anyone who did that. But I didn't. And I ended up forgetting about it. I don't think that I ever told anybody about it, but there was one day where I decided no. I was particularly fond of horses. We had a horse farm and the reason we had it was because of me.

I was on our farm and there was one day I was in the barn, and I was just having this real strong feeling inside to be a nun. And, at that point,

I actually reversed the decision. I was cleaning the barn, and I had that feeling about being a nun and I just said, "Okay, Lord, I will give up everything," and I meant it. Even when I was a child, I knew. I knew that if you were asked to give up everything, at that time you should say, "Yes, alright, Lord, I'll give up everything."

I was twenty-six or twenty-seven years old. I made the choice at that time that I would give up everything. I didn't understand the spiritual part, but the material part, I understood what it meant. It meant giving up the farm and the horses and the dogs and everything else. So I made the promise. And I really knew very little, very little, about my faith, to speak of. I'd been working on it, I think, at that time, but I didn't know that much. I hadn't seen that much of sisters, and I didn't know properly what a nun is because sisters are the ones outside that are active, and nuns are usually the ones in the cloister.

We had quite a few horses, and so it really ended up being five years before I got off the farm after I told my parents that I needed to be a nun. I said, "I need to be a nun and I can't wait two years." Oh, that was good! It was five years before I could finish with the farm.

I read *Diary of Saint Maria Faustina Kowalska*. She wasn't a saint at that time; she wasn't even blessed at that time. There was a community that she felt our Lord was asking her to start. It was a cloistered community. The order that Saint Faustina was asked to found, our Lord said, "Your purpose, and that of your companions, is to unite yourselves as closely as possible. Through love, you will reconcile earth with heaven and soften the just anger of God." I liked that idea. I thought that sounded great—a great purpose! I tried to find out if the Divine Mercy movement existed; it didn't exist. I got into contact with some other girls that were interested in starting the community mentioned in the diary, but we went through years and years of seeing if it would work. We would get together and there would be times where some of us would live together for a while, but it never worked out. We found we didn't really seem to have the same call.

But I still felt called, and I had spiritual directors that thought I really was called to do this. I really needed authentic religious training. I was reading this book, *The Spiritual Legacy of Sister Mary of the Holy Trinity*, about a Poor Clare. In the front and back of the book, there were pictures of *this* monastery with little description of the life. I said, "Gee, that really sounds like Saint Faustina's way of life." I thought it would be a very good place to go for training. It was funny. In about six weeks, I was here. I came here for a visit for a week. I couldn't go in the cloister, but I got to pray the Divine Office. I was in the sacristy and they were in the choir, and I heard that Divine Office being sung and I wanted to get through that grate and get in there and I couldn't! It was the chanting of the Divine Office. I just wanted to get in there and pray with them! I think there were other things, too. I had been feeling in my heart, before I came, a drive to be with community. I really needed to be with community. I couldn't be living alone anymore. I went away for two weeks to think about it, and I was so completely miserable. All I wanted to do was get back here.

I went to another place, a religious-oriented place. I thought maybe I'm called to be there for a while. But it wasn't centered around the Divine Office. I needed my life centered around the Divine Office. We prayed the Divine Office some—once or twice a day together in a group—but I wanted to pray all seven hours of this Divine Office. In order to have the solemn vows, you're supposed to be bound to pray the Divine Office in community; that's a mark of the contemplative cloistered life. I could not stand not to have my life revolving around the Divine Office. And you can see that's mostly a lot of what made me want to get through that grate. Of course, I could get to Mass every day, that wasn't a problem. But if you're doing work, there are other schedules you have to accommodate; I was fitting in the Divine Office in all these odd ways and places. If I was in the back of a truck, I would pray the Divine Office. If I was walking from Point A to Point B, I would be praying the Divine Office. Maybe I wouldn't finish and maybe I would have to pick it up later. And if it was a work period, I couldn't pray it. It would have to wait until later.

So my spiritual director made arrangements for me to come back here for more religious training. The community also had to meet to decide whether or not they would allow this because it was very special if they would allow me to come in. And, of course, I had to have the permission of the bishop to come in for this training, being I wasn't asking to be a member of this community. They decided to let me try for a year. I really liked that and I asked for more time. And they said, "We'll only give you a year. You need to get your vocation going." I was here not the whole year, and I was getting this feeling inside I needed to go away and find my true home. So I left. And I was so completely miserable that in not much over three months, I was back here as a postulant. All I could think about was getting back here. I could pray the Divine Office, but praying it by myself wasn't enough.

In a cloister, a nun is dedicated to our Lord in a special way. An active sister has an apostolate outside, but here 100 percent of our time is supposed to be with our spouse and we are allowed, because of the life we live in here, to spend more time in prayer. It's like a different tool. If you want to do very fine needlework, you're going to need a very fine, little needle. If you have a needle that's too heavy, maybe a very good seamstress could do this wonderful work, but it's easier with the fine needle. This is kind of the purpose of this life—that we are supposed to be dedicated 100 percent to Christ and to being His spouse. Here, we have an opportunity for silence. An active sister has to do a lot of talking with a lot of other people. Here, if you would like to get to know our Lord, it's going to be in silence and it's going to be with Him in quiet. There are a lot of different kinds of noise inside and outside of you. But the silence—there is where you're uncluttered and there is where you're free for God.

For a while, I regretted exploring the Divine Mercy Movement; I thought it was a waste. But maybe it did form me and form my spirituality. And it did form me as a person, too. And I learned more and more about my faith. God has a purpose. I find even here there is so much room for growth in me still. If I hadn't had all of that time being formed, I might not be even as good as I am now. And I really have a lot of room for improvement! God knows what He's doing. And maybe I was deaf and maybe He was trying to tell me a long time ago. But you know, He put that book in front of me, and it wasn't that long after I had that book, that here I was.

The words in the diary of Saint Faustina, it doesn't appear she knew anything about the Franciscans, but our Lord had said to her, "Your life is to be modeled on mine from the crib to the cross." Well, that's very, very Franciscan, very, very Franciscan. And the authorities have many theories about whether Faustina was being asked to start a community; there are a lot of theories on that. And I don't know. It doesn't appear that I'm called to be in that. But I'm called to live what she wrote and I can do that here: "Your purpose and that of your companions is to come into as close of union with me as possible." And that's what we're supposed to do here. It's interesting because the rule that Saint Faustina wrote is very similar to ours: "Through love, you will unite earth with heaven and soften the just anger of God." And, really, that's the job of everyone in the Church: Through love, we will reconcile earth with heaven the more we love and show mercy. My life and really the lives of everyone here and especially contemplative cloistered nuns, we are supposed to be intercessors. We are supposed to mediate.

My family always knew my dedication to wanting to be a sister. They all, in their hearts, kind of thought of me as a sister even before I got here. They knew how badly I wanted this. And they wanted it so badly for me, too. It was so interesting when I received the black veil; my aunt and uncle and my mom said the black veil looked better because they all said, "Now you look like a real Poor Clare." You know they all thought of me as this, and so I guess they're happy to see me becoming what I wanted to be, and what they saw me as. They knew what my desires were. They've read the lives of the saints. They know the needs in the world.

My father died about a year before I came and one of the last things he said was, "Go for it." And I know he thought prayer was the only answer. Yes, it's a sacrifice, but they know why I'm here. And they know that I'm happy here. They want to support that happiness, and they understand this need. The world has a need for this. It was so touching, and I know it's happened more than once since I've gotten here. My aunt Marilyn asked me specially, she was crying and she said, "After I die, pray for me." So few people are prayed for after they die. She knows the need we have for that prayer, and she is counting on me that I will be praying for her.

My family only comes once a year. It's a long way, and my mom is older. It's a sacrifice for them, for assuredly it is. But I am blessed in that my family knows what I'm doing and why I'm doing it, and that's a great blessing; that's a great, great blessing. They, too, saw all the struggles and sufferings I went through with the Divine Mercy thing. They are so happy to see that I'm settled. I'm settled. I'm safe.

They know that I really am the Lord's spouse. And if I have made the promise to give up all I have—I have made these vows to God—can God give me less than He did before, or is He going to give me more? He's got to give me more because I gave more. And so I have opened myself to this relationship and said, "Okay, I am giving up my obedience, my will, my chastity, meaning I am your spouse. I am reserved completely for you. I don't have the freedom, nor do I choose it, to make any other choices. Poverty—I am going to live poor." If I am going to give Him all this and say, "I want to be your spouse," what's He going to do? He's going to have to reciprocate. And of course, He's the one that originated the desire in my heart in the first place. I couldn't have done it without Him. They understand the spousal relationship.

When I was first looking to do this, I was concerned about the family, but I did ask for the family, that the family could receive blessings, too. And there have been blessings to our family. They really believe in that power of prayer. I do, too. If I'm doing what I'm supposed to be doing, then God will bless those in the world and those I'm praying for more than if I was doing something else that might be more direct, hands-on, because I have to be where God wants me to be. We all do. If I'm not where God wants me to be, or doing what He wants me to do, then how can His grace be there?

If I have a person that I love especially, and if I deny myself and deny them our interaction and my presence, is God in justice going to bless that person more or less for that sacrifice that person had to give? He couldn't do anything but bless that person more. I know that they'll get more blessings from God if I'm doing what He wants me to do, even though it might seem less effective, and less gratifying even.

The biggest thing you give up? Your will. Obedience. That's the hardest of all—not to be able to choose what you want to do when you want to be able to do it. It's every day. It's all the time. We have a schedule. And sometimes maybe you're working on a project, and you're supposed to be doing it, but suddenly before you're finished with it they say, "No, stop doing that. We need something else done." That can be hard. You would like to get that thing finished and get it off your shelf. But, no, they said this. In so many little things, the hardest thing is that sacrifice of your will, and this is where your union with God comes in. If you want union with God, you need union with His will.

I need to be doing what I'm supposed to be doing, but not only that, I need to be like Jesus and Mary. Our Lord accepted the will of the Father, not as you like it, not as I like it, and He came to a complete peace with that, no matter what the suffering it entailed—and not to fight the will of God. And the Blessed Mother, you think about how she could be united with the will of God, watching her son die on the cross and not be fighting it inside herself. How united with God's will would she have to have been? And if I can take what I'm supposed to be doing in life and do it, and accept all that comes to me from God's hand with love—because He is all-powerful; everything that happens, he's allowing it to happen—therefore, I have to say,

"Okay, God, take it as Jesus." I should take it as Jesus would. Take it as love from your hand, and give it back as love and use it for what you want to use it for. If I'm united with the will of God, I need to always do what pleases Him and I will have union with God. So what else is there to worry about or to think about? But there it is. It's that will. So I know if I keep working on this will, and if I were ever to get to where I really was united in my will with God, I would have union with God. The closer I am united to the will of God, the more effective I am for me and everybody. The truth is, the more you are united with the will of God, the more you are going to have joy.

They say that the vows crucify you. Yes, they do. It's a crucifixion. Obedience is. If it doesn't cost anything, you know, it doesn't make a very good story, anyway! You want to watch the stories in the movies where someone had to struggle and work hard. If he just went and did everything without any effort, it would be kind of boring. He'd be an unreal Superman! Even Jesus, being God, He didn't show us that way. And it's a good thing He didn't because then we'd never be able to do it. He took our weaknesses and He worked with that human weakness and showed us how to do it. And God will help us to do it. Perfect joy is in receiving bad undeserved treatment with an interior disposition of love and abandonment to God's will, which permits it to happen. And the more I keep trusting in that and His mercy, the more I should be able to receive that mercy, as long as I am able to admit where I'm failing. That's the big thing—admit where I'm failing—because I can't get mercy that I don't think I need. I have to admit that I need mercy. "I'm not obedient, Lord. I'm not obedient." I need to work here. And the less I'm blind and the more I see myself, the more mercy. And I must trust God. See, that's the Divine Mercy message.

I'm doing what I want to do. I think the material things are so much easier to give up than that self-will. You know, the self-will is terribly hard to give up.

Maybe it would have surprised me years ago, before I thought about doing it, because it was hard, because obviously when I was younger it was the complete opposite. I started really realizing where the values were and where the worth was. The horses are wonderful creatures, and they're beautiful. They really are gorgeous creatures, but you know, what's really important and what's really going to help people? Really, let's help people get to heaven. And if you look at that, nothing else is really that important. What is it, whether you train horses, or have horses? It gets to be kind of empty;

if God wanted me to work with horses, that would be the way that I could help bring souls, but even then, Saint Paul talks about using the world as if you're not using it. And then at that point, I would have to have that same detachment of "I'm not here for the horses, I'm here for God, and I'm here for the people, and I'm here to help bring souls to Him and I'll try to be faithful and be a good horse trainer." But there's a detachment. I'm not here for the horses.

People thought that I was alive when I was with the horses. In a sense, it had become more fulfilling because I became better at it and I was better with the people and I was helping bring people to God that way. But the interest wasn't there in that my heart wasn't there. People didn't know that at all, but you know God had other things. Now there's more time for more serious responsibility and for things that can really make a difference and not just be for me. A lot of the time I spent with the horses, it was only for me—for my happiness and gratification. In the end, it wasn't for me anymore, which was a beautiful thing. But I can't live for me.

In the monastery we have a couple dogs, Melody and Harmony, to keep the watch. I take care of them—feed them, groom and trim them, and bathe them when they need it.

You get assigned those kinds of tasks. I really think it's a better policy most of the time to just let the community find out what you can do. If you have an ability, God will let them know if they need to know. It all started with trimming the dogs' nails because they didn't have anyone that could trim the dogs' nails and I could do that. They asked me if I could do it and that's how they found out I worked at a vet's for a while and I did dog training for a while, so they thought it was appropriate.

Before I came into the monastery, I had no real conception of what a religious, or a cloistered religious, or monastic life was like. Only here could I become what God wants me to be, and what I wanted to be, and what I'm called to be. I didn't even know what I wanted to be *was*, so here I found out what it was. The transformation is to become a religious, in this case, for me, to become a monastic, a religious contemplative spouse. I had some ideas of what it was—self-giving and those kinds of things—but to experience the monastic life and to live it, there is no way you could ever describe it without just living it.

It's rich. It's so deep and rich. And it's beautiful. Some people maybe think a lot when they're going to do something, "How's it going to be, how's it going to be?" Well, I didn't do that, and then when I came, I thought, "Wow!" It's like a beautiful old cathedral or an old building. It's almost like a work of art. The *life* is a work of art, this eight-hundred-year-old order. We have old prayers we've been saying from the start, and we have old traditions. We have a refectory! Everybody else has a kitchen but we have a refectory! The refectory is where we eat, and, primarily, the focus is on spiritual reading, not on eating. We happen to eat, but we're reading, doing the spiritual reading at the same time. Collation—the evening meal—that means small portion, so that means a smaller reading, a shorter reading.

It's a culture of its own. The monastic culture is a culture of its own. And we're following eight hundred years of tradition. We have to cook and clean and pick up after ourselves just like everybody else does, only hopefully we can do it for the spiritual reasons and for the love of God. That's what really makes the life because we all have the same needs in the end. But it's the dedication of *why am I here? What are we called to?* The spiritual idea is: I'm here for Jesus Christ and for His people.

We are separated from the world in order to be united with God and we need to have this barrier so that we can have our space to be with our Lord. We need to keep the distractions away, and yet at the same time, the Mother Abbess keeps us very up on what's going on and the needs and the prayers. Before our evening meal, the prayer requests are announced. We are told about all the earthquakes, and all the disasters, and the London bombings in the subway, and all the people who were stampeded and died, and in Iraq a little while ago, all those people were killed, and of course, the hurricanes. We hear about it all. I mean, I hear about this stuff more than when I was out there. We have very good connections.

We've set ourselves apart for God and for others, and from this place we can intercede so that, in the heart, the distance is not there. But there is a physical separation. We have to be wherever we are called to be. A mother, her place is with her children. If she wants to reconcile earth and heaven, she has got to do it where she is with her children. If she tried to go off and neglect her duties, if she spends a lot of time in prayer apart, that's not going to reconcile earth and heaven. It's where God wants you to be; if you're where He wants you to be, and you follow the duties with as much love and fidelity as possible, for love of Him and love of our neighbor, we all can do that reconciling of earth with heaven. But yet we have a special purpose: It's the special tool that our Lord has chosen. Contemplative nuns are supposed to be the heart of the Church. We are supposed to be there praying for and loving everybody.

This is a place dedicated to God. I really believe that's what the people who come here feel. I think that's the sense that the people have when they come here; they can tell this is a place of God. And that's a special and wonderful thing, to have a place that's dedicated to God. If I'm meant to be dedicated to God as His spouse, I need to be in a place like this. And it's got to be in the right place. Okay, we are Poor Clare Colettines, and there are Poor Clare Colettines in Cleveland. But He doesn't call you to be a Poor Clare Colettine even; He calls you to a certain monastery. This is the certain monastery that He decided, in His wisdom, that I belong here, and that this is the place that is the best for me.

I had to find my true home. And I found it, once I came here, because I was so miserable. And I've thought about that recently—I was miserable every other place I'd been. I can't imagine there being anything better than being the spouse of Jesus. I think it's a wonderful thing. And I know it's not for everybody, but I'm really glad that God picked me!

I wanted sisters when I was young. I had three older brothers. I prayed and I asked my mom and begged her and begged her and begged her for sisters. My mom had been told by the doctor, after me, "No more children." I think she almost died with each one of us. She was a person they thought never could have children. It was very hard on her. So the doctor said, "No more children," and my parents abided by that. I must have torn my mother's heart apart. I feel really bad about it now, although I didn't know and they didn't explain it to me. I was begging for a little sister because I wanted a sister to play with, not brothers. I think that was even a call back then, that I have sisters. So now I do!

I would probably be so completely miserable if I was anywhere else. Ever since I met here I've never liked any other place that I've ever been. I'm just not happy or satisfied anywhere else.

I will admit, I count for other people. I do. I think it's a wonderful thing and I think it's exciting. I'll count for other people and I look forward to the time of solemn vows, but I guess I am a real religious now. When you become a nun, when you take the vows of religion, you become a religious, and then every act you do becomes an act of religion, and everything we do in the cloister, or a sister out there who took the vows does, every little tiny act you do is an act of religion and it makes it even more possibly beneficial or detrimental if you don't act well. But I wanted this, to be able to represent God's people and to help God to bless His people, and to be our Lord's spouse—all of this is part of the same thing. I wanted that very badly.

The solemn vows will be a wonderful thing because it's permanent and there is a greater responsibility as far as the Divine Office; that's where you really become bound that you must pray this Divine Office. And then there is the Consecration of Virgins at that time, too. And you receive a ring and that ring says you are our Lord's spouse forever. I look forward to that very much, but my dream was to be a religious, and not just to be a religious, but to be a good religious. I think I have a long way to go to be a good religious, but I am a religious and that's what I wanted so, so, so badly.

I have to say I'm really plain Jane. I think that God speaks to me in the pots and pans. I think God is training me through the everyday life. I just need to be faithful where I am. There was a movie about Saint Faustina. They said she was a true mystic in that she gave up everything to be united with Christ. So there it is. A true mystic is someone who gives up everything to be united with Christ, and so in that way we all can be mystics. I don't think you're going to find a lot of experiences, and I don't think you're going to find many people that would want to talk about them if they did have them.

But the big experiences—let's live the life, and let's love God and neighbor. And I think God talks to me through all the people and through all the experiences, and that's how He teaches me and talks to me. It's not like you hear words. Sometimes you wish you did so that you would know more clearly, but I guess I hear my words through my superior, and in that way I know clearly God's will.

We're all mystics. We give up everything to be united with Christ. Let's just live the spiritual life. We're just simple Franciscans. Let's just live our Franciscan life. It's all about love and it's all about self-giving. And to be serious about living and being what we're supposed to be and about our duties and responsibilities that are very serious. But to me, God speaks to me in the daily life, just what I'm doing and what the people are doing and what I can learn and what I can convert and change in my life.

Now, my focus is on trying to acquire real virtue. And I guess that's maybe why I'm not counting days for myself—because I'm really trying to be authentically what I professed. That's a lot of work, and I need to do a lot of changing so that I am really a good representation as Christ's spouse. "Through love you will reconcile earth with heaven." The more I love, the more that earth and heaven will be brought together. God is love. I need to become like Him. I have a long way to go, so I'm really trying to work on that.

Part I

The Call

1

Community Life

Each person has her own responsibility for how she chooses her attitude toward others. Happiness is a choice, and we can't blame one another if the sister isn't the way I would like her to be. Even if you feel annoyance toward someone, you don't have to let that annoyance wreck your day. We choose how we're going to spend our day, and we can choose to think kindly of another person when we're annoyed. God gave us a free will. I think after living here for thirty-two years, you grow to understand those things better. It's a hard life in many ways. You can choose to live the life joyfully; but you can become bitter, too, because you don't have the things you had before, and it's possible that you make your vows and later you start to regret it, but that's all within yourself. You have to come to the realization that it's my fault if I'm not happy, and I can choose to be happy with this life.

Sister Mary Gemma of Our Lady of the Angels

After an early nomadic life, Sister Joan Marie has aged into adulthood and seniority within the same fourteen-acre enclosure. Decade after decade elapses, and Sister Joan Marie rarely leaves the Corpus Christi Monastery campus. She knows that she will die here, unless, she teases, they kick her out. "They overlook a lot, I hope," she says. "You know you're not under that tension. You know they're not going to send you away. They'd like to . . ." she trails off.

Sister Joan Marie ranks eldest in the community by longevity, having entered the Corpus Christi Monastery in 1950, before any other current member. She moved here at age seventeen; now eighty-one years old, she recounts her first impressions when she walked into the monastery, when life as a Poor Clare began: In the reverential moment when she first approached the tabernacle housing the exposed eucharist in the public chapel, she heard the novices and nuns who had already made temporary vows and final vows singing from their hidden choir chapel, which faces the public chapel but is separated and hidden from it by the sanctuary (past a swinging gold gate at the Communion rail that separates the nave, where the churchgoers sit, from the altar of sacrifice and altar of repose, where the priest offers Mass and the Blessed Sacrament is exposed). Sister Joan Marie and the other aspiring postulants walked single file, past the stained-glass windows that depict scenes from the lives of Christ, Saint Francis, and Saint Clare on both sides of the public chapel and under the frescoes with gold detail. The young women knelt before the Blessed Sacrament. "We were just overawed, and so all you could think about was, 'God and me,'" Sister Joan Marie says. "That's all you saw. I just thought I was in heaven. I just thought, 'There's God and here's me. Nobody else. Nothing else. I left everything.' And in a way it's true, but not quite so romantic. But I was in seventh heaven.

"I thought this is it. Live happily ever after. Oh dear. It was so different than anything you had imagined. When you get here, you realize more and more every day, I've still got a lot to learn."

Virginia (a pseudonym Sister Joan Marie selected for herself to represent life before she was assigned a religious name), was led to her new quarters, a cell that measured eleven feet, eight inches by six feet, nine inches. Seeing little more than a bed with a straw-stuffed mattress, she says, "That woke me up a little bit." She changed into the outfit for first-year postulants and then wound her way back through the corridors from the novitiate wing of the monastery to the parlor, where she met her parents and siblings to say goodbye. For the first time, the metal grille separated Virginia from her family and from the rest of the world. Debuting her uniform further startled the dream. "Here I thought I was all grown up, leaving my home and family," she says. "And when I came in with these cuffs and a big bonnet, I wonder, 'Am I a baby again?'" she laughs. Her mother told her she looked like the Dutch girl from a popular advertising campaign.

Before she entered the monastery, Virginia pictured life as a cloistered nun. She thought of Saint Colette, a hermit. "Of course, I was young and idealistic," she says. "I thought it would just be me and God. Nobody else. I didn't know about community. I had a lot to learn. You're that age, you're pretty idealistic, and even my parents—I don't think they knew exactly what I was getting into. We trusted the Church. We were so enthused by the Church, being converts."

Raised in an environment of upheaval that started with her father's job loss, followed by episodes of migrant family life and then periodic separations from her parents, Virginia believed her mother and father hoped she would choose her own religious preference. She took cues from her spiritual surrogate and stand-in mother figure—her maternal grandmother; Virginia claimed the Protestant faith but, after a successful campaign by her older sister, was baptized into the Catholic Church. Two years later, she joined the Poor Clare Colettine Order. Monastic life—her new life—seemed like a riddle. And she lacked the code to decipher it. "I just never knew what was going to happen next," she says.

Sister Joan Marie did not grasp the meaning of every custom or comprehend the significance of all the events she witnessed or participated in. She shares an anecdote about the predicament of observing monastic silence while adapting to her new culture: Every day, the nuns lined up in the refectory to confess their faults and weaknesses of that day before their community. Sister Joan Marie remembers standing with the other nuns, waiting her turn to step into the center of the room; the Mother Abbess and Vicaress sat at the head table at one end of the room, and the other nuns lined the two tables that ran the lengths of the room, their backs to the walls. Each nun stood before the Mother Abbess and recounted to her community her imperfections—confessing, for instance, if she accidentally broke a dish.

After the public admission, each nun prostrated herself on the floor facing the head table. Because they lived in such close quarters, Sister Joan Marie says, no disclosure was truly a revelation. "They knew anyway," she says. "It wasn't anything new." If a nun confessed that she forgot to perform a duty, she was given a broken clothespin to wear—presumably a symbol of the omission and a visual cue to remember the next time. If a nun was concerned she might have forgotten to mention a sin of omission or commission, she wore a "forget hat." Sister Joan Marie remembers one nun in her eighties always took the forget hat. Habitually, the elder nun recited her list of faults, adding, "Something else I forgot." A few minutes later, when she bent forward to eat her soup, the hat inevitably fell into the soup. "She forgot she had the hat on!" Sister Joan Marie says. "It was so funny!"

Following the communal ritual, one of the nuns walked to a chart and flipped the numbers. Sister Joan Marie assumed the nun was tallying for the scorecard the collective faults and weaknesses confessed that day. "Later on," Sister Joan Marie says, "this other postulant came to me and said, 'What does that number mean?' I said, 'I really don't know.' I said, 'There's some things you just don't ask about.' Well, she was smart enough she asked the superior, which I was afraid to do because everything was so mysterious to me." The postulant relayed to Virginia what she had learned; the number denoted the temperature outdoors so the nuns knew how to layer up for their manual labor in the gardens. "I was amazed it was so simple a thing!" Sister Joan Marie says. "I thought for sure it had to do with those faults or something mysterious!"

Virginia's new home, with its foreign routines and formal construct, baffled her. "It was so different than anything you had imagined," Sister Joan Marie says. "I guess that was good. In a way, if you see all that's coming, you can't adjust very well. I would have liked to have some relaxation. There was none. Like when you go home, you can relax. But there was no going home. There was no time when you could just be yourself. You were kind of on edge every minute. There's advantages to being young. I couldn't have done it later. I would have been too set in my ways by that time." Virginia arrived at the monastery directly from high school. She was accustomed to a structure bracketed by bells, and so she had no trouble responding when the monastery's bells prompted her to move on to the next activity—prayers, or work, or recreation. "You know the schedule is pretty tight," she says. "But in the evening, I would have liked to relax. You know, when you came home from school, you could be yourself, you know. You didn't have to be on edge. Well, there was no relaxing because you had work you were supposed to do. You had something you were always supposed to do—except when you went to bed; you were so tired, you dropped. What got me was there was no free time where you could just be yourself because I felt they were all looking at me, watching every move."

As the youngest member of the novitiate, Virginia led the group's processions into and out of the chapel. Another postulant directed Virginia to pick up all the "dust fuzzies" she saw on the ground, for love of God and mortification. This spiritual act, she was told, would prompt other young women to join the monastery. Whenever the postulant pointed out a dust ball for Virginia to stop and pick up, the line was forced to halt behind her in a pileup of postulants. "I just wasn't ready for all those little things, details," Sister Joan Marie says. "She was trying to help, but it just discouraged me because I couldn't understand why you had to pick them up." Virginia learned the postulants saved the "dust fuzzies" for Feast Days, when they counted them up, and she prayed that each ball of dust represented one woman with a religious vocation who would be called forth and hear her calling to enter a religious community. "I know it seems crazy," Sister Joan Marie says. "It seemed crazy to me, too." Still assimilating her conversion from Protestant to Catholic, Sister Joan Marie was moved by the teachings of Saint Therese of Lisieux, a contemplative nun nicknamed "the Little Flower of Jesus." The canonized Carmelite summarized the vocation of the monastic life not as a series of heroic acts of virtue, but as a process of honoring God in little acts that demonstrated great and steady devotion. "She always did something for souls," Sister Joan Marie said. "That's all we've got to offer—little tiny things. We don't have big martyrdoms."

Still, the senior postulant's unsolicited guidance frustrated Virginia, who eventually took the matter to her Novice Mistress. The Novice Mistress agreed the other novitiate was too "zealous," and she permitted Virginia to overlook the dust fuzzies when she was leading a procession. Virginia could, however, continue the practice of collecting wayward dust for prayers at other times, the Novice Mistress said, when she found her itinerary freer. "I could talk to her," Sister Joan Marie says of her Novice Mistress. "I was close to her because she was like my mother. Especially at that age, I needed somebody."

Sister Joan Marie says she was "ready to be formed" when she arrived, but she was also worn down by notations of her missteps. "They saw all your faults and all your defects," she says. "That's what they wanted to point out. They say the novitiate is the 'seed time' in life. They want to point it out so that you get a little better before you get with the professed nuns. Of course, the professed weren't all saints, either, but it seemed to us they were because we didn't recreate with them much."

Incongruous as this life seemed to Virginia, an outsider to the Catholic faith and a rookie at the monastery, she feared that she would be found lacking and would be asked to leave the premises. "I was just so afraid. They didn't realize how scared I was," Sister Joan Marie says. She witnessed, in Clothing Ceremonies, postulants become novices, receiving the habit and a religious name, only to be asked to leave months or years later. One novice refused to talk during the community's one-hour social recreation each day. The girl was moody, Sister Joan Marie says. "Well, that wouldn't work in a community. She got sent home. When she got sent home, I thought, 'Oh, I'm next!' As a novice, you're supposed to get a little better—at some things, anyway. I didn't either, but they kept me somehow. I guess they knew; they knew I didn't want to go back to what I came from."

Sister Maria Deo Gratias says,

Our love for God spills out, and it spills out on our sisters in community. When you have love, you can't keep it to yourself. We take care of each other's needs, but when we're taking care of each other's needs, we're taking care of the needs of Christ in that person. There's that perception of that other sister as the body of Christ and that whole mystical body idea. In community, we show our love for God by how we love our sisters. We form a happy family, in the sense that the family is a group of adult women responding to God together. And people are different. They have different personalities. But that's kind of like a given. You know you're not going to find a perfect human on earth.

Even in a cloistered monastery, where like-minded women convene, for life, after internalizing their common beliefs, and aiming together toward holiness and perfection, there are conflicts. "You know, each person is so different, unique, and then sometimes we clash on each other; and sometimes we agree," Sister Joan Marie says. "Most of the time we agree."

"I think men religious have different struggles than what women religious would have," says Sister Mary Gemma. "A woman by nature likes to arrange things and have her kitchen the way she wants, but in community you have to learn to let go of that. I think that's one of the hardest things—you aren't the woman of the home. There are twenty other women. That's something you struggle with. It's more of a struggle when you first come. You have to let go of the way you want things to be, otherwise you're just not going to get along." Although Sister Mary Gemma has never heard "a bad word" uttered in the monastery, she adds, "I would say probably what I found most surprising was that once in a while there would be a couple of sisters that would get into it with each other. Then later, I found that there's so much forgiveness here. Later, that's what struck me more than anything."

The inherent tensions that can fester within an enclosed community have been mythologized in oral tradition. The stories are like fables, or parables, with morals. Sister Mary Gemma shares a story passed along from the early days of the Corpus Christi Monastery's founding through the generations of novices and nuns: Two young nuns were assigned to work in the garden together, but they could never agree on anything, namely how they should conduct their work. One day, one of the nuns introduced a novel attempt at diplomacy, to quash the inevitable quarreling. She walked out to the garden and greeted the other nun. She had either filled her pockets with marbles in the monastery, or she picked up stones off the ground. She proceeded to place one marble or stone after another into her mouth, as Sister Mary Gemma says, "so that she would keep her mouth shut, because she had a hard time controlling her temper. In charity, she thought she had better put something in her mouth to remind her to be quiet when she didn't agree with something. She recognized that it was wrong of her to get so upset about things, and since she couldn't control herself that way, she did it another way."

This "real old story that goes way back," Sister Mary Gemma says, has been told and retold. Its themes strike at the core of the nuns' values: Discipline. Obedience. Silence. Love. Selflessness. Peacemaking. It illustrates the virtue of caring for someone else over the desire to express one's own opinions, or get one's own way. "Those are the kind of thing we share at recreation," Sister Mary Gemma says. "The sisters that have been here longer like to tell the stories that bring out the foibles of one another. It's a joyful acknowledgment. We're acknowledging that we're all struggling. You can look back and laugh, even though something was so hard at the time; and yet you can look back and laugh."

Sister Mary Gemma sees humor and truth in this now remote but still poignant teaching moment. "The thing is," she says, "we didn't choose each other. God chose. God chose who we were going to live with the rest of our lives and that's where we say, especially if women can get along together, can struggle together and get along, that shows the grace of God is there. It's God's grace that makes a marriage work. It's God's grace that helps us in community to be faithful and get along. Like marriage, you have to work at it."

"But our response to other people's personality is because of the love of God," says the Vicaress, Sister Maria Deo Gratias. "It's a little different than the divided life of a married another person. For us, we're all looking at God together. That would be a way of picturing it. All of us stand together looking in the same direction, focusing our life in the same direction and it's like a circle. We're all standing in a circle and the center is Christ and the more we come closer to Christ, the closer we are to each other.

"We are different people and we do think differently. But there is that unity—that core unity—that holds us together and it's a beautiful experience to live in community. The give and take that we learned as a kid, we apply that here." Having lived in another religious order before entering the Corpus Christi Monastery, Sister Maria Deo Gratias says this community exhibits a "beautiful grace," embracing the "essentials that we all treasure so much"— the same values and a "centeredness on living the life." "You understand that you're bound to have people make different choices, but our community is very united in our basic values—very, very much so, more than other communities, and I've experienced many of them. And that's a plus for us."

Sister Maria Benedicta first joined an active religious order, living with that community for five years before entering the Corpus Christi Monastery. "God has a special place for everybody," she says. "It's not just—religious life, go join wherever you want. He has a special place and a special purpose. And every community has what is called a charism—it's like their spirit— and you're created to be in that community. You have that spirit. God has given that to you. It's your home. It's where you will fit, where you will become holy. It's where my spirituality matches that of the community so we can strive together to holiness. Not that we're all the same because we're not. But we have the common spirituality and charism to strive together toward God."

Sister Maria Deo Gratias explains:

The higher you come into the spiritual life, the more you're able to accept differences because the spiritual life expands you. Whereas if you have a very narrow way of thinking, it all has to fit in that narrow little package, and if it doesn't, then you break out in some way—impatience, or you submerge yourself, or whatever. But the deeper you come into union with God, you come to accept people the way they are. There doesn't have to be any breakage. You can have union in diversity.

And we know—we certainly know—that our sister is striving to do the best she can. She falls short just like I fall short so therefore we don't take that amiss or against her; it's just we have a greater compassion to say, "I know what you mean, Sister. You fell today. I fell yesterday." And it's just that type of it's no big deal about it, but we do strive together and that's why at times, we hold ourselves accountable to say—every evening before collation, we say—"I'm sorry." We say that as a group because we know that we are human. We annoy. And we may not even know the annoyances we give another person. And it may be that on a particular day I didn't annoy someone, but I say sorry for anytime that I have. And you always are crystal clear with God.

For Sister Joan Marie, monastic life jarred her sense of self. Beyond the enclosure and the grille, in the chaotic world she inhabited until the age of seventeen, she was regarded as upright, a model student, daughter, and sister. "I think the novitiate was awful hard—being young, partly, being in a new culture entirely," Sister Joan Marie says. "Everybody's praising me out there. Before Vatican II, it was like coming to a completely different milieu. Well, when I got here, it seemed like everybody was on me for doing the wrong thing at the wrong time. So it was hard to adjust. In fact I don't know if I ever did. I got sick, mostly. Instead of adjusting, I got sick, the one way to adjust. I didn't do it on purpose, but God works it out."

She had endured much in her youth, upended by her family's many moves, jostled by her father's mental instability and the needs of her mother and siblings; she worked to protect her family from self-destructing. Before her parents married, her maternal grandparents predicted doom for the couple. She learned from her parents that they met when her father eyed her mother, a sorority girl in college, at a social. "I'll take that Kansas girl," he said. They married in a civil union; Sister Joan Marie's maternal grandparents were mortified by their quick pairing. Another daughter had married her high school sweetheart, and they "didn't think this could turn out."

Virginia's early years were sweet enough. She remembers visiting her father's office building in Detroit and looking down on the city below. "He would show me these little cars, and I thought they were toy cars. I soon learned it was because we were high up. I was just a baby," she says. She smiles at the memory and her juvenile mind's attempts to consolidate her perceptions and interpret her world. As a youngster, she and her older brother played the Lone Ranger and Tonto. Virginia always wanted to be the Lone Ranger and say, "Hi-yo, Silver!" Her brother relegated her to the role of Tonto. She aspired to become a "cowboy." The family vacationed at their beach house in Canada, and her father took her into the water to teach her how to "ride the waves." To Virginia, the phrase was married to the world of horseback riding; she tried to mount a wave, as if it were a horse. Her father laughed. Her family was "well off," Sister Joan Marie says, and each year she was proud to add one new doll to her collection, a gift from her parents.

If her grandparents' undisguised displeasure at her parents' union was not an omen, an ill-conceived object lesson at Christmas foreshadowed impending turmoil. A toddler at the time, Virginia watched her mother set the holiday cookies on the kitchen table, out of the child's reach. Virginia realized, though, that if she yanked on the tablecloth, she could get at the cookies. At first, her parents laughed at her cleverness, but they tried to stop it soon enough. "Well, Mother didn't like that because all the dishes came down," she says. "But I kept doing that because I got the cookie." Weeks shy of Christmas, her parents informed Virginia that she would not receive any presents if she kept pulling the cookies and dishes off the table; she would get switches, for spankings, instead. Her mischievous efforts continued to be rewarded, with cookies obtained. So Virginia persisted. And she wreaked havoc on her mother's dishware. On Christmas morning, Virginia watched her father hand presents to her older sister and her older brother. Then he reached behind the tree for a package, swaddled in newspaper, for Virginia. Inside the wrapping were switches. "Mother said she would never do that again to any kid because I was crying all day," Sister Joan Marie says. "Mostly, I was crying because Santa knew my sins. Santa knew how bad I was. I didn't mind the family knowing what was going on because they know me. But a stranger—Santa of all people—knew." Her mother tried to console her daughter with a gift of clothesline and clothespins so that the little girl could be like her mother. "It didn't help at all," she says. "I just cried."

When her father lost his job, Virginia experienced her family's downward spiral as an economic crisis. Her father began to unravel. When he filed for bankruptcy, signs emerged of his fragile grip on reality, his declining mental and emotional state. One day, the family packed their car and abandoned their home and most of their belongings. Her mother sold a few items to neighbors before the move, thinking she would replace what she sold after they resettled; she could not know then that they would never establish a stable family life again. "In those days that was a great disgrace," she says of her father's bankruptcy. Since Sister Joan Marie's older sister helped their father pack the car, Sister Joan Marie remembers they found room for all of her sister's collections. The car packed full, Sister Joan Marie was told to select from her possessions only what she could hold on her lap. She took one doll from her collection.

In time, Sister Joan Marie gleaned the backstory of her father's sad life: He was one of twelve children, and his mother died in childbirth when he was eight years old. His older sisters took care of the infant. Meanwhile, he and the other middle children were neglected. "Nobody loves you but your mother at that age," Sister Joan Marie says. Her paternal grandfather was portrayed in these stories as holding his children to impossible standards; he had overcome the dark years of the Depression in spite of the extra mouths and because of the many hands, his offspring toiling on his potato farm. "He worked them to death," Sister Joan Marie says of her paternal grandfather. Her father bonded with one of his brothers, who got a job on the railroad feeding coal to motor the train. In another tragic blow, her father's favorite brother was killed in a train accident. Still an adolescent, he ran away during World War II, lying about his age so that he could enlist in the military. A country boy with an aversion to rules, he clashed with authority. He made whiskey out of potato peelings and was about to face the expected repercussions from the military for his misbehavior when another brother who was "good to him" testified that he had lied about his age to get into the army. He was discharged.

Like his siblings, Sister Joan Marie's father did not want to work as a farmer, a result of their hard labor in their father's fields. "My father especially wanted to be a big businessman, and that was his ideal," Sister Joan Marie says. "He had worked himself up to this." After the financial collapse, Virginia bounced between the family's temporary shelters, including a campground one summer in Indiana, and her maternal grandmother's home in Kansas. At times, it seemed she was a character in a fairytale, inhabiting a campground complete with a backyard forest to explore, and a Hansel and Gretel–like cottage whose tenant kept pet raccoons and raised a blue jay named "Perculator." The owner trained the bird with milk and bread to land on her finger. "To us it was like a miracle," Sister Joan Marie says. Other times, Virginia was reunited with a patriarch who was succeeding either at business or at drink.

Her mother taught her children the Golden Rule. "As long as we were with her, it was okay," Sister Joan Marie says. Her father often left to search for work; his reappearance disrupted the calm and was "emotionally upsetting," Sister Joan Marie says. "And Mother always said, 'Forgive him. Forgive him.'" Once, her parents left their three children for a few days with a caretaker, maybe a neighbor, Sister Joan Marie says. Her parents did not explain in terms that registered to their youngest child where they were going, or why. "I think they said they'd give us each a quarter if we were good," she says. She doesn't remember receiving a quarter. "I don't think we were good."

Her father, never satisfied as an employee, "wanted to be on his own," Sister Joan Marie says. "He didn't want to be under anybody. He was kind of a tyrant." Virginia was terrified of her father. Her mother, it seemed, could talk to him, even during his rants. She warned her husband she was going to record his outbursts and play them back when he was sober and spent. "She should have," Sister Joan Marie says. "He liked to talk. When he got upset, he liked to talk. Just crazy. Wasn't reasonable. Unreasonable. But she could control him, pretty much. I think she was able to. But I was affected more than she. Because he would take it all out on her, it kind of got me."

Sister Joan Marie believes her father was a complicated figure. "Sometimes he would be so good," she says. "He would always stop on the highway if he saw anyone in trouble; he would stop to help. I guess he must have been real hungry when he was little because he always thought he should feed everybody. He wouldn't give you an ice cream cone unless he gave the whole group a cone. One time it was raining and we were soaked and we had to stay in the tent—we had a big tent that we went around with—and he got us all suckers. I think he came with suckers and it broke the day a little bit. He was real good with children. He always liked children. He had a lot of good points. But the sickness got him. When you're discouraged and it goes into depression, then you seem to take it out on the ones you love the most. It's terrible. But that's what happens. Suffering from Dad, I think we naturally turned more toward God because there was nothing else to turn to. Mother always said, 'Don't tell anybody, don't tell anybody,' because at that time you didn't have these groups—support groups. There was nobody we could talk to."

Sister Joan Marie remembers that her mother loved reading the melancholy Old Testament books of Job (the story of the holiest man alive, who experienced an epic plight, with his loved ones killed and his fortune erased, in a series of temptations to curse God) and Ruth (a widow who refused to follow her mother-in-law to her homeland, found love with a rich relative of her in-laws, and famously said, "Entreat me not to leave you, or to turn back from following you; for wherever you go, I will go; and wherever you lodge, I will lodge; your people shall be my people, and your God, my God").

With no one to talk to, no one to help carry her burdens, Sister Joan Marie turned to her dog, Suzy. She told her pet her worries.

It was in her maternal grandmother's care and in the United Brethren denomination, and their small, poor church with its conspicuous crack in the wall, where Sister Joan Marie felt safe and her faith took root. Sister Joan

Marie says her parents did not want to be "prejudiced," and so they left the matter of religion to their children's efforts. "I think they were hoping that we would choose some religion. My mother said she just thought it would take. She had been brought up in it. In college, I guess she just got that idea, that you should choose your own religion, you should bring your children up to choose. She was religious but she didn't know that she had to train; she didn't realize that you have to get some training."

Virginia was often anxious for her mother. Once, her mom disappeared in the middle of the night. Virginia screamed at her father, demanding to know what he had done to her. He laughed. The following day, Virginia was relieved that her mother had given birth, which explained why her mother had sent Virginia and her brother outdoors and out from underfoot in the previous months. Virginia's fear for her family grew, and this was justi- fied: Her father, without any means and one more mouth to feed, experi- enced a psychological break. He told his family he was going to kill himself. He raged at them. One day, he held his newborn out a second-story window and threatened to drop the boy. He ended up carrying the child outside and walking the boy around the block barefoot. Virginia's mother sent her to follow them. "He went into different cars to try to take them away, but he couldn't get them to start," she says. "He didn't have the key, I guess. But then he came back. Thank God he came back."

Sister Joan Marie thinks now that her father was motivated to upset her mother. One day he held a knife to his wife's throat. He told his children he was going to kill their mother. The police were phoned, and Virginia's father was taken to a mental hospital. Asked if she would allow the institu- tion to perform a surgery—perhaps a lobotomy—"so that he became like a vegetable," as Sister Joan Marie remembers it, "Mother would not allow that. She would not allow that. We all thought she should. She said, 'It changes their personality, and they're no longer human because they've got no pas- sions. They've got no passions.'"

Virginia's mother tried to console her children, saying their father prob- ably would not have acted on his threat to kill her. "Mother said he probably wouldn't have done it, just like he wouldn't have killed himself because he just would threaten. I couldn't understand why she would say that when she was pinned against the wall.

"Her love was too great, I guess. Some said she should have thought of the children. Well, she did think of us. I used to say, 'Divorce him. Divorce him.' She said he would just come after us because that's all he had. He didn't have a mother. His only love was for his family, really. But somehow it went haywire."

Her maternal grandmother's faith was a haven, cushioning Virginia through childhood. When her older sister enrolled in flight school, she converted to Catholicism after long talks with a priest-pilot. Virginia's sister began evangelizing her, which Virginia construed as an assault on her carefully guarded sphere. Virginia cried when her older sister professed she also believed in Darwinism, not the creationism that Virginia's grandparents instilled in her. In retrospect, Sister Joan Marie describes the thirteen-year-old version of herself as having "Protestant prejudice"; she was wary of genuflecting, which looked like the worship of Mary. Invited to attend her sister's Catholic church for Mass with her mother and two brothers, they laughed at the family convert who they said appeared to be swatting at flies as she made the Sign of the Cross. Embarrassed by their inappropriate responses, Virginia's sister said they were not welcome to worship with her anymore.

Aside from the theological disparities, Virginia liked her grandmother's church, a cornerstone of her upbringing. Her sister argued that she should not choose a religion based on feelings, but rather with logic. In the end, she gave up on Virginia and stopped arguing. She advised her little sister to find a priest who had the patience to explain theological matters to her. Virginia did seek out a priest at a local church, who explained genuflecting by association: "Now, you love your own mother," Sister Joan Marie recalls him telling her. The priest said that genuflecting was a sign of respect, that every other religion was founded by men, but Catholicism was founded by Christ. He suggested that Virginia pray, on her knees, for the gift of faith. Virginia walked out of the church, stopped on the sidewalk, a few feet from traffic, and she knelt on the pavement and prayed. She immediately wanted to be baptized into the Catholic faith. Her own religious fervor as a convert—the early risings for Mass and recitations of the rosary—attracted followers in her mother, her brothers, and even her father.

At the age of fifteen, Virginia was baptized. Moved by the poverty and simplicity of Saint Francis and his followers, the high schooler studied Latin at a junior college, took a job her sister lined up working for a two-person chemical company (helping test water on farms to be sure it was safe to drink), and read aloud at nights to her mother about Brother Juniper in *The Little Flowers of St. Francis*. They delighted in the stories of Brother Juniper, who was "always doing odd things," Sister Joan Marie says. As Saint Francis described him: "Would to God, my brothers, I had a whole forest of such Junipers." Once, Friar Juniper was asked to prepare a meal for the rest of his community. But because he considered food preparation an undesirable interruption that took friars away from their prayers, he produced a soup on a massive scale and in a less than conventional manner—"the fowls in their feathers, the eggs in their shells"—in the hopes the food would last two weeks. His time and efforts proved a waste of time; when "he set down his hotch-potch" in front of the other friars, "there was never a hog in the Campagna of Rome so hungry that he could have eaten it," according to *The Little Flowers of St. Francis.* Chastised initially for his abuse of resources, Brother Juniper was later commended for his simplicity and charity. "All those little stories were cute. It struck me, the simplicity of it. I wanted to be like Saint Francis," Sister Joan Marie says. She toted bread to work and then tossed it to the birds in the hopes of communing with nature. Drawn to the contemplative life of Saint Francis that was mirrored by Saint Clare, founder of the Poor Clare Order, Sister Joan Marie says, "I knew I wanted to be a Poor Clare right away."

Virginia's father was, at that point, baptized as a Catholic and focused on his next business venture. He worked two shifts at two newspapers as a linotype operator to raise capital for a system that would render obsolete shoveling coal to power trains—the job his brother had been working when he died. Her father carved the designs for his inventions in potatoes.

Although he was a new convert, Sister Joan Marie remembers that her father tried to dissuade her from a religious vocation. He told his daughter that underground tunnels connected nuns and priests. He drove her to a monastery surrounded by a high wall, and Sister Joan Marie remembers him saying, "You're going to be behind that wall. You won't be able to come out." It did look awful to Virginia. And yet she applied to join four Poor Clare communities. A friend of hers—Sister Rose—had entered the Corpus Christi Monastery in Rockford, Illinois, one year prior, and because Sister Rose was considered by members of the community to be very devout, Sister Joan Marie says she was invited to join without the requisite visit. The Mother Abbess only gave her one mandate: She had to wait two years from her baptism as a Catholic to enter. "They took me, thinking I would be that good," Sister Joan Marie says of the nuns' esteem for Sister Rose. "I wasn't quite that good. She was real vivacious. One sister told me, 'You're just the opposite and you'll never last.' Big help! The ones that didn't want you to go really helped you more." Sister Joan Marie says the harsh words gave her more resolve to endure the trials.

In their cumulative centuries of life within the Corpus Christi Monastery, as adherents to a lifestyle that Sister Mary Monica describes as a "work of art," the nuns have developed philosophies about community living, as well as opinons about who is capable to endure it. Sister Sarah Marie says that the strict rules and intense emotional demands of mandated silence and interrupted sleep would self-select members who must be completely normal, immune from psychological abnormality. "I think when you enter an enclosure, if you're abnormal, it's going to come out if there's something wrong," she says, laughing. "In the active world, you can keep it under for a little bit, if you've got a little psychological disorder. Not here! Not here.

"That's why, I mean, when people think they must be a little bit dingy to be back there, it's just the opposite," she says. "We're more psychologically healthy here than most people out there because you have to be, because you get a little ding-dong here. See, there has to be that calling, there has to be that calling from our Lord for this particular life, this vow of enclosure.

"Sometimes we get ones that come here and think they have a calling. And that's what you should do if you feel that you're being called—well, come!" Sister Sarah Marie says. "Find out if this is where our Lord's calling you. That's the only way you're going to know. And after a couple of days, if they say, 'Gee, I miss going to Wal-Mart,' well, it's kind of an indication, because we're not going to keep someone here if they're dying to go to Wal-Mart, you know! Well, then, maybe this isn't where God is calling you to."

In a separate, later conversation, Mother Miryam says that a young woman called to religious life could really miss Wal-Mart but still belong in a cloistered monastery. Mother Miryam remembers, as a novice, glancing toward the wall encompassing the cloister's acreage, hearing the traffic, and wishing she could hop in a car and drive somewhere. Anywhere. She, too, believes, though, that psychological disorders and emotional issues make for a difficult pairing with religious life. Years might lapse before a disorder emerges or a repressed issue becomes visible, she says, but it will become apparent in the enclosure. Mother Miryam gives an example: Humans, in general, need self-esteem; in the close quarters of a cloister, if a woman has poor self-esteem, she might think another nun is ignoring her, or trying to hurt her, or doing something to get under her skin, when, in fact, the woman has not even registered on the other nun's mental radar. Mother Miryam says that God often works not on the spiritual level, but on the human level.

> It's like in relationships on the human level. You really can romanticize, "I love God, I love God, I love God." But He says if you don't love your neighbor, you don't love me. So on that level, you can't kid yourself. You can't kid yourself, "I'm just going to go pray and I love God so much," if you can't get along. And of course there are going to be times when it's going to be hard to get along. That's just normal, because we're all different. But you have to grow in that. You've got to grow in tolerance. You've got to grow in sensitivity. You've got to grow in gentleness—all these things will make it easier for others. You've got to grow in self-sacrifice. Are these on the human level? Yes, they are. They are on the human level. But you're lifting yourself to another level. That's the only way we can really grow is on this human level. A wounded person—maybe they can't do a lot of that. But maybe God will use them. He'll work with them and sanctify them in their own way. You never know.

It may take years for someone to arrive at a moment of self-honesty and clarity, Mother Miryam says, following a pattern of problems relating to others in community that actually points to a problem that needs to be resolved within oneself. Mother Miryam believes the full picture of these hiccups in relationships can emerge only with an admission of one's own emotional hangups and shortcomings; this acceptance of one's defects can allow one to move past them, no longer under the illusion of perfection, or the powerlessness due to denial.

Those who are mistrustful by nature remain mistrustful in the cloister, and the same holds true with social butterflies, confrontational personalities, and critical spirits. It is easy to conceive of ways that these qualities and imperfections can affect others in the cloister. I became privy to the magnification of such traits creating tensions—with conflict and drama inserted in community life—when one nun pulled me aside in the kitchen during one of my visits to tell me she did not know what Mother Miryam wanted to tell me, but she thought I should learn the story of the statue overlooking the gardens. Mother Miryam happened to walk in as I was trying to clarify what she wanted me to ask the Mother Abbess, and the nun in question was startled and flustered, as if she were being discovered mid-transgression. She put her finger to her lips, indicating silence, and her face turned red. I forgot, in subsequent visits, to ask about the statue. A few months later, the same nun talked with me one-on-one in the parlor and told me that other nuns had a question for me, and so she would take notes and relay my words to them; I suggested, instead, that she retrieve the Mother Abbess, the authority of the community, the elected channel of practically all external communications, so that she could take part in the conversation. The nun informed me she did not want to bother the Mother Abbess. Later, I explained the interaction with Mother Miryam, and I learned that even in an atmosphere of monastic silence the telephone game emerges as a means of moving information, stirring conflict. Mother Miryam told me there is a saying, "the angel afar, and the devil within." I am sure that I appeared shocked by her use of the phrase. Mother Miryam quickly added that each individual possesses her own set of issues that she must contend with; all are fallen. She quoted the Catholic Church's historical perspective, that "holiness is wholeness," a notion that was finally—and rightly, Mother Miryam says—dismissed in light of the examples of "wounded saints" who overcame many weaknesses and flaws in their struggle for, and attainment of, holiness.

Vicaress Maria Deo Gratias suggests another prerequisite for adapting to cloistered communal living: A woman must be able to detach from her own vantage point, her own personal desires. Joining a religious order might imply that a woman is willing to disavow her own interests and cede her will to the vows and the direction of her superiors. But Sister Maria Deo Gratias believes, from her interactions with young women visiting the monastery, that today's youth are deprived of skills such as negotiating relationships, which are essential for community living. "Let's say a person comes in and they find in the novitiate a novitiate sister she clashes with personality-wise. And it isn't that either one of them is causing it, that's just the natural way it is; then because they're not used to living with people, it's like they don't know how to handle it, where it can be handled very well if you have the natural ability and then the grace can build on that."

Negative emotions naturally well up and might spill out, unchecked, she says, but growth in the spiritual life derives from reflection. "What is it, when we fail, that we need to change?" Sister Maria Deo Gratias asks. "Two wrongs don't make a right."

In what might appear to be an inversion of the natural order, Sister Maria Deo Gratias says that if life were to play out smoothly, without trouble, she might make the mistake of believing she possessed more virtue—more patience, for example—than she could actually claim, and she might not concede there was room for improvement. "Then you develop that virtue and you thank God for that opportunity, that I was able to acquire a greater practice of the virtue of patience because there was the opportunity," she says, "and you don't hold it against the person because of whatever it was that tried you. It's just one person will try one person one way. And we all try each other. We all have flaws."

Sister Maria Deo Gratias has transferred to communal living a pattern of relating to others, built upon a childhood dictum she learned from her parents: "You stood for the person you were and you make the person you are. You are who you are because of your own choices." As a high school student in the aspirature, Sister Maria Deo Gratias says she learned that everyone arrives at any given moment from different personal histories and frameworks. If she could not understand the actions of one of her religious sisters, she always asked, "Could you tell me why you did that?" She says she has gleaned, through their disclosures, "My mind didn't go that way at all. But if my mind went that way, I can obviously see her behavior now. It was so clear. Then you say, 'If I had a mind like that, I would come to that conclusion, too.'

"You know, so many things don't matter," Sister Maria Deo Gratias says. "It just matters that we love God. It's just a beautiful way to live. We all strive to live that way." She refers to her visual image of nuns standing in a circle, directing their attention to Christ at the center, and conceding their own rights. "When you have somebody coming in that's not used to that, that's used to everything revolving around them, as center, you have to say, 'You have to step on the side with the rest of us and let Jesus in the center.' But they're not used to living that way because everything has to be around them. That's the way the culture is now. When they come into our community, we're all on this side together and Christ is in the middle. The closer we come to Christ, the closer we come to each other."

In a process of mutual discernment, an aspirant and her community might discover they do not make a suitable match. "I think more women today have a different idea of what it's really about," Sister Maria Benedicta says of religious life and the cloistered monastery. "They are unconsciously seeking something else—acceptance or something else."

When Sister Mary Nicolette, the Novice Mistress, first arrived as a Poor Clare postulant, she was one of thirteen women training together; of those, seven stayed and professed final, solemn vows. She says this is a high ratio; typically, fewer than 50 percent of women who enter as postulants join the order permanently. When a woman comes to the monastery "for the wrong reasons, or the wrong motives," Sister Mary Nicolette says, "then obviously they're not bound to stay, and they can't stay because it wouldn't be right. You know, our intention and our motive is a big thing. We could be doing the correct things, living poverty. But if we're doing it for the wrong reason—'oh, this sister is going to think that I'm really poor and great'—well, that's the complete opposite of what poverty is for. You can be living this life for completely the wrong reasons. Or someone might say, 'I'm going to live perfect poverty,' but not make it interior, and then it's completely pointless."

"Obviously, if you're staying and this is not your expression, it's going to agitate you," Sister Maria Deo Gratias says. "And even if you wouldn't say anything, the atmosphere is there, and so you don't want to contaminate the atmosphere with agitation. If the shoe doesn't fit, you take the shoe off. It's as simple a thing as that."

Asked if she reflects on her experience in the monastery as an entirely different milieu, as Sister Joan Marie experienced it, Mother Miryam says, "I wouldn't see it that way myself at all. I suppose it was. Maybe. Maybe she's right. I just experienced it as a gradual change. I would have to think about it, but I wouldn't make a statement like that myself. I really don't see it that way. I can see it that way and she's a simple soul. She really is a sweet and simple soul. I could see why she... but I couldn't."

Even though Virginia's father detested the notion that his daughter wanted to become a nun, her mother helped usher her to this place, conspiring to keep secret her daughter's plans to enter the Corpus Christi Monastery. The mother and daughter tucked behind the couch a few belongings Virginia planned to bring with her to the monastery. When her father discovered the small stockpile and he registered his daughter's intentions were real, he stopped objecting. "My father—he always said a lot of things, but in the end he brought me up," Sister Joan Marie says. "He was proud of me, really, but he wouldn't let on to it. They had brought us up to choose our own religion, so they couldn't complain when we did."

When she left home, Sister Joan Marie says she did not think at first to pray for the family she left behind. "I'm afraid I was all wrapped up in myself," she says. "It was such a new experience and I thought I was doing something so great. And they all thought I was a saint because I was a teenager and most teenagers were looking for a good time and I wasn't. I wasn't. But I soon got that out of me. It didn't take too long to go out."

Before she embraced monastic living, and the constant alternation between manual labor and prayer, Sister Joan Marie does not remember ever being asked to pitch in with family chores. "To work was a shock," she says of the monastery. Having overcome bronchial pneumonia and the measles shortly before she entered, Sister Joan Marie says, "Mother kind of babied me, I guess, and I just laid around and read books before I came."

Still, she found stability, if not comfort, in the cloister. "I always loved everything about it," Sister Joan Marie says, "because, I guess from having trouble at home, I was so grateful to be away from that—that emotional upset all the time. I think it made it seem like heaven, in comparison, except I was young; that was the trouble. I mistook things. I was afraid. I was scared to death to ask anything. I thought they would send you home. I was scared I would get sent home; mostly, I was scared of that than anything else."

As she struggled to figure out what was expected of her and scrambled to keep up with the physical demands, Sister Joan Marie was stricken with a series of illnesses. "You think the harder you work, maybe they'll keep you," she says. "No."

She enjoyed preparing meals, but she was domestically deficient. Her mother never taught her to cook. Believing she needed a break from their troubled family life, Virginia and her brother were encouraged to play outdoors. When she was assigned to work alongside the monastery's cook of fifty years, she failed to measure up. "I did more or less whatever she told me," Sister Joan Marie says. "I tried. But then I got the pan in the wrong place and there was always something I was doing wrong. I tried to write down everything she was doing to learn to cook. She said 'Sister...' She didn't like it. She wanted me to work, not write things down. She said, 'Sister, you'll never be a cook because there's always somebody that comes that will know how to cook.' And she was right."

In time, Sister Joan Marie learned that for years after she left home, her mother continued to set her place at the dinner table every night in front of a long-vacated chair. Virginia's absence was observed daily. Decades the wiser, Sister Joan Marie interprets the experience of loss from a parent's perspective: "I think what was hard was when they got home and you weren't there. We went to a new life, thinking, 'Each day is new,' you know, and each day you learn something new. And here they are left with an empty nest. It's almost like a death. They're left empty until you write your first letter. I think once they have visits and they come, then they get adjusted, then they realize that you're happy, and then they're happy. But it does take time, I'm sure."

After sixty years in the monastery, Sister Joan Marie cannot say for certain if she has adjusted to monastic living.

When you get older, it gets a little easier. Seems like. I mean, now I'm not too sure yet. I've been sick so long.

I think the beautiful thing is praising God. And you're called to that seven times a day and at night. But that's the hardest. That was the hardest for me because I had to break my sleep. And I couldn't. I had a hard time adjusting to that. In fact, I thought they were going to send me home because of that. I just slept. In fact, I still do at Mass because I couldn't break the sleep. It wasn't my cycle. Anyway, I had a hard time with that. I guess you have a hard time with everything when you first enter. Well, I think you just think more of God, what He got out of you. It wasn't much. And pleasing Him and praising Him—and you're happy that you were able, that He let you do that. Nobody else can take the time. And it's not so much the work; the work is more of a penance. Any poor person has to work, and so that's part of the life. But that's part of the life in the world, too. I would have had the same trouble. Had the same, maybe more....

A lot of it was to find out that you are your biggest enemy. Yourself. To realize that took a long time. I was pretty critical of others, and you think, "Well, they shouldn't be doing that. They shouldn't be doing *that*.'" You have to look, "Well, am I always on time? Am I always...? No." When you really try to see yourself, you realize they're doing pretty good. And, you know, in sickness and everything else, they can keep going. And can you? No.

From within the same fourteen acres, Sister Joan Marie's perspective on the world, herself, and God have changed. "You get a different view of things," she says. "The whole thing is terrific, sort of like what God must feel sometimes. You take in the whole world. I think you kind of get God's view of things, because you see all these terrible things to pray for. There's plenty to pray for. It's a wonder He doesn't destroy us, but He loves us. Loved us all. Love makes it seem easy. And it was easy, when you think of it, compared to what He did for us—the crucifixion. We didn't have to go through that. Nobody could. Nobody could. Really, He spoils us more or less. We're spoiled little children, especially us, because we're in the cloister, because we're His, because we belong to Him entirely. We gave everything up for Him. I guess He spoils us in many ways."

Sister Joan Marie lists what she calls her "consolations": The monastery's pet dogs that "keep us going," along with a cat that turned up in the dumpster. These are some of the ways that God has provided. Sister Joan Marie adds that the nuns do find joy in their lives. "When we celebrate we really celebrate," she says. "There's no limit. I mean, according to our life, there's no limits."

Still, she does not think she can ever expect, in this lifetime, to acclimate to the rigid structure and the severe Rule of Saint Clare. "It's just a supernatural life and it's not natural," Sister Joan Marie says. "You would rather live a natural life. The body would rather sleep when it wants to sleep and forget the bells. It's just so different. You really have to have a supernatural outlook; otherwise, you can't persevere. And you have to keep it. You know, you have to somehow realize that there is an afterlife and you're going to get rewarded. And it's going to be nice. It's going to be wonderful. All your dreams are going to come true, but not until you die. You have to die first."

Sister Maria Deo Gratias of the Most Blessed Sacrament

My mom was a re-weaver. She mended clothes at home. She went to school when she was sixteen in Milwaukee to learn this trade. It wasn't real common. Most of the people that called themselves re-weavers didn't really re-weave the cloth. She was a re-weaver in the true sense of the word, in that she re-wove cloth that she'd take apart from the hem. Under the lining, there would be cloth that she would cut out and she would fray the edges, and then she would re-weave each thread into that so you didn't see the hole. She did a superb job. She had an art that not many people had.

Different customers would go to different re-weavers and they would do a patch. And then it'd come off. She never advertised. She always had enough work because people would see her work, and they'd say, "We'd like ours done." She did it in her own home. She did that purposely because she wanted to be there when the kids came home from school.

She wanted us to take it up and I tried, but I don't have good eyes and you had to have good eyes for that. I was born with a very high nearsightedness. In fact, when I was born, I would scream every time that I was fed, and Mom and Dad were just frantic, trying to figure out what was going on, trying to find out what was wrong. And no doctors could find anything. All of a sudden Dr. French says, "Did you ever check her eyes?" And Mom found out I couldn't see the bottle until it was an inch away from my face, and then I screamed because it was there. That's how they found out that I needed glasses. Of course, I was put in glasses when I was two years old. It was really a real trip for my mom to try to keep glasses on a little kid because I was quite active. I'll never forget, when I was older—I must have been in third or fourth grade—we were helping Mom clean up the attic and we found those glasses and my sister said, "Mom, look at these glasses. Aren't they cute? They're little!" My sister Mickey said, "They're a doll's glasses." She said, "Whose are those?" And Mom said, "Those are *my* dolly's," and then she pointed at me. Those were my glasses that I wore when I was two and three years old. That was kind of clever: "Those are my dolly's."

We came from a very good family. It wasn't overly Catholic. We went to Mass every Sunday. Other than that, we were a very good, very close family, but we weren't overly religious.

My vocation is quite unique because I have the exact day that it started: It was a Friday afternoon at a quarter to three. We were at spelling class in sixth grade. We had just taken our test and we were checking the answers. The teacher had a little extra time, so she was writing on the board the different spellings. At a quarter to three, all of a sudden, I got this inner desire: "Go to church." I didn't pay too much attention. But it was very strong. I looked at the clock and my heart was pounding. It was, "Do I go? Do I don't?" Back and forth.

The inner voice was getting stronger and stronger. "Go to church. After school, go to church." Three o'clock, the school bell was going to ring; we were going to get out. I thought, What am I going to do? So I thought, I'll go.

My sister and I usually walked home together. I thought, "How can I tell her I'm going to church?" I told my sister that I was going to stay after school for a little bit. She said, "Why? Did you get in trouble?" I said, "No, I want to stay after for a little bit." She kept on me, "Well, what's the matter?" I said, "I'm going to go to church." "To church?" I said, "I don't know myself. I don't know anything about this. I'm just going to go to church. So then you just tell Mom that I'm going to be late. I'm just going to go to church for a while."

Well, then I went to church and I knelt down before the Blessed Sacrament. It's very hard to put something like that into words, but two hours went past in just a flash and I experienced God as I had never experienced Him before. It was just awesome to experience God that way. I knew I would be His the moment I knelt down. It's very hard to put into words. It wasn't that I didn't see anything; it was more of an experience of God in one's heart and that you knew He was speaking to you—that inner sense of His presence, there in the Blessed Sacrament. It was very, very, very real. It wasn't so much an emotional trip or an experience. I had experienced God in such a way that I wanted to give my life totally to Him and there was that firm desire to be

His alone. And that was it. It was just that experience with our Lord that I came to know Him as a person and wanted to give my life totally to Him.

When I looked at the clock, it was five o'clock. I had a half-hour walk home. I got home and Mom said, "Where were you?" I said, "I went to church!" Well, she didn't believe me, of course. I'm not going to spend two hours in church!

From that day on, I went to church after school and I developed a deep relationship with our Lord and I felt Him calling me to Himself. We went to a Catholic school and I knew the sisters were always called "the brides of Christ," and so I wanted to let Him know I would give my life totally to Him. I didn't know what that was called; I was only twelve years old. We didn't talk too much about the terms, just that they were the brides of Christ. I promised our Lord I would be a sister. I promised Him that I would be a virgin and never drink or smoke. I just would give Him my whole self, totally.

After this experience, I told Mom I wanted to go to the convent. I went home and told Mom, "Mom, I'd like to be a sister." She said, "Well, you can think about that." She thought I would change my mind. Mom would always say, "You'll change your mind. You'll change your mind." The funny thing, too, she said, "You'll always have to wear a dress." I said, "That doesn't matter. That's a habit, that's not a dress." I wasn't one to wear dresses. I was very active, did all kinds of things. I wasn't one to sit around. The other thing she would say was, "You're going to have to get up at five every morning." Now that was a real stickler because I like to sleep in. But I said, "That doesn't matter," because I just thought it doesn't matter what I have to give up. I didn't think so much about giving up; I just knew that I was going to be His and that was more on my mind. And it's good she did put this other stuff on me. It made me think, "It will all take care of itself."

There must have been something prior to that because when I think back, in fourth grade the principal gave me a nun doll. She called me to the office, and I was scared to death because I didn't know what she was calling me to the principal's office for. The thing was—she wanted to give me this nun doll. She must have seen something in me, but I never formulated it. I always admired the sisters but I never formulated my view that I can consciously remember.

After a few years, in eighth grade, I said, "Mom, I would really like to enter the convent." So she said, "Well, you can do what you want." I wanted to enter right after eighth grade, and I did. I was very interested in the cloistered life but my mother was totally against that. She said, "You can write to different orders." I got a book that had the different orders and I wrote to all kinds and got all kinds of mail back. On one of them, she noticed a Carmelite order on the return address. "Not there," she said. She didn't have any use for cloistered life, and so I had to put all of those aside. I didn't know anything about Poor Clares at that stage. I didn't know they existed.

Mom wanted to make sure I knew what I wanted. There was no doubt in my mind, but she didn't know that. And looking at it from her perspective, that's a little different than looking at it from my perspective, but Mom never believed in the cloistered life. "God never wanted anybody to live a life like that," she thought. And down the road in my story there is that point when I told her I was entering the cloistered life and she just couldn't see that God would call anyone to that life. Teaching, yes; you're serving people. That's fine. But to live in the cloister, no; she couldn't see that at all.

I had an older brother, but I left home first so that was an adjustment for Mom, more than I think I could ever realize at that time because I was just a child.

My dad, he had no problem understanding. Not the cloister—he didn't particularly care for that either—but he never voiced his opinion because he felt that your life is yours; you do what you want with it. The active life, he liked that. He was quite proud of it.

My mom didn't stand in the way because she always felt that, too—our life was our own, and you have to make of your life what you think God is calling you to. So she never stood in the way, except, being young, she wouldn't allow me to enter the cloister. But for active religious life, she wouldn't stand in the way. And so I entered. And I remembered when she said goodbye, I knew it was harder for her than it was for me and I can understand that. I have the vocation. She doesn't. My brothers and sisters would always say, "She kept on setting a place for you to come home." It was very hard for her to adjust because I was the first that left home and I think when the first one leaves home that's always the hardest on parents. And I think part of it, too, is we won't be getting married and having grandchildren for them; I kind of think that might have been behind my mom's mind. She never mentioned anything like that, but I think that might have been something that she probably would have considered. I think Mom said later she didn't want to build it up in me so much that if I decided this wasn't my life, that

I would feel uncomfortable saying that; I think that was her whole idea, you know, "You're always welcome to come home." And that was a good thing for Mom, on her part. I said, "I'm not coming home," but I always appreciated her saying that. And I would tell her, "It's always nice to know that, but don't count on it because I'm really solid in this vocation. I have no qualms. No way am I going to leave."

Of course, I was not the typical type to go into a convent. I only found this out years later: The relatives had a bet on me, whether I would make it or not! They didn't tell me that until my solemn vows, my perpetual vows. They said, "You know, we lost our bet." Whatever they bet, they gave to Mom and Dad.

When I was a kid, I was very active, the daredevil type, and into a lot of things. Most of my friends were boys, growing up, because they did things like build forts and ride stock cars—all kinds of things that I liked to do. I wasn't one to sit around and play with dolls. That's probably why the relatives didn't think I would make it. But Mom had us go over to the relatives' house and stay there for a week so we were used to back and forth; we weren't always home. That was another wisdom that she had, that we could be independent. Later, it was something that I desired; I was just very eager to learn the customs and the way of life in the convent.

We didn't just sit around when we were at my aunt's farm. I would go out with the boys and take turn with the boys riding the pigs to see who could stay on this big pig the longest. We would put the food in a pail and when the pig would put its head down—these were huge pigs, huge sows—then we'd put a rope over the neck and we'd jump on. The other one timed how long you stayed on because this pig would try to buck you off. And then, of course, when you're bucked off you have to get out right away because you'd get mauled to death. My grandpa had a bull. When we were kids we'd watch Toro on *The Lone Ranger*. So I thought I'd try that sometime. I got out there with a bull and I was just fascinated because it worked just like it said on television. He would make his feet like that and the smoke would come up from the dirt in the yard. It would be just like TV. He'd charge at me, and I'd step aside. Then he'd get on the other side and charge. I had a great time. My sister Mickey came and I said, "You try it." Mick got out there and got scared, and the bull almost got her. Of course, she told Grandpa and that ended my fun.

My dad was a prankster, too. He sometimes would tell us the things he would do. He worked until nine o'clock because when you first start a business you have the long hours of work. When Dad came home we always wanted to spend time with him, so we pretended, "Mom, I'm hungry." So then she'd say, "Come out and get something to eat." We just wanted to be with Dad a little bit, and he'd get into telling stories of what he did as a kid. And Mom said, "Frank, don't tell them that; they're going to do it." But none of the pranks were mean; they would just be innocent. One time, when he was at my aunt's restaurant, he said, "Oh, Fran, let me wait on the next customer." She said, "You can't wait on people. You don't know how to do that." He said, "Let me just try." He put on the apron. A couple sat down. She said, "I'll tell you what to do. You give them a menu, and then you..." She didn't want to lose her business. He went to the table, and of course he was a card. He gave them a menu, and then the lady asked, "Do you have frog legs?" And Dad said, "No, ma'am, that's just the way I walk." He's just a joker like that. It ran in the family. Us kids—three girls and three boys—enjoyed life. Cindy was born later, after I entered the convent. But the five of us were kind of close, within a year apart, all the way down. There's the song that was real popular with the line "creeping like a nun." Whenever that was on the radio, my brother blared that real loud, and he said, "That's you, that's you!" I just teased him back. We could tease about it. I don't know that they really took me too seriously until I entered. They just said, "What's the matter with you?"

Just after eighth grade, I entered the convent, the aspirancy. I went to Mass every day from that experience on, and I said the rosary every day. And I looked at religious orders, whenever I saw a sister with a different type of habit. At that time they were all wearing a habit that was distinct to their order so you could distinguish and tell when a sister from a different order came to Mass at your church. I noticed that there was a sister of Saint Agnes and I had never seen that type of sister, and so I went up to her and I asked her if she would be kind to send me some information on their order. And she did. Different ones that I met in church would send things, too. I think that's where I found most of the brochures. I was very taken with the Sisters of Saint Agnes. They were beautiful—their brochures and everything—and I had the sense that's the one that God wanted me to join. They had exposition of the Blessed Sacrament a lot, and that's what I liked. So I think that was the drawing card. In brochures, it said they were a very prayerful community. That's what drew me. I applied and I entered right after eighth grade. It was August of 1968 when I entered their community.

When I entered the aspirancy, I just loved it. We lived at the convent, and we would take a bus to the parochial high school, a Catholic high school in Fond du Lac. We lived a religious life for those four years. After those four years, you went to the next stage, the postulancy. I just told Mom and Dad to take my money out of my banking account and put it in theirs. Other nuns say, "I found this so hard to give up." I didn't. I didn't. In fact, I didn't even think about those things, like my bike; anybody that wanted my belongings could help themselves.

My family was always very eager to have me home and show me stuff. My brother got his license and he bought a car. I didn't even get in the house and he said, "I want to show you this car," and of course he wanted to drive me around. I said, "You think we should say hello to Mom first?" The joy of having me home was always there.

When I was on home visit from the aspirature for the summers, my mom said, "You have to date." I said, "I don't care. I can date. I don't mind." Whenever I went on a date I would say, "I am going to be a sister so it's just a friendship." I would think that was only fair to that other person. It would be kind of hard because sometimes I would come for home visit and my sisters' boyfriends would come to the house and they would want me to come out with them. We joked, so it was like, "Have her come along." Sometimes I would, and sometimes I would say, "You two go."

I always felt comfortable with boys. In high school, when I was home we would go bowling. I wasn't much for just sitting around. Sometimes they would just want to sit around and drink. I remember thinking, "This is just so boring." Then they gave me a drink. I don't like the smell of the stuff, let alone the taste, so I would say, "Oh, look at those stars. Isn't that something?" Then I would pour it in their drink. They didn't know they had a little bit more. I didn't get into drinking or anything. Being serious and expressing love to a date? No, because I loved our Lord and my love was for Him. We were just going out to have fun and we were good friends that way, but there was nothing serious because I had my mind made up.

Mom was really interested in one boy having an interest in me, so she'd invite him up to the cottage. Fine. He was a very nice person. He did ask me to go out. I said, "I have to pray my holy hour first," so he would meet me over at church. One night, he wanted to give me his ring. I said, "Oh, yeah, I'll take your ring." He was quite surprised. Then I took it and I put it by the altar. I said, "Everything I get, I give to Jesus." He went up and he snatched it, and he didn't ask again. He knew where I was at. I said, "I told you at the beginning that I'm not interested in dating in a serious way, like steady, because I'm not for marriage. That isn't where my calling is. We go out, that's fine. But if you give me your ring, I give it to Jesus."

The last year of aspirancy, our aspirancy closed so I was home that last year and went to a public school. Mom said, "You can go to the Catholic school," but I said, "That's a lot of money." I wanted my money to go back into the convent, so I just went to a regular high school for my senior year. I could adjust. I didn't have any trouble with that. When the aspirancy closed, I always considered myself still in the convent. We would go once a month; it was a nonresidency aspirancy for the few of us that were in this program, but it was no problem for me because I had my prayer life. I went to Mass every day, I had a holy hour every day, and I kept the schedule that whole high school year.

We were a close family, a very, very close family and we did a lot together as a family, played together a lot when we were little and even when we were older. We were always very close.

Both Mom and Dad were very easy to talk to. If there were little difficulties, Mom would sit down and talk it out with us. I think that was a very good thing, growing up, that you handled your own problems. She'd sit down and say, "What was the problem here?" And then we had to figure out: What was it? And then you could work it through. You didn't blame the others; you just worked it out yourself. And there was that give and take. We didn't really fight that much, but if there was a disagreement, well, "You work it out. Don't come running to Mom. You work it out." We'd work it out together, and then we'd be friends again. We never held grudges that long. Half the time you forgot about it and you kept going on with life.

Mom was a good psychologist, even though she didn't use that term. She was just very basic in dealing with life. You made the best of it. And she was a good example of that. Both parents were good examples of that. They had good psychology without even knowing what it was. It was just common sense. I think that's what I would say with both parents: They both had good common sense, how to live. If you got upset at what somebody did and you said, "They made me do it because they did this," my parents said, "No. You chose to get upset by what they did. You could have chosen not to. It might take a little virtue." But of course they never used those religious terms. They weren't that type, but they were just very upright and honest, and so they made you responsible for who you were.

They would never say right out, "Do not drink and do not smoke." But they realized we were getting older so one of them once said, "We've got to deal with you. If you don't smoke until you're eighteen, you get a hundred dollars. And if you don't drink until you're eighteen, you get another hundred dollars." That was a motivation for us. And it was a motivation for them. They didn't want us to get into those habits while we were children, so instead of saying, "Be sure you don't take drugs, be sure you don't do that," they did it this way. You were kind of looking forward to the hundred dollars as a kid. Now, when I was eighteen, I was in the convent four years already. So what did that mean to me? My brothers and sisters—that was something for them. But for myself, I made the choice after my experience at the altar; I didn't have the desire to do any of those things, so it wasn't fair. I told Mom it wasn't fair for me because there was no temptation to do it. So, therefore, I said, "You keep your $200. I don't want to take your money."

One time, I was on home visit. There was a school close to us and the kids were walking past our house to go to school. And I thought, boy, those kids are small. And Mom said, "Well, they're in sixth grade." And then it dawned on me that I had made my life decision when I was their age. Other than that, you were just growing up so you didn't think of yourself as so young. You just thought of yourself as yourself! But that's one experience I had where I realized, my gosh those kids are babies and I made my life decision when I was their age!

I've always had the desire to be a cloistered contemplative but because I was only fourteen years old when I entered, twelve when I made the decision, I had to obey my parents and they wouldn't hear of it. And I figured God wouldn't call it if it wasn't granted by my parents. I knew I had to respond because He was calling me to respond now, so I thought maybe He's calling me to a prayerful active community; I entered that and I loved it. I can't say I left that because of anything I didn't love while I was in that community. I was very happy there serving the people in different ways, first as a gym teacher and later as pastoral associate in the hospital. But then God in His way said, "No, I want you to go further." Also, the superiors at that convent would say, "Have you thought of the cloistered life?" They could see it in me that I was probably called to the cloister. They could discern that I have the gifts to be a cloistered contemplative nun. And they said, "It won't be long; you're going to be a cloister." One superior told me that and I said, "If that be, that would be very fine, but I myself I don't know at this point whether He wants me to be a contemplative in action, or truly a contemplative." Did He want it, or did I want it?

My mom wanted to steer me away from a cloistered community. The other community, I think that that was all right with her. You could be a teaching sister; that was all right. She was a re-weaver, and so she had customers come to the door to fix garments, whatever they had holes in. One day, a priest came and he wanted his suit coat fixed. And so Mom said, I'll ask him. In fact she came out and said, "God would never want anyone to enter one of the cloistered kinds of orders," and then the priest said, "Oh, yes, He would." And that helped my mom because she could talk to him and he talked to her about the value of the cloistered life. I just think how humble my mom was to share that with me. Because I wasn't home, I didn't know that that experience had happened. She shared it with me. I think that had helped her. I was here already when she shared that with me.

I think I can do more for people in the cloister than I could ever do out there, even though I did a lot out there, so to speak. Touching people's souls, you do that through your prayers. We don't see the results of that in the hidden life, but we have the faith to know that is what is happening. Here, it's kind of like the powerhouse of prayer going out into the community and touching people's lives in a way that we're not aware of, but that we know it happens. And so to be a part of that, to give yourself totally to God, I think is a real privilege. To be together and have a life provided by the Church—that frees us to do this. There is a real freedom because of our customs; we don't have to follow the protocol that you would have if in the world. We have our own monastic culture here. And we live side-by-side, respecting each sister's union with our Lord. In that living together day in and day out, knowing that we do keep silence and in that silence, she's communing with God, I'm communing with God and somehow developing our own relationships with God. But more than that, that's our apostolate—to pray for others, and God gives graces to others that they would not have had otherwise. That doesn't put it on us. It's not us, it's Him.

That's the purity of the life of being one with Him. It's a union, the contemplative prayer and whatever you're doing outside of chapel; it's not two separate things. It just flows into each other and it's just the life of union.

Now, our life is a perpetual Lent really, and I love it. I love Lent. It's more simple. So in a sense, it's probably my feast day because I love it. The simpler, the better. I just happen to be that type of person that I like that.

I'm only an instrument, as each of us sisters are. But we have the responsibility to be good instruments in our apostolate of prayer. We don't work it through with people like I did when I was a pastoral associate, but I work it through in a different way. I say, "I pray for you, and I asked God to give you the special graces and the nudges you need to think things out." That's what I think my role is now. I think it's a very important role that I can't take for granted.

Even those who don't call us and don't contact us in any way—that don't believe in us—we can touch their hearts.

2

The Claustrophobic Nun

In the monastery, everything is directed for the search for the face of God. Everything is reduced to the essential because the only thing that matters is what leads to Him. Monastic recollection is attention to the presence of God. So when you think of how the media, mass media in the different forms, can distract and be like a noise that can interfere with communion with God, we try to reduce that; most, we reduce to zero. We don't listen to the radio or watch television, but it's not because we're against progress, or we're against information, it's just because of the effect that that can have on an environment that is silent, and what it can do to a recollected mind. It would come in and would just totally disrupt.

Sister Mary Nicolette of the Father of Mercies

To Sister Mary Nicolette, it is a familiar refrain, a now-old family joke: It is for the best that the Corpus Christi Monastery sits on South Main Street and that no mountain can be seen on the flat midwestern landscape; otherwise, the travel-hungry Sister Mary Nicolette might be tempted to run for the hills.

Sister Mary Nicolette laughs when she retells this jest of her relatives, which is funny because it is true. She was a child from Texas who grew up in Europe. The Alps were her backyard. When her family lived in Italy, and she was still known as Monica, she met Pope John Paul II twice. Once, he patted her on the cheek. When her father took a job in Lichtenstein, she learned German. In Austria, she hiked the mountain trails. There, she says, nature spoke to her of God. Her family moved and she thrived in each new culture. Because Sister Mary Nicolette managed to pick up languages like other teenagers pick up boyfriends, she considered studying etymology in college. And then she discovered the perfect outlet for her love of traveling and her talent for languages—a career as a flight attendant. "I had thought of being an airline stewardess because I love travel and wanted to see the world," she says, "and I thought that would be a great way to do it. I knew that wouldn't be a permanent thing, but that was a dream. And I thought, well, maybe I could even be a pilot." At twenty, when she became a postulant of the Poor Clare Colettine Order, Monica was fluent in English, Italian, German, and French.

Although she is allotted up to four family visits each year, her siblings are scattered across the globe; she usually sees only some of her family members once a year. She has a large family: three sisters and two brothers. In their transitory upbringing together as expatriates, the siblings bonded through humor. Once, when her younger brother arrived at the monastery for a family visit with his wife and children, Sister Mary Nicolette reminded her young niece that she is the big sister to the girl's dad. The child did not buy it; her father is six feet tall. Sister Mary Nicolette looks petite, by comparison, especially when seated, talking to her family from the enclosure side of the parlor—a metal grille between Sister Mary Nicolette and her relatives. Sister Mary Nicolette climbed on her chair; her ankle-length habit hid her advantage from her niece's side of the grille. Her niece was fooled and awed.

Sister Mary Nicolette's brother travels for work. He has told his sister that he thinks of her during these trips; when he stood on a mountaintop in Peru, he was startled by the amazing view and the fact that his sister would never have the chance to hike up that mountain or take in that scene. Sister Mary Nicolette remembers him saying that he feels sorry for her because she is missing out. All joking between the siblings stopped then. Sister Mary Nicolette says she told her brother, "That's really sweet to be thinking of me. But you know, I don't think, 'I'm here and I'm never going to be able to go out again.' You don't think of it as something restricting. It's something that's freeing. I'm freed of the worries and of all the exterior things."

Sister Mary Nicolette realizes that the cloistered monastic way of life is difficult to understand, to translate to her own family. She received the calling to this life, she says, and so has been granted a supernatural grace to value and accept the vocation.

Sister Mary Nicolette's journey to this place began, she says, with a lie. Her parents raised their six children Catholic. Sister Mary Nicolette believed she could become whatever she wanted; any path she chose in life, her parents told her, she should do with her whole heart. Her parents encouraged their children to consider any vocation, including the priesthood or sisterhood.

In childhood, Monica encountered religious figures regularly; nuns taught her at Catholic school, and when the family lived in Rome, the birthplace of the Catholic Church, sisters dressed in the full habit were a common sight in public.

From an early age, Monica wanted a family of her own. She planned to get married and have eight children. "It was a beautiful ideal for me to be a mother and a wife and have a lot of children," she says. Above all, she wanted to give her life for others. She says, "I wanted to do something that would really make a difference and help. I always wanted to help." This aspiration fit with her conception of marriage and motherhood.

Monica became what she jokingly refers to as the "black sheep" of the family when, instead of following the path of her two older sisters who had followed in their parents' footsteps and attended the University of Dallas, she enrolled at Franciscan University of Steubenville in Ohio. Her parents' and sisters' alma mater is also a Catholic institution, but Monica heard of its reputation as a party school and she thought the Franciscan university would be the better place to meet someone who shared her beliefs, someone with whom she could spend the rest of her life. "Something in my heart told me this decision was going to be important for the rest of my life—if I was going to meet the man I was going to marry, or if I would discover the vocation God had for me," she says.

During her first year of college, Monica was put off by the religious fanaticism she encountered in the other students. Her father, a Fulbright fellow, had moved his family overseas to teach at universities; during Monica's teenage years at a restored monastery they referred to as the Sistine Chapel of Central Europe, her peers were older philosophy students. At the Franciscan university, Monica befriended but debated a student who believed that every Christian should evangelize the world aggressively, preaching the gospel with the intent to convert people. Monica agreed, to an extent. "His approach was, everyone has got to do this and if you don't do it, you're going to be lost. My approach was, I can save souls and help further the kingdom of God by prayer," Sister Mary Nicolette says.

Back home in Austria the summer after her freshman year, Monica told her mom she was thinking of transferring to another college. Monica was turned off by a polarizing, judgmental message: "You're not good enough and we want to convert you." She says, "They were out to convert everybody," Monica included. She decided to try one more semester at the Franciscan university before making a final decision about transferring. Her sophomore year, Monica had a much different, much better experience. Now, in retrospect, she ascribes the pushiness and zealousness as acts of "misdirected charity."

During her sophomore year, she and two friends worked together in the college's conference office, helping organize a massive event, Pentecost in Pittsburgh. When their work was complete, the three sat in their dormitory, exhausted. They needed a break. One of them said she knew just the place where they could rest—a cloistered monastery in Ohio. She picked up the phone right then and called to arrange a visit. The Mother Abbess said she could not offer a place for young women to stay if they simply wanted a vacation, but the monastery welcomed visits by those interested in the cloistered monastic life. In that case they could stay across the street from the monastery with an active order of nuns, and they were permitted to attend the cloistered nuns' chapel service and Divine Office.

"We were all three sitting on the bed," Sister Mary Nicolette says, "and I remember my friend covered the phone and she said, 'Mother wants to know if we're interested.' We all said, 'Oh, yes, we're interested! We're interested!'" Sister Mary Nicolette laughs. "So this is how I got my vocation—through a lie. I was interested in knowing how Buddhist monks lived, too!"

Sister Mary Nicolette says her two friends "played their part a lot better than I played my part" because they asked for private interviews with Mother Superior. Monica did not. "Uh-uh!" she says.

Sister Mary Nicolette does not question her friends' sincerity in asking for those private talks. "They were very, very, very spiritual so I'm sure they spoke to Mother about spiritual things, their spiritual lives and what-not," she says, adding that the two were not interested in becoming cloistered monastic nuns.

In the monastery's chapel, the Blessed Sacrament was exposed perpetually. Sister Mary Nicolette spent hours praying before the Blessed Sacrament, the host that, once consecrated, Catholics believe becomes the very presence of Jesus. She says, "I remember I was praying there and I felt a strong sense in my heart, not an audible voice, but a voice speaking to my heart, kind of, saying, 'This is where I want you. You don't know where, you don't know how, and you don't know when, but this is where I want you.' And I was shocked. This is not what I was expecting. At all! Not right now. I was expecting to relax from my busy, stressed work and instead God hit me over the head and told me this was really what He wanted for me."

Monica talked with an extern nun, who maintains a unique role in an enclosure, as the one responsible for communicating with the public and with the world on behalf of the cloistered nuns. The nun explained the mission of the Poor Clare Order: Cloistered contemplatives dedicate their entire lives "for the salvation of souls to the complete love of God without any distraction, or without a divided heart." The extern sister told Monica that, in the enclosure, there are no distractions, and so their hearts are not divided because they are separate from the world, devoted to God alone. For Monica, this description—this life—seemed like an answer she did not know she was seeking. "It's all about this deep relationship with God, for your own salvation but also for others," she says. "And I just thought, that's always what I felt deep in my heart. I wanted to live for others. Everything she is saying is what I feel God created me for. I imagine it's what someone would feel when they meet someone they love and want to marry: God created me for this person and this person for me. We were made for each other. It was the same thing for this; everything she was saying, I thought this is the whole reason God created me."

Introspective and reflective Monica took stock of all that the cloister denied—traveling, marriage, motherhood, talking to and visiting her parents and siblings. Hugging her loved ones at will. "It just seemed so radical to me and so drastic," she says, "and I didn't know if I could do that. In my mind at the time, I'm just working through it and I'm just saying, 'I'm really attached to my family.' I'm giving all these reasons to God why this isn't a good idea. I'm like, 'Lord, you know, you *know* me. You know I can't do this!'"

Monica's proficiency with languages offered little solace; rather, it was a lens into yet another obstacle. The words "cloister" and "claustrophobia" both derive from the same Latin root, meaning "to close" or "to lock." "That's where the word 'cloister' comes from—being shut in," Sister Mary Nicolette says. "That was very ironic. I get claustrophobic in an elevator. So I'm like, 'Lord, the cloister? I'm going to get claustrophobic!' That's the word that comes to my mind. You know being shut in and not being able to travel. I just thought, 'How am I going to be able to do this, Lord? You're asking me to do something that's just completely contrary to my nature.'"

Monica never learned if her two friends asked for applications to join the Ohio monastery, or if the Mother Abbess offered the applications during their private meetings. "All I know is that when we walked out of there, they had application papers and I didn't," Sister Mary Nicolette says. "I didn't dare ask for the application papers."

Over the next couple of weeks, Monica wrestled with an unsettling prospect: She might have stumbled, unwittingly, upon her vocation—to be a cloistered monastic nun. "To my human, limited view, this was something that just seemed so contrary to what I was expecting of life," she says. "And it was beautiful; I wasn't against that, but it just seemed so much bigger than what I could do." She told God, "You know, I thought you knew me. Why are you asking this of me? You know me better than I know myself."

Gradually, Monica engaged her own desires and her will in a mental exercise, a question of faith. She became convinced that if God truly called her to this vocation, He would also grant her the ability to embody it. Sister Mary Nicolette says she took a "stab in the dark." She asked one of the two friends for her application papers to the monastery, since neither of the other young women planned to apply, and Monica submitted her own application to join the Poor Clare monastery in Ohio.

She was rejected, though, for health reasons. In childhood, Monica was diagnosed with a rare autoimmune disease after antibodies, which had been called forth to fight a virus as they should have, turned and fought her own body, devastating the healthy muscle cells. The monastic community's physician thought that someone with her disease could not live the physically demanding Poor Clare life of fasting and manual labor and interrupting sleep at midnight for the Divine Office. "I was on medication, but I was stable. I was crushed," Sister Mary Nicolette says.

"I thought, 'This is what God created me for. This is my life,' and I had come to a peaceful acceptance of saying, 'If God wants me to do this, He's going to help me.' And then it was, 'No,' and it was just like everything, my whole world, came down. I just thought, 'Oh my goodness.' "

She says she cried for two days after hearing news of her rejection. Monica worked to interpret the twist; maybe she was mistaken in thinking she was called to the cloistered contemplative life, or maybe the monastery in Ohio was not the right community.

Again, Monica enrolled in college courses at her Franciscan university. She remained open to the possibility that she might be called to become a nun. Sampling religious orders and communities became her weekend pursuit. "There was a group of us at school—seven at first, and twelve by the end of the year—who were interested in a religious life," she says. "We'd go convent-hopping, or make 'nun runs' on weekends and we'd visit these convents."

Monica was impressed when she visited a convent in Kentucky. She was taking everything into consideration. "I loved their habit," she says. "I just thought their habit was so beautiful. It's all black and they had a head covering that doesn't go across the forehead; I think it goes a little bit higher and it covers the ears. But it's all black and they have an insignia of the Sacred Heart of Jesus. The austerity of it attracted me for some reason."

She thought the Poor Clare habit was beautiful, too. "It kind of captured my whole idea of a sister who is consecrated and set apart," she says. "It's a sign, a very tangible sign to me of that. And I loved it."

Monica kept thinking, "The Poor Clares is the place. Poor Clares—it just kept coming back to me." On her birthday, a Sunday, a piece of mail was delivered to Monica's dorm room. She thinks it could have been dropped in the wrong mailbox the day before, then left at her door when the error was detected. The return address on the envelope listed a Poor Clare Colettine Order in Rockford, Illinois. "The fact that it was my birthday and it contained the address of this monastery I don't think is a coincidence," she says. "I think God works through little things like that, just little touches in our life here and there you can see all along the journey. It was just the special touch I needed that day from the Lord. So it was a beautiful birthday present that year." The form letter served a simple function—calling Monica's attention to another Poor Clare monastery—yet Monica felt, because of the unique timing and situation of the letter's arrival, she might be fated to go there.

Monica wrote a letter to the Mother Abbess. She wrote about her visit to the Poor Clare monastery in Ohio, that she had asked to join that community but was turned down because her health was not deemed adequate. Monica thought it prudent to be honest from the outset about any potential obstacle. She informed the Mother Abbess she wanted to live as a Poor Clare. She assumed that this candor about her medical condition and the other monastery's rejection would sabotage her acceptance into the Rockford community.

On Christmas break while home in Austria, Monica received a response. The Mother Abbess explained in her letter that the process of joining a religious community should start with a visit; she invited Monica to spend a few days at the Corpus Christi Monastery. Monica replied that she would love to visit when it could be arranged. She did not mention at the time that on a student's budget she could not afford the $110 round-trip flight from Franciscan University of Steubenville in Ohio to Chicago, or the $98 bus fare. After the holidays, Monica returned to college. About ten days before spring break, while she was working in the conference office, a friend walked in and announced to everyone within earshot, "Does anyone want to go to Chicago?" Monica shouted, "I'll go!" She figured a group was taking a road trip and she could split the cost of gas and tolls. Monica learned the student had found an airline deal called "Friends Fly Free"—two tickets for the price of one. The two split the cost of one ticket, each paying $60 for the round-trip fare. "You wouldn't find that normally so I said, 'this is a godsend,' because I could pay for that," Monica says.

She flew to Chicago. A relative picked her up at the airport and dropped her off at the monastery so she could stay for three days during Holy Week, leading up to Easter. "I spoke to Mother Abbess and a few of the sisters and I was so afraid," she says. "I was just scared to death. I was terrified. I think I just sat in the chair and listened most of the time to what they had to say to me. I didn't say much myself. I was just so terrified. You would never know it, but I'm a shy person!"

Before Monica left the monastery, the Mother Abbess told her she could return to join the community if she wanted. The ease of this acceptance stunned and frightened Monica. "I didn't expect that," she says. "I was like, 'Whoa.' " She told the Mother Abbess she still had a year of college left before she graduated. "I guess I was scared of being hurt again, of it not working out and putting all your hopes in something, and then it's just crushed," Sister Mary Nicolette says. "And I think it was just a defense mechanism; I didn't want to commit myself."

Back at college, Sister Mary Nicolette solicited advice from a priest whom she had sought out earlier to help her discern her vocation. She conveyed her confusion. "This is the life I want," Sister Mary Nicolette remembers telling him, "but when I was there, I felt nothing. It was just, like, blank." She told the priest that maybe God was treating her differently in this situation than during her visit to the monastery in Ohio. "Maybe this time," she told the priest, "he's not going to whisper in my ear, 'This is where I want you.' Maybe he's going to say, 'This time, you make the choice.' "

The priest pointed to a park bench and instructed Monica to sit there until she heard a directive from God. Sister Mary Nicolette says, "It was a lovely day to sit on a park bench!" She explains, "The priest wanted me to come to a conclusion for myself, you know, because he knew he couldn't tell me what to do. He couldn't tell me, 'You go and try.' He thought, 'You have to figure this out on your own.' He was very wise. And I remember just feeling in my heart, 'Now, the first place the door was closed to me. Here, the door is opening to me. So the choice is up to me. What am I going to do? Am I going to give it a try and if it doesn't work out, well, at least I tried? Or am I going to spend the rest of my life wondering if that's where God wanted me?' "

Monica was up from the park bench, decision made, within an hour. She tracked down the priest—with his long white beard, he looked to Monica like a jovial Santa Claus—and she told him she planned to join the monastery. He gave Monica a "bear hug" and congratulated her.

That summer, when her junior year came to a close, Monica flew home to Austria for two final months with her family before joining the Poor Clare Colettine Order. "A lot of people probably think we spend the last month thinking, 'This is the last time I'm going to eat ice cream, walk in the mountains, hug my parents,' " Sister Mary Nicolette says. "And most of that is true. Most of that is true. It is the last time you do a lot of things.

"I had a few minutes where I thought, 'What am I doing? I'm crazy.' I had moments that I wavered. You get cold feet. But when you get past moments like that, there was just a real eagerness; I know this is it, I'm not going to let anything stop me—fear or the uncertainty."

Sister Mary Nicolette repeats and laughs at another nun's joke, that a few of them who did not finish college become members of the Dropouts for Jesus Club at the monastery. Her new life, her hidden life, began when she gave up her shoes and was given a new name. Sister Mary Nicolette is not, in fact, this cloistered contemplative nun's real religious name. Humility is integral to the Franciscan spirit, and anonymity is treasured as a virtue of the enclosure. Sister Mary Nicolette is the name she chose as an alias, a condition for disclosing this story of her life.

Sister Mary Nicolette discovered when she entered the monastery that God indeed equipped her to live as a cloistered monastic nun when He called her. "It's a mystery," she says. "There's really no way to be able to explain that, but when you get the vocation, you get the strength to do it. So it was a sacrifice to leave my family, and it was a sacrifice to leave everything, but at the same time there's something so much deeper that fills you. It's like it makes up for everything else. It makes up for that sacrifice. And you know that it's worth it. There's a reason for it and it makes it all worth it."

Since entering the monastery, Sister Mary Nicolette has heard from the friend she argued with in college about evangelism. He wrote to her that he understands the point she was trying to make: Someone can have an impact on the world quietly, behind the scenes, praying for souls and for the conversion of souls, praying that a missionary will speak the right words at the right time. Sister Mary Nicolette says, "You need both. You need the prayerful support of the religious—of cloistered contemplatives—to support those who go out and evangelize, to prepare the way for them so that people to whom they are speaking will be receptive. And a lot of times that's only going to come from someone praying for them. We don't know who they are, of course, but we can pray that souls will be receptive to God's message."

Ironically, this worldly woman does not know the layout of the city beyond the cloistered grounds. She does not know the neighborhood just past the monastery's stone wall. One winter night, when traffic was light, Sister Mary Nicolette went outside the wall with a novice to shovel the driveway and the parking lot next to the Shrine of Mary. A car stopped. The driver asked the two for directions. Sister Mary Nicolette smiled and told the driver, "We don't get out much!" She imagines the driver might have been searching for a street around the corner from the monastery, but she had no context for her physical environment.

Having embodied her gifts and hopes in a life she did not realize she longed for, Sister Mary Nicolette says that her question to God as she debated, internally, the veracity of her calling—if He really knew her personality, if He might be placing impractical demands on her God-given temperament—has also been resolved. "That's the thing," Sister Mary Nicolette says. "He knows us better than we know ourselves."

Although claustrophobic, Sister Mary Nicolette has never felt restricted in her private seventy-eight-square-foot cell, or in the 25,000-square-foot cloistered monastery, or within the fourteen-acre enclosed complex.

Sister Mary Nicolette, who once hoped to have a family as large as the one she was born into, believes her desire for motherhood was not abandoned, but satisfied in the cloister, which she describes as a "powerhouse of prayer." "I love the whole idea of spiritual motherhood, that we're the spouses of Christ—another name for sisters—and our fruitfulness in the Church is to bear spiritual children," she says.

"That's one of the things that struck me very much, that struck a chord in my heart, is that you're not only responsible for a few souls, like you would be in your own family if you had your own children; you would be responsible for *these* souls. But you're responsible for a multitude. It's something that's very deep in every woman's heart, probably, to give herself for others. I think that's a part of our nature—to give yourself for others, and even that is fulfilled in our vocation. You know, we're not physically mothers, but we are mothers to souls. And that's something that's very fulfilling in our hearts." It's a paradox, Sister Mary Nicolette says: Cloistered nuns leave the world in order to be for the world, albeit absently and anonymously. She has removed herself from the world in order to give herself wholly to others.

During an especially harsh midwestern winter, Sister Mary Nicolette and Sister Maria Benedicta, shoveled for hours to remove piles of snow from the monastery's premises. During communal hour with the other nuns, Sister Mary Nicolette shared a lesson inspired by their manual labor. She showed them a cartoon she had drawn with the caption, "You don't have to go to the North Pole to reach all four corners of the world." It is Sister Maria Benedicta who recalls and tells about the cartoon. "Here," she says, "your heart can expand to the whole world."

In her spare time, Sister Mary Nicolette deploys her language skills to translate religious texts. She is translating into English a compilation of writings by Poor Clare nuns over the centuries. The journeys of this thoughtful, seasoned traveler are now entirely internal.

Sister Mary Michael of the Hearts of Jesus and Mary

Both my father and mother were German. We lived right in town, just a little town—five hundred people, and only eighteen in my high school senior class. My dad owned a garage and filling station. They had a little restaurant with one counter, one booth. My mother worked there. I just got in the way.

My dad could fix almost anything. He was a workaholic. The garage was right next to the house, a few steps down, and he was there at all hours. It was hard to get him to come in and eat; he worked very hard.

We were the first ones in town to get a television set. The neighbors would come over and watch on our "snow TV." You had to put the antennae up high, and all the neighbors would come over when we'd say, "It's good; it's clear tonight. Come on over."

They were good parents. They got along well and it was a good thing my father died first because he couldn't have gotten along without my mother. I couldn't see how he could live alone.

They were just always there. My mother was always home. We came home from school and she was always there. Our home was *everything*. You always wanted to be there. Our Christmases were great; we had our tree and the gifts were way out to the middle of the floor. I'd go to our friends' houses and they didn't have many gifts, but we always had lots of gifts. We weren't wealthy, but I never felt I was lacking anything.

I was a tomboy. I should have learned about fixing cars, but I didn't. And I didn't learn anything about cooking. My older sister's a great cook. I don't know what happened to me. I really don't. My sister would go shopping and see things in the store and bring things home. Not me; whatever was on the list, that's what I came home with.

I think there were thirteen years between my older brother and me. And then my younger brother, he was five years younger. It was like two families.

We were always trying to get away from him, when we were doing things we didn't want him to know, like smoking under the railroad cars. We had a lot of fun. We went swimming down in a crick, a river. We had to track through all this grass and woods to get to this hole—a swimming hole. Then we'd build grass huts down there. Can you imagine? And then we'd crawl in there. I just can't imagine. There must have been snakes. I'm just petrified of snakes. That would be a good place where we would do our smoking, too.

My family was real easygoing. Even friends I played with, we just didn't have all their rules. We were fussy kids with eating, but my mother just tried to fix something we liked. I didn't eat much; I was just in a hurry to go out and play outside. As I was running out the door, I would grab candy. We didn't have to do the dishes or anything like that. They were good parents but they weren't real strict. I'd be running down to get my friends to play and they had to finish dishes. Well, we didn't.

We didn't have a Catholic school because it was just a small town, but we were good practicing Catholics and went to church every Sunday. Some of the nuns came to teach us in the summertime, and I enjoyed going to classes but I didn't have thoughts about becoming a nun. Some of the girls from our town would go there to a boarding school for high school, maybe forty miles away. They stayed the week and then came home. My sister-in-law did that. The thought was too much for me. To be away from home, I couldn't think of doing that at that time. I couldn't see how the other girls could leave home and go there for school; it wasn't something I would ever think of doing. It frightened me. I just couldn't imagine doing that.

During high school, I was a cheerleader. That was fun. We went to all the basketball games and I liked that. In fact, I was a cheerleader all four years.

In high school, I wanted to be a doctor, so I went to the University of Wisconsin–Stevens Point for the first four years. I studied a lot and worked hard to get good grades. I wasn't involved in a lot of things; I was concerned with studies and getting good grades. Then I applied to medical school. At that time, I think there were only seven in the class—just a few—and I was accepted. I guess I had these ideas of helping people and being a missionary doctor. When I went to college, I still went to Mass. Sometimes, I would go during the week. I didn't have any devotion to the Blessed Mother. I didn't even pray the rosary after a while. But that all changed later.

My younger brother lived with me in a small apartment when I was going to medical school. He was completely carefree, and I was working so hard and spending all my time studying and trying to get good grades. Maybe I envied him because he was so carefree. He worked in a florist shop and he had these crazy friends. One drove a hearse!

This was during the Vietnam War, a kind of wild time with a lot of demonstrations. I remember getting involved, and the tear gas, which burns. I went a couple of times when they were hooping and hollering, or they'd be stopping traffic, but I was never that involved. I observed more than I took part. I was against the war at that time. My father was against it because he didn't want my brother to have to go.

In medical school, you're assigned a cadaver. It's in a large container. And to work on it you just crank and it comes up. You start and you work from the outside, every part of the whole body. That wasn't any problem. That didn't bother me. You get kind of cold. You don't think about it too much. It's something you have to learn to work on. It's not like you're thinking this was somebody's father or somebody's brother.

I had a real close friend—Bill—in medical school. We worked on the same cadaver. I can remember when we'd finish at night—the fat tissue it gets under your nails–and I can remember a lot of times we'd go to a restaurant nearby.

It was getting into the clinical work, working with people, that I found hard. I don't think I had the personality for it. I wanted to leave my first year. I was having a hard time and didn't want to go anymore but my older brother came over and talked me into staying. We weren't close. We got along okay but we weren't real close; not like with my younger brother where you can say almost anything and you think along the same lines. My older brother was real nice. He was just trying to help me out.

It was a disappointment for my parents, for my family, because they were going to have a doctor in the family. I don't blame them, I suppose. It was a disappointment. It was hard to say, "I don't want to do this." There was one class I had a hard time with, but I stuck it out. I kept going.

In my third year, I left. It was traumatic. It was hard—the whole thing, telling them you're leaving and quitting medical school. It was a hard time. I mean, I'm glad I left. I mean, I didn't want it, I just didn't want it. In the third year, I guess I was kind of panicky about doing an externship at a hospital. I got panicky over the whole thing and I couldn't take it anymore. It was too much for me, so I said I want to leave. You had to talk with the head of the different departments. They question you up and down. It was awful.

They try to figure out what's going on in your head. And why you really want to leave. And they have other ideas. I can remember one saying something about where I was going to go. He was accusing me of something about my parents. I can't remember—insinuating something about being close to them. I just remember it was upsetting. I guess he thought that maybe I was letting other people control my life; I wasn't in charge, something to that effect. Maybe he thought I was too close to them, that I couldn't do things on my own. I just remember it was an unpleasant conversation.

After med school I went to a technical school for a little while to learn the computer. I went to Milwaukee, and I was going to work on a graduate program, but I didn't carry that through. I stayed in a crummy apartment. Actually, now when I think of it, it was really scary; the apartment I stayed in, they said that somebody was murdered in it. I think it was on a bad side of the city. It was the east side of Milwaukee. Then I went to Chicago and I found work at a large insurance company in the Loop, right on Lake Michigan. You looked out one side and you could see the lake. It was a real good job. I worked there almost eighteen years. That's where I was working when I got this call.

I liked my job. I didn't have any reason to want to leave. I really loved that work. I couldn't wait to get there in the morning. We had "flex time," so we could come in during a range of time in the morning as long as you put in a certain number of hours. You didn't have to be there at seven; you could come between seven and nine. And your lunch break wasn't just boom-boom. Some days it was longer, and some days it was shorter. It was a beautiful job. I just loved it. I was a programmer analyst. We wrote the programs, designed the programs to pay insurance bills.

I've been lucky because the twenty years I worked, I enjoyed it. Not everybody likes their work. If I had it to do over, I wish I had gotten into that right away rather than go to medical school. I had some training in computers already, and the insurance company gave me some training. At the time, women weren't being paid equally with men, so to catch up to make us on the same level, all of a sudden, every little while, I got a pay raise. It was really funny; I would come home and I had another pay raise! They were big chunks!

In the meantime, right across from where I worked there was a Catholic church, and almost every day I went to Mass down there. I had this thought that I should start praying the rosary again. After high school, the rosary was in the back of a drawer in my bedroom and there it sat. I don't think I prayed the rosary at all during college. I don't know where this inspiration came from, but I thought I should start praying the rosary. I started trying to do it when I went to bed. That was a mistake; you start praying these prayers when you get into bed and you just fall asleep. So that didn't work.

One Christmas, I think I was down at my mother's house. She lived a block away. She was in her late seventies. Her brother used to live with her and he had left some books in a cabinet, including *The Song of Bernadette*, a book of fiction about Saint Bernadette of Lourdes.

That's where it all started. I read that book and something just clicked. I got interested in her life, which started a desire to read other spiritual books. I started going to Mass all the time. During the week it was in Chicago, where I worked, but then on the weekend where I lived in Indiana I would go wherever they had Mass early in the morning. I had this real desire to pray. I wanted to pray a lot.

I was so excited about this new thing that was happening to me. At lunchtime, I couldn't wait to get out and go to a Catholic bookstore; I'd spend almost my entire lunch hour browsing the books and buying some new ones. I was just so excited about all this.

I remember that I loved baseball. I loved the Chicago Cubs. My mother did, too. She noticed that I lost interest in that. The Cubs game would be on at her house and I'd be outside reading. Things like that were changing. My family noticed that, and my mother would get upset because I always wanted to be at church. I'd take off to go up and just pray by myself. It was just such a strong desire to do that, to be alone.

One morning as I was coming out of Mass, an older woman came up to me. She noticed I was always at Mass. There is a statue of how the Blessed Mother looked at Fatima. Some people would take that statue into their homes and they'd invite people in to say the rosary and prayers; the statue would stay for a week and then go on to another house. She invited me out to her home because she had it in her home, and so I went out there and then I got to be real friendly with her. She read a lot of spiritual books and biographies of saints and we got to talking a lot. I was having all these desires to read about saints and spiritual things, and so I had someone to talk to and share my experience with. I couldn't share with my family; they were concerned. I couldn't relate this to them because they were upset that I was being so taken away by wanting to go to church all the time and wanting to pray. I had this lady I could talk to. She mentioned one time when I was out there one evening, "Maybe you have a vocation to a religious life." I thought, that's impossible because of my age. I said, "What kind of religious group would I go to?" Sisters that serve the sick with nursing, or that teach—I didn't have any of those qualities. I didn't understand it, but I still had this desire to pray and dedicate myself to God. It went on like that for a while. She knew a priest, and it was a real coincidence because he had just been up to *this* monastery teaching the sisters Gregorian Chant.

I got up enough courage to call him and I went to see him and while we were talking, he just came out after a while and said, "Maybe you're being called to the contemplative life." That wasn't a shock because I had that feeling. One time I was reading a book about monks and the contemplative life. I had this feeling, that's what God was asking me to do. I can't explain how it was; it was interior. Deep down I knew that's what I was supposed to do. It was a real coincidence, the priest had been up to this monastery teaching the sisters here Gregorian Chant. He mentioned this monastery to me. I said, "I'm probably too old, though." He said, 'Well, we'll call." Then I got information.

What impressed me when I got the pamphlet was they all wore long habits and there were pictures of them at night, kneeling before the Blessed Sacrament. I saw all that and said, "That looks great!" It made such an impression on me. I got up enough courage to call here and that was real hard, to pick up that phone to call and make an appointment, because this was all so strange. I had no idea really what the monastic life was all about. It was all new to me. I just knew that God was calling me. I knew for sure. There weren't any doubts. In some ways, I had it easy because a lot of the women that come here are looking; they're searching; they don't know quite what they want. They go to different monasteries, look into the active life. I didn't have that. I knew I was supposed to come to this—to the contemplative life, for sure.

My mother, when I approached her about the contemplative life and showed her the pamphlet, it just really hurt her. She didn't want anything to do with it. That was hard because she was so much against it. She was older. And she was sick. Since I wasn't married, I took care of her a lot. I was close to my mother, and she was getting older. She had a bad heart, but I think she died of some kind of cancer. She was always getting blood transfusions. But I knew God came first. It was really hard, but that was just the way it was. I'm sure now she understands.

The second time I visited the monastery, I just wanted to ask some questions about what I had to do to get here. I was so anxious to come and so afraid they wouldn't take me and it was like, "Let me in!" I kept wanting to know, "What should I do next?"

I had a strong conviction that I knew I belonged at the monastery. I was supposed to come here. It was what I was supposed to do. It was just I had to hurry up and get here. I couldn't wait; I was just real anxious to get here. I really was confident, even though I didn't know much about the life from reading the pamphlets. It's not the same as coming here and living. I can't understand why, but I was very sure that this was it. I knew for sure I was coming. The Mother Abbess gave me a list of things you have to bring and I started on that. It's kind of funny things when you think about it. It was real funny because I needed a white blouse with sleeves and I had the hardest time finding one. I had to go way up the north side of Chicago; a religious store sold them for kids. I made such an effort, such a big thing out of this. They have some of the things at the monastery, and if I didn't get them, it wouldn't have been the end of the world. I needed a blue blouse for working outside in the garden as a postulant. I was wanting to get all this stuff—a sewing kit—exactly what was on the list. It wouldn't have been the end of the world if I hadn't gotten it; they would have gotten it for me.

It's all so interior it's hard to put into words. When you have doubts, you know that. But this was just so clear. You have that inner peace, so you know you're doing the right thing when you don't have turmoil, when you're at peace.

This made my life meaningful. It gave meaning to my life. Such a crooked path. I don't know why it was me. It's hard to understand. God wanted me, so I guess He loves me the way I am, so that's all that counts. It's all past. You can't change it. Not everybody's life is perfect. Things fall into place. Anyway, I'm here and that's something. That's special. Not everyone is called to this life.

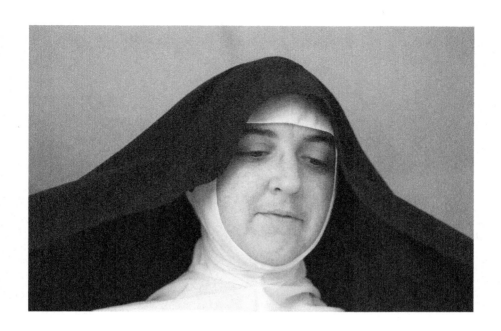

A novice harvests cabbages grown in the monastery's gardens. She smiles, caught using hosiery—a novel gardening method—to protect the vegetables from worms.

In general, the nuns observe monastic silence, a custom in which they speak only what is necessary and in a low tone in order to complete a task. One hour a day, during recreation, they can talk freely.

The Mother Abbess was not particularly pleased to discover the holy graffiti that turned up on the greenhouse. Set on the nuns' cloistered premises, it could only have been their handiwork.

Rockford Poor Clares make and ship the host. Here, a nun stamps out the host after it has been baked.

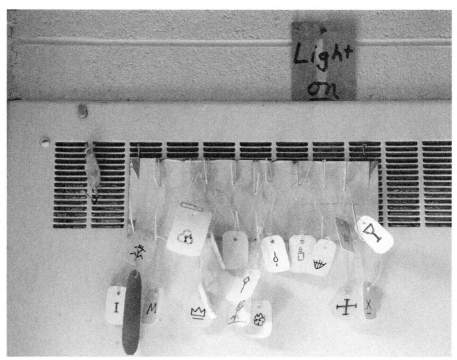

The nuns' marks hang by paperclips on a radiator next to the door. If a nun goes outside, she indicates this to the rest of her community by removing her marker. When a postulant enters the Rockford Poor Clares, the Mother Abbess assigns her a mark.

Part II

The Life

3

Monastic Living in a Throwaway Culture

It is a mystical life. The more that God gives to us, the more we give back to Him. And we are freed, because the structure of our life is such that we don't take on work that is over-encompassing in the mind; the reason for that is so the mind and heart can be with God.

Sister Maria Deo Gratias of the Most Blessed Sacrament

The corridors of the monastery are dark, as usual, the lights off. Mother Miryam walks out of the nuns' private choir chapel after the Divine Office. She opens a closet and finds her mantle—a heavy cloak. The woolen artifact is a vital layer at the Corpus Christi Monastery in the winter; it keeps the nuns warm in the drafty building, which is heated by a boiler that dates to the building's construction in the 1960s. The nuns clean and repair the boiler themselves, as much as possible. Mother Miryam has used this same mantle since she entered the monastery in 1955; green-thread stitching denotes her mark—the letter R. (Mother Miryam was assigned this letter when she first joined the community; the Mother Abbess at that time was partial to giving each postulant a letter for her mark—a letter from the name Jesus, Mary, Joseph, Francis, Clare, or Colette.) The cloth in Mother Miryam's mantle is worn and thin. She jokes about these "old rags" that she loves. The garment has been mended many times, the fabric unraveled and reused; it is precious because she helped make the mantle more than fifty years ago. "I hate to give it up," she says. "Then I wonder why it's worn. That's what amuses me. You wonder, 'Why is it wearing out?' It's been a long time! We expect things to last a long time around here."

According to the Rule of Saint Clare, the Poor Clare Order was granted the "privilege of poverty" so that the individual members as well as the community as a whole would not own property. Sister Mary Gemma quotes the novel credo, "without anything do I own." Literally, this means a nun cannot borrow anything from one of her religious sisters because, she says, "it would acknowledge ownership by the other sister of something." Mother Miryam does not own the mantle; it is for her use. Poor Clare nuns look to God, their superior, and church patrons for sustenance.

This absolute poverty, a pioneering concept at the order's inception, hails from Saint Francis, the forebear of the Franciscan order of Poor Clare nuns. Saint Francis wrote of his community of friars, "Let the brothers not make anything their own, neither house, nor place, nor anything at all. As pilgrims and strangers in this world, serving the Lord in poverty and humility, let them go seeking alms with confidence, and they should not be ashamed because, for our sakes, our Lord made Himself poor in this world. This is that sublime height of most exalted poverty, which has made you, my most beloved brothers, heirs and kings of the Kingdom of Heaven, poor in temporal things, but exalted in virtue."[1]

The future Pope Gregory IX tried to relieve Sister Clare and her followers, the Poor Ladies, of the harsh tenets, but she held fast, earning approval in decree for "Privilegium Paupertatis," issued September 17, 1228:

As is clear, by your desire to be dedicated to the Lord alone you have given up your appetite for temporal matters. For this reason, having sold everything and distributed it to the poor, you propose to have no possessions whatsoever, in every instance clinging to the footsteps of Him, who was made poor for our sakes and is the Way, the Truth, and the Life. The lack of goods from this *propositum* does not frighten you, for the left hand of your heavenly spouse is under your head to uphold the weaknesses of your body that you have submitted to the law of the soul through your well ordered love. Accordingly, He who feeds the birds of the sky and clothes the lilies of the field will not fail you in matters of food and of clothing until, passing among you, He serves Himself to you in eternity when indeed his right arm will more blissfully embrace you in the greatness of His vision. Therefore, just as you have asked, we confirm your *propositum* of most high poverty with apostolic favor, granting to you by the authority of the present document that you cannot be compelled by anyone to receive possessions.[2]

As elected Novice Mistress at the Corpus Christi Monastery, Sister Mary Nicolette is responsible for overseeing the training and formation of postulants and novices; she buffers young women from a cultural clash. Sister Mary Nicolette helps women make the transition from the outside world; she was nominated and then voted into the position because the other nuns recognize she is uniquely situated, as one of the younger members, to understand the current challenges of adapting to monastic life, and to relate to the young women. "The monastic culture is a culture of itself, of its own. Of its own," Sister Mary Nicolette says. "So while we have many different sisters coming from different cultures, we all learn the monastic culture when we come." To this end, Sister Mary Nicolette says an aspiring nun must shed presuppositions and routines, in order to arrive at the monastery with an open disposition to relearn even the simplest of tasks. "When they come we explain to them that you're relearning everything and you just have to be very humble, you know, and willing to listen," Sister Mary Nicolette says. "And teachable. Be very teachable."

Each member of the cultural time capsule that is the cloistered monastery is a product of her upbringing, her familial context, and her geographic framework. Within the enclosure, novices and postulants are integrated gradually into the rest of the community, as required by canon law; they reside in a separate wing from the cells of the professed nuns who have made temporary and permanent vows (typically three and six years, respectively, after entering). Today, the contrast between mainstream culture and the cloistered monastery is so stark, and departure from the world outside to the ancient rules so radical, that novices are given more time than they were given in past decades—one extra year before making final vows—so that they can adapt to monastic life. This steady and gradual immersion is intended to allow them adequate time to discern if they truly are called and to learn if they can adapt to the deliberate environment of unceasing prayer.

"You're just so used to functioning in a normal way," Sister Mary Nicolette says. "Eighteen is the youngest a woman would come. But already, at eighteen, nineteen, twenty, you're used to functioning a certain way. Usually, the younger women find it easier to adapt because they're not as set in their ways as an older woman would be, perhaps, who's had a career and a home. But still, at that age, it's like, 'Hold on!' You know?"

They say only what is necessary, in a low tone, in order to complete a task, and ask another nun to step out into the hall for the conversation so as not to disturb anyone else in the room. Anything a nun says must serve a purpose; otherwise she must refrain from talking (except during the daily evening recreation, when they are allowed to socialize). "Obviously, sometimes we slip," Sister Mary Nicolette says, "but it's a discipline that we try to cultivate and foster, and it's a learning process because when you first come, you're not used to that. So the novitiate is good for that."

As a novice, Sister Maria Benedicta describes the process of integrating into the monastic community as "a time of orientation and learning." "It's really kind of unraveling for everybody," she says. One evening as a postulant, Sister Maria Benedicta took her assigned seat next to her Novice Mistress for collation. When the dish of potatoes was passed, two portions remained—a full potato and half of a potato. Sister Mary Nicolette told her, "You may take a full potato." She was not hungry enough to eat a full potato, though, and thought, "I may, but I may not." She served herself the half-potato. "And then I realized, I think 'may' actually meant, 'Take the full potato,'" she says. "It was like, 'whoops!' You realize what this really means is, I need to give my full consent, but I need to take a full potato. Even though you have the fundamental attitude that I'm coming to do God's will, it's really in the small things. Talk about countercultural from independence and doing things your way, to say, 'Okay, I'll eat a full potato."

Sister Maria Benedicta explains,

It's a life commitment and it's very different from anything in the world, so it's in the wisdom of the Church to say, "Live this life. See if it's for you." In Saint Clare's day, a woman would come for a year and then make final vows. But gradually, the Church has said, "Let's just take our time and say the person can decide over time, the community can decide, Is this person called here? Do they fit? Do they have the right dispositions to strive for holiness, those sorts of things it takes?" So you can take the commitment and have it be informed. It's not just, "I love it! It's great!" I have time to experience the difficulties I'm going to encounter and ask, "Can I live this? Can I make these sacrifices over time?" And it's the wisdom of the community, too. You're gradually incorporated into the community life. We get up at midnight, but when you first come, you don't get up at midnight every night. You would just crash. So it's gradual; everything happens kind of gradually. You lead certain prayers at certain times, with a gradual incorporation into the fullness of the life.

Forty-seven years old when she began to learn the ways of the monastery as a postulant, Sister Mary Michael pondered the unbending peculiarities. Working in the kitchen, she wondered, "Why do the vegetables need to be cut this way? And prepared this way?" But she accepted the structure imposed on her, and she deferred to tradition. She has seen others resist the tutelage. "They might be used to a better way, or may even know more about it than I do," Sister Mary Michael says. "You notice sometimes they find it hard not to say something and to just do it. The work is done a certain way. I think that's what some find hard; they know how to do something but we do it a certain way, and so you should follow the way we're doing it. Maybe they question that, why it's done that way."

Sister Mary Michael attempts to convey the challenge of subjugating one's own volition to the monastic customs: "It's so restrictive, especially starting out. You have to.... You can't.... There's some place you're supposed to be all the time. Somebody's telling you what to do and where to go."

"It's just a different—very different—culture that, at first, you're just like, 'Wow,'" Sister Maria Benedicta says. "You know how to do normal things, but here we do it differently. With monastic life, you do things a certain way so that it doesn't take a lot of conversation to discuss. It's just, there's a way that we do it, but it makes it more peaceful and run more smoothly and we don't have to talk about a lot of things so that our hearts and minds can be on God."

Any domestic idiosyncrasies Sister Maria Benedicta possessed when she entered the enclosure have been undone during her tenure. She has relearned how to make her bed the monastic way, folding the blankets lengthwise in thirds—a symbol of the Trinity and also a practical measure that keeps the blankets from dragging off the low beds, sweeping against the floor, and getting dusty. She has relearned, too, how to hang the laundry outdoors with her Novice Mistress silently, crisscrossing the courtyard in sync; how to clean her plate with her bread, then wash her dishes in a tub on the rolling cart in the center of the refectory, and then replace her dishes in the drawer at her assigned place at the table. "It's like, I thought I knew how to do dishes," she says, remembering her first impressions of the monastery. "But it's like you don't even know how to do dishes anymore! You don't know where anything goes, you don't know how anything is done. We have a very systematic way and it goes very smoothly, you know. But it's like every aspect of your life you're relearning and it's like, 'Wow, you know.' And at first, it's really like, 'How do we do dishes again?' Everything in your day is like this: 'How do we do this? How do we eat? What's the ritual for eating?' You take out your plate at a certain time. You know, it's very, very different."

Failing to register each new instruction, Sister Maria Benedicta told her Novice Mistress, "I know you told me how to do the dishes yesterday, but you also told me how to do five hundred other things. It's really overload at first. My goodness! And you forget. It's like, 'Oh, I heard that, but I forgot.'" Sister Maria Benedicta, the most recent member of the community, is supposed to lead each procession. She recalls her confusion when the Divine Office would end and nuns began leaving the choir chapel. "All of a sudden everybody's up and it's like, 'I'm supposed to be first!' It's like, 'Ahhh!' It's like, 'Bye, God, we're going! I don't know where we're going!' All the time, we're going somewhere and, okay, gotta go, and they're tripping over you. They're coming, they're expecting you to know, but I don't know where we're going!" Confounding the normal routine were the alterations to the schedule for feast days and during certain seasons in the liturgical calendar.

Through the daily upheaval to her own habits, Sister Maria Benedicta slowly became familiar with the monastic customs. She drew consolation by reframing her foibles within the grander schema. "We know it's between us and God," she says. "In Scripture, it says, 'Man looks at appearances, but God looks at the heart.' That's very comforting. I can be messing everything up, I can be doing everything wrong, but trying to do what God wants, and He's pleased with us. And that's very freeing. He doesn't ask us to be these perfect beings all the time. Yes, we try, but He looks in the heart and He knows that we're trying. That's all we have to do. It's so simple to live for Him."

In this built and controlled environment, twenty women with varied experiences and personalities attempt to undertake radical lives. "If you really have the call, you won't feel hedged in," Sister Maria Deo Gratias says. "If you don't have the call, then the rules are burdensome. But, really, the rules are just a loving response to the Lord who called us to the life, and so there have to be some guidelines. That's what the rules are. And there have to be some challenges of, okay, you said 'yes' to God, you said you would give yourself to God, so there has to be something to give." Until making solemn vows, a nun can petition the community to leave the monastery.

Sister Maria Deo Gratias says that the monastery's dwindling population has not altered the community's recruitment strategy or diluted the customs; one exception is the raised age limit for women wanting to join. "The community won't hold onto anybody and say, 'Well, we'd like to have numbers,' because sometimes numbers—if you're not living the life the way you're supposed to live the life—can be a detriment to community," Sister Maria Deo Gratias says. "So adding to our numbers isn't the answer. It's the quality of life. That's the most important thing."

"What draws you here? What makes you stay?" Sister Maria Benedicta asks of the hiccups and frustrations she has encountered. She answers her own question: "Love. At first, it is unsettling, but once you learn it, you can really settle down and really, like, enjoy the benefits of the life, rather than being puzzled by it. Your mind and heart can be on God. It is like a fundamental motive; as much as we can, we think about Him. But the love grows—love for Him, rather than love for ourselves, so that we're not still wanting to say five years later, 'But if we did it my way, it would still be a lot faster!' No. You give that up. Or you may still be thinking about it five years later, but you say, 'Okay, Lord, you can have this again. I'm doing this for you—just for you—not for myself,' even if you don't agree with it. It's all for love."

As Sister Mary Nicolette explains, "We've set our hearts on God—love of God. So even the work that we do, some of it is very common and mundane, you know, cleaning and keeping house. But it's done for the love of God. And when everything is done for the love of God, that sets kind of a higher standard because you won't do it sloppily if you know you're doing it for the Lord and for the love of God. That's what keeps us here and would keep us doing the same things—that desire to love and serve God. And also—this would be secondarily, but it always comes in—is it's for the good of community. We serve community. In Scripture, the two greatest commands are to love the Lord with all your heart and to love your neighbor as yourself. God is first, and then neighbor. But they really go together because our way of expressing our love of God often is in the very common day-to-day life with one another."

Prospective nuns are initiated to the daily rhythm of work and prayer, meals and sleep with the sounding of two bells. One bell is called Peter, for Saint Peter, whom Jesus described as the rock on which the Church would be built; the other bell is named Paul, for Saint Paul, a Jew who persecuted Christians before he was blinded on the road to Damascus and then became a follower of Jesus. "Peter does the most work," Sister Mary Clara says. That bell signals the start of Mass and summons the nuns working outdoors to the chapel for the Divine Office.

In an early lesson in cultural adjustment, postulants and novices are taught that obedience is a free choice. Sister Mary Nicolette explains that a superior—a Novice Mistress in the novitiate, or the Mother Abbess for the entire community—always first "invites" a woman to undertake a task; rarely would a superior need to word the request more strongly or directly by making a command. A superior might ask, for example, "Would you like to go outside today and prune the fruit trees?" "It's an invitation so the person can make the free choice to obey," Sister Mary Nicolette says.

Today, the nuns are amused by anecdotes when previous newcomers simply accepted the strangeness of monastic culture, miscalculated their environment, and exhibited unquestioning obedience to a humorous conclusion.

Sister Joan Marie says that when she first arrived in 1950, the culture was stricter: In the spirit of anonymity, the nuns were not allowed to share personal information about themselves, and they were supposed to begin any verbal exchange with "Dear Sister." "We still try to," Sister Joan Marie says, "but we had to say, 'I humbly beg, sister, would you do this or would you do this?' Or, 'I humbly beg, sister, can I have your pencil, can I borrow your pencil?' We were supposed to say all that. One sister—another postulant— thought that we were saying 'Honey Babe.' She thought the Mother Abbess was saying, 'Honey Babe, would you do this, would you do that?' That was really funny! I knew that right away; I knew she would never say 'Honey Babe!' Well, I knew we were supposed to say, 'humbly beg,' 'humbly beg.' She was older, see, so I think it's harder to come when you're older. I don't know. That's just my theory."

Sister Mary Gemma's all-time favorite story—"the funniest story I've heard since being here," she says—dates to before her arrival, to the 1950s. At the time, the novitiate was on the second story of the building, furnished with a large round table for studying. The Mother Abbess told the postulants and novices that she would like the round table brought to her on the first floor. "So all the novitiate sisters were struggling to get this round table down the stairs," Sister Mary Gemma says. "They were narrow stairways. When they finally got it to the Mother Abbess's office and she saw, she started to laugh so hard tears were coming down her face! She said, 'I meant the book!' There's a book called *The Round Table* that was up in the novitiate. The sisters just love to tell that story. The Mother Abbess laughed and laughed and the tears were just going down her face!"

A chasm has always existed between secular culture and religious communities. In the lapse from the order's founding eight hundred years ago to postmodernity, a continental drift has widened the distance between mainstream popular culture and the cultural oasis that is the Corpus Christi Monastery, described by Mother Miryam as "a whole different secluded world." A fundamental unity of purpose and values prevents any significant culture war within the monastery between women hailing from different eras of the past century and different experiences around the globe. When Sister Mary Nicolette was a novice alongside women her mother's age, she felt an unexpected kinship she does not think would be possible beyond the enclosure. "We shared the same ideals, and we were striving for the same thing—living the same life—and so what was dearest and closest to our heart was what we shared, and so that kind of transcended any kind of generation gap as far as what we were striving for," Sister Mary Nicolette says. And yet it is no small feat to knit together several generations of women from a range of personal experiences, who departed their own versions of contemporary culture. The difficulties have intensified over the centuries for would-be-denizens willing themselves to release their fascination with what popular society suggests is significant.

An oft-stated adage at the monastery is that the nuns know, when they arrive, that they must adapt to monastic culture, and they should not expect the monastery to adapt to their individual desires and personalities. Sister Maria Benedicta embraces the dictum; even if her fresh eyes find room for improvement in the ancient order, she would not presume to suggest the community revamp any customs. "It would be totally contrary to what we're supposed to be," she says. "I'm not coming here to do things my way, you know what I mean? I need to fit into the life. We're fitting in; we're not trying to make the life fit us. And that is something you have to learn. Because you can say it. They can tell you before you come and you can say, 'Oh, yes, that makes perfect sense.' But then it's really in the little details. I have to even fold the laundry the right way, with all the nametags in the same place."

Sister Maria Deo Gratias believes that young women arrive at the Corpus Christi Monastery today from a world of immediacy, with a mind-set of "when I have a headache, I take medicine right away." "It's always instant. They want instant answers, instant gratification. It's like the level of suffering is very low. So, here, say you have a headache, naturally, if you need medicine you take it. But you don't jump to that as your first solution. Sometimes, by just being calm, then it's gone. On the emotional level, it's more a sense of keyed-upness, and I think it's probably because of the fast rate of society—everything at them all at once, everything is always action, action, action. Where, if you come here, it's a different culture, so they have to learn. Not that they can't; most of them that enter are very welcoming of this, but because they don't have the experience from the world, then they have to learn how to slow down, or they have to learn how to combat difficulties or struggles that they may have within themselves in trying to adjust to the silence and to the life."

Seventy-four-year-old Sister Mary Joseph is known as the mechanical nun who fixes what she can and calls in repairmen for the rest, often to teach her how to make the repair herself next time. Born in the aftermath of the Great Depression's financial reserve and material minimalism, Sister Mary Joseph's transition to the monastery felt simple. What she learned at home was reinforced at the monastery; with tools, she was taught to handle possessions "as they should be," she says—leaving them in good condition so that others could use them after her. She joined the Rockford community as an eighteen-year-old in 1957. Her understanding of modernity has developed from watching and listening to the tales of novices. She has seen young women who are the products of emerging technologies—objects she has never encountered in person or virtually—try to assimilate with her religious family. "They're coming from a different world, a different society than we came from," Sister Mary Joseph says. "It's sort of a throwaway society, where you use a thing and throw it out. We use a thing and take care of it, and keep on using it and use it so the next person is able to use it. It's a respect for things, and handling them carefully. And the younger ones weren't taught that. They use a thing and maybe that's the only one that can use it. It's not useable after that." Aghast by postulants' destructive tendencies, Sister Mary Joseph recites a lyric that captures the religious approach: "You can tell a monk by the way he sits and stands, the way he picks a thing up and holds it in his hand." She explains that the monastic way of caring for material possessions means knowing what pressures or demands the tools should take, how they have to be handled—"what they are, and using them for what they are and what they can do, and not pushing them too far. It's something you have to have or learn. And it seems they're coming from a world that just doesn't have that, for the greater part."

As religious communities have discovered that women need more time to adjust to life inside a cloister, Sister Mary Monica says the Rockford Poor Clares have revamped the black-and-white time frame of progressing from postulant to novice one year after entering the monastery; the three-year temporary vows two years later; and then final vows, which are permanent. At the Corpus Christi Monastery, temporary vows can be extended by one-year increments if a nun needs additional time before making solemn vows, which are permanent.

Although Sister Mary Joseph cannot relate to the newcomers' approach to the monastery's equipment, or condone their unrealistic demands on the tools, she does not judge the women. She knows they bring into the monastery only what they learned in the world. "They don't realize it because that's what they did; they just used things and then threw them out, and when they needed it again, got another," Sister Mary Joseph says. "Each generation will have to find their own ways to overcome what distractions are brought about by the people that are living in them at the time, because each person is different; each person comes from a different background."

Sister Mary Clara leafs through the pages of an album; at one time, a superior gave one of these small photo albums to each nun. She has turned hers into a book of memories, filling the transparent folders with cards and mementos, including a prayer card following the 1963 assassination of John F. Kennedy. She has also kept, since 1982, the piece of paper on which she wrote, in precise cursive, the final, solemn vows she made the day she became a Poor Clare. Ever since she made those vows, she has recited them again each day. In another transparent folder in her album is a card, and inside the card is a poem written in calligraphy—a gift from her best friend, Sister Michelle, the last time the two saw each other in 1978. The poem reads: "May you be kept in safety in the hollow of God's hand, no matter where you wander, over sea or over land; under His protection may your life's heights ascend, is the prayer that's offered daily, the benediction of a friend." Sister Michelle and Sister Mary Clara were teachers in an active religious order. Sister Mary Clara lived with that community for more than two decades before she decided to join the cloistered contemplatives at the Corpus Christi Monastery.

Clutching her memory book, she explains how her view on possessions has changed. "It's not that they become less important," she says. "You draw away from them. You know where your treasure is: It's up on the altar and the Tabernacle. If I was asked to give this up, if one of the sisters wanted the book, I would be able to give it to them." She pauses, then adds, "I would take some things out, of course."

When she was a teacher, most of Sister Mary Clara's wages went to her community's operating expenses; she received a ten-dollar monthly allowance, which she spent on the brand of toothpaste she liked. Sometimes, she saved up to buy a book. The more austere lifestyle of the Poor Clares still startles her at times; she believes that the gradual immersion into cloistered monastic life from an active order, in which she could make personal purchases and own a few items, afforded a more fluid transition than she might have experienced otherwise. "That's why the young people have such a difficult time," Sister Mary Clara says; "because they haven't experienced anything religious in their life, and so they have a harder time making the switch giving up things or not being able to hold onto things, not possessing things."

Sister Maria Benedicta's path from college softball pitcher to the youngest member of the Corpus Christi Monastery, when she joined in 2006, might appear unlikely. She knows this and smiles when she explains she was drawn by the poverty. Sister Maria Benedicta was a twentysomething active nun with the Marian Sisters, a Franciscan order, when her religious community made a pilgrimage from Nebraska to Assisi, Italy, where Saint Clare had followed Saint Francis; there they founded the Franciscan Friars and the Poor Clares, respectively. Sister Maria Benedicta toured San Damiano, the run-down church that Saint Francis and the Friars Minor turned over to Saint Clare for her budding order to use as a monastery.

"They were so poor!" Sister Maria Benedicta says. "But they were so happy because they had Jesus, and I thought, 'They never had to do anything but just love Christ.'" She shows a photographic postcard she kept of San Damiano, the Poor Clares' motherhouse where fifty sisters lived together, cramped in the stone quarters. Sister Maria Benedicta muses that she is not sure how they all fit. Some of the nuns must have slept on the floor. "Talk about only staying for the right reasons!" she says. "It's no comforts. But that's like how God puts it in your heart, because I think most people would see this and think, 'Uh, what? Yuck!'"

Sister Maria Benedicta aspired to the life of simplicity that Saint Francis and Saint Clare modeled—the giving of oneself entirely to Christ in utter poverty. In the Franciscan template for monastic living, poverty is not merely an external demonstration, with indifference to physical signs of wealth; poverty in religious life means divesting oneself of other status symbols—power and prestige and looking good to others. "That's the true poverty," Sister Maria Benedicta says. "Yes, it starts with the material things; I don't need all these things that lead me away from God, but it's also in giving up my own self, my selfish ways, my selfish desires in order to just live for Christ. The material poverty is a start; we don't want all these things that are going to lead us away from God because the more you have, the more you want.

"Jesus said, 'Blessed are the poor in spirit; theirs is the kingdom of God.' He didn't just mean, 'If you don't wear shoes, you'll go to heaven,'" Sister Maria Benedicta says. "Obviously, there's something behind it. There's so much more to poverty than not having the latest modern conveniences or the most comfortable whatever in your life. It's being stripped of everything that's not God. It's an interior stripping. The exterior stripping helps to make the interior possible. If I'm always seeking things that are going to help my comfort, it's not going to help me strip of all my selfishness. It's going to feed it. But the purpose is so that God can fill me rather than be filled with self. That's what poverty is: It's not an end in itself. Not wearing shoes is not going to get me to heaven, unless I see the purpose that, you know, it's very selfish that I always want to be comfortable, to seek self."

Her Novice Mistress, Sister Mary Nicolette, teases this concept further: In and of itself, she says, poverty has no value. "Poverty can even be an evil. It can even lead people to be bitter, or away from God. But when it can be used as a means, as an instrument to a deeper reality, then it becomes a good. But never in and of itself—poverty is just a means to something greater."

In what has become her third and, she hopes, final home with her second religious family, Sister Maria Benedicta feels affinity for the older nuns in her community. She senses few hindrances relating to the older nuns because of age differences or generation gaps. All share the same values, motivations, and desire for simplicity. "I think in the world, I wanted *this*, I wanted *this*, then *this*," Sister Maria Benedicta says. "Those things don't satisfy." She reflects on the postcard of the San Damiano Monastery that triggered her countercultural transformation. "Poverty," she says. "It's a good thing. It's not what the world thinks is a good thing."

Although she has not yet made permanent vows as a Poor Clare Colettine, Sister Maria Benedicta is already a zealous protector of her ancient order. Assuming that a new wave or trickle of postulants and novices follows, she will contend with any relics and mind-sets of contemporary culture that disrupt the carefully guarded terrain of the Corpus Christi Monastery.

Sister Mary Joseph
of Our Lady's Joys

Prayer was part of the family. I can't say when I first realized it because it was just part of our life, an integral part of our life. We said the family rosary every day.

I must have been around three when I started telling Mom, "Mom, I want a little sister." I had six older brothers. I wanted a sister, someone like me. She said, "You'll have to pray about it. You'll have to ask God." I prayed to God, and I did have a little sister!

In fact, I only had the little sister until I came here, and then she died ten days after I came. I had a sister while I was at home. Here, I have quite a number of sisters.

With my life, it should start with Mom and Dad.

I don't know as much about my father's family as I do about my mother's. Mom belonged to one of the better families in Milwaukee. And yet she was quite different. She was very advanced in school, and she liked to play with the boys in the sandlot. She'd play baseball with the boys in the sandlot, and she was doing that up until the time she got married. In fact, she said when she was going to Marquette University she still played ball with the boys. The boys asked her where she went to school and she said, "Marquette University." She said they were so hurt that she wouldn't tell them where she went to school because they had told her where they went to high school. They thought she was their age, but she wasn't. She looked much younger than she was. She was only eighteen, but she looked younger. I was always like Mom; I looked way younger than I am. She never looked old until she was really old.

Her father owned his own business—a baker supply business. He went to work every day of his life until he was ninety-one, when he died. Two weeks before he died, he got sick and stayed home. They were nursing him at home. I remember going to see him then. I was in sixth grade. Up until then, he had gone to work every day of his life.

Mom married Dad at eighteen, but she was a very bright, intelligent, young girl. She went to a private school, to Milwaukee University School. She skipped a couple of grades, and so she graduated early. She was not a Catholic at that time but she wanted to go to Marquette University. Her father was a Mason and the Masons are not in favor of the Catholic Church. Her uncle was a High Mason and he told Grandpa he could not send his daughter to Marquette. Mom said she was real happy then; she knew her father would let her go because Grandpa wouldn't let his brother tell him what he couldn't do!

Mom met Dad there at Marquette. Dad was studying; I think he had a fellowship. He was teaching while he was studying. She started going with Dad; my grandparents didn't like that. They offered, if she would quit school—because then she wouldn't go with Dad—to give her a fur coat. So she quit school. And then she got married. She got her fur coat and married Dad. I really don't know why they weren't in favor. It might have been religion. It was a real quiet wedding because they weren't in favor of it and also because she converted to the Catholic faith. She said it wasn't because of Dad—he didn't convert her—but Dad's parents had a good marriage. She didn't want to get married outside the Catholic Church. She saw there what she would want in marriage so she converted before she married Dad.

One of the hardest things for her was she knew when she got married she couldn't play out in the sandlot anymore! She had to stay home and take care of the house and hopefully raise a family. That was one of the hardest things—hearing the kids out in the sandlot playing and she wasn't able to go out.

Dad was studying to be a teacher. Mom read all the books on education, on educating children. She gave Dad the books she thought were worth his reading. Really, she read all of the books and she gave him the best. In a way, she got quite an education even though she never had a degree.

Mom started raising boys and she had boys and boys and boys. She wanted a girl all along. But she kept on getting boys. She wanted twins, too. After she had four boys, she was praying. She prayed to Saint Joseph for twins. The next ones were twins. Mom thought the doctor knew she was going to have twins because he told Ma when she went to visit him, "Sometimes these things happen." He told her what to do and that she wouldn't have to come back as much because he knew how hard it was with four kids out there in the waiting room. He was not expecting twins, but there were twins! They were born at the Deaconess Hospital. One was much smaller than the other; Joe was the smaller of the twins. I guess the nurses decided he wasn't going to live. At that time, the children didn't stay with the mother in the hospital. They were in the nursery after they were born, and so Ma went to the nursery to see the children. They had put Joe up by an open window, no blankets or anything. Mom was really upset. She put covers around him and she insisted he stay in the room with her. When it came time to go, Joe must have been a little underweight. They let Mom and Dad take him home because they were afraid of her reaction. And he survived fine. Mom decided then she would never have a baby in a non-Catholic hospital again so I was born in Concordia, the Catholic hospital.

We moved to Elm Grove, Wisconsin—near Milwaukee—when I was a year old. Before that they were living in Wauwatosa. I think because of the size of the family, they wanted to move out where there was more room for the family.

It was just a very good family life with brothers and my little sister. It was at the time of the Depression, back in the '40s when you didn't do much driving around because the gas was expensive. Mom and Dad saw an ad for a cottage on Lake Michigan that was for sale. They went by bus to see it and they bought it. It was very reasonable at the time because dad was teaching at a Catholic school, where the salary was way less than you'd get at the public school. During the summer, we would go to the lake, back and forth. We were just very frugal. We grew as much of our own food—produce— as we could. I know other children always had allowances. We never had allowances. If we needed money, we'd ask Dad and he'd give us whatever we needed for school, but we didn't ask him unless we really needed it. The boys would sometimes get a job and go bean picking with the migrant workers and the farm children around, or they worked for the cannery in Belgium. That would be their summer job if they didn't work in Elm Grove. Some of them, when they got older, worked at the brewery in the summer. The boys would also get babysitting jobs. I don't know whether other boys babysat, but I know my brothers did and the people liked them. They baby-sat for the family that owned the brewery. The people liked my brothers. They always felt safe with them and they were good boys, so they got a lot of good babysitting jobs. When I was old enough, I babysat, too, but I had my own clients.

I have a lot of memories with my brothers—being with them, playing with them, living with them. We had an acre and a half and we did quite a bit of gardening to raise food for the family as much as possible. We had apple trees, pear trees, plum trees, and cherry trees, and so we spent a lot of our time during the summer months picking fruit or taking care of the garden. My father was a teacher and so during the school year he was going to school when we were going to school, and during the summer he was home with us and working in the garden. His master's degree was in botany and so he was really into gardening. He loved the iris. That was his specialty in the garden—crossing the iris to develop other varieties. Now, when I see the iris today, I think, oh, he would have loved it! They've developed the iris so beautiful now that he would have really delighted in it.

Dad was also very interested in music, and so all of us played instruments. Some of us played piano, but if we played the piano we also played another instrument. A few times we all played together. I think my oldest brother played saxophone; he was twelve years older so I don't remember playing with him. I played flute. My sister played flute. One of my brothers played flute, another played clarinet, and the twins played trumpet. Dad was also the band director at the high school, where he taught chemistry until he had a heart attack.

My sister was four years younger than I was. We had our differences. When she was real little, with our family size, there were a couple of us in each bedroom. It was a big farmhouse and the boys were in two rooms. After Mary grew up enough, she came into the room with me. I must have been five or six by the time she came in. It was just a little room. We quarreled a lot. When the boys began leaving—my oldest brother got married when I was in the seventh grade and my second oldest brother got married when I was in high school—we could move to the bigger bedrooms. When the boys were gone, we had separate rooms and we got along better.

My brothers were everything to me. Since there were so many of us, I can't remember many times when they had friends over. They stuck together, though, so they didn't need a lot of other company. I looked up to them and they were wonderful. There was nothing better than being with my brothers. Being with them meant more to me than anything. Whatever they did, I wanted to do. In a way, my life was sheltered because they took care of me and made sure nothing ever happened to me. I was the youngest in the family for a few years, and that's why, when my sister was born, we didn't always get along; she was the youngest then, and she was the one getting spoiled. I didn't consider myself spoiled but they said I was.

I went to a Catholic school and I admired the sisters. We had the Notre Dame Sisters at the parish school. I got along really well with them and I admired them. Around seventh grade, during noontime, I was just daydreaming and looking out at the country woods near the school. I was praying and looking at the woods, praying about having a big family. I wanted to get married and have a family—a great big family—and one of the sisters came by and said, "Did you ever think about being a sister?" I said, "No," but then I began thinking about it and praying about it and I began to feel the call. My family went to daily Mass, six o'clock Mass every morning after I received Communion in the second grade. With our Lord, you have a daily relationship that you develop in prayer. The sister suggested it, but then in listening to Him, I did feel that He did want me.

The Notre Dame Sisters used to have an aspirature over on the Mississippi River in western Wisconsin. After eighth grade, I said to Mom, "What would you say if I wanted to become a sister and I wanted to go to the aspirature?" Mom didn't want that. She said, "You have a good family life. There's no reason to go over there. Wait until after high school." I would have had to go to a boarding school to go to their aspirature. I went to high school and there were different sisters, the Divine Savior Sisters, a different order than the Notre Dames. In a way, I liked the Divine Savior Sisters more and I admired them; I saw things in them that I liked better. I think the Notre Dame Rule was way stricter than the Divine Saviors', who seemed to have a more personal relationship, a human dimension rather than a focus on the rules. I thought, maybe I'll try the Divine Savior Sisters. I went to a guidance counselor and she encouraged me, but she didn't encourage me to join them.

In high school, I always read a lot. From the time we wanted to read, Mom had signed us up to a Catholic book club for children, so we always had good books to read. She got me books about Saint Therese of Lisieux and Andrew Jackson's daughter. My brother and his wife gave me *A Right to Be Merry*, which is about the Poor Clares. It was that book that sparked my interest in the Poor Clares, especially the chapter about the Rule of Saint Clare. The Rule of Saint Clare was to live the holy gospel. That was what drew me—the simplicity. There weren't any other pious practices, just the simplicity to live the holy gospel in poverty, chastity, and obedience.

And so I became interested in the contemplative life. The guidance counselor had books on the religious orders, and I read through all of the contemplative orders and I didn't like any. Right off, I didn't want to join any that had lay sisters doing the work, and the other sisters praying. I didn't want that; I didn't want someone else doing my work for me. I thought the prayer and work should go together. I didn't think there should be two standards, like the rich and the poor, or the publicans or the peasants and the nobility and more educated socially or elite—all those different standards in social life.

I think the guidance counselor gave me the names and addresses of orders that were already reformed. She thought I should join one that had already reformed. I came down to visit the Poor Clares. That was what I was interested in. The Colettines were reformed Poor Clares and that's what we are—Colettines. I looked at the addresses, and they had monasteries in Chicago and Rockford and Cleveland. Mom said she wouldn't want me to be in Chicago. Even as a contemplative, she didn't want me in Chicago; Chicago is a rough place, so I came to visit Rockford.

In a way, I didn't want it but I did believe it was what God wanted for me. It's where He wanted me to be, and so that's what I wanted.

Before that, I was planning to go to Marquette. I sent in my registration but when I had to finalize it, I said, "Do I need to send this in? I really want to enter the religious life." Dad said, "That's all right if you're sure." When he found out I wanted to come here—to a contemplative order—he wasn't so happy. He said it would be the end of my education. He said I should have more education. He was teaching at a Jesuit high school, and he said all the Jesuits he asked said the same thing: I should go for at least a year of college or university before I entered here. I don't know that anyone here has, but you can take courses by mail; theoretically we could, and I think some do. He didn't realize that. And then it was too late to finalize my registration for Marquette.

A number of my classmates, or in the class ahead, or the class behind entered the religious life. None entered the contemplative life. In a way, I could have been anything I wanted. I could have been a doctor, or I could have been a teacher or a nurse. In fact, they called me a dentist in high school. I knew I was going to enter the religious life but during vocational days for different professions, different people would come to see what you were interested in.

Although I was planning on entering here, I had never been here for an interview. I came down here for an interview at the end of the summer. That was my initial visit. I came down on the bus and I got lost in Rockford. They said to take the bus, and so I got on the bus. The trouble was, the bus I got on went the wrong direction. It went out to *North* Main Street. I was about to get off and I said, "It doesn't look like a monastery." I asked the bus driver, and he said, "Oh, you're in the wrong place," and so he gave me a transfer to come back down to South Main. I can't remember whether I was drawn to the building or repelled by it. I must not have been repelled by it or I wouldn't have come back. I was just happy I got to the right place. I rang the doorbell and it was dinnertime, noon. Wrong time. I was very young and I wasn't used to being out alone, but I wasn't scared either. I was just doing what had to be done before I came. You had to come for an interview, so I came for an interview.

I didn't realize they would make me wait until November before I could enter. They gave me a date in November—the sixteenth—where, if I wanted to come, I could come. It was the novitiate's Patron Saint Day for Saint Agnes of Assisi, Saint Clare's younger sister, who followed her to the religious life. Saint Clare followed Saint Francis, and then a few weeks later, her younger sister followed her.

They gave me a list of things I would need: towels, blankets, underwear, nightgowns, and shoes for the garden. I can remember Dad helped me with that. He took me to the shoe man, and that way I knew what size to get in the Sears catalog for the boys' shoes. The Poor Clares said garden shoes could be high shoes. Back then, girls didn't have high shoes, but I ordered them in the Sears catalog. I got a real nice lightweight pair of shoes for the garden. I don't have them anymore; I think they did give out.

They said you could bring along anything you needed or would want so I brought along a few books and a flute and sheet music. I had time to clean up my room before I left. I can remember everyone was going to school or their jobs. I was still at home. I felt bad because when the boys were cleaning up their things, I always considered it an honor to have their junk; but when I offered Mary some of my things, she wasn't interested. But, of course, she didn't need them. It was at that time that the boys discovered stuffed toys. Mary and I got all these stuffed toys that had character. I got a monkey and a couple of dogs. I had a number of those that they had given me, and so I had Mom give those to my nieces and nephews after I came.

I cleaned everything up and left it in the closet. Later on, Mom said, "If I had known all that you left in that closet, I never would have let you out of the house!" I left some artwork, some sketches, and I had some of Mary's artwork and letters and drawing pictures. She was a better artist than I was. She was very talented, very gifted, both in looks and otherwise. I left some of those in the closet. Mom appreciated those, I think. She didn't appreciate all of the other stuff I left—the *Better Homes and Gardens*. I was interested in architecture and building my dream home. I just didn't know what to do with all of my stuff. It was too good to throw away! And clothes I left because I thought Mary would have needed them sooner or later. But she didn't.

I remember my junior year, I went to a lay apostolate women's group over on the Mississippi River in western Wisconsin for a summer course. They had a lot of good courses for women. I got sick with a gall bladder infection and had to come home. I went to the hospital because our doctor was gone at the time and our substitute would only see me in the hospital. Usually, it was Mary that was in the hospital; she came to see me. She was too young to come in. They didn't allow children to visit in the bedroom, but they allowed her to come in. They were so used to seeing her.

My sister contracted leukemia when she was in sixth grade after she had her tonsils out. Mom thought that somehow her bone marrow had been poisoned by the ether when she had her tonsils out. That was Mom's guess. The type of leukemia she had was pernicious. She shouldn't have lived more than six months or a year at the most, but she did. She lived. Mom and Dad had her go to school, and they kept on her to go to school because they wanted her to have as much of a normal life as possible.

So she went to school and her teacher knew. They let the teacher know because she missed so much school. When she was sick, she was sick and she couldn't go to school. They never told Mary then what she had. We knew; the family knew. But they told Mary she had anemia so if anyone asked her, she said she had anemia. Otherwise, people would have always been asking how she was doing, like people do. But my parents wanted her to have as much of a normal life as possible.

When Mary was feeling well, she'd want to do anything she usually did and the doctor told her she could do whatever she wanted. Of course, he didn't realize she was like me—a tomboy—always wanting to do what my brothers did. She was like that, too, maybe not as much as I was. He didn't know what she was used to doing. She went out and played on the trapeze and when she came in, Mom looked at her—because the blood vessels began bursting—and she knew Mary couldn't do that again.

The thing was, sometimes in the end the disease didn't act like acute leukemia. Sometimes the red blood cells were produced correctly. Mom watched very carefully the medicines the doctors gave her; if she saw any bad reaction, she told Mary not to take it. Mom said the doctor said that, too. She said, "He gives the medicines to others and they take them like candy but they're dead." She'd go back and see that other patients wouldn't be there anymore because the medicines they were experimenting with were poisonous in the end. They had to be very careful. Mom watched very carefully, and so Mary lived. After a while, Mary knew the things she couldn't do because of the reactions. After a while, when we would go out to the cottage she couldn't even go wading because of the difference of the pressure of the water.

Mom and Dad didn't tell her the name of the disease but she understood she was very sick. The bone biopsies she had to have were painful. They weren't anything that you wanted to go through. She had long hair—long beautiful hair from the time she was little. When I was born I didn't have any hair. When I was one year old, they put a ribbon around my head so that people would know I was a girl, not a boy. But Mary had hair when she was born, and by the time she was one or two, she had long hair. She had braids when she was little—just two or three—long blonde braids. She was beautiful. She had pigtails when she started high school. I always had short hair. I never had curly hair. Mom didn't believe in trying to curl your hair if it wasn't curly so I just had a bob. They did give me a permanent once and when I came home, it was curly so my brother, Father Tom, who was in the seminary, told Mary, "You should cut your hair like Josephine." She had long hair and because of the medicine, she was losing it. But because of the braids, you didn't notice. I told her, "Don't pay any attention to him. You're fine." If she cut her hair, it would have been noticeable that she was losing it.

Mary knew she was very sick. And when she was real sick, she knew; she knew she was deathly sick. She knew how she was feeling. At times, when she was very sick she would wake up and say "mercy killing" because she was in so much pain. She was tempted, because of the pain, to want to be killed.

Mom, Dad, and Mary came with me when I entered here, and I remember seeing her in the parlor. I came in and I was dressed as a postulant and I was thinking, "This might be the last time I see her." And it was. I remember the sisters asking her if she wanted to enter the monastery. She, like myself, from the time she received First Holy Communion, went to daily Mass. In fact, I think she might have wanted to be a religious. I can't remember what she said to the nuns, but I knew she wouldn't live that long. I was sort of resentful that they kept asking her because I knew she wasn't going to live long enough to be a religious.

When they went home on Saturday, Mary felt awful sick. She went to school that Monday because she knew she was going to see the doctor that afternoon and she knew he was probably going to put her in the hospital for more transfusions. He put her in the hospital and she never went home after that. Mom was with her in the hospital; she always stayed with her. The day before she died—she died on November 26—Mom said the doctor came, and Mary told him she didn't want any more transfusions. And then she thanked the doctor and she thanked the nurses that had been caring for her because she knew she was going to die.

One of my friends was a nurse's aide in the hospital, and she said to Mom, "What's happening? Everyone's coming out of the room crying." It was because Mary was thanking them all for their help and what they had done. Mom said she didn't want any more transfusions, and so they all came out crying. Mary must have known that she was getting near death. And, no, she didn't resent that. In fact, in the end, she really was longing for it, to go and be with God. In the end, she wanted to die.

Usually, November is our time of Lent of Saint Martin and we don't have family visits or letters from November 2 until Christmas. I entered during that time and so I wasn't expecting any correspondence until after Christmas. But I was told that Mary had died. My family sent word and they told me. I knew she was ready, and I knew she wanted it because she had been so sick. But for Mom and Dad, it was terribly hard for them because I had come here, and then ten days later, Mary died.

I didn't know if I could go home for the funeral. I didn't ask. Usually, once you enter you don't go home for a funeral. I hadn't made a vow of enclosure then, but when you enter you observe it. I think they told me when the funeral would be, and I prayed during the time when she was at the funeral. My parents told me afterwards that Mary's entire class went to the funeral because she was in school until nine days before she died. She was a freshman.

I realized later that it was a good thing that I entered and didn't go home for the funeral because the public opinion would have been very hard. To come back here would have been very difficult; it would have gone against the public pressure. People would have said, "How can you leave when...? How can you leave now that your sister's...?" I think the Lord worked it that way. I asked Him for a sister, He gave me a sister. I came here, and she died right after. He gave me a sister for as long as ...

I prayed for a cure. Really, I did. I wasn't looking forward to entering. I thought it was what He wanted. And I tried to bargain with God: "Well, I'll answer if you make Mary well." But I knew I couldn't bargain.

That Christmas, when my parents came to visit, it was hard for them. It was even harder for them than it was for me. There were very few times I've seen Dad cry. Once was when they came back from the doctor and he knew what Mary had. I saw him reading *The Merck Manual*, and he was crying. And it was hard that Christmas when they came. Dad asked Mother Petra to pray for them because it was like the bottom had dropped out of the family. And it's true. It was like that. The two youngest were gone. But they got through it and so did I. Just remembering, though, it's hard.

But that's the way life is. And, you know, God's ways are not our ways. His thoughts are not our thoughts. And you see that, too, with the crucifix: God's ways are not our ways. That's what His son had to do for love of Him, for love of us, to show His love of us.

I think in every Christian's life, for everyone who's trying to follow Christ, they're going to experience it. It will be according to their vocation, according to whatever state of life they are in—they will all experience it in some way. It's a sacrifice He asks. It's the sharing in His suffering. And it's the share He gives to all of us, to all His followers. You can refuse, but then you're not being like His son, and He sent His son and His son gave us the power to become sons of God, to become God's children through baptism. He makes us like His son and if we're like His son, we'll be like Him in the different experiences of life.

You ask me, "Why the contemplative life?" I felt I could be anything I wanted to be. Really, if I wanted to be a doctor, I had the intelligence; I could have if I wanted—or anything else I wanted to be. Here, I thought, I could help more by praying, I could help people in every walk of life; it wouldn't just be one walk of life. Here, it's helping in all the professions. That's why I chose this.

4

Little House, Big Heart

It's a whole different world that we're living in.
Mother Miryam of Jesus

There is a scene that Sister Mary Gemma conjures easily. She has slipped back to this visual memory many times. When she was nineteen years old, she flew to California to visit her aunt, uncle, and cousins; it was her first—and second to last—trip by airplane. She hoped the vacation might save her from what she believed to be her calling to cloistered monastic life. She had pictured a "romantic encounter" during her trip to the West Coast. Raised in the country, she reveled in her relatives' sophisticated and uninhibited lifestyle; they partied with friends and drank alcohol. The trip ended early, with tears.

It is not this memory that Sister Mary Gemma recalls so vividly, though. Finding language for her experience in California takes time; in her recounting, she stops and starts, she pauses, and then she revises the timeline and events. She has not rehearsed the story with multiple retellings.

The series of images she knows so well, and the feelings resurrected by the visual memory, took place before she visited her relatives in California. The scene is not from her own childhood in northern Illinois, near her monastic home of almost four decades. The memory is her own. The experience is not.

Sister Mary Gemma describes what she sees: An open prairie and a family fighting to survive, uncertain if they will outlast the winter. It is the late nineteenth century. Sister Mary Gemma remembers that the family is waiting out a blizzard in the hope the rails will clear so a train can deliver necessities in time. They grind wheat in a coffee mill all day in order to make bread, which suffices until dinner the next night. The family labors for their daily bread; each day, they grind more wheat and then bake more bread to last one more day. At night, the mother sits with her baby on a rocking chair, unable to fall asleep because of the cries of "natives." Sister Mary Gemma sees the children sweeping the dirt floors of their cabin; because they cannot afford shoes, the children go barefoot from first thaw to first frost.

Sister Mary Gemma loves the dramas of the Ingalls family. She loves reading about Ma and Pa and Laura—the simplicity of their lives, the hard manual labor required to pioneer unsettled territory, the constant threats to their existence, the characters' faith in powers outside themselves, and their closeness and dependence on one another.

As a child, Sister Mary Gemma's family drove west through South Dakota, and so she can imagine the lake the Ingalls lived near, the birds that slept on the lake when it froze, the noises they made in morning. "I can picture it," she says. "I don't know why. It seems I must have seen it or heard it before, heard these birds. It's so real to me." When Sister Mary Gemma first read *Little House on the Prairie* as a child with an active imagination, the books gave shape to her fantasies. They carried her away from sometimes trying family dynamics. In grade school in the late 1960s, her father moved the family from Rockford to a rural village in the next county over. "He thought it would be a healthier bringing up for us if we lived out in the country and had animals to take care of," Sister Mary Gemma says. "He got us into a farming community where the kids were all farming kids and town kids. It was a completely different atmosphere." They had pet cats and dogs. They raised ducks and chickens. They hiked and camped. With this move, Sister Mary Gemma felt more connected to the Ingalls family.

Today, tears surface when she describes the challenges the pioneers faced. She knows that the *Little House* books were written for children. But, she says, "They're so simple and beautiful." Poor Clare Colettines at the Corpus Christi Monastery do not generally read novels. During the limited time that is unscheduled each day, in between meals and chores and prayers, and when they retire to their cells at night, they sew baptismal gowns or make prayer cards using dried flowers plucked from their gardens to be sold in the store. They read biblical and inspirational texts. Sister Mary Gemma assists in the monastery's infirmary; her primary charge is the only full-time resident of the infirmary: Sister Ann Frances, bedridden with advanced Alzheimer's disease. Sister Ann Frances speaks a language the other sisters cannot comprehend. At times, she grows distressed. She demands time and attention, often keeping Sister Mary Gemma from other duties or attending the Divine

Office. To soothe Sister Ann Frances, Sister Mary Gemma reads aloud. Sister Ann Frances smiles—the best smile in the monastery, Mother Miryam says.

At times, it has seemed like Sister Ann Frances might pass away soon, in a matter of months, but each time she has rallied and recovered under Sister Mary Gemma's watchful eye. Meanwhile, as Sister Ann Frances has become more needy, Mother Miryam says she does not know "quite how to entertain her." Mother Miryam says that she is happy to visit with Sister Ann Frances, who "talks back a mile a minute," and even though the nuns do not understand what Sister Ann Frances says, listening appears to comfort her.

"She's mystifying us," Sister Mary Gemma says. "She could last a long time yet. She takes a lot of my time, though. I do spend a lot of time with her because she gets confused and she gets restless and it's best to keep her entertained. I'm good at entertaining, I guess. And I'm pretty good at calming her down if she gets upset. Right now this is the necessity of the community."

Sister Mary Gemma's assistance in the infirmary is a blessing, Mother Miryam says; she does not know what the community would do without her. Maybe Sister Mary Gemma's voice or face suggests a memory. Maybe Sister Mary Gemma remains unfamiliar to Sister Ann Frances, yet she still manages to bring solace.

Like the rest of her community, Sister Ann Frances made lifelong vows to the enclosure. She committed to remaining until she died. And so she stays, even as she no longer knows where she is, no longer understands the symbolism of Communion, or why she must wear the small veil worn by the ill. She may no longer know herself or the vows she made.

Sister Ann Frances enlisted in the Marines during World War II. Ever since she transferred to the contemplative order from an active order, she has depended on others. While the public relies on the Poor Clares for prayers, the nuns pray for donations and gifts for their own sustenance. The cloister's inhabitants depend on benefactors from the outside world. Doctors, dentists, and chiropractors pay house calls to the monastery. Locals donate food. One delivers salmon he buys in Chicago. Other food requires effort to salvage, for instance cutting away the wilted parts of vegetables. All of this supplements fruits and vegetables the nuns grow in their gardens. Sister Joan Marie says the donations sometimes appear to be a miracle of redundancy. "As soon as we eat something, the same thing comes in. So it's miraculous, really!" Sister Joan Marie laughs. "I think, 'We ate that! It's at the door! We ate all that!'"

Just as the nuns hope for provisions, Sister Ann Frances looks to Sister Mary Gemma, who indulges her love of books, especially children's stories. "Sometimes it can seem like if you haven't read the stories for a while, you can tell her mind can't comprehend what you're saying to her," Sister Mary Gemma says. "And of course she can't express herself at all anymore. But when you start reading the stories to her, somehow there's some part of her mind that takes it in. She laughs at the right time. She smiles when I show her the pictures. She's so happy. I show her the picture on the cover: 'I'm going to read this to you today.' She remembers and she gets excited. She doesn't remember what we read exactly, but she remembers the picture when she sees it. It's so good for her. It's probably good for me, too, but I do have the joy to care for her and I do have the gift of gab and that's good for her."

The *Little House* series and Sister Mary Gemma's love for the plots and characters have unfurled a new drama, a present-day conflict for Sister Mary Gemma within her own psyche. "After reading those stories to sister, I get fascinated by the history of it," she says. "So much of the history I never knew before, and so I start looking up things in the encyclopedia, or I'll go look up on the map to see where this Indian Territory was, which was actually Oklahoma. I get so fascinated with it. I have to be very, very careful that I don't let it grip me so much that it takes me away from my relationship with our Lord. You admire this family's faith in Providence. Even though they had these worries, they had a great trust in Providence."

In caring for Sister Ann Frances and trying to keep her own appreciation for the Ingalls family in check, Sister Mary Gemma submits to the hierarchy of the Poor Clare Order: In living out her vows, Sister Mary Gemma waits until Christmas each year to ask the Mother Abbess for permission to ask her parents for one more book in the *Little House* series. "I have to keep asking myself, 'Am I getting these books for myself, or am I getting them for sister?'" Sister Mary Gemma says, "Because I really do love those books very much. That's a struggle for me. I often wonder if I should be asking for something like that. Sister is getting to the point she can't understand anymore anyway. She does all right, but you could keep reading the same book to her over and over again; she doesn't remember that she already heard it, but she enjoys it. That's something I struggle with right now. I love books, and stories like that are so interesting to me."

Even as Sister Mary Gemma recognizes her mixed motives and worries about indulging her imagination, she can hardly wait to read again what happens next, to learn again how the plots are tidied up, the characters evolved, the conflicts resolved. "We don't realize how hard it must have been for people who pioneered the United States and made the beginnings of America," Sister Mary Gemma says.

The Ingalls family left a culture known to them, foregoing comfort and convenience for a life of simplicity and faith. This mirrors her own narrative: Sister Mary Gemma has embraced with monastic life the traditions of a bygone era. Sister Mary Gemma is a pioneer, staking her claim in an unseen world to come. "Here in the monastery, we're living in a different world than what so many people are living in," Sister Mary Gemma says. "Because the Christian message is countercultural. What our Lord teaches us in the gospels is countercultural. There's just no two ways about it. And that's our vocation. Our vocation here is to live the gospel life to the full. We're not distracted here, and we have the vows of poverty, chastity, and obedience, which help us tremendously to live completely for God." Like the Ingalls family, the nuns are usually barefoot.

Sister Mary Gemma was drawn to enact the ideals and virtues in the Ingalls books—to embrace, generations later and voluntarily, a life of poverty. But although a cloistered monastery strips away many material distractions and creates the space to focus on God, Sister Mary Gemma names a vice: She daydreams too much. She always has, she says, and her grades were poor in school because her mind often wandered from the teacher's lesson. She believes she missed out on a lot because of these mental flights. When it was time for her to become a novice, Sister Mary Gemma gave one name to the Mother Abbess as her selection for a religious name, not realizing she was allowed to submit three choices. (She was given the English version of the Italian name she requested.) Sister Mary Gemma struggles to stay focused; when the nuns gather for the Divine Office, she says, "something we're praying will make me think of something else and then my mind will be all over the place before I know it."

Sister Mary Gemma is accustomed to admitting her weaknesses publicly. During the Chapter of Faults, the sisters confess aloud their imperfections and weaknesses that have defied the Poor Clare customs. Sister Mary Gemma often admits that she talks too much. She loves to talk. She has learned to appreciate silence, yet she is often tempted to speak in the company of others because she is, by nature, social. "It is a paradox, I suppose," she says of her calling to observe monastic silence. She adds, "God can call anybody, you know." It has been challenging for Sister Mary Gemma, now fifty-seven, to live decade after decade attempting to adhere to a strict code of speaking only what is necessary outside of the community's one hour of daily recreation, when they can socialize. "I did fail in silence many times, and I still do sometimes," she says.

Sister Mary Gemma entered the order when she was nineteen years old. Before she was Sister Mary Gemma, she was Teresa. As a child, she learned she was placed on earth to love and serve God and that her true home was in heaven. Her father, a strict disciplinarian, imposed many rules on his children. Sister Mary Gemma shares a few of the rules: Do not lie. Sit up straight. "That was one I had trouble with; I was always slouching," Sister Mary Gemma says. Clean the house before their father arrived home from work. Go to bed on time. Say the rosary every day, and if they stayed overnight at a friend's house, her mother told them to say the rosary while they fell asleep.

If Sister Mary Gemma's parents went out and left the children home alone, they were always admonished, "Don't fight!" "We usually did anyway," Sister Mary Gemma says. "So we weren't terribly obedient that way. We weren't supposed to hit each other, which we did all the time. We were good friends, but we picked on each other a lot."

When she was five or six years old, Teresa saw a nun for the first time. She was visiting her older brother at school. She learned then that nuns give themselves completely to God; she felt that she, too, wanted to belong completely to God. "I know that I was attracted to her in some way. I thought that's what God wants me to do," Sister Mary Gemma says. "I don't know why I felt that way. Somehow, I knew I had to give Him everything." Her father approved. "He would have been willing to give all his children to the religious life," Sister Mary Gemma says. "I think that's just the way my dad is."

Her childhood religious inclination waxed and waned through her turbulent teenage years, when desires incompatible with life as a nun stirred. These tensions became tangible when Teresa began sleeping with a photograph under her pillow of a boy she had a crush on, a boy she says did not know she existed.

"I was actually afraid of falling in love because I felt—I felt so sure God was calling me," she says.

As Sister Mary Gemma describes it, she was on the fence, sometimes wanting religious life, sometimes wishing desperately against that fate and crying herself to sleep, hoping it was not her destiny. On Christmas vacation during her sophomore year, Teresa read a spiritual book that served as the tipping point. Sensing that God was "calling me in a deeper way than I felt as a child," she reached under her pillow, tore up the photograph, and threw it in the wastebasket. She felt happy then. This relief stayed with her when Christmas vacation ended, school resumed, and a friend, in tears, told Teresa that her own boyfriend had broken up with her over the holidays. Teresa thought, "Well, Jesus, I know I never have to worry about you turning your back on me." Feeling pulled back and forth by her own unsteady whims until that point, Sister Mary Gemma says, "I knew I didn't know whether I could trust myself, but I knew I could trust Him."

The summer after high school graduation, Teresa went to work at a nursing home. When an aunt—her godmother—invited Teresa to stay at her home in California for the winter holidays, Teresa imagined what the trip might yield, particularly how her life might unfold if she met a young man while visiting her family on the West Coast.

Teresa's aunt was married to a doctor; Teresa admired the family's home, their parties, and their outgoing personalities. Her aunt asked if she was sure about her vocation to the religious life. "Don't you want to get married?" Sister Mary Gemma remembers her aunt asking. "I said, 'Well, I do feel that way,'" Sister Mary Gemma says. Her aunt replied, "That's a sign that you don't have a vocation." Another aunt interjected: "That's not a sign. That's a sign that she's a woman. She could still have a vocation." Asked if she wanted to be home for Christmas Day or stay longer in California, Teresa answered slowly, "I'd like to stay here." Before she finished her sentence with "but I think I should go home," her aunt said, "Well, then, you'll stay here." Teresa was shy, afraid to offend her host. She also felt persuaded to the other side of the fence—the possibility of marriage and a family. "I was hoping something would rescue me from going to the monastery," she says.

Her reverie was temporary. It ended when Teresa phoned her father and explained she planned to stay with the relatives for the holiday. She added she might wait to enter the monastery. Sister Mary Gemma remembers her father saying she should do what she felt she should do. "Somehow, even though I didn't say much, he knew I was struggling and he was afraid I would end up not following my vocation," Sister Mary Gemma says. "He understood me. My dad and I were real close spiritually. We had an understanding."

After talking with her father, Teresa regretted agreeing to stay in California. If she joined the monastery, as planned, this would be her last Christmas with her parents and siblings. Teresa told her aunt she was homesick. An airline strike almost prevented her return home, but the strike lifted on Christmas Eve. One of just a few passengers on the flight, Teresa cried en route to Illinois, knowing she would probably never see her California relatives again.

Her father installed new carpet in her bedroom. Her parents settled on the Christmas gift after considering she might continue living with them and find a job, or leave for the monastery. "I really think this is a temptation," Sister Mary Gemma remembers her father saying. "If you have felt God calling you so often, you should really enter the monastery and just put the temptation behind you. You have felt this call for so long." He may have understood her heart, Sister Mary Gemma says. But in struggling to define her father in precise and charitable terms, she says, "I should say he's Irish. That makes me Irish, too. But he—how shall I say about my dad? He's delightful. Really, we tease him so much. He's overly optimistic, I shall say.

"I told him, 'Dad, I'm a little worried about my laziness, entering the religious life.' " Sister Mary Gemma remembers him replying, "Oh, you can overcome that." "But my dad was a very disciplined person," Sister Mary Gemma says, "and I think he couldn't see why anyone else couldn't be the same way he is. I think in that sense he didn't have an understanding that people were made differently. I think he was a little that way; if he had a headache, we all had a headache and had to go to bed early, something like that. 'We have a headache, let's go to bed.' " Sister Mary Gemma says her hardworking father probably assumed she was, too—or could become that way.

Her mother, meanwhile, thought that Teresa was not equipped for cloistered monastic life. "She saw that I liked to talk," Sister Mary Gemma says. "She saw that I was kind of lazy. In a way, I had a stormy relationship with my mother. I was struggling with myself and I was taking it out on my mother, stomping, slamming doors, and so she had doubts about my vocation. She didn't think I would persevere, quite frankly. She was happy to give me to God, if that's what God wanted. She was just afraid I wasn't being realistic about whether I would be able to live the life."

Three months after returning from California, Teresa entered the Corpus Christi Monastery. Her three years as a postulant and a novice were painful. Sister Mary Gemma attributes the challenges to the age difference between her and the next youngest nun and to the culture gap between her and the rest of the community. When she joined the monastery in 1976, she was the first new postulant in fifteen years. At the time, the nuns still made their own straw beds with rye and wheat that they cut and dried themselves. It was the first time Teresa had slept on a straw mattress. "It was very hard for me in the beginning, I must say. I know I found it hard to wait until recreation when I came. It was just so wonderful when recreation came and I could just start talking." During recreation, Teresa told stories; she asked and answered questions, and the older nuns began to grasp just how different her experiences were from theirs. "The kinds of presents I got for Christmas, the sisters were horrified—'You got *that* many presents for Christmas?'—because they would get one gift," she says. "That just showed them that the culture was already changing. Kids were more spoiled than they were back then because the parents had a little more money than the parents in the generation before. So they felt that I really had to struggle because I had culture shock myself."

Teresa's eagerness to talk did not endear her to one nun, in particular—a teacher in an active order who had transferred to the cloister. "Quiet!" the nun called out, shushing Teresa when she thought she talked too much or too boisterously. "And that used to make me so mad!" Sister Mary Gemma says. "And sometimes I would get impatient with her at recreation. But I always told her I was sorry afterwards. She was always so kind and forgiving and would say, 'I'm sorry, too.'"

Teresa's visits with her family in the parlor exacerbated her loneliness, her longing for her former life. They talked of their camping trips; Teresa missed the outdoors. Her Novice Mistress advised her to take comfort in her surroundings and to look to the sky because the sky is always changing.

Three years after she entered as a postulant, the twenty-two-year-old who had been renamed Sister Mary Gemma panicked. She made temporary vows, then thought, "Oh, my, what have I done? I can't leave for three years. It was like by then I'll be too old to get married. No one will want me." Sister Mary Gemma outlined her anxiety to a priest; she felt "torn both ways," as if she were "fighting God" because she longed to fall in love, get married, and raise a family. "This priest did settle me," she says. "He said, 'You definitely have a vocation. The very fact that you've been fighting God so long and He got you here anyway is a good sign that you have a vocation.' He said he didn't think I would have ever actually entered if I didn't actually have a vocation. And he set my soul completely at peace. And I've never wanted, I've never wanted, I've never wanted anything but this life since then. I just needed that confirmation."

Sister Mary Gemma believes that her yearning for married life was typical, "a normal way a woman would feel," and not necessarily any indication of a true calling to religious life. She discovered, too, a critical precept for understanding her own personality: Verbalizing the inner, conflicted dialogue to a spiritual advisor could set her secret temptations "to flight" and defuse the power of her worries.

Still she struggled. She remembers on two occasions sitting in the choir chapel with the other sisters for the Divine Office and feeling a huge sob forcing its way to the surface. "And I thought, 'Oh, now, not here, not in front of everyone.' I just started sobbing right there in church." Sister Mary Gemma believed the outbursts pointed to self-esteem issues she needed to overcome. "I would say I was still working through them after I made final vows, but the sisters were able to see I was going to be able to be okay in time," Sister Mary Gemma says.

In the southwest wing of the monastery, perpendicular to the corridor of cells where the professed nuns live, Sister Ann Frances's cell in the infirmary overlooks vegetable gardens and a few flowerbeds. Sister Mary Gemma spends much of the day there, as well as part of the night, when the Alzheimer's disease confuses Sister Ann Frances's circadian rhythm and she stays awake all night, then sleeps during the day. The infirmary is the only place in the monastery where nuns are permitted to talk freely.

Sister Ann Frances smiles when Sister Mary Gemma appears in the doorway. Sister Mary Gemma sings and talks and reads to the aging nun. Sister Ann Frances's dependence on Sister Mary Gemma might be poetic justice. Sister Ann Frances is the former teacher who shushed the teenaged Teresa during recreation. Over time, the two nuns developed a close bond, and Sister Mary Gemma has helped care for Sister Ann Frances for almost a decade.

"It's interesting the way God works," Sister Mary Gemma says. "It's just interesting that sometimes the ones that you struggle with the most end up being the ones you love the most." Sister Mary Gemma says a true friendship formed while she was still in the novitiate because they were able to forgive one another so readily. As the talkative Sister Mary Gemma has cared for Sister Ann Frances around the clock over the past couple of years, watching the elder nun respond positively and gratefully to the stories and attempts at conversation, Sister Mary Gemma says, "I just have grown to love her very, very deeply. She's just as sweet as can be."

Sister Mary Gemma does not relish the rare occasions she must leave the silence of the enclosure. The world outside "kind of encroaches on our recollection," she says. "When you're used to this type of environment, it's kind of a shock. It's so different." Once, the extern sister drove Sister Mary Gemma to a doctor's appointment, and then they stopped at a grocery store. Sister Mary Gemma stayed in the car with the window down and was shocked when a man yelled at a stranger for parking at an angle and blocking what could have been his spot. Sister Mary Gemma remembers the society of her youth as polite; she wanted to close her window but could not without the keys. She was aghast when the woman responded in kind to the man.

Sister Mary Gemma prayed silently for the man and the woman and the woman's children, also witnesses. "It brought home to me how important our life of prayer is because our whole life is centered on God and a life of paying reverence and adoration and respect to God," Sister Mary Gemma says. "And you always know there's a lot of people that are living a completely different life, they're not even paying attention to God, and then when you're exposed to it, it brings it home that much stronger. And it's not necessarily their fault if they don't know God. They're just picking up what they heard. You don't blame them or anything. But it's just—it was just very, very sad to me to see how the world has changed since I was in it."

The back section of the monastery's fourteen-acre property is lined with evergreens and landscaped with fruit trees. Sister Mary Gemma misses nature. She rarely has time to walk to the backyard. She remembers the *Little House* characters saying, like her Novice Mistress, "You're with nature all the time." The stories offer a respite, reinforcing values that run counter to popular culture, and offering a mental pilgrimage for a middle-aged nun who still feels like an unfocused soul with a fanciful mind.

Sister Mary Clara
of Our Lady of Sorrows

I was Sister Eucharista with my other order, the Felicians. I was there for twenty-two years as a teacher—a primary grade teacher for first or second grade, and sometimes both. I loved them very much; I loved the little children.

I was from Buffalo, in western New York near Niagara Falls. I was born August 11, 1937—Saint Clare's Day. I also was called Clara. My name was Clare. That's how it all began. The Lord has a plan for everyone's life. As the Lord says, "I have formed you in your mother's womb. I have a plan, and your name is written on the palm of my hand."

The Felician Sisters were always in the long habit; they were just like I am now. Because of the Felician Sisters and because of their relationship with my mom, it grew on me. It was an attraction. Many times, it's an attraction; it's a drawing. I have a drawing for prayer, but it's the Blessed Sacrament that I have the drawing for.

When I was in fourth grade I had rheumatic fever. After that, I had to be careful, walking upstairs and so on. I was restricted. I had to go to school on a special bus for one year, and after the first year I had to be on the first floor; I couldn't walk upstairs. In sixth grade, I had to go upstairs. We were in an annex building because there wasn't enough room, and I remember my sixth-grade teacher talking about vocations, talking about sisters and different orders, but more about the Felicians than anyone else. That's where I really think the initial calling came. That never left me. I can still see where I sat in the classroom. I can still see the classroom. I can still see the building. I can still see sister.

I really wanted to go into the aspirancy after eighth grade. The girls lived in the aspirancy, like a boarding school, for four years. But my mom and dad said I had to live at home and experience life before I entered the community, the religious life. They said if I'm still sure about joining and I still want to be religious, they would let me go. So they did; they kept their promise. It was close to high school graduation, April or May, and I slowly approached my mom. I said, "You remember the deal we had?" She said, "What deal?" I said, "Well, you said if I still want to become a religious, a Felician, you would let me go." She said, "Oh, I thought you had forgotten about it."

They allowed me to go. But one thing Dad said that I will never forget, he said, "If you ever want to come back, the door is always unlocked." He didn't say "open." He said "unlocked." It made such an impression to me. For a door to be open, it has to be unlocked. I took it as they would welcome me home anytime. It meant a lot to me for him to say that. But I stayed.

I entered in July and my mom died in March of the next year; '56 I entered, and she died in '57. She had a stroke. When I went with my Novice Mistress to my dad on the day of death to organize things or to talk about things, I said, "Dad, I'm coming home. I talked to Sister and she said whatever I want to do." And he says, "No. You stay where you are. You chose your life. The Lord called you. We can get along. We're able to be home alone. You can come home, but you don't need to." And I looked at my Mistress. Tears were coming down my face. We were going to bury Mom. I had two younger brothers: one in eighth grade and one in fifth or sixth grade, a couple years behind. It was hard. Difficult. But I accepted it.

I thought, I guess the Lord wants me to stay. But it was hard, it was very hard. Sometimes I would be crying. In the dormitory, sometimes I would be sniffling. The sister across from me used to pull the curtain and put her hand through. We would hold hands, hold onto one another, because she knew what I was going through. It was tough. That was the only time I thought that I wanted to go home, because I wanted to be of help to my father. But he didn't feel that I was needed. He was very strong about that; whatever I chose to do was meant to be for my life.

I came here in '78. About three years before that, I knew something was troubling me. I knew I didn't belong with the Felicians. I was searching already then. I had a calling. I had had it with the teaching. It wasn't that I was dissatisfied with the teaching or my children or what I was doing; it was that I had a different calling. The Lord was saying, "It's time to switch gears." So I went for this weekend retreat. Father was there. I went to confession. I said, "I really need guidance." I said "I'm a sinner, but still I need to talk,

Father." I said, "I think I'd like to go to the cloister." He said, "Oh? Where?" I said, "I don't know."

I said, "I want to switch, but I don't know where." He said, "Do you have any idea?" I said, "No." He said, "Do you have any friends in any communities?" I said, "Not friends, but I know of sisters at different communities." He said, "Do you think you're being drawn there?" I said, "I have no idea. I don't know." I know he was really drawing this, pulling this out. He said, "I don't have time to spend on this. I have to go to another commitment." I said, "I understand." He said, "I want you for the next month to forget all about your vocation as a cloistered sister. Get it out of your mind. Do what you have to do, but don't think about the cloister." I said, "How am I going to do that?" He said, "Just don't think about it." I said, "I'll try." He said, "Just give it a good try." I said, "What if it doesn't work? Then what?" He said, "It'll work if you work at it." I said, "Okay." I tried. That was April. I knew this was important. I was so busy with the children it wasn't hard to forget, really. In May, on Memorial weekend, I went to Father, the Dominican priest at the monastery, and I told him what the priest said, that I should come back and talk to him about a vocation to contemplative life. So we did. We spent about two hours together. We talked about my life as a Felician, sharing things about what was drawing me. Then he said, "Do you know where you want to go?" I said, "No, I have no idea." He said, "I can give you a little bit of help. Not much." He said, "Go to the extern sister; they have pamphlets about cloistered life. Ask her to find one for you and to give it to you. Tell her I asked her to give it to you." She found it in the drawer. And one was a brown paper pamphlet, and it was written by a Poor Clare, the Abbess in New Mexico. She wrote a pamphlet, *With Light Step on Unstumbling Feet*, that was about the contemplative life. It spoke about the whole entire contemplative life as a Poor Clare. So I took that and I read that and I was happy with it. And that was it. And that's why I'm here.

The back of the pamphlet listed six or seven convents of Poor Clares. I had to choose one of the convents. I went to Sister Michelle and she helped me write a form letter. I said, "How am I going to know where I'm supposed to go?" She said, "You'll know. I don't know how, but it will come about." I said, "I trust you, Michelle. I don't know how this is going to happen." So we wrote this introduction to my life, that I was a Felician sister, that I was still teaching, and that I still had a few months to go—in fact, the whole year to go of teaching. "I'm committed to my apostolate here, so I can't promise anything, but I want information about your order." I wrote to Mother Mary Francis in New Mexico, I wrote to two convents in California, and then I wrote to one in Cleveland, Ohio, because I knew that would make my brother happy, in case I was accepted there. Then I wrote here, to Rockford, Illinois. Well, Mother Mary Francis answered and said, "It is our policy not to accept transfer sisters who have another community, especially the many years you spent as a Felician Sister." She said, "We're sorry, sister." I accepted it. In California, they said the same thing: "It is our policy not to accept transfer sisters." The Cleveland, Ohio, monastery had a number of older sisters that needed care, so they really had to devote themselves to the sisters. They said they would pray for me that I would find a suitable place for my vocation. I wrote all these places just after January. Mother Dorothy answered me in February. She said, "We would be happy to meet you and to talk with you." That was it. She put in a few other nice sentences. She wrote again every two weeks, just a short note. In March, she asked me to send my life story, why I wanted to come all the way to Rockford. I didn't know why I wanted to go to Rockford, but I knew I wanted to be a Poor Clare. In March I told her I couldn't come any time except for during my Easter break because that was the only time I wasn't in school. That was March 25th in '78.

I flew here in March; my superior was kind enough. That was the first and only time I flew. My family was not exactly poor, but we didn't think of flying anywhere. We traveled by train because my father used to work on the railroad, so we had passes. We never flew. It was interesting. It was exciting; especially looking at the clouds, it just took the breath out of me. I loved it, I really did. I was hoping I would fly one other time.

I came here for an overnight visit, made my papers, met the community, and they interviewed me. From all the letters, I guess the Mother Abbess knew me quite well. I entered in July that same year.

I went home, finished school, and then I had to go to my superior and close up things and get my records, my baptismal records, and all the other records I needed—physical and dental, like you have to have. Then I went to my brother and he wasn't too pleased about it. My father already had passed away. I knew that when Dad died, I knew that if I wanted to do something drastic like join the cloister, I was free. I wouldn't have to hurt him, or disappoint him, or leave him here alone. I was free. But John just couldn't understand. He was young yet. His kids were young. The girls were just in eighth grade, sixth grade, and then the two little boys were just small. He couldn't get it in his head. My brother was stubborn like a lot of men are. We knew each other, what we were struggling with. He couldn't understand why I came here, all the way over to Illinois. I could have gone to New Jersey or Cleveland, Ohio. I said, "This is my calling. This is where the Lord wants me. He wants me in Illinois. I don't think I'd make it anywhere else." John accepted it. He brought me over, set me up, put my suitcases up, and that was it. It's not that I appeared heartless or cold, but some people are just like that.

My brother passed away in '97. That was a struggle for me. I knew I couldn't go to the funeral. I couldn't go see him. I could talk to him while he was in the hospital before he died. Mother Dorothy allowed that, because that's just compassion for the family and the sister. She said, "Pick up the phone and see if you can reach your brother John." I did, but he wasn't able to talk that night. He said, "I don't feel like talking." That was it. I said, "I'll call another time." I knew John. I knew he wasn't feeling good. He was sick. He was dying. When you have someone that's very close to you and you know the person and you know the struggles, it's not difficult to accept his "no." So then I called my sister-in-law, and I started crying. She said, "Why don't you call tomorrow night and I'll be there. I'll pick up the phone." We agreed, and I called and she picked up the phone and gave it to John and we had our last talk. About two weeks after that, he died. He died in July, the last day of July. I called sometime in May.

I found it difficult to say goodbye this last time when my family left because it might be the last time. You never know, because it's so hard to get here—ten hours from Buffalo, New York. It's a long trip. They write to me. I don't always answer the letters, but I know that their love is always there for me and if ever anything should happen, if the devil gets in the way too much and I get tempted too much, I could be tempted to go back home. And I know that the door is unlocked. But of course I'd have to find a new place, because they're moving. I know the door will still be unlocked somewhere else. I would still be accepted.

5

Mothers of Souls

He has not only redeemed us, He has raised us up to the divine life itself. And He couldn't have done that without becoming human, Himself, because He came to earth. He's taught us that we can live a divine life, because He has shown us how, by taking on our humanity. And, of course, we have to have His life within us because the divine life itself is out of our reach except through Him.

Sister Mary Gemma of Our Lady of the Angels

The phone calls seem to arrive in patterns: requests for prayers for children with brain tumors one week, couples who want babies another week; threats of divorce one day, financial troubles another day.

The cloistered nuns assigned by their superior to answer calls to this prayer hotline of sorts write notes by hand, and then the names and requests are transcribed by typewriter. Sometimes, the Mother Abbess tapes the list to the doorframe outside her office. Each evening before collation, the Mother Abbess reads the day's prayer requests to the members of the community so that together they can "share in their pain a little bit," Mother Miryam says of the callers, and "take it away a little bit by prayer."

Asked if it is burdensome to hear about tragedies day after day, Mother Miryam says, "Sometimes it gets a little heavy." She adds, though, that cloistered nuns consider the callers their wards, in a similar way that nurses and doctors must regard their patients. "That's what we're supposed to do," she says. "You know, if we didn't do that, we wouldn't be faithful. It'd be like if you left your patients in the hospital and didn't bother about them."

And so the nuns intervene on behalf of humanity. They pray for healing, for safe pregnancies and deliveries, for reconciliations, for financial solutions. They are the comforters and caretakers of the world, believing that their own suspended desires and dreams, their directed intentions, their prayers and their penances, can alter the course of history.

Sister Maria Deo Gratias explains that her role as a cloistered contemplative requires that she act as an intermediary, making reparation through prayer or fasting or some other penance for other people's sins. "There's a dimension in the spiritual life; where there is much sin committed, for instance in a city, there has to be reparation from man," she says. "Man committed the sin; man has to make reparation for it. That's a part of our life; we try to balance out the accountability of others living in sin. And so we make reparation and supplication to love God, because they do not love God. That's part of our apostolate: 'They won't stand before you, God, and so we stand before you, God, in their names so that we can praise you in their names.' For the whole city, there's a special spiritual grace that's given because some people have that apostolate to offer up reparation."

The nuns are active agents; each endeavors to call forth God's plan in lives beyond their cloistered grounds. They merely need a prompt—a phone call, a patron's request, news passed through the Mother Abbess of a crisis. "There's a sensitivity that we're kind of the center of the city, trying to supply the spiritual energy that they need along with their own graces, that they receive from God—that extra help to them. They know they have someone backing them up in prayer," says Sister Maria Deo Gratias, the Vicaress.

"I mean, people have so much faith in prayer. It just makes you really humble," Mother Miryam says of those who phone repeatedly to ask for prayers or to report rescues from their troubles. "They say, 'Ever since I asked you to pray for us, everything's been...'" she trails off, explaining the caller says the tide has turned. "And you think, it's their faith," she says. "That's what the Lord said: 'If you have faith, it'll move mountains for you.' It's their faith. They just have wonderful, wonderful faith, and people have so much goodness in them to respond."

"It's just all in God's care," Mother Miryam says of an aging member of the community, though her words could apply to the nuns' outlook in general. "We watch and care, but just wait and see what He has in store, just in case someone would take off for heaven." The cloistered contemplative Saint Therese of Lisieux, a nineteenth-century French Carmelite nun also known as "the Little Flower of Jesus," inspires and directs her spiritual progeny. "She considered our life as contemplatives to be the heart beating, sending out the blood to the other members of the Church," Sister Mary Gemma says. "That was the way she understood our life and I think that's probably the best description that I can think of. We've had so many missionary priests come and tell us how much they appreciate our life, because they know they would not be able to convert souls to Christ if there weren't these contemplative orders. They believe very strongly that the heart of the Church is in these contemplative orders, and that's why the Church has always encouraged this kind of life.

"I've been thinking about these things ever since I was young. I was thinking, 'Gosh, all those people in the world and so many of them don't know God and I would love to help. How can I help people come to know God?'"

Sister Mary Gemma's parents were Catholic. Her family's house in the midwestern countryside was exposed to natural elements, and so Sister Mary Gemma remembers taking shelter, on occasion, from tornados. No one seemed to worry more than she did. She collected the cats and the dogs and made sure that all of her family members found their way to the safety of the basement. "I mostly wanted my family safe, safe in God's arms in heaven, but I used to often think that I have to have that same concern for everyone because everyone is special," she says. "Everyone is special to God. I had to have that same concern not just for my own family, I had to have that for everyone—people I had never heard of. Everyone is special. And there's so much ignorance of God in the world."

Once, as a teenager, Teresa, as she was called then, went to the county fair with a "whole troop of cousins," as she remembers it. The eldest, Teresa, was charged with keeping track of her siblings and cousins. "I was counting everyone all the time," Sister Mary Gemma says. Her mother was unconcerned for the children, Sister Mary Gemma remembers, because Teresa was "taking care." "She knew I was counting. I could not enjoy that fair at all because I was always counting heads making sure we were all together."

In this mayhem, Teresa identified her deepest desire. She remembers thinking, "Dad says prayer is more powerful than anything else. That's what I should do. I should go and pray at the monastery so that I can help all those souls get to heaven. Since I was small, my dad taught us to be concerned about the salvation of souls. He said there's nothing more powerful than prayer. My dad always taught us that, and so it's probably natural that I would kind of be drawn to this kind of life.

"It seemed to me there was no better way to help people find God than to live a life of prayer and just pray for the world continually," she says. "You can touch any soul around the world. And, of course, we don't know who we're praying for actually, but God knows.

"I would guess that's been a big reason to choose this life; it's a love for the world, but in a different way. We don't want anyone to be deprived of the love of God. It was also that I wanted to live an intimate life of prayer with God. But it's not a selfish life since we want to do it to bring as many souls to God as we can." In this life, Sister Mary Gemma feels responsible for all of humanity. "I mean I'm limited, of course," she says, "but I have to do the best I can, at least."

Sister Maria Benedicta acknowledges that prejudices develop in the course of one's upbringing; but a life of prayer can erode an inclination to judge others. "It's called expanding your heart," she says. "The more you allow God to change your heart and open your heart, the more you realize Jesus went to heal sinners and the tax collectors, you know, the people in the world that others would ask, 'Why is He with them?' But you see, God loves everybody. And it does expand your heart to pray. When we hear terrible news stories, we think to pray for the man who did that. I never would have thought of that before. I would have thought, 'How horrible.' But it's like that man really must be suffering to have done that. To realize *that man* has a soul, too. Or woman. And obviously he doesn't know God. But it is a broadening of your heart. I'm not just cleaning the floor; I'm doing it for God. And you think of all the suffering that people endure and I can do this little thing for God. And He can help those who are suffering. I couldn't help people in Africa if I was doing whatever sort of a job. But, here, your heart can expand to the whole world."

Each woman who joins the Poor Clare Colettine Order takes on a new name; embracing anonymity, she performs her duties before the small audience within her community, and for an unseen, immortal God. "The hiddenness is part of our enclosure," Sister Mary Nicolette says, "that we're not to be known to the world, that we are here, we're here for God and it doesn't really matter who we are, you know. There's an anonymity and hiddenness because what matters is what God sees and not necessarily to be known to anyone outside."

The "hiddenness" of the cloistered monastic life empowers others' lives, Sister Sarah Marie says. "It's the little pulled away, hidden, nobody really knows about you, nobody even cares—might not even care to know about you—that does, I think, have tremendous impact."

Before entering the enclosure, Sister Mary Nicolette knew she would be allowed to leave the enclosure's premises only on rare occasions. She had heard the mantra: The metal grille does not keep nuns in an enclosure; it is a sign that keeps the world at bay. Sister Mary Nicolette believed that with this separation she could give herself to God completely, paradoxically. "We leave the world in order to be for the world," Sister Mary Nicolette says. "See, it's like we're removing ourselves from the world so that we can be wholly given over to others."

Residing within these cloistered walls suits Sister Mary Nicolette. "I didn't struggle with that because I understood it so much as part of the vocation and so much a part of what I desired," she says. "So it was something I longed for—to give myself and maybe not be appreciated and maybe known in the world and, like you say, disappear into obscurity. Nature—human nature—obviously loves to be known and seen and appreciated. But as far as the vocation is concerned, it's something that everybody who receives the vocation desires. It's a part of understanding our purpose, that you desire; you're counteracting something that is very natural, that's perhaps not the best to want to be seen and known, and, 'Aren't I great?' You're denying yourself in a certain way. You're counteracting that natural tendency."

"This is where you want the totalness with Him," Sister Sarah Marie says. "I want to be completely with Him, I want to be totally away from anything that would distract me from my life with Him, from my union with Him."

Sister Sarah Marie was introduced to the Rockford Poor Clares when she still answered to the name Tiffany. Her mother, a member of the Third Order of Franciscans, taught her only daughter that no tornado ever touched down within city limits because the Poor Clares' prayers kept the city safe. "My mom, to her dying day, said, 'It's the Poor Clare monastery that's kept Rockford from being hit by a tornado,'" said Sister Sarah Marie. "Now others of more knowledge will say it's the river," she laughs. "So that's debatable, if you want to fight the old Italian lady on that!"

Raised to turn to the Poor Clare nuns for prayers, Sister Sarah Marie says that when one of her brothers was sent to serve in the Vietnam War, the nuns prayed him safely through his military service; when a pregnant sister-in-law nearly miscarried, the nuns prayed her through a safe delivery; and when Tiffany was living in Kansas City and her fiancé broke off their engagement, her mother called the Poor Clares, and the nuns prayed the young woman through that personal devastation. "It was just a constant outlet," Sister Sarah Marie says of her mother's prayer requests of the Poor Clares.

But when Tiffany announced her plans to return from Kansas City to join the Poor Clare Colettine Order in her hometown and become a cloistered contemplative, her mother resisted. It was an assault on her mother's expectations. She knew more than most people what her daughter's choice—what the vows and the enclosure—would cost. "There would be a line that would be drawn," Sister Sarah Marie says. "Jesus would pull me even more. Here, you give it all. You give Jesus everything. Even visiting home. Even going to see Mama when she's sick. Even going to her funeral. Even to go to the wake, just down the street at the cathedral. That's what the enclosure is and that's why we treasure it so much."

Sister Maria Deo Gratias says,

Some people are called to that—to give to a person, and together they give themselves to God, and then they participate in the creation of God in having a family. Others, like ourselves, are asked—or invited, really—to give ourselves to God alone; so chastity, it's a freedom, because we can give ourselves totally to God and we don't have divided responsibilities. It's not a divided love, because you don't have to divide your attention in such a way that a married person has to. In their life, they fall in love with the person and they want to give that love to each other. We fall in love with our Lord and we want to give that love to God, undivided. We can be concerned with the things of the world, where a married person is concerned with their family.

Sister Mary Clara left home at eighteen; she took a religious name, Sister Eucharista, and became a teacher with an active order of religious sisters in upstate New York. The orphanage also housed neglected children and offspring of divorced parents. Sister Eucharista taught first and second graders. She became best friends with another teacher, Sister Michelle, who knew how to drive. The two would ask for permission to take the community's car on drives throughout the countryside, sometimes stopping at a lake to watch the sun set and listening to music on a tape recorder; sometimes they asked along older religious sisters who would not have had the chance to go out otherwise.

After twenty-eight years as a teaching sister, Sister Eucharista sensed she might be called to transfer to an enclosure. She showed Sister Michelle a pamphlet about the Poor Clare Colettines. "Wow," Sister Mary Clara remembers Sister Michelle saying. "That's all she used to say when something struck her as different," Sister Mary Clara says. "She said, 'Wow, that certainly has a lot in it.' I said, 'Isn't it wonderful?' She said, 'Is that what you want?' I said, 'I think so.' She said, 'Really? You won't ever come back.' I said, 'I know.'" Sister Michelle reminded her she might never again see her brother John. At this, Sister Eucharista cried. "She was feeling me out," Sister Mary Clara says. "That's the way we were, the two of us, and so I reread the pamphlet a number of times. Every time I read it, I knew this was where the Lord wanted me."

Since Sister Michelle could not dissuade her friend, she helped her draft an application seeking entry to the Poor Clare community. She was accepted, and Sister Eucharista ferried plants on the cross-country drive. "In class I always had plants in front of the windowsills. We always, I always, enjoyed them, so I came with a planetarium with plants in a little fish tank and I think I brought four plants in a box," she says, remembering the day she arrived more than thirty years ago. "They're floating around in the monastery somewhere. They might be dead already."

"Somehow," Sister Mary Clara says, "it was easy for me to turn my back on the world and just come here." Poor Clare nuns can correspond with loved ones by letter, and Sister Eucharista is always happy to receive updates from her brothers and sisters-in-law. She does not usually reply, though. "That's what they always cry about: 'I'm still waiting for an answer!'" Sister Mary Clara says. "Well, I'm a cloistered sister," she tells them, adding that she's a terrible writer. "They know I pray for them and I think about them. I say, 'You don't need my John Hancock to remind you I'm here.' So we joke around like that."

Her first fall in Rockford, Sister Mary Clara was dispatched to the outdoors to work in the gardens. She remembers picking green beans and tomatoes and strawberries and apples, and then hearing school buses stop, within earshot, to fill with children. "If you spend a quarter of your lifetime in a community, and then the Lord calls you somewhere else, naturally your thoughts will come with you—whatever you were doing there," she says. "That was a special gift I had received from God, to teach the little ones. I just loved them to bits. I really did. Anything I could do for a little child, I would do."

While she was toiling in the green bean patch one day, there seemed to be an unending procession of school buses. "I thought, 'When will they finish?

Why won't they just go somewhere? Just get away!' " Sister Mary Clara says. "And there I was, sitting on the ground, on the grass, and I couldn't hold the tears back. The tears were falling. A sister came behind me and said, 'Are you all right?' " Sister Mary Clara busied herself, pretending she was fine. The other nun persisted. Sister Mary Clara explained that the sound of school buses reminded her of the children she taught. She missed the children, missed teaching them. The other nun told Sister Mary Clara, "By this time next year you'll be so used to us and you'll be so used to your new life that you won't even think of the buses." The prediction was true, Sister Mary Clara says.

Still, Sister Mary Clara says sometimes a group of children from Catholic schools in the diocese visit. Their chatter and laughter provoke her to ask the Mother Abbess if she can peek into the parlor and look at the children on the other side of the metal grille. Sometimes, the Mother Abbess tells her, "Now, now, you have work to do." Sometimes, the Mother Abbess teases, "Aren't you over that yet?" Sister Mary Clara responds, "I'm over it, but I'd still like to see the little kids." Often, Sister Mary Clara is allowed to check in on the children but "not too often," she says, "because it's a distraction for me and it's something that I have given up. I shouldn't be that attached to the children. The Lord wanted me to do that over there, and now He wants me to do this over here. I have an entirely different life now."

Sister Mary Clara thinks the replacement of her work as a teacher with her vocation as a contemplative nun must be similar to the transition from single life to marriage. "It's the same thing with us," Sister Mary Clara says. "There has to be a break for your own peace of mind and love, too, because you can't have two loves. I can love the children, but I can't have my heart over there, wondering what's going on over there—if the kids are still growing up, still good, or whatever—and then be here in the monastery and praying the Divine Office. That doesn't work well."

Sister Maria Deo Gratias explains:

We are spouses of our Lord, and we said "yes" at our profession and then throughout every day of our life we continue to say that "yes" in a practical way because it's one thing to stand at that altar and say "yes," but it's another thing in the daily nitty-gritty of life to continue to say that "yes" with all faithfulness. And we want to be a faithful community because that gives graces. Because our apostolate is prayer, and

God hears the prayer of a holy person, we strive to be holy, to be heard by God, to intercede for all the people of the world, all the diocese, the people of this city and offer reparations for the sins of the world, the sins of the city. So, therefore, in order to be heard by God, we have to be faithful. But it's out of love. It's not like: "I have to do this." It's, "I want to do this because God has called me into that relationship of love with Him." And part of that relationship is taking on the responsibility of the life, in saying "yes" all the time.

Cloistered nuns keep watch while the world sleeps, waking at midnight for the first of seven prayers each day. They pray each day for the worst sinner in the world, believing that the worst sinner cannot desire redemption without supernatural intervention.

Their sacrifices make way for blessings, they believe, and so they welcome hardships because increased suffering can yield greater rewards, submitting to "death for the sake of resurrection," as modeled by Jesus, according to *Verbi Sponsa: Instruction on the Contemplative Life and on the Enclosure of Nuns*.

When her mother died, Sister Sarah Marie was not allowed to leave the monastery. "And it was hard," she says. "I'm not going to sit here and say, 'Oh, no, easy come, easy go. That's the way it goes.' No, of course, it was hard. But I was closer to my mom and the family spiritually than they were physically present at the wake, at the funeral. I was much closer because I was in our chapel while they were at the funeral. The funeral was at 10:30. I was before the Blessed Sacrament. I was before Jesus, physically present there. I was looking at Him. You see, there was a uniting there. Physically, I wasn't there, of course, but spiritually I was there."

She says her family and friends sensed her presence—perhaps a testament to the fervency of her prayers, the faith of her loved ones, and their shared belief that the most trying aspects of her life can be reclaimed. One friend said she felt that if she turned around at the funeral, she would see Sister Sarah Marie sitting behind her.

Sister Sarah Marie's mother had asked the Mother Abbess if her casket could be carried into the monastery's parlor after she died so that her daughter could say one final goodbye. In a departure from the cloistered community's standard protocols, the request was granted. As in life, the two were separated by the metal grille. Sister Sarah Marie could not reach far enough to touch her mother, or to lay the roses that the Mother Abbess gave her in the casket. Sister Sarah Marie cried. She cried in mourning; she cried because of the distance still between them. The priest walked into the parlor then. Silently, he touched Sister Sarah Marie's hand. With his other hand, he held the hand of Sister Sarah Marie's mother. "She was touched by me," Sister Sarah Marie says. "Our Lord works. You give Him all and He gives it all back to you. He's outdone in all His generosity."

When Sister Mary Nicolette prepared herself to enter the enclosure, she believed that she had just enlisted in a lifetime of boredom. In two decades, though, she says she has never once been bored. "I was talking to my family when they just came to visit this summer. They were asking me, 'Have you ever been bored yet?' That's a joke because I've never been bored since I've been here. When I was out in the world, sometimes I was bored to death. But since I've been here, I've never once been bored. It's like you're going from one thing to the next and it's like a peaceful pace and you always know what you're going to need to be doing next and there's never a time when it's like, 'Oh gee, what should I do?'"

Sister Mary Nicolette says,

When you're listening all day long, you're listening for God's voice and every day is new. He'll ask something new of you. He'll put some new situation in your life or ask something different of you. Every day is different. One of the things that I always thought was, "Lord, I'm offering up the great sacrifice of a very monotonous life and I don't know how I'm going to do it, but I'll make the sacrifice, Lord!" But there's no monotony. No monotony. There's a regularity.

Monastic life has presented other challenges. When her family visited for the first time, Sister Mary Nicolette had not seen them for a year. Her first reaction was to hug everyone. "But the grille was there," she says. "And it was just striking. And it made me realize there is a definite, a real separation." The last time she hugged her parents was in 1999, when she made solemn vows. "My mother didn't want to let me go. But they were very good about it. It's always very moving—not just for the sister herself and for the parents, but for all the sisters. You know, everyone starts crying. It's just very moving.

"When it is a sacrifice that costs, you can offer that for someone who's maybe struggling with something," she says, like a mother who cannot hug a child serving in Iraq. "That makes it all worthwhile and bearable, really, and something that you feel this is something that I can offer this for someone," she says. "It's a very heavy burden on them, and so if I say by my offering I can help alleviate that heart of that other person. It's just the idea of helping carry one another's burdens."

In her effort to become a spiritual intermediary, living on behalf of humanity, her novice Sister Maria Benedicta finds herself lacking. "That's the hardest thing—you want to love God," she says. "That's why I'm here. You want to love God with all your heart, all your soul, with all my mind, with all my strength. But I don't always do it. Because when you see how much He loves us, how much He's done for us, to die on the cross for us, to give us the Eucharist, to be in the Tabernacle with us constantly, to forgive all our sins, you just want to give Him everything. But sometimes you just fall into your own selfishness. And you think how could I do that? And He's been so good. It just crushes you."

Not long after Sister Mary Clara arrived at the Corpus Christi Monastery, the three aged extern sisters passed away. Sister Mary Clara offered herself as the next extern sister, to operate as a conduit between the world and the enclosure, communicating with visitors to the gift shop and running errands by car. The Mother Abbess turned her down. "No," Sister Mary Clara remembers being told. "You joined the cloistered sisters, so you will remain cloistered. Your original calling wasn't to be an extern sister, out there. You're supposed to be in the cloister, in here."

Sister Mary Clara's innate social temperament found an outlet at the monastery as one of the few nuns assigned to answer the phone calls for prayers. Every morning, Sister Mary Clara expects to hear from one woman who recites the names of her immediate and extended family; she asks that the nuns pray for their safety and well-being and for her own health, that the cancer remain in remission. Sister Mary Clare does not often speak to the woman directly; her caller prefers leaving a message on the answering machine and will hang up the phone gently if Sister Mary Clare picks up.

Typically, Poor Clare nuns do not reveal to the callers their religious names, even if pressed; the nuns are instructed to say, if asked, that they are just one of the sisters, in keeping with their aspiration for anonymity and separation from the world. This also helps prevent callers from becoming too attached to a particular nun and asking to speak with her. But Sister Mary Clara cannot help but bond with some of the callers.

One elderly woman tells Sister Mary Clara she is nearly blind and lives alone. "I don't know what I would do without you sisters," Sister Mary Clara says the woman tells her. "I know that you're there and I know that you'll pray for me." Sister Mary Clara says she replies, "Keep calling and we'll keep answering. And if we're not here, you just leave it on the answering service. You talk to the answering service and we'll listen." Sister Mary Clara describes the answering machine as the monastery's "salvation" because it allows the nuns assigned to phone duty to participate in the Divine Office.

At times, when Sister Mary Clara answers the phone, a caller reminds her of a previous call and asks if she remembers the conversation. "You have to think, 'Who was it who called?'" she says. "You wrack your brain, 'Who is it that's calling?' But in order to keep peace, you say, 'Of course I remember.'"

Other callers are cautious, reluctant to disclose their names. Sister Mary Clara tells them they do not have to disclose the information. If the person asks how the nuns' prayers will be directed to the appropriate individual, Sister Mary Clara says, "All I know is that God knows. God knows who you are, and He knows your petition, and He'll take care of you. All I'm going to do is pray—pray for all the people that called today and then leave it to Him. That's all we do."

Although Sister Mary Clara revels in her assignment for her delight in interacting with people, the phone calls are a disheartening glimpse into the state of the world. "They're desperate," she says of the callers. "They're very desperate."

One woman phoned after her husband died and asked if the nuns would pray for her daughter, who had turned to drugs and tried to take her own life. The widow still calls, at times after long intervals; she always sounds rushed and always requests prayers for her daughter and herself. "That's one that I feel very close to," Sister Mary Clara says. If she hasn't heard from the woman in a while, Sister Mary Clara asks permission from the Mother Abbess to write the woman a note. "She needs me now and she knows who I am because of the telephone calls," Sister Mary Clara says. "I can write to her and console her, and let her know that I'm praying for her."

Sister Mary Clara ends each phone call with a promise that the nuns will pray and make penances on their behalf. "What kind of sacrifice are you going to make, sister?" Sister Mary Clara remembers one caller asking. "Your life is a sacrifice already." Sister Mary Clara concedes that she cannot give up food, if the nuns are already fasting. "I cannot drink some water, just not take a glass of water when I'm thirsty. That doesn't break my fast, so I can say I will offer that up," Sister Mary Clara says. "The Lord knows who needs something, so He'll take that sacrifice. He'll take that glass of water and give it to somebody who needs water."

As Sister Mary Clara ended one phone call, the woman told her that she would also do something for her. "Alright, you do that," Sister Mary Clara said. "We'll help each other out." Many express their plans to pay back the nuns for their supernatural efforts, offering to buy presents for the nuns during pilgrimages, but Sister Mary Clara tells them the nuns do not need anything; they have enough. "What would we do with all the things they want to bring us anyway?" she asks. She tells the callers that the Poor Clares would welcome prayers or the lighting of candles at shrines or sacred sites. "Everybody tries to remember us because we remember them to the Lord," Sister Mary Clara says. "That's the exchange we make."

Sister Mary Clara says there are days "that you get moods." "I miss going out. I miss going out with a friend like Sister Michelle," she says. "I guess there are days that you just wish you could go out and go for a walk. Well, we can go for a walk because we have the back filled with trees and we can walk around back there. But it's different. The devil's out here saying, 'Aha, I've got her wanting to go out.' If I allow myself to dwell, to think about it, he can win over and he can get me out there. But I think I'm stronger than I was before. I wasn't as strong before, but I'm stronger now. When my family left I found it a little difficult, but now it's okay because I know if I live longer they'll come to visit me again."

In becoming a cloistered contemplative nun, Sister Mary Clara's charges are no longer her students, but the public at large. "I can listen and I can feel for people. I can understand their needs," she says. Answering phone calls connects her with humanity.

"We're a little bit different than anyone imagines," Sister Mary Joseph admits. She recalls her first exposure to manual labor in the novitiate: Performing garden duty, she and another novice, the current Mother Abbess, spent the day plucking strawberries from the patches; nearly sixty years later, they recount their exhaustion and their lighthearted response. Feeling sorry for themselves, they agreed to sing to keep their spirits up; with a hint of irony they borrowed the tune of a Jewish lament. "When we were feeling down we would go, 'Woe, woe, oh woe, is me. Oh woe, oh woe, oh woe, is me,'" Sister Mary Joseph says. "We'd do that for the fun of it."

"People think, 'Oh, you're going to do all this, and you're going to be all disciplined and you're going to accept sufferings, and voluntary mortifications—you're going to be miserable,'" Sister Mary Monica says, citing a stereotype of what she calls the "prune-faced" nun—women in the past who found themselves in cloistered monasteries even if they weren't truly called, or who became teaching sisters even if they did not want to work with youth. "But, no, if you do it right, you're not going to be miserable. You're going to be joyful and nobody's going to know the difference."

Their whimsical outlook appears to have physical benefits. Sister Mary Nicolette was surprised when she first began to learn the ages of the nuns in her religious community. "I remember thinking, 'Oh my goodness, I thought she was like twenty years younger than that,'" Sister Mary Nicolette says. She articulates the phenomenon of extended youthfulness: "Cloistered nuns are removed from the pressures, the fast-paced, go, go, go modern culture that is otherwise a source of twenty-four-hour stress. When you're removed from that, there's a certain peace that your soul is steeped in. It doesn't mean that our lives are stress-free, you know; I don't mean that. Everyone has a certain amount of personal stress that you work through and whatnot. But what I mean is the stress from the outer environment is closed off. This is a very peaceful and like a controlled environment, almost. We cut out the outside noise and all the worldly news and concerns. So I think that has a big, big impact, on our lives in general."

Sister Mary Nicolette, whose family teases that the decades of observing monastic silence have eroded her skills at small talk, jokes that there could be another explanation: "But also there is a secret. The habit covers a lot. It covers the double chin and the gray hair!" Sister Mary Nicolette laughs and says she knows she has just blown "the mystical illusion."

"The whole purpose of sacrifice and penance, " says Sister Maria Benedicta, "is to strengthen your body against wanting all these comforts that aren't good for you, strengthening your mind against all these thoughts that aren't godly thoughts. But if you go beyond that and say, 'I'm going to not sleep, not going to give myself that luxury,' well, then you're going to be so down. When you don't sleep, you don't have any defenses against temptations. It's not strengthening you; it's making it worse. There has to be a balance. There's a saying, 'Virtue is in the middle.'"

In a spiral-bound booklet handmade by the nuns to mark the Golden Jubilee—the Corpus Christi Monastery's 1916 founding—the caption under a photograph of five tombstones in the cemetery states, "Fifty years have passed and only in the annals of eternity can the true record be found of the joys and sorrows, the hard work and many sacrifices of this half century. Five times death came to the monastery forming a closer tie between heaven and earth as God called cloistered and extern sisters to enjoy eternal life and the hundredfold promised to those who leave all to follow Him."[1]

Cloistered nuns serve as intermediaries between the physical world and the unseen, eternal realm. Sister Mary Nicolette enacts her deepest beliefs in an invisible, all-powerful God, laboring on behalf of people she will never meet. This vocation delivers an unknown, intangible harvest. She will not learn in this lifetime the results of her life of devotion and sacrifice. "Sometimes we just have to go by faith that what we're doing really makes a difference," Sister Mary Nicolette says. "Because we don't see the fruits of our lives. I think one of the trials that every cloistered nun goes through at some time is just clinging to that faith to know that, 'Yes, what we're doing makes a difference.' Because you don't see the fruits, and so that's all you have sometimes—to go by that faith, that you believe little sacrifices are going to do something, that your prayers that you don't feel are worthy—your whole life given over, and you don't see the fruits of it."

"She'll never see how many hundreds, thousands of souls receive the fruits of her prayers," says Sister Maria Benedicta of her Novice Mistress.

The nuns assigned to field phone calls share repeat calls that credit the nuns' prayers for keeping a marriage intact or a disease at bay. "Sometimes we get calls like that and it helps us to continue," Sister Mary Nicolette says. "But many times we just go by faith that there is a purpose, that there is a reason, and that it's good."

The Mother Abbess reads the newspaper each day. She chooses which stories to share with the nuns. She always tells them if there has been a murder in Rockford. On occasion, she clips an article to be placed on a table in the library. Sister Mary Clara answers the phone, taking note of personal tragedies and global catastrophes. And then the community takes action: They pray, and then they "wait and see," Mother Miryam says, what God "has in store."

Sister Joan Marie
of the Child Jesus

My mother was home all the time. She was always home. When I was born she got sick. A nurse kept a heating pad on her too long. First her arm got stiff, and then her leg got stiff so they called up my grandmother who lived in Parsons, Kansas—that's where my mother came from—and so she took care of me when I was little, when I was just a baby. I don't remember it, but that's what they tell me. My mother couldn't walk very well because she had that stiff knee. My father took her to a specialist, and he said, "Walk to me. Walk." She said, "I can't." "Walk," he kept saying. "Walk." And so she walked. Evidently, she could walk after that, but with a stiff knee. My brother used to blame me because before that, Mother used to take him on the sled, but when I came along she couldn't do that anymore.

My sister's the oldest, five years older than me. My brother was two and a half years older. The older two would talk for me; I didn't have to say much. I had to have speech therapy because others couldn't understand me. I had a tutor, and I learned the vowels and to pronounce better so they could understand me.

There was a gas station across a big street, but I was kind of little so I took my brother and sister with me. The Overhands owned the gas station—just a little gas station—and they had caramels and things. They would give me penny candy, and so I went there as often as I could. My brother and sister liked to come, too, because they got to share. I used to keep a jar of money— pennies and things I got. Anyway, I would shake that jar, and when it shook like there was enough, I would take them over; they would go with me—my brother and sister and cousin, too. I treated them. I wanted their company because I wanted to go over there, and I couldn't go alone! I was only five or six. The Overhands took the money and said it was enough, and they asked each of us what we wanted; they got Pepsi-Colas and stuff.

The Overhands were wonderful people. They took an interest in me. One Easter, the bell rang and I went to the door. Mother went to the door and I went along. They had a clothesbasket and inside were two bunnies—white bunnies—and they were so cute. They were for me. That's what I mean; they just took an interest in me because I was the baby, I guess, the youngest. That was really something. We kept those bunnies. There was one that lived longer. Mother said when he got to be the size of a milk bottle, we had to get him out of the house. She thought he would give me pink eye, or maybe he did give me pink eye. I don't remember. Anyway, we would have to get him out of the house then, so I would measure him. The bunny would come to the breakfast table and it was so funny. Finally, my father said he would make a fence so we could still keep him outdoors. He made him a fence, but the next morning, the bunny had dug under the fence. We never got him back. I guess they never looked for him.

What really got me as a child was Christmas. I didn't know what Easter was because I didn't know anybody that died, but I knew what Christmas was and I knew that God became a child like me. That just went over and over in my head—that God would become a child. Because what was I? Insignificant as a child.

My mother and father never went to church, but my mother always had good books. I remember this one book she had—the Old Testament story about the little girl that was sold into slavery. They had a picture of the little girl and I always wanted to be that little girl who said, "There is a prophet in Israel!" That influenced me a lot, that book about the leprosy and the girl. She was a slave girl from Israel. It's an interesting story, in Nehemiah or something, I forget where it is in the Bible. We hear it in Mass sometimes. I've read it since, many times. I remember the pictures, too. It's a child's book and the picture of the little girl looked like she was my age.

It always did impact me—that story—that the slave's master would get cured, and the way he got cured. The slave girl said, "There is a prophet in Israel that will cure you." He was her master and she wanted him to go to Israel. He did. He got cured, but it was a roundabout way. The prophet said, "Go plunge in the Jordan seven times." And he said, "What, are not the rivers in Egypt good enough?" He didn't like that. He was mad. He said, "I thought he would come out and lay his hand on me." But the prophet didn't; he just said, "Go." The slaves tried to argue with him, "Now, if he had said something great big, you would have done it. So why not this?" So he plunged seven times in the Jordan and came out clean like a baby's skin.

Ma had a lot of good books she used to read to us because my brother couldn't read. She would read not religious books, but books that boys would like—*The Count of Monte Cristo*. I liked them, too—books about Doctor Dolittle and by Frank Buck, things like that. Because my brother had trouble reading, my parents were supposed to let him stay back; the teacher wanted to keep him back in first grade or kindergarten, but my father wouldn't let him; he wouldn't hear of it. My sister was so smart and he thought that the next one should be that smart, too, so he wouldn't let them. So my brother moved on, but he couldn't pick up the reading; he had trouble with the reading.

I remember staying home from school when I got sick. I mean, I pretended I was sick in order to stay home. A big tree was cut down in our yard and we wanted to have fun in that tree. Mother knew I was just pretending, but she let me stay, so all day we played on that tree. That was fun.

We had to rent a house so we could go to school, but I don't remember school much. I didn't like it. My sister liked school and she was an "A-plus" student in everything. She had to be top in everything, and she was. She studied. She studied hard to get those grades. It wasn't like it came easy, although she was like a genius, I guess. My father was a genius because he could take any job. He could seem to.

My sister had a boy that would come over; he liked her. She played the teacher; she liked to teach, and she would keep him in the corner. He was always in the corner. My mother didn't like that. She didn't think that was right. I don't remember standing in the corner, just him. But he would come back for more. He liked it. Mother thought that was awful. Isn't that funny?

They always expected me to be like my sister. I couldn't match that. I was lucky if I made a "C." My mother always said, "Well, don't worry if you don't get better grades. You can understand others better when you're just normal, average." She tried to console me. But anyway, I guess I just wanted to play all the time.

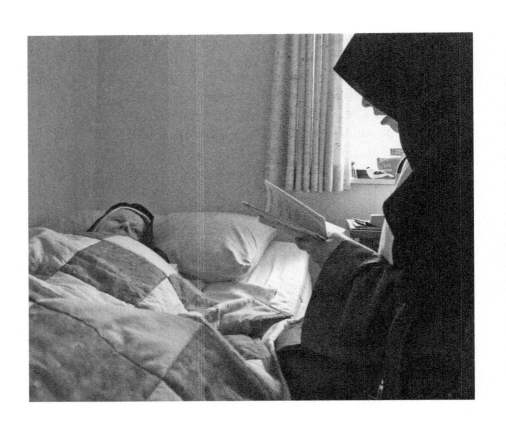

6

The Suffering Servants

In a sense, I think that's what God asks of us—it's that trust element. He's say-
ing, "Are you willing to risk everything for me? Do you really love me? Do you
really love me enough to risk everything for me and trust that I will take care
of you?" And it has to come out of a personal relationship, and a deep personal
relationship with our Lord, knowing that, yes, I can trust Him and He will take
care of me and He won't let me down. He won't just drop me, leave me in the
lurch, or just dump me. But we can really, really trust that He loves us and wants
to give us the best.

Sister Mary Nicolette of the Father of Mercies

When Sister Mary Gemma entered the Corpus Christi Monastery, she left
behind a younger sister poor in health. When her family visited, Mary was
wheeled into the parlor. Sister Mary Gemma says her mother "kept her father
real" and both parents helped Mary learn to contend with her disease: coli-
tis, an ulcerated colon. "She was only in seventh grade when she started to
suffer," Sister Mary Gemma says.

Since the onset of Mary's disease, their father had scoured health journals
and medical books on Mary's behalf, always hopeful of finding new treat-
ments. The pattern continued through Sister Mary Gemma's tenure in the
Corpus Christi Monastery. Her family still lives near the monastery, and so
together they would drive there to see Sister Mary Gemma for each of her
four allotted family visits each year. "I still remember Mary sitting in the
wheelchair and Dad all excited because he was giving her *this* now, and Mom
sitting in the back now going like *this*," Sister Mary Gemma says, shaking
her head.

Mary prayed for her own healing; she wanted to be made well. Still, she
ended each prayer asking that God's will be done in her life. Sister Mary

Gemma says, "Because of the guidance she received from my parents, she learned how to use the suffering, how to offer it to God, how to accept it, and how to unite her suffering with the suffering of Christ. She grew in love with God through all that."

Over the years, Mary's condition changed as the disease advanced, led to joint and spine problems, to open-heart surgery and a full colostomy, but not before an infection poisoned her colon and breached other organs. Mary was an avid needleworker until a rheumatic disease ate away the bones in her hands. Sister Mary Gemma says children gravitated to Mary; she allowed them to play with her deformed fingers, to push them backward and watch the fingers twist and flatten. This did not hurt Mary because her joints and cartilage had completely deteriorated, Sister Mary Gemma says.

As her body self-destructed, Mary appeared to grow lovelier in spirit. "She was one of the happiest persons I ever met," Sister Mary Gemma says. "She always had a smile on her face. She was always joking."

Mother Miryam witnessed the same transformation in Mary—a "lovely little thing" who initially grappled with her "crippled" state until doctors said they had done everything possible and Mary understood she would not recover. Eventually, she believed it was her vocation in life to suffer.

Self-deprecating, Mary joked that a cousin selected her as a wedding attendant, along with two friends who were seven months pregnant, because there was "nothing like two pregnant women and a cripple in a wheelchair to make you look tall and thin." Referring to her electric wheelchair, she called herself the "remote-control cousin."

Mary survived and suffered until a medication thinned her blood, and she had a stroke. She died within twenty-four hours. "I think she was ready for heaven," Sister Mary Gemma says. "I was so happy for her to be with God, where she wanted to be, that I couldn't even cry for her after she died. I think it was harder for my family who were with her all the time, but I only saw her four times a year. And we were very close but I just felt nothing but joy for her. Not that I don't miss her, but I just still feel real happy for her. That's what my parents always taught us—we're living for heaven. We're here on earth to get ready for heaven and that's what we all want, for us all to be together in heaven someday."

After Mary died, Sister Mary Gemma learned about Mary's brush with death a year earlier. Mary told a cousin about the experience and asked her not to share the story with anyone yet. After Mary died, the family read

Mary's own account of the events in an essay she titled "My Journey toward Heaven." "I have had a lot of pain in my life, but this was the worst," Mary wrote at the age of forty-two. "How could a bladder infection cause so much pain?" A tentative diagnosis of a tumor, abscess, or a blood clot was followed by hallucinations—a side effect of the medications and the barium tests. Told she would need to undergo an operation, Mary scheduled a confession with her priest. "I have felt for a long time now that I would never survive another major surgery," she wrote. "My feeling was that I would not be coming back." Friends visited Mary in her hospital room; she told them that if she died she "wouldn't mind." "I felt my life fading away," she wrote.

Four days after she was admitted to the hospital, doctors scheduled a CT scan of her lungs and abdomen to determine the cause of her breathing difficulties. "Before I was taken away for the scan I had an urgency to tell Mom and Dad where my will was. I felt death was very near, but I didn't want to alarm them," she wrote. She told her mom, "I don't want to be kept alive by extraordinary means."

During a CT scan that should have been somewhat routine, Mary could not catch her breath. The technician thought she was hyperventilating and advised slower, deeper breaths, before she realized Mary's system was shutting down. Mary remembered her pushing emergency buttons, remembered the technician screaming for help. "It became extremely painful. With every gasp after gasp I could only think, 'God how long can this go on? God, please take me now, this is torture!' Then it was over. I must have finally passed out."

Later, when Mary described what happened next, she said the pain left her body at that instant. She felt surrounded by a "golden kaleidoscope of a yellow bright light." She believed she had started her journey to heaven. She was ready. But then she heard voices of confusion and panic. A doctor repeated her wishes: She did not want extraordinary measures taken to save her life. She heard a men's choir and she felt soothed. She thought she was about to end her journey. Then Mary saw "black and gray." Her throat hurt. She realized she was alive but worried that the nurses would not know she was. An emergency tracheotomy revived her. "I was not able to finish my journey to heaven," she wrote. "I knew my trials and struggles were not over after all."

"They worked on her for quite a long time and she came back to life again," Sister Mary Gemma says.

After Mary died, her cousin e-mailed family, writing that Mary told her she heard, "not through her ears, just in her heart," a voice asking, "Will you still suffer for the poor souls that have no one to pray for them?" Her cousin replied, "Yes, if you want me to." The emergency tracheotomy that saved Mary was a "cruel twist," the cousin wrote, because it stole her ability to sing—her only remaining creative outlet.

Her family believes that her spiritual encounter consoled Mary for her decades of chronic debilitating diseases. Mary died at forty-three years old. Looking back now, Sister Mary Gemma says of her younger sister's descriptions of approaching heaven, "I honestly can't say what she experienced. Certainly, it was a mystical gift that she received, to hear the angels singing. And you could tell—she always already was a beautiful person to me—but after that, there was so much peace in her. Before that, she always had a certain fear of dying, I think. And that's natural to the human condition—to fear death. In God's original plan, the soul was not meant to be separated from the body."

Sister Mary Gemma believes that suffering can bring good, purifying a person's soul of selfishness and uniting her with the suffering of Christ. Although the reasons for this suffering remain a mystery, Sister Mary Gemma believes that God is an all-powerful being, an "infinite genius."

Daily, Poor Clare nuns pray for those who call the monastery seeking relief from their circumstances. The nuns seek treatment for their own ailments as well. Mother Miryam underwent knee replacement surgery after postponing it several times, insisting she was too busy overseeing the monastery's operations to take a break for the operation and a period of recovery.

"Suffering gives us empathy for others because you're understanding more the suffering of Christ in a certain sense; there's no way He loved us more than suffering on the cross for us," Sister Mary Gemma says. "That kind of gives you an appreciation of what He suffered for you.... It really does have an effect on your love of Christ, if you don't become bitter about suffering, and use it to draw closer to our Lord on the cross. And then you can't help loving Him more. Of course, some people don't have to suffer to have empathy for others.... Actually, what really purifies us for God is love; loving God and loving our neighbors is what really purifies us. But sometimes we have to suffer.... It's how God purges away our selfishness, is through suffering. He can use our suffering for souls, for the salvation of souls. And I know from my experience that your union with Christ deepens through suffering. He allows suffering for a reason. There's two ways that you can handle suffering in your life—either trusting God, or you can turn to bitterness. But your spiritual life deepens when you suffer and you learn how to suffer graciously."

Sister Mary Gemma is not speaking abstractly. Not only did she suffer and empathize as witness to her sister's struggles, but Sister Mary Gemma has also endured her own physical trials. She, along with another member of the Corpus Christi Monastery, are both victims of serious diseases. One of the two nuns is now healed; any sign of the disease has vanished. The other nun continues to wrestle not only with her condition but also with the degree of self-care required to accommodate the affliction. Both reconcile their illnesses, and their present states, through the looking glass of faith.

Sister Mary Nicolette was diagnosed with dermatopolymyositis, a rare autoimmune disease, in childhood; the illness, which causes muscle weakness, flared twice. "I had recovered both times, but it's a hereditary disease that you don't usually ever get over," she says. "You just live with it the rest of your life." A daily regimen of expensive medication stabilized her condition, and Sister Mary Nicolette learned to deal with the symptoms, limiting her physical activity and monitoring her health.

When Sister Mary Nicolette applied to enter a cloistered monastery in Ohio, she mentioned the disease in her application, not expecting it would bar her entry since her condition was stable; she was turned away. In 1993, Sister Mary Nicolette was twenty years old when she was invited to join the Corpus Christi Monastery as a postulant. She brought a year's worth of medication, not wanting her illness to present a financial burden to her new religious community.

She fulfilled her duties, including the sometimes demanding manual labor required of all novitiates, under close medical surveillance; regular blood tests tracked her enzyme levels. Tests revealed that she was stable, but she felt weak, with limited mobility in her muscles and tendons. "If you didn't know that I had this, most people wouldn't notice, but there were some things, like bending, that took a lot of effort to do," Sister Mary Nicolette says.

But the more she worked outdoors, the stronger she felt. Several times during regular consultations with the doctor who makes house calls to the monastery, she said she did not think she needed the medicine anymore. The physician suggested reducing the dosage. "So it was gradual," Sister Mary

Nicolette says. "Very gradual, very gradual, very gradual." Eventually, she was no longer on any medication, "which is very unexpected and very out of the ordinary for this illness because it's not something you're ever cured of."

Today, she has no sign of the illness. She does not take any medicine. She no longer undergoes blood tests. "And I'm as strong as an ox!" she says. Sister Mary Nicolette knows why she was healed. "God," she says. "I just feel like if there's a need in the community, especially with the outdoor work and everything, the older sisters can't do that and I'm here and I can do it," Sister Mary Nicolette says. "And I think God strengthened me to serve community in that way, and do some of the manual work that maybe some of the older sisters can't do."

Asked if she thinks she would have been cured if she had not entered the monastery and assumed the trying duties of a cloistered contemplative nun, Sister Mary Nicolette says, "That's an interesting question I don't know the answer to." She pauses, then adds, "Yeah, I don't know. I don't know. It's something very mysterious to me and perhaps only God knows. But I do feel like there was a purpose at the time when I became sick—to draw me closer to God—and there was a purpose why I was healed, so I that I could help community and be a strong sister in the community."

Sister Mary Gemma grew up in a nearby farming community. In 1975, she entered the monastery. She was nineteen. Assigned the manual tasks of a novitiate, Sister Mary Gemma began experiencing chronic back pain. Seven years after entering the monastery, she experienced a type of pain she had never felt before: a burning sensation that seemed to jump from one area to another, traveling up and down her arms and legs.

The pain began to spread. She did not understand what was happening within her; she had trouble finding words to accurately depict the sensation. Changes in the temperature seemed to trigger discomfort, as did any sort of emotional strain.

After years of pain, punctuated by more tests and a trip to a pain clinic in Chicago, doctors eventually diagnosed her with fibromyalgia. Her condition did not improve with treatment, however, and so doctors conducted more tests. Almost two decades after the pain started, Sister Mary Gemma's hand swelled up and turned blue; this helped the physicians deduce the underlying cause: reflex sympathetic dystrophy (RSD), known also as complex regional pain syndrome. Her doctors believed the previous diagnosis was correct, too, and that she also has fibromyalgia. Possibly the result of a previous injury, RSD had operated with free reign, advancing unchecked for so long before Sister Mary Gemma was diagnosed and treatment started that in spite of potent doses of daily medication, small changes in temperature and minor injuries provoked major flare-ups.

Once, her hands began to ache while she was playing the organ but she kept practicing; it took her a year and a half for the pain to subside. "RSD just takes a long time to quiet down," she says. "It's not a nice disease. I actually have a mild form of it, but the doctor said the problem with me is it's gone into my legs and my arms, and since I've had it so long, it's harder to cure."

Sister Mary Gemma's treatment has included nerve blocks—temporary fixes that limited the pain for less than a year. Through trial and error, Sister Mary Gemma tries to accept her chronic condition and manage it with rest and medication (covered by Social Security disability payments). Even too much excitement or laughing too hard seems to awaken pain signals from hibernation. "Clearly a weird thing," she says.

Doctors have told Sister Mary Gemma that her symptoms will improve if she can avoid cold temperatures as well as heat, which makes her sweat; they suggested she move from Illinois to a more temperate climate. "I just feel this is where God wants me," she says, "and I feel so much that the community here understands my disease. They're so understanding of it. I felt like it would be a burden to put on another community just like that, although I'm sure other communities would be willing to take me. But the sisters have grown with me. They've been with me through the whole thing. They've been supporting me through the whole thing. And I just... this is my home. They provide heat for me and they do everything they can for me to help me."

Sister Mary Gemma believes she would not have been accepted into this religious community if her diagnoses had been made before she asked to join. She does not regret her decision to become a Poor Clare, in spite of the fact that her condition might have been detected and stabilized sooner if she had been living a more "normal life" out in the world, she says. "I think it's a blessing for me that I'm in the monastery because I have a community who—they're all very understanding. There are times where I cannot work at all and I have to rest a lot. I don't know how I would survive if I wasn't in the monastery."

Sister Mary Gemma does not fully comprehend her affliction. She knows her body has failed her. God never intended suffering or death, Sister Mary Gemma says. "Our body and our soul are a unit. He did not make us to be spirit only, like the angels, and He did not make us to be body only, like the animals; He gave us a body and soul and He did not intend, in the original plan, for the body and the soul to be separated."

Like her younger sister, Sister Mary Gemma prays for her own healing. She closes her prayers just as Mary did—that God's will be done. She has not experienced substantial healing, physically. But she believes that suffering can serve a redemptive purpose. And she believes that God has answered her prayers. "I think God has helped me, not with an actual miracle, but He has helped me get the doctors that can help me," she says. Since childhood, Sister Mary Gemma grappled with issues relating to her self-esteem. Once, a few years ago, when she received the Sacrament of the Sick, she says, "I can remember that I was asking our Lord to heal me in whatever way He wanted to, and I felt a great strength emotionally after that." Another time, as Sister Mary Gemma observed her hour of prayer before the exposed Blessed Sacrament, she knelt down and said, "Jesus, I failed you again. And I felt His voice coming from the Blessed Sacrament going right to my heart: 'I love you still.' I was so surprised, I said, 'Jesus did you just talk to me?' " Sister Mary Gemma says. "I didn't hear it again. But I felt it so strong. It felt like an echo in my heart and it was one of those things that kept me going through this tough time of low self-esteem. He loved me anyway. And He loves me anyway."

An assistant in the infirmary, helping watch over Sister Ann Frances as she contended with Alzheimer's, Sister Mary Gemma is thankful that Sister Ann Frances can remain in the monastery and has not been sent to a nursing home, where Sister Mary Gemma thinks she would be even more confused. Working in the infirmary allows her a more flexible schedule. Not wanting to "spoil herself," she has had to learn, repeatedly, not to try to soldier through the early warning signs of RSD; otherwise she will need to be admitted to the hospital to receive intravenous pain medication. A necessary regimen— frequent rest—feels like punishment for the sociable Sister Mary Gemma.

Mother Miryam says it is hard for any of the nuns when they cannot take part in community because they are sick and bedridden, but it has been especially hard for Sister Mary Gemma when she is forced to remove herself to her cell. Mother Miryam says Sister Mary Gemma questions, "Am I giving in to myself?" Mother Miryam describes Sister Mary Gemma as phlegmatic by nature and not prone to push herself; she says Sister Mary Gemma has made great strides in the steep learning curve to know how much she can handle once she feels pain and when she should stop working.

Sister Mary Gemma does not walk barefoot—unlike the fictional Ingalls family, unlike the other Poor Clares. RSD forbids her feet from greeting the cold floor. "That's part of my suffering, too, because I came here to live a life of penance and to live a hard life, and I'm not able to do that because of my health situation," she says. "And yet I am living a hard life within my situation. It's hard for me not to live the life as I thought I was going to. Through spiritual direction, I've learned to accept it; this is how God wants me to suffer. He wants me to suffer by not being what I would call a *Colettine* Poor Clare. We have a very strict penitential life and that is what I came for, but it's God's plan that I'm not able to do that. I suffer in a different way."

A nun works in the monastery's woodshop, equipped with tools of every type after one woman joined the Poor Clares and, in keeping with her vow of poverty, gave up all belongings, donating them to the community.

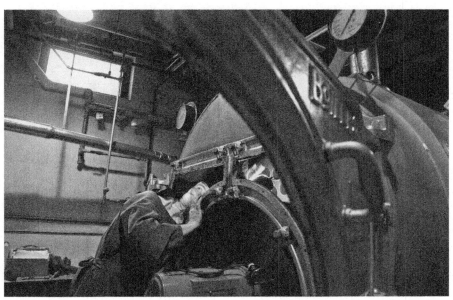

To honor their vow of enclosure and separation from the world, Poor Clares try to maintain themselves as much of the property as possible. Here, a nun cleans the boiler.

A nun and a novice garden together. The Poor Clare day comprises regular alterations between prayer and manual labor.

A John Deere tractor—a rare concession by the Poor Clares to technological advancements—is operated only so that the nuns can mow the acreage more quickly in order to return to prayers. Rather than relying on the tractor for hauling, the nuns use a wheelbarrow and pitchforks in keeping with their life of manual labor. Here, a nun passes the gardens and a storage shed.

A nun has passed away. Her coffin, seen through the grille, is placed on the enclosure side of the parlor before the funeral.

Part III

The Threats

7

Idealism and Reality

It's in self-giving that people find their truest fulfillment. And it's a paradox; it's one of those paradoxes that seem to be a contradiction. Now if you look at something as beautiful as marriage, you see how, when two people sacrifice themselves for one another and give themselves to each other wholly and completely, there is a true fulfillment there. It's the same in religious life and on a supernatural level; when people are able to sacrifice themselves—give themselves up—that's when we can find the deepest fulfillment, not in seeking selfish ends and selfish motives. When we're seeking ourselves, or seeking ourselves in creatures or in creation, it's so finite; we're seeking what it can't give. Only God can fill infinite desire.

Sister Mary Nicolette of the Father of Mercies

After Sister Mary Michael's forty-fifth birthday, her family witnessed a quick transformation, somewhat miraculous, totally disruptive. "It all just happened so fast, out of the sky. I compare it with Paul being knocked off his horse," Sister Mary Michael says.

Her journey from an insurance firm to transcendence took shape in the utterly mundane. When family members borrowed her red car and turned on the engine, they knew to anticipate blaring country tunes; now they were baffled, instead, to find cassette tapes playing spiritual lessons, and her radio tuned to church music. Her young nieces and nephews, who had looked forward to her visits and the spoiling that inevitably ensued, became the objects of her evangelism. Poolside in her backyard and during hikes in the woods near her family's cabin in Wisconsin, the children tired of her efforts to impress on them religious teachings and stories. She taught them the sobering story of the holy children of Fatima, who saw visions of the Virgin Mary in Portugal; two of those youngsters had learned they would not live long, and so they dedicated themselves for the remainder of their days to only what mattered for eternity—prostrating themselves for hours in prayer and practicing acts of self-mortification.

Sister Mary Michael, known then to her relatives as Jenny, told the children that in the story of the Fatima children, an actual modern-day morality play, she could identify with the little boy who quit dancing and stopped singing to contemplate quietly behind a bush. She wanted to spend her life praying, growing closer to God. "Just to be nice to me, they would, but they weren't interested," Sister Mary Michael says. "Of course, they weren't going to understand. They were going to lose me. We were real close." As Jenny's interests and attention tunneled in a religious fervor, her nieces and nephews complained that she was changing; they distanced themselves from her. "It was like I went overboard and they couldn't understand," she says. "I feel sorry for them because I was so excited and I was trying to push this onto them."

At her niece's confirmation party, Jenny stood in the hall with the other celebrants. She felt ignored by the guest of honor, but she was not sure the slight was intentional until her niece apologized. "Later, she told me she was sorry she didn't introduce me to her friends because she was upset," Sister Mary Michael says. "They were just so hurt because what they had was going to be lost. But they were getting older and they were going to have their own lives pretty soon. But at that time they were still quite young, so this was quite hard for them to let go."

On weekends, Jenny typically brought her mother to her nieces' and nephews' basketball games. She remembers that when she first started desiring the cloistered life, she went to one of the games. "You know how it is in the gyms, with those bands playing and the crowd?" she asks. "I had never noticed how loud and how awful the noise was before. It just seemed so horrendous and I didn't want to be there with all that noise. When my mother and I were going home, my brother called my sister and wanted to know what was happening. It went on like that; I went up there again a couple of times, and they'd get upset, and I'd try to talk to them, and they'd try to understand."

Jenny's family was bewildered by the middle-aged woman they once knew as a tomboy who stole cigarettes from her parents' gas station store and swiped the complimentary maps to roll cigars stuffed with weeds.

As a medical student in college, Jenny was impervious to dissecting cadavers and remembers, matter-of-factly, trying to scrub her fingernails free of the fatty tissues that accumulated there before she and her lab partner went to dinner. Jenny dreamed of becoming a missionary doctor, but, fearing interactions with patients and the pressure to diagnose and cure their ailments, she quit medical school after her third year. She says now she might have enjoyed clinical research if she had thought to consider that as an option. Her parents, who had claimed her desire to become a doctor, were distressed by word that she was about to drop out, and they sent her older brother as an emissary on a fruitless mission to dissuade her. An advisor, who mistakenly believed that her parents held too much sway in suggesting that she quit, badgered her to reconsider abandoning the program.

Jenny enrolled in computer classes at a technical school and then began working as a programmer analyst for an insurance firm that overlooked Lake Michigan. For eighteen years, Jenny worked in Chicago, commuting from her home in Indiana to her job. She saved money, bought a house, drove a convertible. "I was fortunate to have such a good job and to have something I enjoyed to do so well," she says.

In her mid-forties, living with her sister and brother-in-law in northwest Indiana, just down the street from her mother, Jenny had a reputation as easygoing and averse to conflict. For the second time in her life, Jenny charted a course in direct opposition to her family's wishes.

The changes in Jenny began with meager gestures—her reading material now consisted of biographies of the saints—that shifted her path completely. "What drew me was just a desire that God put there inside of me," Sister Mary Michael says. "It wasn't anything that I did. It wasn't anything I was searching for. It just happened. I mean I had this desire to love God. It's like I fell in love with God and nothing else mattered anymore. It's like from His side because the desire was put there. I didn't have anything to do with it, and so it just became stronger."

Jenny's family members became bystanders, shocked by her changing values, priorities, and temperament, uncomfortable with the new dynamic in their relationships and their passive status. Jenny's stamina in the face of her family's opposition to her fortified spirituality surprised her. "I was really close to my family and it was grace that I could stand up to my family because normally I would say, 'Well, forget it. They don't want me to do it, I won't.' That was really hard," she says.

Jenny told her sister of her impending first visit to the monastery only "because I lived with her, so she and her husband had to know," she says.

"They weren't real happy about it. It was really hard because they didn't understand. I can understand because it's such a switch, such a shock to say you're going to leave and live a contemplative life. So we didn't tell my mother. I was gone a whole day or so. We just didn't tell her."

Her visit was disappointing: "It seemed like everything was so dark and dingy." She learned from the Mother Abbess for the first time that there are "even priests that don't believe in cloistered life. That was a shock. It got late and I was planning on going home that night, but I stayed overnight. I woke up at midnight for the Mass choir to listen. Then I got up in the morning, they gave me breakfast, and I went home. When I got home, I was just kind of confused. I wasn't impressed," she says. "But there was still that feeling that I wanted this life." Sister Mary Michael remembers that her sister tartly—perhaps hopefully—said of her visit: "You expected to see saints flying around."

Still, she had not thought about home while she was visiting the monastery, and she attributes that to God's grace. "I know it was," she says. "I wasn't wishing I was back there. I was here and I was supposed to be here and that was it. It was like I was real strong inside, I guess, like you're doing the right thing, whatever had to be done."

After Jenny returned home, she informed her mother she planned to enter the Corpus Christi Monastery. "No, you're not," she remembers her mother saying. But Jenny told her mother, who was terminally ill, "I have to."

Jenny was drawn to the radical and idealistic roots of the Poor Clare Colettine Order, and she identified with the original mission; she wanted to live as Jesus lived. Sister Mary Nicolette draws strength today from the simplicity and poverty of Saint Francis, who was initially met with disapproval by the approving body in Rome for his community of contemplative friars. "They said, 'This is just not livable,'" Sister Mary Nicolette says. "'It's just phooft,'" she sweeps her hand over her head, signaling the lofty standards set forth by Saint Francis of Assisi. "And they were saying idealistic is not realistic." Sister Mary Nicolette summarizes the historical account of the exchange that followed and led to the founding of the Poor Clares, the second order of Saint Francis: One wise cardinal stood up and warned the others, "Brethren, beware of saying that we cannot approve this, that it's not livable, because if you say that, you say the gospel is not livable." "And no one could argue with that," Sister Mary Nicolette says, "because Christ gave us the ideal in the gospel. And if you say we can't live that, you're saying that

Christ asked us to live something that's impossible, and that's not true. So it's something that's very on my heart."

Sister Mary Nicolette matured in a breathtaking scene—the rim of the earth's crust that is the Alps. She developed, spiritually, during solo hikes in the Italian mountains. A self-professed woman of high ideals, she says, "It was like nature spoke to me of God and I realized that there was something deeper in life than I had ever experienced." An heir to the eight-hundred-year-old order who still marvels at finding herself free of an incurable disease, Sister Mary Nicolette comes by her romantic outlook rightly.

Sister Mary Nicolette, a visionary, is within prayer's reach of eternity. She, like all cloistered nuns, is "entirely dedicated to God," according to the book *Verbi Sponsa: Instruction on the Contemplative Life and on the Enclosure of Nuns*, which is given to each new postulant at the Corpus Christi Monastery to assist in her formation and training. Called to renounce not only "things" but also "space" and "contacts" and the other "benefits of creation" in a "ceaseless straining towards the heavenly Jerusalem," the cloistered contemplative yearns for fulfillment in God, alone, "in an uninterrupted nostalgia of the heart" toward "the realization of this sublime contemplative ideal."[1]

Those who abide by Franciscan virtues submit themselves to a radical way of life. Sister Maria Deo Gratias explains her aim in elementary, yet incredible, terms: "The challenge is to become a saint in the life. That's the challenge—to give 100 percent each moment of the day no matter how I feel—100 percent in the virtue of charity, 100 percent response in the virtue of my own prayer life, and giving God totally all the facets of our life. If I can just give 100 percent, that's the challenge that I see."

Sister Mary Nicolette believes the same hands that struggle against nature's restrictions should reach for perfection. Sister Mary Nicolette says the gospels give readers the example of Jesus' flawlessness; the saints proved that it is possible for men and women—nondeities, who are not God incarnate—to attain this: "They made it. They got there. Now it doesn't mean that they didn't struggle, but we know with certainty that they reached the goal that they were striving for. And we have their example and that's why the Church raises them up as examples. That's all the Church is saying, is that they lived heroic virtue and it's possible, and that you can arrive at this. And it's going to be a struggle; it's going to take your whole life, but it's not impossible and it's not in conflict with reality."

Not everyone—not even all of the monastic nuns at the Corpus Christi Monastery—believes that idealism and a full acceptance of reality can be reconciled. Sister Mary Nicolette describes a recent theological exchange. "We were talking about reality versus ideals," she says. Sister Mary Nicolette does not place the two concepts on opposite ends of a spectrum or regard them as mutually exclusive, "because I really believe that the reality is the vehicle that leads us to the ideal. I don't believe that being idealistic is being unrealistic. I wed them together. I believe that the reality that we live should be such that we're growing toward the ideal and that the ideal is something that can be reached. We're going to be short; most of the time we're going to be living short of the ideal because we have a lot of growth to go through before we get there, but I personally reject the idea that being idealistic is being unrealistic. I think the two go together. I think you're on your way if you're idealistic."

The reality of the cloister can conspire to subvert the spiritual pursuit of ideals. Some women are simply not equipped for cloistered monastic life. The principled—and arduous—quest is for those who can cope with reality, who can reconcile the impossible standards and their own limitations with the rigors of the cloister. "When you enter the monastery, the life is structured," Sister Maria Deo Gratias says. "And so I don't just say, okay, I'm just going to 'x' it out and I'm going off to spend the time walking in the woods. It's a total giving of yourself. And that time is not yours to 'x' off. That's part of your poverty—that we don't own anything. And we don't own the time that we have either."

Interrupting one's sleep at midnight for the Divine Office, never again hugging one's family—all of this is "not natural," Sister Maria Benedicta says. "God chooses the weak to make them strong. He gives them His power to be able to do it. And it's like, okay, I can do it. And you realize your utter weakness because He has to come in and He has to do it, because we can't. It's beyond our own capacity."

When she was a postulant, in training and learning about the ancient customs, Sister Mary Gemma was nonplussed by her fellow spiritual travelers. "You are very idealistic and you want to keep that idealism, but you're not quite realistic when you first come because you see the beauty of the monastic life and you expect that everyone's going to be a saint," Sister Mary Gemma says. "And then you find out more about yourself. As time goes on, you find out that you have a lot to work on, too. You understand when you notice faults in others, as you grow in the spiritual life and you grow with your own struggles with your faults, it makes you more compassionate with your sisters. You realize this life is hard; striving for a life of perfection is going to be hard, even though there's so much joy—so much joy living in community. But it's hard, too. The religious life is a life of perfection. But you're striving for perfection. You don't come perfect; you're striving for perfection. That's what you promise when you make your vows. You're promising to strive to follow Christ, and to become perfect, like He said: 'Be perfect as your heavenly father is perfect.' So our life is a striving for that. But we fail and we get up and we keep trying because we're human and we have that tendency to fail. That's just the way life is. The important thing is to get up and to keep trying."

Sister Maria Deo Gratias believes that the monastic island within a crime-ridden urban area is "a suburb of heaven." "Our destination is heaven," Sister Maria Deo Gratias says. "We're not camping out forever. We're passing through. Even in this suburb of heaven, it's not heaven yet. So, therefore, I'm traveling. We're all pilgrims and coming to that perfect union, which is heaven."

Disarming in her frankness, Sister Maria Deo Gratias personifies two competing interests: a compulsive industriousness to embody her ideals, and an acceptance of her present circumstances. She sacrifices daily for her beliefs; she also detaches from that which she believes she cannot or should not control or change. Sister Maria Deo Gratias's last assignment in an active order—working in the psychiatric unit of a Chicago hospital—illustrates her willingness to bend herself, but not her beliefs, to each situation. When this former teacher was asked to work in the psychiatric unit, another religious sister offered to lend Sister Maria Deo Gratias "civilian" clothes, because she thought the modified habit of her active order, which did not cover her ankles, would create conflict with the patients. Sister Maria Deo Gratias dismissed the suggestion; she felt the other nun was already "putting the expectations on" that she could not come into the unit as she was. When Sister Maria Deo Gratias was interviewed by the director of the psychiatric unit, he, too, raised the topic of her hospital uniform. She said she would wear her habit. "I said, 'If you want me to come into the unit, I'm wearing the habit. If you don't want me to wear the habit, then I don't come in.' I just said it like that because that's how I felt," Sister Maria Deo Gratias says. She remembers the director replying, "No, I want you to come in. I'll give you space." Sister

Maria Deo Gratias, who says the uniform issue was "rigamarole," told the other religious sister in the unit that she would just try the post and leave if it did not work.

Sister Maria Deo Gratias recalls that once, possibly on her first day in the psychiatric ward, she was told that a woman, accompanied by police officers into the emergency room, had been found "running around on a billboard, hardly any clothes on, just really drugged up." "They brought her into the unit and then, like dummies, they took the cuffs off. She ran all over and I'm trying to calm her down." When the woman was finally subdued, the woman asked Sister Maria Deo Gratias, "Why aren't you wearing a long habit like the sisters used to wear?" Sister Maria Deo Gratias laughs. "I said, 'See! See! Now I'm getting into trouble because I don't have a habit long enough!'"

Raised in a Catholic family that built their own cottage together, stone by stone, Sister Maria Deo Gratias was an independent child who defied her mother when she announced in the sixth grade that she intended to become a nun. Today, she appears to be a well-adjusted cloistered monastic nun, casually indifferent to whatever might fall in her path. "When I enter a new experience, I guess I don't expect anything," she says. "I just say, 'What is there? I'll find out what is there when I get there and I'll go with the punches, go with the flow.'" Sister Maria Deo Gratias might be a spiritual pragmatist in her efforts to participate in the redemptive work of Jesus on behalf of humanity. "I just fell in love with God, and said, 'Whatever you want, I do,'" Sister Maria Deo Gratias says. "That's just the way I came about it." She says that since she didn't have any expectations when she came to the monastery, no hopes were ever dashed. "There was nothing to get disappointed about," she says, "because I didn't know what the life is. But I just know that I'm called to be a cloistered contemplative in this particular community. And so I entered and whatever unfolds in my training as to what it means to be a cloistered contemplative nun, I'm learning that."

More than two decades after entering the Corpus Christi Monastery, Sister Maria Deo Gratias says she still catches herself walking too fast in the corridors at the alert pace she kept in the psychiatric unit. She reminds herself to slow down, to enter into the silence that is the presence of God: "Wait. Where I have to go isn't an emergency."

In Sister Maria Deo Gratias's life devoted to prayer, she asks God to "give the special graces and the nudges you need to think things out. And I think it's a very important role that I can't take for granted. I'm only an instrument, as each of us sisters are; but we have the responsibility to be good instruments in our apostolate of prayer. And God does give extra graces when you ask, but a lot of people don't think about asking. So even those who don't call us and don't contact us in any way, that don't believe in us, we can touch their hearts. It's really a privilege to live this life and I think we get more than we give. That's definitely true. He didn't have to call me, but He did, and I wouldn't want anything other, so I'm really grateful God called me! You know, I would not choose another life."

Aware that she is subject to "the human condition," a fragile and imperfect state, Sister Maria Deo Gratias does not cling to anything too tightly, including her own perceptions of life, others, and herself. She readily accepts that she will not see the full, or completely clear, picture this side of heaven. "You stand in the truth. And the truth sets you free," Sister Maria Deo Gratias says. "I am who I am regardless of whether you think I am that way, or not that way. I am who I am. And I may even come to realize I am not who I think I am, and that's where my growth comes in—you know, I'm fooling myself, and I've got deeper growth to go because I'm seeing the truth that isn't the truth. So I have to be humble enough to say, you know, I don't have it all together here. I have to go back to the drawing board and say, 'Lord, help me to know myself so that I can know you more.' There's that sense of openness that even though we stand in the truth, I still may not be seeing the whole truth. We should always, until maybe ten minutes after we die, always see ourselves with that possibility—that we may not have the whole truth, that we still have things to learn. And be open to life, whatever comes your way—to be open and respond in a charitable way, in a virtuous way, in response, no matter what it is. I think that's where true poverty lies.

"So we always live like on the pilgrimage to heaven. Then, in heaven, I'll say, 'I've arrived.' But until that, I haven't arrived yet. I still have growing to do."

Sister Mary Nicolette says,

Like we always say, the Church is composed of human beings who have faults and are sinful, so naturally there's going to be a little bit of that in religion. We're all fallen, so to speak. But I think looking at the life as we strive to live it, our rule of life is really living the gospel so if you look at Christ in the gospel, there's nothing narrow-minded about Him. That's the ideal. That's what we're trying to live and what we're trying to imitate and take on. And it's very simple—the gospel life. That's our Rule. Our rule of life is to live the gospel for our Lord Jesus Christ, of our Lord Jesus Christ, and plain and simple without any alterations, without any adaptations. And what it comes down to is that—there won't be a narrow-mindedness the more and more converted and the more and more changed deep in our heart we become, because, naturally, we all come like that. But the more we grow in Christ the more we shed that off and become more embracing and more loving.

The maximum age for women entering the Corpus Christi Monastery is forty years old. This criterion was raised in recent years on account of the dwindling population. After she first visited the Corpus Christi Monastery, Jenny called one other monastery in the hope of scheduling a visit, but she was turned off by what sounded like a standoffish tone when the nun learned her age. She was welcomed into the fold at Corpus Christi, which made an exception in accepting her when she was forty-seven.

Believing quite fervently that she belonged in this foreign subculture, Jenny gave her family everything, including her Oldsmobile and control of her checking account and retirement savings. "When I came I didn't have any questions. I didn't have any doubts: 'Did I do the right thing?'" Sister Mary Michael says. "It was really funny. I didn't understand it. I didn't have any doubts—from the day I came. And it was awkward. I had to learn to chant the Office. I didn't know how to chant the Office and I had to learn to do all that. I stuck it out. I just knew I was supposed to be here so whatever happened, happened. I never had any doubts. I felt so much inside of me that God wanted me here. I knew this. I don't know why, I just knew this. So everything that came along, I just accepted this was the way of life. This must be what God wants because He asked me to come here. I just didn't question things. However they lived it, that was fine. It didn't bother me. But I do know some that come and they want to know, do we do this, do we do that, and it makes a difference to them. Well, I didn't. I just knew I was supposed to be here and so I accepted things. I know for some it was harder, but for me that was an advantage because I didn't question everything: 'Why do they do things that way?'"

In adjusting to the pace and purpose of the monastery, Sister Mary Michael exhibited the same easygoing temperament her family expected from her. She admits, "If God didn't really call us here we couldn't live this life. You can't live it unless you're really being called. Because it's so different—countercultural—especially today when so many people are so self-centered. You give up everything, really."

The transition was excruciating for her family and her colleagues. Sister Mary Michael remembers them asking her, "Why do you want to throw your life away? What will you do all day?" "It was just like somebody died when I came here. It was that hard," she says. "And I can see it because if it was the other way around I would feel the same way, I'm sure, because it's hard to understand. You're cut off. You don't go home anymore. It's very hard to understand. It's all faith."

Her colleagues did not want her to leave and phoned her sister for updates. Still, they celebrated with her at a going-away party, eating a cake decorated with a depiction of a nun.

Sister Mary Michael's younger brother, whose children struggled to comprehend her metaphysical changes, yielded eventually when she insisted that she belonged in the monastery. "They thought they should let me go and try, that I'd probably come back home, I knew I wanted to come here," she says. For years, every time they visited, Sister Mary Michael remembers their tears. "They depended on me in some ways, financially—not totally, but I did help them a lot because they had three kids. They missed me, too, but financially it was hard for them." "You can come live with us," she remembers her brother telling her. "Why don't you come and live with us?" Eventually, her brother, sister-in-law, and their children seemed to understand; they yielded their resistance to her choices. "They know that I am real happy here and they even said, 'We know that you belong here,'" Sister Mary Michael says. Her brother's family, although scattered geographically, with families of their own now, visit once a year. "I marvel at it," she says. "They're real faithful. They write all the time."

Her sister still writes in every letter, almost twenty years after she joined the monastery, that she misses her little sister a lot. "I feel sorry for her," she says.

Her older brother and sister-in-law visit the monastery but Sister Mary Michael does not think he has made peace with her religious vocation, although his opinion has improved; she remembers that during an early visit he said, "You're living in the Dark Ages."

Sister Mary Michael's mother visited her several times after she became a postulant. "It was hard," she says, "because she would come and sit here and say, 'Are you happy?' And she looked miserable. Of course, she was sick. And

I was content. But it was hard for her." The two did not talk much during those visits, just sat awkwardly, she says. She learned from her older sister that her mother became "gloomy and grumpy" back home, upset over Sister Mary Michael's absence. When her sister informed their mother that the situation was not going to change, she says her mother "snapped out of it." Her health digressed, though, and she moved in with her other daughter. "It wasn't like I was leaving her uncared for," Sister Mary Michael says, "because that you wouldn't do." Her mother died four months after she joined the monastery. "And again, the grace was there because I didn't fall apart or anything," she says.

Sister Mary Michael remembers, as a child, overhearing a conversation between her parents: a neighbor's daughter had joined a Carmelite order of cloistered nuns. When family brought food to the girl at the monastery, they could not even see her because a curtain covered the metal grille. "That's the only time I ever heard of contemplative life and it was this kind of on the negative side," Sister Mary Michael says. "They couldn't understand it, how she could do that." Asked if this influenced her mother's ability to accept her new life, she admits, "It could be." Asked if this life feels natural to her, she says, "Oh, yes."

Today, Sister Mary Michael reflects on what she perceives to be the few negative aspects of her life. "What makes a bad day? Let's see," she says. "I think it's mostly community living. You live with the same people in a small area and I think it's marvelous how we are able to get along that well. You have normal problems and sometimes they seem like mountains, but they're not—I mean, different personalities. We're all not the same. So I mean, sometimes you might get on each other's nerves, little things that are annoying. A lot of that is just living in community and normal problems of community life and struggling with that."

Sister Mary Michael has considered that she might have wanted to leave the monastery after her whirlwind arrival. "Just think—if I went back, if I went back soon enough, I probably could have gotten the same job I had, but I don't know that for sure, either," she says. "At that time, I was forty-seven. That isn't that ancient. That isn't *that* ancient, but the longer you stay here, that gets to be scary because what are you going to do, especially with computers where everything keeps advancing and if you don't keep up with it you're going to be lost? It keeps changing. So that would be a real problem. It would be scary. What would I be doing if I was in the world? I would be retired, I'm sure. You retire early. I'm sure I wouldn't be working. I'm glad I'm here because what would I be doing?"

Sister Ann Marie
of His Holy Wounds

God never tells you, "I want you to go here, go to Rockford" or "This is where I want you." It's an inner feeling. And the call is there. You can feel it. You can feel like you can hear it, and yet if it's true, why can't I see?

I just liked to know if God is really calling me or not. That's the thing. It's in me, and yet is it? Is it? You don't see any calling to join this community. You want to see a tangible answer. But God is playing hide-and-seek, you know; it's kind of like that.

I was born in the Philippines, and I was born in my mother's hometown, where my father and mother met. And then we moved to Manila, and that's where my family still is.

I'm the oldest. I have three brothers and one sister. I remember my three brothers were super-active. They loved to play. As soon as we'd get home from school, they'd just throw their things out and go out and play. And my sister used to stay home and the two of us would play with dolls.

When we were young, my father had to go to Vietnam, to work there to help support our family. He's a civil engineer. He was hired by part of the US government to work in Vietnam. He worked there for eight years, and so my mother was the one who took care of us. One time, my father got sick; they found that he's diabetic. He was hospitalized there, and so my mother had to be with him; she brought my two youngest siblings with her to Vietnam, and I was left with my brother, the next younger one, because we were both school age. He was in kindergarten and I was in first grade, so we stayed with my grandmother—my father's mother—in my father's hometown. It was only a year or so, I think, and then my mother came back, and we were back together. My father continued to work in Vietnam. He came home once in a while, once a year, or every three years. I can't remember how many times he came home; I was so small then.

I can't even remember when he left. All I remember is I was seven when my brother and I had to stay with my grandmother and my aunt. You miss your parents and younger siblings. My grandmother was kind of strict; she was kind of sickly then, but she was kind of strict, but I guess she had to be because we were super-active kids then. She was older then and could not take too much.

I was thinking of religious life even when I was little but I never had a calling. You have to know where God wants you. So when I was in the Philippines, I never really felt any calling to any communities there. We had a Poor Clare monastery in the Philippines, only fifteen minutes away from us, and my mother used to take me there. We always went there for prayers, but I never felt I was called there.

I told all my classmates I wanted to be a sister. Everyone else would get a crush or like "this person," but I never really got involved with anybody— just like a movie star, whom you like because he's handsome or because you like her hairstyle. I admire beauty in people so I feel like I'm quite normal, but still in me it's not something that's satisfying. It fades away. It doesn't give me peace; it's more a passing joy, you know what I mean?

Since I was little, I felt that God was calling me but since I don't know where, I didn't know if what I was feeling was really real. I had this constant seeking: What does God want of me? It was an interior struggle, if God is really calling me, or not. If yes, why doesn't He show me where I should go?

I was a nurse. There was an agency in the Philippines that contacts hospitals here that need nurses. At that time there were a lot of hospitals that needed nurses, so the hospitals hired this agency and then the agency put an advertisement in the newspaper and then we went there for an interview, and they sent our papers to the hospital here. I went to work in New York.

Before I left the Philippines I talked to our parish priest, and I said, "You know, my desire to serve God is, like, bursting in me, or bubbling in me. But I really don't know where to go, and I've already committed to go to the States. I really would rather stay in the Philippines and serve God wherever He wants me. I really would answer God, if He just tells me where He wants me to go." But our parish priest told me, "Since you have all the papers done, since you've already committed yourself, just go. That's God's will."

I also talked to a nun in the Philippines, a Poor Clare nun; she's dead now—Mother Rosa. I had talked to her before; I didn't plan to enter the Poor Clares, I just went there because when I was little and my mother had problems, she went to talk to the sisters. She gave the same advice. "You go." She didn't invite me to join the monastery. I didn't really feel called to their monastery. They saw that my papers and everything was settled. They just said, "Maybe it's God's will that you go."

I never thought it was bad advice. I felt kind of nervous going to a foreign country away from my family. I guess my thinking was, "I'll serve God close to my family." My own premonition, inner desire, is that if I'm going to serve God, I really want to be close to my family. God had another kind of way of putting it. He wanted me to be away from my family. I never thought that I would enter here in the States. I thought after I finish work here, then I would go back to the Philippines and find and see where God wants me, that kind of mentality. I never thought God would call me here.

I worked in a nursing home in New York, with the Carmelite Sisters of the Eucharist. They petitioned me, and I worked there for one year and a half before I entered here.

The Carmelites wear a full habit. I always went to church. They have a chapel in their nursing home, and I always went there before work and after work to pray. One of their sisters—she was the youngest in the community—one time stopped me after I prayed and said, "Do you want to be a sister?" It just struck me because the other Filipino nurses would do the same thing, you know, and they were also religious, but some of them were married. So when she asked me, I said, "Yes, but I don't know where God wants me." So she said, "Oh, I'll pray for you." Even the superior thought that I would like to join them. Well, I really didn't feel called to join them. You have to feel a call. I never felt really called here, too—I mean to a monastic life. In the Philippines, a monastic life means you'll never see your family again. Well, I knew that would be quite hard for me and I knew it would be quite hard for my family.

We had a mission in New York at the parish church. They call it a mission because it's a calling back of lax Catholics to their faith, or strengthening their faith. I think it was laypeople proclaiming, sharing how God touched their lives. I went to Mass that day; I decided to stay and listen, and then that stirred me up and I went to confession and for spiritual direction. After that

I became restless. That surfaced the call within me. I felt that God was calling me, but I still didn't know where. I said to the parish priest, "You know, Father, I feel like I'm being called to religious life, but I really don't know where I should go, it's just strong in me. I don't know where to go." And he said, "Well, where are you from?" I said, "I'm working at Saint Teresa's Nursing Home under the Carmelites."

The parish priest I talked to said, "Why don't you join them?" I said, "I don't feel called to join them," because I was a nurse and working there with the sisters, but most of them are administrative, not nurses like me.

I have an aunt—my father's sister—and she and her husband are kind of rich; they support some religious organizations, including a retired home for sisters in the Philippines. One time my aunt and uncle visited our family, and they took us to visit their friends, these sisters who are retired in their motherhouse. One of the retired sisters, when she learned that I was here in the States, she wrote to me. She would send me letters and inside her letters were letters that I should mail here in the States. One of the letters was for the Poor Clares here in Rockford. She was asking them questions—how to make rosaries, I think. I copied the address because I wanted to ask for prayers because I was taking my nursing board exam. I asked the Poor Clares for prayers, and then they wrote back and said they would pray for me to pass my board exam.

I still felt uneasy. Like I told you, when my mother was low, she always brought me to the Poor Clares in the Philippines to ask prayers when she had problems. So I told myself, "I'll try to call them." Well, there was no telephone number in the letter, so I called the operator and she tried to find their number. Finally, I got it and I called the sister and asked for prayers. I said, "Sister, can you pray for me? I feel like I have a vocation, but I really don't know where God is calling me." The sister immediately said she was going to get Mother Dorothy to talk to me. Mother Dorothy was the Abbess then. I said, "I wonder what Sister's doing? I just asked her to pray for me. I didn't tell them I want to come, you know. I'm not inquiring about their life, you know."

I really just called the monastery to ask them to pray for me. I had already taken my board and I was asking for prayers that I passed it. Passing the board was the only way that my visa would be extended because I was on a working visa. That's the main thing—to pass the board so that I can stay here longer so that I can work; that was just a means for me to keep working here.

But that was not my life's goal. My life's goal, which I was more interested in, was to find out if my real vocation was to enter the monastery because that would answer the questions within me: Am I called, or not?

I talked to Mother Dorothy, and she said, "Well, I think you have a vocation, but would you like to come and visit?" I said, "I really don't have time to visit because my friend is going to the Philippines and I'm doing her shift, I'm going to work overtime. I really can't." She said, "Well, just take your time. When you have time, just give us a call."

That made me speechless. I felt like I really wouldn't have time because my friend was going to stay there for a month or longer; I knew it would be a long time before I could visit. Still bugging my mind was why she was asking me to visit. But I became restless again. I felt like I had to do something. My friend was leaving the next week, so I only had one weekend free. Anyway, I finally arranged it; I came here on a Sunday, I left on Wednesday.

It's amazing. When I came here, everything was perfect. Everything fell into place. I called the airline. The plane flight was so cheap then—just $89 back and forth—the first time when I came for my visit. I was surprised because the next time I came here, it was double. And the bus—as soon as I got out of O'Hare, there was the bus going to Rockford. And then when I was here, I felt God. I felt so much peace. I felt that God was calling me here. Before I left, I committed myself already. I had my entrance day. The place felt like a presence.

I always carried with me a picture of the Sacred Heart of Jesus. It's a picture of Jesus with the Sacred Heart exposed. When I left, I left that picture here where I slept downstairs. Mother Dorothy called me and said, "You know you left your picture?" I said, "Yes, I left it intentionally because I told Him I'll be back." When I was here, I just had that peace, that searching, that I finally found it. I didn't hear Jesus, like the saints said, "This is where I want you," but I just feel like that inner call, that calling in you, finally: "This is it."

I think that other girls feel that same way—applicants that come here and didn't feel that when they came here. They feel it in another monastery. After they visit another monastery, they write back, "When I went to that monastery, I just felt at home."

When I came back from my visit, as soon as I got to our house, my friend said, "Oh, wow! Congratulations! You passed your board!"

As soon as I came back to New York, I settled everything quick. I told the nursing home, and they said I could have two weeks." The Mother Abbess gave me all the requirements—towels and things—so I bought everything.

Then I called my family. I said, "I think I have good news and bad news for you. The good news is I passed my board. My bad news is I think I'm going to enter the monastery." My mother said, "Oh, no. Don't enter yet." I said, "I think I have to, Ma, because God's calling me now and I want to know. I don't want to wait. If God is calling me now, I really want to answer now." I was just afraid. I was twenty-five then and I felt like I was really old. In the Philippines, they enter at sixteen. They entered young—sixteen, seventeen, eighteen, and sometimes after college. So at twenty-five, I felt like I was ancient.

It was hard for my parents. Well, it was hard for my whole family, but especially my mother. My father said, "If that's what you want..." But my mother said, "No." But I said, "Ma, I'm twenty-five." I had to decide, you know. And like I said, this longing to serve God has been with me since I was a child; I just don't know where to go. Once I knew, I said, "Ma, I really have to know if this is God's will. I'd rather know it now than later." My father said, "Oh, your mother cries every night." She wanted to see me.

I visited here May 26 and I entered July 16. I entered that quickly. The second time was hard because the plane ticket went up and different things. But it was fine. I felt like when I had come here before; I felt so much peace that God was calling me here. It's where He wants me.

My father died a year after my profession. I was solemnly professed in 1991 and he died in 1992. But I'm glad, though, because I always wanted to see him, and I saw him before he died. I hadn't seen him since I came to the States. I came here in 1983. From 1983 to 1991 I hadn't seen him; I hadn't gone home to the Philippines. That was the first and last time I saw him after I left the Philippines.

He had worked for the Americans, so he spoke English well. It was funny because when he came here for my Solemn Profession, he was interviewed by the US Immigration in the Philippines, and the interviewer said, "Is that all you're going to do there?"—you know, to see my profession? He said, "No, we're going to see the whole country, your beautiful country." They were so impressed when my father said that. The thing is, my father was diabetic then, and he really couldn't travel that much. Even when they were here for two weeks, or a week, I could tell he was kind of tired. He loved to travel before, when I was young. But when he was here, he didn't travel, really. But they did go to California because my mother has lots of relatives there.

When I entered everything was fine with me. I didn't have a hard time, except the cheese. I can't eat cheese. I am lactose-intolerant. I didn't know that then, because in the Philippines we don't eat that much cheese. When I came here, we had cheese every night for supper—two pieces of bread, cheese, and an apple—and I was just getting sicker and sicker from it, I could hardly sleep. Well, I got through it. I knew they wouldn't change the whole diet just for me! I knew that. So I tried everything. I put jelly in it. I put margarine in it. I mean I tried. I was willing to do as much as I could do because I felt if it was God's will that I stay here, He will give me everything I need to endure it.

I didn't think I was lactose-intolerant. I knew milk bothered me, but I just keep going. After a few years, it got real bad. I had really bad diarrhea. My doctor then told me I might be lactose-intolerant. I said, "No, I can't be, I'm eating all this milky food." And then she said, "I'll put you on the test." So she put me on the test, and then I found that I'm really lactose-intolerant. Since then, I ask permission not to take any milk at night, because I learned my lesson; I just have trouble with digestion and it keeps me awake at night. Sometimes I take a little bit and then I have to deal with the result. But I still take some. I still drink milk. I eat everything. I'm pretty good. In the morning and in the afternoon for lunch, I can take it; I take a little.

For the night vigils, it can be hard to get up, but it's something that I want to do and I have to do it. It's for the Lord. You know what I mean? I just have to think that what I'm doing is for the Lord; it's not for me, it's His will. I think that's the main thing; if you're doing things for the Lord, He gives you the grace. I still have that peace. I still miss my family, but I just have to keep trusting that God will see me through. Although I had peace within me, I mean, I still was kind of unstable, like a temptation: 'This life is hard for you, you can't do it, your family is suffering.' All these kinds of things. I didn't think I could live it. But it's all in God's grace. I just kept praying, I only want to do God's will. That's all I prayed every day was to do God's will. And that's what I think kept me going is that it's His will.

You know, to tell you the truth, I really didn't know what to expect. I was just trusting that this is where God wants me. There was a mixed feeling: It's kind of exciting because this is all I wanted all my life and I feel I've been called since I was little, and then still there's kind of pain because I hurt my family and still felt the uncertainty—is this really for me?

I struggle being away from family and the culture. Even when I was working in New York, we ate Filipino food, but here I have to eat regular food—mashed potatoes and other things, which we never had there. We always ate rice. They won't eat the fish with the head here; the way we cooked fish is different than the way we cook here. That's the way I grew up. We fried the fish with the head and tail and everything. We cleaned the insides but left the skin on. And the language—it was hard for the sisters to understand me, at first, but I got slang, I got adapted to the way they speak. I'm not saying my English is perfect. I'm just saying I had to adjust so that they can understand me better.

You have different traditions here. Our Christmas is very simple, and here you have lots of decorations. And the climate—we don't have snow in the Philippines. It's always hot. It's different, not to be able to talk to a Filipino. My Tagalog is kind of broken, and even now when I pray, I pray in English. I don't pray in Tagalog anymore. It's kind of hard to remember all of my Tagalog words.

I'm in charge of getting the applicants their books. I have felt so many of them were called, but they have to do this, they had to do that, and then they lost their call. They end up in different things. I mean, if she's not called here, that's fine; she could be called to another community, but what I mean is answering God's call. All I know is sometimes I feel, I wish that young women would really open their hearts because I know that there are a lot of young women that are called to our life. It's just they have to really trust in God, really trust in God's call to them.

Some of the women I've talked to have told me, "Oh, yes, when I was a little girl I also wanted to be a nun. I felt like I was called." But they got married. And they're happily married. But it's like, is it a real call for them, or not? Or is it like, "The nuns are so pretty, aren't they, in their habit"? Maybe God was calling them, I don't know what. But they mostly said, "Even when I was a little girl, I felt called, too." Some are benefactors. They're older now. They said that when they were younger, they thought that they were called to the religious life, but they got married. They found out it's not really a call; they were called to get married.

Some women are called. I'm not saying that everybody is, but a lot of women, I think, are called to the religious life, but it's kind of a struggle between themselves and God's call. There's so many things that influence them in choosing whether they want to follow God's call, or they want to do what the world thinks they should be. The only thing I could advise them is to have a deep prayer life because whatever they choose in life depends so much on the salvation of their souls. I think if they could have a deeper prayer life, go on retreat, have prayer before the Blessed Sacrament, or go to Mass more often, to listen—because I think therein lies their strength in choosing what they should be. If they're really for marriage life or single life, then that's something that will give them health and strength; they will be light if it's God's will. Whatever is God's will, that's our salvation because that's what God created us for, to do His will.

My main thing is I feel like God is calling me. My main thing is, I was thinking of myself being called here as a Poor Clare to a more deeper life of prayer, intimate prayer with our Lord, though with all my duties and all my distractions sometimes.... But that's my main thing, I feel like an inner call within me, to deeper prayer life, communion with Jesus. You know, it's like to enter that prayer life to draw people to it. Do you know what I mean by grateful prayer? Grateful for all that God has done for us and grateful for all the people that have supported our life. We owe so much for our friends and benefactors; they support our life and so I feel so much gratefulness for them. I feel like I really have to pray for them, remember them every day in my prayers for their needs, but also so they know God and grow closer to Him.

I can't remember her words, but Saint Clare was so close to God, her heart was full of joy being close to God, and she wanted others to feel that, too. She wanted everybody to feel that joy and closeness to God. I feel like that's kind of something that God wants me to do. Each sister is different. Some pray more for priests and religious; that's more of their calling. Everybody's different, you know.

We are all called to be holy, to holiness. Jesus said, "Be holy as my father is holy." I think a lot of women thirst for that intimate union with God, but it seems that the world offers them more options to be happy. But real happiness really doesn't consist of what you have, or what you do, if it's not God's will and it's not for the sanctification of souls.

It isn't a perfect life. We still have struggles like everybody else with temptations, personal difficulties—challenges that we should really continuously change our attitudes toward being a better person, being a better Christian, relationships with each other. We don't have many temptations like in the world—cars to fight with, or dresses. We have the same habit. We don't have to wear earrings. We don't have all these things—temptations that the world could offer; we don't have that here.

The spirit of our founder, the Holy Father Saint Francis and Saint Clare, is poverty, which is living in simplicity. I guess in here I just have more time for prayer and to reflect, to meditate, and in everything I do, in everything that happens, God is more present, more close.

I can feel the difference. When I was still with my family and during the part of my life before I entered, I could feel God taking care of me and He was with me. But now my entering is like a fulfillment. It's closer now. Before, it was like a calling, a calling to be more intimate with Him. Now that I have answered the call, it's more close with Him now. I still struggle with all my human weaknesses, you know, but God in our life provides me all the things. In this environment, we all strive for the same goal, closer union with God, and to answer His call for more closer intimacy. All our works—our prayer, everything we do—should grow us more closely to Him.

I think that before I used to do things just for the sake of doing, but now I'm doing everything for God and I always offer up everything I do for God. And when you do things for God and you love God, you do it with joy. There are things that are hard to do, but if you accept it as God's will, then you know God transforms that and He gives you peace to carry it out.

It's not just cloistered nuns who are called to holiness. Everybody is. You are. Your family. Your friends. All our benefactors' families. All are called to holiness, whatever the vocation. It's Monsignor's homily, too, that whatever state of life we are in, we are all called to holiness; if all people of whatever religion only answer that call to live a holy life, to purify our hearts from all the hatred and revenge—the evil that's in our heart—if we could only purify that and put God's love in it, this world would be a better place. Everybody has their own perception of God, but one thing that's true is God is a holy God. He is a pure God.

I still sometimes doubt. I still doubt sometimes. I guess it's more of my human nature and my human weaknesses, that maybe this is hard and not for me. But always God's grace triumphs. I always have to end prayer, whatever God wants. Sometimes I say, "This is hard," but then, "Whatever you want," because I only want what His will is. That gives me strength.

Sometimes, you can feel it's from the devil when you have trials, when you have a misunderstanding with a sister, or when you feel sick and all these things come up to you.

8

Erased from the Landscape

I think every vocation story is a love story of how God has really shown that soul His infinite love for her. He's invited her to live in that love in a very special and intimate way. Just like all young girls who dream of love, you know, of a husband or something, some of us are blessed, through nothing that we've done on our own. But somehow God has given this divine invitation, this special look of love, and invited us to live with Him. And it's beyond what we dream of, of finding the perfect husband or whatever in life—perfect happiness. It's so much beyond what you can dream of when God shows you how much He loves you. It's no question, "Absolutely, of course I'll do it, God," because He shows that love, and it's just beyond anything.

Sister Maria Benedicta of Saint Joseph

The youngest nun in the Corpus Christi Monastery, Sister Maria Benedicta grew up—in her words—in "Secular, USA." This assessment of her upbringing in a Catholic family that prayed daily together and never neglected Sunday Mass might be influenced by the stories she has collected in brief discussions with her new family members. Compared to her Novice Mistress, whose adolescence brought her into the company of the Pope, Sister Maria Benedicta's experiences seem more conventional, if not secular. Her family did not say the rosary together, and because there was no Catholic school in the vicinity of her rural town, she attended a public school. Sister Maria Benedicta, still called Maria at that time, did not see a nun—in person, or on television—until the fourth grade.

When Maria finally did see a nun for the first time, the impression was indelible. Her youth group stayed overnight at a Benedictine abbey, a prelude to their trip to an amusement park, and each child was paired to sit with a nun for the Divine Office; Sister Maria Benedicta says she was matched with "the cutest little old thing." She did not understand what the sister was praying, or grasp the symbolism of what she was witnessing, but she thought the incense-stained atmosphere exotic and appealing. Sister Maria Benedicta says, "I remember looking at her and thinking, 'She prays with God all day. She has the perfect life. Oh, I could really do that.' And then it was reality: 'That was the weirdest thing I've ever thought in my life. Forget it.' And I really did forget about it. It wasn't always in the back of my mind, 'Oh, she has the perfect life. I should do that.' No. I completely forgot about it until years later."

Sister Maria Benedicta's first contact with a nun could be described as a signpost. "God puts it in your heart," Sister Maria Benedicta says. "Somehow He showed me the beauty of it, even though I was like, 'What are we praying? Where are we going?' But I remember thinking, 'This is the house of God and this is the perfect life, living for the perfect God.'" Today, Sister Maria Benedicta enters, seven times a day for the Divine Office, a chapel similar to the one that awed her as a child. The prayer stall that seemed, to her grade-school eyes, straight out of a movie set, is now characteristic of her daily routine. From fourth grade through college, Sister Maria Benedicta says she did not reflect again on her first encounter with a nun; she did not see any other religious sisters. "How we can just push that out of our mind and not think about it? What's real life about? That's the true reality that lasts forever. But I forgot about it for years. It's terrible. But God works, here and there; you can see how he's planting the seeds."

While some of the cloistered nuns struggle to recall memories during oral history interviews, sifting the decades to frame and share their experiences after a lifetime of anonymity and perpetual silence, Sister Maria Benedicta considers such retrospection a gift. A recent arrival to the monastery, her memories are still at attention; it is easy to pull emotionally charged strings to each phase of her former life, find the corresponding anecdotes and conversations, and connect themes to the events. "It's a good principle in the spiritual, religious life, you know, when prayer is difficult or there are hard times or suffering in your life, to look back and see what God has done, look how He's loved me, look how He's shown me His love," she says.

Calling memories to the surface of her consciousness reinforces the lessons of her life, and it reminds Sister Maria Benedicta how God has provided for her. With hindsight, she sees now what she did not always discern at the time—the ways that God was directing her to a cloistered contemplative life. Looking back, Sister Maria Benedicta is surprised she did not recognize sooner that she was intended for this otherworldly realm, although she can pinpoint the moments when God opened up before her the path He wanted her to take, showing it to her step by step, at her own pace. "It's not coincidences. He's guiding everyone," she says, "but we have to listen to Him to experience Him."

Sister Maria Benedicta was a softball pitcher, coached through high school by her father and admitted to a Catholic college on a full softball scholarship, when she detected her life would evolve in a dramatically different way than she had dreamed about. There was a turning point: Before she signed away her only means of paying for college, before she accepted her religious calling, she was working at Wal-Mart. One ordinary day, Sister Maria Benedicta remembers, she was working the first of forty-five cash registers; the line to her register was backed up. An hour into a very busy, very trying day, it occurred to Sister Maria Benedicta for the first time ever to introduce her prayer life into her workplace. "I said, 'Lord, help me. Just help me. I can't do this,'" she says. "The next customer handed me this wooden cross. He said, 'I want you to have this, and remember Jesus loves you.' And I thought, 'Oh my! God just answered my prayer.' He could have handed that to anyone and it could have meant nothing." Naturally attuned to serendipity, Sister Maria Benedicta became increasingly aware of the spiritual mysteries in her life. She believed that God was telling her, through the cross the stranger handed her, "I love you. I'm going to help you. I'm answering your prayer. I know you're crying out for me. I'm going to help you through this day." "That's true mysticism," she says, "seeing that God is there, even in Wal-Mart."

The youngest member of the Corpus Christi Monastery, Sister Maria Benedicta swam upstream to reach this place. "It's amazing that God can, in these days, break through all the noise to get to the heart," she says, "which is so crowded with so many things. But He's all-powerful so I guess He can do it. But you have to allow Him."

As a child, Sister Maria Benedicta's faith was relegated to church life on Sunday, not integrated into her daily life with her family or school. She did not know then, she says, that saints were in her midst, that angels were praying for her, and that "God is everywhere." The idea that a spiritual realm eclipses any physical reality dawned on her in college. Her dorm room was above the chapel, and she could hear the Mass below. One day, she attended chapel. She still remembers a visiting priest's homily about the Eucharist: "Jesus Christ comes down into this chapel every day. What is more important than that?" "Wow," Sister Maria Benedicta thought. "He's right. I was thinking, in college you're searching for answers about your life, and the purpose of your life. The purpose of life is to love and to get to heaven, you know? When he said that—'what is more important than God coming down to be with you?'—I said, 'Yeah, there's nothing more important than that.' It was so clear this is the purpose of life. This is why we're here. Everything else is to lead us to God and to heaven."

She contemplated the Blessed Sacrament and realized, "That is God. That is almighty God right there in the form of bread. That is so unbelievable. Why would He make himself so small in this little host? It's unfathomable. The only reason why He would do that is because of His immense deep love for humanity. I kept thinking how much He loves us, to do this."

Despite the unanswerable questions, Sister Maria Benedicta had received the gift of faith. She thought about God descending to earth every day into what she describes as an "obscure chapel" in a dormitory building because He loved her completely. "Everything changed," she says. Her perspective and priorities shifted. She began to think, "Now what's more important, God coming down to earth, or this phone conversation, or this math assignment? My friends told me I was falling in love," Sister Maria Benedicta says. "I was. I was falling in love with Jesus! They laughed. And I said, 'I'm sorry. I just can't get enough!' I was a fanatic, falling in love with Jesus."

Soon afterward, the dorm director invited her on a group outing to a convent; the trip conflicted with her softball practice schedule, though, and so Sister Maria Benedicta said she could not make it. "It was true, but I was glad I had an excuse," Sister Maria Benedicta says. "I thought, 'She's crazy. I'm not a nun.' I didn't know anything about the religious life. You have in your mind it really is not fun." A week later, the dormitory director told her she had signed Sister Maria Benedicta up for the road trip. "It was terrible," Sister Maria Benedicta says. She thought, "I can't tell my coach I'm going to visit a convent. Good grief! 'Where are your priorities?'" Although the softball team practiced every weekend, the coach happened to cancel practice, and so Sister Maria Benedicta rode with a van full of girls for an "eye-opening" weekend. The nuns laughed. They played tennis. Their convent rested on beautiful grounds. "Oh," Sister Maria Benedicta says she thought, "these are real people." Sister Maria Benedicta remembers the superior singling her out to ask what she thought and if Sister Maria Benedicta might be called to religious life. Sister Maria Benedicta said she did not think so. The Mother Superior replied, "If God calls, He will turn your heart to only want that." On the drive back to her college campus, Sister Maria Benedicta thought, "My heart does not want that, so I'm off the hook." She prayed that if she did desire more than anything to live as a nun, she would know that desire was from God, "and I would do it because I knew it wasn't coming from me."

After the visit to the convent, the dormitory director offered Sister Maria Benedicta a ticket to hear Pope John Paul II speak in St. Louis. "Absolutely!" Sister Maria Benedicta said. "It was no longer, 'I have softball practice.' It was, 'Absolutely, I'm going.'" Once in St. Louis, every conversation, every occurrence seemed a message sent directly from God. "It's the way God turns your heart," she says. Standing in line for the restroom, a nun handing out literature bypassed dozens of women to give Sister Maria Benedicta a pamphlet about the religious life. "It's a sign," her friend told her. Then, emerging from the masses, Sister Maria Benedicta saw a nun from the convent she had recently visited. Inside the bag of freebies, which included a flag to wave when the Pope appeared, she found a prayer for discerning one's vocation. Sister Maria Benedicta dropped the prayer back in the bag. She was startled to pull out yet another prayer to discern her vocation. Then Pope John Paul II, stricken with Parkinson's disease at the time, took the stage. "He was on fire. We saw the Church was alive and young," Sister Maria Benedicta says. She remembers listening to the Vicar of Christ—the voice of Christ on earth—say, "'Go now, don't wait, God needs you.' He was so emphatic that God uses human beings. God could do it Himself, but He has chosen to use human beings. I just knew that what I was called for was to love God in a special way in a religious life. That's a special grace, too," she says, "because everyone else heard it, too."

Sister Maria Benedicta was convinced that God was giving her the confirmation she needed. "God knows every soul and what's going to get them—what one person can say to you to turn your heart," she says. "He inspires that person. It's really amazing." When a friend asked Sister Maria Benedicta to travel with her to another convent, an active religious order of Marian Sisters in Lincoln, Nebraska, Sister Maria Benedicta intended to decline. She had procrastinated on an assignment to read a three-hundred-page book, and she planned to cram that weekend. But when she opened her mouth to say "no," she heard herself instead agreeing to go. "It was the weirdest thing," Sister Maria Benedicta says. "I've never experienced that before. I don't know what happened." When she visited the Marian Sisters, she was smitten. "Everything about the life was so beautiful," Sister Maria Benedicta says. "Everything was for God—the sacrifices they make. It was all so beautiful." In the convent's chapel, Sister Maria Benedicta prayed, "I don't know what you want, but this is what I want more than anything." She remembered then her prayer following her first visit to a convent—that if she desired the life of a nun, she would know it came from God and not herself. "And so I knew this was what God wanted," she says.

When Sister Maria Benedicta returned to college, her best friend told her she seemed like a different person. Sister Maria Benedicta confided that she wanted to become a Marian sister. Her best friend told her that she was going to miss her at college and on the softball team, but Sister Maria Benedicta explained she wanted to complete her two final years of college. In the days that followed, Sister Maria Benedicta fished out her notes from the St. Louis speech by Pope John Paul II. She read, "Don't wait, God needs you now."

"I said, 'Lord, let me know,'" she says. "'I will do what you want, but you better let me know, because I'm not going to do something crazy, quit school, leave everything, scholarship, my whole livelihood. But if you let me know, I will do it.' Boy! Ask and you shall receive!"

Like an allegory, Sister Maria Benedicta faced three obstacles in quick succession. First, she felt pain in her pitching shoulder. She asked her father, her lifelong coach, to watch while she pitched to see what she was doing wrong to trigger the pain; he could not see a problem. "I thought, I've been doing it for fifteen years," she says. "Maybe it's wearing out. But if I can't play, I don't have my scholarship, I can't come here." Next, when Sister Maria Benedicta tried to sign up for a full load of classes for the following semester, she was not able to schedule more than nine hours—which would be part-time status. "I couldn't graduate with this type of a schedule," she says. And then, when two sets of friends were sorting out lodging, separately, both groups assumed she was planning to live with the other group, and Sister Maria Benedicta realized she did not have anyone to live with. "God was showing me through the very ordinary circumstances what His will was. It was not to be there," she says.

Her thoughts were starting to anchor beyond the physical sphere. She remembers standing on the pitcher's mound in the last inning of one game, a high-pressure situation that should have prompted her to focus and perform well, she says. Instead, her mind drifted: "This really isn't important compared to eternity." "I'm thinking about this at the strangest times!" she says. Hearing her astronomy professor lecture on the expanding universe, Sister Maria Benedicta thought that although "billions and trillions and gazillions" of years had passed since the earth began, "compared to eternity that is just a drop. I mean, eternity is so far beyond what we can imagine and this life is so small compared to that eternity, which a gazillion years is just a fraction; it's just a second compared to that. This life is just so short we have to do all we can to get all these people to heaven."

Sister Maria Benedicta adopted the philosophy of a college friend who said that she lived thinking about her deathbed. "I realized I have one life—one life—and you're not reincarnated," Sister Maria Benedicta says. "We live this one life, and we either go to heaven, or we go to hell. We have one life. I remember thinking, 'If I'm laying on my deathbed, if I'm eighty or ninety, what will I wish I had done in life? Will I wish I had that car? Probably not. Will I wish I had a better house? Probably not. You know, when you're dying, you want to know you're going to heaven. That's the purpose of your life." At twenty, Sister Maria Benedicta asked herself, "Would I rather have said, 'I finished my two years of school and had fun and was on the softball team,' or would I rather say, 'I did the will of God'? It was, what is more important? What is the most important thing in my life? It's doing God's will."

When Sister Maria Benedicta received an invitation from the Marian Sisters to attend a retreat, she told her best friend it conflicted with the upcoming softball tournament. "I made a commitment to the team," Sister Maria Benedicta said. Her friend replied, "Don't you dare miss that retreat. You know you're supposed to go." "She was so good in helping me keep perspective," Sister Maria Benedicta says. "She was a very good friend because we truly were striving to be holy. We had our priorities: It was God, family, friends, school. There's a hierarchy of what's important, and if you obscure that, if I put softball above God, that's wrong," she says.

Her coach agreed, reluctantly, that she could skip the tournament. "I knew that was God because I had prayed, 'God just show me,' and it was the answer. He had closed the door to the next year of school. But He showed me right there, 'This is what I want,'" Sister Maria Benedicta says. She prepared to inform her parents, who attended all of her softball games, that she would not be at the tournament because she would be on a retreat at a convent. This first shock would be a mere segue to another revelation: She planned to ask the Marian Sisters if she could return and join their community.

In Sister Maria Benedicta's master plan, she would tell her parents after the final game before the softball tournament. "I was so nervous the whole game, I didn't think a bit about the game," she says. "Afterwards I was so nervous; I was stalling. Usually, we would just jump in the car and go to Sonic or McDonald's. I said, 'Oh, just let me jump in the shower real quick first.' So I was really stalling and taking my time. Usually, I would throw my hair up; I was blow-drying my hair—really stalling. My parents were thinking, 'What has gotten into her?' It was just so countercultural and I knew it was going to be a shock. We were in my dorm room. My parents were very patiently waiting. At my dad's work, they had old computers on sale and he said, 'I bought you a computer.' I was thinking, 'Oh, boy, I don't need it.' I said, 'Oh, Dad, that's really nice.' I didn't ask anything about it; I didn't care. I'm sure he thought that was kind of rude. I was just so focused. So we get in the car and it was a Sunday and the school was in a small town and everything was closed. I was panicking, 'Oh, no, what if we don't find anything open?' So finally we walk into the one place still open and all the softball team is there with their parents. I thought, 'What a disaster! I can't tell them with all these people here.' But I had stalled so long they were almost finished eating and they were leaving. So finally I said, 'I've got to tell them.' My dad said, 'For that game before Easter, can we just take you home, or do you have to come back to school?' I said, 'I'm not actually going to go to that game.' I said, 'I'm going to go on this retreat and ask these sisters if I can join them.' Dead silence. You want to kill a conversation, that's the way to do it! Oh. Oh. Shocked!"

While Sister Maria Benedicta was agonizing about the retreat—"I was just in knots," she says; "how do you ask someone to join their family?"—her family asked if dropping out of college to enter a convent seemed like the hallmark of a stable and secure life. They asked if she would have health insurance at the convent. She did not know. She remembers telling her family, "I just love Him and I'm going to live for Him and that's it. That's all I know about it, really." It was as if, for the first time, Sister Maria Benedicta and her family were speaking different languages. "We have the highest security—in God, who's all powerful, all loving, all knowing," she says. "But it's looking beyond the visible to the true reality." In retrospect, Sister Maria

Benedicta understands her parents' concern and bewilderment. They wanted her to explain her logic and the rationale for her livelihood. Maybe, she says, it also felt like she was rejecting her family's values. "They want you to be happy and they can't imagine you being happy living a life of poverty, obedience, and chastity, because they found happiness in marriage and through children and they think you're giving that up," she says. "That's where they found happiness and they think you're not going to be happy. It's just a different way that God leads you to find your true happiness and fulfillment, and once they realize that, then gradually they're okay because you've found what they wanted you to find, which is happiness and your purpose in life."

Word spread that Sister Maria Benedicta wanted to join a convent, which came as no surprise to friends and teammates, even though she says she only shared her interest with her best friend. "They said, 'We knew that,'" Sister Maria Benedicta says. "I said, 'Why didn't you tell me? It would've been a lot easier!'"

The day she signed away her softball scholarship, Sister Maria Benedicta walked outside and thought, "What have I done? Honestly!" She knew she would never be able to afford college without a scholarship, and she had the nagging suspicion that her plan was not only contrary to what she thought she wanted for her life, it simply was not the way she thought "life is done."

"I realized, Lord, I'm giving you everything. I'm putting my trust in you. I'm going to take a leap of faith because I don't know. Give me a sign, a word, anything," she says. Sister Maria Benedicta opened her Bible to Psalm 119. She read the word "nun," which gave her the assurance she wanted that she was making the right move. Later, she learned she had merely stumbled upon a man's name in a biblical genealogy, as in Joshua, son of Nun. "I thought, 'Oh, isn't God funny? Some man's name, and I'm like, 'I'm supposed to be a nun!' I just needed a direct answer. That gave me the courage to leave everything for Him." Upon reflection, Sister Maria Benedicta is not put off by the message she accepted as divine direction for her life from that one word; despite her ignorance of the proper context, she does not believe she was mistaken in interpreting the meaning. Sister Maria Benedicta believes her naïveté reflects the gospel message: Jesus told His disciples they must become like children in order to enter the kingdom of heaven. "In so many ways, He was just saying, 'You're such a child," she says, "and I think I was in the hands of the Father saying, 'Okay, here you go. I don't know anything.'"

Sister Maria Benedicta became a Marian Sister, and the community became her family. Almost six years later, when she appeared to her parents to be at home in the order of active sisters, with the stable and secure life they desired for her, Sister Maria Benedicta informed her family that she planned to transfer to the even stricter, more removed world of a cloistered monastery. The notion began to percolate when, as a twenty-one-year-old pilgrim with the Marian Sisters to Assisi, Italy, the spiritual birthplace of Saint Francis's Friars Minor and Saint Clare's Poor Ladies, she toured the Poor Clares' motherhouse, San Damiano. When she saw the abject poverty of their lodgings, that they "had nothing," it reminded her of Jesus, who was so poor He had no place to lay His head. "I just fell in love with Saint Clare. But I just loved where I was, and so it didn't enter my mind to do something crazy like enter the Poor Clares."

Several years passed. Less than a year remained before she was to make final vows as a Marian sister. "It was a sense of this isn't fitting," she says of the other religious community. "Saint Augustine says, 'Our hearts are restless until they rest in you, my God.' And it's that way; once you finally discover what God is asking, there's a peace and, yes, there are struggles, but it's okay. 'This is what God wants and he's going to help me.' There's a peace. If you join any community, everything is not going to be perfect all the time. That's a given. There are going to be sacrifices. But there should also be a peace. You fit; it's just like a peacefulness, you are at home, you fit with the apostolate."

Sister Maria Benedicta had tried various jobs with the active religious order. She taught catechism. She studied nursing. "Nothing ever really fit," she says. "So that kind of added to the unsettling, the searching. It was just like He wasn't asking me to make this sacrifice. It was, like, that's not the sacrifice He was asking me to make.

"Looking back, I can see God was asking something of me that I couldn't quite put my finger on," Sister Maria Benedicta says. "I thought, 'I think I can just do more by praying.'"

It became increasingly clear to Sister Maria Benedicta that she was meant to take a path away from the Marian Sisters. She felt unsettled, thinking that God was asking something of her that she did not yet know, and so she went on a retreat and met with a priest to seek spiritual direction. She said she could not fathom leaving her community. Then she said, "I just love Saint Clare and I want to live like her." "I just threw that in there," she says. The priest asked if Sister Maria Benedicta was considering the contemplative life.

The question surprised Sister Maria Benedicta, although she says now that if someone wants to live like Saint Clare, it is likely she would choose to withdraw from the world and contemplate God in a cloister. "When he said it, it was like, 'Oh, oh,' like a light bulb."

Still, Sister Maria Benedicta struggled to reconcile her calling. She did not want to leave her close-knit community in Nebraska. "I couldn't believe it because I was so happy," she says. Plus, when she was called to the Marian Sisters, she says "it was so obvious that God was calling me there. It was tangible almost. 'This is what God wants.' Being in a community is different. You can't just go visit these Poor Clare convents whenever you want. It took me a couple of years to come to terms with it and to discover what God was showing. I prayed about it a lot; really, it has to be through prayer."

Sister Maria Benedicta learned of the Corpus Christi Monastery through a search on the Internet. She prayed for guidance from the Holy Spirit before she went online. "Oh, this is it," she thought when she read about the Rockford Poor Clares. "This is it. I can't even describe it, but I just knew. God was speaking to my heart, I guess, 'This is how I want you to love me. This is the way it should be.'" Every day for several months, she heard one of three words: Illinois, Clare, contemplative. "You can hear those words a lot, but something jabbed in my heart like, 'Are you listening? There it is. There it is.' Day after day after day after day, it was God showing me. He was asking me every time, 'Are you going to go? Are you going to wait? Are you going to serve me? Are you going to love me?' It was always, 'I should do this.'"

"When God asks that of you, you kind of really make sure that's what He's really asking," Sister Maria Benedicta says. "It's a commitment and you really have to believe with all your heart that this is what God wants. It's for life—not five years down the line, 'Whoops!'" After the novitiate, the Marian Sisters renew their temporary vows every year for five years until they make final, permanent vows. "I knew I had to find out before making that commitment," she says. "I think that's a human thing, 'Are you sure, God?' I think He really did show me." Halfway through the year before she was to make final vows as a Marian Sister, before she even visited the Rockford monastery, Sister Maria Benedicta determined she would leave when her yearlong commitment ended in order to embrace the Rule of Saint Clare.

During her visit to the Corpus Christi Monastery, she heard the same Scripture reading that "flipped everything upside down" in college, when she made her first retreat with the Marian Sisters. Sister Maria Benedicta paraphrases: "Jesus said to Saint Peter, 'Put out for the deep for a catch of fish.' And then he said, 'From now on, you will be catching men, souls.' That really struck me. Put out into the deep; go out, go to where you've never experienced the deep, deep things of God. Go deeper." When she returned to Nebraska, another biblical passage, read in Mass, cut to the core of her decision. Two sisters, Martha and Mary, were friends of Jesus and hosted Him at their home. While Martha served Jesus and His disciples, Mary sat at Jesus' feet and listened. Martha complained to Jesus, "Tell her to help me," but Jesus replied, "Mary has chosen the better part and it will not be taken from her." "The better part was to sit at the feet of Jesus, to love Him, to contemplate Him, and I just knew that was what He was asking of me," Sister Maria Benedicta says.

"Yes, it was so difficult to leave my family the first time to join the convent," Sister Maria Benedicta says, "but that's what we're made to do; we're made to leave our home and our family and pursue our vocation, whether it's marriage or the religious life. But once you're in the religious life, you think, 'This is where I am.' It's difficult to leave." Sister Maria Benedicta knew that if she left the Marian Sisters, her decision would hurt her religious sisters. "When you're on the deeper and the spiritual level and you share things that are very important to you, it's very hard to break those ties," she says. The decision would also affect her family, who had grown to love the Marian Sisters when they saw how happy she was there.

Her parents insisted on traveling with Sister Maria Benedicta on her first visit to the Corpus Christi Monastery; they hoped to participate in her decision-making process. After the trip, her father was disappointed. "It seems you already made up your mind before you visited," she remembers him saying. "That was hard," Sister Maria Benedicta says, "but God had already given me that assurance, through prayer, that this was what He wanted."

Her parents tried to dissuade her, knowing that the cloistered monastery would erase any last vestige of normalcy they had managed to retain: She would never be granted another home visit; they could not hug her; she would never hold her niece again. "They didn't understand why," Sister Maria Benedicta says. "They said, 'You have so much. Why would you give it up?' I said, 'I would only give it up for one thing, and that's for God.' I told them, 'I've already given my life to God. I'm going to do what He wants. When I made my vows, that's what I meant: I give my life to God completely for whatever He wants. I had no idea He would ask that, but He did.' I said, 'I'm sorry. I've already given my life to God. He asks, I say, 'Yes' because I've already given it. He asks something else and I give it in a different way.' That was difficult for them, very, very difficult."

Other voices—of reason, skepticism, and antagonism—weighed in, unsolicited. Sister Maria Benedicta remembers feeling as if her college softball coach was grilling her: "What are you thinking? Have you lost your mind? Wasting your life? What are you doing?"

The decision-making process—refuting the outside world, a world her loved ones would remain part of—was not without temptations. At a family reunion several months before she planned to join the Poor Clares, Sister Maria Benedicta looked around at her relatives. "In my mind, it went over and over, 'Can you give this up forever?' And it was like ugh, ugh," she sighs. "I love my family. But it just kept going in my mind, 'Can you.... ?' And I was like ugh. It was like, 'I can't, but God can.' You know, God can do it because I cannot."

Another scene tested her resolve. She was completing her training to be a nurse; she felt constant pressure, always worried she was about to make a mistake. Tending to a newborn in the maternity ward, she considered a sacrifice she had not thought of before. When she first made her vows to the Marian Sisters, she says, "I was just so swept away with Jesus." Six years later, while carrying an infant to his first-time parents, Sister Maria Benedicta says, "I just saw their love, and it was like God was saying to me, 'Look what you're giving up. Will you give this up for me?'"

She says she believed she was being called, "But it's like He does require that leap of faith, too. It's not like you're 100 percent sure all the time. He does give it, but He also asks for the leap of faith, 'Do you trust me enough to do it?' It's such a hard time, particularly, because everything is bombarding you. You're giving stuff up in your heart, but you're still there. It can be hard."

Sister Maria Benedicta's college volleyball coach cried when she learned of her impending move to a cloistered contemplative order, which she thought conveyed a rare act of selflessness. "If you realize that the giving of yourself is the ultimate fulfillment, it really does strike something," Sister Maria Benedicta says. "It's really something that people see, that God is the fulfillment, but we can let everything get in the way and say, 'That's what's most important,' and forget about Him."

On April 6, 2006, the day Sister Maria Benedicta graduated from nursing school, her parents drove from Kansas for her pinning ceremony. They picked her up in Lincoln, Nebraska, and with her two sisters, drove her to Rockford, Illinois, so that she could join the Poor Clare Colettine Order.

"Now I have this wonderful family here. Now I have two wonderful religious families," Sister Maria Benedicta says. The Marian Sisters in her first religious community still write to her. "There were no hard feelings. It was beautiful how they prayed for me."

In the six years before a nun makes permanent vows as a Poor Clare, several events indicate her progress, a sequence that ends when she dons a ring during her solemn profession of final vows. At the Clothing Ceremony one year after she arrived, Sister Maria Benedicta put on a habit for the first time. Her hair was cut short. "It really struck me that I'm a new person," she says. "You turn away from the things of the world. A woman's hair, I think Saint Paul says, it's her adornment, and we just chop it off. We just offer everything. It's not important to us. We come to be holy, and so we give everything. It's really, really something—that you're just a new person." For the second time, Sister Maria Benedicta was given a new religious name.

Forty-year-old Sister Mary Nicolette, the second youngest nun in the Corpus Christi Monastery, instructs Sister Maria Benedicta as her Novice Mistress. Although there is just seven years' difference in age between the two, Sister Mary Nicolette knows that she was exposed to an America that changed radically while Sister Maria Benedicta was still experiencing it. When Sister Mary Nicolette entered the monastery in 1993, she had heard rumors of the Internet, but she had never used it, and she has never sent or received e-mail. "I have a very basic understanding of how that functions, how that works," she says. "And even, like, cell phones, most of the women who come to visit bring their cell phones with them; that's something that I never experienced." Only a few years after Sister Maria Benedicta departed popular culture, Sister Mary Nicolette thinks that elements of America might be unrecognizable to her pupil today. Sister Maria Benedicta agrees. She has heard family members discuss iPods and texting, devices and modes of communication she cannot picture. "It's changing so fast," Sister Maria Benedicta says. "I mean, we can't even keep up with it. And we do choose, thankfully, to give it up."

Sister Maria Benedicta thinks the technological upgrades, intended to save time, instead are "filling, filling, filling the time, filling the silence with noise, filling all these things with the things that really distract from what's really important." She shares an anecdote depicting the unnecessary technologies: A friend, after buying a cell phone, told Sister Maria Benedicta, "I thought a lot more people would call me!" Sister Maria Benedicta laughs. "You really don't need it! You know what I mean? It's really not a need; it's superfluous and it's not leading to God.

"The world sees freedom as, 'I can do what I want, when I want, how I want.' That's not freedom," she says. "True freedom is to give yourself to God, to be taken in by His love and His truth. I think it was Saint Augustine who said, 'Love, and do what you will.' He doesn't mean do what you want. It means if you truly love God, everything you do is for God and you're not going to do what He doesn't want you to do. The world sees freedom as doing whatever you want, but how many of those things are not what God wants, and they're not what God wants because they're not for our good? If you're in line with that, it's just a free existence. It's authentic. It kind of is a lightheartedness, an authenticity, like we don't have to worry about so many things, either about the world or about what's going on, or what others think of us, or how others see us."

The technological regression and the slower pace of the monastery agree with Sister Maria Benedicta. She associates "technology" now with the monastery's John Deere tractor, a convenience the nuns only operate to mow the yard, enabling the nuns' pursuit of union with God. "If we're able to get the mowing done more quickly, then we can go in and pray," Sister Maria Benedicta says. Rather than motoring the tractor to transport mulch for the gardens, the nuns instead push the mulch in wheelbarrows and heft it with pitchforks. "I mean, no one would think to do that, you know," Sister Maria Benedicta says. "You have a tractor sitting in the garage, and we're out there with wheelbarrows and shovels. People would think we're crazy, but the manual labor is such a good balance for our life. A lot of our day we're sitting and praying. We need exercise and work and to get our mind off things."

As the distance grows between Sister Maria Benedicta and the culture that she once identified with, the values of her adopted home have created—or perhaps revealed—fissures between Sister Maria Benedicta and her loved ones. A sports fanatic from cradle to college, Sister Maria Benedicta has lost interest in college and professional athletics, once hallmarks of her quality of life. Loved ones, meanwhile, scarcely recognize her for who she once was.

During visits, they ask, "You don't care that *this* team beat *this* team? Or that *they're* going to the Super Bowl?" "But it's like, oh!" Sister Maria Benedicta says. "There's so much more, you know what I mean? There is a huge difference in what you realize is important." She shares these impressions from the enclosure side of the parlor, where she sits with her Novice Mistress. Their sparse environment—and lack of televisions—reinforces a disregard for her former hobbies, she says. "You think about it and you're like, 'Oh, they're still doing that?'"

"What a quaint tradition!" I tease. Both laugh.

"I know!" Sister Maria Benedicta says. "They're still doing that? The world still goes on without me? Are you sure? If I'm not watching it, they're still going to put it on TV? They still have TV? I'm kidding. You realize that's still going on, but you're immersed in a higher reality, not because of anything we've done. It's not because of anything we've done. It's purely the grace of God. But the reality is, you realize what is important."

Sister Maria Benedicta recognizes her calling is contrary to the way that the rest of the world lives, and it is at times contrary to the beliefs of fellow Catholics. Just before Sister Maria Benedicta transferred from the active order of nuns to the Corpus Christi Monastery, a woman at her parents' church asked Sister Maria Benedicta about the cloister. "Girls still do that these days?" Sister Maria Benedicta says she responded, "Yes, they do! This one does."

Sister Mary Nicolette can appreciate the woman's disbelief. When she visited a cloistered monastery for the first time with two college friends, intent on a relaxing weekend holiday, Sister Mary Nicolette was awestruck; she did not realize anyone still lived like that, but she was thrilled to find a place that epitomized the life she wanted. Still, she had mixed emotions. "Is this reality?" Sister Mary Nicolette asked herself. "I must be crazy. Nobody does this anymore." "All of that floods through your head, even if God's calling you," she says. Quiet time in prayer moved her through the discernment process into acceptance.

Sister Maria Benedicta reflects on the differences between life outside and inside the monastery. "There is a retreat when you go away and you just focus on God. That's our whole life. We're not always on retreat. We have work to do, but in a sense we are separated so that we can focus our whole lives on God. If I had a job or was in the world, I wouldn't be able to think of these things. But here, it's all focused on God, and we do it all for Him. We're made body and soul, and we're called to sanctify both. So even the physical things we do—eating, sweeping the floor, everything—we bring that mystical dimension into it. God. We do it all for God. I'm not going out like the missionaries and converting the world, but I put my faith in God that everything I do, I do because it's His will. I have a set schedule, so I'm constantly doing the will of God at every moment, if I'm doing what I'm supposed to do. And He will use that obedience for something that I don't even know and that we can sanctify, even the normal bodily things. 'Lord, I'm going to eat this meal so that I have strength so that I can serve you. I'm going to sleep so that I can be awake and pray to you.' You can do even that for God. It's really amazing to think that even in the normal things, that you can experience God in every aspect."

When Sister Maria Benedicta played the hand she believed she had been dealt, and dropped out of college to become a religious sister, she says, "Everything you've ever believed in, you're giving up; or everything you've dreamed of, it's not important anymore.

"It is a sacrifice," she says. "The Church says it's such a gift—these lives that God has given grace—that these people are for God alone. It's so precious to the Church, because the prayers and the sacrifices are what keep the Church going; it's prayer. And we've chosen this and we know that these are going to be the sacrifices."

Sister Maria Benedicta says families should not wonder what they have done wrong when daughters heed the religious vocation, rather than marrying and starting their own families. She thinks families should ask, "What did we do right?" The answer, she submits, is that "we showed them God, that somehow in the family it was fostered that God is important." "It is very hard for them," she says. "When we first enter, we receive the grace of the vocation, we are in love with God, we're wrapped in Him. We have our new life, all these wonderful things that happen to us, all these experiences behind these walls. They just see the empty table, the empty chair at the dinner table, or Christmas without us. It's harder for them to see how missing a family Christmas brings you happiness, but there's more to it than that. We find our love. They find God through their love of husband and wife and family. We find our love directly to Him in the religious life. There's just that difference. And it is hard. They haven't experienced it to know it is real. It's real."

Sister Maria Benedicta prays daily for her parents. "I owe them my life," she says. "They gave me my life and they gave me, taught me God—taught me who God is. I owe them so much; and I repay them with my prayers. I think that through prayer we're a lot closer, because we're on that spiritual relationship."

As her relationship with her family settles on a spiritual plane, she notes that God relates to her differently. "Before, God was showing me these signs and what I needed," she says. "I hope now our relationship is deeper. When He called me to the Poor Clares it was more prayer and the silence of the heart. There was that growth, where He didn't have to show me 'nun' in the Bible, or all these little signs. You hope there's growth when you look back. But look how God takes you where you are. He knew what I needed when I needed it. I needed that little cross at Wal-Mart that day. Now, He might just let me receive His consolation in prayer and let that be enough. I know that that is true. I may have sufferings now, but I know He's faithful and this is for my good. Maybe it's for my purification or maybe it's so I will offer it with Him on the cross for some other souls, but I know there's a reason for it."

Once, a friend told Sister Maria Benedicta that she has it so good; her spouse is always perfect. Sister Maria Benedicta agreed: "I said, 'You're right. He can never let me down. He's all good, all loving, all powerful. He will always do what's best for me.' I said, 'You're absolutely right. But if there's ever a problem with our relationship, it's me. I can't blame it on anybody else. It's my fault.'"

Monastic life demands constant assessment and an awareness that there will always be room for improvement. Sister Maria Benedicta says, "Perseverance in the religious life isn't just, 'I will stay here until I die.' It is, 'I will strive to live perfect charity and to become holy.' That's what perseverance is; it's not just staying here and 'I made final vows, smooth sailing until I die.' Or a comfortable life. No. It is striving to perfection and to live charity and to give of yourself. That's hard. To dedicate your life to that, it's serious. It's a life commitment. I know that to not let it die—your love for God—does take work. You can't just come and live a luxurious life and grow in the love of God. It takes work, like any human relationship. If you get married, you wouldn't say on your marriage day, 'We're done.' Relationships are work. But to believe that God is really alive, He's living, He's alive and present here—it's not an abstract idea. He's personal and He's living and in the sacraments, and especially in the Eucharist, I receive Him into my body.

Those are the ways that we, with God, foster that relationship and grow. We have to continually work at prayer. We have to fight distractions. We have to fight our imagination wandering. Like any relationship, it takes work. It is a commitment. I will do this for the rest of my life."

Days before making temporary vows, Sister Maria Benedicta sits with Sister Mary Nicolette at the metal grille and attempts to express during an interview with me the significance of her impending ceremony. After a few years of observing monastic silence, albeit with more opportunities for dialogue because she has been in training in the novitiate, she verbalizes her thoughts tentatively. "God wants little me," she says. "And it's not like any…it's just really…I don't even know what to say about it. It's incredible, really."

Her Novice Mistress shares her own reflections from the same experience seventeen years prior. "I just remember the overwhelming feeling was the condescension of God—the condescension of God, that He would take a broken and fallen human creature to be His spouse," Sister Mary Nicolette says. "And like, 'Who am I?' The fact that He would do something like that was just very overwhelming and moving and overpowering."

Sister Maria Benedicta chimes in then: "When you first come, you have to get over your normal, big things. But then God shows you all the little things, and you see how much you're corrupted. You see how poor and weak you really are because the mentality in the world is, 'I can do it,' but when you're face to face with God and you see what you really are, you say, 'Does God really want this?' Humbling. But my goodness, He shows you what you are."

"He still loves you," Sister Mary Nicolette says.

"Yeah, you think, 'Is He crazy or what?' I don't know. It's hard to even describe. You see how much work there is to be done. Every bride wants to give her love something, but then you see, 'Here I am, Lord. Sorry! This is all I can give. It's everything, but boy is it little, you know what I mean? But anyway, I'm excited, but it's very humbling."

A few weeks later, on April 19, 2009, her family reunites for Sister Maria Benedicta's ceremony of profession, to watch her make temporary vows. Relatives fly in from Kansas. Members of her second family, the Marian Sisters, drive from Nebraska to Rockford. After a somber ceremony, Sister Maria Benedicta's loved ones gather on the other side of the grille, talking, laughing, crying.

Sister Maria Benedicta's purpose in life is clear: "I just have to live like Saint Clare. That's my way to God—just to live like this. He creates you for a purpose and He'll direct you there." She prays and she makes sacrifices and she asks God to deliver graces to those in need. In her hidden life in the enclosure, Sister Maria Benedicta is a silent witness to the world.

As one of the few people to whom God has broken through, Sister Maria Benedicta explains simply, "His love was so compelling I couldn't resist." "I think a lot of people have the notion this life is dying out or that girls don't do this anymore. It's very sad that people don't realize God is calling young women to the religious life, to join these religious communities." The culture beyond the monastery's premises is so loud, with radios and television and cell phones—"all these things I don't know about anymore," she says. "They can't hear God calling them anymore. God whispers in the heart; if there's no silence, they don't hear Him speak."

When passersby see the monastery or learn about the cloistered nuns, Sister Mary Nicolette hopes people pause to wonder, "Why would someone do this in our day and age?" Sister Maria Benedicta, who almost majored in Spanish so that she could become a missionary "because I wanted to go out and help people," believes she would have reached a limited number of people that way. "But here, I can reach the whole world through prayer and offering everything to God and Him using it as He wants," she says. "I don't say now, 'Only use this penance for my mom, or for my sister,' but I let Him use it as He wants and He can reach the whole world that way because He knows who needs it the most. He's not going to abandon my mother and my sister. He's going to give them graces, too, because it's united with Jesus' infinite merits.

"No one ever sees us go to pray. They don't see us because we're behind the wall, but they know we live our life just for God, that we pray, and it's to be a witness that God is worth giving everything for. God must exist if people are willing to give their whole life for this through a sustained effort. Some people give their lives for things that are not right, like the terrorists; it wasn't right. But a sustained effort—he has kept the Poor Clares going eight hundred years since Saint Clare lived. God has sustained that. It's from the grace of God. People must think there's something there that's worth it, that's worth giving up everything for. It's a sign of the world to come. We hope when people think of us, see us, or experience something of us, 'They're living for heaven,' to think, to grasp, to pull themselves out of the secular world they're living, and ask, 'Why am I living? What's important?'

That's what we hope to be a witness of. Through our prayers and sacrifices, God is going to use those to give those graces to people."

When Sister Maria Benedicta makes her final vows as a Poor Clare Colettine, she will then wear the silver ring of a solemnly professed nun. The community will have accepted her as a permanent member. And on the rare occasion that she must leave the enclosure, for an appointment or to vote, Sister Maria Benedicta will find herself a stranger in her homeland.

Sister Mary Veronica

You're a postulant for the first year, and you keep your original name at that time; at that time, you're not really a nun, you're hoping. Not until you take vows would you really be considered a nun, properly speaking. And then you become a novice when you're clothed. You become a novice, a sister, and from then on you are *Sister So-and-So*. When you take the vows—when the Church accepts you, and then you are representing the Church—it's ratification, and it's spousal at that point.

Mother Abbess chooses both parts of your name—your title and your name. Before you receive the habit, after your postulancy and you've been accepted, you present three choices, if you want, of possible names. And you might get those, or you might get one completely different. Or some people say to Mother Abbess, "Just pick."

I had had it inside me to tell her just pick, but I didn't go along with it, so I wrote down three names. It was really interesting because I said, "Holy Spirit, you're letting me know I should have trusted," because when she gave me the name, she said, "I knew what I was going to call you for months." She knew what she was going to give me before I ever gave her the names. It was actually one of the names I gave to her—Veronica. It's very interesting because Mother Abbess is very intuitive, but the Holy Spirit works through her, so we both had that name. But I should have just trusted and I think God would have given me more grace if I had.

I don't think it would make any difference in the name, but I think I would have more grace to be more faithful to interior inspirations and have more confidence—just trust God and have confidence, and be open and trust in other people, too. And the more you trust, the more you will receive from God. The more faithful you are, grace builds upon grace. And the more faithful you are to graces, the more God gives you. Saint Peter said to our Lord, "Ask me to walk on the water." His immediate reaction was that he stepped out of the boat and he was walking on the water, but then he started doubting and wondering, and he sank. Our Lord still saved him and pulled him up. But what would the graces have been if he had the faith not to look at the waves and to really trust Jesus? He could have walked all the way to Jesus on the water. Not only would he have done that physical thing, which is a miracle, how would God have blessed his faith? That is what God really wants; it's not really the outside, it's the inside, and how would He have strengthened Peter's faith?

In secular things, let's say you're learning how to do something. If you do it halfway, you're not going to make as much progress as when you put your whole effort into it, your whole heart into it. I think God works in those things, too, in the secular things. He wants to give us graces, but how much effort am I going to put into it? The measure of the effort I put into it, I will receive—I will be capable of receiving. I can't receive what I don't embrace or what I won't accept.

I think it would have given me more grace to be more faithful. I think that people lack the confidence to follow what they really believe is right. They end up doubting, like Peter, and they sink. It's not like it's anything that would hurt. And it's really a thing of trust in God. If I say, "I'll leave it to Mother Abbess to pick and I'll know it's God's will," then I should trust God. And if it doesn't come out that way, that's not what He wanted.

I would probably have more of a tendency now to say, "No, let's trust and do it," rather than doubt, doubt. I think a lot of us could do much more if we didn't doubt and waver over what we really feel inside. I think we get stopped a lot. I know I have. And I've met other people, too, that have said that kind of thing. I mean if you don't try, you'll never know! You'll never know. I don't know if a person can see that many results in themselves; maybe other people can see the results better than you can. I know if I just keep trying to be faithful, God will help me to trust more and more and more. I trust in that.

Veronica means "true image." She was the one who, when our Lord was carrying His cross, and His face was so bloody and He couldn't see from all the sweat and blood in His eyes, she was brave enough to break through the guards and she gave her veil to Him to wipe His face on. After she did this, He wiped His face and His face came onto the veil. They have, in Rome, the actual veil. I have always been fascinated by that Station of the Cross. Of course, I am to pray to and imitate Veronica—Saint Veronica and her boldness. It took a lot for her to do that, so hopefully I, too, can make reparation to our Lord and wipe His face for all the harms and all the bad things done by all of us. I do many bad things, too, but at the same time, our Lord accepts from sinners. You know, He accepts beautiful gifts from sinners. He imprinted His image on her veil for her act. And not only did He imprint His image on her veil, at the same time He imprints His image on her soul. So each time I or someone else does an act of love or reparation to our Lord, then His image gets imprinted on our soul, and then if we're doing this on behalf of not only ourselves but for everyone, then His image gets imprinted on everybody.

A novice has a white veil and traditionally, like in the old times, a white veil was for a woman who was a fiancée; she changed to a black veil when she got married. When you take your vows, you are truly becoming Christ's spouse and becoming married to Him. You are completely set aside and dedicated to Him at that time, and then you wear the black veil. There are other responsibilities that come with that, because I am supposed to live for Him and on behalf of His people, and that's supposed to be my entire life. If I'm faithful, and do well, then God will bless the world more.

It is a big responsibility. It's a very serious responsibility. And that's why it would usually take you three years before you could take your vows, and then I have three years of temporary vows. So I have at least three years of temporary vows, and then in three years I could take the solemn vows, which is permanent. That will be wonderful.

Epilogue

When I first approached the Mother Abbess with my request to engage with the community, she told me the nuns would need to pray and get back to me.

In reflecting on the contours of this project, I see that it has unfolded at a peculiar pace. That I adopted to a rate more akin to the monastery than to the fast-paced culture beyond the enclosure was key. About a year after the nuns agreed to let me work with them on this oral history and photography project, I moved a little farther away from the monastery. (Before that, I had lived an hour's drive from the Poor Clares.) There were longer lulls between my visits and phone calls. There were lulls between my visits and phone calls to the monastery, and I received more handwritten letters from the Mother Abbess, who informed me that I was welcome when I had the time. In retrospect, I believe my absence prompted the nuns' greater commitment to this project. The dynamics shifted; the Mother Abbess solicited my visits.

This was not a conscious strategy to withdraw so that they would solicit me, but I believe that it established a tenor that the community was comfortable with. A few years later, my engagement again waned. I think that this pace suited the slower pace of the monastery, and it led to greater buy-in and engagement from both parties. The project unfolded at a deliberate pace, on terms that were mutually agreeable.

Just as I choose potential subjects, they choose me. After multiple visits, Mother Miryam elaborated on the community's prayers regarding this project; they believed that God had sent me.

I rarely repeated any details conveyed to me in the one-on-one interviews in subsequent interviews with other nuns. Once, though, I asked Mother Miryam about a comment made by one of the nuns; Sister Sarah Marie said that if a young woman thinks she has a calling, she should visit the monastery to see if she belongs and if, after a couple of days, she starts to miss Wal-Mart, "well, we aren't going to keep them if they're missing Wal-Mart!"

I asked Mother Miryam about this comment and was surprised to hear strong dissent. Mother Miryam stated that she missed certain activities, including drives, when she first joined the community. Working outdoors in the monastery's gardens, she heard the traffic beyond the enclosure's wall and she wanted out; she wanted to go somewhere, anywhere. "You can miss all those things," Mother Miryam said. Until that moment, the two nuns did not know that they embraced such divergent views on Wal-Mart—of all things—or on the mega-chain's impact on a religious vocation. In the nuns' lives, they would not find occasion or opportunity to discuss philosophical differences of a cloistered calling.

In general, in keeping with their values of anonymity and hiddenness, I believe it was prudent to repeat little of what was shared during those interviews. Yet it revealed a complex perspective of the monastery's population to learn about these spectrums of opinions.

Early on, I learned that when a member of the community passes away, a biography is written of that nun's life for the monastery's records. Mother Miryam told me that it is challenging to draft a nun's biography, given that they rarely have occasion to tell one another their life stories. I told her that I would give the nuns transcripts of the interviews for their archives, as well as for the nuns to review their own interviews with the option of scheduling an additional oral history session if a nun wanted to clarify anything in her own transcript. The Mother Abbess stated the transcripts would be included in the monastery's archives and she was grateful for this exchange. I delivered heaps of transcripts in 2009 and 2010. Later, one nun gave me a scrap of paper with the correct spellings of several pronouns she had mentioned in her interview. Another handwrote six pages of clarifications on scrap paper (the blank side of a handout for a capital campaign).

In the spring of 2011, one of the aged nuns died. A World War II veteran, Sister Ann Frances had been bedridden in the infirmary for years; her health declined as her Alzheimer's disease advanced. I interviewed Sister Maria Deo Gratias, who entered the monastery at the same time as Sister Ann Frances; they went through the novitiate together, and Sister Maria Deo Gratias knew her life story better than the other members because they experienced the training, the transition into monastic silence, together. The Mother Abbess asked if I would like to make photographs of the funeral procession from the rooftop. I did. I think it was critical that I made myself available when they made these offers and suggestions and requests.

Looking back, I wish that I attended more of the events they invited me to—the ceremonies for those who were progressing from postulants to novices to making temporary vows to final vows, and the Jubilee celebrations for those who had made their vows fifty years prior. In retrospect, I think it would have been beneficial if I had been a quicker study of the liturgical calendar, and more cognizant of the impact of my requests and visits on their schedule. All of the nuns knew from experience, though, that it takes time to be socialized into a cloistered community, where communication is abbreviated and silence is observed, and they were patient and gracious. Because of their indirect style of communication, it took a while to realize that they would not ask me if they could take a break in the interviews for a glass of water. I regret that I did not think to bring water for them and that I did not ask permission from the Mother Abbess to bring a special drink for the sometimes-lengthy interviews. (When it occurred to me that although the nuns lead lives of sacrifice, they are allowed to accept donations, I brought them homemade cookies and muffins. One evening, I stopped at the monastery with a delivery of baked goods; my nephew met the Mother Abbess, who greeted us outside, at a side door.)

A few months after photographing the procession from the rooftop, I met with Sister Maria Deo Gratias and told her that I was still realizing their trust in me. I explained that when others learned of this project, I was often asked if I wanted to become a nun. Not missing a beat, Sister Maria Deo Gratias exclaimed, "You would have to become Catholic first!" I said that I had felt no such pressures from the nuns. Then I asked why the community decided to let me in. Sister Maria Deo Gratias told me what others in her community had said before—that it was a major exception. A few months later, the community held elections. Mother Miryam had served her term limit as Mother Abbess, and she needed to take a break from her position. The Vicaress, Sister Maria Deo Gratias, was elected Mother Abbess. She mailed me a card with a drawing of Saint Francis on the front. Inside, she articulated the answer to the question that so many had posed: Why did they allow me in? Mother Deo Gratias says,

You have a beautiful way of making people feel "at home" with you. Being a good listener, you are able to pick up and perceive what is being said in a true way and are not afraid to ask about what you might not understand. You have a genuine sensitivity to handle precious things shared with you in a respectful and reverent way. In interviewing you have a good way of drawing out what may be of interest for your project without doing it in a prying manner. If the person hesitates in sharing something, you are very good about leaving it go, even if you would have wished otherwise. You are so careful not to intrude—so sensitive to the situation at the time. We were so impressed with you when you came into the enclosure—our sacred space—in keeping the atmosphere of silence. In choir and in the refectory you took the pictures in such a wonderful way, wishing not to disturb what was going on in there. In all the places you had a way of going about it that did not draw attention to yourself.

Sister Maria Deo Gratias has mentioned that a true friendship formed in the aftermath of my car accident en route to the monastery in 2009. While driving on icy roads to the monastery early one foggy winter morning, I was in a head-on collision; I broke my back, sustaining a compression fracture to my vertebrae. The nuns could offer support through prayers, she told me; this was their mission.

In my first visit to the monastery several weeks after that car accident, it dawned on me the concessions the nuns had made to allow me to undertake this project. In the hallway of the cloister, Sister Sarah Marie told me the nuns were praying for me. (A young woman I knew during the six years that she considered joining this monastic community told me that she never entered the cloistered monastery until the day she became a postulant.) "I know," I told Sister Sarah Marie. "You're wonderful. Thank you." I repeated what I had told a friend: If I'm going to be in an accident, I'm glad it happened en route to the monastery because the nuns would suspect something amiss, and pray. Or, I told Sister Sarah Marie, maybe you just assumed I was running late, as usual. Sister Sarah Marie smiled, tears in her eyes. She told me that the morning of my accident she had prayed to the Archangel Raphael, patron of travelers. She said that she always prayed to the Archangel Raphael when she knew I was traveling. In fact, she said, she and the other nuns prayed for me every day since my first visit to the monastery. I was stunned.

Mother Miryam found me in the hall a moment later. She underwent knee replacement surgery the same day as my car accident; she phoned me several times from her hospital room as we both recuperated. Mother Miryam told me by phone that she was eager to start physical therapy, eager to progress, eager to return to the monastery, eager to see the community's cat, which she admitted she spoiled. She shared all this, and then she told me we would learn patience together as we contended with our limitations.

In the monastery that day, the Mother Abbess and I walked slowly down the dark corridor together. If she noticed my tears, she did not mention them. "Two cripples," she said. We laughed.

Acknowledgments

At times as I have worked on this project, my life has begun to mirror aspects of the cloistered nuns' lives. I appreciate silence, find myself withdrawing from aspects of popular culture, and realize that I have adopted the nuns' dedication and devotion.

A constellation of individuals—mentors, friends, and family—and organizations have been instrumental in the development of this work as I ride these phases of retreat and engagement with the outside world.

I am incredibly grateful to Steve Rowland, who not only is technically astute but also has an empathetic spirit that is a source of inspiration and guidance. He values the nuns' ideals. I trust his counsel.

Peter Maguire availed himself to inquiries throughout the process of interviews, writing, and the book contract. His input was precise and substantial.

Anthony Bannon enabled me to articulate my vision for the images and to refine my photographic approach.

In the early stages of the manuscript, Carlee Tressel Alson was reliable and tenacious; her gracious feedback improved the work and her friendship is invaluable.

Friar Benet Fonck OFM and Sister Joan Mueller, both authors with busy schedules, made time to explain the intricacies of the Franciscan lineage and the Poor Clare Colettine order, Mueller having entered the Rockford Poor Clares' Corpus Christi Monastery and experienced cloistered monastic life.

I am very thankful for all project support, including from the Illinois Arts Council, the Foundation for Contemporary Arts, the Puffin Foundation, and SHURE, Inc.

Anna Belle Nimmo has been like a fairy godmother.

After the car accident en route to the monastery, a number of foundations that assist visual artists and writers intervened, creating a very welcome safety net.

Months after that accident, the women I met on a writers' retreat at Ghost Ranch became my lovely and supportive community.

With the manuscript complete, Cynthia Read rallied forces. Donald A. Ritchie opened doors. And Nancy Toff blazed the final trail to bring this book into being, moving the manuscript from acceptance through production, and correcting, with mild amusement, my penchant for malapropisms.

It seems now that a clear line can be drawn between this book and my high school teacher, Pat Toth, who fed my interest in writing and other cultures, supplying me with reading material such as folklore from around the world.

Throughout adolescence, my sister Fairlight was like a highly specialized film librarian; she screened—and sometimes even let me join her in viewing—Jean-Claude Van Damme flicks, musicals, and classics. *The Nun's Story*, with Audrey Hepburn, made a lasting impact on me, and probably ignited my desire to understand the religious vocation and the women who heed that calling. Fairlight's perspective helped shape the way I processed and produced this book.

I have also been aided by the expertise of Eric J. Palmer; the generosity of my newest sister, Angela Angelovska Wilson; and the presence of Julie Swanson, Kimberly Lamm, Laura Turner, Megan Coleman, Alicia Eisenbise, and Clare Rosean.

My parents introduced me to religion—sharing their childhood encounters with Judaism and Catholicism, and the Protestant faith they chose to embrace. Because of them, I learned moxie and humility, qualities integral to my approach to ethnography, art, and life.

I am especially appreciative of my two creative younger brothers, Isaac and Aaron, for their unrelenting assistance and support.

Finally, this ongoing eight-year endeavor is only possible because the Poor Clare Colettine nuns in Rockford, Illinois, allowed me to enter their world on occasion. Because of them I have been "changed for good" and "for the better."

Appendix: Interviewees

The nuns selected pseudonyms to be used in place of their actual religious names. The nuns also chose pseudonyms for their childhood names, which are used instead of their actual birth names.

Interview Date	Religious Pseudonym	Childhood Pseudonym
March 18, 2005	Mother Miryam	Catherine
August 25, 2005	Mother Miryam	Catherine
September 15, 2005	Sister Mary Clara	Klarka
September 15, 2005	Sister Mary Joseph	Josephine
September 15, 2005	Sister Sarah Marie	Tiffany
September 18, 2005	Sisters Mary Nicolette	Monica
	Maria Benedicta	Maria
September 18, 2005	Sister Mary Monica	Mary
October 29, 2005	Mother Miryam	Catherine
July 25, 2008	Sister Mary Joseph	Josephine
November 14, 2008	Mother Miryam	Catherine
November 14, 2008	Sister Maria Deo Gratias	Clare
November 14, 2008	Sister Mary Michael	Jenny
November 29, 2008	Sister Mary Gemma	Teresa
December 5, 2008	Sister Mary Gemma	Teresa
January 2, 2009	Mother Miryam	Catherine
February 6, 2009	Sister Joan Marie	Virginia
February 19, 2009	Sister Joan Marie	Virginia
February 19, 2009	Sister Sarah Marie	Tiffany
February 25, 2009	Sister Maria Deo Gratias	Clare
April 1, 2009	Sisters Mary Nicolette	Monica
	Maria Benedicta	Maria
August 4, 2009	Sister Maria Benedicta	Maria
August 4, 2009	Sister Mary Nicolette	Monica

(*Continued*)

Continued

Interview Date	Religious Pseudonym	Childhood Pseudonym
	Mother Miryam	Catherine
September 24, 2009	Mother Miryam	Catherine
September 24, 2009	Sister Ann Marie	Lisa
September 24, 2009	Sister Mary Michael	Jenny
December 16, 2009	Sister Ann Marie	Lisa
January 26, 2010	Mother Miryam	Catherine
January 26, 2010	Sisters Mary Nicolette	Monica
	Maria Benedicta	Maria
March 12, 2011	Mother Miryam	Catherine
March 21, 2011	Funeral for Sister Ann Frances	
April 5, 2011	Mother Miryam	Catherine
May 26, 2011	Sister Maria Deo Gratias, on the life of Sister Ann Frances	
July 30, 2011	Mother Miryam	Catherine

Notes

Preface

1. Michael Frisch, *A Shared Authority: Essays on the Craft and Meaning of Oral and Public History* (Albany: State University of New York Press, 1990).

2. "Displacement and Community," Oral History in the Mid-Atlantic Region annual conference, April 20, 2011.

3. Antjie Krog, *Country of My Skull: Guilt, Sorrow, and the Limits of Forgiveness in the New South Africa* (New York: Three Rivers Press, 1998), 64.

Introduction

1. *Verbi Sponsa: Instruction on the Contemplative Life and on the Enclosure of the Nun* (Libreria Editrice Vaticana, Vatican City, Congregation for Institutes of Consecrated Life and for Societies of Apostolic Life; May 13, 1999), 13.

2. *Post-Synodal Apostolic Exhortation Vita Consecrata of the Holy Father John Paul II to the Bishops and Clergy Religious Orders and Congregations Societies of Apostolic Life Secular Institutes and All the Faithful on the Consecrated Life and its Mission in the Church and in the World*, Rome, March 25, 1996, http://www.vatican.va/holy_father/john_paul_ii/apost_exhortations/documents/hf_jp-ii_exh_25031996_vita-consecrata-en.html.

3. *Verbi Sponsa*, 10.

4. Ibid., 27.

5. Pope Benedict XVI, *Biographical Sketch of St. Clare of Assisi*, September 15, 2010, http://www.vatican.va/holy_father/benedict_xvi/audiences/2010/documents/hf_ben-xvi_aud_20100915_en.html.

6. Ibid.

7. Colettine Poor Clare Nuns, *Golden Jubilee: 1916–1966* (Rockford, Ill.: Corpus Christi Monastery, June 29, 1966), 6.

8. Ibid., 5.

9. Ibid., 10.

10. *Come Follow Me*, a brochure written and published by the Poor Clare Colettine nuns at the Corpus Christi Monastery.

11. Ibid.

12. Friar Benet Fonck, e-mail message to author, September 3, 2011.

13. Ibid.

14. "Frequently Requested Church Statistics," Center for Applied Research in the Apostolate, a Georgetown University affiliated national not-for-profit research center on Catholic data, Catholic statistics, and Catholic research, accessed on June 19, 2013, http://cara.georgetown.edu/CARAServices/requestedchurchstats.html.

Chapter 3

1. Editors Regis J. Armstrong, J. A. Wayne Hellmann, and William J. Short. Francis of Assisi—The Saint: Early Documents, *Volume 1*. New York: New City Press, 1999. Page 103.

2. Bullarium Franciscanum I:771. Translation in Joan Mueller. *Clare's Letters to Agnes: Texts and Sources*. St. Bonaventure, NY: The Franciscan Institute, 2001. Page 208. Also, Joan Mueller, e-mail message to author, July 31, 2013.

Chapter 5

1. Poor Clare Colettine Nuns, *Golden Jubilee: 1916–1966* (Rockford, Ill.: Corpus Christi Monastery, June 29, 1966), 25.

Chapter 7

1. *Verbi Sponsa: Instruction on the Contemplative Life and the Enclosure of the Nun* (Libreria Editrice Vaticana, Vatican City, Congregation for Institutes of Consecrated Life and for Societies of Apostolic Life, May 13, 1999).

Further Reading

Fonck, Benet A. *To Cling With All Her Heart to Him: The Spirituality of St. Clare of Assisi*. Cincinnati, OH: St. Anthony Messenger Press, 1996.

Fonck, Benet A. *Ritual of the Secular Franciscan Order*. Cincinnati, OH: St. Anthony Messenger Press, 1995.

Fonck, Benet A. *Called to Make Present the Charism: Ongoing Formation for Secular Franciscans Based on the Footnotes of the Sfo Rule*. Cincinnati, OH: St. Anthony Messenger Press, 2001.

Fonck, Benet A. *Called to Build a More Fraternal and Evangelical World: Commentary on the Rule of the Secular Franciscan Order*. Cincinnati, OH: St. Anthony Messenger Press, 2002.

Mueller, Joan. *Clare of Assisi: The Letters to Agnes*. Collegeville, MN: Liturgical Press, 2003.

Mueller, Joan. *Clare's Letters to Agnes: Texts and Sources (Clare resources series)*. St. Bonaventure, NY: Franciscan Institute Publications, 2012.

Mueller, Joan. *The Privilege of Poverty: Clare of Assisi, Agnes of Prague, and the Struggle for a Franciscan Rule for Women*. Philadelphia: Pennsylvania State University Press, 2008.

Norris, Kathleen. *The Cloister Walk*. New York: Riverhead Books, 1997.

Rogers, Carole Garibaldi. *Habits of Change: An Oral History of American Nuns*. New York: Oxford University Press, 2011.

Index

THE OXFORD ORAL HISTORY SERIES

J. Todd Moye (University of North Texas)
Kathryn Nasstrom (University of San Francisco)
Robert Perks (The British Library Sound Archive)
Series Editors

Donald A. Ritchie
Senior Advisor

A Hand In Time

ISBN-13: 978-1540881243
ISBN-10: 1540881245

Table of Contents

Also by Louis Rogers

Coming Alive: Accessing the Healing Power of the Universe
Writer's Club Press, 2000

Mirror of the Unseen: The Complete Discourses of Jalal al-Din Rumi
ToExcel, 2002

The Fire of Love: The Love Story of Layla and Majnun
Writer's Club Press, 2002

Call and Response: The Wisdom of Rumi
iUniverse, 2006

The Age of Spirit
CreateSpace, 2013

Ladder to the Sky
CreateSpace, 2014

Tales of Immortality
CreateSpace, 2015

What Do You Expect God To Be?
CreateSpace, 2015

Where Do We Go From Here?
CreateSpace, 2015

Bridging The Gap
CreateSpace, 2015

Who Do You Think You Are?
CreateSpace, 2015

Kissing The Spider
CreateSpace, 2016

That Which You Wish To Be
CreateSpace, 2016

What Next May Come
CreateSpace, 2016

The Face In The Mirror
CreateSpace, 2016

Rebel In The Mind
CreateSpace, 2016

As Always

For Jennifer, Andrew and Peter

And now, for Ashley, Laura, Zoe and Madison.

And whoever next may come …

ONE

Time to begin

We seem to have arrived at a point in our evolutionary journey at which many of us, very many of us in fact, have lost faith in the traditional supports that our familiar religious traditions have offered us in our journey towards wholeness.

We have evolved so far for so long now, in terms of our extraordinary technological and material progress, that we have assumed those changes represent the functionally-automatic manner in which civilizations progress and we along with it.

But assumptions can be not only misleading, but a complete waste of time when time and experience prove them wrong, Assumptions are not proof of anything, and neither are they adequate substitutions for evidence when evidence is lacking.

We must begin to change those assumptions and search for the truth of our existence, and now is the time to start. Now is the only time to begin anything. The now moment is the voice of eternity calling us from beyond to act in the present moment, the only time in which we *can* act.

The past is finished, over and done with, and cannot be revived or resuscitated. The future is only a possibility, at least according to our conventional assumptions about existence,

even if, one day in the far off future, some branch of as-yet unnamed physics may prove those assumptions incorrect.

But as we typically experience it, time structures our reality, the way we think about life, and the unknown duration of our existence of physical being.

And because of our limited span of existence within time, the uncertain length of our stay, we are necessarily obliged to make full use of whatever opportunities come our way through deliberate planning or the ministrations of fate.

Whatever comes our way may or may not be a matter of chance, fate or destiny. And it may also be possible that no matter how many potential opportunities for anything come our way, the problem lies as much in our ability to recognize them for what they actually are, as it is in our abilities to seize them and bring them under our conscious control.

Whatever the case may be, what is always an absolute necessity for meaningful existence is our understanding and experience of time. And the way we use or misuse it.

What we do and how we do it is the real issue of course. The material world is the physical arena in which our efforts are played out, and time is the eternal referee for the duration of our engagement with physical reality.

Some of us know what we want to do and want out of life from an early age, while others discover something along those lines as they move through time, making choices in regard to the exigencies of the moment. Still others drift through life, occasionally happy and content, often frustrated and occasionally flirting with despair or worse.

Their unhappiness may grow until, as Henry David Thoreau observed in his seminal book "Walden" written in 1854, *The mass of men lead lives of quiet desperation. What is called resignation is confirmed desperation.*

What is shocking is the realization that what was true in 1854 and before is just as true today, and may unhappily be one of those truths universally acknowledged of which Jane Austen was so adept at describing.

Time for a change in the way we do business, and the way we make use of our time now. Unless we take serious charge of our evolutionary prospects, there will only be more of the same, and possibly even worse.

We are due for a shift in our understanding of who and what we are, a great awakening in our spiritual awareness. The sooner this change comes about the better off this world and all that it contains will be on Planet Earth, and that includes us as well.

If we want to remain a vital and active creative presence in this world we must act, or become a handful of miserable survivors of some planetary series of disasters huddling in the back of caves. And burning whatever scraps we can find for warmth and light. Hungry and thirsty.

Scant comfort in a world of already scant comfort. But this may become reality for our descendants unless we accept true responsibility for the stewardship of our environment, and correct what we have done to despoil it.

We have given in to the inherent duality of life and our lower human nature. Instead of being protectors of our world we have become a world-wide force of environmental destruction. So many of us have become enslaved by the profit motive, blind to anything that does not turn an immediate profit or with the potential to enrich us.

And then there is also our urge to possess whatever comes into our line of sight. And thus so many of us are heavily laden with objects of desire, weighed down by obsessive needs and material possessions to such an extent that we can hardly breathe.

This, rather than an honest evaluation of our place in creation, and the need for personal responsibility. Without that we cannot continue on the path of selfish self-indulgence indefinitely without unsustainable damage taking place.

Our natural resources are fast becoming depleted. The environment so near-catastrophically changed by unquestionably man-made activities that the ability of our planetary home to sustain life itself may be in danger.

We have so undermined the ability of the planet to heal itself that, if the planet was a conscious entity, it might well consider ridding itself of the incredibly destructive human species of life. Mark Twain once said that God made man because He was disappointed in the monkeys.

He might well be considering another change of mind. We've had our shot at creation, and may have bungled the job permanently. And this time there may not be enough wood lying around to build another ark.

In one respect time itself may be on the brink of losing all positive meaning. We will not be leading lives of quiet desperation. The despair will be loud and hard and clear in spite of the air and other forms of pollution that has already fast become a world-wide phenomenon.

Changing the nature of existence in all the wrong ways in the process, and because of that adding a terrible emphasis to our experience of duality, even the duality of time.

Time can be our friend when things are going well, when we lead lives of joyful existence in a safe, secure and happy environment, But when that changes, and this is, in fact, a world in which change is the only thing that never changes, the duality of physical existence will assert its privileges.

Negative and painful encounters with reality will be on the agenda, and time may become a suffocating, worrisome and unendurable fact of existence. We may find ourselves

dreading what will come down the pike with yawning jaws with every passing moment.

And if that should happen, we will all find ourselves seeing the elephant in every negative sense that implies. Time always has the potential of becoming a constant and ever-present reminder of what we have achieved, or fail to have achieved in life.

Time can certainly be our friend when we lead lives of joyful existence in a safe, happy and contented environment. Every moment a prolonged experience of joyful existence, stretched out as long as possible, cherishing a love of life, and wishing it would never end.

But time changes everything when it comes time for sad farewells and unasked for new beginnings. Everything comes to an inevitable end. And when change takes place and the duality of existence asserts its influence in negative and painful ways, time can become a suffocating presence and unendurable tyrant with dictatorial power over our lives when it threatens us with more of the same.

We may suddenly find ourselves dreading every moment of every day, even of our very existence when things go wrong and we see the elephant in the room. Fear of change and what new terrors time will add to the mixture, re-arranging our personal agenda, adds a new dimension of terrified apprehension in our lives. And then there is the problem of death.

Time is the constant and ever-present reminder that we are all mortal beings bound by the deadly limitations of material being in the most profound way we can imagine. Death is waiting in the wings waiting for its moment to strike us down.

We are all fated to die, personal extinction perhaps, our existence coming to an end as we know it without also knowing if in some way we go on. Or fall into the deep, endless and bottomless sleep of death and non-existence.

Death, which knows no glories and admits nothing of creature comforts or human cheer into its company or its domain. Death, which knows no warmth of heart or thrill of existence in the physical realm. *The graves a fine and private place,* wrote the English metaphysical poet John Donne, *but none, I think, do there embrace.*

Death may welcome us with open arms, but who among us willingly returns the embrace. Death, which holds us fast to its bosom, but not in mutually-endearing companionship.

Death, in whose company spring shoots do not thrust their budding heads through their earthly womb to add their glories and their flowery blossoms into the air we gladly breathe in, and just as happily breathe out.

Death, which comforts no one except, perhaps, the terminally suffering, and afflicts us all with the sorrows it brings. Which takes by force what it would always be denied by choice except for the most desperate or callous among us.

Those whom illness lies low and in despair, and those who choose war over peace. Forgetful that they themselves are destined to face the same hopeless encounter they so willingly inflict on others.

Death, the final chapter in the book of life. The last battle, the doorway into unknown regions through which most of us are terrified of passing. The great beginning that will inevitably see a final ending.

Or so we imagine when we face the bleakness of our mortal fears, inwardly cringing at the nightmares we imagine when we feel our body begin to slip away from our conscious control, unresponsive to our instinctual commands.

Bit by bit, little by little, limb by limb we slip away until, once again, as we once were when we were newly-born, helpless and crib-bound, once again we become nearly the same as strangers in a strange land.

For want of better information from informed sources, *for want of a nail,* we imagine terrible scenarios and horrible consequences when death strikes. Our imagination a powerful tool when we are afraid, beyond our conscious control when it is activated by fear and everything we are or possess is up for grabs, auctioned off to unknown bidders by the final embrace of death.

The price we pay for our willful ignorance is astounding, and we pay it willingly because we are so ignorant of our options. We can do far more than close our eyes to our future, cross our fingers and hope for the best.

The most thoughtful things we can do among our options, the most prominent among them, is clearly to learn more about the processes of mortality and physical existence from spiritual traditions that have devoted so much time and energy to exploring our human condition.

We could investigate what lies beyond the veil that separates the finite from the infinite. And if anyone is in the mood to mock or deny that, it is simply a dead-end which we could easily avoid if we did our homework. Just as those instinctual nay-sayers have not done theirs.

Impossible to know this say the rationalists and the literalists, forgetful that they were not there at the creation themselves and had no say in the matter.

But they are nevertheless correct in that it is impossible for them to consider anything in their deliberations that exceeds the boundaries of what they consider to be reasonable, rational and within the scope of their vision of the creation.

Which may in actuality be nothing more than their personal customs or habits, but which for the literalists take on the appearance of reality. They accept nothing that suggests anything other than the absolute literalism according to which they define existence. And beyond which their imaginations will not allow them to roam.

This is a logical but hopeless dead-end in their thinking, a living death for those who hope for a richer and more expansive experience of existence.

While reason and logic are fundamental and essential tools in the exploration of material reality and physical existence, crucial elements in our evolutionary progress, they do not define the whole of reality or the full nature of human potential.

Nor should they be thought of as encapsulating the entirety of who and what we are and what we are about. We are not animated protoplasmic slugs capable of some slight degree of self-organization with limited physical abilities, doomed to the finality and uncertainty of material existence.

This is when fear is born again and takes over, re-defining the shape of our reality by subverting into emotional retreat our natural impulses towards joy and the inherent bliss of existence.

This is the mind, and the ego, asserting its only-assumed mastery over our lives, dictating the terms of our existence and surrender through its assumptions about life. What we encounter and the implications that ensue according to our self-obsessed imaginations.

But assumptions are not evidence. They are how we respond when we are confused or do not want to take the time to understand something, or anything, in a reasonable and mature fashion according to direct evidence.

We make them when we have no evidence or direct knowledge, and our impatience wants us to take its word for it. Which also happens when we are unable, for many reasons, to admit that we are ignorant of something. This may tend to leave us feeling weak or vulnerable. And unstable, so we make assumptions to overcome our fear of ignorance, and then have to live with the results.

When those assumptions prove to be accurate we call them insight or intuition. But when they are incorrect, way off base, we tend to ignore our errors and write them off as chance, fate or a case of mistaken identity.

It is nothing of the kind, but something of a hit or miss proposition for which we are not willing to take responsibility. If we think about it. But then again, if we had taken the time to think about it and seriously looked into the matter we might never have been willing to make such quick and easy, but ultimately incorrect, assumptions. And then have to clean up the mess that resulted.

The problem of time again, so often at the bottom of so much of the how and why of our decision-making processes. Time forces our hand in often the most unconscious and unexpected ways, and takes a hand in every earthly game we play. And makes reality the ultimate game show.

Time is the invisible player in the game of life, a natural force of existence, as implacable as any of the three other dimensions that define the boundaries of the material plane.

Time surely is the fourth dimension of our existence, along with breadth, height and width. Time extends those expressions of physical reality, directions in a sense, by adding its own emphasis.

Duration, time, defines one aspect of our existence, the length of our visit to this small green planet in an expanding universe which is so unknown, and the physical conditions of our existence so uncertain. Time, the length of our earthly stay, is all we have, over which we have absolutely no control.

Time is a natural breeding ground for fear in all its forms. There is so much uncertainty in every aspect of our existence; so much is unknown that it accelerates our instincts for survival at the expense of our delight at being here in the first place, immersed in the bliss of self-conscious existence.

In so many ways we plead for time when we are in doubt or unprepared. We blame time, or the lack of it, for our mistakes and errors of judgment. We excuse ourselves for our poor timing when we are guilty of having rushed to judgment, simply because we did not want to take the time beforehand for careful evaluation. Our attention span may be in doubt.

When time runs out we will jump through hoops if action is called for or a decision has to be made in a time of crises. But when we have abundant time to research a problem we will all too often take an easy way out, and devote ourselves to leisure-time activities. For which, oddly enough, we always do our best to make time.

And then blame time again, and once more the lack of it, when our borrowed time again runs out and we are forced into the bankruptcy of bad decisions and the unpleasant consequences that eventually result.

Indecision and the assumptions that characterize the pressure to act in life go hand in hand. And both result from the misuse and careless waste of the time allotted to us for the completion of whatever task it is in which we are engaged.

When we approach the end of our lives, through age or illness, we come to realize the reality of how much time we have wasted in the pursuit of frivolous things or frivolous activities. Or simply sheer indolence.

We come to understand how precious time is, and how much we have taken it for granted. Almost like background noise in our lives to which we pay little or no serious attention. Once again, the limitations of our attention span.

This is a lesson we learn the hard way, through hard experience, and it takes us well beyond the formerly elementary understanding of our earthly activities. It calls for a re-evaluation and change of what we consider to be the spiritual dimension of our lives. And it can be painful.

We tend to think of ourselves as conscious beings taking advantage of our time here, and this is what we are in terms of our physical being. But in terms of our inner awareness, that is only one aspect of who and what we are. We are immortal beings, we are informed, who exist within time in one aspect of our experience, but outside of time in another.

In terms of our spiritual existence that is exactly what we are, immortal spirits whose true existence is not ruled by time, not subject to the limitations of physical reality, and not doomed to extinction in the way of all our previously material bodies.

We are told by spiritually-informed teachers that we have several energy bodies, each one inhabiting a separate reality. The material body simply being the most dense in terms of frequency and energy inter-action. And as we know from experience, our bodies are subject to massive deterioration, pain and suffering.

Even to have access to this information has traditionally been beyond the scope of most people for many centuries now. It has traditionally, at least in the occidental world, been denigrated as esoteric teachings, associated with all manner of foolish enterprises of dubious or little value.

Truly esoteric teachings are a golden treasure beyond evaluation, traditionally reserved for a select few characterized by high intelligence, moral rectitude, and emotional stability with a serious and mature understanding of human existence.

Those requirements have loosened somewhat, perhaps out of necessity considering the threats mankind now faces from every direction. Time now for change before time runs out. In this new age of information we all have easy access to esoteric principles and teachings, and the mystical traditions in which they are explicated in further detail.

Anyone with access to the Internet can find information that had traditionally been kept secret from previous

generations because of the strict requirements a spiritual aspirant was expected to master. And the problem to be dealt with here is that there is no effective control over the use, or misuse, of that information.

One reason may have been that most people in the ancient and medieval worlds were uneducated, ruled by superstition and fear, and consequently intellectual and emotional slaves to the ruling authorities that dominated the landscape.

Most were constitutionally unfit for any form of inner exploration, responsible practices of self-awareness, lacking the inner freedom to go beyond conventional beliefs of the day, and temperamentally unsuited for the rigors that resulted from intense spiritual practices. And superstitious to the extreme since so many lived in such intense fear due to the dangers and rigors of ancient and medieval existence.

Widespread education and information has changed the inner landscape of our minds. Modern man is better able to understand esoteric teachings and mystical practices than his medieval predecessors, which might have mistaken them for witchcraft and taken the witch-burning stakes out of storage.

This is possibly one reason that we now have such easy access to information that was previously so hidden or disguised. Fear of torture or a death from being burned at the stake can have a powerful impact on a questioning mind.

There might be other reasons as well, one being that the human race has not generally been ready or willing to think along the lines of higher consciousness. Another being the need to maintain the integrity of the teachings.

That, along with the readiness and fitness of spiritual aspirants to make proper use of more advanced abilities and higher knowledge in a world where violent men with swords and spears occupied seats of power.

In our age we might be on the cusp of a great awakening to our spiritual potential. Perhaps we are ready to make that giant leap forward in our understanding and experience of material reality, and where the stairway to heaven is really located.

But then perhaps, in this world of duality, there is another reason as well. Whether we are ready for that leap of faith or not may not matter quite as much as the reality that we are slowly destroying our world.

We are desecrating our planetary home in virtually every way we can imagine and that our lawmakers will allow. And denial of this essential fact of our existence is a foolish waste of time, for which, over time, succeeding generations and the planet will pay dearly.

Consciencelessly and remorselessly, we are responsible for the destruction of our planetary home through widespread pollution, destructive environmental practices, endless warfare, rising sea levels as the result of global warming, and the dangers we bring on ourselves by our potentially crippling and deadly nuclear policies.

This may have forced the hand of whatever spiritual authorities may be looking out for us to inform us of the precarious situation we are in, and the imminent dangers we face.

All of which we are responsible for through our mindless pursuit of wealth. This is the situation in which we have placed ourselves. We must find a way to dig ourselves out of the mess we have made of this pleasure planet and center of learning.

The relatively sudden outburst of widespread spiritual information may offer us a way to save ourselves, each other and the planet by accelerating our evolution so that those with eyes to see and ears to hear, the best among us, can both

see and hear more clearly. And take action in concert to address the problems we all face.

The problem is survival, nothing less than how we can find the ways and means to develop and articulate potential solutions to issues that not only haunt us, but threaten our continued existence.

When existence itself is at stake anything is possible, anything can be achieved, and who knows what can be accomplished by a dedicated band of researchers. And the awakening of awareness and conscience.

And an educated population aware of the issues, mindful of the deadly consequences of delay and obfuscation, ready to vote the rascals out of office whose mindless inaction only adds to the difficulty and willfully ignores the consequences.

Nothing will change unless we, the people, change our way of thinking by incorporating the values and message that true spirituality brings into the discussion through our own informed thoughts and effective actions.

Or we go extinct, not because nature selected us for extinction, but because one by one, we and the ruling powers that be have eliminated our chances for survival through sheer stupidity.

We have ruled the roost for so long, and had our way to such an extent that we have categorically demonstrated our unfitness for stewardship of the planet. Our loyalties can be bought, our allegiance allied to selfish self-interest, and our commitment, not to human progress and the demands of matured identity, but to economic security and political safety.

We are a relatively young species, often extremely immature in our decision-making processes. We are subject to inferior influences, often unable to overcome the burden of

unmotivated fear and emotional insecurity that inflects almost everything we do and every action we take.

This is profoundly unnerving to the noble picture we would prefer to paint of our self-image, and of course there are exceptions. Even so, by enlarged it is an accurate summary.

We may be heading down the road of virtual extinction if we keep poisoning everything in the natural world because of economic greed, political totalitarianism, religious intolerance and the destructive force of hatred in all its forms.

More than enough to destroy our chances for survival, at a time in our history when we have multiple means of destroying ourselves in a world-wide mutually-assured suicide pact as nation after nation plays off the vulnerabilities of its neighbors for its own advantage.

Trading bombs with each other instead of a peaceful exchange of views is not a good trade or a profitable way of doing business in the matter of survival. In the long run, what we are engaging in is immature thinking.

Rash actions, provocations that result from destructive impulses, and the expansion of basically imperialistic policies on all sides may prove to be of value to no one when they result in inflamed passions and declarations of war.

War, the most insane activity of which we are capable. We are no longer in charge of our destiny when our elected leaders are not really elected, but chosen by unknown powers whose motives may also be unknown. But which might generally be supposed to be in their own private or corporate interests. Even war can turn a profit for the war profiteers.

We have so relatively little say in the electoral process, from nominating candidates on down to funding their campaigns that we hardly have any ability to correct what is being done to the democratic process. Other than mourn for what we have lost, and for what has been taken from us.

Nor have we much to say about the hidden loyalties of our elected officials, what they owe and to whom they owe it. Whose interests they serve, to what influences they respond, what they truly believe and who, really, do they serve. Not us, certainly not we, the people.

This is fast becoming our permanent reality, and we all know it. *We know it*. But it is also true that we have done relatively little to change that process. Not that these changes have flown beneath the radar of our collective conscience, or that very many of us have been engaged in political activity other than to bemoan our fate over a cup of coffee or a glass of beer.

We have heroes and heroines among us, but not enough to change the system and fight against the corruption that has infested the American political process. Unless the voice of American justice emerges from under the blanket of invisibility that has covered it in recent decades, and rings out loud and clear in this land of liberty.

Which is in danger of being destroyed from within by corporate mercenaries, and the endless and constant barrage of intimidation in every form that threatens our fundamental freedoms. Even the liberty to voice opposition.

We are in danger of becoming a totalitarian state, one among many in this brave, new world of economic fascism run by international cartels flying under corporate flags but with private loyalties to a relative handful of powerful people. Like dominos falling one by one until their perfect alignment of economic servitude is the very cause of their downfall. One after another they topple over in despair and defeat.

The world is in danger of falling on its face as international plundering by international plunderers picks over the dried-out bones of fallen and ripe-for-the-pickings nation states. They use their economic, political and legal powers to bully the vulnerable, intimidating them into economic slavery.

And we will then reach a world-wide condition of such concentrated financial power that a new age of medieval feudalism will begin. And formerly-independent nation states will become little more than economic vassals in the hands of their international financial overlords.

The experiment in freedom and democratic traditions has been exploited by those who act only in their own interests. We are in danger now of becoming unwilling and unknowing servants of multi-national forces seeking world domination through the power of economic repression and suppression.

Financial power is an international legalized weapon of mass destruction, and legislative action on an inter-national basis will legally ensure the risen of a world-wide police state of unfathomable power and control.

This horror may well be in our near-immediate future unless we wake up to the danger, rub the sleep out of our eyes and take action before action is legislated out of existence.

This has all the earmarks of an enormous crisis sneaking up on us year after year, in one country after another, through each offensive action taken in defense of 'liberty' after the preceding one. And limiting our rights until, under this new wave of legislative imperialism, we will no longer have any rights left to defend.

It is a nearly invisible process, precipitated by faceless and souless political and economic mercenaries whose allegiance has long-since been bought and paid for by their masters.

Anonymous all, as are their masters, but more powerful in the effects they produce than the government officials they helped to elect. And in the process forced their will on the people. They serve, not at the pleasure of the people, but on the orders of their handlers.

This could not be accomplished in a spiritually-enlivened atmosphere in which our priorities were in appropriate order. And our allegiance was to the growth and maturity of our species as a whole, rather than to selected portions of the financial elite and social hierarchy.

This is not the direction in which we should be moving, not into economic slavery and subjugation by international corporate forces that seek world domination through the legislation of financial restrictions, with international trade agreements that set the terms and conditions of our slavery.

Spiritual self-knowledge is the most effective solution to these problems, the most long-lasting way we can overcome the barriers of fear and insecurity. And band together in mutual assurance for purposes related to the common good.

When we know who we are, what we are about, from where we have come and where we are going there will be nothing to hide and little to fear merely on account of the difference of an opinion.

Difference among us will most likely always exist, but they need not lead to war and there need not always be warmongers. And there also need not be the hatred that comes about when we are suspicious of our neighbors or dissatisfied with this, that or something else.

Hatred towards strangers will no longer have a secure base of operation within our psyche, within our psychological awareness or our anxious assumptions about existence. We may no longer find ourselves dancing in the dark while all about us there are things that go bump in the night.

Two

Things that go bump in the night

We have no time left to continue in our old ways, for the powers that would-be seek world control and their domination will no longer leave us alone. They have gathered, concentrated, and are all about us. *If we have eyes to see and ears to hear,* we can see them and their minions on the march.

We will face challenges to our freedom, our health and our economic stability on every side, and many of us will be confused by unfamiliar tactics that seek to exploit the confusion they have created.

To such an extreme degree that some of us may no longer be able to tell the difference between friend and foe, while others will confuse populist rhetoric for truth-telling. Even when it comes out of the mouths of those who are least suited for popular support, and most guilty themselves of the crimes and misdemeanors they shamelessly accuse others of committing. Diverting attention from themselves.

The power of the people to create and enforce change when we act together, in brotherhood and sisterhood, is a force to be reckoned with and the way of the future. If we have not lost that essential spirit of democracy that sustained our founding fathers, and inspired the most brilliant political writings in history.

But that future may be a long way off if we do not begin now, and it is beginning to look as though many of us are on

an extended vacation from reality. These are themes that visionaries in every field of human activity have envisioned and promoted for many years, but may be falling now on tone deaf ears considering the volume of insincere and politically-motivated populist rhetoric.

The seeds of freedom have been here for a very long time, planted deeply in our psyche, waiting to germinate and unfold in our collective consciousness.

If we will act in our best interests now and avoid the delay and obfuscation that results only in stagnation, we can find the inner strength and determination to act in concert in meaningful cause. To act in responsible ways and overcome the challenges of economic totalitarianism and environmental destruction that awaits us all.

There is no escaping this conclusion, nowhere to run, no place to hide our heads in fear and shame, even in our dreams. We cannot live in our dreams, but we can make them happen if we are determined to succeed. Unless we prefer to keep dreaming, which so many of us choose to do.

But when we awaken we must live in reality, *that which is*, and our reality is in serious danger and threatened from all directions. Wake up, which we are still able to do as long as we have the opportunity to escape the dismal possibilities that are gathering energy and waiting for their day in the sun.

We are falling asleep at the wheel to so much of what is going on around us that it nearly justifies the claim by a noted scientist that human beings are nothing much more than lumbering robots.

We so often function in an automatic mode or semi-automatic fashion, similar to the way we drive a car when we adjust the wheel automatically, without consciously thinking about what we are doing. Paying almost no conscious attention to the mechanical details of what we are doing, aware in a fashion, but unaware that we are aware.

Familiarity may occasionally breed a kind of non-specific contempt, but a more frequent occurrence occurs when we tend to lose the spontaneous involvement and appreciation of the absolute wonder of existence. And our ability to live in a free, healthy and joyful engagement with reality.

The sights and sounds of the material world are a truly breath-taking adventure when we are conscious of who we are and what we are doing on this pleasure planet, amid this nearly infinite garden of existence.

We lose sight of this as we unconsciously go about the daily business of living. And it will be gone forever if we allow those who seek ownership of the entire planet for themselves to succeed. With the rest of us bound in chains of every type and variety. This is not an appealing idea unless we are comfortable in chains.

When we take our freedoms for granted, as many of us do, and take the breathless beauty and overwhelming splendors of nature equally for granted, their loss, as we begin to lose each of them one by one, little by little, will pass nearly unnoticed beneath our conscious level of attention. We will see without truly seeing; hear without truly hearing. We will continue to speak, but our words will be empty of meaning: bland, pointless, powerless and with no redeeming qualities.

Or if some of us do notice it, we might just let it pass with a shrug of helplessness. No big deal, we will think with the recognition that we are essentially powerless to oppose changes that disenfranchise us from power.

And we may become forgetful, after significant time has passed since we knew what life was like before we adapted to the chains that had now bound us to our invisible overlords. We might not even notice the absence of the extraordinary beauty of the material world, which we will no longer be able to enjoy because of the bars on our prison cell windows limiting the view.

In a terribly inevitable way, this would almost appear to be a predictably automatic outcome if we do not pay attention to the actions of those among us who seek power and control at any price.

We have the numbers in terms of the general populace, but they have money and power. And the loyalty of those, in the words of the Roman Emperor Claudius according to Robert Graves, *who would sell their souls for the tail-end of an anchovy.*

Our individual duties and responsibilities all too often submerge us in the necessities of fulfilling whatever requirements are demanded of us, and which inevitably engage our full attention.

But as a direct result, our attention is diverted from the larger stage around us. We lose touch with the fundamental experiences of existence, the tactile, sensory relationship with organic life. And we will also have destroyed our imaginative abilities to create new experiences and novel alternatives to familiar patterns. Our habits, not life, become the reality in which we live unsustainable yet unchangeable.

Our imagination will atrophy through misuse or lack of use, dulled as though by novocaine. Our physical senses no longer a source of joy and pleasure, without our even recognizing the loss until it is upon us, leading our lives indeed as lumbering robots.

If we can become so unconscious to the beauty in which we live, what wonder then that we also pay so little attention to the freedoms that once we took for granted. And the dangers that confront us as well, which some of us have become too bloated with pointless diversions and miniscule self-satisfactions to notice loom larger than ever on the horizon.

Time only serves to emphasize those dangers when we sense the sands of time are running out. And we as well,

running away from the stress and anxiety of contemporary existence.

And that is the power of strict fundamentalism and mindless conservatism, the attempt to reverse the flow of time by the futile attempt to return to an earlier time when difficult questions had quick and easy answers. Or so we imagine, those of us who think in this childish way.

An imaginary time of stability through mental inertia and the willful giving over of control. A time of narrow sensibilities strictly enforced. A time in which power is concentrated in the hands of the few, while the many are content to remain sheltered in their own imaginary castles. In which they are only-imaginary lords of the realm, temporarily ensconced in their mortgaged lives.

A time that never actually was but might well come into being when the fevered imaginations of those who cannot live in the present moment with present-day realities give themselves over to the dark dreams of those who can. Those who cannot live in the reality of whatever time brings are fated to suffer, and suffer they will.

But no matter how often, or in how many ways we are reminded of this by those whose job it is to remind us of our fate, there is ultimately no time left now to stall or delay. Or endorse political obfuscation and similar tactics because we cannot find an easy way out of our dilemmas.

We may not like or approve of what we have, but if we do not take a hand in the deal we lose our right to complain. And we will have to get used to accepting the consequences, whatever they turn out to be.

We need a miracle, *a hand in time,* before our time run out. If we can send our fellow humans flying through space in a tiny tin can, land on the moon and leaves our footprints in moon dust, can we not create our own miracles here on earth.

Do we no longer have it in us to change the face of our deteriorating reality and live in preparation for the needs of tomorrow, which we must prepare for today.

As a society we have become bloated on our own past successes, so some social critics maintain. And when that happens it suggests that we have lost the energy, confidence, desire and momentum that earned previous generations those victories.

Those are the qualities that prompted our ancestors, with great urgency, to seek out and face challenges everywhere with the necessary emphasis to succeed. Their continued health and well-being, their very lives, depended on them succeeding. And succeed they did.

We have reached the point that we are consciously avoiding the current circumstances of our lives that desperately need to be addressed. But instead of taking the bull by the horns, as pioneering generations had to do along with the necessity of self-responsibility, we have inexorably been ceding power and authority to those who serve, not in our interests, but in the interests of the high and the mighty.

Our tendency now has been to content ourselves with what we have, or what little we have, rather than venture forth into unknown territories and risk the dangers of the unknown for a better life. We have lost the pioneering spirit that once made us great, and we have stalled in all manner of ways.

Middle age spread significantly reduces the athletic abilities we now only dimly remember of our youth, even sending us off on a downward-sloping path that encourages only inertia, sloth and a reluctance to engage in active life.

Our visionary capabilities and imaginative hopes for projects of note, or adventures that stimulate and encourage us to cross over strange borders into unknown territory, have gone underground and are nowhere now to be seen. We have grown stale and weary, where once we felt safe and secure.

A few of us are waiting for our own second coming before we can even begin to feel alive again, for surely something is waiting to be come to life within us. Something out of time, something unaffected by the deadliness and lifelessness of inertia and stagnation.

A renaissance, perhaps, of thinking and feeling, when our old patterns of thinking and feeling are refreshed and revitalized in accordance with some great visionary experience. However that might occur does not really matter as long as it does. Some new fact, a fuller understanding or reinterpretation of existence that comes in like a hurricane and takes us all by storm.

We may all be waiting for that rebirth of conscience and creativity now, like a modern-day phoenix rising out of the fiery ashes of its own innate self-destructive impulses.

The stasis in which we are now stuck may be running out of the last few remaining vestiges of energy that has sustained its inertia, a closed energy system running out of steam.

Which signals that change is coming, if not already here. What that change will be, and if it will be in the best interests of all concerned, is a matter of visionary abilities and a well-defined sense of reality

In this dimension time reflects change, like a giant pendulum is carried in the direction of one arc of its swing by its own momentum, from one extreme to the other, until the momentum runs out of energy. And stasis ensues.

The internal changes our culture has been undergoing may represent an extreme shift in direction towards repression of the creative imagination in all the varied forms through which it is experienced. Time will tell, but the signs are already here.

The enormous changes in our culture, the clashes that have occurred in recent years between various groups that identify with one particular cause or another, along with the endless

conflicts that have made warfare a constant and perpetual presence in our lives have all contributed to destabilizing what once appeared to be, but in reality was not, a healthy, stable and secure culture. We know it and we resent it. And there may be worse to come. We have lost the feeling of safety, and the security and confidence that comes with being a pre-eminent and admired world culture.

What once was unthinkable has now become reality. It has shaken our society to its core, and given fascist powerbrokers an opening to stake their claim in world affairs, both here and abroad. Virtual reality is not an acceptable substitute for life.

There is no future in that for the mass of mankind, for *nothing beside remains of that colossal wreck*, no towering architectural monuments, no glorious new works of art, and most significantly, no thirst for new experiences or hunger to seek out adventures. And that has shaken our self-image, along with our economic viability.

Nothing but the futile attempt to hold on to whatever we individually have by any means. Even if need be by repression of freedom, or suppression of the creative impulse if in any way, real or imaginary, it appears to threaten a way of life that can no longer be sustained by its own momentum. We may be a culture that is running out of steam.

Civilizations begin to deteriorate from within and crumble from without of their own weight, lack of ambition, loss of courage and failure of nerve. And when competing civilizations begin to take stock of their own strengths and act on their own ambitions, Rome is once again invaded when the barbarians are at the gates.

Cultures rise then fall when they run out of the energy that once activated their ambitions and fueled their progress. And when people begin to lose touch with the ideals and aspirations that first inspired them to action, the downhill slide begins. They content themselves with playing in the

ruins that surround them, rather than starting over and building anew.

We in the western world may fast be approaching the apex of our swing unless we find a way to sustain ourselves by either new adventures or artificial means of preservation. Repression in any form is one indication that artificial means are being employed to keep the ship of state from sinking, the rest of us treading water and still afloat.

Nevertheless, our influence in world affairs is still so overpowering that the west is most likely not in immediate danger of collapsing, as the Roman Empire died to its previous form before morphing into its current state in present-day Rome.

But if one day, for whatever reason, western culture should begin to collapse, it would very likely initiate a world-wide momentum from which there would be no escape for anyone for generations to come, if at all.

The rise and fall of empires throughout history has been documented many times by eminent scholars, well researched and well written. What is consistent in their reports appears to be that once a civilization falls it is never resuscitated in the same form, never resumes its former place in history in the same shape, the same manner or with the same influence.

There is a fundamental lesson for us in that, and we must remain aware, if uncomfortably so, that we may be in danger of losing the energy, influence and momentum that enabled us to rise to our present state of comfort and prominence.

If the current state of education of our young people, especially in mathematics and science, is an indication of the state of their enthusiasm for the wonders of exploration and adventure, then we are very possibly heading for a sorry state of affairs, if not already there.

Many of us are not enthusiastic about science and the technological miracles that have come our way, and many of us have long since given up on our mathematical education.

It might be also true that many of our young people, as a general rule of thumb, have fallen far behind many other more progressive world cultures in their academic progress other than passing general exams and the like. *Would you like fries with that sir?* might very likely become a standard refrain in their job resumes and direct work environment after high school.

It appears that many have gone no further than that in their imaginations, demonstrating a profound lack of appetite for education at higher levels. But more significantly, lacking in enthusiasm for science and technology. Not all by any means, but enough so that in the general state of affairs it makes a difference.

The challenges of the many rapidly growing fields of scientific research are breath-taking and awe-inspiring. But to succeed in these areas of study demands that students be dedicated, alert, disciplined, intelligent, determined and awake to the challenges of the adventure of scientific discovery.

One does not generally prepare oneself for a career in science by proficiency in video gaming, social media expertise or the many possibilities for mastering the intrigues of Rubik's Cube.

A life devoted to personal pleasure and anonymous Internet companionship my not lead to a life of discovery and achievement in ways that will last longer and be of more use that yesterday's headlines.

This is clearly obvious, and so why is it that the same standards of responsible academic behavior do not apply to our familiar traditions of religious education and training. What exactly is the evolutionary point of conventional

Bronze Age themed religious education? How far from the tree does the fruit fall before it rots?

Why really is it we so easily content ourselves with the false comfort that tends only to reinforce our separate identities from the source of all being. Traditional stereotypical concepts keep us in isolation from the divine, instead of teaching practices and offering techniques that affirm the true nature of mankind and the spiritual state of affairs. And the true nature of our consciousness, our inner identification with infinite spirit.

Is it a question of spiritual sloth and sheer laziness that keeps us in the shadow of our enlightenment, especially when the demands of material being take up so much of our time and energy. We hardly even have time for a little fun. A standard response, but also a standard cop out. Most of us are quite simply not interested in higher consciousness.

That might be because of the way religious institutions have been set up. Their internal structures and dogmas reflect something more akin to a power-structured corporate headquarters, with authority coming from the top down instead of from the inside out.

But not an educational organization whose purpose is the transformation of consciousness, resulting in the enlightenment of as many as possible. This is the mystical approach, and it is hard to fundraise for that when potential donors might expect something more along traditional lines of architectural improvements or social programs. All to the good perhaps, but also all avoiding the essential nature of spiritual progress and progressive enlightenment.

We are not set up to learn by current standards concerning the education of the spirit. We are set up to learn what institutional thinking wants us to learn. To obey when commands are given and orders are issued. To follow the leader and the direction of appointed authority, but not leaders chosen by us. We, the people.

And where we are lead is only within the spiritual prison of conventional religious rules, traditions, dogmatic regulations, and the various forms of theological mind control that eliminate unconventional or alternate ideas as against the wishes of the institution. So far, the divine has not yet made its preferences known in the matter of personal freedom, unless free will is the eleventh commandment. *Thou shalt have free will.*

Spirit is free or is meant to be, but when we follow the inarticulate and inchoate rules that other people have devised for their own purposes, according to their own beliefs, and concordantly sanctify them with names representing spiritual authority, we are no longer free to be ourselves. We are slaves to fashion and fashion's God, whatever the times demand and chance or opportunity sets down on the table before us.

And then there is the matter of the direction in which we are guided, which tend to place undue emphasis on the institutions of this world and the standards which the social world applies. And are generally meant to accelerate their economic stability and worldly success, but not necessarily ours. Institutions may survive their times, but people do not.

We have few options available to us when we follow a path so many have traveled and achieved nothing for their efforts. The Silk Road we follow in traditional religious studies, and the caravan in which we travel, makes no unscheduled stops for spiritual refreshment. And all too often worships at the subtle and hidden altars of sex and gold.

If we have become dissatisfied with our general progress in terms of the enlightenment of our hearts and minds, and our soul's progress through time, we will have to stop our daydreaming. Which very likely is what we may be doing.

We will have to take stock of where we are, what we are doing, what we ultimately want, and then simply get on with it. Stop the stalling. Turn the computer off, turn off the television, unhook the cable wire. And meditate.

Which might very well mean leaving the caravan for a bit if it has become top heavy with the baggage of despair and disillusion, until we are firmly established in a new and productive spiritual practice. Overloaded with material goods, dreaming of increased possessions, overwhelmed by desire. Ambitions that grant us no peace

Is it up to us to determine the path we want to travel when it comes to our spiritual interests, or do we leave that for others to decide, higher religiously-contrived authorities whose hands, not ours, are in control.

A question each age must decide for itself, that we must decide for ourselves, or a question already answered and decided for us by those higher authorities whose authority is not for us to question. Or so they say.

Where we go and what we do is generally assumed to be our own business, our fate in our own hands, as is what we choose to study and how we earn our living.

Do those same assumptions not apply as well to our religious interests and the direction of our spiritual studies. Are we to be bound to the supposed authority of appointed officials in this regard, unable to study what interests us on our own without prior ecclesiastical consent and approval.

At what point in our evolutionary journey do we spread our own spiritual wings, take charge of our own evolution, study what we want and learn what interests us. And fly where before we had only meekly stood in line, bowed our heads and supplicated before clay idols and stony statues.

The journey we must ultimately make is not out there, it is within, to the source of all being, the consciousness of universal being, so that we can meet ourselves, the self as it truly is. And then meet others where they are, with the same purpose of engendered endearment.

Too much is at stake before we dare risk crossing the borders of enclosed humanity, much less inter-species encounters in space. Too many of us are in a state of emotional insecurity, weighed down by immature and feckless general attitudes.

We must face up to where and what we really see when we gaze into the mirror, unnerving as that might be. And potentially so self-shattering that it is a wonder the collective mirror does not crack from the weight of our reflection.

And we might reflect on that as we read the day's headlines, and take in the immediate and full impact of what our collective activities have been, where they have led us, and what our leaders are doing, if anything, to get us out of the mess that has been made that we are always having to clean up at our own expense. And never quite manage to do.

Spiritual advancement is not compulsory, or a required course in any field of study. And not necessarily so in formal religious training either. It is a voluntary activity, free will in action, and there is no question but that it makes its demands.

To follow seriously the footprints of a genuine spiritual tradition requires the utmost of our attention and devotion, along with the demands it makes that cannot easily be satisfied by token demonstrations of faith or faithless supplications in support of our earnestness.

Progress is what is called for, the only evidence that matters, not pacifying rituals of adornment or elementary rites of passage that entertain no further notions of spiritual integrity or advancement in self-knowledge.

Beyond the redistricting of our wants and desires along less conventional lines of possession, spiritual enlightenment calls for the transformation of consciousness itself. Even beyond the rudimentary levels of consciousness on which so many of us seem to be permanently encamped, and which so few of us have advanced beyond.

Spiritual stagnation has unquestionably become a permanent fixture of the interior landscape, and it is fast becoming a nightmare as it deteriorates to extraordinary low levels of extraordinarily confused fundamentalism. A nightmare from which all of us must awaken, but in which many of us appear to be trapped. Misery longs for company.

World-wide forces of repression, whose weapons in this regard are regressive social and political attitudes, often preached from dubious pulpits as holy writ, are intent on spreading their message to center stage. Even infiltrating the educational arena, inflecting prejudicial and immature educational standards in all fields with the simple beliefs of a child-like religious fundamentalism that denies the verifiable findings of science.

Which will set the evolutionary clock back five hundred years as they hold center stage and monologue the issues. Center stage they want, and they are intent on holding it by any means available for purposes that will inevitably bring on another intellectual and social dark age. And resulting from that process of infinite regression, the world-wide nightmare of a dark night of the soul.

So dismal a scenario as this *is* being thrust at us, not necessarily as an expression of religious fundamentalism on its own merits as has generally been supposed. Although that is the flag under which it generally flies, there is more hidden than has been publically revealed. It is simple political opportunism skillfully enacted by greedy forces of economic imperialism with their own private agendas.

It may perhaps also result in the incredible frustration so many of us are now feeling, that they have no secure and rightful place in a world they do not understand, a world they never made.

They live in an economic/political system in which they feel disenfranchised, and a world of technological progress

which they do not understand and in which they feel they are inept, unnecessary, untrained and even insignificant.

It frightens them, and they are mad. They want to return to a safer world, a world with conditions and containers in which people of differences are set apart and do not have to interact. A world in which inherited privilege endures and rules.

But if they are aware, each knows and keeps his place and adheres to those conditions. They want to return to a vanished world of simple ideas, elementary thoughts, and common diversions of harmless amusements where troubles melt like lemon drops. A world that never existed, and never will.

In a sense, they have been banished from the marketplace of ideas by the ongoing advances of science, historical scholarship, and technological progress which they are unable to comprehend on their own.

And the continuing revelation that what skills they have by which they might have gotten along several generations ago, are now anachronisms in the business community, unneeded and unwanted as are they themselves.

They are laborers now, nothing more, and it has cost them their dignity. Left behind, they have become mere pawns in the world-wide economic systems that worship a separate god, one who in ancient days was known as Mammon, the devil of covetousness.

Religious hypocrites generally try to persuade themselves, as they attempt to persuade others, that the god they worship is a god of love. While the more Regan and Goneril-like among them proclaim in ringing tones their absolute devotion in terms of near-total enslavement and near-total love to a mythical incarnation of their version of the divine presence.

But when their social, political and religious rhetoric includes expressions of contempt, verbal abuse and sheer hatred for others of different political views, social attitudes, economic achievement, religious preference or sundry and essentially meaningless distractions such as skin color or food preferences, it is not the god of infinite love they worship but the adversary.

There are only two fundamental choices in this world of duality, love or fear. It all comes down to one or the other. According to some eastern teachings, all emotions begin their original impulse in an expression of either love or fear, hence hatred, and gradually descend to their various and multitudinous forms. But they are all subtle variations of the original impulse.

Hatred in any of its secondary forms can neither be tolerated nor justified in accordance with any spiritual principles of modern-day sensibilities. But uncomfortable as we may be in admitting this, the sensibilities of Bronze Age people may not have been as enlightened as we would hope or believe. Why would their thoughts be more evolved than ours, or is faith enough to justify a conventional non-answer.

Many forms of hate can easily be found in biblical writings, many forms of intolerance, destruction, slavery, state-sponsored murder and open warfare even encouraged. True, it would be incorrect and unfair to take those events out of their biblical context, or ignore the conditions that applied in those times.

But still, biblical events that would or should not be tolerated today by more enlightened minds might need further explication than has traditionally been given. And clearly should not be seen as biblically-sanctioned spiritual approval for overt acts of war or hatred.

In much the same way, the horrible events at Hiroshima and Nagasaki that ended World War Two should never be seen as a blanket endorsement to use nuclear weapons, but

understood in terms of the necessity of the times. It may be a matter of debate if the use of those weapons was justified, but the debate should include the context of the times, not that of latter generations.

Any extremely destructive or negative emotional responses to life could never be justified as the word of God, and there are many who are absolutely confident that violence for its own sake is never advocated by genuine spiritual teachings in any tradition. Not necessarily in agreement by those who defend violence in the name of their religious beliefs, but not necessarily in the name of God.

Explanations for biblical violence vary, and biblical exegeses roam all over the landscape. But for those who are concerned with moral implications and the consequences, it might be helpful to think of man and his works as an unfinished work of art from the hands of a celestial creative force, metaphorically speaking.

Divine inspiration in the manner of an ancient Greek rhapsode may be as useful, and accurate, a manner of biblical interpretation as any other. While not in denial of the spiritual values of biblical teachings, those ancient Bronze Age books of religious pseudo-history might also be considered to be unfinished works of art as well.

Generation after generation has worked hard to bridge the gaps by excavating and then revealing additional truths of existence from the spiritual domain. Revelation can come in many forms, and by no means are finished with teachings that are still to come from the far side of eternity.

Here it is necessary to emphasis that conjecture is not evidence, speculation is not revelation, and biblical exegesis is open to many levels of interpretation and separate modes of understanding.

The deeper we go, the more is revealed and the greater our understanding. Such that what we learnt on a more literal and

shallow level takes on a much greater depth of understanding and spiritual maturity when interpreted in a more sophisticated manner. And according to better evidence than simply word of mouth.

It has frequently been said that we are taught according to the level of our understanding and our ability to learn. And conversely, we understand according to what we have been taught and the level of the teaching.

Viveka, a Hindu term for discrimination, is said to be among the first, if not the first, principle we must learn on a spiritual path. We must seek out, study and choose the path we wish to follow. And we must choose wisely lest we discover, after considerable time has passed, that we have placed our ladder against the wrong house and climbed to the top of the wrong roof.

If this is what some of us are or have been in the process of discovering, the painful recognition is waiting for us that it is due to our lack of discrimination, for whatever reason notwithstanding. We have wasted our opportunities and that most precious of resources. Time.

Our time here is more precious than gold, and once gone, the same experiences here of classroom Earth may not come again when our lifetime ends. There are hard choices to make when our suspicions are aroused about the usefulness of any form of religious orthodoxy in our private lives, or when the tradition to which we adhere comes under scrutiny. This will most likely be a lonely battle we fight as we engage in silent inter-mural debate with the many voices in our heads in conflict with each other.

Armed forces will clash by day and skirmish at night in endless warfare as we debate with our various selves the meaning of this or that, the implications of one way of interpreting something over another. And the spiritual slaughter that could result, or the direction we might take that most satisfies our minds and hearts.

This can be and very often is a bitter battle, often with no clear resolution so that is might be fought many times in many ways. When emotions are involved and loyalties are questioned or thrown open for debate, our inherited traditions may take a beating in the process, may occasionally be abandoned, and we begin the education of our spirit anew.

The deeper our understanding of ourselves the deeper our understanding of spirit. And the more we understand of other traditions, particularly the esoteric and eastern traditions based on Advaita, non-duality, that the soul is not different from God, the better we might understand that all the distemperate theorizing we engage in is simply indulging in our continuously recurring cyclical patterns of behavior.

We constantly repeat that famous formulation *God is One*. If that is so, as has generally been supposed, then again, in its essence that is the generic principle of Advaita, non-duality. Nothing there is that cannot be apart from God, including we ourselves. If indeed *God is One*.

And it must therefore be true, if that basic premise is correct, that the true function of religious studies should not be focused on establishing a relationship with a purely mythic idea of a celestial diety, that which is wholly other.

Otherness implies something with which there can be no points in common, and therefore there cannot be any relationship of personal identity. There can only be separation.

This will not do if we stop to consider our options. Are we to believe that the universe is set up as a master-slave relationship, an inscrutable force of existence against which there can only be independent origination.

And no sense of identity that we have come out of the universe in the natural course of events, and are children of the creative force of existence. The very opposite of what we have traditionally been taught in the west.

We have been taught that in essence we are merely toys which the creator is said to love, but who demonstrates that His love is strange, unpredictable and often displayed in picayune ways about which we have little or nothing to say. Much less understand.

No, the true value of religious studies cannot merely be in the study of religious history. It must be, if God is One, to find the God-force within our own being. And that too is Advaita, non-duality, and must be experienced to be understood and appreciated. Enlightenment is for all.

Appreciation is too mild a word here because the true description for this process of self-recognition is enlightenment. The most glorious achievement of which mankind is capable, which supersedes all other dimensions of experience and fields of knowledge.

In this regard we are compulsive under-achievers, contenting ourselves as lambs when we might be shepherds. *Why be content to be nothing, when there's nothing you couldn't be?*, a lyrical refrain from "Kismet," a Broadway musical of long-ago.

A haunting refrain, a deeply thoughtful Broadway koan, one that encapsulates the spirit of human potential, offering us a landmark direction in which to head our caravan in our evolutionary journey. And the fulfillment of our spiritual ambitions.

We are all fellow-travelers on the path of self-knowledge. And where that ultimately leads, if we are willing to listen to the words of those who have gone before us, the spiritual masters of history, we may find is within our own hearts. We may find ourselves in contact with a greater glory than we have ever known, or could ever have imagined. *And we, dear ones, are that.*

THREE

A greater glory

We sometimes think of ourselves as small and meek when we are troubled or filled with doubt, intimidated strangers in the Land of Oz. Where miraculous events occur, difficulties abound, and strange sights reveal themselves before our startled eyes.

And yet the magical encounter we anticipate with the mighty wizard turns out to be nothing more than an encounter with innocent fraud and inept deception by those who are themselves troubled and filled with doubt.

Or so we imagine when the mighty wizard is revealed to be just another myth, a simple man pulling chains and grabbing levers behind a flimsy curtain, hoping himself for a miracle to come his way and deliver him from an unwanted fate.

But in the movie, all Dorothy had to do was think of home, click her heels three times and back she went on her return trip to her true home.

Would that we all might do the same thing, find our own Shangri-La by clicking our heels three times and returning to the source of all being from whence we came. If only we knew where and what that was, and how we might book passage on that return voyage.

But just as the good witch Glinda told Dorothy that she always had the power to return home, so too we as well have consistently been informed of the same thing by our elder

brothers and sisters of high spiritual attainment. We have always had the power to find our true home, the source of our being, which is always and ever within us.

The enlightenment of our soul promises us infinitely more than a return trip to Kansas. It offers us the secrets of inner illumination, the descent of grace until our awareness consciously radiates with original nature, now fully cognizant and mindful of itself in the earthly realm.

The bliss of being in corporeal existence, the fulfillment of our earthly affairs in material reality and the promise of what things may come when we return to our original state as pure, conscious energy.

But energy is too vague a word to be anything more than a convenient metaphorical analogy. And at this point in our evolution, any attempt to define consciousness in such vague, insubstantial and indefinable terms as 'energy' might be a mistaken or misleading notion.

What consciousness is and how it comes about is unknown, but that knowledge is not of critical importance in practicing a spiritual technique. The only thing that matters is that we *do* practice a spiritual technique leading to transcendence.

We must find a way to shed our doubts, cast aside our fears, love everybody and everything as the incarnation of the divine presence, and let go of our perpetual need for control. In that way we will find ourselves in love with the divine force and serving the Creator, which is to serve the creation, in which we are an integral part. We are one way in which the God-force knows itself.

There will come a point for each of us when we will finally begin to realize that try as we may, we are not ultimately in control of anything much beyond what we will eat today and what we will wear tomorrow. And even that might change. We never have been, and never will be in total control of

anything. That is the illusion that takes us by the hand and leads us down the garden path.

We are temporary occupants on a revolving organic spaceship, traveling through our own galaxy among the infinitude of star systems, just as we always wanted to do when we were children. Only not in fancy tin cans with gadgets and wings as we once imagined. On our own planet!

Not at all what we imagined, although traveling on a life-sustaining planet with its own food and water supply, its own air, in a beautiful landscape with seasonal variations and flora and fauna beyond compare is not such an inconvenient way to fly through space. And there is one other advantage as we continue our space voyage, and that is we are also traveling through time.

We are time travelers, not from outside of time, or jumping backwards and forwards from this point to that, but traveling lineally with time marking the way for the full benefit of the adventure. Enjoying the actual experience of being in time and exploring three-dimensional space. A trip to Disneyland for the soul, which each of us must experience from within.

With time functioning as the fourth dimension of our experience. We are voyagers moving through time, visitors from eternity intent on exploring and experiencing this reality and the challenges of material existence within a physical body.

What a glorious way to look at our human experience and an even greater glory awaiting us. Not as the small and weak, meek and mild, timid and afraid frail creatures that lived in fear and huddled together for warmth and shelter in the backs of cold, damp caves that once we were.

Fear takes a hand and changes the foundation of our being in the template of our earthly experience, inflecting everything we think about and do with its disruptive colorations and machinations.

When fear takes us by the hand, strangers in a strange land that we are, we are being deceived. Not by a mythical great deceiver in rebellion against God, but by our own limited nature that has been corrupted by danger and illusion. Deception is an enemy that often pretends to be a friend.

Fear uses time as an unwitting ally, pretending that the inexorable pressures of time force us to take shortcuts around time when we must face an issue and take action. We have no time to do anything else but follow the dictates of wherever fear may lead us. But then face the consequences. In time.

Fear promises us its way is better than any other because time is too short to inform ourselves properly of the alternatives, and the full measure of the issues involved. But in truth, there are no shortcuts through time, no shortcuts about anything when they might very well lead us through a potentially explosive minefield, or over a hidden patch of quicksand.

Time is the invisible clock ticking away in the background of our lives. But no matter how we may try to take a detour around time we cannot avoid reality, and reality will not accept shortcuts or give up any of its demands. Karma will see to that, if not in this life then in the next.

There are no shortcuts to eternity, no stairway to heaven, no roadmaps to enlightenment with unmarked side streets that will help get us there faster. Nothing that can help us escape the tick-tick-tock of the hands of time ticking away in the background, the celestial alarm clock.

We must either take a conscious and principled evolutionary stand, or make-do with what we have and where we are. But we will not move faster through time to our evolutionary rendezvous, we will instead simply stagnate in time. And once again, miss the main chance.

Fear leads us only to waste time, stalling and delaying as we heed the call to retreat when trouble looms. We may listen to

its clarion call and urgent entreaties, its plots and plans, its schemes and shibboleths. But we will still stagnate.

When we listen to the voice of fear, when we give in to its machinations that force us to deviate from our spiritual path we rob ourselves of our opportunities. And when we do that, we also cheat ourselves out of our rightful time here on Earth.

Our precious time here on Earth is meant to realize what we came here to achieve, to actualize what is in our destiny to achieve. Fear will only destroy our opportunities to advance if we give in to its presence and hide from the light.

Why would we trust fear to guide us? And why would we ignore the entreaties of divine love to join with it in the reality of its presence, establish our own presence in enlightened consciousness, and free ourselves from the needs, anxieties and from the terrors that have plagued mankind from time immemorial.

The only thing we have to fear is fear itself, proclaimed Franklin Delano Roosevelt in his 1933 Inaugural Address, when the nation was at the height of the Great Depression and suffering the depths of despair.

The great change the depression had brought over a once prosperous economy was devastating to most people. We lived in fear then, fear of loss, fear of joblessness and poverty, fear of hunger and thirst, fear of homelessness.

Matters of substance they were and still are, as was the fear they instilled in most of us. A nation of fearful people cannot live through an experience like that and come out unscathed, without a permanent shift having taken place in their collective consciousness and national memory.

That and the horrors inflicted on the world and families everywhere by the catastrophe that was World War Two. Along with succeeding wars and economic setbacks, many of

them severe, that have left us in a semi-permanent state of uncomfortable wariness, suspicion and doubt concerning the reliability of our economic institutions and the stability of our way of life. In that regard, we may not have left the need for our primitive instincts for sheer survival that far behind on the plains of Africa.

We may even have become somewhat wary of the good intentions of the divine force of existence itself. We may have become a nation of stressed-out and anxiety ridden people, indulging ourselves with alcohol, drugs, and nonsensical so-called social media entertainments and mindless escapism.

Not to mention the so-called reality shows that have one foot in the grave and the other in the twilight zone of bad taste, social media mindlessness and all manner of expatriate, pseudo-intelligent attitudes and worthless activities.

While we still can, we should rid ourselves of our addiction to these mind-numbing activities before our internal self-phone shuts down on this plane and blinks out of existence.

We have not only lost significant faith in our traditions, cultural and religious, we have reached the ridiculous point in our cynicism that Thanksgiving, a traditional time for family and the joy of reunion, is mockingly known as Turkey Day. We are a people who no longer know how to give thanks.

We may no longer believe in the historical accuracy of many of our religious celebrations, but it is the spirit we should be celebrating, if not a mythic event. The ways in which those myths inspire us to come together, which is what matters, is what myths and metaphors are concerned to render. They are not meant to be history, they serve as reflections of our social conscience and cultural awareness.

When we mock our participation in significant cultural and religious celebrations, or find reasons to avoid them, it is our need for spiritual cohesion and cultural unity we are deriding. And almost always with little or nothing to offer in its place.

What purpose does this kind of negativity, these forms of cynical behavior serve that has empowered the cynics, and turned us against traditions that unified us as a people and a nation of immigrants.

Fear, perhaps, first that we have been deceived. That we are celebrating an historic event that never happened in the way it has traditionally been described, as history rather than myth. And that may be because myths are often so much more inspiring, because they are artificial man-made creations rather than actual history.

Some of us may be embarrassed in that regard, that we have been caught off guard and unwary. And may have pledged our allegiance to a false flag flying under the radar of our general level of rational apprehension. And thus insulting our intelligence while mocking the openness of our hearts. We will not be made fools of when our ego is bruised.

There may be another reason as well, which is that we have collectively been betrayed so often, and in so many ways over the decades. How often have we placed our trust in individuals and institutions that betrayed us, for which there was no accountability and no moral or ethical restitutions.

Many of us no longer know in what or whom to believe, and it shows itself in the collective rise in cynicism, skepticism and outright despair that things will never be made right again. For many of us, the American Dream has become an American Nightmare.

And so we have grown careful, skeptical and filled with doubt, eventually leading to self-deception. It has spread like a contagious infection from coast to coast, around the globe, and we are all susceptible because we live in such close proximity.

Not necessarily in close physical contact, but through various forms of media, especially social media. Ideas and attitudes spring into existence and go viral on the Internet in

a matter of days now, sometimes even hours. And there are no longer any effective media filters to contain the spread of damaging or malicious lies and deceptions.

Which are plentiful enough considering the enormous amount of misinformation that finds its way through public venues, accidently or deliberately infecting the modern-day world-mind, the Internet.

And this especially by Internet trolls, whose malicious activities may be the only life they have, and the only source of pleasure, vicious pleasure at that, they take in what may be an otherwise malodorous existence.

That aside, the willingness, if not eagerness of people to embrace the dark side of life may indicate a fundamental change in the American psyche, in which cheerful optimism is being replaced by a sense of subdued despair.

We may unconsciously be trying to stay ahead of the Bell Curve of social expectation by anticipating that things will not go well or are destined to fail, instead of joyfully participating in the sorrows and struggles of existence.

And joining in with others in the thrill of the adventure, rather than withdrawing from fear of failure and failure of nerve. We may have reached the breaking point of the cultural expression of our yang energies, the outgoing, expansive force of existence.

And consequently, experiencing the manifest beginning of the dominating expression of our yin energies, the energy of contraction, withdrawal and decline. Which in its current incarnation is assuming the force of regressive political obstructionism.

The conscious withdrawal from any rational exegesis of difficult political complexity, and the turning away from every form of communal welfare to endorsing lives of selfish self-interest at the expense of the common good.

This is certainly not true of all of us, but it *is* true of enough of us so that it has taken a cumulative toll on our national will. It has inflected our sense of fairness and justice. It has damaged the national identity in which we once took such enormous pride, and which is now fast becoming only a far-fetched and distant idea in the minds and memories of our older generations.

We do not strive for excellence as once we did. Perhaps an answer may be found in that we have learnt through hard experience that those at the top of the food chain take the choicest cuts. And what is left is expected to trickle down and feed the masses. Economic fantasy masquerading as practical economics, but skimming off the top.

We can usually expect that those on the top levels of every human activity will all too often enrich themselves through countless schemes, in every way they can with whatever means at their disposal.

Or that hired underlings will invent money-making or money-laundering schemes for them, for whatever purpose that continues to enrich their already over-flowing pockets. And with very little or nothing filtering down to the rest of us on the general level of existence.

This is the old familiar dog eat dog mentality that has once again consumed the realm of our natural affections. And in the process, alienating us from our cultural institutions, national traditions, and the sense of communal well-being that unifies a people in common. And which serves us well in times of stress, when danger threatens, and we are called on to band together to make common purpose.

When we cannot find or have abandoned common ground, we are forced to live and act solely on our own behalf, and no longer share the same ground of being in a social or psychological sense. We are once again lost among the stars, divorced from collective reality, alienated from the fundamental force of social cohesion.

Things fall apart when that happens. And in so many ways things *have* fallen apart as American life disintegrates on a daily basis one way or another.

How this can be turned around is questionable. Heaven forbid, a moot point when a civilization or culture begins to disintegrate, when the worst impulses and the worst among us act out their loathsome scenarios in the full light of day with passionate intensity and the disinterest of the public.

Barely able to disguise the frauds that they are. Hypocrites and liars, con men and frauds, they are the disease for which they pretend to be the cure. They have names, and those with eyes to see and ears to hear know who they are. They are the worst among us because they seek power to carry out their loathsome agendas. They are relentless, they are everywhere and they are unstoppable as long as we look the other way.

And the pity, or the shame of it is that so many of us are so willing to believe the lies and falsehoods that should by rights fill us with disbelief. But which so inflames the passions of those who may have nearly reached the end of their individual ropes and life trajectories that they act out their silent rage even against their best impulses and best interests.

We are no longer a nation of immigrants, we are a nation of refugees. Perhaps we always were. The difference now being that so many of us are not turning toward something new in hope and eager anticipation, but running away from something that is old and fearful. And which may have found a new home in the new land, now not so new.

Even those of us whose families have been here for many generations are feeling this force of discomfort in their lives. Many of us have begun acting as though the enemy was at the gates, forcing its way into our very hearths and homes.

Talking points, nothing more, used by talking heads to terrify and intimidate those of us who are already primed and ready to fire away in hopes of hitting something, anything,

that threatens our existence. Nothing more than a constant volley of Hail Mary passes hurtling through the dark night of the soul and the despair of disillusion.

This is a socio-political attitude more than simply physical reality, although nowadays it has become both. There are indeed real dangers in this dangerous world of dangerous people who already live among us.

But it has now become an attitude of fear and suspicion that indoctrinates the mass of men through public-relations techniques that prey on their weaknesses. And making them even more susceptible to manipulation and distortion.

And consequently easier to guide along pre-planned and pre-ordained lines of political maneuvering and economic exploitation, along the invisibly authoritative lines of impenetrable global authority.

Once we allow fear to make inroads in our collective psyche the stragglers among us will begin to fall in line one by one, little by little. Fear will take possession of our inner faculties and we are lost to our better selves. This is when we become most vulnerable to a collective take-over by the forces of tyranny and repression.

Not by accident does this take place. It happens by design on the part of those who intend to benefit from the consolation of power, the acquisition of natural resources, and the subjugation of the masses by those whose contempt for those self-same masses is a palpable reality.

We know this and them from their policies, and the brittle contempt they display towards pain and suffering. Ours, not theirs. They take care of their own and each other.

They, the true powers that be, may be invisible but their political shills and economic hit men are well-known. And have generally adopted public postures that very nearly indemnifies them from criticism by endorsing the principles

of democratic ideas and democratic policies in unworthy causes. Their own.

Unless we begin to pay serious attention to their serious policies, we will never understand who stands to benefit and who stands to suffer. And that is the very reason they try so hard to keep us off guard, separated, divided and in conflict with each other.

So that we will not see through their charades, their spin doctors, and so that we will not stand united. We will not pay careful attention to the politics of economic and political servitude that threaten to destroy whatever is left of the dwindling American middle-level consumer class.

Divide and conquer served the Roman Empire well in its time of imperialistic expansion, when it began the change from the Roman Republic to the Roman Empire. And we may indeed begin to wonder if we have not already begun that same change ourselves, from an American Republic to an American Empire.

We have traditionally thought of ourselves as a republic, and sing songs praising that *for which we stand*. But has that reality changed with changing times, as we begin leading lives of quiet desperation and social discord under the multi-national rules of the American Empire, for which we do not stand.

The difference is like working as a partner in a small but flourishing business with limited liability, to working in a small cubicle in a windowless office building with only one small family portrait allowed to remind us of home. And that we are still human beings.

But that is not the only choice we have. We are in a sink or swim environment, publish or perish, do or die, now or never situation with bleak alternatives in this age of neo-political despotism with economic and political hit men a dime a

dozen. We have become infected by greed, despair and hopelessness. Our nation is in peril, and so are we.

Courage is what is called for to find our way through the forests and jungles of modern civilized existence, and courage is what is missing. *The end of living,* in a speech attributed to Chief Seattle in 1854, *and the beginning of survival.*

Ghost dancing could not forestall the aggressive, deadly activities of armed invaders in the homelands of Native Americans in the nineteenth century. And now we, faced with a similar situation, must find a way to begin to live again.

And not retreat, as we are now doing, into survival mode as we horde what little remains after corporate greed has stripped us to the bone. With little to remind us that the liberties we once so cherished, but now will not stop to defend and fight for if need be, are beginning to vanish into the pre-dawn mists of history.

History is replete with the end stories of vanished civilizations and the mystery of how and why many of them died. At the height of their full power, most probably never imagined that one day, one era, it would all come to an inevitable end. It would all be for naught, and what then would remain as its legacy?

And neither can we imagine the same fate for ourselves, but it might come sooner than we imagine. And one day, as is the way of all created things, it will. But it does not have to be today, or tomorrow, or next year or even the decade after that. Even if the folks half-way around the world are already preparing for the day, once the barbarians are at our gates, when their sun will be in the ascendant.

We live in perilous times, as seems to be the case at this stage in human development. We know it unconsciously, even when it is flying below our radar. But it is darkening the skies above us, and many of us are flying blind when we

should be paying careful attention with our eyes wide open and our vision keenly on the alert.

That we do not do so might be an indication that we have unconsciously accepted our inability to change ourselves, our situation and our society. We have accepted failure as a viable option to achievement, a failure of nerve and the total abnegation of responsibility due to a massive lack of courage.

We do not call out and punish those who are raping the environment or the economy for their own gains with anything other than a mild slap on the wrist. And an inconsequential fine considering the wealth they are reaping from their destructive efforts and mindless behavior.

We do not legislate laws that would take power back from embedded special interests and return it where it belongs. In the hands of democratic and just traditions, interpreted and carried out to a fair and equitable fulfillment by fair and just men and women of unquestionable integrity. Those who care more for our democratic traditions and responsibilities than they do for their own pockets.

We have not abolished war and violence, which includes economic violence against the defenseless and helpless, as legitimate methods for settling disputes. War as a weapon of public policy solves nothing, usually only enriching the private pockets of arms dealers. Or ambitious despots with dreams of empire building. Or rash politicians with a grudge.

We have not taken action to redress the wrongs and inequities of social circumstance. The homeless remain unsheltered. The hungry remain with empty stomachs. The sick become sicker, and then they die. We all die.

We do not stop conscienceless executives of pharmaceutical companies from gouging the desperately ill by over-inflating the costs of life-saving medications. All for the shameful purpose of filling their already overflowing pockets

while barely noticing the loss of their souls as they count the profits from their ill-gotten gains.

The sounds they may hear, when they open the windows of their mansions to let a fresh breeze into the foul air they breathe, is not the whistling of a summer breeze through plush gardens and heavy-laden orchards.

What they should be hearing, and do not, are the cries and moans of sick people, children among them, who cannot afford the medicines whose prices have skyrocketed at the hands of these despicable mercenaries of greed and callous indifference.

Among the sounds they do not hear is the sobbing of grieving parents who cannot afford to buy the medicine their children desperately need to stay alive. And have no one to turn to for help. The terror they face is blood on the hands of those merciless individuals who continually enrich themselves by feeding on the blood of children.

We have not effectively abolished unfair and unnecessary restrictions on individual liberties. We have not effectively abolished discrimination of any sort, in any way, against any person or people.

And most of us do not rise in protest against politically-inspired congressional delay or obfuscation in matters of national importance by individuals who only act promptly and efficiently when the interests of their corporate masters are involved.

We do not take any of these necessary and critical actions because we have become meek and mild, bullied into submission by bullies whose actions are determined by the system, not personal prejudices, or so they would have us believe. We heard that before at the Nuremburg Trials.

All too many of us are afraid of asserting ourselves, taking risks for fear of losing what little remains to be lost, afraid of

reprisals for truth-telling and whistle-blowing when the truth needs to be told, and the factory whistles have gone silent because the jobs were shipped off overseas, along with the corporate American conscience.

All too many of us have lost the courage of the convictions that once were ours, or so we thought when nothing serious was at stake. When protests effortlessly took place on college campuses, but which we have now sadly realized turned out to be only of the passing moment. Time and tide.

We must regain those treasures of the human potential movement before they fade into history, now mocked, ignored and nearly-forgotten history at that. We must renew our friendship with courage, and affirm the convictions that once made us great and dewy-eyed with pride. And when renewed, if we can find the time before that world is lost to us for ages still to come, will do so once again.

But until that happens there is no getting around the fact that we have lost something essential for the matured growth of a civilized society of free and independent citizens.

We must stand together and act in a unified manner, shoulder to shoulder, secure in the absolute and firm knowledge that we share common beliefs, enlightened convictions and the absolute knowledge, in which we can all trust, that spiritually, if not necessarily biologically, we are all brothers and sisters. The family of man.

We are all members of the same human family, and in that knowledge we will find our most sincere courage and renew our fundamentally humane convictions affirming our communal right to liberty, our communal right to justice, and our communal right to live peacefully in the planetary community that is mankind.

We may not all be equal to the same standards, but all men were created with equal rights. We must do everything possible to insure for ourselves and our posterity that nothing

is ever done to abridge those rights or corrupt the fundamental principles of American democracy.

Serious inroads have already been made towards abridging those rights, and for those who have been busy with other matters, our rights and privileges have already been breached. Our liberties are seriously at risk of undergoing intense and critical scrutiny by those who have keenly noticed that most of us are not really paying serious attention to what is going on around us.

We may think we are, but we have been deceived. We have been deliberately misinformed by organizations with the serious intent of shaping the contents of our future. That future has been pre-planned along the lines of corporate domination in world affairs. *The end of living and the beginning of survival.*

This is the sworn enemy of the individual expression of liberty, and against the freedom to think and act outside the party line. With no talking points to dominate our thinking, except what we ourselves wish to express.

We absolutely must affirm the inalienable rights that the Declaration of Independence inspires us to believe in, asserting that they are self-evident, and that among them are life, liberty, and the pursuit of happiness.

Those were the days! By adding the phrase *among them,* the framers most certainly intended that man was indeed endowed by our creator with many inalienable rights, of which only a few, life, liberty and the pursuit of happiness, were articulated in that document. There are more, which it is our inalienable right to secure for ourselves, and the pursuit of future investigation and justice.

Other rights are described in our constitution, which analyzes and articulates the details of our freedoms, our rights and our obligations under the law of the land. And for it to remain a living document, it must continually be examined,

referred to, amended and adjusted to fit the contours of the times. This is most certainly in accord with the original intent of the founders, which was inarguably and unquestionably to assert and maintain our freedoms for all time

We will grow into those inalienable rights as we come into them over time, as we debate issues which the framers had no way to anticipate or imagine in their own time during those colonial years.

And this is why these two founding documents of our national conscience, the Declaration of Independence and the Constitution of the United States, must continually be interpreted and re-interpreted by succeeding generations to address the realities of changing times according to the needs of the moment without losing sight of our national purpose or our inalienable rights.

This recapitulates the truth that Ralph Waldo Emerson affirmed when he wrote that *each age must write its own books.* Each age is different from its predecessor. Every generation of men is faced with problems different from previous generations.

The landscape of human existence is continually undergoing change and re-evaluation, and each age must scrutinize what is worth keeping and what must be re-invented along more useful or contemporary lines.

A new generation might have to deal with issues that no previous generation had ever faced, and therefore could not have found solutions that might have been handed down through time and tradition.

We are in this sense on our own, and have the dual task of solving the problems of the day while also keeping faith with the founding principles of our democratic traditions. Every generation has faced this same problem, which is another reason why the constitution cannot be treated as though it had been written in stone and inscribed in concrete.

If that were the case it would not still remain a living document. It would be a tombstone, a memorial to the hopes and aspirations of other men, long since dead, as are the ideals in which they believed. And this cannot be allowed.

Existing laws must be re-examined or re-interpreted should the need arise or an occasion demand when the conditions that made those laws necessary are no longer appropriate, or perhaps even necessary in the same format.

What is necessary is that we take nothing for granted, make no easy or unwarranted assumptions about the safety or security of our republic and our national and individual interests. Freedom and liberty must always be defended from enemies within as well as enemies outside our national borders.

And this above all. We must constantly affirm through determined, peaceful and pubic action that we are a nation of fair and equitable laws. A nation of people who will not tolerate the infringement of our freedoms or laws that empower economic or public tyranny in any form.

A nation of people who will not tolerate the intentional and ongoing threats by organized interests to seize control of our national institutions, instituting a ruling principle of economic slavery. And in doing so, control the legislative process with elected officials acting on behalf of those powerful, special interests and disempowering the rights of we, the people.

We have disregarded or abused the most fundamental force for freedom we possess in our arsenal of righteous ideals and cherished principles. What unites us as a people is our fundamental identity as human beings with the same basic needs and desires.

And beyond that, our common identity as the incarnation of the divine consciousness of the universe. We are the very ground of existence in our essential being that we pray to in

our houses of worship, and which we idolize and worship through external forms.

This has been unacknowledged or de-emphasized by many religious traditions, and it is a colossal blunder in modern times. A total and complete misreading of spiritual history, spiritual teachings, and the meaning behind the spiritual traditions we celebrate but do not understand as our innate heritage of inner knowledge. We have short-changed ourselves, and the results have been appalling.

This must be acknowledged by those who know and know that they know, but accede to incomplete doctrines and fail to refute the errors of fact or omission that reduce our spiritual potential to a minor footnote in history. And in the process, disavow the true heritage of mankind as the rightful inheritors of our genuine and evolutionary impactful spiritual history.

We are not only enacting history through our presence here on the earth plane, we are simultaneously the disembodied witness-observers that reside in our bodies as our conscious awareness, but whose true home is the spiritual dimension.

But we are really not separate beings, we identify ourselves as ego-minds that only imagine we have a separate identity. We are one with our deeper selves, which is one teaching that we came here to understand through enlightenment.

The life we now lead is only one among the many we have already led, and those yet to come. We are witnesses to the evolution of our own being, inheritors of the human condition. We belong to the universe and beyond.

We are the universe, the eternal consciousness within all dimensional appearances that seeks the fullest possible expression of its being. And this is what the Declaration of Independence most truly implies along spiritual lines of interpretation.

The God-given inalienable right to be all that we can be. This is the heritage that most truly empowers humanity, and in which we will all find our greatest glory, and our deepest and most authentic source of power.

It is what unites us beyond even the most basic rights and most material impulses of the human condition. In it resides our truest moral courage, and the antidote to the failure of nerve that characterizes so many of us when we are most troubled and faced with a conflict of interest.

When all else fails, our spiritual beliefs and practices are there to sustain us if we can find the means to renew our acquaintanceship with our soul and soul destiny.

Our fears may make us foolish in that regard, and in our fear we may disregard the opportunity to commune consciously with our innate spiritual nature when there are no diversions to distract us.

Nothing left to attract our attention, compel us by appealing to our obsessive curiosity, and nowhere to hide in our daily prognostications. No way to hide from ourselves. And that is when we confront the one remaining option we have left to identify the bottom-level spiritual nature of our being, our true identity, that which we genuinely are.

And if we can do that, we can then consciously reside permanently in that which we have always been, that which we always and ever will be. The divine force of existence, the god within, true being itself, the source of all being which is the joy of existence and the bliss of eternal being. The Self.

We incarnate within ourselves that which we have always been, as do all our brothers and sisters in our world-wide human family. This is the truest meaning of giving thanks for our most complete sense of safety and security, the power of humanity, and our most basic and universal frame of reference. It is the ground of our communal being.

When one day we finally acknowledge this as reality, and act in ways that incarnate our inner being, we will have immeasurably accelerated the course of our evolution. We will enjoy a more matured perception of the realities in which we have our multi-dimensional existence. We will live in bliss.

We are far more than physical beings in a material universe. We are spiritual beings enjoying a brief visit to this temporary earthly home. We are voyagers through time on our trip through the heavens. We keep forgetting that each time we incarnate.

Earth is home, for a while at least. We should treat it as such and disengage from any activities in which we soil our own nest, which would certainly not leave a comfortable environment in which to live and raise our children and enjoy our grandchildren.

As we are now finding out because of climate change, our world is on the verge of becoming an extremely difficult environment in which to live. But the realization of our spiritual nature is the destiny we serve, the empowerment of our fullest human identity. The pollution of our environment will only disrupt the goal for which we will one day make common purpose.

There is also the realization and incarnation of unmotivated love with which to be concerned. When we are centered in our inner being, our spiritual selves, there is nothing real to fear. Nothing other than what we ourselves empower.

We will find ourselves secure in that realization, whole and unafraid of the rigors of physical existence which we encounter on a daily basis. We will have finally realized that we are not physical beings, the body only a material shell for the incarnation of the soul. Only our bodies can be affected by material existence, never we ourselves for we are not material beings.

The fingernail we cut off, that once seemed to be such an integral part of our being, so necessary to the completeness of our appearance, now seems like the useless artifact of a previous existence as it lies alone and neglected on the bathroom floor. Once it was part of our being, now no longer. And yet we, the witness-observers, still remain.

Nothing there is that can threaten our primal and essential understanding of self when we realize ourselves as the Self of the universe. Not even the death of the physical body can threaten our spiritual existence, or shift our identification from the spiritual ground of being which we have finally come to understand is none other than what we really are.

The enlightenment to our true nature is our evolutionary goal, the radical means by which we will find a secure and effective way to join with others in overcoming the many challenges we face in physical existence that hinders our evolutionary purpose.

Enlightenment is now, and has always been the true meaning and purpose of our human existence It is what we strive to achieve, consciously or not, and the goal of all humanity throughout all of time. Nothing less than that, and that is everything.

FOUR

Nothing less than that

We set all manner of goals for ourselves in pursuit of our individual purposes and in furthering the work trajectory of our lives. Some of us work hard to achieve the fulfillment of those dreams and desires, others find themselves drifting along from one thing to another, but never truly feeling the satisfaction of achievement.

Most of us have probably felt a little of both, and so we know the fear of failure and the thrill of success. Knowing both, it is easy to understand why success motivates us so much more than failure ever could. Although there are those among us who are as much motivated by fear of success as others are by fear of failure.

There is another attitude that surreptitiously creeps into our consciousness with enormous stealth when we have generally stagnated in our activities. This we might recognize as a state of being characterized by a lack of energy, lack of will power, lack of imagination and lack of motivation.

We resist the urge to begin new adventures or explore fresh opportunities. We stall, delay or drag our feet before returning to older ventures we thought we had only temporarily delayed, but which now appear we might have permanently abandoned.

Something within us appears to be damaged or corrupted, like a computer program that failed to close properly and

refuses to start up unless its damaged files have either been repaired or replaced.

Something similar to that happens which results in our having stalled in our general evolutionary progress. We go so far but then no further, with the often devastating consequence that we accept where we have stalled as though it was a genuine achievement in our general progress.

Not only having accepted our inability to move past that point in our progress, but even worse, accepting our failure as both natural and inevitable, the true state of our affairs with nothing further to be gained by additional thought, research or experience. Again, the result of a lack of imagination and a failure of nerve.

This is a nightmare of failure and frustration from which we must awaken or begin a backward slide into another dark age. A dark night of the soul from which it will be difficult to emerge, with the inevitable collapse of civilized thought and action to weigh us down. Only this time not simply the recapitulation of another medieval period of stupid men with thirsty swords and superstitious beliefs masquerading as power and knowledge.

Considering the destruction of our environment, diminishing natural resources, and poisonous industrial practices that are stripping our planet bare of its natural beauty, we might one day be living on a prison planet with a life sentence and no possibility of parole except through death.

This cannot be allowed. Those many of us with an empowered conscience, and the ability to engage our willpower, must begin to re-energize the stultifying inertia that has infected so many of our human companions. We must do all that we can now to avoid the fatal consequences that are fast descending on our world.

We must find a way to emphasis the many traits we share in common, and accentuate the many issues of planetary distress that place us all in danger and threaten our very existence. Our collective backs are up against the wall, and that existential wall cuts across all real and imaginary international borders.

Nothing can be allowed to interfere with the collective need to save ourselves and our planet from the impending disasters that have been thrust upon us by the tragedies of our time. We are faced with the urgency of the moment, and what will inevitably become the very formidable results of our destructive practices.

Our general political unwillingness to act in responsible ways now, for all manner of reasons, is nevertheless completely unjustified if we consciously begin thinking about the long-term consequences of a race of beings effectively committing planetary suicide. Mankind.

If we knowingly refuse to accept responsibility for what is being done to poison our air and water, and laying waste to the landscape in the process, we are knowingly committing suicide. We cannot continue to go along in order to get along, which is simply furthering our own skewed interests in spite of what the greater costs are inevitably going to be.

Our children and grand-children will face a world they never made, but which we, through our inaction, indifference and cowardice helped to destroy. We may not be the architects of that destruction, but indirectly we share some of the responsibility and the burden of the blame. They have the power and the money. We have the numbers, and we are clueless how to use that to our best advantage. This may be why they have the power and the money.

If we do not act others will, the conscienceless profiteers whose worship of money and what money will buy is more than enough to overwhelm the demands of what little conscience they still have remaining. And which is basically as

inert and dead as granite boulders lining the sides of mountain trails.

Direct action now is what is required. But if we suspend our conscience and postpone our responses to the environmental, social and financial crises that are fast approaching, if not already upon us in a latent or beginning stage, we will have allowed the deterioration to begin under our very eyes.

And it will continue, no matter how often we avert our eyes or simply choose to look away and turn the other cheek. We may look away with sadness, but sadness is not an effective weapon for the processes of change, growth and maturation.

We may not have initiated the destructive environmental practices that are dooming our planet, but if we know and do nothing, we are as much to blame as those who conceived of those deadly practices for their own ends.

Our individual voices may not reach very far down the road, but collectively we are the voice of the planet and the planet wants to be heard. And it will make its message known as the streets of our low-lying cities slowly begin to flood with sea water.

As nearby oceans begin to bubble up through the front and back lawns of suburbs that should never have been built on porous foundations in the first place. As species after species reach near extinction levels and go out of business entirely due to man-made environmental catastrophes.

The earth will speak to us by treating us like a world-wide infection, a hostile species that continually fouls its own nest, the planet. In truth, it is we who are the cause of nature's responses to environmentally unsound earth-changing practices. When profit is the motive, conscience is inevitably among the first casualties.

Short-term gain does not justify long-term loss, and in that regard we are all going to lose when the game is called because of acid rain. A metaphor that, God forbid, might one day turn into a genuine weather forecast. *Sunday will be cancelled because of acid rain.*

If courage is what is called for, *and it is,* why should it be so difficult for so many to find the courage to commit to sanity? How and where do we find the root cause to which all of us can wholeheartedly subscribe? Why do we not recognize the common cause, our mutual humanity, which will allow us to treat strangers as friends, brothers and sisters all.

United we should stand, without regard for the inconsequential differences of race, skin color and religion. Or any of the ridiculously pathetic excuses we fall back on to justify the self-defensive positions we adopt to keep the play-groups to which we belong' uniform, selective and free of differences.

Suspicion, exclusivity or any other form of prejudice will avail us nothing when the metaphysical boat we are all in springs a leak. Off we will go, frantically rowing our little boat, merrily, merrily, and finally, not so merrily after all. Adrift on a sea of consequences and an ocean of despair.

When inconsequential things happen, inconsequential men and women seize the opportunity to rise to the occasion, a tragedy that must be averted by thinking men and women of good standing and good heart.

Heart is what separates the good from the bad, the ability to think and act from the spiritual heart for the benefit of all. None of us are perfect, so perfection cannot be the imaginary standard according to which we measure our productivity or our record of moral and ethical behavior.

As the mythical story teaches, *let those among you cast the first stone.* Unfortunately there are stone throwers among us, cynics and skeptics everywhere, on every street, lounging on every

corner and hanging out under every street lamp. They may have nothing useful to do, but their hands and their stones are at the ready.

They may serve an important function, which is to weed out the frauds and fallacies from taking hold and spreading their roots underground until they have established a visible presence.

And soon enough, if we are not on our guard against the malicious behavior they endorse, they and their activities will soon take on the legitimate appearance of conventional and traditional behavior.

But familiarity does not legitimize any activity. Time eventually takes a hand in any enterprise whose purpose is not to *enrich* the general coffers, no matter how *enrich* may be defined. But to defend the indefensible, by so-called 'spin doctors' skilled in justifying the lies and deceptions of those who sign the checks and pay the bills.

Time offers us the benefit of perspective, .which might also be thought of as the maturity that age brings. That kind of maturity takes time to develop, but oftentimes there is no time to wait for the maturity of age before reaching and acting on a decision.

There are no shortcuts to maturity, but there are ways we can find substitutes for the kind of earned knowledge and inherent wisdom that the self-awareness, insight and experience of age brings to those who have earned their share of the rewards of self-observance.

Having made their mistakes, recognized and paid for them one way or another, there are those among us whose words carry genuine worth, and ought to be consulted and listened to with some measure of regard.

The elders among us carry within them one psychological trait that their younger brethren have not yet attained, and

that is the wisdom of age. And our spiritual teachers go even one, or many steps further, which is the wisdom of the ages.

Sometime they are one and the same thing, although our genuine spiritual teachers can generally be regarded as having something close to the final word on matters of the heart and soul.

Not in the sense of a celestial dictator giving orders that must be obeyed and faithfully followed, but in the sense that wisdom carries its own earned authority. The authority of experience and informed knowledge, tested by time and tribulation.

There are those among us who aspire to spiritual wisdom which others may disregard, those who follow a path of lesser wisdom. Which is their choice, which is their freedom, and which must be respected. It is their freedom of will to choose the direction they most wish to follow, as it is ours.

Wisdom may be a difficult path to follow when it calls for restraint, thoughtful consideration and postponing the immediate satisfaction of voicing an opinion. Which calls into existence the fallacy of making premature decisions, reaching specious conclusions based on faulty reasoning or the lack of serious evidence.

Wisdom teachings point out the seriousness of judging prematurely in any situation, and attendant on that is the wisdom of or necessity for judging others at all.

Not necessarily refraining from judging others on matters of great and mutual importance, but in the everyday judgments we make that tend to dismiss or diminish others based on the most superficial aspects of their being.

Compassion and understanding offer infinitely greater rewards in our relationships with other people than do suspicion and hostility. This represents a changing over from fear, which is the contraction of energy, as the basic substrate

of our attitudes about life to uninflected love, the expansion of energy, which is more in line with the spiritual undertone of our existence.

This is a difficult lesson to learn, requiring us to examine all our conscious and unconscious attitudes, which we might better understand from the effects they produce in our thinking and behavior.

In this way we might be able to determine the true and authentic reasons for what we do, why we do it, and how satisfied we ultimately are with the results that accrue from those attitudes.

If we are not satisfied we have the freedom of will to change, much as we could change the formatting in a word processing program. If we feel attached to faulty programing we will have to suffer the consequences, but who among us would feel that kind of attachment to a word processing program whose features need adjusting.

An analogy can be made between the flawed formatting of a computer program and an individual whose ego structure is flawed and in need of repair or readjustment. This is in the province of psychology and psychiatry to repair or readjust.

But if the problems any of us face require more than either simple or complex ego-oriented adjustments, no matter how serious those problems may be, it might also be a question of a fundamental orientation towards life that is the true underlying issue.

This may be more in the nature of a spiritual dilemma than a psychologically-oriented personality issue. The answer might not necessarily lie within the domain of psychology, or any of the various approaches that psychiatrists use in understanding and evaluating for therapy the make-up of an individual human psyche.

Not that there are any simple answers to this fundamental dilemma, for there are not. Only that there are those issues that require more than a medical opinion, valuable though that may be in a general regard for the nobility and usefulness of that profession.

So many of us suffer in some degree from the general condition of unenlightened presence in our earthly affairs. A sense that we are flying blind, unaware of the truth of our existence and unsure of where answers might be found. If, indeed, they are to be found in this life by those who do not appear particularly involved or interested in the search.

This is a kind of widespread spiritual malaise, often an unconscious and unrecognized condition of modern life about which we many of us do absolutely nothing. Even when it is brought to our attention, we shrug off the metaphysical implications and go on about our business.

But we do not have a smile on our faces and a song in our hearts when we do that. We do not hear the song of the muse and we do not respond to the metaphysical lure of nature. If not actually indifferent to the spirituality of existence, we tend to relegate it to a background condition of our lives while our wounded egos take center stage and call our very existence into question.

We have been told countless times by beings of high spiritual attainment that our natural condition is the state of joy. We hear but we do not listen; neither with our minds nor with our hearts.

If we admire those beings, the authentic saints, genuine spiritual masters and enlightened beings of world traditions, cultures, religions and history, why then does not admiration lead us to accept and undertake their teachings.

Some of us are taught to substitute a philosophy of imitation for direct experience, as if such a thing were

possible. One cannot truly know a thing through imitation, but only through direct experience.

To believe otherwise may generally lead one on a foolish and naïve misadventure. But then, those who do embark on such a course may find out for themselves that they have gained nothing but sentimental attachment to an image for their efforts.

If we admire the achievements of great beings, if we are thrilled by the message and encouraged by their deep insights into human nature and the destiny of mankind, why in the world do we ignore them, forgetful of their message by the time we reach our cars and drive off to the next adventure in wonderland.

Because that is exactly what we tend to do, drive off into the darkness of night and the dark night of the soul. And in that sleep of forgetfulness, immersed in the waking dream we mistake for life, ignore the enlightenment of our minds and hearts.

This is the choice we continually make, and the most likely culprit that influences that choice is our attachment to material reality and the physicality of experience.

In effect, we are simply postponing our day of reckoning, the day or night when we finally make the most profound decision we will ever make. When we make the choice to follow the impulses of our spiritual heart and seek entrance to the domain of spirit. Instead of following the impulses of the mind and body, and where those impulses have traditionally led us which so often led us nowhere.

If we have not yet had our fill of cherries and chocolates we will continue doing what we have always done, and with the same obvious results. We will continue on the path to oblivion, rather than the path to self-knowledge, which is another way of saying the path of self-realization.

Some of us may be completely unaware of the choices we can make in our understanding, fulfillment and any philosophical/religious approach to existence we undertake in our lives.

Some of us may be aware and choose a course of least resistance, carrying out the requirements of traditional duties and making conventional choices. Of course, that is their choice, and if that is where they are in their evolutionary journey, then God speed and best wishes that the trip be happy and satisfy the goals they wish to achieve. What else is there to say.

But there are those of us who are aware, and aware that they are aware. And it is that awareness that prevents them from falling back to sleep and endorsing the illusion of material reality, and commitment to physical existence alone.

Not that they have experienced and entered into a steady state of non-local reality, or that they are permanently established in a state of higher consciousness. They have become aware, though various means of education, that a higher order of reality awaits them. A beginning, not an ending.

What sustains them in their earthly endeavors now, aside from the immediate rewards of their material lives, is the realization that their course of existence has only just begun. We are all incomplete beings, having only partially achieved the fullness of the human experience in addition to our enormous progress in so many fields of knowledge and human endeavor.

There is so much more to come in material being, and so much more than that in our true nature as spiritual beings that there are no laurels for us to rest on. This is merely a rest stop on our journey to eternity, a temporary dwelling place for us to have adventures in the physical plane, understand them, cherish them, but then move on.

Attachment eventually breeds only dissatisfaction and stagnation. The sooner we recognize those vacations from reality for what they are, setbacks in our spiritual education, the sooner we will get back on track and resume our evolutionary journey.

The education of the spirit is the truest and most important course of knowledge that will ever serve to soothe our existential anxieties, and pacify the troubled human spirit that so inflects our experience of reality.

Our natural state is the state of bliss, but how many of us ever experience bliss, for even the most fleeting of moments, before the countless anxieties and generic stress to which we have pathologically become accustomed assert their traditional controls over our minds and hearts, and suffocating us with their presence.

When we leave the safety and security of home, which is our true spiritual state of unmotivated bliss, we fall prey to the demands and dangers of material reality. And when we identify ourselves only as physical beings, we succumb to the illusions of physical existence and act as though our essential being was under threat and in danger of extinction.

That is the illusion that permeates our material being and threatens the other illusions under which we live. But nothing real can be threatened, nothing concerning the truth of our existence. The reality of our spiritual existence is how we should define ourselves, and so seldom do. And which can never be threatened by the illusions of the material plane.

The material plane is the dimension of physical experience, but nothing more permanent than that. It is not, as has generally been supposed, the beginning and end all of our existence. It is only one aspect of our eternal reality, separate self-existing entities floating through time, united by our common origins and truest identity, manifestations of the divine source of all being.

The material plane has only given birth to this impermanent state of our material existence, but it is not the source. And when one day our temporary span of physical existence is over, and our visit to the earthly realm has reached an end, the physical doors to material reality will close shut. But that will not be where we end.

We will pass through the dimensional veil that opens, when the processes of physical death have reached an end, into another dimension of being. There to resume our adventures in another form, with new challenges to undergo on our voyage to further enlightenment and reunion with the source.

We may or may not be ready when this new stage of our existence begins, but that is an event for which we can consciously prepare. We have already been given a great deal of information for how to prepare for this culminating event of our lives. If we will pay attention, we will become aware and informed of what only haunts our imagination now, and consequently filling us with dread and apprehension.

It would only be to our advantage to begin this phase of our education while we are able, so that when it does come, we will know what must be done and will be able to act according to the other-worldly teachings available to us now from many spiritual traditions.

Most of our education has been concerned with how to live a human life, but hardly anything, and usually nothing, about how to face the ending of it. Death comes when it will come, but it *will* come, inevitably, to everyone.

And just as inevitably, few of us have prepared ourselves to face that looming possibility with anything other than a pseudo-religious expression of spiritual endurance or stoic contempt. Or in a worst case scenario, existential panic and mortal fear.

Perhaps a metaphysical shrug by some, which might be meant to suggest or actually be a minor act of moral courage,

but it might also only be that some of us cannot face the most profound threat to what we imagine is our true being, our physical existence and mental presence.

But courage is not the same as confidence, and confidence only comes when we are sure of our ground and certain of the direction we are heading. Neither may very likely be true for most of us if we were pressed on the issue. And having to live with that terrifying uncertainty is what gives rise to so much of the existential anxieties that plague our existence.

Fear of death gives rise to the complementary fear of life, preventing us from living joyously in the fullness of our existence. We live with the fear that anything or everything we do can be the cause of something that might diminish our being. We could die at any moment, and eventually, at one moment in time or another, we will.

And which consequentially results in our holding something of ourselves back from plunging headlong into an unrestricted experience of the whole of life with joy, humility and gratitude for the thrill of being. Fear is the mind-killer.

Everything that exists is grist for our existential mill, part of who and what we are, including differences to be respected certainly as much as there are dangers to be avoided. But it is all part of the passing show, as are we ourselves. All things will pass, this too and that and all else to come.

It is all the story of the creation, the play of the eternal consciousness in which we, just as we are, are principal actors unaware of the true nature of their performance. Unaware of the true audience for their endeavors.

Which tends to make the performance all the more exciting for the actors and the audience, the witness-observer who revels in the authenticity of the actor's beliefs. And understands, from the point of view of eternity, that the nature of the performance is the play of consciousness.

This makes the performance all that much more genuine, uninflected as it is by the creator's obvious presence. And therefore empowering the illusion that the creator, participating through the observations of the interior witness-consciousness, is not actively directing the play throughout all the varying dimensions of existence.

Free will adds the element of chance, the instability of the material world, the emergent factors of novelty, spontaneity and adventure. Adding to the variety and beauty of the creation, with the ability to delight the observing witness-creator by acting on its own according to the given templates of existence.

We live in a growing universe, an expanding universe, a universe evolving into its infinite potential and we along with it. We are not captive creatures in a gilded cage at all, but the creative force enjoying and participating in its own creation from an aesthetic distance.

But of course the creator, or creative source, is always here, always the force behind the movements of all and everything that is. Always there to witness and observe that which is always and ever itself participating in the dramas, melodramas and comedies of existence.

That we are unaware of the full dimensions of our existence is the evolutionary challenge we must and will one day meet, but the game of creation does not end there. This material plane is only one dimension of experience. There are others, to which most of us do not, as yet, have access.

And that is the four-dimensional game we play, perhaps not at all limited to four, but encapsulating the idea that beyond this realm of physical being there are other more advanced realms in which we exists purely as energy beings with varying degrees of diverse capabilities.

And what would we be doing in the spiritual realm with no work to perform, no families to support, no recreational

activities or mindless entertainments to capture our attention and waste that most precious of all resources, time.

We might find ourselves, as energy beings, learning to understand and control the energies of the universe for the purpose of furthering the creation by becoming co-creators with the divine. We might find ourselves learning to create for the sheer joy of creation, on a scale unimaginable to our former human mentality.

We might, in fact, discover the truth of what it means to be created in the creator's image. That we ourselves, as we might be in an evolving and evolved state of being, have within us the potential to co-create along with the creative force of existence.

To use our creative potential to activate deeper and more profound creative forces within and outside ourselves, adding our individual and collective efforts to the design of this and other universes. But why limit our thinking to just this universe when there might well be others.

Modifiers of existence perhaps, in those initial beginnings as students and advanced adepts in the halls of learning of the spiritual domain. But why not eventually becoming creators of our own realities, our own universes, children of the divine coming into the fullness of their own creative maturity.

And in doing so, fulfilling the additional promise of our creation and the fulfillment of our potential as the sentient, self-organizing and self-determining children of the universe, which is what we are.

Surely this is another message of the creation to itself, the message the advanced ones among us, the enlightened beings from all traditions, have been pouring forth in all their writings, all their actions, all their efforts throughout all of time.

We ignore it at our own peril, and we foolishly imperil the education of our spirit when we stall, delay and generally disregard the advances that our human potential is capable of achieving.

Why should this be so, when in so many other fields of knowledge and experience we eagerly race forward in hot and feverish pursuit of new ideas, competing with each other to attain our dreams. Eager for new achievements for our private pleasures and public purposes.

One probable reason might be that on the material plane we resonate most fully with things that are material in nature. We live in the physical and we live for the physical, and that which is spiritual in nature does not innately satisfy our most basic impulses as we perceive them.

Which is why we must evolve past our attachment to the physical, to the things of this world, this plane of reality, before we can continue our evolutionary journey towards fulfilling the purposes for our separate self-regarding existence.

We must shape our own future, and we can only do this by understanding our past and living fully in the present moment. The only time and place we can take a hand in time towards fulfilling our destiny.

Understanding ourselves is more than simply a matter of unearthing past achievements of archeological significance, or memorializing significant gains in our economic, religious, social, psychological or political status. All these are important indexes of our civilized achievements and cultural attainments, but they are all simply on the human level, and the discourse is limited.

Not that there is anything wrong about that, simply that the human stage is only one level of our eternal existence. Most of us do not know this as fact, which may be why most of us

ignore it, focusing our attention almost completely on the physical, the human stage of our development.

This is a strange concept to take in, that humanity is only one level of our fundamental being, and a materially-based one at that. And nearly impossible to conceive that it is a level we are meant to pass through, and not stay behind to become attached to the compulsions and attractions that seemingly come with the territory, making it so attractive and diverting.

We are attracted to them because they mirror the nature of our mental attractions and compulsions on the material plane. Overcoming those attachments is the journey of a lifetime, and essentially requires that we fight against the most basic impulses of our physical nature.

In this regard we are fighting ourselves, our own innate nature, when we begin our engagement with a spiritual path. Everything we thought we were, everything we think we are is up for debate and subject to change. This is more than an existential threat; it is a threat to our very self-identity, our sense of who and what we are.

And even the thrill of learning that what we thought and think is inaccurate. That we are far more than what we have become conditioned to think and how we identify ourselves is still not enough to allow us to go forward with confidence, enthusiasm and the thrill of self-discovery.

We hold back, afraid of what that internal change might bring, afraid that if we are wrong we will suffer inconsolable losses. This, despite the assurances by those who have gone before us to the contrary, those who have completed the human stage of their journey.

There is nothing to fear, and yet fear is so powerful an experience on the human plane that it has become an inherent aspect of our psyche. And it must be overcome, or we will remain subject to its activities.

We are human prey for dangers that, even when they are non-existent in our physical reality, have become a psychological trait that endures within our being. We have become used to fear, and so we continue being afraid.

A trait that regularly surfaces as a generic aspect of our general approach to life unless we are extraordinarily self-aware and self-observant. And can take immediate control of our thoughts and actions when it is called for.

And this is when we automatically react in fear and loathing instead of sympathy and compassion. We can be vulnerable when we express sympathy or compassion, but most generally only vulnerable in the sense that our hearts may be awakened to the plight of others, as well as their pain and suffering.

And which can cause our conscience and the compassion of our spiritual hearts to awaken, requiring us to act on the behalf of those in need and our own spiritual selves. This is an inner force to be reckoned with, the power of compassion.

If we are willing to do that, all well and good. But if we are not, and are essentially self-defensive in an existential posture towards life, we might face a crisis of conscience that will cause us to suffer, and adversely inflect the contents of our consciousness.

This sets up an existential dilemma of our own, a Hamlet-like situation in which, knowing we should act, we are nevertheless unable to meet the requirements of conscience and duty, falling backward into stagnation and delay.

The only proper course of evolutionary and humane action is to act with sympathy and compassion. And this is when fear makes an appearance, for when we open ourselves to those powerful emotions we open our hearts, and when we do that we are vulnerable in so many ways. And thus begins an ongoing crisis of conscience.

There are always those who are eager to take advantage of the goodwill of others, just as there are always situations in which, if we become involved, we may find ourselves on the losing end of a somewhat debatable proposition.

That might be one of the chances we take, one among many, in which we find ourselves at a disadvantage by acting with sympathy and compassion. We take risks in everything we do, but the most painful among any of them is when we risk being spiritually wounded.

When we are not yet ready to open our inner being to genuine, heart-inflected spirituality, the opening of the heart, not quite matured and self-knowledgeable enough to understand how to handle the inequities the world can present, we are in danger of being prematurely wounded.

A spiritual wound goes directly to the heart, adversely inflecting our emotions before we are able to maturely handle the suffering that results. The suffering can be intense and of long-standing duration, and some of us know this from painful experience.

And all too often, we, the walking wounded, are unable to recover quickly or appropriately. However awkwardly, running the risk of becoming permanently scarred. Perhaps even unable or unwilling to ever again risk the encounter that compassionate intimacy offers.

Even more difficult, the engraved and newly-innate sense that the opening of the heart, which any truly spiritual tradition encourages and is concerned to render through its teachings, is somewhat threatening in that regard. Not something with which the disheartened among us might want to be involved for fear of becoming vulnerable again, perhaps even on a permanent basis.

And that might be enough for those who so fear the loss of their perceived autonomy over the undisciplined freedom to indulge or express their emotional states that they continually

resist the impulse to accept the invitation when a spiritual tradition makes an appearance and spiritual thinking comes calling.

This is when the harmony of the universe makes overtures into our conscious awareness. Gentle urgings towards peace and harmony waft through the atmosphere like clouds of incense drifting across the heavily-laden and already fragrant air of an enclosed meditation chamber.

All of which makes some of us unfit and unready for duty and intense adventures in the spiritual realm. Some of us turning tail and running out the back door without even stopping to open it like a Tom and Jerry cartoon. All this so that they will find and protect their freedom to fight another day. And fight they will, one way or another, for one reason or another.

True spirituality is not a call to move on to other spheres of activity. It is above all a manual of different perspectives, within reach of the different sensibilities of all mankind, for how to live a decent and honorable human life.

And do so in the gentlest possible way, according to humane standards of behavior, in accord with the most profound potential for enlightened living within our ability. With freedom for all, justice for all, compassion, sympathy and a little looking out for the other fellow.

Fear would find ways around those teachings if so empowered, but teachings they are, found in every spiritual tradition alive in the hearts and souls of men and women of good will everywhere. In every village, every city, every community, nation, continent, religion and gathering of more than one person.

Make no mistake on that score. These qualities of enlightened living are not teachings external to the human race that need to be imported from some outside source. They have their home and origin in the unmotivated bliss that

is the natural state of mankind. A deep and thoughtful glance in the mirror at one's inner being, and we will know these words are true.

Anything other or less than that state of incomparable bliss is just a responsive act we put on, a comedy, drama or melodrama, in response to whatever stimuli has come our way and to which we responded. We are far more in our inner being that what we pretend to be on the outside when we respond to the demands the world makes on us.

Forgetful that when we do that and live according to the changing conditions of that changed state, we also lose direct contact with our inner self. Through attachment to and identification with our external state, and the compelling processes of change itself, we circle around the deepest nature of our essential being. We are rarely at home with ourselves.

Which sometimes suggests that we are often only itinerant actors playing out whatever earthly drama comes our way. Even so, we have only temporarily departed from our original state. We are the self of the universe, the state of unmotivated bliss, the music of the universe, the harmony of the spheres, the universe in accord with itself. *We are that.*

FIVE

The universe in accord with itself

Western biblical traditions and many eastern teachings have a great deal in common, in spite of the obvious surface differences in teachings and techniques.

Moral and ethical beliefs are cut from the same cloth when they are humane in nature and concerned with truth, justice and absolute fairness in the equal application of community laws in service to the communal good.

Religious practices differ, although always necessary to keep us mindful of who we are, where we are, what we are doing, and how our hearts and minds should responsibly react to the difficulties and challenges of life.

Practices are different, but what does it matter who stands where or why, who eats what and when, or any of the relatively superficial differences that encapsulate the enormous and beautiful variety in the human experience.

But still, there is an extraordinarily similar belief in both biblical teachings and eastern teachings. One particular Zen koan illustrates extraordinarily similar implications in each. A koan is a puzzle of sorts that Zen Buddhist practitioners meditate on to help them unravel greater truths about the world and about themselves.

It is a different way of reaching a deep understanding of the world and human nature, usually non-linear in its teachings, and can often be expressed through the realization of a

metaphor more directly than through the literal-minded rational exegesis which is more typical of a western approach.

A well-known biblical saying is generally expressed as *God is One*. This biblical and contemporary belief implies the harmony and unity of the divine presence, which according to one level of interpretation is that there is one God and one God only.

And on another deeper and more mystical level, the implication is that *everything that exists is God*. Nothing that exists can be separate from God. Not the smallest creature crawling on the deepest level at the bottom of the ocean; not high-flying passengers seated comfortably on giant air ships crossing through the ocean of air that floats above us.

The well-known Zen koan referred to is: *What is the sound of one hand clapping?* Students meditate on the possible meaning of this seemingly irrational phrase, whose solution does not lie in rational exegesis.

The solution to a koan lies in the intuitive understanding of the meaning to which it points, usually arrived at through often long, prolonged and painful wrestling with the rational mind's intent on having its own way through logical analysis, rather than the Zen way of direct perception.

The solution might be phrased in this way. *The sound of one hand clapping* is *the sound the universe makes when it is in harmony with itself*. And as a sound, might be thought of as the syllable Om, which is called the four-syllable sound, the sound the universe makes when it is in harmony with itself. Om.

The meaning of the koan lies in the intuitive understanding that a greater harmony in the universe exists than can be glimpsed in the scattered fragments of this and that, bits and pieces of cosmic debris, energy flows and material manifestations, all of which we take to be the fundamental level of reality.

And then try to make philosophical sense of the earthly nonsense we have egged each other on in each other's company, which we then frantically try to unscramble even though they are already bubbling away in the frying pan.

The reality we perceive is not the ultimate truth. What we call reality is only the surface interpretation of what lies beneath the façade of existence. To delve beneath the surface levels of reality empowers one to hear the sound the universe makes when it is in harmony with itself.

There is an underlying harmony in the cosmos. It is within all existence, within the creation, within the universe. And if one person wants to call it God, go ahead and call it God. Call it by any name you like, and let her call it by any name she likes. Why argue about names? Names mean nothing in the immensity of the universe, signposts in infinity.

Naming only points towards a direction, it is not essence. Naming something solves nothing and demonstrates nothing beyond an ability to create names. What difference does it possibly make what we call the underlying harmony of the universe, whether by this name, or that, anything other or anything else?

Just as a finger pointing at the moon is not the moon, just so using one name instead of another explains absolutely nothing and adds absolutely nothing to the essential experience of existence. The universe is in accord with itself whether or not we give it our blessing. And a blessing itself implies that the universe is in need of our help.

It is not. It got here with neither our help nor our permission. We should be directing our efforts towards finding that harmony within ourselves instead of glorifying and sanctifying the only-imagined differences that separate and tear us apart through negativity and fear.

And do so only according to one name or another, one cause or another, one moment of spontaneous emotional

combustion over another that reverberates through time, eventually to take on the imprimatur of fact and history.

What difference does it make what name we use to justify the murder of Abel by Cain, or the nearly infinite number of Abels who have been murdered over time by the same nearly infinite number of Cains.

Killing is bad enough, and murder almost always difficult if not impossible to justify, but to kill without reason in an impersonal course of events, or because of a difference in names or spelling, is an unthinkable act of savagery for which we must all, as a race of sentient beings, be taken to account.

Instead of finding ways to act in loving and peaceful accord, which is always the message of a genuine religious or spiritual tradition and those who interpret its meaning, we have so often chosen the route of discord and violence. We listen to the voice, or voices, of ego when we do that, rather than the organ tone of the spiritual heart.

Perhaps this is because we are a relatively young and immature species. But perhaps there is something inherent in our genetic make-up that authorizes violence as an acceptable expression for the disappointments and frustrations we experience in life. Are we a violent species because violence is in our genetic make-up, or have we just not yet grown out of the adolescent phase of our existence?

And perhaps also this may have resulted in many of us closing down access to our spiritual hearts for fear of becoming vulnerable to what Hamlet describes as *the slings and arrows of outrageous fortune.*

Life is hard, sometime harsh, often cruel and we must all learn to defend ourselves when we are attacked or in danger. This is an inescapable fact of material reality, an inescapable fact of life no matter what the religious persuasion, spiritual belief or lack of either may be.

We can control only the way we respond to life, never life itself or the causes which impel us to take action or run for cover. Disciplined self-control may not come naturally or easily to those of us with hearts made heavy by sadness, or worse, filled with the hot air of steamy passions.

This is one reason why following the reasoned logic and subdued passions of a spiritual tradition can wreck such havoc in the inner senate chambers of the mind. The voice we listen to may at any given moment only be the loudest voice in the room.

The mind is like various software programs that interpret and organize the energies of the brain and the experiences we encounter. It can easily be inflamed or confused by the mental clarion calls of inner standard bearers for one cause or another. Those who speak with passionate intensity, but little in the way of informed understanding.

The resulting chaos can be of violently conflicting ideas that clash by night, causing nightmares which can and do easily inflame our energies. Or we must deal with the fallout from reasoned arguments that openly conflict with one another, whose intricate and complicated truths might be difficult to decipher by uninformed or untutored minds.

This is the message we are meant to hear and reflect on by our spiritual teachers, but which we tend to avoid because we are usually so caught up in the business of living that some of us often refuse to hear or see more than we are prepared to understand in the business of living.

But life should not be lived like a business enterprise when it could be an ecstatic experience of unmotivated bliss. Bliss is the natural state of our inner being so we are told, again and again, and yet again. But if we are not ready to hear we will not hear, and if we are not ready to see, we will not see.

We may look back one day, in as far off a future as fate will allow, when the light of consciousness begins to dim and we

can sense the journey is nearing its end. We may look back, when the inevitable processes of age and decline approach the final culmination, and realize then that we have squandered our opportunities to advance our evolution.

We never did begin the process of a sincere and profound spiritual training, we may realize, which we might always have wanted or meant to do. But which we never did seem to have the time, energy or true desire to accomplish. And when that day of reckoning finally dawns, we may realize, with a shock of recognition, that we have run out of time and the experience is over.

This is not merely within the realm of possibility, it is inevitable if we have a moment or two to reflect on our lives as the end approaches. But if we retain clarity of mind, have undergone some period of training and are not panic-stricken at the approach of death, we may have the presence of mind to leave the past behind joyfully and enter the next stage of our evolution as an adventure in consciousness.

If we are prepared, this will happen. If we are not, we might find ourselves sending *Hail Mary* passes into the universe in our final moments. This might not be the ending we hope for now, and it will certainly not be a situation we will be happy to find ourselves in should that be the case.

That is when we might most wish we had anticipated and paid serious attention to this avoidable destiny, and been better able to advance our spiritual interests as we enter the realm of spirit. That we had taken life, and death, more seriously as companion fates we can expect to encounter on the human journey.

Life and death are the two complementary realities we have no choice but to explore to the fullest. Yet of the two, which one is hardest to bear is most probably a matter of individual maturity and philosophical preparation.

Life does not necessarily have the advantage in the matter of a long-terms prognosis for those who are suffering and in pain. And there are all kinds of suffering and all degrees of pain.

This will fall into accord with the necessities of personal experience and self-motivation. Any thoughtful proclivity towards self-reflection and self-recognition we might have developed will serve us well in our culminating reflections on mortality.

For many of us death is not necessarily a reality, but only a far-off possibility we do not wish to actively explore. About which we have no desire to either understand through readings or teachings on the subject, or prepare for through the education of the spirit and the practices and meditative techniques of a spiritual training.

Many of us simply make a conscious choice to postpone either approach, resting comfortably or uncomfortably in the moment to moment experience of life with no further thought in the matter unless we, or someone we know, become seriously ill.

This is a choice some of us make. For others it is the default position we fall back on when we are unable, unwilling or uninterested in choosing how we will deal with the most profound dilemma we will most likely ever face.

Death. The apparent ending of all we know, all we love, all our hopes and that which we fear more than anything we have ever consciously known. Personal extinction. We ignore this when we are young and have ages ahead of us. But when we reach an advanced age it becomes an ever-present reality, not to be taken carelessly or lightly as it was in our youth.

What will be, will be is not a particularly useful philosophy to live by, and certainly of even lesser value when reflecting on the human adventure. If we choose not to think in these ways we are fundamentally simply avoiding the painful awakening

of our conscious self-awareness to the realities of physical existence on the material plane.

How long will we continue to live according to this partial existence. Enjoying some of the satisfactions of life as long as we are able, as long as our health, wealth and energy hold up? Avoiding the sum total of our existence for fear of facing greater challenges to our awareness of the limitations of our self-knowledge? Avoiding the formidable secrets of self-recognition that we are not yet prepared to deal with?

But deal with them we must at some point in our journey if we ever hope to break out of the stagnation that binds us fast to the merely physical phase of our evolutionary progress. If we can find the courage to deal with life's impossible ending, and compassion for the human dilemma, which most of us are not quite ready to explore through a spiritual awakening.

The secret of self-recognition yields a treasure-house of riches beyond compare, among which are the inestimable virtues of courage and compassion. In a sense, both are by-products of an enlightened mind since both remove the residual aspects of the many forms of self-defensive posturing that fear engenders in the human psyche.

The kind of courage that empowers us in this unveiling of our true nature comes about when we recognize that fear is the illusion for which it pretends to be a proper response. Fear may be a state of mind, but it is not the natural state of our minds, it is only a reaction to a genuine or perceived threat that is all too willing to take up permanent residence in our psyche.

When the threat disappears so should the fear. But when it does not, and makes itself at home, we have substituted false gold for the real thing. And when we live under those conditions, we are living in an illusion that pretends to be life. In reality, it is only a waking dream.

A dream from which we must awaken, which is when we can take the support that comes with the promise of inner freedom that spiritual enlightenment offers. The courage to be that which we have always been, which we always, already and ever are. The self of the universe in human form, the immortal consciousness that we worship as the divine source of existence. *That which we are, for we are that.*

Compassion also makes itself at home in our spiritual hearts as self-recognition awakens us to the reality that we are essentially alike. We all come from and belong to the infinite source of existence. We are all part of the same fundamental ground of being. We all share in the same existence according to the same rules of nature, and in this particular sense what happens to one happens to all.

We all share the same pleasures and pains of human existence, and nothing in the human experience can be foreign to any of us. And this calls forth compassion in that we can identify with all the burdens of life, share all the experiences of joy and pleasure.

If we can feel compassion for our individual human plight when we suffer and are in physical or mental pain, we can also feel the same sense of compassion for others in the same or similar situation. We all share in the voyage of earthly existence.

We can identify with others in terms of basic human emotions, since at some point in our lives we have probably experienced most of them. And while we each have our individual episodes of pain and suffering, we all know what it is to be in pain. And we all know what it is to suffer.

Courage is what allows us to break-free of our fears and join in the fellowship of our human community. And compassion is what allows us to identify with and support others, even complete strangers. This is when we live up to our potential, when we are reaching a higher peak in our

humanity. When we are most humane at the level of the spiritual heart.

Knowing these same emotions in the privacy of our separate being allows us to reveal ourselves, and demonstrate that we and others are not alone in our private sorrows and public presence. We are all joined together even in the most seemingly impersonal ways since we have all had intimate access to the same emotional and mental states.

Nothing human can be foreign to our nature if we are aware, awakened and alive to our essential being. We know this to be true through the experiences in life we have. Through the insight that illuminates the inner landscape when we integrate those enlightening experiences into our hearts and minds.

We all share in that essential unity and it is the bedrock of our existence. We do not consciously share in a group mind like a hive-mentality, but we all share the essential experiences of being alive. And we all have the common experience of what mental and physical consequences we may expect from our actions as we live our daily lives.

We share membership in a social scale of values as well, in the learned moral and ethical evaluations of the dilemmas we encounter. We share in our hopes for a peaceful and harmonious future. The vast majority of us can peacefully resonate in harmonious accord with enlightened goals of existence.

We can all subscribe to these beliefs with no reservations, for there is nothing to fear, no hidden agendas, no political repercussions unless we live under a totalitarian system and the tyranny of dictatorship.

Which if we are not vigilant can come seemingly without warning, even in a previously democratic system whose citizens have become complaisant and take their freedoms for granted. Freedom requires vigilance.

We pay a price for freedom, which is eternal vigilance. And along with that, the necessary actions that must be activated and made manifest by those willing and able to take a stand. It takes time, it takes energy and it takes commitment. And more than that, it takes heart to fight when fighting is the last thing we want to do.

We must actively fight against wrongdoing, not only for our own liberty, but for the liberty of others as well. Freedom for one must be freedom for all, or it is not freedom we endorse but simply an individual escape from the hive mentality of social and political conformity.

That same hive mentality is what has been suffocating the individual quest for religious freedom and spiritual enlightenment. The relatively new public western search for meaning has become a prevalent but often underground fixture in the social façade of religious appearances in recent years.

Mocked by some public religious figures, carelessly condemned by careless social critics, but it is an undeniably authentic call from the spiritually frustrated in the outlying regions of western cultures. Even in the very heartland of our nation.

The face of western culture has been changing from within for decades now, an inexorably slow process of attention and intention. Many of us are and have been searching for some way for legitimate acknowledgment of an innate hunger for religious meaning and a secure inner connection to spirit.

And for some technique or method for expressing the existence of or enhancing the spiritual experience they hope to attain. It is a matter of belief now, what to believe and most importantly, not to rest on the presumptive value of those beliefs but how to act on them and activate the message they carry within.

If it is higher consciousness they want, *and it is,* the problem is how to attain it. And then, who is there to legitimize it when the churches of all denomination appear to have closed their doors to the inner experience of enlightenment.

The quest for enlightenment is not a passing fad, or an historical footnote to the exigencies of decades ago when the world was young and we along with it. The joyful parade of spiritual teachers from every corner of the globe that landed on American shores in the sixties and seventies is not a misty memory, but has established itself in the background landscape of our lives.

Many of us may not be aware of it, others dimly so or taken for granted as a fringe movement that has lost its inertia. But none of that is accurate. What is true is that seeds have been planted, they have sprouted and their roots have established themselves in the soil of western culture.

The belief in biblical traditions has become something of a stagnating force in our spiritual awareness, but for many of us there is nothing vital or energizing in ancient, medieval, traditional and conventional beliefs.

We might wish we knew more about the founders of those religions. What their training was, what they believed, and what they taught in their own unmistakably and historically accurate words to their immediate followers.

We have records of their lives and teachings of course. Some of it mythologized, some of it invented, some of it seemingly authentic, but not written down and witnessed in their own words. Only accounts by others who are basically repeating what they heard and believed, but not what they knew according to factual evidence.

Many messengers bearing glad tidings of spiritual enlightenment have been lost in time and over history, but the essence of their messages appear to have survived. Taken together, they might supply us with a new syncretic gospel for

humanity, addressing various levels of human understanding and ability with teachings appropriate to that particular stage of learning.

And act as a comparative source of thoughtful contemplation for those who wish to rise above the differences that separate and keep us immersed in duality and illusion, and leading us even further into disillusion and despair.

And in terms of the vast influences that the awakening presence of world religions has had on western culture, live now according to what the family of man aspires to achieve. This is a contemplative reflection in terms of our spiritual destiny, the enlightenment of our hearts and minds.

And yet, we are so caught up in the exigencies of the human experience that we forget we are essentially spiritual beings. We have forgotten what is referred to in Zen teachings as our original nature. The face we had before we were born.

Ideas like these are not meant to be paradoxical for the sake of paradox. They are meant to so frustrate the rational mind that it has to look elsewhere for the correct interpretation. Which may occur in a breakthrough moment that penetrates the barriers of reason and logic via an insight that abruptly points the way towards truth.

A sometimes difficult teaching for the western mind generally immersed in logic and reason as fundamental tools for understanding reality. But perhaps it is a good thing to discover that insight and intuition are extraordinarily valuable tools in the human arsenal.

Anything that serves as a useful guide for piercing through the illusions and fantasies in life is deserving of respect and consideration, which is one reason that we are generally cautious before jumping to premature conclusions when

faced with something new or foreign to our standard perceptions about life. Some of us, at least.

But some of us might tend to forget that the life conditions, and the social and religious teachings in which we were raised represent only a limited set of perceptions about existence. And might not be the most useful filter through which to view the world. We do not work and play well with others when we do that.

However, if taken as universal philosophical statements about the whole of existence, any parochial views of life we adhere to, despite any evidence to the contrary, might present a standard barrier of such enormous limitations to a genuinely thoughtful, worldly and sophisticated education that it must be deeply penetrated to be understood.

If we are caught up in the dilemma of trying to fit the world into the little nutshell of our childhood training and inherited beliefs, we might find that the hard shell that encapsulates those beliefs might crack under the strain of its own forceful being, which is most likely inauthentic to experience and existence.

This is an inevitable outcome as the enormity of the universe transcends our limited abilities to take in the whole of existence. And then try to squeeze it into conventional ideas and traditional beliefs, along with the problematically relatively narrow focus of human perceptual ability.

Ancient books of religious belief are useful when understood in the context of their time. But this is more in the province of biblical scholars who understand these distinctions than the dubious authority of street corner evangelists and fundamentalist-oriented YouTube religious advocates whose biblical knowledge is scant, shallow, distortingly-illiterate and filled with radical misunderstanding, if not entirely missing any semblance of truthfulness.

The point here is that, as Ralph Waldo Emerson famously wrote, *each age must write its own books*. We must focus on our own needs in the here and now, as every age must do, rather than pretend that there are unchanging rules of existence and eternal interpretations of reality that are set in concrete, written in stone and engraved in granite.

There are not, and no such rules exist or have ever existed. Like everything else on the material plane, and most likely in the entire universe, workable rules for existence and authentically useful interpretations of reality are relative to physical conditions and whatever state of informed knowledge is available. And like every form of knowledge, they will change with changing circumstances and adapt to changing times.

It is no use pretending that one ancient book from one tradition or another can solve the problems of modern-day existence, or are anything other than the best attempts by ancient peoples to solve the riddles they had to deal with in their own times.

This is precisely what we must do, once we get past our fixation on the pseudo-historical, mythologized so-called revelations acclaimed and passed down through history by Bronze Age and succeeding people. Who may have genuinely believed that what they were writing was divinely inspired, written in accord with the authority of God. If only their beliefs were in accord with reality.

This is the tradition we have inherited. What should concern us now is whether those beliefs actually hold true for us, living as we do in the age of technology. And perched as we are on the precipice of the age of space exploration, are those ancient beliefs truly suited for our forthcoming expansion into the solar system and beyond.

Perhaps the concretized mythologized themes we understand as religion are not what the ancient masters, of whom these stories are told, actually experienced and

believed. But have come down to us as living history through the efforts of latter generations, who interpreted ancient events according to their own particular ideas and religious concepts of the divine and its activities in human history.

We may be accepting as revealed truth only the beliefs of succeeding generations of religious clerics, creating their own interpretations of ancient myths and legends during the Dark Ages of European history. Who used those ancient myths as a means of formalizing their own religious hopes and impulses, but with no experiential knowledge of their own to add to the discussion.

We must add more contemporary knowledge, more accurate information and a greater depth of spiritual experience to the debate. We should have faith in our own ability to further our knowledge of existence in far greater detail than mankind has ever known.

We can plunge ourselves whole-heartedly into the investigation of our evolutionary promise with calm assurance. We can move forward, past the superstitious or ill-informed beliefs of our ancestors, rather than fall back on and seek shelter in conventional notions whose authority is now seriously under intense scrutiny.

Times have changed in every conceivable way, and our spiritual beliefs and practices should move us forward in line with our increasing knowledge of our world, the universe, scientific advances and the deeper knowledge we have attained into our own human nature.

And now, and most importantly, the spiritual nature of our species that ought to awaken us to the fullest possibilities that are inherent in our genetic make-up, central to the evolution of our species as spiritual entities.

That may be a strange notion considering that most of us identify ourselves as material beings, according to the perceptions of our physical senses. Which is understandable if

that were all we had to go on, but to any informed observer that is simply not the case.

If it were there would be no point to religion, no point to religious faith, no point to any of the beliefs and practices that have sustained and empowered human existence through the ages. Those who have stagnated in terms of their religious beliefs and spiritual advancement may not have done their homework properly, reaching conclusions based on inadequate preparation and spotty research. Theirs did not appear to be a hands-on approach to spiritual experience.

This is a serious matter of serious concern, and without serious knowledge of the spiritual potential and demonstrated abilities of mankind, judgment of any sort ought to be held in reserve. The subject of mankind's spiritual potential is a matter of the deepest concern, and holds enormous promise for ourselves and future generations.

It ought to be treated with that kind of respect, neither dismissed as superstitious nonsense that holds human progress back from serious forward momentum. Nor should it be held in stagnant abeyance, relying on conventional answers and traditional responses that do nothing to further the conversation or add to the storehouse of human knowledge.

Our spiritual stagnation has become so profoundly disempowering that even to broach the subject with disinterested or otherwise uncommitted individuals is to subject oneself to ridicule, if not contemptuous abuse.

Which is one reason the subject of our spiritual destiny remains under the table, not usually a matter for public discussion and all too often dismissed out of hand for fear of the possible repercussions that may accrue.

Fear of what lies behind that particular red-flagged door has kept it closed for many generations now. And rightly so perhaps, considering the horrific history of religious conflict.

That, along with the innumerable imperialistic wars of conquest carried out under the flag of religious proselytizing.

A meaningless waste of time and energy, clearly antithetical to the best interests of mankind. Clearly encapsulating the worst instincts of individuals too aggrieved by the innumerable assaults on their fixed and immovable beliefs by reality to think coherently about our future progress as a race of sentient, ambient beings.

What is it any of us mean when using the word "God?" Setting aside all metaphorical analogies or specific historical references, there are, in truth, no specific or useful analyses or descriptions that make clear what it is we are actually talking about.

Would it were otherwise, but that state of intellectual passivity is the clear and simple truth. We do not know what we mean when we talk about God, and we are apparently content, most of us, to rest comfortably in our ignorance.

How long we can continue to remain fixated in this stultifying expression of our spiritual curiosity, failure of nerve and lack of courage is a matter of debate. But the problem is that there is no debate, virtually no public discussion of this most important matter. And with apparently little or no reflection in the public conscience of the disparity between our public beliefs and private doubts.

And certainly little analysis of the enormous gulf between our general theological philosophies and dogmatic beliefs, and the state of knowledge, or lack of it, which those beliefs and assertions actually mean in specific detail, and with attendant and verifiable proof.

The elephant in the room is that the only certifiable proof of the ultimate purpose of religion and a spiritual tradition is the transformed consciousness of the individual practitioner.

Who do we point to as exemplars in this regard? Who are the spiritual savants and enlightened saviors whose examples illuminate our lives in this modern world.

Who are they whose individual attainments are of such high regard that they stand ready to open the doorway to advanced learning and inner attainment.

Where do we go for help and who is there to help us. This is an enormously significant problem that requires the greatest diligence in our unfolding awareness of the spiritual recognition of our inner self.

These have always been significant issues in the world of spiritual thought and training, and the answers seem always to come in the form of a long-awaited spiritual messiah whose presence and teachings will redeem the world.

That is a great deal to believe, and a great deal to ask from any one person, for history attests to the achievements a great leader can accomplish. There is no denying the effect a luminous presence can have in the public arena, or that there are many individuals who look for leadership to determine the direction they hope to move in.

This may be because there is always a need for leadership to represent the voice of the many, but it might also be because so many of us are more than willing to fill in an absentee ballot rather than endure the stress of getting out to vote.

And it may also be true that many of us do not have the will or inclination to inform ourselves of the subject under discussion. Or the determination and energy to follow the trail of informed opinion when it requires more of us than we are willing to give, or follow the facts of any matter to the truth of the situation.

We are willing to leave that to others, who are willing to follow their own star for one reason or another. Or a combination of reasons, and sometimes for the most

extraordinary of reasons. But the unpleasant truth is that many of us are unable or unwilling to research and engage in the decision-making process, and prefer to leave that to others.

We will too often settle for an engaging smile, a reassuring presence, a catalog of slogans that satisfy us in shallow or superficial ways, and the qualified appeals that are meant to engage our attention in an unconscious transfer of power.

This is true in the political process, and even in a democracy it is an effective strategy when people are not willing to accept personal responsibility for the decisions they made and the process they underwent in reaching their conclusions.

It is a fact of human nature. There are those who step forward to accept and take on the challenges of life, and those who advance to the rear while others do the hard work of furthering our evolutionary progress.

And it is equally as true in our religious traditions, which should rightfully be addressing the needs of the body, mind and spirit. But which should also provide the means for the transformation of human consciousness so that we may all become incarnations of divine wisdom.

We should all become that which we seek to be, and nothing less than that should be the focus of our spiritual attention. That is a goal it should be easy enough for many of us to admire and even accept in our personal lives.

How we do it is another matter, and the spiritual problem mankind has to deal with in a responsible manner. Institutions have been founded and organized with this in mind, but over time became more concerned with maintaining their corporate presence than in advancing the integrity of the human soul.

The individual tends to get overlooked when that happens. Institutions can become top-heavy with administrators and procedures, and the more important issue is that it is not the institution that really matters but the spiritual teachings the institution is created to actualize.

And so the problem is that when enlightened masters are not available, as is often the case, and the institutional organization that is meant to embody the teachings is unable to interface with the individual spiritual seeker in a personal way, what are we to do to achieve our goal of a transformed and enlightened consciousness.

There is an approach that might be useful in this regard. In truth, the leader we seek is within, and the teaching we so highly regard as the incarnation of divine wisdom is and should be regarded as the field of being in which we should firmly be at rest.

If we can accept the possibility that we are ultimate reality come into physical existence through the template of human form, then we should be able to access that wisdom in some way that satisfies our spiritual needs. And which also allows the teachings to be brought forth in a specific context that addresses our individual needs.

We must therefore enlarge our concept of a spiritual teacher while at the same time minimizing the development of institutional control and a secular hierarchy of spiritual authority. Religion should be brought down to a human level, and spirituality should be the backbone that holds the effort together.

And so we should talk with one another, reach out to make common cause and bring forth the teachings from within. Let the voice of communal wisdom be the leader we seek, and let a teaching be the focal point of the discussion.

Let voices of mutual support and friendly interaction create an environment in which the earnestness of the effort, with

goodwill and heart-felt sincerity, becomes the leader we seek. And which collectively we can all manifest from within.

If we speak and act with integrity, willing to listen to each other with respect and genuine regard, we might indeed stand a better chance of furthering our spiritual evolution than simply acting on our own in private, while submitting meekly to institutional anonymity and social conformity in public.

Perhaps now is the time for individual initiative to replace group indifference to the spiritual matters that consume us. If, that is, we are involved in the movement towards becoming self-aware and self-organizing in all our activities. If we are interested in furthering our evolution, we can learn to take a direct hand in the process.

We have the example of those who have gone before us on the path of enlightenment. And we have records of their teachings to guide us in our own efforts. It is for us now to sift through those records and find that with which we resonate.

We ought to be uncovering what satisfies our own needs, and yet still retains, in Wordsworth's famous phrase although set in a different context, intimations of immortality. Yesterday's leftovers will not do to satisfy today's spiritual hunger and empty stomachs.

Or satisfy our contemporary psyches that have been shaped by far different influences, the social and psychological realities that ancient people could never have imagined, much less been aware of existing and rendering through their writings.

We are who we are now, in this time and this place. Our spiritual energies should be directed towards finding our own path through the wilderness. But not in fruitlessly resuscitating the beliefs of past peoples from past eras.

We should absolutely admire the achievements of those who attained enlightenment and left records of their struggles and discoveries, but it is up to us now to find our own answers.

The past should be a guide for those activities. What we achieve will not lie in resuscitating the past, but in enlivening our spirit through the direct apprehension of spiritual reality and the spiritual domain. The answers, as all traditions of enlightened inquiry affirm, lie within our being.

Six

The answers are within

What do we expect God to be? Who do we expect God to be? An other-worldly visitation? An infinitely powerful being whose existence transcends this physical world of material being, whose wonders astound the eyes?

A supernatural presence of epic-like biblical proportions whose kindness and charity, at least according to oft-quoted western biblically-inspired thought, can frequently appear to roam freely through an infinite catalog of human-like responses?

Whatever we can imagine, if we look closely through our religious memories and memorabilia, there we will find some tradition that closely approximates that which we might have thought we had only imagined.

It has been said that man creates God in his own image, as if that bit of literary creativity demonstrates that the divine is merely a figment of man's imagination. But that is not the only way in which that saying can be interpreted. There is another side of that dark coin, as there is always a reverse meaning in this world of duality.

If we think about the divine as the substrate of all existence, the force of creation from which nothing can be apart, then the faces of God that appear throughout human history are all true in that generically-universal sense. They all represent the infinite face, or faces, of the divine presence.

If God is God, let Him be God. Why would we believe that the divine can be limited to only one aspect of our understanding of His presence, or Her presence, or Its presence. Why would the limited power of human invention supersede the unlimited power of the divine to manifest, when or where, according to whatever agenda the divine authorizes on its own behalf?

Who are any of us to decree what God is or is not, what God may do or refrain from doing, how and when God should manifest or apparently remain hidden from our view.

Or perhaps *our limited perception* might be a more approachable way of thinking about this. Perhaps God is in plain sight, but it is we who are blind to the divine presence. It might be more a matter of how we are disposed to think about the divine than what our physical organs of perception are able to reveal.

Do we interpret reality according to the evidence of our senses, or does our perception of reality influence how we interpret whatever information comes into our awareness. Which comes first, the concept of a chair or the actual chair?

And possibly another interpretation of this dilemma is that the necessity for something to come into existence might precede both the imaginative concept of its existence, its physical manifestation or both.

Some may believe that our emotional needs call the belief in a divine being into our imaginative reality, but as Carl Jung, the Swiss psychiatrist noted, *Vocatus non vocatus, Deus aderit. Called or not called,* the teaching reminds us in Latin, *God will be present.*

Some religious traditions so quantify divine reality that it almost appears as though they are trying to bring the infinite into to our earthly reality by immersing it in concrete blocks of dogma and theology. And in that entombing process of

spiritual mortification, removing all possibility for divine spontaneity.

It might be more appropriate for us to reach upwards toward the spiritual heavens and raise ourselves to higher levels of thought and perception, than reduce the divine emergence into comfortable and familiar human terms.

We must learn to live with the mystery rather than turn it into a spiritual cartoon with cardboard-like characters. This, rather than enforcing the opposite approach, trying to force the divine into our human level of perception and understanding. This is an approach that has never worked and never will.

It is we, our earthly selves, who should be reaching towards a higher perception of reality. We who should enlarge our understanding of existence, and avoid the temptation to encapsulate the divine in familiar but nevertheless still arbitrary sets of rules and restrictions.

When we do this we are merely playing another in an apparently endless series of human games, with human rules and human methods of judgment and evaluation. We may be at our best when we do this in our only-assumed ownership of Planet Earth, but when we apply these same methods to the spiritual realm we are doing nothing more than trying to impose our will on the divine reality.

It is our duty as self-responsible beings to learn before we attempt to teach. But when we teach, or attempt to impose our will on others without a solid and substantial base of knowledge, we are fools playing a foolish game.

And with no discernible results, other than an apparently endless series of façades that mimic spiritual authority. Pseudo-spiritual traditions that impose many rules, but little in the way of inspired revelations about the human condition.

And most importantly, no legitimate methods or techniques for transcending the self-imposed limitations of the egoic mentality that help a spiritual aspirant rise above lesser standards of self-absorbed self-existence.

Where we should be humble we are arrogant, not in necessarily aggressive or hostile behavior, but in our inherent assumption that it is we who are the final arbiters of what is, what should be, what is not and what should not be.

And this might be the cause of our inability to extend our evolutionary reach and move past standard barriers of penetration, which only our arrogance has erected, that forestalls the transcendent experience that can occur in the divine and human encounter.

And which only humility, an enormously useful learning tool in our arsenal of achievements, might allow us to penetrate our ignorance and respond to the divine as beginners in the universe, which is what we truly are.

We are on a steep learning curve, which is what self-conscious evolution is in an educational sense. And which when we are fully engaged in exploring can open vast vistas of knowledge and experience about the cosmos.

What is equally as important is the understanding of our rightful place in the evolution of being and consciousness. We should be as open to knowledge of our essential being as we are to so many other fields of knowledge and experience. And yet, it is so often the profit motive that determines so much of where we will invest our mental and emotional resources.

This is understandable when it comes to the private sector, which must conscientiously weigh the pros and cons of any investment, and carefully balance the appropriate allocation of financial and other resources. But life is not an adventure in venture-capitalism, nor should it be.

Our federal government allocates so much of public resources to the defense industry that it sometimes appears as though our elected representatives are making an investment in war-related industries rather than a necessary expenditure in defense of home and hearth.

So much of what we can understand about the defense budget appears to be fundamentally in the service of the defense industry and private contractors, and those who represent them in the halls of government one way or another.

As though the government, aside from essential defense spending, was drumming up business and investing our public resources in the interests of specific private sectors, rather than funding more usefully-direct opportunities for enhancing the public good.

We should be debating these issues openly and with serious interest, rather than collectively shrugging our shoulders and dismissing the ridiculous over-expenditure of public resources, financial and otherwise, in the service of war. How many multiples of times must we boast that we have the most powerful armed forces that have ever existed.

To what point, when our country is in such economic distress and social peril. When our infrastructure is rapidly deteriorating. When financial institutions are essentially raping the economy, and when our educational standards are falling far behind the achievements of other countries.

We are in the position of having to play catch-up ball now, and catching-up is what we should be doing. So much of our thinking has fallen into habitual patterns of decay and deterioration, without imagination, without the scientific curiosity and technical knowledge that promotes new ideas and new inventions that can invigorate our economy and improve our general health and well-being

All this is the wave of our future, and it is how things should be going if we could rejuvenate our thinking and elect responsible and visionary leaders who are capable of reasonably responding to the challenges that confront us now and await us the day after tomorrow.

Paramount among those challenges at any time is the mystery of who and what we are as a species. Our spiritual potential has been ignored, and we ignore this at our peril. But if we look thoughtfully, honestly and with absolute integrity around us, we are already imperiled in every general aspect of our existence.

We need to rejuvenate our fundamental understanding of life and experience of existence. We need to reinvigorate our enthusiasm for life, and along the way find ways to re-evaluate our social presence as a race of inter-active sentient beings. This will never happen as long as the inmates are running the sanitarium.

We can no longer afford to identify ourselves simply through membership in exclusionary groups composed of political, religious or social adversaries with competing agendas, intent on hostile take-overs of adjacent territories.

We need to move on from the decaying age of competition to the visionary age of cooperation. And this absolutely requires a renewed sense of purpose, and an enhanced understanding of the meaning and purpose of our existence.

We must find a way to incorporate the spiritual dimension in our lives as a participatory relationship, instead of the conventional concept of the divine as wholly-other and an inconvenient truth in the corporate mentality.

We are the sensory organs of the universe as it awakens to itself in physical reality, the eyes and ears of the cosmos. We are the way the God-force comes to know itself on the material plane, and we should finally accept this as the truth

of our existence. Existential anxiety has no rightful place in this understanding of creation.

We should know this deeply, and never lose sight of it as we go about the daily business of living. It is this knowledge of our innate being that will sustain us through the daily stress of organic existence. This is not a way *out* of living; it is a way *to* live our lives to the fullest capacity.

But even more than an enhanced view of existence, it connects us deeply to the essence of being, the truth of our consciousness and the salvation of our mortal being. To know the truth we must become the truth, and no amount of sublime supplication or profoundly-beautiful prayerful accessories can ever substitute for the authentic and direct experience of who and what we humans really are.

We tend to avoid the difficult business of investigating our inner nature, particularly when it involves the initial boredom of practicing a technique of spiritual investigation such as meditation. But like it or not, there is no easy path to the divine, no express elevator to higher consciousness. And we all start at the bottom of the mountain on our climb to the summit.

This process of self-organizing spiritual evolution might be considerably easier for us if we learned to disengage ourselves from the normal activities of and identification with ego consciousness. As though we were temporarily closing down a computer software program which was no longer of immediate use in order to move on to a more sophisticated program.

Not permanently, for the ego helps us navigate through the treacherous shoals and hidden obstructions of life. But the ego is a tool our higher consciousness uses in our earthly sojourn. The ego is not the permanent reality of our being. It is the shadow self which takes itself to be the whole.

It only appears to be the fixed state of our being because we identify our existence based on the functions and decisions of our ego-oriented awareness. But the ego is only a temporary and ever-changing construction, a subtle fiction in consciousness, a self-organizing operating system which organizes and coordinates many of the mental and physical faculties through which we inter-act with the world.

And according to which we react and respond to the influences that shape our physical and mental realities. The ego pretends to be the master, but in reality it is only a servant that has forgotten its origins in self-awareness.

The ego is a house built on sand. Always and forever subject to shifting winds and incoming tides that force us, as defenders of the realm and loyal subjects of the faith, to manipulate our words and actions to keep the ego intact. To keep it safe and floating free above the flotsam and jetsam of ordinary existence. A project foredoomed to failure.

Anything that threatens the nearly-always precarious and shaky state of the ego-structure making its way through the world is either subject to intense scrutiny, or subjected to adverse reactions through any of the numerous means the ego has at its disposal to defend its only-imagined self-existence.

The ego is only a method our conscious awareness uses to inter-act in the material realm. A method of organizing information for effective action of any sort in physical reality. Nothing more than that, and certainly not an authentic statement of what human existence represents in terms of the most complete expansion of our being.

We are told this endlessly by spiritual teachers. It is most consistently the meaning of realization in our spiritual traditions, particularly the inward-focusing meditative traditions of which we should all be aware, but which, unhappily, most of us are not.

One aspect most spiritual trainings have in communal regard is the awareness that we are *not* the ego, we are *observing* the ego. We, the self within the embodied form, usually act in the material world from the mental position of self-sufficient awareness. And the ego is the mechanism through which we balance our multiple perspectives and engage in action when action is called for.

And action is what *is* called for in physical reality, and we cannot distance ourselves from that necessity through any form of self-medicating pseudo-nirvana. We must perform actions of every sort in order to survive, and this is perfectly clear to all of us.

Meditation is a tool through which we can find the appropriate relationship between the doer of the action and the witness-observer of the doer *and* the action. We can do what needs to be done without identifying ourselves as either the doer *or* the action.

We can find the space within our awareness in which we experience complete and authentic being. And then, secure within, can act in the world without losing the knowledge of our essential identity as the embodied spirit we truly are.

This is one technique we can explore to disengage ourselves from the mechanisms of the mind and the manipulations of the ego as it attempts to assert its needs and desires. There comes a point in every life when we have reached a certain limit, when we have had our fill of whatever thought or desire most attracts us, to which we have been beholden for a very long period of time.

But when that point in our personal evolution comes about we may become aware that we have been scraping the bottom of the barrel. The desire that we once found so compelling, over which we waxed so enthusiastically in our dreams and frustrating nightmares, no longer satisfies or amuses us as once it did.

We have moved on. To greener pastures if we have matured and come to a deeper level of self-knowledge. Or to another desire if we have not. In the immature mind desire recapitulates desire, and there is no end to desire in a world of material attachment and trivial amusements sanctified by social acceptance or communal pressure.

If we can watch those processes occur from a place of detached inner awareness, we might see with crystal clarity the confusion of impulses that sends us chasing off after endless phantoms of desire. And the flighty illusions that material attachment attracts us to with obsessive-compulsive regularity and no possibility of fulfillment.

This might be regarded as a regular fixation of human existence, the obsessive-compulsive attachment to the affairs and activities of the lower self. The part of us that actively engages with the world. That aspect of our awareness that inter-acts with earthly affairs and regulates all our worldly activities. That part of us that willfully ignores the higher aspects of its existence.

There is a lower level of our awareness that thinks it represents the whole but which, in reality, is only a part. And that is who we think we are, and what it is we are generally so intent on satisfying and protecting.

The illusion that does not recognize it is only an illusion because it knows no other course of being or dimension of existence, and cannot therefore break out of the nightmare fantasy under whose spell we have bad dreams.

We may be engaged with the world under those conditions, but we are not engaged with ultimate reality. Reality has outdistanced us in this regard, or to put it another way, we have not lived up to the expectations evolution has engraved within our spirit.

We are living in what may be nothing more than a fantastically elaborate holographic illusion in which energy, in

a multi-aspected inter-weave of forms, creates the substrate of our physical existence. Inter-active energy is the ocean in which we swim, and we are unaware that we exist in an ocean of energy. Or that we are swimming for our lives.

Life, physical existence, is only a finite part of our infinite existence. That is the secret many of us have yet to learn, and which we struggle to realize without truly knowing what it is we are searching for. Or where the answers may be found.

The answers are within, where else? The secret for which we metaphysically search is the secret of self-recognition, the breaking through the self-defensive mechanisms of the mind and ego to find the conscious awareness that exists on a deeper level than the egoic mind.

We are visitors to this beautiful world and fascinating reality, painful though it may sometimes be. But that is the nature of physical being, and it is part of the vacation package that comes with the excursion.

This plane of material being is only one dimension of our total existence, but we imagine that our vacation itinerary is our permanent home. We have forgotten our original nature, pure consciousness without an object of being. Without content and without identification as anything other than the self, that which we most authentically are.

We are all one on the deepest level of our consciousness. This is the lesson we must learn from our spiritual aspirations, which we must incorporate within our psyche. This is the spiritual belief that will eventually lead to a new frontier in consciousness, something ancients in the eastern world knew and passed on to succeeding generations through mystical traditions.

The success of those spiritual enterprises resulted from the emphasis on experience, rather than any oblique insistence on painfully artificial dogma and rigid theology. Both of which avail us nothing on the road to salvation.

Dogma and theology are artificial constructs of the mind, laid out in service to an idea or belief that satisfies sentimental attachments of the ego. In this sense, both dogma and theology are inauthentic because they do not reflect a genuine experience and understanding of spiritual reality.

Dogmas and theologies only provide interpretations of reality, usually based on little more than inherited opinions. They reflect only a set of beliefs that do not necessarily result from a permanent construction in reality, or a condition of infinite spiritual existence. They are pseudo-spiritual dreams made finite by the insistence on finite interpretations and historical misinterpretations.

Informed experience is the best way to understand reality, along with the proper interpretation of the evidence for whatever conclusions may be reached. Experience is how we learn in any field of endeavor. It is the most singularly profound teaching, for experience does not exist only in the mental field but comes from the world around us.

Experience is centered in the world while dogma and theology are centered in the mind and attendant belief systems. Belief is not the same as knowledge. Belief is essentially a passive state of being if the evidence for that belief is missing or simply a matter of speculation.

Experience may be subject to interpretation, but the evidence for experience is based on facts. Experience clearly reflects an active state of being. And the more conclusive the evidence and better defined the facts, the more accurate the interpretations of both will be.

This is not to say that dogma and theology are irrelevant, only that they suggest a direction in which the higher reality those theologies suggest exist might be found. But most importantly, experienced.

It is unlikely, highly unlikely, that only one of the many religious traditions we follow is the only true path to the

divine. There is only the reality of what is best for each one of us individually. What is appropriate for one might be inappropriate for another.

We are all obviously different in one degree or another. What satisfies the person we are today might not, in fact, satisfy the person we were yesterday. Or the person we will be tomorrow.

Most of us are generally flexible in terms of the fulfillment of our needs, to which the accumulated experiences of our lives offers clear testimony. Why should this not be equally valid when it comes to our spiritual needs and preferences. But if we wish to achieve the fulfillment of any spiritual tradition we must be prepared to dig deeply, rather than flit around on the surface of things.

We are not biological drones pre-programmed with fixed patterns of thought and action. We are not lumbering robots, but frequently respond with either dynamic enthusiasm or the extremes that immobilizing despair incarnates in our minds and hearts to whatever life brings before us.

But respond we do to the needs of the moment, to past experiences, to future possibilities. And we are not therefore legitimately subject to adverse criticism for evaluating the needs of the moment and judging how best we might respond. And the same applies to choosing a spiritual tradition that best excites our potential for action.

And so to extend the analogy even further, it would be pointless to insist that any one religion or spiritual teaching is better than any other. All that truly matters is which is best suited for our needs, how deeply we are able to delve into the teachings, and how profoundly we are transformed by our engagement in the process for a richer and more spiritually-energizing experience of existence.

What matters most is reaching the goal, not especially the means by which we arrive there. A boat that crosses a river

with passengers in it is still only a boat when the passengers depart. The boat is the useful means, nothing less, but in this particular sense, nothing more. What matters is that the passengers cross the river and arrive at their destination.

Ultimately, it is the journey that matters, not the vehicle that helps us arrive at our destination. And we could not arrive at the summit of spiritual enlightenment if the method we choose to follow is anything less than appropriate to the occasion. And contains within it the resources to add to or fulfill the needs of our spiritual evolution.

We must choose and choose carefully, and that may be subject to our discrimination and spiritual virtue. And just as likely, it may be a choice we make dictated by the heart, rather than any method of rational exegesis or philosophical determinism.

We may not necessarily know the absolute truth of anything in this world since this is the realm of duality, but we do have to make choices, and we do have to act. And we do have to be conscientious in our actions so that our conscience is at ease and we can proceed with full vigor. *Remember these words when I am dead,* said Davy Crockett. *First be sure you're right, then go ahead.*

We may make mistakes, and we most probably will, but that is part of the evolutionary process of coming into physical being and growing to and into maturity. We all know this to be true.

There is a Tibetan Buddhist injunction we might consider in this regard, which is *to joyfully participate in the sorrows of existence.* We learn as we go along, and we must live with our mistakes and learn from them as well as rejoice in whatever success or happiness comes our way.

The evil that men do lives after them, eulogized Mark Anthony after Caesar's assassination wrote Shakespeare, *the good is oft interred with their bones.* This may be true for some, but it is also

true that we can correct the mistakes we make while we are still alive and capable of correcting our course.

And then again, the good we do need not necessarily be interred with our bones. We need not boast about the charitable acts we perform according to our sense of what is right and just. Or, to paraphrase Mathew 6:3, when we do merciful deeds, we do not have to let our left hand know what our right hand is doing.

We can simply to our very best, this one in that way, that one in hers. We may fail in our judgments or actions, or we may pass the course with full marks, but if we have done our best there will be no karmic indebtedness to follow us as we proceed in our evolution. Which might well be a secondary theme in our lives, and which phrased differently might be something along the lines of cleaning up our act.

This may fall under the rubric of the consolation of philosophy for some. For others it is a statement of the way things actually are in a spiritually-derived multi-dimensional universe of cause and effect. What position we take is clearly an indication of our spiritual leanings, and most likely the way we view reality.

Whatever spiritual path we follow, whatever religion best suits our minds and hearts, we should do our very best to satisfy the demands of our conscience and the needs of our spiritual hearts. And follow wherever the path may lead.

If we are sure and certain that what we believe and do reflects the honesty of our being and the fair judgment of our conscience, then whether that agrees with official dogma and the doctrine of authority or not, like Davy Crockett, we might just simply go ahead as a matter of conscience.

Which, if we encounter adversity or institutional disapproval, might prove to be the most singular act of spiritual courage of which we are capable. To consciously go

against authority solely according to the dictates of our minds, hearts and conscience.

Becoming mindful along the way that human beings are imperfect creatures. Although we may do our best at any given moment, our best at any given moment is not necessarily the best we are capable of doing. Our actions and our potential are not synonymous, just as wisdom and knowledge do not refer to the same information we refer to in evaluating reality.

Knowledge is simply the accumulation of information, whereas wisdom is the proper understanding and implementation of knowledge, along with fair and impartial judgment in the application of ideas and actions. Knowing what to do and how to go about doing it.

These are often separate realms, although when they are conjoined they provide the most useful means of interpreting reality and living according to the merits of any spiritual path. We should have faith in the spiritual potential that lies dormant within us, and confidence that there is a way we can activate it and manifest the wisdom that is within us.

That wisdom lives in our spiritual heart, a sacred repository of lifetimes of experience and learning, the inner temple of understanding which we can all access when we learn to trust the wisdom of our inherent spiritual potential.

We know this to be true when we have listened to and trusted our spiritual instincts. But when we insist that the mechanisms of the mind's rational resources are the only true measure of wisdom, we sell ourselves short.

And this leads to doubt and disarray, which in turn leads to a confusion of choices and an evolutionary dead-end. This does not serve us well in the ongoing struggles of life, and can effectively cut us off from the source of light and wisdom within us all.

It separates us from our true self, the divine light within our being. The enlightened consciousness that we truly are, not the pale light of unreason the ego embodies when it assumes total control over our activities without even a by-your-leave or consultation.

Which is another reason why a spiritual teaching is of such paramount importance. It is the way of return, the way home to our essential state of being. Our original face before we were born. The truth of our spiritual nature.

Beyond the physical we are spiritual beings. The spiritual realm where we have come from and where, when our time here is ended, we will one day return. We lose nothing of our true essence when this life comes to an end except our physical bodies. Other than that, all that will happen will be a change in location.

We can learn to make that change-over consciously with full control over our awareness. Or we can face the hazards of the unknown in a existentially panic-stricken mode, unable to comprehend the shifting landscape of our environment and newly-conscious arena. And the various ways in which the subliminal energies of the mind make their presence known and reflect the fading echoes of the ego in its death throes and final embrace.

In a somewhat morbid interpretation, it might be inferred that a spiritual teaching is a preparation for death. Perhaps a gentler way of saying that is a preparation for conscious dying, teaching us to disengage from the false reality of ego-orientation and the energy-based illusions of physical reality for the enduring presence of our spiritual nature.

This is one way of describing what enlightenment can mean for us. The revelation of the truth of our being, and a necessary aid in the conscious transition between this physical world and the world of spirit.

Another way of thinking about enlightenment is the transcendence of the gravity of worldly influences while we are still alive and actively engaged in worldly affairs. To be in the world but not of it. To consciously awaken from the illusions of life to the greater reality, which is both in this world and beyond it. In it, but not of it.

This is clearly what we are told, over and over again, by spiritual teachers from all traditions, and yet we do not hear because we listen with our minds, but not our hearts. Our minds are not necessarily interested in the transformation process because desire and attachment are deeply implanted within our mental reservoir of love and affection. The message is so clear, but our confusion of identities blinds us to the real choices we have in living this existence.

We are capable of so much more than simply *getting, spending and laying waste our powers,* to paraphrase Wordsworth. And yet, time and again we submit ourselves to the authority of our physical senses and the desires of material reality. We do not hear the clarion call of spirit because we refuse to listen to the inner muse within us.

We know the truth, all of us know truth in our spiritual heart, but we refuse to listen to our inner knowing. We dismiss our inner knowing for one reason or another, but none of them worth listening to and acting on. We act instead on our material impulses, and often with abandon. And we turn a blind eye and deaf ear to our spiritual instincts.

Perhaps one reason is that some of us are more intent on getting material rewards for our actions than we are willing to admit, and are not certain that leading lives of spiritual integrity will earn us anything more than gratitude. Not worth substituting what might turn out only to be a feel-good mentality for the hard nitty-gritty of a non-apologetic competitive reality we must overcome on its own terms.

In this age of material gain and endless consumption which passes itself off as conventional wisdom, or what passes for

wisdom when the marketplace dominates our thinking and subverts our better instincts, what else is to be expected?

But then again, another reason may very possibly be that in our hearts, many of us do not truly believe in the spiritual realm. We cannot find our way out of the essential loneliness, frustration and isolation we feel when our eyes close to the world's presence and power to attract. And consequently leading lives of conscious spiritual integrity is much more than a worldly choice, it is a moral, ethical and spiritual imperative.

We are part of something grand and glorious, the universe awakening to itself in all dimensions of creative being and becoming. And yet here we are, bounded by the physical, forgetful of our true nature and thinking ourselves afraid and isolated with death the final exit that awaits us all.

A dismal reality if it were true, and nothing to inspire confidence or long-term enthusiasm for the human adventure. But none of us passes a final exam if we have not paid attention all semester, handed in our term papers, studied for the tests and showed up for and passed the final exams.

This is what spiritual traditions prepare us to achieve. And if we have not thought about it before, time now to change our thinking. If we need a hand in time, as some of us do, we can take the friendly hand that a spiritual tradition holds out and learn the truth of our existence.

If doubt or skepticism inhibits direct action, it might be useful to remember that we may never get what we want unless we actively go after it. If we hold back or wait for an easier time to make our ambitions known, it might also be good to remember this as well.

There is most often never a better time to act on our needs than now, not tomorrow or tomorrow or tomorrow. There is no other time but the now moment in which to live. Putting

something off until a latter date only means that in the now moment we do not have what it is we truly want. Why wait? Wait for what?

And the answer to that is most probably we are waiting for the courage to act. But if not you, who? And if not now, then when? Time, as we all know, is not a renewable resource. And come to think of it, neither are you. There will never be another you, exactly as you are, in the whole of creation.

Why not be the best version of you that you can possibly be. Why not bring forth what is within you, that which yearns to manifest in outer reality. That which haunts your dreams, fires your imagination and fills your heart with joy.

That inert aspect of your being is the unmanifest self within you, the part of you in communion with your spiritual self. We all have within us a gnostic intermediary that reflects the spiritual integrity of our soul's presence.

We could learn to listen to that inner voice without allowing fear to deceive us by questioning the authority of that inner source of wisdom. What matters is the truth within us, not the judgmental mind that questions everything, even its own existence.

We could learn to trust our inner self and act on our own earned wisdom rather than stall, delay or judge by default instead of on the merits of what we have to say from the inner wisdom of our spiritual hearts.

We are truth tellers not nay sayers when we listen to our conscience and act from the depths of our hearts. It is such a fundamental truth about our inner nature, so profoundly important to our well-being and evolutionary growth.

It is what our spiritual teachers have been saying and what they have been demonstrating through their lives, and yet it so often goes unnoticed or ignored.

Our inner nature is bliss and nothing but bliss. It is the mind and ego that colors our inner reality with varying shades of morbid confusion and self-doubt. *Everything is dust,* said Bhagwan Nityananda, a great meditation master of the last century. *Our natural state is the state of joy.*

Experience is the only teacher, and the only way to know the truth of what Bhagwan Nityananda said is to go within and experience that inner state of being for ourselves. Experience is not only the best teacher; but for many of us, it is the only teacher. The only way we truly learn.

Clearly this is true for all other fields of human endeavor. Why hold back when it comes to our spiritual well-being, our salvation as immortal beings trapped in endless rounds of incarnation after incarnation.

Unable to move on to higher realms of being. Unable to evolve further than as beings embodied in mortal flesh. Doomed to experience frustration after frustration as we stall and stagnate due to a lack of creative imagination, a failure of nerve, and a paucity of spiritual courage.

SEVEN

Love Everybody

Evolve and change. Fail to adapt to changing conditions and perish. Live or face extinction. Change is the mechanism by which evolution proceeds, and on the purely physical level, quantity of numbers usually leads to survival, and determines the inevitable outcome of remorseless change.

In the age of competition, quantity of numbers casts the winning vote. In the age of competition, ethics and morality take a secondary, although selectively necessary role. If enough individuals reflect the same or similar changes, that, as they say, is the whole ball game.

That being said, and reflective of general truths, in present-day circumstances the spiritual nature of evolutionary human change remains firmly connected to and limited by the material plane. But the reality is that the spiritual realm cannot be stormed by incendiary voices, brutally fundamentalist fantasies, or hearts hardened by competitive religiously-oriented bull-fighting.

Entrance into higher realms of being, before and after physical death, depends to a very great extent on the unmotivated tenderness of the heart. It depends on virtue in all aspects of its glory. It depends on the clarity and purity of a spiritual aspirant's motivations, intentions and perceptions.

All in all, entrance into even outlying districts of higher realms of being depends on love. Only a heart that embodies

the non-discriminating virtues of a forthcoming age of cooperation, individual or collective, is free from the downward pull of material forces. In this sense, even spirituality is subject to the force of gravity, metaphysical though it may be.

How we prepare for the expansion of consciousness into higher realms of being depends on adjusting the way we resonate with life. And the resonating frequency that most enables us to move on in our evolutionary journey is the force of love. Love is a frequency, a state of being.

This is not simply personal love, and certainly nothing comparable to lust, but the uninflected love we feel that has no cause, needs no commitment and exists for the sake of its own being. Love for the sake of love reflects the spirituality of a heart unintimidated by secondary considerations or external influences. And which cannot be bribed.

The uninflected state of love, spirituality in action, allows us access to higher realms when we focus our attention on the state of infinite being within us. In that state there are no potent negative forces holding us back. Nothing exists in that inner realm to pull us down into the inflections of the ego-persona. Nothing that holds Agape, spiritual love, hostage and in abeyance for its own ends.

When we are taught that we should love everybody it does not mean being forced to love individuals from whom we would normally shy away. It does not mean forcing a loving smile on our faces, pretending to something we do not feel and which is therefore inauthentic to our being, our inner self and our conscience.

It does not mean doing anything that violates our sense of right thinking and right action, nor does it suggest we pretend an unwanted intimacy with any individual whose thoughts and actions we might rightfully despise. Or companionship with a loathsome ego whose very presence offends.

Neither this nor that, but what it does mean is that we hold in the highest regard the eternal and infinite consciousness that exists beyond the individual personas we imagine ourselves to be. Which is what exists in all of us, which is what we all are in our innermost being, the witness-observer of our individual experience in material reality.

And with which, in our highest moments of enlightened being, we most devotedly wish to return to and reunite with in the state of infinite love. What we learn to love, through the fullness of self-knowledge, is the light of consciousness itself. That which informs all sentient being. Our inner self, the consciousness of the universe.

And we might also learn to love the infinite variety that does not stagnate, and which does not go stale with time. Change assures us of that metaphoric comparison, as does the perspective of the changeless state. It is the flow of life we trust, and the evolutionary thrust that keeps us consciously within the downward flow of supernal energy.

The only true spiritual teaching is to love everybody as the light of consciousness. The problem is how to do it, but that kind of loving attention does not originate from the conscious mind. It comes from the spiritual self, and it is the natural and uninflected expression of self because it is the natural and uninflected state of original being.

Bliss is the natural state of our being, and when it is expressed in human terms we know it as love. We understand it as love, we feel it as love, we respond to it as love and when that happens it calls forth the same response from us.

Like always attracts like, and love speaks from a heart uninflected by the negativity that often comes from the mind's attachment to worldly affairs. But when the heart speaks, another heart that listens knows it can respond openly, without fear of harmful intent, and with resonating empathy.

In the way of original being, love is a force of sublime mutual assurance that can metaphorically heal all wounds and bind the sentient, self-organizing universe together in one harmonious whole.

This is the original state of self-awareness from which we have all descended. And to which, in the depths of our inner being, we all hope one day to return in our evolutionary journey from the inner darkness of the nafs, the lower self, to the light of universal consciousness.

The return to love is the unconscious drive that inflects our social, philosophical and religious agendas. But experience demonstrates that the bliss of self-existence has been suborned from within by individuals acting solely on their own agendas, all in the mistaken belief that they truly are individuals with separate agendas.

Such a state of assumptive being misses out on the truth of our conscious universe. It encourages the self-aware monad to act solely from the philosophical position of self-existent individuality, rather than find within its nature the cohesive experience of being.

We take for granted who we think we are, what we imagine ourselves as being, but the truth is we are all relatively ignorant of the actual truth of our existence. We accept easy answers to difficult questions when we assume that the questions being so inconvenient and difficult suggests the answers may be beyond our ability to grasp or our ability to understand.

And that may be true, but understanding is not the tremendous road block we imagine it to be. The real issue here is not understanding, but the actual tactile experience of the inner depths of our being. Understanding is the booby-trap the ego adopts to avoid displacement. Which prevents us from having the actual experience of higher consciousness.

We do not have to understand how things come about or why things are the way they are in order to move on in our evolutionary journey. Understanding how things work will come in its own time and in its own way. But until that happens we do not have to automatically look away or accept trite responses because we do not have all the answers.

This is especially true when it comes to living a spiritually-awakened life. There are steps we must take, some involving self-discipline, others engaging in intellectual and emotional activities whose purpose is to broaden our understanding by expanding the frontiers of our inner experiences.

We might find, as we investigate these matters hoping for direct experience, that we are denied what we have read about and hoped for from the writings of advanced spiritual initiates. It might be that we are not yet ready for those kinds of deeply profound inner experiences through the inflections of pure consciousness.

There are many spiritual adventures that strongly appeal to our sense of the numinous and the mysterious, but may require more of us then we are capable of giving. And we might be unable to access those inner realms and understand their significance if our minds and egos are not yet ready, or able, to assimilate those investigations. Some of us can be easily frightened by inner experiences that threaten our only-imagined sense of well-being.

We might be unable to leave behind the preferences and assumptions of the lesser state of being in which we are most comfortable, and which we imagine to be our emotional or intellectual home. And if something falls outside that familiar territory, some of us might panic or feel extraordinarily threatened. Or at the very least, extremely ill at ease.

This does not advance spiritual progress, and in some cases, may even retard progress. If we are not yet ready to advance, our time might be better spent cultivating the ground we currently occupy. In its own way, the mundane world is

equally miraculous, and can lead to more profound experiences during the natural course of events.

To venture too far afield of our comfort level might leave some of us gasping for metaphysical air. And discomfort in this regard inhibits understanding, preventing us from absorbing new information into whatever paradigm for reality we have previously chosen to subscribe.

Which is one reason that a genuine spiritual teaching can often be so difficult to follow, if not actually threatening, as it may tend to move us far afield of our familiar levels of reality. And in a sense, that is exactly what evolution does. Force us to expand into unfamiliar territory if we expect to survive when the world around us begins to close in and infringe on our territory.

To be told to love everybody by a spiritual master, as a particular example, carries an extraordinary authority and is clearly meant to be taken seriously. And it is no easy task, as we soon find out when we begin to take it seriously.

There is something or someone around every corner that challenges our expectations, ultimately forcing us to submit our judgments to a higher authority for evaluation. Not out of fear, but because there will be times when we are simply over our heads, unsure of what the next step is or should be.

The manner in which we listen for the answers tells us how far we have come, or how much we have stalled in our personal evolution. And just exactly what does it mean to submit our judgments to a higher authority, and how do we expect the answers to come to us?

Many of us may be struggling in the dark waiting for answers to our hopes and prayers that never seem to come in a timely manner. And which may leave us alone and perhaps even in near-despair. Thrown back on our own resources without the consolation of a heavenly father taking over for us since our own efforts have seemingly come to naught.

In those moments we may feel as though we have been blocked in all our earthly activities, left with nowhere to turn and without any reasonable hope of resolving whatever the particular situation is we are in that so troubles us.

When this occurs, it may signal to some of us that it is time to turn within for a spiritually-direct consultation for the answers, and the answers may come in a different format than we could possibly have anticipated. And that might be in response to an entirely different question, or anything we might have imagined in advance.

There is a traditional Judaic saying, *If God is God, let Him be God.* Which is also to suggest a different way of looking at the problem. What is it we expect God to be? What expectations do we have about divine reality, and how that eternal consciousness can function in an individual life?

And then again, how are we to relate to a divine, eternal source of being from an ordinary earthly perspective. If we appeal to the divine for help in our earthly affairs, on what level and in what form do we anticipate the answer may come. How do we expect the divine to answer our prayers, and from which perspective do we expect to respond.

Which is also to suggest that we want the divine to give us what we want, but without thought for how the divine might want to give us what it wants. And taking the occasion to do so when we are vulnerable and potentially open to guidance. When we might be capable of opening to the infinite source of power within us, the true solution to all our earthly dilemmas.

Which choice would we make beforehand, and what option would we choose, if that were the way the situation was presented to us. Choose the divine response, or hope for a solution that only satisfies the problems of today, but leaves tomorrow's issues to be faced when tomorrow, or the day after tomorrow, comes. And then another appeal for help or guidance, and another period of waiting and near-despair.

But here we are now, in the present moment, with the philosophical knowledge that today is yesterday's tomorrow. And how do we handle that in our moments of immediate issue, knowing that we are appealing for help in the immediacy of the moment, knowing also that the now moment is always in the process of change.

The now moment comes and goes, problems arise and disappear, and life brings endless change, some of it good, some unfortunate. If we are left with only our own ego-mind resources to fall back on, how deep do those resources go and how profoundly helpful will the answers we find actually be.

If we are forced by circumstance to search within, our earthly self, the persona we present to the world and with which we so completely identify, may feel short-changed in the sense of missing worldly experiences according to the results.

But our spiritual self may recognize the enormous gift that earthly difficulties may spiritually bring us when we are forced to find a deeper level of our consciousness in which to reside. And attendant with that, a richer level of understanding the diverse elements of the human experience.

The deeper within we go the more we will find the experience and understanding of love becomes the ever-present state of being that inflects all our moods. And consequently determines the way we will choose to inter-act with material reality.

We do not simply experience love as an impartial witness and occasionally direct participant. We become love itself. In everything we do we become the infinite and ever-present reality of unmotivated, selfless love.

And this is the state that spiritual masters have attained, the most singular achievement of the human adventure. The highest earthly level of our evolutionary adventure.

The single most necessary state of being that grants us the spiritual keys to the heavenly kingdom. And which allows us entry into higher states of consciousness, love being the essential preparation for the inner changes that will occur as we advance our experience of consciousness.

Love is the antithesis of fear. The very presence of love eliminates fear from our compulsive daily diet of endless material desires with which we console ourselves. And tends to make the physical challenges that await us all in the earthly adventure more bearable.

Spiritual traditions teach that we can learn to love whatever comes our way because that is the way things are in the essential nature of existence. The spiritual reality of our inner self, in which the love that exists eternally comes from unmotivated tenderness of the selfless, infinite and eternal heart. In the eyes of the divine, to paraphrase numerous teachings from many spiritual traditions, all things are right and good.

We can either respond to whatever comes before us with love or recoil in fear. Expansion or contraction is the heartbeat of the universe, and the resonating emotional rhythm of mankind's existence.

We can choose to accept life as it is, without regard for the need to control or dominate in accord only with our personal agenda. Or we can do the opposite, and make the anxious effort to challenge life according to our preferences and desires. Forgetful that everything that exists is all still part of the human experience, never really subject to our personal will.

No matter how valiant our efforts or sincere our desires, ultimately we will find that life is bigger than anything we had previously imagined within the confines of our fevered imaginations. And far beyond our best and most determined efforts to change the flow of events that surround us.

We do not have to choose to react in fear, even though life, glorious as it is, always involves pain and suffering. Life is suffering, said Buddha in his first of four noble truths, and who could disprove him.

Suffering too is part of the human adventure. It comes with the territory and cannot be ignored, not even by the most devout or fanciful among us. There is a story about a man who saw his friend banging his head against a wall. *Why are you doing that?* he asked. *Because it feels so good when I stop,* his friend replied.

Not necessarily a comforting thought in this vale of pain and suffering, but nevertheless there is a truth there that cannot be denied. How many of us are banging our heads against a wall we create out of our own fears and sorrows. And when, if ever, does it stop?

We are informed by those who know, the spiritual masters of mankind, that our original nature is nothing other than everlasting, never-ending, endless, perpetual, undying, immortal, abiding, permanent, enduring, infinite, boundless and timeless bliss. Bliss is not a word we generally find or use in our everyday experience or vocabulary. But it could be.

The trouble begins when we shift our awareness in a different direction. When we begin a thought or make a movement of any sort that takes us out of the field of bliss, the essentially unmanifested nature of our consciousness.

Individuation, in the sense of separation from our original nature, consciousness without external objects of identification, which introduces duality into our experience of existence. And then begins the forgetfulness of our original nature. And then comes pain, and thence comes suffering.

Everything we experience on the plane of duality comes with an opposite experience: thought, emotion or action. As long as we remain attached to material being, as long as we

are addicted to those experiences of duality, *here we stay and here we burn.*

Here we stay and here we burn, because of attachment to the material world, is an ancient Egyptian teaching re-framed into contemporary language by the Egyptologist Bika Reed in her translation of a papyrus spiritual text, "Rebel In The Soul." But it is as true today as it was in ancient Egypt because it is still the typical everyday experience of human existence.

As we all know from the tremendous suffering that addicts with all kinds of material attachments experience, addiction can overpower any of us, from the weakest to the strongest.

But never do we think or imagine that our various attachments to physical existence make us all addicts, each in our own way. There is simply no denying the attractions of physical existence.

Nor the obsessive-compulsive nature of the mind that entertains its inner awareness with non-stop fantasies and endless desires. And lives in anticipation of the rewards it will reap from the rich harvest of material seeds it plants in the fields of desire.

But those holographic-entertainments never seem to end, always promising far more than any actual experience can ever deliver. Only a greater and more sublime experience of inner awareness can shift the center of our attention from the imaginary world the mind creates, colored in by egoic needs and sensory preferences.

A greater reality awaits us all if we can learn to discipline the mind and subordinate the ego. How to do that is the problem to be addressed, and in that regard, yogic traditions have a traditional method of addressing the issue.

Yoga, as has been most usefully defined, *is the intentional stopping of the spontaneous activity of the mind stuff.* The reason for learning to do that is to stop the mind from creating the

endless fantasies that send us scurrying here and there in search of this or that, in essentially a mental merry-go-round of continuous and all too often fruitless activity.

Some of it may be meaningful, but much of it may probably be little more than endless activity for the sake of endless activity. And how much of that takes place on an unconscious level? We are drawn into a particular action resulting from a continuously unbroken inner monologue that is simply one association after another with attendant details to fill in what is essentially a waking-dream scenario.

We all know from first-hand experience what that inner stream of consciousness is. How engrossing it can be even if essentially irrelevant to whatever activity we are engaged in fulfilling, even when the details of the fantasy are completely insignificant.

But none of those imaginary scenarios seem to matter, nor do the specific details we visualize in any of those fantasies. They all appear to merge into the stark bleakness of forgetfulness, one after another. All episodic clips of endlessly imaginative fantasy lives that quickly disappear into the mental void of non-existence.

All chasing after some phantom purpose, which may be nothing more than the mind entertaining itself in its endless search for amusement. Diverting itself from the endless boredom of a mental existence that is unable to recognize the bliss of its true and essential nature.

We identify with that apparently endless flow of thoughts and images, and the mountain stream of contiguous flow which is what we imagine we are. And we will act on it, defend it and preserve is as if it were our historical heritage. More fundamental to our being than our bodies, the consciousness within or the life force that animates all its activities.

Expansion and contraction, attraction and withdrawal, being and non-being. The identification with and repulsion from are all aspects of the experience of duality, the emotional and intellectual ways in which we decorate the front yards of our minds. Those inner illusions are the furniture we collect that comfort us when we are afflicted, assuring us some measure of inner security and stability. Eventually some of them will be moved up to the attic, others to the basement as a fresh crop of indigenous artifacts takes their place.

They come and go, those ideas and influences, secured by nothing and attached to little more than the moods and emotions that course through our inner being like a mountain stream raging out of control during a flood and overflowing its banks.

This is the familiar territory we inhabit when we move or are moved from our true center, the organic inner core of perpetual and never-ending bliss. In that we are all alike, most of us. Except for those determined few who have taken their evolution in hand, and returned their attention to its rightful center of attention. They have returned to their spiritual home.

When we reside in bliss all else fades in comparison. Nothing can distract us from the fundamental experience of all-engrossing being. That which completely occupies our awareness when we have awakened from the sleep of illusion, the waking dream which is our daily life.

The inner experience of enlightenment is the true experience of awareness, the center in which we all reside when we are spiritually activated. This is the direction in which we are all eventually fated to travel. It is the return to an authentic state of being, the enlightened presence of the individual monad to its eternal existence.

It is where love exists in the fullest measure of its presence. All our activities, when we are centered on that profound

inner level of our being, are inflected by the presence of spiritual love and infinite bliss. Everything we think, everything we do all come from the same place of secure, changeless and abiding presence.

And when that occurs, we become fully authentic to who and what we really are. Having attained to the royal presence within, nothing and no one can move us from that authentic experience of existence. We are secure within, lonely no more, fear is recognized as nothing more than an illusion. Love the only reality, and bliss the landscape of being.

No longer victims of chance, *or nature's changing course untrimmed,* we have become what we were always capable of becoming and never were. We have finally realized the true experience of life, the awareness within that flows beneath the senses. And which does not depend on physical existence or emotional support for its happiness.

The eternal being within us is the true source of our existence, the inner reality which never succumbs to the ravages of time. Or submits its authority to the erratic indoctrination of the senses, or the challenges of physical existence.

All of which confuse us by virtue of the powerful influences of shifting moods, leaving us vulnerable to the ever-changing tides of time. All of which deny us access to our spiritual birthright, to the legacy of immortal being which is rightly ours. And which we mercilessly deny ourselves through our addiction to external experience.

All kinds of experiences, mental as well as physical. Anything that moves us out of our essential nature is an addiction or an infatuation within time. A false longing we only imagine is a more potent and informing force than the bliss of self-conscious existence.

The secret of self-recognition is that we are already saved, already beyond the need for rites and rituals of initiation. We

need only achieve the realization of what we already and always are, but have only temporarily forgotten.

Anything that aids in the spiritual search may be useful, but the so-called spiritual search is itself only a distraction from remembrance of our inner nature. In this regard, the spiritual search can itself become a barrier we must overcome. There is an implied assumption the search affirms that we are essentially without that which we wish to become.

But again, what we already are and have only forgotten. Which may be why we so deny our true nature as we search in the world for the satisfaction of desire. We are missing out on the true experience of being when we succumb to desire, substituting the relatively inert experiences of physical encounters for the all-consuming bliss of true being.

The truth of desire is that it can be so potent a force that it blinds us to the trap in which it enfolds us. The attraction to any object of desire can have an obsessive-compulsive quality about it from which we cannot easily escape. There is simply no end of repeating this until finally, at long last, it sinks in and we recognize the truth.

Unless a more powerful experience comes into our awareness that enables us to escape the lure of desire. It is a cheap and easy victory when desire takes control over our minds and hearts. And when that happens, we have essentially sold our birthright for something of infinitely lesser value and virtually no attainment.

When a desire is satisfied with nothing left over to fulfill our needs, we are once again left where we first began. And must start over again in search of something else that will make us feel whole and complete, but never can.

Pain and suffering begin when we are forced to endure the agony of withdrawal from physical and mental addictions, with only the sensation of emptiness and loneliness to occupy our awareness.

The only wholeness we will ever know is the recognition of and identification with that which lies within. Nothing in the external world can ever satisfy the deep inner yearning to reunite with spirit. This is a yearning within us all for the experience of completeness, and the satisfaction of being totally informed about the nature of our existence.

We all want, some of us on a deeply unconscious level, to experience the enlightenment of our soul. And that is another problem, for many of us never recognize that the existential anxiety we feel, but never quite come close to naming or understanding, is our yearning for spirit. For the experience of integral wholeness.

Nothing else can ever fully and completely abnegate our sense of loneliness and alienation. Nothing we can experience with our physical senses or through mental imagery will ever fill our hearts with joy, or immerse our inner being in bliss and the joy of existence. Nothing less than the absolute truth of our existence will ever calm the implacable yearnings of our restless hearts.

Which is the reason that a spiritual teaching, and a spiritual master, is the way out of suffering. The teaching, because it gives order and meaning to our spiritual existence, and because it clearly defines the parameters of our lives.

A spiritual teaching offers us an authentic sense of being and belonging, a method by which we can absorb the suffering of existence. Something to cling to when we have gone astray, or when we are swept away by the often uncontrollable time and tides of mortal existence.

When we are buffeted about by the storms of existence, a spiritual teaching gives us something to cling to when all else fails. The teachings may themselves be only a higher form of illusion, but they are necessary steps on the ladder to the sky. Anything created by man is destined to fade away over time, as anything that appears will one day disappear. All created

forms eventually return to the undifferentiated energy of the universe.

And if we are fortunate, a spiritual master in our lives offers us a confirming presence and the authority of true being. The calm, placid and peaceful existence of an individual centered in the inner bliss of authentic being. Unshakeable and unmovable, immersed in the center of conscious awareness. That which we long to be and which we have forgotten is our original and natural state of being.

To awaken from the sleep of illusion is the essential teaching of any spiritual tradition. *Awaken, dear one, from the sleep of illusion,* the ancient Indian teachings cry out through time. We have the examples of so many men and women from every corner of the globe to guide us, yet we resist the call in every way we can.

Content with so little compared to what has been revealed about our human potential by spiritually-enlightened beings, we remain captive-slaves of a subordinate state of conscious-awareness. We remain wholly captivated by the light show within the holographic inner fields of our imagination.

We are in search of so many emotional and physical sources of worldly pleasure, but at the core of our desire system we are all fundamentally in search of love. Love is what motivates us because love if the essential nature of our being. It is home, and we are homeward-bound.

Bliss is the state of our spiritual nature, and love is the way it manifests on the earth plane. In that state of original being there is no negativity, nothing other than love, nothing to divert our attention from what that great incarnation of divine being, Bhagwan Nityananda, referred to as pure mind, steady mind, big mind and pure feeling.

Everything is dust, he would say again and again, *our natural state is the state of joy.* But are we so afraid of joy, one might suppose, or is it simply that our uninformed and automatic

attachment to physical experiences is so profoundly all-engrossing.

If the purpose of attachment to various physical and emotional experiences is meant to result in the pleasure we only-temporarily obtain from them, what then would be the purpose of any of the painful processes of achieving those ends if that state of bliss is always and forever what we essentially are in our original nature. Why would we be willing to settle so easily for a lesser state of being?

It would appear that the choices we make in this regard have more to do with the immediate or near-immediate sensations of pleasure we can more easily and quickly attain. And it does not appear to matter how temporary or short-term those experiences actually are, as long as we satisfy the immediate but momentary satisfaction of desire.

Desire is not a permanent state of being as might generally be supposed. It is only an inflection of consciousness towards something that only temporarily attracts our attention. In that sense, desire is a descent from the awareness of higher consciousness. Only a temporary fixture in the abode of consciousness, a secondary consideration no matter how powerfully it draws us to the center of its fixation and attention.

Desire may be understood as a reflection of the obsessive-compulsive aspect of our earthy experience, but need not necessarily be thought of as an inescapable fact of our existence. We can not only learn to live with and reasonably accommodate the desire-nature of our consciousness, we can go much further and learn to overcome it. One touch of bliss and we understand where we are and what we are doing.

And thereby eliminate its influence in our daily affairs, which is what genuine maturity is about. To respond to life by choice, rather than automatically through any pre-programmed system of thought or action that reflect only a lower state of awareness.

And in accord with that uncoordinated line of thinking and runaway train of behavior, an inability to control the lower levels of our awareness, resulting in a lesser state of being. Acting in life in a manner similar to pre-programmed lumbering robots, not especially high on the evolutionary scale.

The more advanced we are on an evolutionary scale of being, the more we recognize the necessity of expanding our ability to both give and receive love. Not simply from and with those with whom we are intimate, but as a necessary condition of life.

Love is not the luxury some of us think it is, and it has nothing to do with the merely physical satisfaction of a biological function. Nor is it solely a matter of preference. Love is an absolute necessity for advancing both our emotional experience of life, and our ability to access the spiritual dimension during and after our brief span of existence.

The experience of love resonates throughout our being, putting us in accord with every dimension of our existence. It resonates in the echo-chambers of the heart as well as fulfilling the needs of our soul in any incarnation. It allies us with the highest expression of transcendent bearing.

Love is what gives ultimate meaning to life, to existence on all levels of being. And when we are absorbed in love, when we resonate from the fullness of our heart, we hear the sound of one hand clapping throughout our field of awareness. We are in harmony with ourselves.

Love puts us in accord with the universe and all that is in it, the most sublime force in existence. The ultimate purpose of life and the reason the universe was called into being. The total and absolute expression of the universal field of being in the field of time and space.

We are called on to love everybody by the highest spiritual teachings. And whatever name we call the source behind those teachings matters not a bit. What matters is that we invoke that universal injunction to re-unite with that sublime expression of ultimate resonance and highest being.

And in that regard, specific forms of spiritual teachings may come and go, as do all forms of creation. But what always stays with us is the truth of those teachings, and that is where we ought to put our faith.

Truth resonates through time. When a particular incarnation of truth depends on a specific context for its existence, that truth will eventually become relative and potentially lose its ability to inform as conditions change.

But when truth emerges as a necessary and inevitable condition of life, it attains an immortality that is no longer subject to the vicissitudes of time, nor to the ever-changing conditions of existence.

Spiritual truth is susceptible neither to change, nor to re-interpretation according to any shifting mood based on personal whim, political or social correctness. Love, and the injunction to love everybody, is the yellow brick road we must all one day travel.

Eight

Serve God

Some of us may be concerned that to serve God in the conventional manner would essentially mean having to endure enforced intellectual and emotional servitude to the arbitrary rules of some oversized, personally-indifferent religious organization. And in this regard, there is little difference between spiritual service and slavery.

Having to obey the artificial rules, spiritual regimentation and strict regulations of a biased earthly-institution is not an enticing prospect to the modern mind. And being forced to go along with the restrictions, dogmas, theologies and placard-waving sentimentalist and fundamentalist right-wing policies of a group-conscience stripped of so many humane considerations is not an appealing prospect either.

But be assured, that is not what it means to serve the divine. Whatever any individual consideration of the divine presence might suggest, there is a general sense that the divine resides in the human heart, the spiritual heart. And that God, or the power of infinite spirit, is within our very being.

Not that all that many of us would necessarily understand what that might specifically mean, nor that we fully understand the theological assumptions, which of themselves no longer seem to be of such paramount importance in our lives. Theology no longer leaves us trembling with awe and wonder. Nor does it fill our hearts with an experience of love so profound that all other considerations seem pale besides it.

Usually when we speak of God we associate the divine imprint with love, the love that resides in the heart, not to be confused with lesser forms of love usually significant of attachment or biological sensations.

And when this becomes the medium suggestive of the divine presence, it also suggests that the light of love that exists in one spiritual heart exists also in another. What is true here is also true there, for who would have either the wisdom or the arrogance to attempt to place restrictions on what the divine presence might be. Or where it might be located.

There is a well-known truth in real estate concerning the value of a property. It comes in three parts: location, location, and location. A property is most highly valued according to its physical location. This is not news.

But in this sense, one value of love is where it resides and with what we identify it. If it is located in the loins, we mistake lust for love, and consequently suffer a sensation of loss and disempowerment when the experience ends. And we are left where we began when the event is over, only partially satisfied if at all.

Only then to begin the processes of unreachable fulfillment over and over again each time the sensation of desire arises. Never to know the genuine experience of blissful self-awareness. Never to understand the true nature of love, and the infinite depths it reaches when we are centered in the heart and experiencing the fullness of which it is capable.

Relying on the inevitably declining faculties of physical empowerment to re-experience the merely-physical sensations we mistakenly identified as love is a losing game, and a waste of irreplaceable time and energy.

In this sense, time may be among the greatest motivations we will ever have when we search within for the mystery of being. Time lost is always a losing venture in every sense, and there is no such thing as time regained. When the sands of

time have run out, there is no way to replace or regain what has been lost forever.

Time suggests hope, and without hope all is lost. Nothing we are or have ever been can change for the better without hope. And when our allotted span of time runs out, who and what we imagine ourselves as being can evolve no further in its current incarnation.

Love centered in the heart is true love, and love centered in the spiritual heart is nothing less than Agape, spiritual love. This is the love that never fears an ending, never loses its appeal, and never descends into the lower reaches of human emotional states.

And because it is infinite and comes from infinite spirit, there is no need for hope since we have already arrived at our destination. There is only the intensity and fullness of the present moment of now. Where are you? *Here.* What time is it? *Now.*

Location is indeed everything; it separates earthly chaff from spiritual wheat. And it suggests an all-important fact, that we are each worthy of love because there already exists a love that transcends all human emotions located deeply within us all, deeply within our essential being. We are all incarnation of love because we are all incarnations of the divine presence.

For some it shines forth brightly and illuminates the inner landscape and outer appearance of that person's presence. For others that light has been polluted by sundry forms of abuse, some of it self-inflicted. And whatever light they shed is consequently dim, feeble and subject to interpretation, change and re-evaluation. A fertile field for stress, anxiety and despair to flourish and grow.

But that same light of consciousness nevertheless shines in each of us. And deep within our spiritual hearts resides the same essence of divine love that inflects the whole of

creation. Neither created nor an emergent factor of existence, it is the light of the divine, of infinite spirit as it inter-acts with the universe. The energy, power, or force of the universal and infinite source of being.

It is this inner light and archetypal staging area of love that we are meant to enter and embrace. The divine source that we are meant to worship and adore out of love, self-recognition and gratitude that we are not and never have been alone.

We are not lost among the stars. We are individual incarnations of the divine examining and experiencing the stars, as well as the whole of creation. We are the spiritual light of the universe radiating through self-conscious and sentient material forms, the physical templates of human bodies.

In this deeply spiritual and enlightened sense we are simply worshiping ourselves for what lies within, and which it is our function to bring to the full light of consciousness. This is not ego masquerading as self-knowledge, it is the enlightenment of the soul to its true nature.

The closer we come to that inner experience of self-regard and self-recognition through any spiritual practice of high regard, the closer we come to a fundamental understanding of the universe and our rightful place in it.

And having embraced the truth of this spiritual injunction, we can see our way towards accepting that the same spiritual reality that lies within us also lies within another, and another, and then another. What is true for one in this sense is true for all.

To love everyone and everything is to most truly serve God, to recognize the divine presence within all sentient beings and all existence. And whatever the state of an individual consciousness may be, this same understanding is

nevertheless true and available for all through spiritual evolution and the practice of self-recognition.

The light of consciousness shines forth from within all sentient beings. The spiritual nature of their inner being, no matter how dim or distorted any individual condition may be, is still there however unmanifest it may appear.

This is the problem to be solved, the reason that spiritual traditions exist. How to switch the light on of true consciousness, focusing spiritual light on the darkness within. Illuminating through conscious awareness those areas of inner being of which we are still relatively ignorant and unaware.

And which not only escape our attention, but due to varying circumstances some of us may utterly deny our spiritual potential exists at all. Ignorance may speak with a loud voice, but it is nevertheless still only ignorance. Bullying voices may occasionally make the most noise, but there is no victory in their achievement.

It is absolutely hypocritical and utterly preposterous to deny within any individual manifestation the spiritual reality that so many of us supposedly worship in our conventional Sunday morning adventures devoted to religious affirmation.

Which of themselves may or may not produce a useful and lasting effect, but which generally do not address the fundamental issues that serious and inner-directed spiritual teachings examine in any authentic meditative tradition.

We are taught to love everybody as a primary method of serving the divine light of existence, but we are not always taught how to do that. The closest some of us generally come in traditional western Christianity, for one example among many, is the injunction to hate the sin but love the sinner.

How useful hate is in any context is debatable however, and subject to intense scrutiny as a viable teaching method.

Where is the rightful place of hate in any spiritual tradition, and under what heading would it be found in any index of divine attributes of a God of Love?

The deeper we go into the experience of love, the less room there is for anything other than love. And certainly hate is a violation of that canon if we are to consider the fullest possible measure of what love means.

Spiritual teachers have long maintained that when one seriously sets foot on a spiritual path, God will remove all that is not God until only God is left. And if that is true, where in that process can hate find a secure sinecure for its existence and continued influence in the affairs of mankind.

Perhaps this is where we part company with the true saints and sages of mankind, individuals who have found within themselves more than simply a relationship with the divine, but who identify their essential being *as* the divine.

Many of whom, in all traditions, were crucified in various forms by ignorant souls who could not endure the challenge that spiritual enlightenment brought into their lives. Rejection was their only response to the offer of the enlightened education of the spirit.

Those great souls who attained to enlightenment recognized through the internal processes of self-realization that their essential being *is* the divine. They *are* that, and that inner force of conscious self-aware existence is exactly what they and we and all of us are.

But they also took care along the way not to allow their ego-structure to hyper-inflate to the extent that they identified their personal existence as the only and ultimate source. This is usually accomplished through the various trials and tribulations they, and we, all undergo in the process of evolutionary growth and spiritual transformation.

This would only be the ego trying to take back control rather than accepting what we all are, incarnations through individuated forms of infinite spirit. To which the ego-structure is simply a bonded-servant, rather than acting as if it were the master of the universe, and which it would like to pretend it is. The rule of ego is only another endless variation of Casey at the bat.

This can be a difficult maneuver if one is overwhelmed by the inner riches of enhanced consciousness, but still subject to the well-lubricated structures of the ego. The inner path is often subject to temptation and attachment, and if one is not careful what should be understood in one way might be carelessly misunderstood in another.

What should be clearly understood as a statement of universal being, when understood from the point of view of ego, might be mistakenly seen and acted on as the evolution of personal power. Eventually inducing the narcissism and self-regard of an uninformed and immature mind.

Great wisdom is needed to separate these two extremes of self-understanding when the appeal of self-empowerment can be so profoundly over-reaching to an immature ego. But that is why the spiritual path requires not only maturity, but mature guidance.

Such guidance is not as easily available as might often be thought or needed, which may be one utterly profound and widespread reason we have faltered as a race of evolving individuals only occasionally following or paying solecistic lip-service to a spiritual path.

But it is still true that the wisdom and discrimination needed to follow any path of the heart is painfully and agonizingly slow. No matter how compelling the rewards of the path may be to those moving towards that unknown inner reality, it nevertheless requires full attention to detail. Inattention to detail can be time-consuming to correct, as well as disastrous to experience.

Hoping, wishing and dreaming will not necessarily put food on the table, and neither will intercessory prayers, heart-felt pleas of penitude or supplications to the divine. These may all be useful in transforming one's spiritual demeanor, but we must generally work hard and labor skillfully to achieve our ends. There are no shortcuts to enlightenment.

We usually put our hopes, wishes and dreams into direct action through thoughtful and skillful means. Miracles may indeed occur, but if miracles happen it is more likely according to a higher power than simply our own desires influencing the universe and made manifest.

Our prayers, pleas and supplications must be accompanied by right action and right regard. To follow a spiritual path demands hard work and the integration of all aspects of the personality structure into one meaningful and united whole. A spiritual path is not an escape from reality, but instead helps the aspirant fulfill the conditions of true being.

Easy it is to say *Yes,* but difficult to do. And when that is based on spiritual injunctions to serve God and love everybody, the problem is magnified immeasurably. We no longer have the luxury of scapegoating any one person or any one group in order to let off steam, releasing frustration and pressure with everyone and everything by attacking an easy, available or convenient target.

We are no longer justified, we are never justified, in targeting convenient or powerless targets, victimizing them for the difficulties we experience in life. But to be told so powerfully and directly that we must learn to relate to everyone through love, rather than through hate, can force some of us into an early retirement from a spiritual path.

The readiness is all is the great realization that comes to Hamlet when he finally recognizes that *there is a divinity that shapes our ends, rough hew them how we will.* This is not a stray thought that somehow enters his awareness, it is the direct realization of a fundamental truth of higher consciousness.

And the impact of this is that it frees Hamlet from indecision, obviating the inability to act that has plagued him throughout his adult career.

His new-found spiritual awareness has integrated a central spiritually-oriented authority within him from which to act, a psychological position that informs his activities and allows him a free range of choice, movement and fulfillment.

There is no higher authority than the integrity of God. Once realized and fully accepted, one then acts in accord, as best one can, with the divine will. In the enlightened sage there is no separation between the personal will and the divine will.

Inattention to detail disappears as there is no longer the conflict that results from a confusion of choices, the disillusionment of mortal affairs, or the distractions of the ego-oriented decision-making processes. One is in accord with the universe and at peace within oneself.

Individuals who have attained that experience of wholeness act from the integrity of their unified being, rather than listening to the confused voices of the various personae within them, each of which seeks the full measure of action and authority on its own behalf.

The more serious issue is not really whether or not to love everybody, the problem is how to do it. And it then becomes clear that we cannot change the world or force others to do our bidding. The best we can do, all that we can do, is to work on ourselves so that we ourselves become the loving incarnation of divine spirit. *We* are *that,* made manifest through our earthly presence. In every aspect of our being we become transparent to the divine.

Which means we must learn to search out those dark places within us in which negative emotions and restless attitudes reside. Fear has its own fortress of solitude within us. It hides

within our hearts. It manifests through the ego-structures that determine the shape and content of our thoughts and actions.

When we act from love we do not have to go through the give-and-take processes of deciding how something will benefit or harm us. What we stand to gain though one course of action, and what we stand to lose through another merge into an all-encompassing spiritual love of creation that flows through us like a supernal force of nature.

When we act from love as the full measure of our incarnation, we act naturally and without any forethought of malice. We have become authentic to the truth of our spiritual nature. We have been freed from the incessant plotting, and all too often ineffectual planning, that so often attend decision-making processes.

When we act from love we are freed from the doubt and insecurity that so often trails our actions, lingers in our memory and invokes our conscience. And when our conscience is activated it is a sure and certain sign that something somewhere is clearly amiss.

When our conscience is disturbed we usually share some serious measure of blame for whatever situation we are in. Whatever the actual circumstances may be or whatever the circumstances are that affect us even if they are only imaginary.

Imaginary though they may be, the effects they create, if we believe in what are essentially only-phantom causes, are as real as the effect that would be produced by splitting a two-by-four over our collective heads.

Real or imaginary, either one can produce a result and the result can be either substantial or insubstantial, depending often on the depth and integrity of the belief system that initially brought them into being.

Love as a fundamental force of existence may on occasion be subject in its influence on us by the inherent power of our belief system. What we accept we may easily cherish, but if we are subject to the fragmentary impulses of our moods and desires, we may find the integrity of our belief system flawed.

Or worse, begins to disintegrate due to the confusion that results when inner fields of interest collide and then conflict. When rational considerations, philosophical indexes of authentic measurement, or psychological adjustments based on genuine standards of physical and mental well-being encounter resistance from powerful emotions that defy rhyme, rhythm and reason.

Our beliefs may shape our response to reality and the way we react to the endless change that reality brings into our lives, but that does not necessarily suggest that our beliefs are an accurate reflection of reality. Only that to some extent we all try to shape physical existence towards meeting our own ends.

Physical reality may be malleable to some degree, but to imagine that we have ultimate or final control over any aspect of existence is to live a foolish dream, an immature illusion. We are not in control, aside from our merely personal likes and dislikes.

We are only disinvolved spectators when we consider our brief span of existence and the sheer immensity of the space/time continuum. We clearly leave behind only a small, finite and relatively insignificant imprint, temporary manipulators of some aspects of our physical existence. We are here for an indefinite period of time, and then we move on.

Our beliefs, combined with our physical and intellectual prowess, may allow us to shape-shift within our material surroundings, but at some point in time it all ends as even our best efforts are foredoomed to eventual failure.

What we call reality is perhaps only a holographic playground of explicate forms unfolding from the implicate energies of the universe. Our beliefs allow us entry into some particular but still finite playgrounds. But whatever games we play, whatever forms we create, they and we are nevertheless still subject to the immutable laws of the space/time continuum.

Those beliefs, such as they are or might be, may or may not allow for the power of love, particularly spiritual love, called Agape by the ancient Greeks, to dominate the market-place of our inner lives. When the ego is in charge of our affairs it all too frequently makes use of the various forms through which love incarnates for the fulfillment of its own ends.

What some of us take to be love frequently appears in the form of Eros, often defined as the zeal of the loins for each other. And often takes the form of Amor, personal love, the opening of one heart to another.

These are both vital for the health and well-being of the incarnated soul, as are other forms of love between individuals, family members, friends and even social institutions. Love in whatever form it appears is generally regarded as a worthwhile and highly cherished emotion.

Most of those multiple forms of Eros and Amor rest on personal preferences, and the relationship between involved participants. They may not necessarily invoke a permanent state of being, or a relationship of such profound depth that it defies gravity.

Not even physical force can pull lovers away from their appointed paths. Nor the inherent mental, physical and emotional limitations of the space/time continuum, or so it seems to those under the spell of the beloved.

Agape is said to be beyond all that. Powerful though the force of Agape is in an individual heart, it does not depend on personal preferences for its existence. It is not limited by

duration, choice or any mental, physical or emotional characteristics.

Agape is so powerful a force of love, almost an impersonal expression of existence, that it appears to be without the necessity of any specific object of attention. The content of Agape-consciousness appears to be love, love, nothing but love.

As though swept away by a tidal wave of such infinitely loving-and attentive attraction that the atypical egoic self is taken over, and without moving an inch, resides forever in the abode of infinite and everlasting bliss.

When that happens we exist authentically within the loving contours of our spiritual hearts, the abode of love which is the true center of our inner attention. We are that which lies most truly, most deeply and most eternally within the sacred ground upon which we all walk on an inner path.

And from which we all learn to act in our relation to the whole of existence, including first uncovering and then exposing the darker side of our own nature to the light of spiritual growth and compassionate understanding.

It is within our own hearts that the first impulse must come if we are to follow the spiritual injunctions to serve God and love one another. That is one impulse that will not lead us astray of its own, particularly when our matured experiences of life teach us to act with the integrity of full-being as we respond to the world. Or sit in silence, informed by the enlightening experiences of life that come our way on a spiritual path.

At some point in our evolution there will no longer be a difference between daily life with its mundane activities and a spiritual path. Some of us may mistakenly imagine a spiritual path as something outside the normal ebb and flow of our existence, but it is not.

It is an inner path we travel when we follow the dictates of the heart, and submit our egoic impulses to the modulations and impulses of our immortal soul. They come to us through insight and intuition, as much as a lightning bolt descends from the heavens. Or a finger writing on a wall in a long ignored or generally forgotten spiritually-oriented metaphoric poem.

Life and love, one and the same in their essential nature. Differing only in the intensity of love present and available, or the lack of it. Without that presence we live in an emotional void. With it, we swim in an ocean of love. We exist within the fullness and certitude of eternal being.

The choices we make obviously determine our future to a considerable degree, but they do not necessarily suggest a necessary, radical and permanent change in our essential being. Our essential being is never under duress.

But to choose love, to follow the injunction to love everybody, unlike most other earthly decisions does not involve an escape clause. And because it is a spiritual injunction, there is no earthly court of appeal, no additional fine print, and no further amendments to be made.

To love everybody means to love *everybody*. And from that there is no alternate implication that frees us from the extraordinary challenge of embracing the whole of existence without preferential or exclusionary exceptions. Personal preferences must be set aside until they no longer exist, or have a significant impact on our thoughts or actions.

To love everybody is to serve God. Neither reading a lilting scripture, reciting a beautiful passage from a book held in sacred reverence, nor attending religious services with some degree of regularity can substitute for this one essential, fundamental and only serious requirement on a spiritual journey.

The only way to truly serve God is by knowing God. We cannot imitate God through secondary practices that absent us from the presence of the divine. The only true way to know God is to become God. Only God can know God, and in this cause the only goal of any spiritual path is enlightenment to the presence of the divine.

And then there is this consideration, that if the divine exists, does it exist only here but not there? Now, but not then? In this direction, but not that, this way but no other, in this one, but not those others.

Who is there with the wisdom and knowledge to place man-made limits on how the creative force behind the universe may or may not manifest its presence and its power? Who is there to justify that determination?

Who dares attempt to enforce that only-assumed absolute authority on mankind? Who would imagine forcing the universe into alignment with such an arbitrary decision? And all based on scant evidence, personal opinion taken in the name of religious certitude about the origins of man, the universe, and the creator. Who would dare such a preposterous undertaking and call it by the name of revealed religion?

If the divine force of existence is real and actual, then where or when could it not be found? And if that is so, why look away when we should truly be looking within? How better to serve God then to find God. And once found, rejoin the infinite, divine source of existence and merge individual being into the divinity from which it first came

The only thing that separates us from knowledge of the Beloved is the illusion in the beginning that we were ever separated from the divine source when first we came into the individuated light of personal consciousness. This is the game the universe plays with itself, from which the goal of personal existence is to awaken to the imprisoned splendor.

We are asleep to the true nature of our existence, and awaken we must or we will keep playing the game until our time runs out. It is all, according to the by now well-known phrase made famous many years ago by Swami Muktananda, the play of consciousness.

How conscious are we of what really goes on beneath the surface level of our awareness is the problem to be addressed. How aware are we of the nature and trajectory of our thoughts, our emotions, and the stream of conscious awareness that informs our movements and awakens us to the dawning of inner light.

Time begins when duality begins, when we first feel ourselves lost and alone, separated from the creation and faced with the mystery of existence. Try as we might, we have yet to find a truly meaningful philosophical or scientific approach that solves the problem of existence.

Nothing we know of our own creation presents a unifying conjunction between man and the cosmos. We have justified our aloneness as a cosmic act of fate, whatever that might mean to those who believe it. And even those who do not.

And in place of a trans-dimensional working postulation between ourselves and the spiritual realm, we have substituted a series of reigning deities of varying incarnations whose existence, or non-existence in terms of physical being, purportedly explains the universe and our place in it.

But they do not. We are as lost and alone as ever when we continually substitute a ruling deity, any ruling deity, for direct knowledge and a genuine experience of spiritual reality and the spiritual realm.

And the same idea holds true for scientific explanations of the beginnings of the universe, the big-bang theory, which asks for a free pass on the origins of the initial explosion that brought the universe into being. The god-like miracle we are asked to accept as science.

Our comfort level, such as we are aware of it, may be as secure as ever when we simply conform to whatever spiritual expectations our social circumstances place on us. But our souls are restless and aware that they have not been served well through their incarnated presence within and as us.

We have not risen to the spiritual task set before us when we took birth. To find and express ourselves in this earthly realm of great and enormous beauty, tremendous hardship, and the company of like-minded and dissimilar souls.

To pass through the physical realm and emerge unscathed by attachment and aversion into the light of full consciousness. To be that which, in true reality, we already and always are.

There are endless detours on the path to personal salvation. Some of us have taken many of them ourselves along the way rather than face the harsh necessity of truly facing the illusions we have so carefully maintained throughout our lives. Not that it is the easiest way out, but some of us are reluctant to question our existence too deeply, or assert our private lack of faith in the institutions to which we publicly and of necessity often subscribe.

Instead of faith in our own existence and love of life, we substitute faith in our own suffering as the common-ground of our being. We are the water of the water, but identify ourselves as the froth bubbling on the foamy surface of the sea. The choice we so often make is to be neither the light, nor the mirror that reflects the light.

Instead of serving God through love, we serve the dark side of our own nature through suffering. One is a permanent state of affairs, the other is not. The other only a temporary detour through eternity that unfortunately, in the human scale of things, can last a lifetime.

But we cannot live in the spiritual realm. Being human, we can only be aware of its existence within us, and do what we

can to respond from that deep place of safety and security. And love.

We can serve the divine within us by finding ways to love as we go about the daily affairs of life. Whatever they may be, wherever we are, whatever we are doing, we can still find ways to be of divine and loving service to creation.

That includes us as well. We have the means within us to end our suffering, which is also within us. The road to salvation is not measured in miles, and in truth, there is no distance between the lover and the divine beloved.

There is only the frantic urgency of self-separation, the need to seek the expression and fulfillment of one's own individuality. And that is the illusion in which we are caught up, that we are all separate beings in quest of our own autonomy.

Such autonomy does not exist. How could it? First, because we are all dependent on so much outside ourselves, and second, and above all, because we are all expressions of the one reality. We are all manifestations of the one consciousness that informs the universe, inflected through our own being.

Autonomy will come to us when we merge back into the oneness from which we came. When we recognize that fundamental truth, instead of automatically subscribing to and endorsing through forgetfulness the traditional and fundamental error of self-separation.

The spiritual heart is the only human realm in which the conjunction of divine autonomy may be found. To look elsewhere is to empower the illusion of separation, prolonging suffering until suffering, and consequently life, have lost their appeal.

When we are hungry we eat; when we are thirty we drink. When we, or others, want to punish us for mistakes in

judgment we allow suffering to come into our sphere of experience. And when finally we are tired of suffering we end the game. We look deeply within, past the debris field of personal history, like what we see in the depth of our being, and take charge of our own evolution. We move on into love.

We do that by ending the illusion, waking up from the dream, ending the nightmare of loneliness from which, in our hearts, we all suffer. In our minds we are alone with our thoughts, perennially untangling ourselves from the Sargasso Sea of personal debris that fills our awareness with a mental minefield of images, ideas, memories, dreams and reflections.

And the result is we lose ourselves in a never-ending train of thoughts, such that whatever we imagine our destination may be, we never arrive at a secure location in our inner world. Some of us know this, some do not. But those who do understand the dilemma we all face when our minds are out of control and we along with them.

Obsessive-compulsive control is not the issue most of us face, but the problem of a secure psychological center from which to act is. The central problem is one of identity, the absolute and certain knowledge of exactly who and what we really are. Our minds harbor so many negative imprints that cynicism and despair have established firm footholds in our philosophical thinking during the natural course of contemporary events.

Some of this reflects the lack of certitude many of us feel about the spiritual direction of our lives. And more importantly, the loss of faith we have experienced in this modern age of doubt and disbelief. We may have killed our expectations from a personal God in our daily lives, but that does not mean that God is dead.

Philosophical despair can never regain for us the confidence and spiritual accord that once was ours, however incomplete or fragmentary that position may have been when

we first recognized or intuited the divine nature of the universe.

The ground of being quickly shifted under our feet when we succumbed to the alienation and isolation of philosophical nihilism. And the advance of science and the scientific method incorporated ideas and methodologies that were perfectly attuned to the material world, but which had no place in the structure of our thinking or belief system when investigating the spiritual realm.

Perhaps that was a necessary stage in our collective evolution, to rid ourselves of false notions about existence. And to investigate as well the immature and even irrational impulses within our psyches that seek certitude where there is only quicksand.

Science may presume to have the proper approach to these questions, but science applies the rules of the material world to the spirit world, with which the same rules of evidence do not apply. Spirit is not bound or limited by material existence, and to think otherwise is to misunderstand the implicate nature of the spiritual dimension.

To believe in the divine structure of the universe does not necessarily suggest the renaissance figure of a bearded father-figure extending a finger-pointing arm towards man. Such anthropomorphic thinking extends back throughout history, but it is not a necessary or fruitful way of thinking about the divine presence and spiritual authority.

That kind of ancient and medieval thinking creates and re-creates God in endless ways in man's image or through man's imagination, as has been pointed out many times.

But any concept of the divine reality worth thinking about should consider that God, or the God-force, cannot be limited to any one particular manifestation or inflected in some localized group consciousness grown familiar to us over time and through historical representations.

We need to revisit our thinking, if we can set aside our various emotional attachments and traditional religious affiliations. We may not be able to define infinite spirit now, and probably not in the foreseeable future, but we can revise the convention beliefs that place limits on the infinite ability of the divine manifestation.

When we do that, as so many of us do, we are essentially dancing in the dark and bumping into the furniture. Clarity does not mean a clear vision and understanding of the divine, it means seeing through the mind-created and emotionally-sustained illusions we create to certify our place in the universe. And in that process of spiritually-oriented self-justification, calm our restless minds and troubled hearts when we contemplate the mysteries and tragedies of existence. When we wish to commune with the divine, many of us travel to stone buildings, sacred sites in our imagination.

But when we do that, light our candles, say our prayers, knees bent towards whatever image of the divine resides within the architecture of the building, do we then imagine that the presence of the divine ends when we step outside the sacred confines of the building?

For some the answer might be yes, others might not think all that much of the question. Perhaps the question is fundamentally without meaning, and they might be correct. An imaginary line on a map separates one state from another, but it is all part of the same landscape, all part of one planet. In the same way, neither a wall nor an institution itself could divide the divine into separate parts.

The God-force exists everywhere, in everyone and everything, in the air we breathe and the thoughts we think. There is no place and nothing in existence that is not filled with the plenitude of the divine. This is where any philosophy of gloom and despair serves nothing and no one but the morose ruminations of those who cannot see their way through the cynicism and philosophical determinism of their personal lives.

Experience is everything in this reality, shaping our thinking and expression of self. The problem we run into here is the nature of the experiences we have, what we must deal with and how we manage the encounter. The result may be soup or dishwater, but whatever the results we may or may not benefit from the outcome. And if our spiritual or philosophical inclinations are derived from whatever obstacles we encounter, and whatever results may accrue, we might still find ourselves at the mercy of duality and the world of form.

Which is where we live, but which is not the abode of true being. We come from the spiritual realm, and there we should be placing our true allegiance. We acknowledge this when we understand the truth of the injunction to serve God. And in doing so we serve ourselves, those we love, our friends, neighbors, the planet and our future.

Home is where the heart is, the spiritual heart, and service to the divine puts us firmly on the path of personal illumination and saving grace. There is no other way to reach the fullness of being which is our spiritual heritage and divine right.

To serve God is not to become an unchained slave to an imaginary celestial monarch, but to free ourselves from the limitations, misunderstandings and constrictions of false allegiance to the material realm and physical dimension.

We are more than that, and we should make the time for that realization to come home to us and transform our conscious-awareness. In our essential being, we are that which we worship. We should be happy that this, and not eternally indentured servitude, is our true fate and spiritual destiny.

Nine

Don't Be Afraid

Fear, not only conscience, makes cowards of us all. Whether facing our environment, the ambitions of others, the difficulties of physical existence, the inevitable declines in life, ourselves and our future prospects, fear inflects so much of what we think and do.

Fear may be the price we pay for material existence, the inevitable cost of doing business in a physical environment which inflicts so much damage, real and potential, on our plans and ambitions. We even suffer from the fear of change, when change implies the onset of unfortunate consequences.

Wear and tear on the human body after a significant length of time has passed can be extraordinarily difficult to deal with, eventually impossible to overcome. The physical challenges we must face and endure can be overwhelming, and eventually, none of us are fated to survive the ordeal.

Those of us who have moved past the mid-point of our years already know this. Those who have not can easily observe the effect of age on others. There is no escaping the ravages that age and disease bring on the human body. And that is clearly one way in which fear can inflect our daily existence.

Age brings a daily measure of fear into our lives. We tend to be wary of the physical movements which, in our earlier years, we unconsciously took for granted. Moving easily from here to there, quick-step marching through life, we were oblivious to gravity, which to our older companions can drag us down to certain defeat with one careless misstep.

We learn to monitor our bodily functions with care and regularity less some unfortunate circumstance creep up on us and take us unawares. When we become ill we discover that we cannot depend on our bodies to heal with the same nearly-automatic precision of our youth.

Nothing of youth remains with the exception of a few scattered memories. Even yesterday is only a memory today. The present is all we have, and even that cannot be held onto no matter how we try to escape the oblivion that time rains down on us all.

Time is change, and we fear change when it threatens to rob us of our safety, undermine our security, pollute our environment, destroy our health and well-being, harm our loved ones and steal our youth. The future belongs to the young, but the elderly among us are aware that they are living their future. And their days are numbered.

We fear death, for who knows for sure what lies behind the closed door that signifies the end of this existence. We fear the pain and suffering that attends the deaths of many of us, and we fear the end of everything we thought we were, everything we cherished, everything we believe we are.

The end of living is a terrifying thought, the possibility that when our eyes close for the last time it really will be for the last time. That there will never be another tomorrow, and what could be more terrifying than the thought that for each of us, at some unspecified point in time, it will all end.

Today or tomorrow, this moment, the next or the one after that, none of us know when that final event will occur. And we are forced to live with that fear, not nameless but one for which we truly cannot prepare. As Hamlet recognizes, *the readiness is all.*

But when we think about that, exactly how *do* we prepare for death. Or for that matter, how do we prepare for anything we may or will unexpectedly encounter in life. How do we

learn to live in a state of perpetual readiness this moment, the next and the one after that.

Fear of what may come can provide an energizing momentum for some of us, but it can also create an emotional numbness within us from which it is difficult to recover. We may wish to come out of emotional hiding when we have that experience, but when it becomes a habit it is engraved in our souls with adamantine brilliance.

Fear can deaden us to the adventure of life, numb us with sorrow and challenge our willingness to engage with life on anything other than our own strictly-limited terms of engagement.

Fear forces us to insist on control, but voluntary control carries with it an impossible agenda. It supersedes anything of the spontaneity and willful eagerness of joyful existence. It overshadows the radiance of life, and that will inevitably keep us entombed in a state of perpetual spiritual darkness.

Better to reign in Hell than serve in Heaven, screams Milton's Satan, and that is a call to which most of us would likely not respond. It is the call of a wounded ego as much as a defiant rebel. It resonates throughout our being when we are called on to sacrifice or suffer, and it can chill us to the bone when we recognize that life can be a tragedy as much as anything else.

Fear chills us to the bone, no matter what the cause or circumstance. Fear drains the energy flows within our body, dissipates our energy reserves and serves life up cold and already quartered. We are entombed in the icy mountain caves of our inner fears.

We have all felt this along with similar experiences. And we may often find ourselves holding tightly together, constricting our muscles and restricting our breathing to the upper chest in shallow draughts as our voices rise and grow shrill.

The physiological effects of fear are well documented. While it may be useful to be reminded of them when we neglect its presence or fail to recognize that fear has taken hold of us, for some of us it may be that, however unconsciously, we do not want to recognize that we are afraid and dealing with the after-effects of fear.

We may believe that feeling or acknowledging fear is a sign of weakness, but true weakness is when we refuse to acknowledge reality because we are afraid of what we might discover. No matter how we try or what we do, reality always wins out in the end.

And this is another way that fear extends its rule over us. On a deep inner level, we all know we are destined to lose everything we love and everything we have. We are here only for a short while before the curtain descends and we make our final exit.

There is and never can be genuine comfort or true security on the material plane. If our personal philosophy suggests there is nothing beyond this mortal realm, the more time passes the more we will become psychologically agitated as the end of time, our personal time here, approaches.

We fear so much that comes our way, and the more and deeper we love others, the more we fear for their safety and security, their health and well-being. And there is no way around this problem.

We are informed by spiritual authorities to love everybody, and then not to be afraid. And yet it seems paradoxical that the more we love the more reasons we have to feel fear. Love and fear, diametrically opposing human emotions from which all other human emotions are direct descendants. Attraction and repulsion, expansion and contraction, love and fear ... the duality of existence.

This is the nature of the effects the mental and physical landscape of human existence have on our being. We must

deal with them before we become adversely attached to the effects of either, which if we do can seriously alter the spiritual trajectory of our lives.

Even love, when it descends into possessiveness and uninhibited control over another, has its darker side. Just as fear, when we ignore its rightful implications, can leave us at the mercy of desperate forces when we ignore our fear of them at our peril, our eyes closed in denial.

Everything on this earthly plane is subject to duality, and there is no escaping that essential fact of existence. Which clearly means that eternal vigilance is an absolute necessity while we are here on earth. This may not be news to many of us who have had some seriously conscious experience of life.

But eternal vigilance, although a necessity in this dimension of existential anxiety, contributes its own share of pain and suffering. Anxiety, stress and the physical and mental suffering that dance in tandem and in attendance ring out in sonorous tones when we are forced to scrutinize too much and too soon.

Duality brings joy and suffering in abundance to us all, and from this there is no escaping the consequences. We will suffer. Yet there is still hope, for one spiritual solution to the problem of duality is literally to rise above it.

To establish oneself in a state of higher consciousness such that the bliss we seek external to ourselves may be found within our own being, rather than in the things of this world which are all fated to pass away with time

Why wait? Why succumb to the immediacy of any worldly pleasure which will never, and can never, offer us anything of permanent value. Like a bright, shiny lure that attracts a hungry and gullible fish, we too fall victim to the lure of the bright and the shiny.

And eventually, like a hooked fish, we too will find ourselves hanging upside down and dangling in the air, having fallen victim to something that did not have our best interests at heart.

If we are told not to be afraid as a spiritual injunction, how are we to manage when our earthly interests conflict with our spiritual beliefs. Which do we choose, which *should* we choose, or is it all a matter of convenience and expediency?

There is a well-known story about a man standing at the edge of a cliff who lost his balance and began to slip over the edge. Frantic to save himself, he reached out desperately as he was about to go over and managed to grab hold of an exposed root of a nearby tree.

There he dangled, his fingers clutching the life-saving root but swiftly becoming numb as his strength began slipping away, along with his life. Realizing that he would not be able to hold on much longer, he screamed out with all his might, *"Help! Help!"*

Suddenly he heard a heavenly voice calling down to him from the sky directly above him. He looked up but could see nothing, and what the voice said shook him even his more. The voice said, *"Let go my son, let go."*

The man could not follow so terrifying a command. *"No, no,"* he responded. But the voice insisted. *"Let go my son, let go.'*

At the edge of exhaustion and nearing death, his fingers too numb to feel, his mind and body frozen with fear, the man considered what fate awaited him and what the voice had said. He pondered all his options.

He looked up at the heavens for what he feared was the last time, then made up his mind. *"Is there anyone else up there?"* he cried.

The voice, of course, was God. And what God knew, and the man did not, was that there was a ledge only a few feet directly below the man which would have broken his fall had he followed God's suggestion. The man chose differently. Free will is, by definition, free and costs nothing. But in earthly terms, you get what you pay for.

This may or may not be a true story, depending on one's point of view, but if it is not historically true, it is still true as a metaphor for human existence. And is there any significant difference between them as long as truth is revealed?

For the professional cynics and rational skeptics among us, might this not be a more useful and universal way of understanding the underlying truths of what religious history has long-since literally mis-termed revelation. But which, in the light of contemporary historical scholarship, might not pass the test of historical accuracy.

Information of any sort should usually be verified before it is acted on, at least in accord with any responsible point of view and course of action. But that does not mean that if something is unverified it is necessarily incorrect.

It only suggests that we cannot vouchsafe its accuracy, and more prudent measures would suggest that any decision based on uncertain information should not automatically be acted on. It does not suggest the information is inaccurate.

Sometimes this is when intuition is a vital ingredient in the decision-making process. And sometimes, when spiritual matters are involved, this is when we must learn to trust in a higher power. Something, again, which many of us fear to do because we are uncertain how and when to do it.

The problem to be addressed is the discrimination and wisdom to know how to do that, how to know when a higher power may be involved. And how to understand and interpret whatever guidance may be found to our best advantage. This is not an easy matter to resolve.

Discrimination is absolutely a subject for greater wisdom to adjudicate, and how we approach the spiritual wisdom we have at hand is a matter of the utmost care. This is absolutely not to be addressed lightly, for the spiritual choices we make not only can help shape our future, but justify our past as well.

Everything we have become can be on the line when we make choices, and when we make spiritual choices we reach deeply into alternate possibilities for our future well-being. Fear can hold us back from making the correct choices, but it can also keep us aware of the seriousness of the matter.

We can hang on with a failing grip to whatever stray root is within our grasp, knowing that at some point we will have no choice but to let go and accept whatever happens next.

Or we can accept the wisdom that comes from above, from God, from our higher consciousness through the intuition that flows through the heart, or from the wisdom teachings of established spiritual traditions.

Mature discrimination will help guide us through the dilemmas we face in our earthly sojourn. But fear in any of its forms and disguises will always make an appearance and confront us by questioning our choices. And thereby devaluing the merit of our spiritual intuition and innate wisdom.

This can be a nightmare scenario, or it can challenge us in such a way that we finally learn to accept the soul wisdom within us. And then, secure within ourselves, trust the life we are spiritually leading and in which we are trying to find the bliss of being. Something to look forward to when we have taken charge of our own evolution.

Every challenge we face has within it the opportunity for growth, and the truth of that may simply depend on the way we understand and evaluate the challenges we face.

Everything that comes our way is an opportunity for affirmation of our innate standing, for spiritual growth if we have learned to see through the surface illusions that obscure our way.

Fear can blind us to those opportunities, paralyzing us into despair and inaction. Our mental fingers can become numb, just like the man desperately holding on to that tree root while dangling over the side of a cliff.

And this is a condition many of us may be familiar with in our own lives. Unable to retrace our steps and faced with an apparently insurmountably unacceptable present, we hold on to what little we have with ferocious indifference to any higher call that comes from belief and leads to action.

Many of us do not really trust that, and therefore cannot act according to any higher calling. We are so caught up in our attachments and aversions that at times it appears as though there is little more we can do than watch the feverish goings on in the holographic movie-screens within our brains. And with a sometime mixture of sorrow and heartbreak that we are no longer in control of our mental activities.

And that is just exactly the point, that we are not in control of the sweep and sway of our mental images and ideas. Like a non-stop internal carnival parade, they float before us in an apparently endless flow of mental imagery, even in sleep.

But they are not *our* mental images and ideas, they come from and belong to the spontaneous activity of the mind's energies. We watch them from a privileged and intimate point of view, and we identify those inner visions as we ourselves. We own them when we do that, and when we own something we have to be responsible for them and responsive to them.

And that is a fundamental error we make. We are not those images. They do not belong to us unless we choose to believe they do. And we do not belong to them, again, unless we choose to believe we do. We are free to pick and choose what

we will and what we will not do or believe. And what we will avoid, and what we will fully engage in. The choice is ours.

The mind is our servant, the mental means through which we communicate and survive on the earth plane, somewhat like the workings of a personal computer with software programs that occasionally go astray or become corrupted through improper usage.

But we are not our minds, they are the mental filters through which we engage physical reality. And when we choose to believe we are only our minds and holographic mental projections, we indenture ourselves in constant servitude to the biological computer within us that runs the body.

What we truly are is the witness-observer within, the consciousness which incarnates on the earth plane through the human biological template, and of which the mind and body are simply temporary vehicles for manifestation.

We do not have to have to believe anything unless we choose to, and because of that we are always and essentially free. No longer identifying as the mind, but as the observing consciousness within, we are free to accept or reject anything and everything that appears within our inner vision or outer reality. Taking care, of course, not to step on anything that might rise up in anger.

This world and everything in it is altogether external to our true being, eternal consciousness. And we are also free to change beliefs, accept any orientation we choose, believe or disbelieve what we want, and be whatever satisfies and fulfills the chosen conditions of our own existence.

It is all the mind stuff going about the business of creation in its own way, personal creation through mental ideation and physical expression. But like all created things on the plane of material being, whatever we think and do is fated to undergo the process of change one way or another.

Everything has a beginning on the earth plane and everything has an ending, and the ultimate tragedy in life that we fear and dread is that we too will one day have our own ending.

As long as we identify ourselves as our physical bodies and the contents of our consciousness, this is what we will believe, and this will be the primary cause of our suffering. Sometimes, suffering is nothing more than a choice we make out of ignorance and an addictive way of understanding things to which we are completely imprisoned without even the possibility of parole.

We create our nightmare in the image of what we fear, just as we create a multitude of deities in our own image, according to our own preferences and addictions. All of them aspects of divine reality, but all still reflecting anthropomorphic perspectives of generically-derived meaning and pseudo-universal purpose.

This, the collective sum of conscious-awareness within the collective body of mankind, and which originates from the common source of consciousness, is what we are, all that we are, and everything that we are. *We are that.* Consciousness exploring itself within the field of time and space. All else is illusion.

Obsessive and compelling as this world is capable of being, it is the mind that is caught in these detours from fundamental being. There is nothing either good or bad, muses Hamlet, but thinking makes it so.

We think we are these bodies and the minds and egos caught up in the hypnotic spell of physical existence. Our vocabularies, our philosophies, our normal day-to-day activities and all else that goes into the making of the human experience reflects this divergence of opinion and experience from the state of oneness with the universe.

Those among us whose teachings are meant to awaken mankind from the sleep of unawakened consciousness may be revered by some, but they are unhappily ignored by the many. There may come a day when the reverse will be true, but enlightened individuals are in the nearly infinitesimal minority, while the vastly greater majority ignores those teachers and their teachings.

And do so at their peril, for unenlightened man is a creature of conflict and internecine warfare. Fear of change often implies sacrifice and loss, and here again fear deals a powerful hand. Fear of the unknown is an open-ended affair, subject to endless imaginative and emotional speculation.

Fear closes the door on reality but leaves open the infinite possibilities the mind can create that keep us entombed in traditional and conventional ways of life without the possibility of meaningful change. Frantically trying to hold on to what can never be held onto.

We organize ourselves around the comfortable and familiar, no matter how uncomfortable the familiar has become. We do not change our ways because everything, including language itself, supports the traditions that time and history affirm for us as right and purposeful.

That they are not matters little when the preponderance of belief supports continuing our existence in the same conventional mold. This is death to the creative imagination, but when tradition subverts the imagination and fear keeps it busy creating internal ghosts and external goblins, the best we usually do is shrug our collective shoulders and get on with the business of living in fear.

Don't be afraid, advise those teachers who have themselves moved beyond fear. On the other side of fear, they counsel, you will find God. But fear rises before us like a Himalayan mountain peak partially obscured by early morning mists on a cloudy and overcast day.

Fear creates monumental apparitions that loom up out of the morning fog and daylight hours when consciousness is still in the business of recognizing and organizing itself. We are a work-in-progress at this stage of our earthly evolution, and because of that, we are still learning to respect, aid and comfort each other in our dawning years as evolving beings.

Of course we will fear and respond to fear at this stage of our evolution, which when danger threatens is an entirely appropriate response. And when action is called for, act we must, and act we will.

But coming as it does in so many forms and in so many guises, fear can manifest as much more than a response to a real or perceived threat. Fear can become a virtual way of life, a philosophical reality of its own genesis.

Fear takes mental and emotional support not only when a genuine danger confronts our well-being, but takes non-local support from fundamental assumptions about existence that we take to be facts instead of what they really are, assumptions.

That those assumptions are familiar to us does not prove the truth they purport to represent. Fear of death can haunt us when we are in our last years, or, in fact, at any time in our lives when our thoughts turn to mortality and the end of being.

The undiscover'd country from whose bourn No traveller returns, says Hamlet in regard to the mystery and fear of death. And yet, somewhat paradoxically, he maintains this position in spite of his recent confrontation with his father's ghost, who informs him of both the facts of his death and his penance on the other side. Denial is often a powerful pseudo-defensive force we invoke when we are threatened.

In our own way, similar to Hamlet, we as well ponder the mysteries of life and death while still ignoring the messages of spiritual teachers and spiritual traditions of what generally

awaits us on the other side of life. And then how to prepare for our final exit and the ultimate encounter.

Fear keeps us so hard at work worrying about these matters that there is nothing left over with which to focus more creatively on the problem. We are entering strange and unknown territory if we choose to do that, but if we do, we must learn to leave the toys of childhood behind.

No easy task if we are still intent on remaining children. No easy task if we are not, but the alternative is to remain child-like with no hope of ever escaping the inlaid traps that fear conceals before us like entombed minefields on a darkling plain.

Fear can censor our every thought and action, blinding us to the light and the activity of spontaneous creativity within us. We become creatures of habit, rather than creative incarnations of thought and action.

Our beliefs are shaped by social conventions and traditions, but at some point we will begin to realize for ourselves that even those are assumptions we and others make and accept about reality.

They are traditional and conventional only when we identify ourselves at that egoic level of human responsiveness, but of themselves they merely float about in the inventory of man's hopes, aspiration and unmanifest potential.

Those responses may not extend much further than that static level of activity when the transformation of consciousness takes over the evolutionary process, making us aware of deeper and more profoundly spiritual aspects of creation and human potential.

If we are fortunate enough to have that kind of spiritual experience we may find that our formerly practical, pragmatic and realistic philosophies are of little value. Those beliefs that deny anything that does not fit comfortably within the

conventions of culturally-affirmed normality begin to fall apart on closer examination. Reality tends to provide an ongoing series of check-posts along the way, if, that is, we are paying serious attention.

This process of continuous revitalization begins when spiritually-orientated experiences refresh our stale and orthodox sense of what is to be expected and what is acceptable in life. Doors and windows will appear and open in our lives, to paraphrase Joseph Campbell, where once we did not know there were doors or windows.

A fresh breeze will blow thorough our minds and hearts, invigorating our sense of what reality may actually be and no longer is thought to be according to past beliefs. We will have moved beyond the reactions of childhood to the multitude of mysteries that surround us.

And our typical response to all of this is fear, which begins in childhood, when we were small, weak, powerless and ultimately defenseless. The imprint that makes can last a lifetime, and morph into philosophical positions we try to justify with complex and unyielding defensiveness that may never have truly moved us all that far beyond our childhood terrors.

This presents a standard barrier of penetration through which advanced spiritual practitioners among us have already passed. Many of whom have returned to inform us that our fears have made us foolish, especially when we linger in our emotional pasts, continually trying to right the wrongs we have accumulated from which we can neither let go nor move on.

Many of those beings have remained behind to teach, guide and inspire. The sacrifice in personal evolution they made, again called the Bodhisattva Vow in Buddhist traditions, means the postponement of their final enlightenment, remaining behind to teach for the sake of all sentient beings.

Were any of us in that spiritually enviable position, how many would willingly sacrifice the bliss of enlightenment for the sake of our fellow beings. And the truth here is that many of us would neither know nor appreciate the sacrifice that had been made for them in the name of humanity. God may be thought to move in mysterious ways, but then again, so does humanity.

What is so often notable about those precious souls is the lack of fear in their lives and teachings. Those who have written about their trials have done so without bitterness or malice, and many of them have first-hand experience of the causes of both.

As do we, this one in one way, that one in another. We all face trials and we all face suffering and defeat. And always in our lives, hidden in one form or another, there is the presence of fear and the mystery of death.

To find ourselves secure and sheltered within the adamantine brilliance of the spiritual heart is to act from a sure and certain psychological/spiritual center, the sheltering abode we all seek to enter and embrace.

Fear shuts down that possibility, closing us off to that inner center from which we can all act with complete confidence. And the welcoming assurance that Dame Julien of Norwich, the fourteenth century English anchoress, expressed in her book "Revelations of Divine Love," that *all shall be well, and all shall be well, and all manner of thing shall be well.*

This is the first book written in English known to have been authored by a woman, and it explores the human perception of the divine influence in terms of a mother's embrace.

What is most important is the confidence and assurance Dame Julien reveals in her trust in God, and the lack of fear it represents for the ultimate outcome.

This may appear naïve and unrealistic to those who seek some form of practical in-hand evidence that goes beyond accepting the word of another, but to others it offers a form of comfort and security that reaches a deeper and more informing foothold than merely textbook sermonizing. The power of faith, combined with the authority of belief, form a powerful and cohesive force in mankind's ability to evolve in the cosmos.

And that exemplifies the profound nature of trust. The first response we generally experience to creation is in terms of physical evidence, which is not without its merits in a court of law or last appeal. But the second reaches deeper into spirit because it calls for the soul's involvement, rather than a literal-minded response bespoken in terms of worldly affairs.

If we believe we are simply physical beings enjoined by a limited span of existence, we need never concern ourselves with spiritual concerns. According to any standard material definition of being, such matters are unreal because conventionally unproven and unprovable.

Any such beliefs in spiritual matters are merely illusions, critics maintain, created in response to various forms of insecurity festering in immature minds.

Morality and ethical standards are, of course, matters of the deepest concern, but spiritual affairs are no less real than dreams, so the skeptics say, and vanish when we awaken to a new day. So the literalists dismissively maintain, and so they believe according to the evidence of their own words.

But if we understand ourselves to be spiritual beings, the situation takes on a different ambience. We could instead learn to evaluate and act from the spiritual position of immortal being, rather than simply according to a physical definition of existence based only on the limited duration of time and being.

Perhaps being should no longer be defined solely in terms of a temporary state of physical existence, but understood as consciousness itself, the conscious-awareness which all sentient self-aware beings experience as their inner reality. True being is the subtle awareness of the surface awareness that floats within the level of sensory phenomena.

Thinking and acting from that psychological/spiritual position does not necessarily provide a way out of physical suffering, but it does tend to limit the effects and after-effects of fear itself. It offers hope that indeed, as Dame Julien maintains, *all shall be well.*

But more than that, it aids our evolutionary progression from intellectually benumbed upright creatures engaged in a brief but life-long desperate struggle to survive.

And over time, with evolving physical and mental abilities, becoming sentient beings engaged in a spiritual struggle to plumb the depths of consciousness and recognize, through experience, the fundamental nature of the cosmos.

In that towering process, overcoming the many forms of fear that plague the lower stages of our evolution. With each step in the spiritual growth of mankind, with successive and more illuminating ways of understanding whatever particular form fear takes that haunts our sleeping and waking dreams, we become aware that they are only illusions in the grand scheme of things, as is the "so-called" conscious state.

There may indeed be forms of physical reality that do not change and are not illusory, and so we learn to identify and avoid those particular challenges. But any form of fear that remains in our minds and petrifies our thinking and acting does not and cannot affect our essential being. It has only become a habit, from which we suffer the consequences.

We are consciousness, not the physicality of our being, and consciousness is not a function of our body but an expression of our soul. This may be difficult to remember when danger

threatens, but if we identify with fear we become a product of fear, and that is well worth remembering and avoiding.

To know the truth we must first recognize the truth. But in the matter of recognizing our fundamental being, we are already that which we have failed to recognize. Our lack of understanding inevitably leads to illusion, and illusion invariably ends in suffering.

And so we suffer, stuck in the illusion that we are all separate beings incarnate here on Earth for an unknown and limited span of time. Doomed, some of us believe, to final extinction when the body dies or the brain is no longer functional.

Some may believe this supports the conclusion that when the time comes that, for whatever reason, we are no longer able to think, then the time has come when we no longer are.

This is not an inescapable fact as has generally been supposed, but an assumption based on incomplete evidence that should be, but is usually not, investigated to the fullest extent possible through cross-cultural fields of study.

Our mystical traditions address this issue through the direct investigation of consciousness by the only available functional means, the meditative process of direct knowledge. As far as can be determined, this is the only functional method of reaching deeply into the human psyche to pierce through the barriers that separate us from the source of being.

This cannot as yet be accomplished in a laboratory setting through any known method of investigation. At some point, in some way, science might find a way of adapting its methods of investigation to accelerate the process of transformation and the evolution of consciousness. And monitoring the results.

This might be something to look forward to, but it might also simply be just another illusion in the annals of time.

Time, as usually expectable, will reveal the truth. But in the meantime, our best and only hope to enjoy the evolutionary rewards of an enhanced and transformed consciousness may only be through our mystical and meditative traditions.

The truth of that will become evident when we have engaged in the process of self-examination, experiencing for ourselves the reality of deeper and more profound states of consciousness and awareness.

The proof of the pudding, as the saying goes, is in the eating. The knowledge of true being we seek lies within, and meditation is the direction in which we must now travel to find the answers and the experiences that define our being.

TEN

Meditate

Why meditate? We can speculate about its value, but from a distance the truth is that the best and most useful information we find will be through the teachings and guidance of a meditation master. This is not an easy task in the western world, where meditative traditions have traditionally never been as easily available as in the eastern world.

Nor are there as many accomplished teachers, although things have changed considerably in the last few decades. Our opportunities for spiritual growth and maturation have changed for the better, but meditation is not yet generally regarded as the most significant and useful guide to spiritual illumination.

Here we sit, in our own best time, our minds trying to focus with laser-like precision on the interior depths of our being, our memories scourged by the lingering debris of time and experience. Back and forth we roam uncontrollably over the free range of memories, dreams and reflections that fill our mind's awareness. We are trying to meditate.

Submerged within this mental debris field, we fight the force of out attachments and the flow of our aversions like a swimmer caught in a raging rip-tide desperate to break free for calmer waters.

Something we can never do as long as we remain who we are and what we imagine ourselves as being. That is the

inviolate web that illusion casts over us, from which we struggle so desperately to escape. The warp of that web is composed of our attachments, and the woof woven from our aversions to the world we imagine of duality, joy and shame.

Together they inter-weave the fabric of our lives, for without them nothing would remain to signify individual existence. Taken together they weave divergent elements into an often fragmented personality that defines who we are on the egoic level but leaves the rest untouched.

Our attachments and aversions form the token presence of our mental being, while our physical presence is signified by our bodies. Meditation is meant to take us beyond the perimeters and definitions of our existence on the material plane. It is a voluntary voyage, and the price we pay is top-heavy with fear and aversion, as well as the sublime joy of the discoveries of the inner exploration of the psyche.

To sit in silent meditation is essentially the attempt to break free from the life-long and familiar outposts of our humanity into territory that at first glance appears altogether strange and intimidating. In which anticipation lurks under cover and in disguise.

This is how it may appear to our human self, but to our spiritual self we are going home. It is where we have come from and where, one day, we will be returning in full awareness of the meaning and message of the journey.

But not quite yet. Whatever intellectual illumination we experience may only be the interior revelation of a spiritual message. New thoughts for a new day.

Tomorrow they will have aged, need replacing and once again, as always, we will set out on the path to enlightenment. Convinced that we still have much to experience before passing the torch of experience on to those more easily adaptable to the physical hardships of existence.

In a sense, life is a process of endurance, but it is not necessarily true that those who endure, or endure the most, are best qualified for success in the inward journey to the center of the earth.

There are no automatic qualifications for enlightenment when enough time has passed, enough experience assimilated or we have a change of mind about our spiritual priorities. Nothing will come of nothing in this regard. No bread will ever bake from this dough.

New crops will grow only from the actual seeds we have planted, never from the seeds that flourish only in our imagination or the fantasy world of conventional religiosity.

Meditation will most likely begin when we sit quietly and calmly, casting aside the toys of childhood. When we ignore our preferences, forget our attachments, embrace our aversions. When we simply let go and let be.

When we sit for meditation, so we are informed by those who know, all that exists outside the witness-observer of our inner consciousness is nothing less and nothing more than simply more grist for the mill. The inner light show from which we are trying to escape.

As has been so frequently maintained, if not now, when? And if not us, who? It is always the right time to begin the practice of meditation. Now is the only time, and we are the ones to do it.

Yesterday has come and gone, and we did not do it. The future has not yet arrived, and we know we cannot live in the promise of things to come. Even though we do try, we are inevitably only postponing the day of spiritual reckoning that meditation encourages to some undefined future point when we will begin the beginning.

We may not yet be there, but it is in our eventual destiny, if not in this life then the next. But at some point we will have

had enough of this physical phase of our existence, turned inward, and found there the next, best direction for our evolutionary presence.

Whether we begin within the religious tradition into which we have been born or chosen, or if we take up a meditative practice from some other source, the reality is that none of that truly matters when we have pierced through the debris field of mind and ego.

And once accomplished, tapped into the underlying reality of essential being, there to recognize the illusions that formerly dominated our thinking and awareness. They cast their spell over us, subdued the expression of our original nature and carried us off into slavery.

Free will allowed us to make that choice, but once we begin to live under the spell of our physical and mental attachments we live in slavery to the fulfillment of those essentially adopted needs and desires.

Those preferences, good or bad, helpful or unhelpful, become innate habits over time by which we define who and what we are. And most of us live according to our habits. The preferences of our existence are merely arbitrary rules of existence, not permanent elements of essential being.

We can change, moderate or eliminate those preferences if we wish, and meditation is one way we can accomplish that inner revolution. Seeing through the illusions of existence to the interior reality of spirit awakens us to the unreality of the surface world of appearances.

And why should we want to do that when the illusions, if illusions they truly are, can be so pleasant, so satisfying, so stimulating and so necessary to our actual physical and mental existence. They are the only game in town, or so we think.

But they are still only illusions, no matter how pleasant they may be, and many are very definitely unpleasant as well. The

experiences we undergo in this world are phantom-shapes that quickly vanish in the clear light of truth. They may be pleasant, they may be painful, but illusions they are and illusions they will nevertheless remain.

The experiences of our incarnate existence quickly become memories over time, while in our essential being we are beyond time. Which reality we recognize is the proper subject of our spiritual endeavors, and which one we choose to accelerate contains the shape of our future and the content of our lives.

The essential issue we face is the undeniable truth of existence, and the choices we make in service to this ideal. Do we justify and continue with our attachments in life, or do we reach beyond our various addictions to this or that, whatever they are, that indulge our sensory appetites. Do we, in truth, have the courage to overcome and conquer our physical and mental appetites.

A difficult series of choices we must make when we undergo the commitment to a spiritual path. But then, if we want to find God we cannot allow ourselves to become distracted by and attached to the various phenomena we encounter along the way.

It is said that when He chooses a devotee He removes everything that is not God until only God remains. This is difficult even to conceptualize by those of us who remain fixated on our attachments to physical phenomena, and those of us whose addictions to the things of this world are paramount in our conscious-awareness.

And to such a pervasive extent that we are not even aware that we willingly allow ourselves to become material slaves, creatures of habit, so addicted to those habits that we inwardly identify ourselves as those habits.

We *are* that which we love to eat. We *are* that which we choose to do during our waking hours. We *are* that about

which we obsessively think or act out in the various roles we play or personas we adapt during the daily business of our lives.

So many of us are always unconscious and unaware of what we are really doing as we go about playing roles to face the various situations we encounter. Or doing our best to satisfy our addictions with a straight and corporate demeanor so that we do not reveal the truths of our inner world to outsiders.

We do our best to keep our addictions private lest the truths of our inner life be exposed, and we stand revealed and naked before the prying eyes and judgmental glances of others. The truths of which are, of course, that we are addicts satisfying our addictions on the material plane.

We first begin to see the truth of this when we sit for meditation. Various discomforts will begin to assert themselves and dominate our self-awareness. When we pay serious attention to the nature of those discomforts we might begin to understand how our attachments and addictions have shaped our physical and mental well-being.

And to such an impossible extent that in every sense we finally recognize we have lost control of our lives. We have allowed ourselves to succumb to the lure of the physical, and we accept that as the essential way of things in the material world.

We have shaped ourselves according to the template of the world, instead of witnessing the processes of existence while still remaining the observing consciousness within. We have become something of a lumbering robot, as has already famously been said, recapitulating the habits of its ancestors and the standard, conventional worldly addictions to which it has succumbed and fallen victim.

Meditation increases this state of self-awareness because while we are sitting quietly within ourselves, we are continuously faced with the essential truths of our existence.

They will not be denied, but the various personas we have adapted and which remain fixed within our psyches will begin to unpeel themselves from the frozen walls that surround our inner being.

Close examination of the inner impulses that arise when we sit in meditation, determined to pierce through our inner defenses, will reveal that those imprints with which we have so continuously identified have no power of their own to shape our existence.

We are not under their power and immobilized victims of their spell, we empower them to assert control over our free will by lending them whatever energies they need to manifest their presence. This is one revelation that meditation can lead to, that we are not our habitual ways of responding to the world, nor are we the addictions that control our behavior.

We, the essential subjective self, are simply observing the way our minds and bodies function, and witnessing those processes as a detached observer. Except that we are not detached from either our bodies or our minds as long as we identify ourselves as either or both.

We must go very deep indeed to understand what we truly are and not what we only imagine ourselves as being. Beneath all that we think we are, imagine ourselves as being, enjoying the ways in which we enjoy the enormous variety of experiences of physical being, we are the Self and nothing but the Self.

We think about those thoughts, images and our inner reactions endlessly as that constant stream of thoughts and images absorbs our attention. We examine, explore and interpret the images that come into the interior awareness of our mind.

The holographic movie screen that dominates our attention, and with which we so identify, encourages us to believe and accept that true happiness will only come when

we satisfy the desires and cravings that so easily capture our attention.

We think about these things to such an extent that we forget that thinking is itself only a form of non-sensory phenomena. Thinking is a function of the brain, similar to the mental arena, in this sense, as our physical senses are to our physical being. The means we incorporate for interpreting and understanding the data we perceive.

Thinking is the mental means of interpreting and understanding information, relating and collating ideas and experiences. It is a tool we use, and so powerful is the thinking process that we assume, because of its inevitability, its incredible usefulness and the necessity of the process, that we are the thoughts we think as well as the various secondary processes of the thinking mind.

We witness those activities, we respond to them, we are informed by them and we act on them. But we are simply not our thoughts. And more importantly, we are not the thinking process either.

We are far more than that. And when we begin to meditate the realization hits home with enormous force that we have been taken over by the mind and all its activities. We sit in silence contemplating our inner being, and we are faced with the enormous task of sorting through our personal history, which will not be denied, will not retreat into silence, and will not stop tormenting us with the wishes and wants of success and failure.

We are tormented by the experiences we had and the experiences that escaped us. We are plagued by the hurts we suffered and the insults we endured, just as we remember our triumphs, the praise we earned, and the comedies and tragedies that informed our existence.

Praise or shame, both extremes plague the inner silence into which we wish to retreat for further exploration. In the sense

of spiritual exploration we are spelunkers of inner space. The light we shine on our interior darkness is the light that comes from our concentrated awareness and focused consciousness.

Intention and practice determine the degree of concentration we are able to maintain, but constant and daily practice is essential if we are to ever see through the mental apparitions that fill our minds and distract us from our stated purpose.

Meditation is the way, so the sages maintain, to escape from the illusions of existence. This is something many of us either do not believe, or do not choose to devote time to the inner exploration of their consciousness.

Ignorance may be bliss for some, but for others it is not true bliss, but a challenge to overcome in the pursuit of what is real and everlasting. Faith in the goal is essential, as is the genuine teaching of a spiritual path. How to choose a path, and how to follow a meditative technique is a genuine problem to be addressed.

The answer for one may not be an appropriate answer for another, and here discrimination is of the utmost value. One guideline that may be useful is to choose a path with a heart, and for many that might involve an enormous amount of time, effort and energy.

And especially the discrimination, inner knowledge and the wisdom to know intuitively what is right for us in any current moment of our lives. And conversely, what may not be appropriate, what we should avoid or what we ought to postpone thinking about until a later time.

We are the sole judges in this matter, and report to no one for confirmation that we have made the correct or any choice. Advice we may seek, but the decision ultimately belongs to us. No one and nothing has authority over us when it comes to our spiritual life, although others might

propose themselves or the institutions to which they belong and represent as the sole and only arbiters of our destiny.

But they are not, and they are wrong when they do that. Our life belongs to us and none other. The choices we make and how we make them belong to us and fall on our heads alone. That is the reason we ought to be, as many of us already are, fully functional when it comes to our spiritual existence and the method or methods we choose to explore our being.

Meditation is one way to do that, perhaps the most effective and direct, but who can say with any degree of certainty what works best for any one individual. All we do know for certain is that we must move beyond Bronze Age dualistic theologies.

In this now-known to be universe of quantum uncertainty, we must recognize the existence of non-local influences from the implicate, unmanifest spiritual order involved in our evolution.

The mind and its activities present a standard barrier which we all must penetrate to energize our inner knowing. This is neither intuition nor instinct, but the direct perception of our inner being. And beneath the surface of our habits of constant ideation, to reach the depths of what we truly are beyond the familiar and spell-binding egoic level of mind

Meditation can break the spell of that addiction by freeing us from voluntary servitude to the thinking process. And when we recognize that formerly unknown dilemma, meditation can help us overcome the newer stage of recognizably involuntary servitude.

The mind is addicted to experience and rumination, and we are addicted to the mind's activities in all its forms. In a way, we are confronted by an addiction within an addiction. We empower those addictions continuously when we allow them to take over the surface functions of our thinking and activity,

which is when we become creatures of habit rather than free-thinking individuals capable of spontaneous immersion in the activity of the moment.

In that now famous phrase, *Be Here Now*, we are often anywhere but here, in the now moment of our existence and the depth of that moment. We are like fishermen trolling the surface of the sea, unaware of what lies below the waves or the depth beneath the surface.

Which, again, is why we are informed by those who know, who have passed this way before, that we must meditate to understand who we really are. Meditation can get us past the doorway of the mind into the interior chambers of consciousness.

Once there, we are told that experiences will come which will convince us that we have only scratched the surface of our being in our daily activities. Experience is the best teacher, and in this case, the only teacher.

No books of pious moralizing or abstract theology could possibly convince us that a golden treasure awaits us within our being unless we had some evidence of the truth of that proposition.

The purpose of meditation leads us to that truth. When inner experiences begin to manifest from the depths of our inner being, we finally understand that the spiritual domain exists and is within us.

And this is when a different form of addiction arises and which this too we must overcome. We can become attached to inner experiences, especially when they invoke intense feelings of pleasure, comfort and security.

Joy, harmony, pleasure and various forms of inner happiness can all become nearly insurmountable obstacles, as can the inner lights, sounds and visual apparitions that may

arise. They capture our curiosity, excite the imagination and fixate our mind on these inner phenomena.

They are noteworthy, and in the sense of inner progress they can be extraordinarily encouraging. But they are all still merely phenomena, and gross phenomena at that. Those visions, apparitions and inner movements of often emotionally-oriented inner energies are not the goal of our meditative efforts.

If we indulge them they can become roadblocks to our inner progress, and if that occurs, we can easily become fixated on those more subtle inner experiences. They can so capture our inner attention that, in essence, our inner awareness stagnates if we obsessively contemplate these revelations of our inner self.

We are informed by those who have passed through these trials that so marvelous are the sights and sounds of the meditative voyage within our consciousness that we can become compulsively addicted to this newly-found source of pleasure.

This may be difficult to believe and even harder to accept, much less conceptualize. But said by those in whom we have placed our trust, and accepted their belief systems as worthy of investigation, we have little choice but to recognize the validity of what they say. Or what would be the purpose of following their examples.

Here too, even if we have made some inner progress in our meditations, we must be wary lest we fall into another devious trap of addiction. Both the outer world of physical experience and the inner world of energy experiences on a more subtle level can keep us from reaching our true being. Addiction and attachment to whatever it is they offer keeps us enthralled and in chains.

The mind is still always in search of entertainment, usually pleasure, and for some, even in pain there is some form of

pleasure. Addiction to either can assume an infinite variety of forms.

But we are assured that meditation leads to a place beyond either pain or pleasure, and that is the inner unfolding of which we are in search. A secure inner connection to an infinite and eternal reality beyond the secondary influences of time, place or circumstance.

When we begin excavating beneath the surface features of our awareness, even when we start to make progress, we will quickly discover there is still a long way to travel on the inner journey. That so few of us among so many have made it to full enlightenment should come as no surprise.

There is still this hopeful reality to face. As a collective race of sentient beings we have barely begun to recognize the necessity of the inner awakening, even though the inner unfolding of our spiritual nature is frustrating and often discouraging.

This is the goal towards which our spiritual activities ought to be directed, the revelation of all revelations, the unfolding and manifestation of the divine God-force of existence within and as our essential nature. All else is fluffery, no matter how well-dressed the enterprise may be.

The ultimate purpose of all spiritual traditions and formal religions should be to unite the manifest, outer being with the unmanifest, inner being into a non-dualistic holistic entity. The enlightenment of the phenomenal being into an undivided whole, the manifest expression of pure consciousness in human form.

This is where we should be directing our efforts, not in justifying cultural concerns by deifying them and the attendant ceremonies and circumstances that attend them. This is simply religious tribalism dressed up for a new day, and can offer nothing of hope or purpose when it comes to

the fundamental issue of the transformation of human consciousness.

Transformation is the game of life we should be playing to our utmost ability, not the transmogrification of ancient ideas and medieval beliefs in the vain and fore-doomed to failure attempt to breathe new life into old or dying traditions. When we do that we are forgetful of reality, that life is change and nothing but.

We cannot hold on to the past, just as we cannot step into the same stream twice. Life changes beyond anyone's ability to assert our preferences and hold life accountable to our personal wishes and desires. The past if dead and cannot be revived, and no amount of high-minded bribery will breathe life into a dead horse.

And so we must change in keeping with reality, and find for ourselves, in our own way, according to our contemporary environment and always in the present moment that which we admired, cherished and hoped to find for ourselves from past teachings, past experiences and past teachers.

We keep them alive in our hearts when we practice what they preached, not by enshrining them in marble halls and gilded statues. We keep their memories and teachings alive when we incorporate all that into our own hearts and minds, making every effort to open our consciousness to the wonders within and the miracle of consciousness

We are all united when we cross those inner borders in meditation. Of one heart, one mind, and ultimately of one supreme consciousness which seeks, though us, only to know and experience itself.

Home is where the heart is, the spiritual heart, the wonder of wonders from which the bounty of heaven and the fruits of the earth meet and blossom through the innate spirituality of the enlightened soul.

Spiritual realization is the fruit of the meditative process, and as in any similar earthly analogy, the matured result of any organic process takes time, energy and genuine effort before reaching fruition. Spirituality is the actualization and bouquet of the meaning and purpose of life.

We come from the earth as do all things which spring from the native soil of this planet. We grow in our mother's wombs just as our landscape is filled with vegetable and organic life forms that came from their own particular sources. None sprang forth into existence whole, well-formed and independently suited for individual existence.

Everything requires a period of growth and maturation in order to reach full development and survive in often difficult and perilous environmental conditions. This is obvious to all, and it is the experience of existence on the physical plane.

But unlike the companion life forms with which we share the planet, our full development does not come when we are simply physically fit, nor when we have attained to child-bearing years.

There is a spiritual component to our existence, the inner development we must undergo to reach our full potential and matured humanity. This, of course, is the maturation of our conscious awareness and the self-realization that comes when we recognize, through our inner meditations, the power, strength and internal, eternal, ever-lasting bliss at the most profound level of our inner self.

We are that, we are that, we are nothing less than that. We truly are the omniscient, omnipotent consciousness of the universal mind. The self-aware, self-conscious, unmanifest universal field of being, expressing itself in every possible way, through every possible means and method, in everything that exists, organic or inorganic, conscious or unconscious, in time and beyond time. *We are that.*

And we should find the truth of that for ourselves in our own lives, through our own experiences, before out time runs out and the process must begin again from where we left off here. We should recognize this enormous gift of grace we have been given, that has essentially been implanted within us to both aid and accelerate our evolution. We are not isolated creatures left alone in the dark.

We have the ability to achieve self-realization in any given lifetime. We are not now, nor have we ever been, condemned by an indifferent fate to suffer lifetime after lifetime in ignorance of our true destiny and rightful place in the universe. We are free, and always have been.

We might begin now to re-think our separatist notions about ourselves and our place in the universe. We might begin to re-think our separatist notions about God, the divine force of the creation and the purpose of the whole adventure.

And we might also begin to think about the universe and ourselves as complex products created from the recombinant energies of divine manifestation. The method or methods by which that occurred none of us could possibly even imagine or guess at, but which the enriched consciousnesses of the spiritually informed among us, the mystics and meditation masters, have informed us is the true origin of the creation.

God created the cosmos, they say, so that He could be here Himself to experience it. And then witness Himself experiencing it first-hand from within the space/time continuum. And that includes suffering as well as joy, pain as well as pleasure, victory, defeat and all the tribulations that life entails.

The game of existence must be played with all the rules intact else where would be the fun of it? How else to experience and understand the suspense, the drama, and the enormous variety of physical, mental and emotional responses to whatever comes with incarnation. God has not kept Himself separate and apart from His creation.

Once a pattern emerges from the inchoate field of divine energy and forms a template for existence, the template re-orders the structural unity of the inherent energies that produced it through which a material form emerges.

The form follows the energetic rules of order of that template, determined by the innate architectural unity. This is deterministic in that sense, but that the template was first created is arbitrary, the play of consciousness and the welcomed gift of divinely-ordained creative free will.

This is not God playing dice with the universe, it is God watching the universe order itself into formative patterns or non-patterns, contenting Himself with the play of existence before entering the universe as part of the creation, the unitive consciousness beneath the surface appearance of things.

The witness-observer within. The blank slate upon which the universe is engraved, with no agenda other than the fullest expression of being in every possible direction. The expansion of universal consciousness through and into material creation. Over which there hangs no spectre of death.

Past events are now only history, while future possibilities have not as yet unfolded, unless our understanding of time is incomplete and time is non-linear. All we believe we have is the present, here and now moment of existence in which to actively explore our existence. And in accord with a more conscious way of existence, exploring the meaning, purpose and ultimate unfolding of our life potential.

Why waste additional time and precious energy on maintaining the out-sized beliefs of past ages and decoding their possible meaning. They were meant for another people in another time. Why continue accepting doctrines that do not satisfy our spiritual needs and soul requirements, which may also be inauthentic to our present state of becoming. Life changes and so must we along with it.

The flow of existence rushes past us in raging torrents, but many of us automatically cling to our battered little boats, flooding and in danger of capsizing in the immensity of the universe. Better information is needed, along with the willingness and energy to examine conventional beliefs that present a standard barrier which can only be penetrated by a discerning and believing mind.

This takes courage when we defy convention, especially when we look deeply into the spiritual beliefs that have sustained others in previous eras but seem to have lost their power to inform us.

Time is not a guarantee of authenticity, it only authenticates the long-term history of those traditions with which we have become familiar. Or which, through attrition, we may have tentatively accepted into our individual belief systems on a semi-permanent basis.

Spiritual beliefs should not be relegated to mere habits, a last-man standing pseudo-philosophical attitude, or conventional ways of thinking while experiencing nothing other than the sentimental comforts of seasonal celebrations.

Traditions are comforting and often life-affirming, but without hard evidence they are usually little more than myths and legends. We endorse them often because they generally comfort us when we are in need of comforting.

But our essential consciousness remains the same, fixated on our individual destinies and general well-being. In search of material comforts and all too frequently praise for whatever we have managed to accomplish.

Without appearing to be impulsively judgmental, some of us have generally stagnated in terms of the collective search for the miraculous within us. If, that is, any more than a relative handful of us are still in search of understanding and illumination, beyond simply pleading for heavenly assistance

and whatever bounty may come our way as a result of what some of us might term a gift of grace.

This is the nature of the human adventure, caught in the conflict between the needs, attachments and addictions of the mind and body set against the needs of the spirit, whose gratification is so often apparently uncertain.

When those conditions prevail, we are much more willing to postpone the investigation. So much easier it is to simply adhere to standard beliefs and conventional traditions. So much simpler to go along with the social flow of things than find the truth of any of those mysteries for ourselves, according to our own direct experience.

We have become used to the immediate or near-immediate gratification of our interests and endeavors. And when that possibility is indeterminate we quickly lose interest in any long-term adventure with only an uncertain future in view.

Progress on a spiritual path requires many qualities and attributes, and commitment is high on any list. If we are not willing to commit ourselves to a teaching and a practice with serious devotion, the probability of success may border along the lines of the highly improbable.

We may hope for a miracle, and so we often do when trouble comes our way, but a spiritual practice offers us a far better and more pragmatic opportunity to reach our inner goals. Our traditional western concerns about this may be murky and not well-defined, but in recent decades light from eastern spiritual traditions has illuminated the landscape for those in search of illumination.

Our culture has been changed in subtle ways, but in contrast our western religious traditions have tended to retreat into the battered bastions of mythic expression and historical interpretation related to archetypal projections. They have been faced, as they will continue to be faced, with

alternate visions of reality based on eastern and inner-directed traditions.

But any conflict based on different approaches to the spiritual domain is foolish and nonsensical. All that really matters is what is useful and what is not. We should not be concerned with religious pedigrees, nor bothered with uncertain alliances to interpretive medieval commandments in which we no longer believe. And for good reasons.

Or in individuals with formalized status whose spiritual authority we do not accept, and who command neither our loyalty nor our affection. The choice is always ours, but if we are choosing a spiritual path, we can make that choice without exhibiting any form of discourtesy to traditions to which we do not adhere.

Generosity, respect and goodwill for others are what are called for here, not condemnation or conversion because of the difference of an opinion. Unless we can authentically verify through direct perception the truth of our beliefs, they will remain only our beliefs.

We should keep them where they are most at home, in the privacy of our minds and the seclusion of our hearts until they reach full maturity.

Proselytizing rightfully belongs to those with the genuine experience of divine enchantment, not merely holding beliefs and opinions they insist on sharing with others, even at the point of a sword.

Set in concrete though those fevered imaginations may be, the proof of that particular pudding still lies in the eating. It does not rely simply on personal hopes, sincere wishes or heart-felt desires. Opinions in the matter are only opinions, and do not put bread on the table. We are that which we seek to know, so say the sages, the saints and mystics throughout time. Any belief less than that disrespects our true being.

Those beings provided the proof of their teachings through their lives, their experiences, the traditions they left behind for others to experience, and the techniques for transforming consciousness they developed and perfected. And this, not unproven beliefs and unfounded opinions is the direction in which we must all, one day, learn to travel.

That is the legacy of the mystics of mankind. Our contemporary spiritual vision should now be broadened to include them all, with respect, admiration and gratitude. And meditation is one of the methods they discovered, developed and perfected for the welfare and benefit of all.

No matter what superficial differences there may be of color, caste or social condition, we are all men and women in the service of life. We are all subject to our emotions, we all suffer, and we all cherish our hopes for the future.

These, among so many other things, unite us all in the struggles of life. We could better our fortunes when we search within ourselves for the answers we have traditionally sought outside our own being.

We should take the advice of our spiritual elder brothers and sisters, and turn within for the answers of which we are all so desperately in need. And we will all be the better for it.

◆

ABOUT THE AUTHOR

Louis Rogers was the host and producer of the television interview series Turning Inward, and the founding publisher and executive editor of Inner Paths Magazine, both in New York. He was also the founding publisher and executive editor of Pir Publications and Sufi Review located in Westport, Connecticut and New York City.

Professor Rogers began his career as an instructor at Hunter College in New York, then turned his attention towards publishing spiritual teachings. He has written numerous books, articles, editorials, book and magazine introductions and prefaces. His short story, The Zhikr of the Heart, first appeared in the London-based magazine, Sufi Journal.

In 2001, he returned to university teaching as an Adjunct Professor in the Department of Languages, Literature and Media Studies at Sacred Heart University in Fairfield and Stamford Connecticut, and later as an Affiliate Professor at Fairfield University, also in Fairfield, Connecticut.

His previous books include: Ladder to the Sky, an adventure novel set against a modern and mythological background of Taoist energy teachings and legends. Coming Alive: Accessing the Healing Energies of the Universe, Mirror of the Unseen: The Complete Discourses of Jalal al-Din Rumi, The Fire of Love: The Love Story of Layla and Majnun, Call and Response: The Wisdom of Rumi, The Age of Spirit, Tales of Immortality, What Do You Expect God To Be?, Where Do We Go From Here?, Bridging The Gap, Who Do You Think You Are?, Kissing The Spider, That Which You Wish To Be, What Next May Come, The Face In The Mirror and most recently, Rebel In The Mind. A Hand In Time is his eighteenth book.

Louis Rogers

A HAND IN TIME

For the man on the end of the couch;
I hope you played for me.

There is no such thing as a perfect life,
unless we make it so.

In that split second when the gunpowder bursts...the next second when the gun at the end of my hand blasts the room with light, jerking my arm back...in that time out of time, I cannot say whom I truly aim for.

GINEVRA
1899

The air reeks of gunpowder...and fresh blood.

I push the limp body off me. Someone's sobs, mine no doubt, I hear as if from far away. Dropping my skirts, my eyes skirt the room, to the body on the floor, to her standing in the doorway. I've never seen her so pale, so...blighted. I see the gun on the floor. Tendrils of smoke snake upwards from the barrel as if beckoned by the notes of a magic flute.

I hear the voices, the footsteps. They're coming. I hear my heart in my ears; I feel the snuffs of air from my nose.

What I do, I do without thought.

It takes me only a few steps to snatch the gun from the floor and cross the room to her side.

"What?"

Eyes glazed with fear find me.

I reach up and tuck a stray strand of her gleaming raven hair back into her perfectly coiffed Gibson Girl.

"Go."

"What?" she asks again, this time her luminescent brow furrows, growing awareness in the moment returns, a spark of denial simmers.

"You must get out of here, Pearl." I take her hand; one I remember having held more than any other in my life. "You have far more to lose, too much to lose."

I shake my head, tangles of thoughts rattle. The words accusing me, the voices that will say I somehow brought this on myself, part of me believes. That part knows I cannot let her take any blame, for this, for him.

I lie to her for the first time in all of our years together.

"They will believe me. They'll believe I could do such a thing, why I could do such a thing. Look there is blood on my clothes, but none on yours."

Her gaze flits over my dark uniform before resting on her bright, silk gown.

I look at her face, I flash to the memory of the first time I saw her face, the young one, one so like mine.

"My papa is nothing in this world, and yours is devoted to him. Mine cannot be hurt by this. Your *famiglia* ... it will disgrace them forever."

"No. No, I must tell them," Pearl shakes her head. There is little focus in eyes that try to focus everywhere. "I came to protect you. It's my fault. If I had believed you, trusted you, he wouldn't—" she babbles. I understand it all.

Now both of our almost black eyes drop to the floor, to the body slumped upon it, to the growing puddle of blood around it, to the face so dashing even in death.

"They'll execute you," she whispers.

I grab her by the shoulders and shake her. "You did protect me. You came. You gave me time to..." I shudder, the words I must say—fleeting through the sliver of mind still capable of thinking—feel as if they are a rag shoved down my throat, and I gag on them. "...we didn't have time to finish." My gaze grabs her harder than my hands. "He always wanted me more, you know that don't you—"

Pearl shakes her head, covers her ears with trembling hands.

"He desired me." I slap her with a thin thread of truth. It is enough.

The slap of her hand spins my head; the sting of it stays long after her hand retreats.

I clench my eyes tightly.

"He always desired me more than you."

This time it is no slap. Curled fingers and knuckles meet my face. All that I had done to her feeds the strength of her arm.

I stammer back from the blow. My shoulder collides with the wall. The corner of the table digs deep into my buttock. I drop to the floor.

Pearl is blurry through my teary eyes. I can feel the sadness in the wane smile I force upon my face.

Hers creases like crumpled paper.

"My bruises," I totter back upon my feet, "these bruises will tell their own tale."

The shutters flap open; Pearl gasps.

"You made me..." She wants to speak of it. There is no time.

The voices from above grow louder, the stomping upon the stairs insistent.

"You came in time; it is all that matters." I pull her to me; hold her close. "Now we must act quickly."

With a graceful movement, grace acquired from the dance lessons she herself had given me, I twirl our bodies round, open the door, and push her out.

"Ginevra—!"

I shut the door on her face. I turn to the dead man who had ruined our lives, lives that had been better, truer, and richer, for the existence of the other, and await my fate.

PEARL
1895

If that afternoon was different from the many others that came before, I could not tell.

My father, mother, and I sat in awkward repose in the Conservatory, sipping afternoon tea, waiting for the hour of the coaching parade to approach. I detested coaching almost as much as tea. I sat apart from them by the fountain, apart from them in this room. We were all just pieces even when together, never a whole.

Thin, silk curtains fluttered in the salty breezes off Newport Harbor. The smell beckoned to me, whispering softly to me in the waves of air wafting toward me, that I was still young enough to play in it, to run in it, bathe in it. Those days had passed, or so they said, but not in my mind.

Water trickled brightly from the rouge fountain tiered with cupids, filling the heavy pauses, so many of them. I loved this room, where house fused with garden, but only when alone. I was rarely alone.

My brother, Clarence, was off playing tennis at the Casino or gadding about town with his friends, as he did more and more often of late. He still 'played.' While I, caught in the nowhere between childhood and adulthood, was rarely allowed to go anywhere without my parents. I so longed to go somewhere without my parents. But what would they be without me, the small piece of jetsam floating untethered in gloomy thickness of their marriage?

My mother prattled on and on, savoring her gossip with the same relish as she did her tea.

"Alva refuses to speak of anything but the additions to Marble House, how very grand it will be. She doesn't say it, but we all know. She expects it to be the grandest of all the cottages."

Whenever my mother spoke of Alva Vanderbilt, her voice chirped with admiration, her face twisted as if she'd bitten into a lemon. How she reminded me of the catty girls from school, the girls who made fun of me for my dedication to my studies as if that made me inferior to them in some way. How happier my mother would have been with one of them as her daughter. How often I wished one of them were.

Mother pestered my father, invisible behind his newspaper.

"Orin, we must think of expanding. The Beeches has been at the top of the list for a year. We cannot be usurped." She sat bolt straight, spine never touching the back of the chair, the lace of her day dress unfurled precisely from her small lap, and not a single strand slithered out of place from her upswept crown of red hair.

I slumped lower in my chair, crumpling my skirts in my fists.

"We will do no such thing," my father mumbled from behind his wall of paper. "It is perfect as it is. Do not forget our agreement, Millicent."

Their agreement. How it plagued Mother to have conceded to it. Father had made it plain to her; I remembered it well. Her pleading for a summer 'cottage' in the newly chic island off the New England coast, his own desire for how it should be built rising out of his love for art and architecture. He had put it to her straight, if she wanted a home in Newport, it would be constructed to my father's specifications. He demanded; she surrendered.

I sipped, gazed down in my cup, wondering why my mother could find no joy in this glorious building. Perhaps she had had little say save for the wall coverings and the furniture and such, but it was still one of the most splendid places I had ever seen, and still one of the grandest places I had ever lived. Our tour of Europe two years ago had had a profound effect on my father; and it was here, in every curved banister, coffered ceiling, and marbled column.

"But Orin, dear..."

She called him 'dear.' *Oh, here it comes,* I thought, my eyes rolling to the painted ceiling. It didn't.

With his characteristic throat clearing, Mr. Birch took a single step into the room, denying my mother her cajoling.

"There is a man here, Sir, and a girl." Our butler, as stiff as his shirt, proclaimed as if he announced the delivery of a parcel of manure.

"They claim you are expecting them. Costa, I believe she said their name is."

My father jumped up; newspaper scattered with a rustle to the floor. My mother and I balked at his quickness, at the rare glimpse of his smile beneath his bushy mustache.

"Wonderful, Mr. Birch," said he, rushing from the room.

Spilling tea as I quickly dropped my cup in its saucer, I rose and followed.

"Pearl, stay. It is your father's business."

I ignored her. Monotony had become my most constant companion. No matter how inconsequential, I ran toward anything to run away from it.

I stopped at the top of the white marble stairs leading down to the grand doors of our summer home, half hiding behind one set of double breche marble columns crowned with gold capitals. Just inside the small vestibule between the arched wood doors and the inner ones of grill and glass, I could see only their silhouettes against the bright afternoon light, so very small in the massive aperture. I saw Birch had left the outer doors open as if he would shoo the visitors out like pesky insects at the first opportunity.

The man was tall. A short hat and long suit jacket enshrouded him. The girl was no girl, at least not a little one. The slight curves of her body, sheathed in what I could only see as a dark-colored, single-layered dress, were those of a young woman, or a girl on her way to becoming one.

"Welcome, Mr. Costa, Miss. Welcome."

My head popped farther around the marble pillar, not to see the visitors, but my father. To see if this enthusiastic man *was* my father. He rushed toward the man, hand held out, a swath of his black hair, hair he had given me, falling upon his slightly wrinkled forehead. Reaching behind them, my father closed the doors. I could see them more clearly now.

The man looked my father's age, perhaps older, or perhaps simply more aged. It was the face of the girl, an older girl as I had thought, which held me. If not for her deeper complexion, olive I believe such skin was called, we could be sisters, for her eyes were the same nut-brown as mine though more almond-shaped, cheekbones high, mouth full, chin narrowed her face to a point.

Mr. Costa replied with a hesitant good day, but upon his tongue, it came as "gooda day." The distinct addition of a vowel gave them away. Italians. I had never met any real Italians. I studied them as I would a painting I had never seen.

My father pulled the man deeper into our home by the hand still in his, beyond the grilled doors, and into the marble foyer. He straightened his shoulders, gathered himself. Zeal still beamed from him; a bright spark glinting in his dark eyes. His voice dropped to its normal deep timbre, words spaced ever so, with aristocratic nonchalance.

"How was your journey? Fine, I hope."

The man turned to the girl beside him with a particular look I could see she read well.

"Fine, Sir," she replied. Better than the man's, the girl's English was a trifle more fluid.

"Glad to hear it." My father was a man of intelligence and pride; he could see it in others. Though the girl had answered, my father directed his reply to the man. "I hope you will be comfortable here. It is a fine house."

As the girl softly translated my father's words, I smirked. *A fine house, Father, really?*

Would he tell these people the ocean was but a puddle?

To them, our summer home must have seemed a palace, a fantasy functioning as a home, a four-story mansion designed after the chateau d'Asnieres in France, the home of the Marquis de Voyer, sitting on ten acres of land. A 'house' indeed.

"Mr. Birch, please show our new guests to their quarters, if you would." With a gestured hand and a small dip of his head, my father encouraged these 'guests' up the few steps and into the grand gallery spanning the entire length of the house from north to south.

They followed slowly. Their eyes widened at the grandeur, the enormity of our 'cottage,' the thirty-foot-high walls of white Caen stone, the ancient oil paintings, the length of the walls framed by gilt moldings that greeted every entrant. How pretentious such opulence must have looked. Their slight bodies cried out for good meals, not flamboyant affluence. My cheeks burned as I looked at them looking.

"And which would those be, Sir?" Birch sent a blast of cold through the warm room.

"Mr. Costa here is to have the luggage room. I've had Mr. Grayson refurbish it into a living space and a workshop. This is the man who has come to teach Clarence violin and to make us some one-of-kind furniture. Aren't you, Mr. Costa?"

The man nodded, but it was to my father's ebullience. His expression blank, hesitant; he understood little of my father's words.

"He and his lovely daughter will also be staying over in the winter as members of our off-season caretakers." My father turned back to Mr. Costa. "And for that I say *grazie.*"

"T...thank you, Mr. Worthington," the young woman said. "My papa, he is excited, to work."

My father took her hand in both of his.

"Ah, Geenahva, so glad to have you here as well, of course."

She smiled, and it was lovely. "It is Ginevra, Gin-*eh*-v-ruh," she pronounced her name correctly, slowly, for my father's behalf, and perhaps for mine, for I had seen her gaze flash to me with the same curiosity with which I perused her. Gin, like the drink my mother would say; emphasis on eh; rush through the v, to end low with the ruh. I said it over and over in my mind. I would say it correctly when the chance came. I swore to myself the chance would come. I would banish monotony not just from this moment.

"Yes, Ginevra," my father did a passable imitation of her name. "You will be housed with other young ladies such as yourself..." servants, he meant, of course, "...on the top floor. I'm sure we will find something productive for you to do soon."

"Sew," she said without hesitation. I smiled. "I sew."

I saw my father's grin. "Wonderful. There is plenty of sewing to do in this house. Isn't that right, Mr. Birch?"

Birch nodded. It looked as if it hurt him to do so. He held out a hand, pointing toward the right, toward the back stairs, those belonging to the servants.

"*Vieni*, Papa," Ginevra put a hand on her father's arm as she reached down for a battered valise. Mr. Costa nodded silently, picked up the two beside him, having never released a glossy leather violin case from beneath his arm, and followed Birch's lead.

As she brushed past, our eyes met. Did she see it in mine, or I in hers? Regardless, it was a fine beginning.

I feigned a headache to dismiss myself from the coaching parade, illness being the only acceptable excuse. We came to 'summer' in Newport, but our lives were as rigid here as they were in New York.

My head did throb, but with thoughts of the newcomers. I tried to whoosh them away with my reading, but they refused to depart. I lay upon my bed until it was time to get ready for dinner.

* * *

It was a rare evening during summers at Newport where we neither entertained nor were entertained, for doing so was the sole purpose of this small colony of the very rich.

It was only the family for dinner that night, just the four of us at the vast square table for ten. The large room and all its grandeur swallowed us, or so it felt to me at the time, but my mother insisted we dine there, rather than the intimate breakfast room, whether we entertained or not.

I lost myself to the light of the chandeliers and the paintings they illuminated; the ancient figures that hovered over me, over us, ever listening. More than once, I wished they would shower their wisdom down upon us. Their presence was my panacea, or perhaps it was merely the art itself. Like my father, so much of what fed me was art. Fitting that the room where we ate should be so full of it.

I missed many a tiresome conversation in the study of these paintings. Not that evening.

"Really, Clarence, is it so very difficult for you to arrive on time?" My mother chided my brother as he rushed in, still straightening his cravat, no more than two minutes past seven.

Clarence, eighteen and dashing, fulfilled his role as my mother's pet with relish; he scudded a step at her tone, one that did not typically belong to him.

"Darling, Mother, I'm only late because I wanted to look perfect for you." He glided to her chair beside mine with elegance. He had my father's height and my mother's thinness, my father's thick hair, tones of dark and light gold, like Mother's used to be. He leaned over and plucked a kiss upon her cheek.

The magic wand flicked; her earrings, much like the shape of the lights above her, tinkled and glittered, though far truer than she did.

"Don't be silly, dear, you always look lovely," she twittered like a nuzzled bird. It would have been my pleasure to stick a cracker in her mouth.

My brother came around and sat opposite Mother, to my father's left.

"Pop," he greeted my father with the stylish slang becoming so popular among the young men of his set, the young and newly on the marriage market, the athletic and always busy sparks that crowed about Bellevue Avenue like the roosters they were. Father nodded in silence, as was his way. Clarence sat, catching my eye, tossing me a sly wink. His practiced charm, so like the many other young men, had little effect on me. He should have been my hero, as he had been when we were little. I should have looked up to him with worship and adoration. Resentment was far more powerful.

He looked at the opulent façades of our homes and those like it and believed. It was more than the color of our eyes that differed. He and my mother were a matched pair. My father and I, a pair ourselves, but of a different sort.

Clarence pulled in his chair and Birch, having been standing guard at the small door leading to the pantry, gave a nod of his balding head.

The footmen entered the room, silver trays balanced perfectly on perfectly manicured hands. James, the first footman brought the soup, while Charles, the second, brought the wine. Both were amazingly handsome. I always asked for more of whatever James was serving, bringing his dazzling smile and sparkling blue eyes closer to me again and again, though I squirmed in my seat every time he did.

It was a peculiarity, of the life here in Newport, that the footmen were undeniably attractive, not only of face but of physique, for oftentimes they wore livery with breeches and stockings. They must possess, then, a 'well-turned calf' as the silly saying went. And they must be tall, six feet being the minimum height.

It became a social occasion, a real cat's party, when a woman of any house had to hire a new footman. Friends were invited over, drinks were served as handsome young men walked by, displaying their features. The women spoke of them as if they spoke of jewels, of how they glittered, how they were desired. They laughed and giggled as little girls did over their dolls. As was my way then, I hid in a secret hallway to watch and listen. My mother always enjoyed the occasion in a fine mood, enjoyed it a great deal. Admitting my own enjoyment was something I denied, even to myself.

Mother was not in such a mood at this moment. She took one silent sip of her soup, dabbed the sides of her mouth with a starched serviette, and then it started.

"Orin, please explain to me these new servants you've brought into our home. It was never part of our agreement." She put her spoon down with deliberation; she would not pick it up until he answered her to satisfaction. In truth, she had a valid point, the hiring of all the servants—as she called them, my father called them the staff, it was a telling distinction those days—was under the purview of the woman of the house.

My father didn't lower his spoon save for another helping of soup.

"I told you all about them, Millicent, when we were in Italy."

"Tell me again. I don't remember."

I thought she did though, from the look on her face. My mother's face always gave her truth away. Did mine? I hardly knew my own truth then, but I knew I wanted no one to see it. I wanted nothing of my mother, that truth was irrefutable.

"Felice is a violin maestro. Not only does he play like…," my father did look up from his soup then, a bit of rapture on his rough features, "…like a virtuoso. He is also a master artisan. He makes violins, violas, as well as magnificent furniture. Don't you remember my promising he would make you furniture none of your friends would have, like nothing they could compare it to?"

He knew how to mine my mother for gold. I hid my smug smile behind my napkin.

My mother picked up her spoon. "Oh, well, yes, that part I do remember. But I thought he would make the furniture in Italy and send it to us."

My father looked like he would throw his spoon. It was a mean notion, but it would have given me quite the chuckle if he had.

"No, that was never discussed. He is primarily here to teach Clarence how to play."

"The violin?" I hadn't heard my brother's voice crack in many years.

"Yes, Clarence. It is a wonderful talent to have." My father spoke to Clarence much as he did my mother, always with a sigh in his words.

"I have no interest in playing the violin," it was my brother's turn to put down his spoon, "or any instrument for that matter."

My mouth fell open, words needing saying hung there. How could Clarence not be thrilled at such an opportunity? How could he be so ungrateful for it?

"I'll do it, Father." I heard the words for the first time myself; they came without thought. I heard too the squeak in my voice; it thrummed through me like the slide of a bow down taut strings. "I'd love to learn to play the violin."

The silence appalled. I would have preferred it stayed that way rather than be assaulted by my mother's response.

She laughed.

"Oh, Pearl, don't be ridiculous," she chuckled with cruel dismissiveness. She dismissed me often unless I served her purpose.

"Why? Why would it be ridiculous?" My hands balled into fists in my lap. The fragrance of the fresh lobster bisque suddenly smelled like rotted mushrooms.

Mother's face twisted tightly; her sneer devoured me. In that moment, I hoped my face did reveal my truth. I hoped I held up a mirror to her. "Such things are for men. Have you ever seen a woman play in the symphony?"

"No, but that doesn't mean there couldn't be."

"Clarence is so busy, after all, Orin." Mother carried on as if I hadn't said a word. It wasn't the first time. "He has his tennis and his sailing, and so many other activities. Isn't that why we bought a membership to the Casino?"

The Casino had been an establishment in Newport for ten years before we arrived. I had heard a little of the silly tale that brought about its creation. James Gordon Bennett, the man who owned the New York Herald and another newspaper in Paris I think, was the man who built it and made its rules. Before the Casino, and even now, most of the Newport men went to the Reading Room, a 'gentlemen's club,' they called it. I'd heard it was a very serious, a very stodgy place. I had walked past it, of course, for it was just down Bellevue Avenue, not far from our home. Past it, never to enter.

The rumor, as it went, claims Mr. Bennett invited one of his friends to the Reading Room. That friend, an Englishman by the name of Captain Candy, a name which sounded quite fake to me, Mr. Bennett had challenged to do something outlandish at the Reading Room, wake things up a bit. Captain Candy complied. He jumped on his horse, rode it up the stairs, and into the hall.

Imagine the outcry, the madness; I imagined the hilarity. The Board of the Reading Room censured Mr. Bennett and retracted Captain Candy's guest privileges. Mr. Bennett's response...the construction of the Newport Casino.

This club was far from stodgy. With much more modern architecture, it took up the entire end block on Bellevue Avenue on the northeast corner of Memorial Boulevard. There were tennis courts and polo courts and lovely porches where, wonder of wonders, women were welcomed to sit and socialize and watch. There were balls and banquets and musicales held there as well; I loved those most of all. Membership was exclusive but no match for my mother's determination or my father's credentials.

"I have no wish to deny Clarence all those past-times, Millicent, but a well-rounded man possesses other talents than the ability to hit a ball well over a net or excel at other sorts of sports." My father gave my brother a look; there was something in it I didn't understand at the time. Clarence blushed. "He should know of music and literature and art. Such things are what make a man a gentleman."

It was quite a lengthy speech for my father, an impassioned one at that, though, in that moment, I could find no joy in it.

"Well then," Mother said between spoonfuls, "as long as he has time for his other pursuits, ones that will bring him into the good graces of our neighbors, I suppose it wouldn't be terrible." She reached across the table to take my brother's hand, quite the stretch at this table. "Perhaps you will be able to serenade our guests sometime soon. That would make quite the impression. Wouldn't it, Orin?"

My mother brokered a deal with the high craftiness of any of the wealthy industrialists who populated our small summer community. My father knew it as surely as I did. He made the deal; he, too, was a master businessman. Clarence was quick to agree but I caught the look that passed between him and my mother; only they knew the code to decipher their message. Yet I knew my brother would still spend more time at the Casino than at any other place. I believe my father saw it as well, as I saw the ends of his bushy mustache hang lower.

I knew then there would be no violin lessons for me. It didn't matter. I knew what I truly wanted. I stopped listening, stopped eating, and remembered.

* * *

I remembered that day as if it was yesterday, not four years ago.

We were in the home of Henry Havemeyer. Miss Mary Cassatt's dearest friend was married to one of his cousins and the occasion was a homecoming of sorts for the woman painter. It was a showing as well, for her astounding works stood on easels propped up around the circumference of the room. I must have walked round at least five times.

My father, so much taller then as I stood by his side, spoke to her. He preferred the work of the grand masters of the Renaissance, but I could tell he was curious about this woman.

"Your style, Miss Cassatt, it is very unique," he'd said to her upon proper introduction.

The round-faced woman's thin lips almost broke into a smile, almost. My lips tried to form the same knowing, slight curve.

"Not so, sir," she said. "Perhaps here in America, yes. Nevertheless, it has been flourishing in France for some time. It is called Impressionism."

My father tilted his head at the unfamiliar term.

"When I traveled to Paris in 1875," Miss Cassatt continued, "the technique was burgeoning. Especially by Degas. I used to go and flatten my nose against an art dealer's window, a window full of Degas' work, and absorb all I could of his technique."

She looked up at my father; simple features no longer simple as they bloomed. "It changed my life. I saw art then as I wanted to see it."

"And your family, Miss Cassatt," my mother had chimed in with what she thought was an important question. "Do they encourage your...work?"

Miss Cassatt's face returned to its stoic self. It broke only for a moment, when her gaze turned down to me; I saw her smile for the first time that day. The smile faded like the moon with the coming of dawn as she returned her attention to my mother.

"I will tell you this, Madam. I enrolled myself in the Pennsylvania Academy of Fine Arts at the age of fifteen." She said no more, but her eyes held my mother's with a fierce grip.

Mother laughed her tinny, fake laugh. "How courageous of you," she said flatly. "Well, we will let you greet the other guests."

My mother had yanked my father away then, me with them, and brought her mouth close to his ear, but not so close I didn't hear her disparaging condemnation, "A new woman."

I didn't know then what she meant, but I learned. I didn't know what a tangled path would lay before me for it, but I, too, wanted to be a new woman. Most of all, I wanted to be an artist. I thought I had the talent, as Miss Cassatt did, but did I have her courage?

GINEVRA

The man called Birch led us through the marble hall. I walked on tip-toes. I walked as I once had through a grand cathedral back in Italy.

He hurried us along. I had only seconds to glimpse a dining room, one so large it could have served as a great hall in a castle from long ago. It glittered; gold sparkled everywhere. Across from it, an alcove, each end flanked by glass and gold cabinets. On display were more treasures of silver and gold, china and porcelain. I slowed; if I could, I would have run.

The man hurried us along.

We passed through two dark, carved doors; we passed into another world. Inside these doors, we entered a small landing.

"This is a ladies' powder room," Mr. Birch finally decided to speak to us. "The Beeches has some of the most modern plumbing in all of Newport." He turned hard eyes on me. "Family and guests only."

I returned his look. Nothing more.

The snobby man spoke with such pride; you would think this enormous place belonged to him. I suppose in a way he thought it did.

Everything about Birch was stiff, his perfectly pressed cut-away, pristine white shirt, large black puff tie with its big, fancy knot bobbing as he spoke, but especially the stiff tone of his voice. Did he speak to everyone with such cold flatness or did such a chill frost only my father and me? Time would tell.

My father nudged my arm and gave me 'the look.' I translated.

Such looks came constantly during our journey to America. I saw more of them than I did the passing ocean.

Mr. Worthington had paid our fare, thirty dollars each... thirty dollars to travel in the bowels of one of the great steamships crossing the ocean faster than the wind. It was a week living in hell.

Not allowed on deck, I had begun to dream of fresh air before the journey ended. They fed us little else but soup or stew, we slept in huddled masses on the floor in our clothes beside our luggage and had only salt water to wash ourselves.

Few of the others understood the sharply delivered instructions of the ship's crew given only in English. I was one of the few.

My role as translator had started then, and though I tried to teach Papa the language through the long empty hours on the ship, he had learned to say only a few words; he understood even less. Instead, he would give me 'the look' and I would translate as best I could.

The ship docked in New York. We rose up from our burial place and saw the sky, breathing deep. The sight of the giant lady and her torch overwhelmed us. We had heard of her, her welcoming. The people who worked at her feet were not so kind. I feared, despised, and pitied them. Their jobs were difficult; they could not show us too much kindness. To them, we were no different from the colored, what Italians called *mulignane*. The nastiness of it became my reality. They stripped away our humanity; we could have been heads of lettuce. Yet they were just doing their work.

They tagged us like cattle, put us in rooms to stand, waiting. We stood in lines for hours, herded through, telling our names over and over.

So many lost their real names. If they couldn't write, those who registered us went by sound alone, mangling many, wrong names these newcomers would carry for the rest of their lives. Worse were the ones they sent back. They had endured for nothing.

Then the inspections…our clothes, our hair, our mouths, our bodies. Endless invasions making us feel less than human. The constant questions, the same again and again. Thorough and hurried at the same time. They hurried us so fast, often I didn't have time to understand myself. They hurried us, as the butler did now, as if they couldn't wait to get us to a place where they could not see us.

Birch pointed to his left.

"This pantry here serves both the breakfast room just behind it and the dining room. A marvelous convenience for the family."

He said mahvelous as if he were one of them.

He opened another door, plain wood and frosted glass. Into another foyer, a simple if bright one of windows and white tile. The floor, the walls, the ceiling, all of small white squares of tile. Then to the stair-case.

It rose and fell away from us. I looked up and down; I could see the white grillwork and polished wood banister spiral away in perfect symmetry. I stood in the middle, moving neither up nor down. It was a landing named nowhere.

"This is the servants' staircase. It is the only staircase you shall ever use."

Birch stopped and turned to us. "Ever."

My father needed no translation to understand.

"They may use it from time to time." He said "they" as if the word referred to a king or a queen. "But rarely. Downstairs, if you please," he instructed.

I had known we traveled to a rich man's house, but I never imagined a place like this. I became aware of our ragged appearance, clothes old and worn before the hard journey, now so very much worse, our ragged suitcases holding only more ragged clothes. The coarse wool scratched me for the first time in my life. My foot shrunk away from the top step; I could not see where they led.

Before he closed the door to the marble hallway—though I didn't know then it must never be called a hallway—I looked back.

The girl still stood at her place by the pillars; she could have been a sculpture at its feet. Her clothing was so fine. Her dress was short, hem falling between knees and ankles; it puffed all around her from something that lay underneath. It seemed to hover about her, fabric as fine as angel's wings.

Something nameless, a creature I had never met, was born in me that was to live within, eating away, for many years.

She stared at us still, but it wasn't a mean stare. Curious, yes, and something else, I thought. Perhaps that something else was just my own hope.

"Wait right here." Birch instructed me, pointing to a distinct spot at the bottom of the stairs in a large foyer of the same white tile.

"Right…here." He pointed again. I did not know which I was more compelled to do, curtsey to him or slap him.

He took my father by the arm and led him through another frosted door and then another, their footsteps growing ever fainter, their silhouettes fuzzy as if they walked out of this world to another. With each step they took, the churning in my gullet twisted tighter. I found myself standing alone amid people in constant motion. My feet once more pestered me to run.

Most were women, some middle-aged, most young. Their features as alike as their uniforms: fair-haired, light-skinned, blonde or soft brown hair, most with blue eyes like pieces of glass with pointed edges.

I stared too.

All wore black blouses buttoned to the top, sleeves puffed at the shoulders, and full black skirts. All wore crisp white aprons; some aprons covered their whole body, others only their skirts. Atop their pinned hair, some white caps covered whole heads, while others wore dainty lace headdresses. The differences were small. I thought them particular to a precise position in the household. I did not know which was which. They were as strange to me as this new country—new world—I found myself in.

They hurried past, carrying all sorts of items: dishes, linens, mixing bowls. To the one, all stumbled a step at the sight of me. I shivered beneath cold glares. Eyes racked me from top to bottom. They were uniform in their quick dismissal.

A few men passed me. Like the women, their clothes told of their positions. Two men, one young and one old, wore dark suits, full jackets, and pants, while three others, all young and handsome, wore waistcoats and fancy shirts and ties like Birch. One of these men, really a boy not much older than me, winked as he walked past. I pursed my lips as I tilted my nose up and away from him.

Two others stood out, incomparable to the rest, as was Mr. Birch.

I glimpsed the man through a wide archway into a kitchen as large as a cavern filled with a huge wood table topped with copper, cast iron ovens all in a row, and everywhere copper pots and pans, and strange devices I had never seen. He stood, vibrant, in all white, a double-breasted white jacket, a white kerchief tied about his neck, and the strangest hat I'd ever seen; it had no brim, just a band of white circled about his head. The rest rose high, a pleated puff of fabric, like a crown. This man issued orders; he did not yell but spoke strong and firm. His accent was strange to my ears. It wasn't Italian but there was something similar about it. Those he spoke to jumped, with a quick, "Yes, Monsieur le Chef." Their response explained his speech.

"And who might you be?" She stood before me, hands curled fists on near non-existent hips. She wore all black as well, yet no apron. Her blouse boasted sharply pressed pleats, her skirt was fuller; both had a shine to the fabric, clearly finer than those of the other women. From her waistband hung a circle of keys, a huge ring of them, more than I had ever seen.

She spoke as Mr. Birch did, with such emphasis on the 't's' and the long 'o' sound. English.

While northern Italians disliked southern Italians, no one disliked Italians as much as the English and the Irish. Hope, what there was of it, fluttered out the window as quickly as a trapped bird once released.

This was my introduction to Mrs. Briggs, the housekeeper. She was as thin as a fire poker and just as hotly sharp. I learned quickly that she ruled this roost as well and as cruelly as any general ruled an army.

"Well don't just stand there, girl, ansah me?"

Squinty black eyes bore into me; lips pinched into a tight line.

"I'm-a...," My clipped nails dug into my palms, my legs beneath my tattered skirts quivered. "I am..." I rushed to correct my mistake. Too late.

"You ah an I-talian," she announced, face twisting with her displeasure. "Why are you in this house?"

I opened my mouth, nothing. Yet salvation came.

"Not to worry, Mrs. Briggs," Birch called out to us from the doorway, striding fast, my father no longer with him. My relief had a sharp bite of worry to it.

"A word, if you will, Mrs." He called her Mrs. though she wore no wedding ring. Mr. Birch motioned his large head to a room just off the hall to my right. He unlocked the door and they rushed inside; I had only a glimpse of what looked like a nice, simple sitting room, the kind I grew up playing in back home. The twang of loss and longing struck me as the clock does midnight; it stung my eyes with tears.

At first, I heard nothing, then murmurs that grew to voices raised, none too pleased. Then, finally, unhappy acceptance.

They rushed out as fast as they rushed in. They stood before me. The woman's face was far more curdled than it had been when she went in.

"So, you ah to be a new seamstress," Mrs. Briggs didn't say my name. I'm sure she knew it by then, knew all about me. "You had better be good, for the mistress and our young lady wear only the finest."

"Good, *si*, I am." The words flew from my lips. Too fast. Nerves flapped my mouth faster than my mind could stop them.

"Yes, well, we shall see about that." Mrs. Briggs turned to Mr. Birch. "I'll show the girl to her room then."

"Thank you, Mrs. Briggs." Mr. Birch blustered air, shoulders dropping.

"Up with you," the sharp-boned woman waved a hand at the stairs.

I hesitated. I wanted my father, wanted to know where he was. If I took a single step away, it would be a step away from him.

Mrs. Briggs's bony fingers pinched my shoulders, clamping, she turned me and nudged upward. There was no heaven waiting for me there.

When Papa and I had first stood outside this mansion they called a 'cottage,' we stood shivering from cold fear. Scrolled columns and statues surrounded us, beside us, above us. They threatened, guarding even though they were stone. It looked like the *palazzos* of the wealthy *signori* built on the mountainsides of Italy. From our home, we could see them hovering on the horizon like clouds. Like clouds, always out of our reach.

My father's shoulders had turned, turned back toward the path on which we approached. If minds had hands, mine would have pushed him there. He faced the door once more. I held my silence. As we looked at what would be our future home—no, that wasn't right. It would never be our home, but the place we lived; my true home would ever haunt me, becoming grander as each spectral memory invaded my mind. As we looked at it, we thought it was a two-storied building. It was not.

The basement, from where Mrs. Briggs and I started to climb, hid from the outside, and there was another subbasement below the first, she told me so, as if this *were* her home, though I hoped never to see it, just as I hadn't seen it from the outside. Yes, the floors where the most work took place lay beneath the ground's surface.

As we continued upward, Mrs. Briggs took it upon herself to inform me of all the servants in the house. I couldn't keep up with such a list.

I stopped listening and started counting; there were more than forty people here to serve four. If she meant to overwhelm me, she succeeded. If she meant to make me feel like nothing, she succeeded there too.

I grew dizzy, nauseous, as she rattled on as to who did what, or more importantly, what some didn't do.

"Mr. Birch, Chef Pasquel, and I rule this roost. Howeva, the personal maids and valets are far superior to the footmen, the stable boys, or the upstairs maids. Mr. Birch does not serve dinner or empty ashtrays, nor is he expected to answer the door. The mistress's maid does not clean her room, does not even make the bed."

She babbled, layering rule upon rule like frosting on a cake. Too many to remember; too confusing not to break. It would only be a matter of time. Did all of America live by such rules?

As we climbed, I found yet another surprise, another hidden floor. Here were the servants' quarters. From the outside, this floor looked like a row of carved vertical indents held up by carved brackets, all of the same peach-colored stone, a parapet not to keep marauders out, but the servants hidden.

As we hurtled the last step, I stopped mid-stride. I found myself not in a dungeon as I expected, led there by the fiery dragon that was Mrs.

Briggs, but in a simple dormitory of rooms. I didn't know then that the constant juggling and fighting for good servants were part of the life of the rich, 'the servant problem,' I would later hear it called. Mr. Worthington had built a nice servants' floor, hoping to keep his staff pleased and in his employ.

A wide hallway with polished wood floors stretched the length of the house. In two places, my head dropped, eyes widening at the large rectangles of glass squares etched with stars. I saw the light of the sun and my gaze flew upward. Above them, windows in the roof matched their size and shape. Sunlight flowed through the very floors and ceilings as if the owner could command the sun above him as well and as easily as he did all the people beneath him.

On each side of the hall, numbered doors led us on.

Mrs. Briggs brought me into the one that would be my room.

"All the single rooms are occupied," she informed me. "You shall have to share." Were a single room available it would not be mine to have. I knew which rung on the ladder I stood; I had not yet stepped off the ground. Whenever she looked at me, her eyes started at my face, but always moved downward, always darkened with distaste.

The room was far larger than I expected. Two beds hugged the walls, each with a large white steel headrail, a smaller one at the foot. There were two closets, two chests of drawers, two chairs, and a large dressing table that sat before the window between the beds. It was far more than I had ever had at home; it did not make me miss home any less. Home was not a place or things.

The windows were a surprise, the secret of this floor revealed. Through the mullioned panes, I spied a small roof, level with the bottom of the window, a roof of small rectangles of stone. Just beyond, a grey high-shingled wall, the wall that on the outside appeared as carved stone, the wall hiding us away. At least the windows let in the natural light, but it came from nowhere. I could not see the sun or it me.

"You shall be sharin' this room with Greta," she told me, accidentally dropping her 'g,' not so superior in truth after all. "You shan't see her much. A kitchen maid works the longest hours."

She turned her back to me, yet I heard her mumble, "And that's what you should be."

I pretended not to hear, though I did it badly. I would become a master at it soon enough.

Greta's side of the room was bright and alive. A merrily squared quilt covered her bed, pictures hung from the wood rail circling the room painted pale yellow, a lovely, embroidered pillow sat on the chair. The other side looked barren and empty; my side.

"Put your things away." She pointed to the chest and the closet. "I'll be right back with bedding and something decent for you to wear." She looked offended as her gaze scratch over me.

She left me there. I sat on my bed, wondering if I would ever breathe again.

My father had promised me this would be a better life for us, as he had promised my aunts it would be. He had filled my head with the wonder that was life in America. I did not know them then as the fairy tales they were. This room was to be "my home" for the rest of my days. My skill with a needle put to use keeping the fancy clothes of the very rich in perfect condition.

I heaved a gulp of air.

In Italy, I would not have such a fine house. I would have married a simple boy from our simple town, and we would have lived in a simple house. But it would have belonged to us, to me. I would have made clothing for my husband and myself and, if blessed, our children. The clothes would have belonged to us. I would have earned a few *lira* sewing for others in the village, money for my family.

Here nothing would belong to me. I would take no pride in my work, for the people who wore the clothes would never notice it. I would make a little money, but with no family to share it.

I could no longer call my life my own.

* * *

When I finally saw my father again, he was sitting at the far end of the long table in the servants' dining room just off the kitchen, another small and cramped rectangle. He sat alone. There were at least three empty chairs on either side of him; the other servants bunched themselves together at the other end like grapes.

There was another table, a small round one, in the back, right corner. At that table sat Mr. Birch, Mrs. Briggs, the chef, and another man whose face I hadn't seen yet. No one need tell me why. One day I would learn they—the rulers of the ruled—were called the "Swell Set;" I would have another name for them. The real "servants" belonged at the long table. There were ranks within the ranks; I was in a maze with no clue of which path to take.

I rushed to my father, but his guarded look buffeted me. I slowed, sat beside him. In hushed Italian, we told each other of our day. He had fared better than I had. He had his own small room to sleep in and work in, a space of his own, filled with the incredible tools and wood Mr. Worthington had waiting for my father and his talented hands.

As he told me of it all, his eyes gleamed; he rubbed his hands together in anticipation. I hated Papa for a sharp moment—a sharply jealous moment—hated he should be so pleased.

Yet I couldn't break him of it; I hadn't seen him happy since before Mama grew ill. What sort of daughter would I be to deny him this? One that would surely and sharply have displeased my mother.

I told him of my room and that I would share it with another girl. Though I hadn't met her yet, I was sure she sat somewhere along this table. When I told my father of the sewing room Mrs. Briggs had shown me, my enthusiasm—what there was of it—was true, a truth I found easy to exaggerate; a small gift to him. The equipment was the best I had ever seen, some I had never seen. My fingers, so skilled with a needle, guided and trained by my mother when I was a young child, longed to begin work, which I would in the morning.

I watched my father's eyes as they took all of me in them.

"Your clothes, they are fine," he said in Italian.

My uniform would be the same as most of the other women: a simple black, puffed sleeved blouse, a simple black full skirt, both of cheap cotton. I would wear no apron or cap of any kind. My short-heeled, ankle boots were my own. Though their cracks and worn spots had insulted Mrs. Briggs, there were no others in the house to fit me.

"Shine them up," she had ordered me, telling me where the shoeshine room was. "I'll get you new ones when I have the time."

Who knew when that would be? I had rubbed my boots for a half-hour with some linseed oil and a rag.

"Yes," I responded flatly, hearing my own indifference, "fine."

His thin lips drooped at the corners until he opened them. Before he could say more, the staff room maid began her parade into the room. In and out, in and out she came, with dish after dish, simple fare of chicken and potatoes and peas. It was the best meal my father and I had eaten since we left Italy.

We sat among the rest of the house staff, as we would at every meal, among them but not with them. They were all there, all the inside servants Mrs. Briggs had named, yet I had no idea who was who. I knew my father hated to reveal his thick accent in the few words of English he could speak. Though one of the most talented and creative people I had ever known, he would not let his speech reveal a false truth. How strange it was for a man with such a great mind, and me, who possessed one as well, to be thought of as simple, simply because we spoke with an accent. Accents sit upon the lips, not in minds, but small minds could not know the difference.

For his sake, I followed his lead, eating without a word. Though I did not speak, I did more than my fair share of listening. I convinced myself it was to learn the language better, a feeble disguise. I fed upon their gossip as I did the meal. My naughty eavesdropping would make my yenta aunts proud. The thought almost made me giggle.

"The mistress has instructed me to find out what the Astor woman has ordered for her fall gowns." I heard Mrs. Briggs say to Mr. Birch. With a quick glance, I saw she ate her fill, more than I would have imagined from the look of her. Perhaps her meanness devoured the food long before her body.

"You cannot wear that dress at yer wedding, Edna!" The outcry came from a parlor or chambermaid. I knew them by then as those who wore the dainty lace on their heads.

"What?" The sweet-looking girl beside her, Edna no doubt, grew paler, though I didn't think it possible. She looked to one of the footmen closer to my end of the table. He shrugged his shoulders, a groom-to-be unaffected by such nonsense. The bride turned back to the woman. "Why ever not, Beatrice? You know I cannot buy my own."

"It is bad luck, thas what it is," the outraged girl, Beatrice, hissed.

"But dear Mrs. O'Brennan has made such a kind offer."

"Indeed, I have," chimed in one of the older women, by her all-white clothing, the assistant chef.

A gasp came from the other table. Mrs. Briggs grew ever-sharper dripping in overly dramatic horror. "You cannot do it, Edna. It will be the death of you."

With her sharp tongue, she told a tale of her niece, one who was to wed on the very day some man shot the president named Lincoln. The ceremony canceled; the bride gave her dress and veil away. The woman who wore it to her wedding died within a week.

Old world suspicious came into the room, beside it fear in a range of tones bouncing off the hard stone like church bells. Their voices told me another tale as well.

We were in a company of mostly English, Irish, and a few Germans. They came from countries where service had been an accepted form of occupation for hundreds of years, where accepting one's rank was a natural order of life. There was not another Italian among them, nor a single American.

I whispered softly to my father who listened with no expression. I'm not sure if it was the story or his shame that he could not understand which kept him so stone-like.

"Ya'd best believe it," this from another woman.

"I knew you'd agree with me, Nettie," Mrs. Briggs garbled, her mouth full. They said Italians had no manners.

Nettie sat tall in her chair. Her uniform was much finer than those of the other women, even that of Mrs. Briggs. Her silk black blouse was edged in white lace and cut with fine tailoring. Her black skirt wasn't nearly so full and yet, when she moved, I thought I heard the swish of a petticoat or whatever these women wore as fine undergarments. Her hair was done up smartly and her hands were clean and without callouses. A ladies' maid; *the* lady's maid.

"Doon' ya know the story of Mrs. Belmont's wedding dress?" she asked the table at large, her voice thick with Ireland. When all at the table shook their heads, she almost seemed to smile as she began to tell.

"Well, Mrs. Belmont had ordered her dress from Worth's, of course."

I did not know who Worth was, so I did not understand her "of course." I felt pulled into her tale no matter. I felt I should know more about who this Worth was.

"She ordered it late though and feared it wouldn't arrive in time. So," Nettie waved a hand, "she had another made in New York. Which she ended up wearin'. When the exquisite Worth dress arrived, she gave it to a friend, I forget which, who had just announced her engagement."

She paused, whether for effect or breath I couldn't tell.

"And...?" one of the footmen prodded her. The men too were well into the story, but they had no patience for her dramatics.

"And the woman accepted it. Within a few days, the engagement was broken."

"No!" Edna gasped. She thought twice now about accepting Mrs. O'Brennan's offering, the wariness ran all over her face. I looked upon her heartbreak with sad eyes.

"Oh, but it doesn't end there," Nettie enjoyed herself now. "That poor broken-hearted woman gave the same dress to another friend. Hers was a sad, unhappy marriage."

"So are a lot of marriages," a man whose name I didn't know muttered with a nasty grin.

"Doon' be smart with me, Silas," Nettie scolded. "For that is not the worst of her story. Not only was she unhappy, but she died. In child-birth. Within a year."

Nettie sat back in her chair, her pleasure at shocking the room as evident as the shine on her skin.

The room filled with noise once more, allowing me to translate to my father without much notice. They chattered like the *gazza*, the, how you say, magpies, that filled the cypress trees back home, their never-ending chirping a constant sound, a wonderful sound there. Was this the entertainment in these servants' lives? As if there was so little true living in them, they filled the holes with the lives of others.

"Do you believe in such silliness?" I asked my father at the end of the tale.

He turned a gloomy gaze on me. Nodding, in his low voice he told me, "I have heard such tales before. Never doubt, Daughter, either bad luck or good."

He called me daughter, as he always did—my name rarely touched his lips—but it was few occasions when I heard him speak so seriously, gave me advice of any sort.

Mr. Birch stood and everyone at the table followed. My father and I hurried to do the same. "Ten minutes, ladies and gentlemen."

It was a call to order. I would quickly come to learn the privileged lived an odd sort of free, even when it came to their hunger. Staff ate dinner at six, the family at seven. If there was a dinner party, service was precisely at eight.

My father patted me on my shoulder as he left, returning to the workshop he already loved. A pat here and there was all I received, no matter my need for more. I knew it should be enough, knew it was the best he could give, but it was sparse to the many hugs and kisses my mother had gifted me with during our years together. How I longed for them now. I shivered in my skin.

I stood at my place as others rushed into action. I had no idea what the second seamstress did during the family's dinner.

"Back to the sewing room with you," Mrs. Briggs was quick to educate me, even as she walked away, Nettie at her side. "And wash your hands and face. The mistress or the young lady may come to you if they spill on themselves. I surely hope you know how to treat stains."

I nodded, though I didn't. The other seamstress was also a laundress. I had washed my fair share and more of coarse wools, but never of silks or satins.

Mrs. Briggs grunted at me and turned to her company. She leaned down, closer to Nettie's ear, whispering. Not quietly enough.

"How many nights has it been?"

I heard. I listened, taking my time to leave the room.

Nettie rolled blue eyes. "Every night since we arrived. He in his bed, she in hers, every night."

Mrs. Briggs clucked her tongue. "It's not good."

"It's worse," Nettie hissed. "They bicker, collie shangles for hours, almost every day."

I had no idea what *collie shangles* were, but they did not sound a good thing.

A pucker-faced Mrs. Briggs shook her head in small, tight snaps. "A man of his prestige should not be with such a vulgarian. She has no idea how to behave." Her hands tossed her frustration in the air. "She has no idea how to run this house."

"All the better for me." Nettie snickered.

"They *have* to work it out," Mrs. Briggs sounded fierce. "If they split, who knows where we would end up?"

I left them then, hurrying by. The words made me sad. What a pity to hear Mr. Worthington suffered a bad marriage. A part of me, the part longing for home, felt a small spark of hope. I saw a way back. I couldn't have been more wrong.

* * *

I saw nothing of my roommate that night—I was already asleep by the time she came into our room, exhaustion overpowered the fearfully unfamiliar, the roiling of thoughts and emotions—and she was gone before I woke up. Just as well, for I would not have wanted her to see the sweat of my dreams—running after my mother but never catching her, trapped in the bowels of the ship as it sunk, locked in a room with no latch.

I got up and lit the lamp by my bed. My room on the back of the house, the west side, was as dark as it had been when I went to bed. Little light found us here in the service tower. Even with the window shutters open, the barricaded wall deprived us of the sun's cheery light until it traversed its path over the top of the mansion.

Or did I see only gloom? Like a silly little girl, I thought I would wake once more in my bed, where the sun streamed in as it crested the rolling hills along with the smells of the waking earth, rich and thick, full of life.

I left my room for my turn in the bathroom; there were three in all for the servants.

I stumbled down the hall as I passed one of the male servants, his body clad only in his robe. My eyes sought the floor as fast as I could force them, though they fought me. Heat burned upon my cheeks. I had never even seen my father in such a state of undress. I did not expect to find the men and women's rooms so intermingled as they were here. I didn't realize what it meant. How could I? My world, the one I still longed for, was a well-guarded one, especially for young women.

Mr. Birch roomed at one end and Mrs. Briggs at the other, in large rooms they shared with no one. I hoped any sort of misbehavior, despite such moments as these, might be difficult to do. Difficult, but not impossible. A person may be young and inexperienced, but it doesn't make them a fool.

I scurried along and gratefully shut myself in the bathroom. One large, well-equipped, and always spotlessly clean bathroom. I dropped myself against the closed door finding my breath, eased by the soft pale pink of this women's bathroom at the north end of the hall. It washed my discomfort away as I washed.

Mrs. Briggs had been strict in her instructions for the use of this room.

"We are allowed to use the facilities only when it is our scheduled time." She said the word oddly, sheeduuled. "Get your business done quickly and get out. Most importantly, you must always, always clean up after yourself. Dry the tub, the sink, and the soap."

Drying soap was by far one of the silliest things I had ever done. I saw my head shake in the glass above the sink; my lips formed a smirk.

I dressed and sat on my bed, a lifeless statue chiseled by fear and uncertainty. Shadows of loneliness surrounded me. I was untethered, adrift in a house—a world—I knew nothing of. Tears tickled the back of my throat, but I swallowed them away. I stared at the wall, seeing the rolling hills of home in the streaks of paint. The sight did not cheer. My leg bounced; my hands wrung. I needed to do something.

When the bell rang in the hall, I jumped up, opened my door, and poked my head out, eyes wide and searching.

"Come along with ya'." Beatrice fluttered a hand at me. "Thas the bell for breakfast."

I followed her; relieved someone had spoken to me, relieved to learn something of the ways of the house. There were three bells to tell us what to do. A cowbell to start the day, a jingle bell for meals, and a tea bell alerting us if a family member needed service. Shrill and jarring, one would jump whether they needed to or not. The bells sat atop a box, a strange contraption with squares and flags.

If the silence and stillness of my room was a crypt, below stairs was a storm of frantic life. So many of the servants went about their work, lighting fires, as they would through the day, though a glimpse through the many windows on the narrow staircase showed the sky hinted at coming sunshine through the fog, promising some warmth. Summer mornings by the sea were a different kind of daybreak.

Farther below stairs, I heard metal tinkering, gruff male voices barking brashly.

The kitchen was as busy as a hive. Chef Pasquel gave precise instructions to the crowd of scullery maids helping him prepare breakfast for the families and the servants.

We had fifteen minutes to eat a bowl of porridge, some tea—a strange pale drink in comparison to the espresso I used to start my days with—and some bread and butter.

"To your sewing room, girl."

I jumped, turned. She stood behind me. I hadn't heard her come near me, not a step. I'd barely had a few bites.

"Yes, Ma'am," I stood, gave my silent father a silent nod, and rushed off.

I climbed two flights of stairs back to the sewing room, entered with a surprising rush of pleasure…it was empty, save for its magic tools…and me. This room seemed to hold me within it, the me I knew. In there, I looked at it as mine. My ownership was short-lived.

The large woman rushed in, the bunch of clothes in her arms almost as big as she.

"You can sew, can ya'?" she asked, a lovely greeting.

"I can," I said, giving back the gruff I got.

"Well, there's plenty, so get on about it."

On the table against the wall, she plucked down the pile she carried with a sigh of relief.

"There's some simple work here," she hurried on as she separated the clothes, throwing them in smaller piles here and there. "Some buttons missing, some socks need darnin'. But…" here she stopped her busy hands and turned to me, her round, pale face was flushed with pink, wiry red strands poked out of her faded blue cap "…one of the mistress's dresses has lost some beads and must be replaced." She pointed a chubby finger at me. "This work requires great care. She will see, oh you can bet she will, if it's not done right. Believe you me."

Her plump face puckered; it looked as if she tasted a bad memory. I quaked, never stopping to think why they entrusted me with this task.

"You'll find buttons and beads in that cupboard there." She pointed at a tall piece of furniture set in the back corner; there were at least thirty small drawers in this large oak piece. "They must be perfect."

"Yes, Ma'am," I said, again, feeling sure they would be words I would say often.

With a clipped nod, chins appeared in the plump flesh of her neck. She spun on her heel and made for the door, a busy woman.

"*Scusi.*" I could have bit my tongue. "Excuse me, please. Who you are?"

I knew that wasn't right either, but it was too late.

"I'm Mrs. Brown, head laundress and seamstress," she said, chest rising, a quirk of a smile. "Well, I guess I'm simply the head laundress now."

She looked over her shoulder into the hall and skipped back to me faster than I thought a woman of her size could move. "And between you, me, and the wall, I'm mad as hops that you're here."

My lips opened and closed; a fish caught in a hook. Her words confused me. They were not the first, would not be the last, to make me feel like the foreigner everyone saw me as. The wall could hear us? No, that couldn't be right. "Mad as hops" frightened me. Was she angry with me? I hadn't done anything yet. She looked anything but angry. She read me well.

Mrs. Brown pinched my cheek. "I'm glad you're here, gel, the work was too much for me." She smiled then. I had never seen a smile belong on a face so well. "Mind me, do good work or I'll hear about it."

At the door, she flung her last words over her shoulder, "When you're done with the Mrs.'s dress, just lay it on her bed."

With that, she was gone. I was on my own. This tiny room with a window facing the small front garden was mine, all mine. I volleyed between fear and excitement.

I set to work. The buttons, the darning, went fast and smooth. I saved the dress for last, a treat for myself, wanting my fingers limbered up before I tackled it. I put it on the curved, dress form. It was wonderful, perhaps the finest dress I had ever seen; never had I worked on such a garment. It was nothing like the simple, rough-clothed dresses I had learned to make by my mother's side. It was a frock like those that filled my daydreams; the fantasies where I designed and made such dresses. For more moments than I should, I simply stared at it, walking round it to see all its glory. I circled it as I would a great piece of art.

It was all silk, lace, beads, and pearls. It hugged the form tightly through the bodice and the upper legs, then flared wide and long, draping the floor. The puffed sleeves, much larger versions of those I wore, were sheer and had the trickiest design of beads, a floral pattern on the largest part, the stem and leaves flowing down to long cuffs buttoned with more pearls. It was there, in the long curling stem, that I found the open spaces, the beads' missing places.

It took me ages to find the right beads to match, even longer to sew them in perfectly. My pace slowed by my eagerness to do the work perfectly. The sun rose above the tree line, had started to make its way to my window, and the room grew brighter and brighter as I worked. I was as thankful for the window and its glimpse of sky and trees as I was for the work my hands did. The noises in my mind silenced by purpose and gratitude.

I finished and stood back, pleased. Not the slightest stitch revealed where the new joined with the old. I wanted to carry the dress through the house. I longed to show Mrs. Briggs and everyone who doubted me—which was probably everyone—that I was true to my word. I could sew, and very well. I wanted to scream at them. Though I spoke with a heavy accent, spoke slowly, my mind was quick and sure, as were my hands. I had been the smartest girl in school, the most talented sewer too. I longed to be that girl again, known as that girl here. Vanity and pride are not virtues, but they were mine in that moment. I claimed them reluctantly. If no one here would know me, at least I would, the all of me, good and bad.

I knew I couldn't parade the dress, parade my prideful self through the house. I knew I had to return the dress to Mrs. Worthington's room and nothing more.

I took the dress off the form slowly, draped it delicately across my forearms, and poked my head out the door. I saw no one and entered the small foyer outside the room and through another door into the hall. Through all the sewing, my hands were still and sure. Now they shook. My pride and vanity and the sureness they gave me betrayed me and stayed behind. I was once more the lost, uncertain girl. I had no idea which room belonged to the woman of the house.

The doors across from me stood closed, but I didn't think Mrs. Worthington's room would be so close to the sewing room, or the servant's stairs beside it. Along the wide hallway, of the same cream marble as on the floor below, across the wide foyer at the top of the double staircases, those the family used, I saw doors opened at that end.

I tiptoed to them, past tapestries larger than I had ever seen, older still. I smelled my own sweat along with the fresh flowers blooming on every table in every room I passed. I peeked in the first door. It opened to a narrow hall, long and dark and secret, and then two more doors. Both stood open. The first room was rich and dark, deep maroon silk covered the bed, the walls, the curtains. A man's jacket hung on some sort of contraption in the corner. Mr. Worthington's room, I thought, or the son's.

I saw a bathing room at the end of the hall, the door to its foyer and the door to the inner room both open. Inside was a bathing room like none I had ever seen. My unworldliness slapped me good and hard; knowing there were those who lived better lives was one thing, seeing it another. Within its square dimensions lay a deep tub, pure white tile, a marble sink painted with a garland and topped with a faucet of gold, and the strangest toilet, hidden by a cane-covered box. Another basin stood next to the toilet, something shaped like a miniature tub, though I had no idea what it was. The dressing table held every sort of grooming device, delicate ones—combs, brushes, mirrors, and more—all made of tortoiseshell. My mother had a tortoise comb; it was all she had. It was now mine. I held it often but never used it.

I couldn't go in, couldn't keep staring, though I wanted to. Such a bathroom belonged to a woman.

The door closest to it stood opened too. I stepped in and knew at once it was Mrs. Worthington's room. Never had I seen such a place. Rich, thick, light green silk was everywhere, delicate furniture, scrolled and gilded, and lace, lots of lace.

I could have stood there forever staring into this room, this world, unlike anything I had ever imagined. Delight and envy tangled with anger, a knot of rough yarn. How could so few have so much when so many had so little? I criticized it even as I longed for it.

The voices stopped me.

They echoed up the stone stairs, bounced against marble walls, coming closer.

I laid the dress carefully on the bed, as instructed, and rushed out.

I slipped to a stop. The voices were upon me. I heard footsteps now too.

I ducked out a side door by the main door. I found myself in a tiny hallway leading to another tiny hallway. I turned 'round and 'round, not knowing which of the three doors would lead to the best hiding place. The voices grew closer. I spun like a top, the string one of dizzying confusion.

I found a narrow corner, a cubby of space. I jammed myself in, back to the wall, and slipped down. I huddled in a ball as the voices grew louder and closer. I stayed there even as they grew softer and farther away again. Lost became redefined in so many ways. I couldn't stop the tears then.

PEARL

I was up early, eager for the day. Barefoot and in my nightdress, large windows in my large room thrown open for the warm, salty breeze to greet me. I stood before my easel, as I did most days. I know now that I did not see the glory of it all, all which was mine. I never questioned its beauty or my possession of it, not as I should have.

My gaze drifted out those large windows, my mind followed, across the vast lawn of rolling slopes that led to the grove of feathered trees. My trees. I closed my eyes then, opening my artistic vision. With it, I saw a small child, a girl, barefoot and giggling, ringlets bouncing and flying behind her, pudgy hands flapping with the freedom.

I opened my eyes, turned back to the self-portrait—that portrait—before me on the canvas.

Mother had grudgingly allowed me the "hobby," an appropriate one for a young lady of means. "Appropriate" from her meant acceptable to society, her most critical gauge. Little did she know I had no intention for it to be a hobby. Not since that day. Not since I had met Mary Cassatt. Was there a part of me that set my course simply because it would upset my mother? I would not be the first daughter to rebel in such a manner. I only knew the burning passion compelled me to it—my art. Denying it would be to deny myself.

As I brushed on broad strokes of vibrant colors, pigments pure and unmixed, I remembered Mary Cassatt's indomitable expression in the face of my mother's barely concealed disapproval. I strove for more than her talent.

I put my brush down, pleased with the morning's work. Perhaps the memories had helped. I turned my attention then to my next project.

I hoped I might catch a glimpse of the new arrivals to our home.

They were so unique to my world. Filled with such people, people who lived to serve us, Mr. Costa and his daughter were the only Italian people I had ever seen in one of my homes. That sounded dreadfully snobbish, I know that now, but there it was, the truth of my life. Though Mother and her friends, indeed all of the powerful women who ruled domestic life, complained about the lack of good servants—the opening of factories and shops had found many of those who thought servant life worthy before, now found it was no longer worthy enough—few looked to Italy and other countries to fill the void. Did they carry some disease? I thought that unlikely. Did they smell? I giggled. I thought that simply foolish.

Their novelty intrigued me. Ginevra with her sharp eyes and her quick tongue, particularly so. There was more to her, I had seen it in the fleeting few minutes I had to study her. I wanted to learn more. I suppose it was not well done of me, to think of her as an object of curiosity and not as a person. How often we strive to break the shackles of breeding. How very difficult it could be.

It would be a feat to spend time with her as I had few interactions with the staff, but I would try my best. It would be a little easier as I walked through my life so unnoticed. My father had his work; like the other men of this summer colony, he would often be here only on the weekends, perhaps coming back on a Thursday rather than Friday. My brother had so many activities, I rarely saw him. My mother had her events, tons of them throughout the day, all of which she would change her clothes for. Mother rarely sought me out save for the times she longed to look like a doting mother or when, even at my age, she aimed to put me in front of the eye of eligible men.

"It's never too soon to make an impression," she said to me so often it was like a prayer.

We were an incestuous bunch of a sort; it was rare for anyone of the "set" to marry outside it. We played together, bowed to each other as we took dance lessons together. It seemed only natural to find a mate with those we spent the most time. Yet, if one should become a widow or a widower, it was often that the surviving partner married the deceased partner's dearest friend. It was like the quadrille, the most popular dance of the time; they changed partners in life with the same ease and frequency that they did in the dance. My nose crinkled at such couples. I turned from them and such couplings that made me long for a bath.

I knew most of the morning would be mine, especially if Mother chose not to go to the Casino. As the fog still hung thick around the house, clinging to the trees, shrouding the statues all over the grounds, the typical morning spent seeing and being seen would not be in the offing today. For the first time, I was quite glad for it. All the better for my hunting about.

I would not wear his distinctive hat or carry his pipe, but I relished with childish delight playing the role of Sherlock Holmes. It had not been so long ago that playing, pretending, was something I did all the time; the freedom of childhood is hard to relinquish. I confess I was more than a little smugly pleased to do something my mother would absolutely detest. Doing so had become as important to me as 'fitting in' was to her. We were equally misguided and wholly oblivious to it.

As I was not yet old enough to wear a corset, I was allowed to dress myself for I had not yet been assigned my own maid. My governess, nearly obsolete in my maturing eyes, supervised my choice of morning dress when I called for her, helped with the long line of buttons down the back, checked my stockings and my low-heeled slippers.

"You'll do," she said as I stood before her for the final inspection. It was all she ever said.

Thank you ever so much, I longed to respond with a dash of my mother's stinging sarcasm.

A spinster who had never known much of life, Miss Jameson seemed excessively concerned with my education, my father's doing I was sure, but not so with my grooming, though she tolerated it, my mother's instructions no doubt.

Many of the girls my age had wonderful relationships with their governesses, asking questions about life as well as about their studies or comportment. I was never sure whether I was glad or sad I had no such familiarity with Miss Jameson. It would have been wonderful to have a grown woman with whom I could confide, to whom I could ask questions, questions growing increasingly more complex as I grew older. There was only emptiness there, a void of womanly wisdom, a terrible void for a girl trying to become a woman.

On the other hand, our distant relationship allowed me more freedom than my friends enjoyed. Freedom I was especially thankful for that morning. I rushed from my room and her.

As I surmised, I was alone in the breakfast room. Nonetheless, Birch stood guard at the pantry door, a door hidden behind a black and gold Chinese screen matching the exotic décor of the room. He looked less formal in his morning suit, though the informality never made its way within him, while James piled the sideboard with enough food for ten people. One can truly see abundance only if they have seen its lack. I never had.

I ate a few bites, wiped my mouth with the thick linen napkin, and pushed back my chair with a squawk against the parquet floor.

"Thank you," I chirped to the men as I scampered from the room.

"But Miss..." I heard Mr. Birch call out. He rarely saw me eat so little; he may have thought me unwell. The staff knew so much about us, so much more than we would ever know about them.

"I'm fine, Mr. Birch, not to worry," I called as I rushed out into the gallery, my low-heeled ankle boots clicking upon the cold stone floor, disturbing the silence of the house.

Ginevra had said she could sew, but I doubted if the indomitable Mrs. Briggs would allow her to, or if the housekeeper would put the new girl—a foreign girl—to work at some other menial job. I thought the latter more likely, so set I out to find chambermaids and kitchen sculleries at work.

I searched room after room. Ginevra was not in a one.

* * *

Her quiet sobs, thick with sadness, helped me to find her at last.

It had taken far longer than I expected. I had even made a most fictitious excuse to go below stairs to the steamy laundry room—knowing if my mother found out it would not go well for me—but Ginevra was not there either. Nor could I ask for her. I knew, even then, how the staff would look down on me if I did.

These hard-working people, ever at the whim of others who deemed themselves better, had as many notions of what was proper and what was not as those they served. They could be as ruthless about the rules of this life as the wealthiest of families. Anyone who had lived with servants for the whole of their lives knew we were great fodder for their spiky tongues, though my mother ever denied it. She did little to worry about what they said of her. She revealed too much of what should never be revealed.

They must have allowed Ginevra to fill the position of seamstress after all. I ran through the hall, up two flights on the main stairs. I ran like the child I had been, enjoying myself far too much, or like the boys who enjoyed sports whom I envied so. No one saw me, thankfully.

There was no one in the sewing room, but there had been. The lone gas lamp was on, a sure sign of detailed work, drawers were open, needles and thread and scissors littered the room, tools of the trade looking recently used.

When I heard my father's soft voice, with Geoffrey, his valet, a quiet sort of man as well, I hid behind the door of the sewing room. Should they pass this way, though they had no reason to, I had no desire for them to see me, to answer the questions that would surely come. In truth, I had launched myself into the role of spy and had no desire for the gambit to be broken, for the juvenile amusement of it to end.

They spoke of trivialities, of coming and going, of what to take and what to leave behind.

They moved on quickly, into my father's room, and back out, back down the stairs. The quiet, the most common sound in my house, ruled once more. That's when I heard it, the crying. Any game I played ended abruptly.

There are many sorts of crying. Joyful tears had laughter mixed with them. Deep loss, the pain of grief, came from a dark, desperate place. I had heard that sort of crying only once—had heard my mother crying only once—when her mother passed away. The quiet sobbing I heard now was not like either; they were the tears of a lost child.

I followed the sound toward the south of the house, near the rooms of my parents and brother. The sound was as muffled as the pain they evoked. Melancholy spoken without a word. To cry was a release, as much as was laughter and affection. To contain it, whatever sort, was to deny it. Without release, there could be no overcoming. I may have been young, but I had cried enough to know.

I stood at the end of the hallway, hearing it, but not finding it. It was as if I played another game, one of hide and seek, though the one hidden clearly had no desire to be found. She played no game. A few steps this way, and suddenly I knew.

The odd construction of the house, with its individual foyers and hidden hallways, created a wealth of small empty spaces. I found her there, in the hall within the hall between my parents' room.

Huddled in a ball, her dark dress enveloping her, her head hidden beneath a shield of her arms, she didn't hear my approach.

"Ginevra," I said quietly, as I might to a small animal I had no wish to frighten. She flinched but didn't look up. She retreated further into the narrow corner in which she had lodged herself.

"It's all right, Ginevra, I've not come to chastise you," I cooed at her. "I've been looking for you all day."

At last, her eyes found mine. Almond-shaped yet red-rimmed and swollen, the beleaguered depth of her nut-brown eyes belonged on a life-weary adult, not a child. She looked no more than twelve or thirteen though I would soon learn she was older.

"Tell me what's wrong, dear?"

She stared at me.

I scrunched down, squatted beside her, wrapping my skirts over my legs as she had done, crooking my arms just like hers. I said not another word.

Ginevra stared as hard at me as I did her. I waited. I would wait as long as need be. I don't know what she saw on my face, but it was enough.

Her words came then, hesitant at first, then like from a faucet at full open. Her sobs faded as she found release in the telling. Her knowledge of English was greater than I expected, though she stumbled and mangled the words in odd arrangements. She told me of Mrs. Brown. She told me of the work she'd done that day, how proud she was of her work on Mother's dress, of finding her room, of the voices, of how she came to be where she was.

She told me nothing of her tears.

"Then why are you crying, dear girl?" I asked her, unable to see as she did. "You've done nothing wrong. In fact, it sounds like you've done quite well for your first day."

Her full bottom lip began to quiver. "F...father, your father."

I shook my head at my revelation, chastising myself for not seeing it sooner.

"My father would not have been angry with you." I tried to assure her even more. "Nor even my mother. It was your job. Servants are in and out of our rooms at all times of the day and night."

Ginevra blinked; eyes wide. "It true?"

"It is true," I corrected without making it obvious. "As long as you have a valid reason to be there, you will never be in any trouble when you go in any room."

Her chest rose and fell with a deep breath, her shoulders shook with its quivers. She leaned her head down, but not to hide in the valley of her arms, but to rest her chin upon them. She looked better. I was so glad of it, for I had made her so.

We sat in silence for a few more minutes. I dared to reach out, to place a hand on her shoulder, to rub it softly. A stray tear, a leftover, trickled down her cheek. She turned to me.

"I lost, very lost."

If she meant in the house or in her life, it made no matter to me. I knew how she felt.

She was a servant, a member of the staff, a non-entity my breeding decreed. It was the pervasive attitude of my set. Yet if I was more than who I was born to be—allowed to be—as I believed I was, couldn't she be as well? Could a lifetime of habitual integrations be nothing less than habit? Mary Cassatt thought so. I vowed then to help Ginevra find whatever she felt she needed. I knew exactly where to start.

"Come with me." I took her by the hand and pulled her up. She answered with a drawn-out moan. I ignored it.

Peeking out the door to the hall, seeing no one, I pulled her again, even as she uttered soft mutters of protest that I continued to ignore. With the same excited energy with which I had searched for her all morning, I pulled her through the house, to the south end, down the back stairs, through the Conservatory—ever so grateful we passed no other member of the household—and out onto the side terrace.

Ginevra no longer moaned. The resistance of her arm voiced her hesitance. I smiled back at her, hoping to reassure her. Enjoying myself too much at the sly mission I had undertaken, one so very not in keeping with the decorum of my world, I was blind to her. I did not once ask myself whom I served, her, or me.

Our destination was one I had been to so many times since we had moved to The Beeches. I spent more hours there than I did in the house. I had fallen in love, fallen for its magic, from the very first moment I stepped into it. I knew she would as well. I knew it was exactly what she needed at this minute. As if I could know what resided in another's mind. The arrogance of my world was contagious.

I pulled her to me at the back corner of the house, flattened us against the wall as I looked over the two terraces running the entire width of the building, across the vast lawn stretching from the terraces to our destination, falling further into the delusion of espionage I played at. I would have laughed with the joy of it would it not confuse Ginevra more. It was a huge open space, grass-like green velvet flowing in low rolls away from the house, those I attempted to recreate upon my canvas. Usually, I would simply walk straight through. I couldn't be so flagrant with Ginevra by my side.

I saw no one on this side of the estate. I spied a few men at the far side gardens tending to the hydrangeas and rhododendrons. But there was no one on our side.

"Come. Quickly," I hissed, once more pulling her along.

She pulled back this time. This time she found her voice. "I find trouble. Mrs. Briggs, she..."

"She won't be looking for you at this time of day. She'll be far too busy with my mother, planning menus and other such nonsense." I bounced on my toes, grinning ear to ear, believing I could infest her with what I felt.

I pulled again. She came. We ran.

From the terrace, we ran straight north, until we ran through a line of maple trees. Behind them, a small path ran the length of the property, between the high stone wall that kept others out. I often averted my eyes from the sight of it, for it gave me the shivers.

As the carriage house came into view, I stuck my head out from between two trees, once more looking for prying eyes, once more finding none.

With one more pull, I led her onto the end of the vast lawn and into the trees, the weeping beech trees.

"Duck," I called as we came to one of the small entryways of branches and leaves. I crouched and as did she behind me. We were inside.

I stopped, as did Ginevra. Her hand dropped from mine; her mouth dropped as well as she raised wide eyes at the cathedral within. My cathedral.

GINEVRA

I entered a world not even my imagination had ever taken me to, not even in the words of a fairy tale. I couldn't stop myself from staring up and around, seeing the branches twisting and tangling over my head, reaching far up as if to touch the sky. There were so many others curling right down to the ground as if bowing to us, as if asking us to step on them, to climb up them.

As if not allowed, any thoughts of duty or Mrs. Briggs slammed against the hidden entry, barred from this magical place.

Pearl stepped upon a lumpy root without a moment's hesitation, her face changing; for the first time, I thought I glimpsed her unmasked truth. As if a monkey trained to dance, she climbed. To watch her lithe movements was a gift in itself.

She looked back at me, a mischievous wood nymph.

"Well, come on." Her hand waved me toward her.

I couldn't stop myself from following, couldn't even if I wanted to. I didn't.

She led me up and around, but not too high, until we came to a branch sticking out straight and sure from the thick trunk of the tree. Now both monkeys, we used hands and feet as we made our way to the middle of it. It was a tricky act, especially for me with my floor-length skirt, but we both wore low-heeled boots, so our footing was sure. There we perched, birds on a clothesline. It was the most charmed moment of my life. It was a moment that has, that will, stay with me forever.

PEARL

For a while, we said nothing, for nothing should be said when first entering such a place as that. The spirit of nature precluded all words, glorified by one's silence. That same spirit engulfed us as did the trees. They grew as tall as a grand cavern, a cave for giants, yet its delicate, almost ethereal leaves flowed down to the ground like trickles of water into the ocean. Unseen creatures scurried upon the leaf-strewn ground. Birds fluttered, though few chirped; even they honored that sacrosanct spot with their softness. I'd learned here, beneath the weeping beeches, that there are greater sacred places in nature than in any building man could construct. Ginevra broke the silence.

"*Bellisimo,*" it was a whispered prayer. "B...beautiful," she stumbled on the English word. "You lucky...you *are* lucky living here."

I didn't know how to answer her. For all the things in my life, I thought there was little luck to it. It had just always...been, been what it was, filled with all it was filled with. Did I feel lucky? Most often, it felt as if the skin I was born in didn't quite fit; perhaps it had been tailored improperly. But the why of it eluded me. Was I truly just "difficult," as my mother so often called me? I didn't know. Here I knew myself or at the least had no need to scramble for my name. Yes, for *this* place, I was indeed very lucky.

"Have you seen any of the other cottages, Ginevra?" I asked a question devoid of emotion, neutral ground upon which to start.

She nodded, eyes still wide. "We walked, from corner." She pointed north. "There was other...cottages?" I understood the question in the word. It was a silly word the community used. They lived in mansions. "But none like you...yours."

I patted her hand. She tried so hard to use proper English, but it was not an easy language to learn, and I had a feeling she had taught herself most of it.

"Someday soon, we'll walk up Bellevue and on the Cliff Walk," I promised her. "You'll see more cottages." My lips fell in a cynical frown.

"They only call them cottages because the Europeans do, to label them as their summer homes. There are some just as grand as this, if not more so."

"No?" Her brows rose crookedly upon her moist brow.

I nodded, smirking. "Oh, yes. Much more grand." Though she hadn't explained what she denied, what she questioned, I had understood immediately. It had been easy.

Ginevra's shoulders rose to her ears. She lifted a hand from the tree and made a circle round her head. "Why? Why here?"

"Well, as I have overheard the tale, there was this man, a tailor named Smith, born and raised here in Newport, who believed so much in the beauty of this place, that he and another man started buying up all the land. This place was very famous; men of the Revolution came here, came from here, one who even signed our Declaration of Independence. But there was also a great deal of slave trading that went on here as well." I looked out of my history books and back to Ginevra. Her eyes seemed stuck upon an unblinking gaze. "Well, sure enough, this Smith fellow was right. Somehow, many of those rich, southern plantation owners heard about the place, from the slave trade no doubt, and they started traveling here in the summer to escape the awful heat of their own climate. One plantation owner, Daniel Parrish, came first and built Beechwood. Then Mr. Wetmore, a very rich man who trades goods with China, built Chateau-sur-Mer, By the Sea," I translated for her, my hands fluttering like the wings of the birds that flew over our heads, adding their soft twitters to mine. "And then it all grew faster and faster. More families built cottages, each one larger than the last, the Astors and the Vanderbilts, the Van Rensselaers and the Stuyvesants."

I turned a serious gaze upon her. Could I trust her with my thoughts, even the darkest of them? I stared at that lost girl I had found in the cubby who had shared her fear. Yes, I could trust that girl.

"They are like children, I think. If one has a toy, the other must have a bigger, better toy, and the next, and the next." She watched my mouth as I spoke. "Do you understand?"

"*Si*, yes, I think, yes," she said, her words hesitant, but not her tone.

I didn't know, or perhaps I didn't want to tell her, the full truth of things. At least the way I saw them. These powerful men, some of "old" money, some of new, who had made their riches after the War of Secession, had made their fortunes in coal mines and the spread of the railroad across the country. They made so much they didn't know what else to do with all their riches. They gave their over-bearing wives—women who were the true power of this small, re-markably privileged community—carte blanche. It became a hobby, in truth a convoluted competition of sorts, the creation of these minia-ture palaces. Those who lived in them became the chess pieces upon the checkered board of a highly structured way of life.

"The men spend millions of dollars—"

"M...millions?" Ginevra gasped, almost slipping from our branch.

I grabbed her, steadied her, and huffed a laugh cynical to my own ears. "Yes, millions, to build these cottages. And they give even more millions to their wives, to decorate, to entertain."

I looked off to the west. From this high up, I could see the lowering sun glinting off the harbor away down the hill. "I know this world is run by men, Ginevra, but this place, Newport? Here women rule. You will see."

She looked away, a furrow on her brow, a frown upon her lips. "I do not think I want...to see."

I laid a hand softly upon her shoulder. "I do not think you have a choice."

Ginevra turned sad eyes on me. There was something in them so familiar I could have been looking in a mirror. She simply shook her head.

"It is entertaining, I will tell you that," I said lightly, as lightly as I could. "Especially thanks to Mr. McAllister—Ward McAllister. He's a snooty little man who has deemed himself the king of good manners. He hisses in the women's ear, and they listen." I plucked a feathery leaf off the tree, released it, and watched it float to the ground below us. "Oh, yes, thanks to him life is all very scheduled, very coordinated." I no longer knew if I spoke to Ginevra, if she understood. I only knew I said thoughts I had longed to say for so long, with no one to say them to.

I had many acquaintances but far fewer true friends. Among them, there was not a one who was not enraptured with our privilege, our opulent life. None who questioned it. They danced merrily to the tune forever played, marionettes on their strings. They would not understand the things I said to Ginevra. They would, in truth, shun me for them as the girls in school shunned me. Except perhaps Consuelo Vanderbilt, but she had far too much to deal with herself. I couldn't burden her with my confused and contrary thoughts. Here, with Ginevra, the lock upon them was broken.

"There is so much to do, but every day they are the same things to do. In the mornings, everyone gathers at the Casino to show off their latest fineries. Then we go to the beach, then luncheon, which can often be with fifty people or more. Then for me, there are still lessons with the governess, though I am the smartest in my classes during school term."

Ginevra brightened, poking her chest with her own finger. "Me, too. Smartest of all." She grimaced at her own words, at how far from smart they sounded.

"I can tell, Ginevra, do not worry, I can." I could. It was there, plain to see, as though someone had painted intelligence upon her face.

The creases upon her skin smoothed, a churning sea coming once more to rest.

"And then we go coaching, a grand coaching parade." I continued.

"A p...parade? Whata is parade?"

"We all dress up—very fancy—get in our coaches and all drive up and down the streets, Bellevue Avenue and Ocean Drive, and then we drive back."

"Up and back," she repeated, but not because she couldn't understand the words.

"We do it every day. Everybody does," I giggled. "I don't know why they started it or why they keep doing it. Don't tell anyone, will you?

You will see. We do many things for no reason at all. No good reason."
These last words slipped from my mouth before I could close it.

Ginevra's hard stare burned my face. My hands twitched to cover
it, but it was far too late for that.

"And we leave our calling cards. Well, we don't deliver them. We
drive to each other's house and send our coachman to deliver them to
each other's door." I blathered on as if I was not unmasked. "There's
teatime in the afternoons. The women call on each other, taking turns
at each other's cottages, and then return home for a rest. Then dinner. For my parents and Clarence, it is often at someone else's house,
sometimes with over a hundred people in attendance."

"No? Hundreds?" With each response, each question, Ginevra's
voice pitched higher and higher.

"Oh yes, sometimes hundreds," I said, and then muttered, "The Four
Hundred."

"Eh?"

I put my hand on hers. "That, I will explain another time." I did not
want to speak of it now. "It is all rather gay and fun and light. Two
months of play before we go back home."

Ginevra pulled back her chin. "Back home? This not home?"

I shook my head; not only at her question, but at the answer I must
give.

"No, Ginevra, we only stay here during the summer. We arrive a
little earlier than most, so we can celebrate my birthday. It's only a
few days away."

Her eyes lit up and with them her face. "Mine too is soon."

"When?" I cried.

"The third of *Luglio*. Ju...Ju...,"

"July?" I blurt, incredulous. "Mine is the second. How old will you
be?"

"Eh... *sedici*...eh." She held up one finger, then six.

"Sixteen?! Me too!"

We smiled together then.

My smile stayed with me as I finished telling her of my living arrangements.

"We have another home in New York City. Do you know where that is?"

"*Si*, we came," she closed her eyes, looking for the English words she needed as if they were written in her mind, "our ship came there."

"Oh, yes, of course it would," I said quickly. "We live there most of the year."

I could feel the frown form on my face. I didn't like to think of New York. Our house there was not nearly as grand as The Beeches, but then again, every house on the upper east side of Manhattan was grand, just of a different sort. I shook New York away. The summer was just beginning.

"But here is where we come to play. And you will play with me."

Ginevra grinned through her head shook. "No, I not play. I must work."

I sighed. "Yes, I suppose you must."

It was my turn to look at her, peer into her. I had been talking of myself, of this privileged way of life far too long. It was not well done of me; it was not in keeping with the manners drilled into me. I cared not for propriety, but I did for how I treated Ginevra. Did I seek this girl out only as an outlet for words I could not say elsewhere? Was my intent only to use her so? To shatter my bored monotony?

"Enough about us. What about you? Where in Italy did you come from? Why are you here, Ginevra? Your father, you? Where is your mother?"

I had gone too far. I saw it immediately. I wanted to know all about her, but like so many people in my life, they didn't want me to know. I thought she would leave. Instead, she began to talk. She told me her story.

GINEVRA

Pearl shared so much with me, it was as if she had taken off all the layers of her clothing. It was a simple act and yet not. How strange the only gestures of kindness should come from one I was to serve. She was of a rank so far above me in a country where rank meant everything, I knew in truth I shouldn't even be there with her, talking with her. Ours was a smudged line from the start.

When she asked me, "Tell me about you, Ginevra. Where in Italy did you come from? Where is your mother?" I had to answer her; I wanted to, wanted someone in this place to know, to care enough to want to know. Those we live with are more than companions or colleagues or even those we serve; they are a witness to our lives. Until that moment, I walked invisible with not a witness in sight.

GINEVRA
1886

My aunts had always come and gone as they pleased, barging into our home, entering without a knock, barging into conversations between Papa and Mama, never a thought to what was and wasn't their business. It was the way of us, of life there. Until they started coming more often. Until my mother's stomach started to expand. The innocent child I was watched it grow gleefully, a child hoping for a brother or sister.

Mama started changing, eyes sunk, skin turned grey. She seemed to be losing weight, arms and legs becoming spindly sticks, even as her stomach enlarged.

As the doctors started coming, as my mother's beautiful young face grew old, forever pained, I knew there would be no baby.

She took to her bed and still they told me nothing. They passed me as they did the small oil lamp and table in the corner by the door.

They came to our house day after day. The women brought food by the armfuls. The men sat beside my father, all as silent as he. They filled our small home, but it still felt empty. I sat on the floor beside my mother's bedroom door, watching the doctor come and go, my aunts as well. They looked down on me, offering me forced smiles, light pats on the head. Their touch turned me cold. They wouldn't let me in to see her. Until that day.

"Ginevra." The voice of my Zia Domenica, my mother's sister, woke me as I dozed, though such sleep had crept up on me unnoticed. When I opened my eyes, I found her knelt down before me. Her red-rimmed eyes told me. "Come, Ginevra, come see your mama."

I had been longing for such words for days. It was the last thing I wanted to do. I knew what it meant. My cowardice was a shameful thing.

I took the hand she offered, felt my own tremble as I took it.

Shadows blanketed the room. Closed shutters blocked the sun, the air. I could barely breathe. I could barely see the small being my mama had become. Her skin lay thin on her cheeks, fell in the deep hollows of her sunken face. Her swollen stomach protruded from her body. Whatever lay in there grew ever stronger as she grew weaker. I closed my eyes to the sight, my mind replacing it with the beautiful woman who had smiled with the twinkle of stars whenever she looked at me.

My aunt nudged me forward and I moved on feet brushing the floor. I sat in the chair by her bed and stared, wondering where my mama had gone, where she was going, for I knew she was going.

Reaching out, I put my small hand in the unmoving one lying on the bed in front of me. The cold of it was one I had never felt before. My hand trembled as it took hers and gave it a squeeze. My fingers sank into her skin like toes in the sand.

"Mama?" I thought I shouted but knew it was no more than a whisper. I swallowed; my tight throat hurt. "Mama?" I tried again.

Her head moved, barely. Her eyelids fluttered, opened only to slits.

"Ginevra," her voice was a pale sound of the one I had always known, yet my heart warmed to hear her say my name. "You must take care of Ginevra. He—" she coughed, frail body quaking with it. My aunt rushed to the other side of the bed, held mama's head, and held a cup of water to her lips. Most ran down Mama's cheeks. Only a few drops made it past her dry, cracked lips. The coughing stopped.

"Ginevra," she said again.

"I'm here, mama, right here." I squeezed her hand harder. She turned her head toward me.

"You must take care of Ginevra," she croaked. "He doesn't know how."

She spoke of me, but she didn't know me. She didn't know me but in her frightening words, I knew she loved me. I had little as a child, little in the way of clothes or toys. Though my father's talent as a musician was great, there was little place in this small town on the east coast of Italy for it to shine. He made the most beautiful violins. His hands made magic out of wood. Few here could pay much for them. What I always had was her love. I would have it still. She had just told me it was so.

Her sick face swam in my sight. Her eyes closed as breath rattled in her chest.

Zia Domenica came to me. Her hand on my shoulder pulled me. I shrugged it off, leaned over, and kissed my mother's cold cheek. Our last kiss.

After she died, he left all her things exactly where they were: plain dresses hung limp in the wardrobe, small trinket boxes stood open on her bureau, her few simple pieces of jewelry gathered tarnish.

I would find him, sometimes, staring at the boxes and their lowly treasures. Did he look at them with regret, hearing my mother's unspoken desire for more, or perhaps his need to have given her more? Or did guilt hold him there, relieved that he would hear such silent need no more?

For months, my father and I simply existed, living together in a purgatory of nothing. We ate at the same table, slept in rooms beside each other, saying only words that needed to be said.

"Dinner," he would announce as I sat at the table doing schoolwork. I cleared my papers, placed the dishes, and we'd sit over them, feeding our bellies but nothing else. Not the grief eating at us both.

I wanted—needed—him to help me through it. I know now he simply didn't know how.

Like dreams that kept repeating, so were our days, days that stretched to months, to years. Until the fancy man came.

I had been in my room reading...or trying to. Mostly I stared out the window. I spent many hours this way since I lost her. I thought I saw her in the sky, the clouds, in the trees, in the sound of the ocean in the distance. I searched for her in every waking moment. I dreamt of her as I slept.

The tie binding me to the world was gone, and I floated aimlessly. Did I want to return, or did I want to let go? I was so young, only eight, and yet I knew my loss would be a part of me for the rest of my life. I didn't know if I could live this.

I heard someone come in but didn't care who it was. Until I heard their voices grow louder, harsher. I snuck out of my room, sat on the top step, and listened.

"We are going to America. A very rich man wants me there, wants me to work for him. He is paying good money, a lot of money, for me and Ginevra." They were more words than I had heard my father speak in months, and with more strength and determination than in my whole lifetime.

"Who is this man?" Zia Domenica sounded just as determined.

I listened as my father told my aunt of the man who had come to our home before...when mother was still well, or so we thought. I remember the man's clothes, like nothing I had ever seen, a coat and a jacket and a waistcoat, some sort of scarf wrapped intricately around his neck, a hat tall upon his head. So fancy and precise. My father told her of their conversation, of the money he had paid for one of my father's violins. I remember the meal that night, more meat than I had ever seen on our table.

"He has sent me a letter. He wants me to teach his son the way of the violin now that he is old enough. To make some for him. He believes I could make other things too, furniture."

"Furniture." It was a huff. "You are no simple furniture maker."

"I don't believe he wants simple furniture. He is a grand man. His home, he says it is quite grand."

Silence settled until he broke it, shattered it.

"He believes in me, Domenica."

A sigh. "Ah, so, yes. I know what that must mean to you. She believed in you too. Always."

My father said nothing. He knew my mother had always allowed him his work. Never once did she pester him to do something else, something to make more money. Never once did she question him as an artist, though it kept us always struggling. Her family was not always as kind.

"And what of Ginevra?"

"He said there will be a place for her always, as long as I am there. Even longer should the need arise. He has promised me of it."

"She will be a servant then?" I could taste the bitterness of my aunt's thoughts on the matter.

"A servant in a very wealthy household. It is better than I can do for her here. What would she become here but a servant to whichever man she married? It is all that is here for her."

"And what is wrong with such a life?" huffed my aunt who lived one. "She needs us, her aunts. She needs women to grow into a woman."

I heard his low grumble. I'd heard it so many times before. In this meager way, he would voice his displeasure.

"There will be women there."

"What? Other servants? *Dio mio.*" My aunt did not hide her irritation as he did. "They will not love her."

"I love her."

My hands gripped the railing. How strange to hear him say those words about me. I can't remember when he had said them to me.

"*Si*, you do, I know you do." Her voice softened as a chair scrapped on the floor. Did she stand beside him? "But do you love her enough?"

She asked the question as if she stole it from my mind.

"It is the best I can do for her."

I heard footsteps, a door opened, sounds of birds entered.

Before it shut, I heard, "Promise me, Felice, that when she is old enough to decide, if Ginevra wants to return, you will let her."

I didn't breathe as I waited, as I wondered whether this life my father spoke of in America would be better than the one I lived now. I wondered, when the time came, what I would want. I could not know.

"I promise," he'd said. My fate had been sealed.

GINEVRA
1895

"He kept promise." I shrugged a shoulder. "He think he kept promise."

"I won't ask you if you're happy to be here," Pearl fretted. How silent she had been through my story, even when I floundered and grasped for the correct words. Her face had changed many times. Each change spoke its own tale. "How could you be?"

She did not speak as if she gave advice to a servant; we spoke as travel mates on a winding, bumpy road. To be understood by someone else is sometimes the best we can hope for in life.

"My papa, he happy, is happy," I told her. I did not want her to feel badly about my life in her home, in this home.

Pearl looked at me; her eyes were so like mine, as was our hair, though hers was not quite as curly. She smiled with half her mouth. "Fathers and mothers."

I nodded. The day grew long, but there was no time within our leafy cave.

"They make us who we are," she said, to me, to the tree. "In the good and bad ways."

I nodded again. I understood her as well as she did me.

"Your papa, he is happy?" I remembered the conversation I had over-heard last night. I wouldn't tell her. Such things would pass between us, but not yet.

"In his way, I suppose he is, yes." Was she trying to convince herself or me? I thought she wouldn't say more about him. I was wrong.

PEARL

The moment had come. Would I trifle with this girl or truly befriend her? My eyes closed for a moment, my stark vision drawn inward, seeking truth, looking for what was right, what I wanted against the consequences of wanting it. With my words came the answer. No one reveals their dark truths to trivial acquaintances.

"My father is a railroad baron, as so—"

"Bar-ron?" Ginevra said the word strange to her as if it were two.

"A businessman, a very successful businessman, like most of the men who come here in the summer. But he is also a descendant of..." I would have to watch my language, not because of Ginevra's mind, but because of her lack of knowing all the words. "He was born into a great family, with a descent that can be traced back to the Mayflower. They became very rich. But my great-grandfather had somehow—Father has never told me; I think he is ashamed—lost the family fortune. My father earned it back, doubled it. Now he is on both sides of the line."

Ginevra lifted her shoulders. I scoured the branches above to see if the words I needed sat upon them. In the end, I shrugged and spoke plainly.

"Not a real line, there is a line, among the people, an invisible line, marking where their money came from. Does that make sense?"

"*Si*," she rolled her big brown eyes as she nodded. "Mr. Birch, Mrs. Briggs, Chef," she raised a hand and drew a line in the air, "me and the others."

"Yes," I laughed a little. There were all sorts of lines in our lives in those days. Ginevra learned about them quickly. Perhaps there were lines everywhere, even in Italy. All of life seemed a blurry line as I dithered for my dot upon it. "Well, this line is drawn in the roads and in the cottages. On one side, there are the 'Nobs,' people who inherited money, came down in the family. 'Old' money, they call it."

I looked at her. She nodded, still with me.

"On the other, there are the 'Swells,' people rich now, but not before, people who made their money in business and industry. 'Nouveau riche,' they are called."

I didn't bother to explain that it had been Mr. McAllister, *again*, who had made such distinctions, and such distinctions important, who had, somehow, become judge and jury of all. I judged harshly those who judge others. I was too young to see my own contrariness.

"Because my father came from money *and* made a lot of money, he stands alone in a way, in the middle."

"It not... it is not easy for him." I heard tenderness in Ginevra's voice as she summed up her father so well.

I shook my drooping head. "No, it isn't. And she doesn't make it any easier for him."

"She? Mother?"

I sniffed an ugly little laugh. "Yes, my mother. She is twelve years younger than he is, you know. I think she was his prize for making the family rich again. They met before he went off to serve in the War of Secession."

"Ah," Ginevra breathed, "the scars."

I frowned. "Yes, the scars. They had married when she was only sixteen, but she made sure they were bound together before he left, securing his affections lest he fall for some southern belle. I think she meant to secure his fortune for her own. Her family had had money once, but not very much when they met. She was, is I suppose, one of the great beauties of Society. Beauty is as powerful as money here."

I stopped for a moment, my mother's words buzzing in my ear, a bee with a harsh stinger, *You will have beauty and money, Pearl. You know what Ward says, 'beauty before brains, brains before money.' You will move us even higher up.* I didn't care about climbing as she did, save perhaps in this tree.

"Well, she never imagined he would return 'deformed.' Her word, one she bandied, threw at him, cruelly," I continued. The words rushed from me as if they were in control, not I; to say them was a need I did not know I carried. Here, with Ginevra, they seemed to know better than I, know they were safe. "The scars are shrapnel marks—bullet pieces—dotting his left cheek like stars on a clear night. When he talks to people, he always looks over their left shoulder, showing them mostly the other side of his face. My mother always stays on his right, at the table, standing at social gatherings, or on afternoon strolls, if she stays with him at all."

This time Ginevra took my hand. "He handsome, manly."

I stared at a face that I had only just met, yet one I knew. She did not speak words merely to pacify; she said what she thought was true. Gratitude warmed me like the shafts of light sneaking through the leaves. I would feel more of its warmth.

"I think so," I said with truth. "When I sneak into his study or slip through the dark to climb into his bed for a reassuring cuddle," my head dropped sheepishly, heat crept up my neck, "I know I'm too old to keep doing it, but he doesn't seem to mind." I waggled my head as if to waggle away my childishness. "When I do, he is so very generous with them, with his cuddles. I always do so on his left side. I often reach up and touch his scars." I giggled, head tall upon my straight neck once more. "I remember one time I took a little finger and traced a line, connecting the dots on his face."

" 'I've made a giraffe, Father,' I remember saying. I remember most his soft smile."

With a shake, I came back to this place beneath the beeches. I looked at my attentive listener with a sidelong glance. Sympathy etched her face, the chisel one of my own sad making.

"But then he brought her here," I said, my tone rose as did the tide. "She's better here. It's such a small community. She gets to rub elbows with queens nearly every day."

Ginevra's face opened, brown eyes flashed and hid as her eyelids opened and closed, open and closed. "Queens? You have queens here? Queen of America?"

I laughed, taking her hand as I saw the hurt my laughter caused her.

"No, no, of course not. Not real queens, only those who think they are. Those women I told you about."

I picked another fluffy leaf from a nearby branch, picked at its fronds as I tried to explain these people, "The Four Hundred" as the world knew them, to this unworldly girl. How did one explain the three unusual women—rebel, perfectionist, loose cannon—who sat on their thrones, Alva Vanderbilt, Tessie Oelrichs, and Mamie Fish? Of course, the true leader was Mrs. Astor; no one dared rival her decisions. Between the three of them, they could not knock her off the one true throne.

I straightened my back until I was almost bending backward, puffed up my cheeks, stuck my nose in the air, and tightened my throat, "If you want to be fashionable, always be in the company of fashionable people."

Ginevra laughed a real laugh. It sounded like the seagulls forever wafting above our heads while on this tiny island.

"Who that?"

I laughed too, knowing my imitation was a laughable caricature. "*The* Mrs. Astor," I told her through our giggles. "She thinks she really *is* the Queen of America."

"But how," Ginevra struggled. I sat quietly, encouraging her with stillness and a smile. "How these women come to...?"

She was stuck. I helped, but I did so with a bit of a laugh. "Rule?"

"*Si*, rule," Ginevra, though she didn't fully understand our language, she understood queens rule, by whatever means, in whatever forms.

It was my turn to pull my shoulders up to my ears. "I really don't know, Ginevra. I haven't figured it out yet." Oh, how youth misinforms us of our own knowledge. Yet there were things beyond my keen then. I saw them even through my own self-importance. "I only know when they started coming to Newport, when they started building their 'cottages' here, my mother had to have one too. Of course, Mrs. Astor had to approve of our taking a residence here."

Ginevra gave me that look, one I would come to recognize. She tilted her head to one side, one brow rose on her smooth tawny skin, her mouth puckered as if she'd eaten something bitter.

"Yes, these women rule. They decide who can and who can't have a cottage here."

"Where do others go?"

I pointed west as if we could see across the harbor. "They have lovely homes in Narragansett, near a long, long, beautiful beach." I hesitated. I had been to Narragansett once. In some ways, I thought it prettier than Newport, simpler, more elegant and the enormous stretch of beach could have come straight from the Riviera. "*If* they are ever invited to an event here in Newport, and that is a very big if, they take the ferry over from Narragansett Pier."

I took a hard look at my cottage, the palace that was my summer home. In comparison to some of the other mansions, it was rather austere, just as much marble but far less glittering gilt. My father's words came back to me, as they did yesterday at dinner, "If you insist we build in Newport, then it shall be where and how I say."

"I was shocked, almost as much as my mother," I told Ginevra. "It was one of the few times I had heard him so decidedly firm. Nor did he back down, even when Mother screeched that this plot of land was on the wrong side, on the landside of Bellevue Avenue, not the side perched atop the rocky bluffs, overlooking the Cliff Walk and the sea."

" 'We shall be a laughingstock,' " Mother pined with tinny truculence.

My father grabbed Mother's hand and walked her along the thin dirt path leading left around a thick grove of oaks and maples. On the other side, the trees thinned. A clearing sloped gently away before us, striking for the punctuation of its end by three magnificent beeches, these beeches. Their spindly branches intertwined as if they embraced while others arched and twisted, reaching for the ground, their feathery leaves fluffy as cotton. Even then, I could see the cubbies of space beneath them and longed to enter its haven.

My father stopped, turned west, and pointed.

"Look," he said simply.

"And there it was... the sea my mother craved. Over the tops of the beeches, we saw Newport Harbor."

Yachts at anchor bobbed on little waves. The orange summer sun dipped down drawing ever closer to the deep blue sea, glowing brighter with each tick of descent. Its glow lit the thin wisps of clouds daring to draw near, turning them to licks of flame.

In the face of such beauty, my mother became mute.

I shimmied closer to my father, tucking my small hand in his, smiling when he gave it a squeeze.

" 'What shall we call it, my Pearl?' "

"All the cottages have names, Chateau Sur Mer, Marble house, Wakehurst, Rough Point."

As the lowest tip of the sun slithered beneath the ocean horizon, its tangerine rays struck the beeches, filling the cave-like spaces with light. They glowed as if lit from within. I was captivated.

"The Beeches," I said.

My father grinned as he does, with a nod and a grunt.

"Beeches," he repeated. "One might know it for the trees, for we shall write it that way. But others might think it's for the beautiful shore all around us."

He looked down at me with his somber brown gaze.

" 'How very clever of you, my Pearl. Well done.' "

"Though I had not thought of the double meaning of the word, I felt clever nonetheless. I always want my father to think of me as a clever girl, not the kind of girl my mother is."

"Your mother, she is…snotflea," Ginevra attempted. I laughed. She said it wrong, but she got it right. I didn't want to speak of my mother. Or Ginevra's mother. They were both absent in our lives, though a different sort of absent. I'm not sure if it made a difference, or which was worse.

"The first thing we need to do is to improve your English," I announced, then immediately felt sorry for my words. Had I insulted her? It was the last thing I would wish to do to this new friend of mine, for I did feel that we would become friends. We can never know when a similar soul will pass our way, or what sort of dress it may hide behind. My fears fled with her rapid nodding, the spark bursting in her dark eyes.

My taut shoulders dropped; I breathed again. "I think you should start with reading. If you read out loud, it will help when you speak."

I saw the truth then in the slump of her shoulders and the slow slide of her features lower down her face.

"You don't know how to read, do you?" I asked softly.

"*Si*, Italian." She screwed up her shoulders along with her pride.

"Well, that's wonderful," I praised. She needed me to. "Then I shall teach you to read in English and to write, of course. Would you like that?"

"Yes. Very much." Her words were simple; her smile was so much more.

* * *

I scampered down from our perch on the tree. I ducked out, like Alice from the rabbit hole, and onto the lawn. On my own, there was no reason to hide, and I made for the house, crossing the vast yard at a leisurely pace. I skipped as I did so often when I was younger. The shadow of Ginevra, the smiling one, skipped beside me. Her ethereal, unsuspected place beside me made the summer sun brighter. Summer had just begun. I looked forward to the days of it quite differently than I had done when we first arrived in Newport that year.

Was I silly to think of Ginevra so fondly already? Perhaps. Was I wrong about the affectionate connection so quickly forming between us? No, not at all. The resemblance of us—not of the physical sort—was far more powerful than the contradiction.

I looked up to the house, past the two sets of stone stairs, the two wide terraces, the statues rising up at the ends and anchoring the middle. I looked up to the windows, the windows to my room. I saw a curtain fall back into place.

My steps quickened as I groaned.

I rushed into the house, through the Conservatory, and up the main stairs to my room.

She stood there waiting.

"You've kept me waiting, again." Miss Jameson stood with her fisted hands on her narrow hips. "This time for more than an hour."

"I'm dreadfully sorry," I said, and I was. For all that I treasured the time beneath the beeches with Ginevra, my manners were ingrained. To keep someone waiting so long was simply not done.

"Do you think I have nothing better to do than to wait for you?" she demanded.

From across the hall and through the foyer I heard voices, words spoken with the same sharp tone. Ginevra, in the sewing room, received the same sort of greeting as did I.

"No, of course, not Miss Jameson," I lied. In truth, she didn't have anything better to do. She was there to teach me, to add to the regular lessons of school, nothing else. The nothing else, reminded by my absence, was where her anger truly lay. "I do apologize. I will try to do better."

"Oh, you will do better." There was a threat to her words. "What were you doing?"

"I...I...," I stumbled, "I was out in the gardens sketching."

Miss Jameson knew of my love for drawing, for painting. My façade was a believable one.

"Where is your sketchbook?"

I looked down at my empty hands. I was a terrible liar.

I laughed. I didn't fake that any better.

"Well, silly me, I must have left it in the garden," I tried to laugh again. Again, I failed. "I'll go get it."

"You'll do no such thing."

I knew that would be her answer and sighed with relief. My sketchbook was in the small desk, in front of which she stood, statue-like, with arms crossed, a foot tapping.

"You will sit yourself down and work on these math problems." She pointed to my desk chair and the papers waiting there for me.

I quickly did. As I struggled with the numbers—for working them didn't come easily to me—she paced behind me, watching me work, sharply instructing me when I did my figuring wrong.

Her patience, already worn thin, nearly disappeared.

"Such a waste of time," she muttered as she paced, lips so tight all she could do was mutter, arms crossed equally as tight across her scrawny chest, "these girls have no need for such knowledge. They'll never use it. No, not these girls."

It was a condemnation not only of me, but of all the girls of families such as mine, girls whose only goal in life—decided for them—was to marry the right man, have children, and become the next cog in this exclusive machine that was the social life of the rich. They told us this truth, verbally beat it into us, from the moment we could start listening. I listened, merely listened. We choose what we truly wish to hear.

I was smarter than my brother...my brother who was pushed to learn about business and railroads and running large companies. Learning he had no interest in. His was a life so full of promises, of potential. He took for granted what I longed for.

"How dare you?!"

The thunder raged not from the sky, but my door, and my mother standing in it.

I jumped up from my chair, my feet twisting on themselves, stumbling as my words did. "I...I'm sorry, Mother. I lost track of time. I've apologized to Miss Jameson."

My governess stood casually, her fingers tapped merrily upon her folded arms; a smirk slithered across her lips, splitting her face. She showed no surprise to see my mother.

"I saw you!" Mother screamed, lunging toward me with a pointed finger. I backed away, my buttocks slamming hard against my desk. If I could have climbed over it, put it between us, I would have. "I saw you with that girl, that foreign servant. How dare you?"

The monster of anger that was my mother chased away my thoughts, my words. I was the fox, and she was on the hunt.

"Do you know what they would say if they saw you?"

"They" could be any number of people.

"You could ruin us. I will not allow it!"

A gust of wind blundered through the open window, pushing against my back, pushing me forward.

"But, Mother, she is...she is in a strange land. I thought only to be kind and—"

"Do not speak to me." Mother's face was just inches from mine, yet I hardly recognized her. "You will only listen. You will never, ever, see that girl again, never spend a second with her. Do you understand me?"

I understood too well; such understanding did not serve her cause.

"You're being cruel, Mother. Such people deserve our—"

"Enough!" Mother bellowed; her gentile veneer, one she practiced with such constancy, broke like a thin crystal champagne flute under the crunch of a heavy boot. "You refuse to listen to me, don't you? As you always do."

Her enraged gaze scoured my room. Fiery eyes latched and held.

"Well, I shall make you listen."

Faster than I ever saw her move, Mother flashed across my room, grabbed my kit and paints and brushes, grabbed my canvas, and made for the door.

Grief did not belong only to death.

"Where are you taking those?" Desperation plunged me toward her.

Mother stopped at the door, turned back. Evil shattered her beautiful face into grotesque shards.

"If you spend time with trash, then to the trash these will go."

"No!" I pleaded. It didn't matter.

"The rest of it, Miss Jameson," Mother instructed, "be sure it all goes."

That woman's pinched face lit with satisfaction. "Yes, Madam."

Far too happily, Miss Jameson quickly gathered what was left of my supplies and made her way to the door, stopping at the threshold.

"You, return to your work."

I fell into my desk chair, battered as if beaten. Mother had never gone this far to bring me in line. Or had I stepped too far from it? I dropped my face to the papers before me but could see nothing past my tears, nothing but the loss of my most precious items.

* * *

Another night, another dinner alone. I sat in the dark room, lacquered black walls made glorious by the use of gold fleck paint and bright reds of the colorful Chinese figures. My only companion was my pain. I was as dark as the walls, with not a speck of gold in sight.

Mother and Father walked in, both resplendently dressed; he in his waistcoat atop his white shirt and tie, swallowtail coat cut short in front, top hat in hand. She with a beaded frothy dress whose tail shushed along the polished floor, her wide-brimmed laced and flowered hat perched at just the perfect tilt upon the pile of her red hair.

My fork stopped halfway to my mouth.

"I hope you have learned a valuable lesson today." My mother stood by my side, looking down her straight, pert nose at me.

I put the fork down.

"I have." I lied. "I'm sorry, Mother," I said truthfully. I was, very sorry she had seen me with Ginevra; sorry I had not been more careful.

I looked to my father knowing he knew, knowing my mother had informed him of every little tidbit of the day. I searched his face, looking for what I needed, not finding it.

He said nothing.

Mother sniffed at me, unconvinced. "You've lost your painting, and I'm not sure you should continue your lessons either." That dig was for my father, not me.

She circled away from me as she drew on one long satin glove, head shaking, but just slightly, so as not to upset the creation on her head. "Dancing, etiquette, managing a household, now those topics should command your attention, not math, or science, or art."

I longed to pick my fork back up and poke her with it, not hard, just enough to prick some sense into her. My fingers gripped it until my knuckles turned white.

I turned to my father. The frustration returned. I knew it was by his instruction I partook in such lessons, why would he not defend them, defend me.

I closed my eyes and sighed. Father did all he could not to anger his young wife, not to feed the fire of her ire.

He looked at me, at my thunderous thoughts darkening my face. My skin was pale but worse ridiculously opaque, no matter how I practiced the stony countenance of my set, of my station. It was nothing but time wasted. I didn't know how to be anything but me, a me of confusion and contradiction.

"I see no reason to go that far, Millicent." Finally, Father spoke, softly but firmly. My frozen heart melted, a drip. "I do believe the Vanderbilt girls are receiving the same tutelage, are they not?"

It was rare for Father to speak against my mother's dictates; thoughts created fewer arguments. When he did, he did with great keenness. I would have rather he fought for my painting supplies to be returned, but this was enough, for now. He had hit her tender spot, for my mother cared about nothing more than doing what the leading families did, including my brother and me.

"Well, yes, Orin, I do believe they are." Mother's face, blackened like a storm cloud, turned to look out the window. I could see the hold she had on her other glove; the white knuckles of her grasp were just like mine.

"Then I believe it best...," my father began.

"Yes, yes. It is best." Mother pulled on the glove with sharp irritation, the same clipped edge in her voice.

"Continue on then, Pearl." She could not have said my name with more disdain. "But if I catch you with that peasant again, you will lose all. Am I clear?"

"Yes, Mother." In truth, I did not want to lose my lessons. I treasured learning as my mother did her jewels. I simply wanted more.

"Come along, Orin." Mother sashayed quickly from the room. My father lingered. He stood by my chair and leaned down to me, a hand on my shoulder.

"I understand you, my Pearl, I see you," he spoke softly, whether to offer me solace or so that Mother would not hear, I didn't know. "But I can only protect you from her so much. I can't protect you when I'm not here."

He stopped. Closed his eyes for a moment.

"And I can't protect you from the world. Our world can be a hard place. Do you understand?"

I nodded, though I didn't understand fully, not yet. I understood only his comfort.

My father gave my shoulder and squeeze and left me.

* * *

I woke from the nightmare gasping. My face wet from tears and sweat. The shadows in my room had taken on the shapes of the awful dream. I needed my father.

I slipped from my bed, shivering from the cold in the stillness of the hot summer night. I didn't knock but entered my father's room in a rush. His bed was empty and as cold as I. I couldn't bear searching for him, too afraid of what lay in the dark parts of the house, there were so many of them, too many and of all sorts.

I would go to my mother. Is that not where all children go when in need? She could give comfort when she wanted, though she rarely wanted to. Perhaps I needed it from her especially. I knew her door to the corridor would be locked, it always was. I hurried through my father's room, through the bathroom between, and reached for the door connecting her room to his.

The doorknob would not turn. This door too was locked. She locked out not only me but him as well.

GINEVRA

I slipped away from Pearl, slipped away from our place beneath the beeches, though I didn't want to. Everything looked different—felt different—after being in there with Pearl. Surprises came in the strangest of packages. There were no words, in my language or hers, that could describe it. I no longer walked through life quite as alone, though I was very alone as I followed her directions to the side of the house and the servants' entrance there.

As I wandered into the circular drive, its canopy of wisteria and wrought iron, though beautiful, felt like a trap closing down on me, but now I could see the holes in its teeth. Happiness seemed to die when Mama died. Beneath the Beeches, I thought I had glimpsed it again, at the least the shimmering promise of it.

Pearl promised me, before I left, that this was not the first and last time we would be together beneath the beeches, rather it would only be the first of many. She promised to find a way to let me know when we could meet, if I could get away to meet her. A promise such like that of the buds of spring.

I slipped in the door to another white tiled foyer. I could see the cold kitchen just beyond another frosted door. I could hear the voices of many at work. But no one saw me. I quickly stepped to the stairs on my left, the servant stairs, pleased with myself for slipping back into the house unnoticed. Too soon.

"*Figlia?*" My father was there, just as I rounded the landing to the next set of stairs. "Daughter," he said again in Italian, there was none of his sparse affection in his tone or upon his face.

"Where have you been? That Mrs. Briggs came to me, looking for you."

"I...I...," I stumbled. "I had to put a dress, in the lady's room. I got lost." It was the truth, but only some. I lied poorly, whether this was a bad or good thing, I wasn't sure, I was only certain it was my way, a way beyond changing.

"Tell me the truth." He was as stony as the statues posing every-where in and out of this house.

I told him everything, fixing the dress, hiding, and being found. I told him of Pearl and my time with her beneath the beeches. Happiness chirped in my voice. None of it showed on his face.

He said nothing for a very long time. When he spoke, I wished he hadn't. His words fanned the sparks of my own doubts.

"It will never last," he said flatly. "We will never be friends with these people. Do your chores and stay out of sight."

It was a cruel scolding. He walked around me, walked away from me, and back down the stairs.

Stay out of sight, he had said.

Stay out of mine, it was cruel thought my mind flung at him, but I didn't put it there. The little between us, the little I received from him, with such coldness, it almost chased away the joy Pearl had given me. Almost.

I hurried up the next flight of stairs, through one door, to the sewing room.

She stood there, waiting.

"Where were you?" Mrs. Briggs' pale face turned as red as the walls in Mr. Worthington's rooms.

"I...," I started, stopped, not knowing my way.

"Never mind, shut your bone box. I really don't care. And I don't care how young you ah. In this house, everyone works."

From the foyer, the yelling reached us. Mrs. Briggs fell silent, listen-ing, as I did. We heard every word. My heart ached. It was my fault. Nothing Mrs. Briggs could do to me now would punish me more than what had happened to Pearl. Though she tried her best.

Her long bony fingers grabbed my upper arm and with a hard yank, pushing me down in the chair before the long sewing table. For the first time, I saw what was on it.

Socks. Piles and piles of socks.

"These are the servants' hosiery, almost all of it. You are to match them up, see which needs fixing, and fix them."

There were enough socks to keep two sets of hands busy for hours. I sat before the piles unable to say a word.

A bony finger poked my shoulder.

"Get to it," she sneered, "and don't come out until you've finished, not even when you hear the dinner bell."

* * *

For hours, I sat there until my hands hurt. The flickering light of the gas lamps showed every painful, red pinprick dotting my hands. My stomach grumbled, angry with me for not tending to it, but I still had so much to do. I wanted to cry again, like this morning, but within my empty gut, only anger grumbled.

Without pushing back my chair, I slipped from it. Stopping at the edge of the opened door, I peered out, seeing no one. I slipped downstairs, past Chef Pasquel and the kitchen maids, still hard at work.

I had missed dinner long ago. Not another servant was in sight, not a sign of Mrs. Briggs either. All had made for their beds save those who waited to serve their masters—the valets and Mrs. Worthington's maid, and those finishing the kitchen cleaning. I slipped past them unnoticed.

The long, narrow workroom they had given my father smelled like the forest I played in back in Foggia, and the idea of tears came back to me with the memory. Fresh wood of every sort and size stood in piles against the wall. In the corner, on a table of polished oak, my father worked, making the violin for the young man of the house. He stroked the wood as if it were alive and could feel the caress of his hand.

"I need help, Papa," I said in Italian.

Without looking up, my father shook his head, light found his skin through the thinning grey hair. "English."

My jaw jutted forward. I struggled for words in my own language that would convey my struggles.

"H...help, Papa," the word came to me on the memory of Pearl and her offer of it.

At last, he looked at me, his gaze as dead as my mother. He shrugged. He didn't understand. It was an admission he hated to make. In our language, I told him of the housekeeper and the socks and the lack of dinner.

He turned to me. Nothing in his features gave me any hope.

In Italian, he told me, "Do what they tell you. Finish the work. You will eat tomorrow."

I shivered at the cold, in his words, in this house. I turned without a word.

"Ginevra." He called me back and I turned out of duty.

He thrust his head to a small table in the opposite corner. "*Pane.*"

My mouth watered at the sight. On the table sat a chunk of bread, large beside the crumbs of what looked like cheese and perhaps some sort of meat. I ran to it, and with two hands held it to my mouth, tore at it with my teeth.

With my treasure in hand, with at least ten more bites left, I made for the door. I turned to thank him, but my father had already turned back to his work, to the sanding of wood, the stroking of it. I left him, still devouring my bread, focused on the food hitting my angry belly. But not so focused that I didn't see the trash bin in the laundry room and what lay in it.

* * *

My mission complete, I slowly climbed the stairs, my aches my only companions.

The hall was empty, almost dark. I slipped into my room, for the first time so grateful for it.

And for the first time, I found Greta in her bed. From beneath her nightcap, I could see thick curly red hair, a deep, dark red. Beneath the covers, she faced the wall, her small body curled in a ball. Her hair and her small build I remembered as one of those at table, one who had not said a word to me, though she must have known, both last night and that day at breakfast, who I was, that I was to share her room.

I tiptoed in, not wanting to disturb her, and began to unbutton my dress, each press of my punctured fingers bringing another stab of pain.

"She don' want ya here."

I jumped with a small gasp and spun round.

Greta's startling blue eyes pierced me; hatred glowed brightly in the gloom. She'd turned under the covers to face me without a sound.

"None of us do, ya know, no really." Her accent was as thick as her meanness. "But I'll tell ya this, do what she says, or we'll all pay fer it. Then you'll really see what it can be like here, fer the likes of you." She turned her back to me once more.

With such a tender "good-night," I silently shrugged off my dress, and in my chemise, slipped beneath the covers of my bed, shivering in the hot night.

PEARL

But often through the singing broke
A burst of laughter gay,
So young were we, so glad and free,
That happy Summer day!
And hand in hand would linger long,
As through the dance we moved,
For some of us were lovers then,
And some of us were loved.

I lay back on my bed with a sigh. Such beautiful words and written by a woman. I had obtained a copy of *Verses*, a book of poetry by a Newport resident, a young woman by the name of Edith Wharton. She was only sixteen when she wrote them, the same age as I was now. Her proud father had had them privately published fifteen years ago, but I had found a copy in the Astor library a few years ago, while there for the birthday party for Pauline, *The* Mrs. Astor's daughter who was near my age.

I had smuggled it out, snuggled it near me ever since. Read it when I should have—

"What in heaven's name are you doing?"

Mother's voice shattered my reverence. I jumped up, shoved the book of poetry beneath me.

"I...I was just about to get ready."

It was a glorious summer day and the hour for the beach had fast approached.

Her grey eyes narrowed. She held out a hand. Though she did not admire intelligence, hers was sharp. There was nothing for it. I slipped the book out from beneath me and handed it to her.

"How many times must you read this?" Mother tossed the book on the floor as she would a piece of rubbish. "Aren't you supposed to be reading another book, the one I gave you?"

Now I wanted to squint at her. I didn't.

I scrambled to pick up the ignored book—*The Ladies' Book of Etiquette, and Manual of Politeness: a Complete Hand Book for the Use of The Lady in Polite Society,* by a woman named Florence Hartley. The title alone repulsed me—before she could see the turned-down corner clearly marking my place, still stranded in the middle.

"But I am, Mother. It's always right here, by my bed." Yes, always there, always forgotten.

She snatched it from my hand. It fell open, the traitor.

"This is the same page you were on when I asked you last week."

This book she also threw, at me. It landed on my lap, far heavier than it actually was.

"There will be no beach for you today. When I return, I expect to see progress made. I *will* question you."

Oh, I was sure she would. What she didn't know was the punishment she adjudged was no punishment at all. No beach, the whole family gone, I could think only one thought... more time with Ginevra beneath the beeches. Mother had already taken my most treasured possessions. In my mind, I had little else to lose and far too much to gain by being with Ginevra.

"Yes, Mother." I did my very best act of contrition. It worked now as it always did.

She left me with a huff, thankfully, before she could see the smile beginning to blossom on my face.

I listened as I heard her agitated steps wander away from me, growing fainter as they trudged down the stairs.

Like a child, I bounced on my bed. In the joyful frivolity, I wasted precious time. I picked up the dreaded book, and another, and made for the door fast.

It was a portent, in my mind, that my room, on the other wing of the house than my parents, was just steps away from the sewing room. Through one frosted glass door and into a foyer, I stood beside the door.

Ever so slowly, I peeked my head around the threshold.

I had never noticed how dark the room was before. Dark brown, textured cloth covered the walls, the furniture, the rugs. All dark—save her smile—when she saw me there.

"Are you alone?" I whispered to Ginevra.

She nodded, pulling her needle and its tail of thread.

I held the book up before me, grinning like a little girl, my brows dancing up and down on my forehead. She grinned as well.

Ginevra lifted her shoulders, splayed her hands to show me the piles of work before her.

I rubbed my stomach and made a ridiculously sickly face. *Maybe I should be an actress*, I thought, *my mother would die of apoplexy*. I choked back the guffaw longing to be barked.

Ginevra bit her lip, bit back her own laughter I could tell, nodded, and dropped her face back to her work, but not before I saw another grin.

I made my way back to the family portion of the house unhurried. My mother was gone; there was little need to hide. Reaching the first floor, I heard the sound of drawers opening and closing from my father's library. Servants were to clean in there, but never to invade any of it. I strode off, ready to reprimand the offender. I've since heard it said that no matter how hard we try, we eventually become our mothers. I fought against it even then. My righteous indignation in that moment was hers, all hers.

But there was no offender, only my father.

"Hello, my Pearl," he greeted me with the endearment that had been mine since before I could remember. I stepped into the room forever thick with wood, leather, and man.

"Hello, Father." I tossed back casually, a camouflage. I didn't know if my mother had told him of my continued wayward behavior. She hated when I did not attend the days at the beach. At my age, she already paraded me before the sons of like years from the best families, already tried to push us together. She must have complained to him. She was always complaining to him.

"What are you up to this fine day?" he asked, still rummaging in his desk. Mother hadn't told. "No beach for you?"

I shook my head. "No, not today. I have some studying to do." He didn't need to know more.

"Study is always good," he said with half his attention.

My father valued education and learning. The thought struck me like a hammer blow. Would he approve of what I was about? That it contradicted my mother so grossly could swing him decidedly one way or the other. Once more, I dared to push against one of the many fences that surrounded me.

"Actually, Father," I stepped closer to his desk, he looked up at me, "I'm going to teach Ginevra to read and write in English."

He stared at me with his sad brown eyes. The sadness he could not hide, everything else hid behind it. After what had happened, I wasn't sure he would still be on my side.

"Can she read and write in her own language?"

He surprised me. It was a surprise whenever he did.

"Yes. Yes, she can," I said happily.

Father studied me for the length of a breath. "Good. It will be easier to teach her then."

He gave his form of approval, as he had learned to do safely, given but not outright. It was enough, more than enough.

I leaned down and squeezed his hand. "Thank you, Father," I said, squeezing harder at the sight of his pleasure.

I dashed away and out of the house, filled with joy, to await my friend beneath the beeches.

"My Pearl?" Father stopped me cold. I turned. "Don't get caught."

GINEVRA

It had been a few days since we were able to meet again. Though Pearl would sometimes pass the sewing room, an unnatural path for her to take when coming from the downstairs ladies' bathroom, but one easily explained if she had to.

For my needs, I had to climb either to the third floor or down to the basement.

On days when we could meet, she would flick her brows up, flick her head out toward the trees, but I dared not go again at first. I worked very hard for a few days. Red pinpricks on my fingers told the truth of it, as did the ache from an always bent neck. That day—having become an established part of Mrs. Brigg's well-run household—found me courageous.

I waited a few minutes after Pearl disappeared from the door and made my way to the laundry room. I told Mrs. Brown I felt unwell and needed to use the facilities, holding my stomach while holding my face in a scrunched way—the way the Pearl had done—silly but convincing.

Instead of making my way to my room as I told her I would, I slipped down the stairs, out to the side terrace, and ran the path behind the maple trees to cut across to the beeches.

Stepping through the curtain of flowing leaves and branches, I stepped into that other world once more. Here, no work would bend my body until it ached; no harshness could reach through the softness.

Pearl had brought books, one by a woman and one by a man. She flapped them in her hands as if they were wings and their words would give us the power of flight.

"Let's start with this one on etiquette. It's dreadfully boring but the language is a little simpler than Mr. Twain's is, though not nearly as interesting. But I think it a good place for you to start."

Start we did. Slowly, ever so slowly. With the tip of her finger, she scrolled across each line, only moving it when I had learned the word. The movement marked our passage through the work, my passage into the language. The shadows shifted upon the pages beginning to look less like gibberish and more like words.

Don't hold your parasol so close to your face, nor so low down. You cannot see your way clear, and you will run against somebody. Always hold an umbrella or parasol so that it will clear your bonnet, and leave the space before your face open, that you may see your way clearly.

I read it well, happy with my progress. Comprehension filtered through recognition, the meaning ridiculous.

"Do you not understand it?" Pearl asked me, her face florid at whatever she saw upon mine.

"No, I understand." I shrugged with a shake of my head. "But this, this how you live?" I stabbed the page with an accusing finger.

She frowned. When she frowned it was like a dark cloud passing in front of the sun. Such a frown—and one I put there—put something new in our floral cavern. It was an awkward, uncomfortable thing.

"Well, this is how we are made to live."

I began to understand even if she did not.

"Believe it or not, how you hold a parasol is seen as a sign." She lectured with words she spat from puckered lips.

"A sign-a?" I shook my head at the added vowel sound, the part of my accent I had so much trouble erasing from my speech.

"Oh, yes." Pearl chirped, the other Pearl. "Let's say a young lady is walking down the street and she sees a man she likes approaching her. Raising her parasol as he passes tells him she's interested." Pearl taught me much more than how to read and write. "If she wants him to follow her, she would close the parasol and hold it in her right hand. One must be very careful though, the wrong signal can lead to the most dreadful misunderstandings."

I stared at her. She studied my scrunched face.

"Women are not alone in such things." She plucked at her skirt as if she plucked words from an out-of-tune violin. "The men do as well. They must know the right flowers to send and to whom. Red roses, of course, are a sign of true love, while yellow speaks of jealousy or of favor once held lost. Yes, the men must know the language of flowers and how to speak it with...their...florist."

Her words fell away beneath my lengthened stare. She shrugged dismissively, though not without her pale cheeks blushing pink. I couldn't stop myself, though I wish I had.

"These things are...are...*importante*?" I faltered for the English pronunciation.

"Important," Pearl corrected me kindly, as a friend, not a teacher.

"Ah, *si*, important." I held the book out toward her. "These things are important to you?"

To this day, I'm unsure if it was the question or the cynical way I asked her that offended, or whether seeing it through my eyes allowed her to see things all too clearly.

She snatched the book from my lap.

"Well, yes, of course they are important," she said, imitating her mother. "One must live gracefully." She faltered. She didn't like the sound of her mother's voice coming from her mouth any more than I did. "Well, you know."

I grabbed her gaze with mine and held it. She lowered her face against its penetration. We had journeyed to places better left alone, places that disrupted ourselves, and what we were becoming together. Such a journey needed to end.

"Maybe they important, are important," I said, barely keeping the smile from my face. "But not to you. I know what important is to you."

This time I grabbed *her* hand, pulling her down the tree clumsily.

"You will make us fall," she warned as her free arm pin wheeled like a rudder to my engine.

I kept pulling, straight out of our hideaway.

"Ginevra?" Pearl sputtered, stumbling along behind me, gaze flashing this way and that, looking for lookers. I took us into a run toward the carriage house.

No one was there. The grooms were either driving the family or exercising the horses. It was the perfect time.

"Ginevra?" Pearl stammered on thickening confusion, scudding to a stop, pulling her hand from mine. "What are we doing here? Yes, I like to ride but it's not that important to me."

I laughed. I couldn't help myself. I took possession and pulled her again, pulled her up the side stairs on the outside of the carriage house, to the small loft above. I opened the door, stepped back, and thrust her in. Her gasp echoed upon the rafters.

Pearl slapped her hands to her cheeks, walked into the room with slow deliberate steps. She spun to look at me, then spun back. She couldn't take her eyes off the items in the corner by the back, bay window. There stood her easel, a canvas already on it. On a table at its side lay all her paints and brushes.

She spun back again, her face slack with wonder. "Goodness gracious. Ginevra, what have you done?"

It sounded like she scolded me. She didn't. Her smile brimmed and quivered, as did her tears.

I scuffed my toe into the roughhewn wood floor. "I only did what you would do for me."

She came to me and wrapped her arms around me. It was our first embrace. It would not be the last. I had been in her world only a short time, but even then, I knew how rare such an embrace was, an embrace between the privileged and those who served them.

With me still in her arms, Pearl jumped up and down. I had no choice but to jump with her, laugh with her. She jumped and laughed her way to her paints and her easel.

The next time we met, when Pearl came for our reading time, we read *The Adventures of Huckleberry Finn* by Mark Twain.

* * *

I whirled through days in a haze of work and salty breezes. Each day a little of the strangeness of this strange place became familiar. Every morning I woke up to a different me, no matter how tightly I held onto the old.

I saw people of such riches come and go, carrying their wealth with little thought of its treasure. I saw meals served to crowds and intimate parties, food fit for a king's table and his court.

I saw little of Pearl. She had the whirl of society and I my work and my studies. I did both to my best. I almost came into Mrs. Briggs' good graces. Almost.

"Turn the light out already," Greta grumbled at me that night. It was not the first time; it wouldn't be the last. The late-night hours were often the only time I had to do my reading, practice my writing. A servant's day was ten to twelve hours long, even a seamstress, even if all she did was sit in a room in case she was needed, back growing stiff, fingers actually longing for work, and a mind unoccupied to wander adrift. I preferred the nicks of needles in constant motion to the tedium. I didn't know what bothered Greta more, the light or what I did within it. The louder she grumbled, the louder I turned pages.

"Just a few more minutes," I muttered without looking up from my book.

With a huff, she threw off her thin summer bed linen and stomped out.

"I need a wee," she announced as if I asked.

I heard her stomp down the hall. I forgot her as her outraged footsteps faded to soft thumps, becoming as faint as the tick of a clock.

The pictures in the magazine, a copy of Harper's Bazaar I had stolen from the trash bin, set my mind on fire. The glossy pages were filled with fashion, articles on fashion, pictures of fashion, I lost myself to it. I learned who Worth was. I studied each picture, each sleeve, each skirt, picturing how I would change things, imagining how I would design such creations. I left this room, this world, and went to the place of my dreams.

The dream shattered.

"What do you think you are doing?"

Mrs. Briggs stood in the threshold. I hadn't heard her steps, hers and Greta's, hadn't heard the door open. My body and my face tightened, almost painfully.

"Well, I-a reading." Nerves invited back the accent I tried so hard to lose.

She marched across the room to my bed; robe wrapped and tied as tightly around her as her anger, dark ash blonde and gray hair falling in a frazzle down her back. Mrs. Briggs grabbed the magazine from my hands with such force, without warning, the page in my hands ripped. The sound made me flinch.

"Harper's Bazaar? Hah!" she laughed at me, so did Greta, standing behind her, smirking with satisfaction. "Why does a girl like you need to be reading such a thing?"

"I thought…good for my work."

"Your work is to mend and fix, nothing more. Your kind will never be anything more."

My gaping mouth snapped closed. Pain stabbed my jaw as my teeth ground together. I longed for a sharp tongue in full possession of English with which to whip her.

"Go to bed, go to sleep this minute," Mrs. Briggs ordered, stomping out of the room with the same anger in which she had entered, taking the magazine with her.

Greta slipped back into her bed, "Nighty, night, Geeneeva," she twittered at me.

I stared at her back. There was an English word for her, I had heard the men in the basement use it. It began with a 'b,' though that was all I could remember. In my language, under my breath, I called her a *puttana*.

* * *

Somehow, one of Mrs. Worthington's day dresses, one of her favorites, had become ripped at two seams, long stretches of them. I spent the entire morning fixing them, every stitch I made, I made with the best of care.

"Ah you done yet?"

I jumped. Once more Mrs. Briggs stood in the threshold.

"Almost," I replied, unable to keep a note of pride out of my voice.

Within a flash, she stood before me and my table perched before the window. Mrs. Briggs picked up the dress, scoured it with mean eyes. Her two hands traveled down the length of one seam, all the way to the hem. She pulled.

The rip was like a scream, it screeched through my head. In seconds, she destroyed hours of my work; in truth, she longed to destroy my strength.

"Not good enough." She dropped the dress on the desk. "Do it again. Better this time."

She left as she came. I barely noticed.

The clanging in my head wouldn't stop. My hands shook. I gripped the edge of the table until my knuckles blazed white-hot. She had made the damage worse; she had made my job harder. I almost thought to throw it away, almost.

I picked it up and began again. If the battle continued, I would not fall to it.

* * *

I had had no lunch, thanks to Mrs. Briggs and her destruction. I skipped it to finish the work, just barely making it to the dinner table in time.

I sat beside my father as always. He rarely saw me, saw my truth, for he rarely looked for it, but not that night. He raised his shoulders at me, face scrunched by question and confusion. I just shook my head, sat, and began to eat.

As my hunger ebbed so did my anger. Not for long.

"Faleece!" From the senior staff table, Mrs. Briggs bellowed at my father.

He sat upright, stopped chewing.

"The sideboard door has broken, again. You will fix it after dinner. Do not go to your bed until you do." It was an ungracious order, in truth, one Mr. Birch should have given. Mrs. Briggs brought her displeasure with me crashing down upon my father. Hatred is a poisonous thing; we do not often have the antidote for our own. My back stiffened. My fingers turned white as I strangled the fork in my hand.

"It is Felice, feh-LEE-cheh," I said with more force than I had said anything in my life.

"Eh, what's that you say, girl?" Mrs. Briggs grumbled, nearly growled.

I didn't even turn my gaze to her.

"My father's name is Felice," I said with the correct pronunciation, my softer exclamation did not diminish my stern intent. "We been here almost two months. I think it polite you say it right. I believe he has, eh, earn it."

Before she or anyone could say more, I thrust my chair back and stomped away.

In the quiet I left the room in, I heard her bellow, "Why you... come back here, girl!"

I neither went back nor turned back. I never heard my father's name pronounced incorrectly ever again.

* * *

I didn't go far. I sat in my father's room waiting for him. He came in for his tools to fix the wretched sideboard.

"You should ask for more money," I said in English as he took a step in the door.

He hesitated, whether by my presence or my words, I don't know. In the few moments we had here and there, he had started speaking more and more English, though his accent was still heavy, heavier than my own. Only with me, would he practice it.

"*É basta.* It enough," he answered, stepping to his tools, picking through them. "We have home, we have food, what-a more you want?"

I didn't blink. "Freedom."

For one of the few times in my life, his eyes found mine with a snap. "I have my pride," he said in Italian.

Without letting him go, I said, "Pride is a luxury."

I stood. I would try no more. If he had answered me differently—if there had been but a smidgen of empathy, of support—each day that would come after this day might have been different. The fight ebbed out of me as water swirls down a drain, leaving the sink empty.

I went to stand by him at his worktable. I saw huge pieces of mahogany set beside smaller, already cut pieces. In one of those, I glimpsed the basic figure of a woman, the start of scrolls.

"This is not for violin, Papa." My voice squeaked with surprise. "What are you making?"

He picked up one of the pieces, his hands caressing it lovingly. Without looking away, without releasing his hold on the wood, he said in Italian, "The master has asked for a cabinet. He called it some-thing else, an English word for it…broken front?" It wasn't a question, merely his unknowing. "A display piece, for the violins I make for him."

I was pleased for my father. I could see how this newfound purpose did much to bring him back to life, out of the limbo he had been stuck in since my mother's passing.

I meant to tell him, tell him how happy I was for him, but his ab-sorption with his work, his caressing of the wood, had commenced once more. I longed for such a touch from him. A longing never to be fulfilled, save for one time yet to come.

"You don't belong here, girl." Once more Mrs. Briggs had found me, once more her cruelty slapped me. "Get back to work."

"*Buona notte*," I whispered to my father. He nodded silently.

* * *

My father shuffled into my room the next afternoon, head hung low, hat still in hand. He said nothing but quirked his head outward.

I stood in the same murky silence.

"*Cofano*," he muttered and turned from the doorway.

I grabbed my bonnet as instructed and followed.

He took me on a rare outing that Sunday afternoon. It was our turn to have this particular time off, one so coveted by every servant in this gilded world. Every servant was allowed one evening and one afternoon off from work; my father rarely stopped working.

It was his apology, though I had to listen to the underneath of the silence to hear it.

Though my father rarely took days off as the rest of the staff did—on a regular, rotating, strictly followed schedule—there were a few times when we had ventured from the estate, mostly when something was happening my father deemed worthy—an historical re-enactment on the commons, a performance by the small orchestra Newport boasted. I'm still unsure what prevented him—something deep within him—from simply having fun.

I could still remember our days back in Foggia, when a festival filled the small piazza, burst its seams with music and laughter, food and wine.

My father would stand on the outskirts. Not alone, but with a few men of similar reserve, little more than a few words passing between them as we played and danced. Perhaps he simply loved to watch my mother, the beauty in the center who charmed us children, who danced with such grace her limbs moved with the same magical floating as her long, dark hair.

Yes, perhaps he wanted nothing more than to watch her, for his eyes hardly ever left her.

I accepted his apology in the same silence that he offered it.

PEARL

The summer was passing quickly, too quickly. I wanted more time, time with Ginevra under the beeches. Yes, her strangeness had infatuated me at first, but soon, very soon, it was our likeness that captured me, a deeper likeness that broke the boundaries of our shallow differences. I longed for our unique conversations, teaching her, learning from her. I blessed her presence in my life every time I snuck off to the carriage house loft. Thanks to her, my hands still knew the tingle when I held a brush. I still dreamed; it didn't matter that it was in secret.

The cottages on Newport took up but a small tip of the small island, and yet it was a whirlwind, a prevailing vortex that sucked us in, holding us there with its intangible but potent seizure. My youth did not exempt me from it. It had been days and days of events, days without any time with Ginevra, yet I dared not make excuses for not attending today's event. In truth, I was intrigued.

Alva Erskine Smith Vanderbilt, one of the leading ladies of Newport, one of three that formed a powerful trio that determined not only proper behavior but who would and would not be accepted into our world. She was a woman I took pains to avoid. Yet when Mother informed me that Mrs. Vanderbilt was hosting a party where a special speaker would attend—a speaker for women *and* young women—I was eager, for once, to accompany her.

I had been in Marble House before, yet it never failed to amaze me. Considered the most striking of all the cottages, Mrs. Vanderbilt reminded everyone whenever possible. I remember my father talking about it when we were in Paris, how it was modeled after the Petit Trianon of Versailles. I had heard others compare it to the White House or the Temple of Apollo as well. Regardless of its origins, it was the very essence of opulence and grandeur captured by the cottages of Newport.

As was Mrs. Vanderbilt herself. She dominated Newport society with willpower and boldness, not beauty or charm, for she possessed little of either. Frizzy mouse-brown hair sat atop a plump face, a round-ness matching her body, her bulbous nose turned up at the least provocation.

What she did have was a sophisticated French boarding school education and a lineage of southern aristocracy. She had been summering in Newport since before the Civil War; perhaps that's why she thought it belonged to her, and none of these Yankee newcomers. There were rumors about the hard times of her life, when her father lost his money, when her mother lost her life. A gruff exterior builds a great wall for shielding pain, for hiding it in a world where truths were so often hidden. What she also had was her husband, one of the richest men in the world.

Mother and I entered the Gold Ballroom, not the largest in New-port but by far the most ornate, to find every woman—young and old—of standing in attendance. The buzz of excited voices echoed off the carved gilt wall panels and huge painted ceiling.

"Well, how odd," Mother said sotto voce, whether to me or herself, I wasn't sure. "Alva is not greeting her guests."

She wasn't. Instead, the indomitable presence of Mrs. Vanderbilt stood grandly at the front of the room. Beside her, a very serious-looking woman, the speaker, no doubt. She wore a simple black dress, though corseted, it bore none of the frills and lace and embellishments *en vogue*. Even her hair spoke of her; it was not curled and piled but flattened and held back in a tight bun. I was already curious.

"Ladies, ladies, to order please." Mrs. Vanderbilt clapped her hands with a crack, her voice boomed over the twittering. Mother and I quickly sat in two of the sea of chairs, as did all the others. The room fell into an abyss of expectant silence.

"I'm so pleased to see you all here today," Mrs. Vanderbilt began. I almost laughed, as if we had a choice. When Alva Vanderbilt called, everyone answered, or they would know her chill for years to come. "And I am so proud to introduce you to a new friend of mine, Miss Lucy Stone."

As a small round of applause ensued, the serious woman stepped up beside Mrs. Vanderbilt.

"Miss Stone, here, is the first woman from Massachusetts to earn a college degree."

Lighting struck me; the tips of my fingers tingled. Mother released a huff. I sat up straighter.

"With others, she helped organize the first National Women's Rights Convention as well as the formation of the American Woman Suffrage Association," Mrs. Vanderbilt continued her introduction. My mother continued her mews of displeasure. "And she is a regular contributor to the *Woman's Journal*. You will all find a copy of the latest issue beneath your seats."

Like many, but not all, I reached quickly for the slim broadsheet beneath my chair as Miss Stone began to speak.

"Thank you, Alva." Miss Stone's voice was a whisper in comparison to her sponsor, yet most ears hung on every word. "And thank you all for coming today. I know there are some here that may not be receptive to the things I have to say. To those of you, I first want to say that I do believe that a woman's truest place is in a home, with a husband and with children. However, their lives should also include large freedom, pecuniary freedom, personal freedom, and the right to vote."

Murmurs of all sorts shuddered through the room. Lucy Stone was not daunted.

"Half a century ago women were at an infinite disadvantage in regard to their occupations. The idea that their sphere was at home, and only at home, was like a band of steel on society. But the spinning wheel and the loom, which had given employment to women, had been superseded by machinery, and something else had to take their places. The taking care of the house and children, and the family sewing, and teaching the little summer school at a dollar per week, could not supply the needs nor fill the aspirations of women. But every departure from these conceded things was met with the cry, 'You want to get out of your sphere,' or, 'To take women out of their sphere;' and that was to fly in the face of Providence, to unsex yourself in short, to be monstrous women, women who, while they orated in public, wanted men to rock the cradle and wash the dishes. We pleaded that whatever was fit to be done at all might with propriety be done by anybody who did it well; that the tools belonged to those who could use them; that the possession of a power presupposed a right to its use."

A few of the older women stood, their noses thrown into the air as they left the room. Mother pulled on my arm; I shook it off with a vengeance. Miss Stone continued without a care for those departing; clearly, it was not the first time she and her message had received such a reaction.

"We believe that personal independence and equal human rights can never be forfeited, except for crime; that marriage should be an equal and permanent partnership, and so recognized by law; that until it is so recognized, married partners should provide against the radical injustice of present laws, by every means in their power."

"We are leaving, Pearl, this minute. You should not hear this non-sense," Mother hissed at me as she stood, pinching my arm until I stood up beside her. She grabbed the journal in my hand and tossed it on the floor. I had no choice but to follow. The room was long, and we were at its front. It was impossible not to hear more as we made our way out.

"A wife should no more take her husband's name than he should hers. My name is my identity and must not be lost."

They say lightning never strikes the same place twice, yet I was once more struck. "My identity." The words followed me, came with me, stayed with me, as they would for years to come. Mother might have taken me from the woman's presence. She might have robbed me of the journal I so wanted to read—though I knew I would find a way to reclaim it. She may have tried to renounce all I had heard, insist I give it no credence as she did the whole ride home, but I gave no credence to my mother's words. That belonged to Lucy Stone and those of her ilk. I couldn't wait to share them all with Ginevra.

* * *

The footmen packed the line of carriages to overflowing. The high heat and humidity of August had given way to cooler nights and foggier mornings. It was time for us to leave. Last year, I packed my personal bag with a rush, hurried to the carriage. This year, I dallied and lingered.

I was eager to return to school, to regular studies of depth, unlike those of the irksome Miss Jameson. Yet the thought of not seeing Ginevra again for ten months tainted my eagerness. Our conversations beneath the beeches had only grown more intense after telling her of Lucy Stone, as we read the copies of the *Woman's Journal* I had had her purchase and secret away to our spot. We were Pearl and Ginevra, the same girls who had met beneath the beeches, but that Pearl and that Ginevra were no longer.

"Come along, Pearl," my mother called up the stairs to me. In the quiet already taking up its winter residence, I could hear the tap, tap, tap of her fancy shoes upon the marble floor of the foyer.

"Coming, Mother," I called out from my door, but instead of heading to the family stairs, I snuck across the hall, and into the sewing room.

I found her there, back to the door, standing at the window looking down at the carriages.

"It is time," was all she said.

I said nothing.

Without thought, I went to her and wrapped my arms around her waist. She put her arms around mine.

"Will you go the whole way in those?" She pointed down at the carriages, said 'those' as if they were something she despised. I suppose she did.

"No," I replied, though I smiled at how well she spoke, how far she had come in just our short time together. "We'll sail home on the steamer, out of Fall River."

Her brows crinkled as she looked back at me. "A falling river?"

I giggled. It made her smile, a little. "No, dear, Fall River. It is a town in Massachusetts, the next state from here. They have ships that go back and forth between New York and Newport. It is how all the men travel from week to week, back and forth."

"Ah," she said, nodding.

Ginevra turned. We faced each other.

"I am but a breath of time away. You'll see," I whispered.

I ran out, not from her, but our sadness.

GINEVRA

She was gone. Life became pale as the winter sun, marked by the dry, scraping sound of dead leaves as the wind rattled them along empty streets.

I kept busy. Only four of us stayed behind. The general caretaker, Bruce Grayson was a crabby and sullen man who saw to things such as the plumbing and the heating, as well as the grounds. Staying seemed to suit him just fine. He rarely strayed from his rooms in the carriage house, joining us only for meals, still sitting at the senior staff table, though he was the only one remaining.

Mrs. O'Brennan stayed behind, the middle-aged widow who, during the season, served as second to the chef. She cooked for us as well as taking on housekeeping chores, as did I. What there were of them.

At first, our days were a rush to return all to perfection, though the perfection would stand unnoticed, a woman dressed beautifully to stay in her room, unseen. We covered the furniture with yards and yards of white fabric. We shuttered the windows of all the family's rooms as if we closed our eyes to them, blocking out the sight of them.

As the winter stretched out, the months like years, I often snuck onto the family floors to walk about the ghosts, the beautiful furnishings and sculptures covered in their protective linens. I feared and worshipped them.

They were so like the ghosts in stories I read with Pearl, like those Charlotte Bronte wrote of in *Jane Eyre*. Yet they gave me hope, for their very presence insured that they—that she—would be coming back. Their company was far better than the silent sullenness of Mrs. O'Brennan.

She swept floors every day, one floor a day from bottom to top, and then started again. I helped her, dusting away the cobwebs. I helped with meals as well, and though we were side by side for many hours, an ocean lay between us, never to be crossed. She stayed within the emptiness of her life. Any attempts to bring her out of it was like trying to pull out a weed whose roots were buried far too deep in the ground.

I remember the day she was making tarts, delicious tarts I found irresistible, eating seconds even when my full belly told me not to.

"These is…are wonderful, Mrs. O'Brennan." I went and stood beside her by the nearly empty countertop. "Where you learn to cook so well?"

She kept on kneading the dough. "Here and there."

She might as well have not answered. I tried again.

"You from." I stopped, corrected myself, Pearl's voice in my ear. "Are you from here, Newport?"

Mrs. O'Brennan nodded. "A Rhody, born and raised."

"So, your family, they are here too?"

Her hands hesitated their manipulation. It was so quick I was lucky to see it.

"I've been in service to the Worthington's since I was a child," she said in an accent I had come to learn belonged to the people of this region. The "Rhody," a mixture of the English so many were descended from, but far less lyrical. "They are my family."

What a sad statement; what could I say in response? I said nothing. Nor did I try to talk with her again. I had made my attempt, told her I would be a companion, should she want one. I could do nothing more. Day after day, we spent side-by-side draped in silence as the cloths draped the furniture.

I continued my studies, reading with the thirst of a dried sponge, conjuring up headaches as I tried to improve my cyphering skills. I made great headway in the uninterrupted world that had become my life, with no Greta to grumble at me, no Mrs. Briggs and her reprimands.

Other servants, the others left behind in other cottages, came to visit now again. They talked much about the lives of their masters rather than their own lives.

There was so much rain. Minute drips clung to everything like a dotted web; colors—flowers, lush lawn, stone beauties—were a grayer shade of themselves. As was I.

Then came the snow. My father and I had never seen snow. I found an old coat in the carriage house, a man's far too big for me, but I put it on anyway and went out in it. It looked so different from how it felt. It looked like a layer of thick icing, but when I picked it up, it fluttered through my fingers. Yet, after a big storm hit, when the snow came up to my knees, walking through it was like walking through thick mud. I laughed every time I went out. It was one of the few joys of winter in Newport.

Once, I caught my father watching me. That once, I saw a real smile on his face.

When May hit, it hit like the storms of winter.

The house woke up. The same was true for all the cottages. Everywhere there was rushing in preparation for the return of the families. Such madness for four people, when a different four—the four of us—had been living so simply, without any fuss, for so long. Mrs. O'Brennan kept me busy from dawn to dusk and well after. The beds were made, fresh towels put on the racks, lampshades dusted. We freed the furniture from their slumber beneath the draperies.

In the final days before the Worthington's return, fresh flowers—purple hyacinths with their deeply floral scent...the prickly beautiful forsythia and their waxing aroma—filled every room in the house, bunches and bunches on every table, sometimes four or five to a room. Fresh fruit sat expectantly in bowls beneath. We polished everything to a glittering gleam.

I polished myself as well. For her.

PEARL
1896

Nothing had changed, and I had never been so grateful.

The hectic life in New York had pushed through the months with a fury. As I watched them flitter by, I felt nothing but gratitude.

The frantic activity of arrival erupted in the house on Bellevue. The staff brought in trunk after trunk, even their own, which they had to haul up to the hidden third floor.

I entered my room, breathed a sigh. Contentment awaited me in my pale green room with its silk linens and its pink accent lace. I sat primly while my trunks were brought in, while one of the chambermaids unpacked for me.

There was so much more to unpack this year. Just a few days away from turning seventeen, I put away forever the short pinafore dresses of a child with their sailor collars, and the plain bonnets, and now wore the long dresses of a woman. True, they weren't as adorned or as flamboyant as those of a true adult, a woman of eighteen who had had her coming out. Nor was I allowed to pin my hair up in the twisting, complication coifs so in vogue, but the long dresses brought me to the beginning of a crossroad, one that lay many divergent paths before me.

The chambermaid retreated. I counted her steps. As soon as they were gone, I made for the door, for her.

She was already there.

Ginevra's head poked out the frosted glass door separating the family quarters from those of the staff. On her face was the sweetest smile I had ever seen.

I rushed out my door, she out of hers. We threw ourselves together.

GINEVRA

With summer, she came, and my life filled with color. With her arrival, I leaned out to the floor forbidden to me, daring to bring the disapproval and scorn from the others below. I didn't care at all.

To feel Pearl's arms around me was as if to feel my mother's, one arm of tenderness, one of belonging.

"Come, let me show you my new gowns," she cried, her first words to me after she hugged me. I smelled her expensive perfume and hoped it would stick to me as the smoke of the kitchen always did.

There was no showing off in her showing, only the thrill of fashion we both shared. I inspected every garment, seeing the change in designs to the more-sporty looks I had studied all winter.

The postman had continued to deliver *Harper's Bazaar* to the cottage and there was no one to read them but me, no one to stop me from reading them. I had practically memorized the designs as I had the new words I discovered in the books I borrowed from Mr. Worthington's library.

Mrs. Worthington had her own library as well, but it was a children's library compared to that of her husband. Like many women of the day, she abided by the practice of separating the books by male and female authors, not allowing one to touch the other. That alone squashed any enthusiasm for the tomes I might have found there.

"They are beautiful, Pearl," I said. "And you will look even more beautiful than ever wearing them."

"Ginevra!" The dress in Pearl's hand fluttered to the ground; her head spun. "Your speech! You sound wonderful, almost American."

I glowed beneath her praise; a longed-for thing so absent in my life. We mirrored each other's smiles.

She hadn't changed much in our months apart. Pearl was a little taller, but then so was I. Her face had thinned. I could see a true change in it, a true glimpse of the woman she would become. I wondered if my face had changed in any way. The three people I had been alone with for all these months would not have told me if it had. My mirror showed me only what I thought I could—should—see.

"Thank you, Pearl. I am so very glad you are home." To her, this was her summer getaway. To me, it was her home as well as mine. "You should hear me read."

"I must," she chirped with delight, "right now. You know where we must go."

The beeches. I sighed.

In the months of spring, I had watched their spindly skeletons grow fuzzy with buds then burst with fluffy leaves. I imagined they grew thicker and thicker for us, to make our hiding place more hidden than ever. I never went, not even in the warmer months. Her absence there would have made her absence too complete.

"I...," I wanted to go there with her, more than anything. Such desire could not erase my truth. "Mrs. Briggs will—"

"Mrs. Briggs will be in a frightful tizzy," Pearl said, putting her gowns back in the splendid wardrobe of dark wood and white porcelain trimming. "Come," she insisted, grabbing my hand, pulling me through the house and out to the trees as she had the first time. She truly was home.

PEARL

My long dress tangled around my ankles, my feet stumbled and slipped, my balance tested.

"Now you know how it is for me," Ginevra giggled behind me as I struggled to hold on to my skirts and hold on to the tree. I laughed with her.

Ginevra read to me for a bit, astounding me with her progress, she barely faltered, and when she did, it was on words many Americans would stumble upon as well. She changed my opinion of her intellect to fact. She grasped our language quickly, making me laugh with her few bumbles and misses, for she laughed at them as well. How I loved people who could laugh at themselves.

She was my Ginevra, but she wasn't. She was a year older, yes, and her physical form had changed a bit: her cheekbones were so much more prominent as were her budding breasts. Her voice was different; it was no longer a whisper.

As we had made our way to our beeches, she didn't hide behind me, didn't seem to care about hiding, about slipping unnoticed through these trees, this life. Her eyes didn't dart about; she looked straight ahead. She was no longer a dog fearing its brutal master. It made her even more beautiful. All my life I've known women for whom another's beauty would make friendship impossible. I wondered how the footmen would look at her now.

"Oh!" The thought of Ginevra and men brought another thought, another something to share. "I met a boy, well, a young man."

Ginevra's smile ran up her face, into her almond-shaped eyes. "A boy?! Tell me, tell me everything."

I did. I told her how I had met Frederick Havemeyer at the opera.

"His mother is an Astor, so you can imagine how happy that makes my mother."

I laughed as Ginevra rolled her eyes.

He sought me out at other affairs, always chatting with me, asking me about school. He was a friend of my brother's and much like him.

I gave that little thought, for they seemed reserved for the strange feeling he wrought from the pit of my stomach, how shy I became in his presence.

"You, shy?" Ginevra squeaked. "I do not believe."

I dropped my chin though I grinned. "Well, he is four years older than I, a real young gentleman. He could have his pick of girls already out."

But he didn't. He chose to talk to me more than any of them. He crept into my thoughts far too often.

"He is here?" Ginevra asked with still a hint of her accent, its sound now exotic somehow. "Will you see him here, in Newport?"

I nodded, again dropping my chin, hiding the flush warming my face.

To speak of him gave flight to whatever it was that fluttered in my stomach so. "Oh, yes. His family has a lovely English cottage, right at the start of the Cliff Walk. I've heard it has the most amazing view."

"Perhaps you will get to see this view." Ginevra waggled her brows at me. I giggled.

"I think I will, I hope I will," It was my truth, and it was safe in her keeping.

Her open heart and mind opened my own. Friendships among the set were puddles, shallow and reflective of what lay only on the surface. Friendship with Ginevra was a deep ocean, full of exotic creatures and life, full of things to discover.

"The last time I saw him was at a musicale. Just before he left me, he leaned down," I leaned toward Ginevra as he had, my lips close to her ear. "He's very tall, very broad, with sparkling blue eyes beneath golden hair—and he whispered, 'I'll see you again, my dear, soon.' "

Ginevra sucked in her breath. It brought it all back with a hiccup of my own. I shivered as if I could still feel his warm breath on my skin. Never had a boy—a young man—affected me so. It felt much as it had when I put on my very first full-length dress.

I did not share the dreams of a pristine white wedding dress, of running a home, as did all my other friends. After listening to Lucy Stone, reading more of her articles, I knew there was the promise of more on the horizon. In his presence, I forgot all those words I had read.

I looked up. Her eyes were waiting for mine.

"Have you been reading *Women's Journal?*" she asked, quietly as if it were a sin.

I simply smiled, as did she. But then…

"Oh!" I cried as I pulled the folded and creased bit of newspaper from my pocket. "I know you didn't see this; you couldn't have, it was in the *New York Times.*"

Ginevra snatched it from my hands, ever hungry for more reading, for more news of the hurtling journey women seemed to be traveling. I read with her, leaning over her shoulder:

WOMEN CAST MOCK BALLOT

New York, Nov. 3—Women will today have their first opportunity to voice in New York. Of course, their votes will not be officially counted, but they will vote just the same.

The suffragettes have arranged for receiving ballot boxes and polling places in various theaters, and the suffragettes will have their own voting places.

"To vote?" Ginevra kept her gaze firmly upon the tatter of paper in her hands.

"Yes, Ginevra," I whispered, as one did in church. "To cast a vote is to decide which man will be president, or senator, which man the voter wants to make decisions on government issues. To vote is a right and a privilege only men have had." I tapped the paper in her hand. "If this continues, it may not be much longer until we get the same rights."

"Until we get to decide," she whispered as I did.

I nodded. Our eyes locked; together we looked at the future. "I have heard rumors that there may be a mock vote held here, right in New-port."

"Would you do it?" she asked me.

"Would you?"

"Yes," we answered together.

Her gaze dropped back to the powerful words immortalized on the paper. "It changes much," she said.

I shook my head, "It changes everything."

We chewed on that for a while, but it was like taking a small bite out of a feast for four hundred.

"Do you want to marry, Ginevra?" I asked her after a time.

She said not a word. She looked up. My gaze followed hers. The sun had reached its apex. Through the straggle that was the beeches' limbs, its form, bright warm rays scurried through the gaps, dappled our faces with its light. We both stared at the limitless sky.

"Yes, I think I do." Her eyes remained upon the sky; she shared a thing we see in the firmament.

"You think?" I prodded.

"I want children and a home. I want love, yes." She turned to me, her lovely features twisting; her thoughts, like mine, resembled the branches of our beeches. There are few thoughts that did not twist upon others. "It is what we are meant to do, *si?*"

I looked to the ground below us. Down there was where we lived; the sky was where we dreamed.

"Yes, it is what we are told we are meant to do."

Her head bobbed slowly. "The world, it shows us our, eh, path, yes? But what if we want another path or a wider path?"

"A wider path?"

"*Si*, I want a husband who loves me, children to care for, a house to call my own. But there is something in me that wants more. Something mine alone."

"Mine alone," I murmured. She was a thief skulking through my mind. We were of an impressionable age in an age of change, change especially for those our age. "If only there could be a man to love who would let us have such a thing." I looked at her dead on. "Do you think there is something wrong with us?"

Her face crinkled. "Wrong?"

I nodded with dispirit. "Yes, wrong. Is it wrong that we want other things than simply marriage and children? My mother says it's wrong, says these 'new women' are wrong."

Ginevra chewed on my words. Her gaze dotted my face, but I did not think it was my face she saw.

"It's no wrong, it's different," she said.

Ginevra raised her face to the crepuscular rays of the sun finding us through the patchwork of the beeches, brushing the long, thick chocolate hair from her face. She closed her eyes; her full lips had just the slightest upturn at their corners. Without moving, she spoke the truth, a hard, irrevocable truth, "Yes, different. It is a good thing, no? But I think we will pay for it anyway."

The changing way of life, of women, was a part of us, as we were a part of it; another tie that bound us. We would try to have it all, the "more" that itched at us, and love, just as Lucy Stone had said. Neither of us knew how we would, only that we had to try.

She took my hand. "To find such a man, a man that could support us, the true us, that would be the best, but I am no sure there are such men."

"Oh!" I cried, thinking of Frederick, wondering if he was such a man. I suddenly remembered I might see him that very afternoon. "I have to go. Mrs. Fish is throwing a party for Marion, her daughter. She's a few years younger than I, but it should be a wonderful party."

"Maybe he will be there," Ginevra said. Her eyes sparkled as the corners of her mouth twitched upward. She made my hope her own.

I took her hand.

"I'm so glad to be back with you." Truer words I had never spoken. She squeezed my hand and nodded.

"We will spend more time together this summer," I promised her. "It may be a struggle," I warned her. "Mother is fanatical about my push into society. She's obsessed with plans for my birthday party. But I will not let so many things take away from our time. It is too precious to me."

"And to me," Ginevra said softly. "But you are right, it may be hard. I saw Mrs. Briggs for a few minutes earlier. She made it clear she will work me to the bone. Your seamstress in New York, she was no good?"

"She was fair," I answered truthfully. My first long dresses had been purchased from the House of Worth. Englishman Charles Worth had become a couture phenomenon in Napoleon Paris. Anyone who was anyone wore his clothes. Any alternations, any repairs, were left to the woman's seamstress.

"Mrs. Briggs said she was not, eh, up to standards."

My eyes bulged. "What a wonderful compliment."

Ginevra stared at me; one brow raised in silly cynicism. Oh, how I had missed her.

"Don't you see? She was implying, though I'm sure she would cut out her tongue if she knew she did so, it was *your* standards the girl in New York couldn't live up to."

Ginevra's eyes flew open, blinked rapidly. Her small smile was a gift I had not received in far too long.

A thought—a seed—was planted in my mind then. I sniffed a laugh as it grew.

"There may be a way we can see each other more." I leaned over and planted a kiss on her smooth cheek. I picked up my skirts and made my way down. "I shall see you soon."

I hurried away before she could ask the questions writ upon her face. I left her in perplexity, shrouded in my mysterious words. I would say no more, not until I was sure.

GINEVRA

I returned to the house, made my way to my room to change before dinner. Try though I might, I could not seem to force the corners of my mouth downward. They dropped as I walked in the door.

There was Greta returned once more, once more to share the room I had had all to myself for so many months. She hadn't changed. Her freckled face still pinched with displeasure at the sight of me.

"Oh," she said, "it's you."

"It is me," I said, pleased to see her surprise at my diction, "and it is you. We are together again. But no worry, I do most of my reading out there now."

I pointed to the small landing between our window and the inside of the false outer wall.

As winter had warmed to spring, I had found myself there more and more. I had seen many of the staff do the same last summer but had never found the courage to go myself. With them gone, I had made it mine as well. Sometimes I climbed out the window instead of using the door at the far end of the hall. I followed the sun around the landing as it made its way up and over the house, like a flower following its glowing warmth. I couldn't see over the false wall; it was taller than I was. The sun and the tops of the trees and the smell of the ocean, those found me. Contented by their company, I would sit and read, and pretend I was back in Italy. It was a place almost as dear as the place beneath the beeches.

Greta laughed her mean laugh, shook her head at me. "Still reading. Whatcha' doin' all that readin' for? Ye don' need it sewing buttons."

I didn't answer. My words would be as lost in her mind as a guppy is in the ocean. I could think only of what Pearl's last words could mean.

PEARL

The day was so extraordinary fair, so warm and brilliant with sunshine, the non-conformist that was Mrs. Mamie Fish, decided to stage her daughter's party on the front lawn of Crossways, a Colonial-style mansion overlooking the harbor. How her peers had teased her, in their biting way, for not building on the more fashionable Bellevue Avenue rather than on the west side of the tip of the island, on Ocean Avenue.

"We're not rich, pet," she called a lot of people "pet," mostly because she was terrible at remembering names, "we only have a few million." It was a statement only one of the great trio of women could make. Women, who, besides Mrs. Astor, sat at the top of the social pyramid of this life defined by where one sat.

As soon as we arrived, my mother swiftly ran off to find our hostess, to kowtow, to praise. She should have just begged; it would have been faster for the truth to find her.

I should have done the same, simply greeting Mrs. Fish, but I didn't. Nor did I seek out any of my acquaintances, not even Consuelo, my true friend among a set of those who pretended to be. My eyes scanned the jubilant crowd for Frederick and none other. I needed to see him, his true self, removing the blinders attached to me since birth. I did not know how often I wore those blinders were it not for my conversations with Ginevra. Frederick was everything my mother would wish for me. That thought alone made me question my own.

The crowd of people milling about the lawn, dapper in their frothy day dresses and striped blazers, was in fine spirits. The sun here was different from in the city; its glow and warmth penetrated deeper, finding the us deep inside, the us that hid behind heavy coats of pretension and pomposity. The smell of the ocean and the sound of waves crashing on shore infused us with their potent energy. The rules of our lives didn't change, but the happiness to be in this remarkable place changed how we lived within them.

I wandered about, merrily returning the many merry greetings cast my way, looking, always looking. Just when I had given up hope, there he was. He looked even more dashing in his casual navy-blue sack coat and striped pants, his white shirt, collar pressed pristinely down over the matching navy tie. His blue eyes blazed beneath his straw boater.

He saw me then, too. His roving eyes passed me, returned, and stopped on me, stopped and smiled. He offered me a wink and, once more, my stomach tumbled, like the children tumbling down the hill of grass.

In a circle of other such young, dashing men, including my brother, his hands flew, his lips turned up and down as the surf came in and out, his laughter joined theirs as it crashed onshore. Frederick could have been any of the others he stood with; perhaps he wasn't or perhaps that was simply a wish.

Another within this circle, a handsome one I had to admit, locked his gaze upon me as well. I could not hear his voice, though I saw his lips move, nor could I hear his laughter though his head tipped back with the boisterousness of it. His clothes, clearly expensive, did not flash as the others did. His was not a gaze I had experienced before. I pulled from it, its unfathomable hold upon me, demurely nodding my head at Frederick—hoping it was demure—letting him know, without a word, I would be waiting when he could detach himself.

I could dally no longer; it was time I paid my respects to my hostess. Mother would hunt me down if I did not do so soon. I made my way to the front of the house.

There they sat, the three who would one day be known as the Great Triumvirate.

Like queens on three high-backed cane chairs, they perched and possessed the shade beneath the front portico held aloft by four giant Corinthian columns, their pastel afternoon dresses vivid against the pure white house.

Alva Vanderbilt sat in the center, for she was the core of them.

As I approached, my steps growing shorter the closer I crept, I remembered Mother's drilling of how, and how not, to address Mamie

Fish. She would oust anyone who said, "pleased to meet you," instead of "how do you do," "pardon me" instead of "I beg your pardon," or "I presume" instead of "I suppose." Those who faltered would never step a foot near Crossways again.

I was only a few of those steps away from them when I heard her voice—her low, raspy sort of voice—speak my name. It was a closed door that magically appeared, stopped me cold. I turned my back, not taking a single step away.

"I see the Worthington girl is here, Pearl, I believe it is," Mrs. Vanderbilt said in that practiced tone of hers; it was both flat and haughty. Did she really think I couldn't hear her though I was only a few steps away? Or did she think herself so above me it didn't matter?

"Yes, she is. As well as her brother." Marion Graves Anthon Fish—known to those whom she allowed as Mamie—cast her sharp, deep eyes set in her long, dour face about. "Just there."

She was the strangest of the three, I thought. At times her behavior bordered on the outrageous, kicking sand in the face of the milieu in which she surrounded herself, yet known for the most innovative and extravagant of parties. Her balls and dinners were often the highlights of the season, and yet she deigned the whirl of teas, card-calling, coaching parades, operas, and musicales that were so much a part of this life. A true dichotomous personality, though perhaps I think there were other words for it, words not so polite.

Her rudimentary upbringing and limited education resounded in every one of her, "Howdy-do, howdy-do", her favorite greeting. Yet her ambition was a force to be reckoned with—that few dared reckon with—determined to not only reach social prominence but to rule it, all the while appearing as if she detested it. There were many faces to Mamie Fish, as they were to most who summered in Newport. They exchanged them as they did calling cards.

I often heard my father talking to Mr. Fish—Mr. Stuyvesant Fish—calling him an angel. For all of Mamie's outward acrimony, theirs was a love match, one that endured, as he endured, her fluctuating moods with patience and unruffled manners.

Mrs. Fish, however, was best known for her mouth, not its beauty or what she put it in, but what came out of it. My mother had actually heard her call Alva Vanderbilt a toad once, but that was the least of it.

We had been in the receiving line of one of her parties once, and I had heard her sharp tongue for myself.

"Make yourselves at home," she told the couple entering before us, "and believe me, there is no one who wishes you were there more than I do."

I shuddered to imagine her turning that tongue upon me. I held my breath as I waited for the next words.

"You surprise me, Mamie." Mrs. Vanderbilt sipped her lemonade without a sound.

"Well, yes, I suppose it would surprise you," Mrs. Fish's cackle dripped with the same sarcastic tone. "But they are dear children. My Marion adores Pearl so. And their father is utterly mahvelous."

"Oh, I agree wholeheartedly about Mr. Worthington," Mrs. Oelrichs, the final point in the triangle, said her piece. "His war record, his quiet grace, his intelligence. Yes, a wonderful man is our Mr. Worthington."

Of the three, Mrs. Herman Oelrichs, formerly known as Theresa Fair, called Tessie by most, had the most mundane heritage of the triumvirate. While she was now mistress of one of the grandest cottages on the island—Rosecliff—she was born in a California mining camp, the daughter of an Irish immigrant, an immigrant who made millions at Comstock, the famous silver mine. The man who made the American dream come true was also a debauched womanizer. When Tessie's mother divorced him, though a scandal, it was the best thing that could have happened for Tessie and her husband Herman, son of a wealthy German shipping magnate.

One of her brothers had committed suicide, another—with his wife—perishing in a high-speed accident in Paris. Tessie and her sister inherited their father's fortune. They purchased Rosecliff just a few years ago. Herman Oelrichs was more than happy to let her. He was also more than happy to let her have her full social life; he had his own. It was lively but far from public. They performed their pretense of intimacy with a skill worthy of any Shakespearean actor.

Tessie had married a man much like her father. Many wondered if she filled her bed with others as well and as often as her husband did, for she was the beauty of the group, a classic Irish beauty, crowned by regal grace. Hers was a true hourglass figure, with or without a corset, displayed to perfection beneath her huge hats and lace dresses, her creamy skin, and luxuriously thick chestnut hair.

"Yes, yes, yes, Mr. Worthington can be all that, but he can be such a bore," Mrs. Vanderbilt vomited cutting words as she so often did, never once stopping to wipe her mouth. "A gracious bore, I will give you that. But that...that woman."

As if suddenly struck with the same illness, the triumvirate groaned as one.

"She is so, so very...crass," Mrs. Oelrichs struggled, but not more than I did. It was hard enough to hear them call my father a bore, no matter the other things they said of him. I knew anything they said of my mother, "that woman" as they called her, would be scathing. For all my own condemnation of my mother, I loathed hearing these women speak of her so poorly. Only I could, for she was my mother.

"She must have read every one of those silly how-to guides and puts on a ghastly performance of their suggestions," Mrs. Fish pursed her lips, looking heavenward for salvation from my mother and her antics.

"And all at once," Mrs. Vanderbilt quipped, chortling with amused condemnation. "Did you see her the other night in New York, when she twirled her parasol, fluttered her fan, and dipped her hat, all at the same time?"

"Or tried to," Mrs. Oelrichs chimed in on the demolition of my mother merrily. "And the way she throws herself at young men. A horrible flirt."

"Are you sure all she does is flirt?" Mrs. Fish's dribbled snidely.

"Deplorable, simply deplorable," Mrs. Oelrichs muttered as a snake hissed and lashed out its venom. Perhaps she had cause.

"You can put a jeweled gown on a dead body," Mrs. Fish suggested, "but it doesn't mean it isn't a corpse."

Mrs. Oelrichs tittered into her cup. "We shan't be taking her up then?"

Mrs. Vanderbilt slapped the small white wicker table before them with a gloved hand. "Honestly, Tessie, must you even question it?"

"No." Tessie hung her head a bit, but just a bit. "But what of Mr. Worthington and the children?"

"Humph." Mrs. Fish clearly deplored her friend's obvious mixed feelings. "Well, we won't shut them out. Stu would be furious with me. Mr. Worthington is one of the few he truly enjoys. We shall simply have to tolerate the hen for the rest of the coop."

"More like a crow," Mrs. Astor said. The women applauded her with the scandalized laughter she craved.

I had heard enough; I heard too much, no matter who these women were. I spun round and stabbed her with the disgust fuming inside me. If she saw it, she gave no sign. I walked away, my back ramrod straight, just as Mother had taught me.

* * *

We returned home at teatime and the four of us sat in the wicker chairs of the Conservatory, almost as still and stony as the nine statues perched in the sunroom, their hard grace somehow apropos in the full windowed walls and the delicate lace curtains. I sat with my back to the view. I could see it just as well in the two mirrors on the inner wall, mirrors reflecting the panoramic vista of the yard. The reflection of the four of us stripped us of our social disguises.

Anger still seethed in me, pumped by the women's words that echoed in my head as if it were an empty cave. Though I had spent some time in Frederick's company, my good manners, and whatever acumen of flirtation I possessed at the time, were as flimsy and elusive as a single layer of chiffon. Or perhaps it was his friend who joined us, Butterworth his name was. How off-kilter his presence made me;

he was so unlike the other young men. Perhaps something within me knew, even then.

As I sat and sipped my tea in the awful silence that was a family fractured by more than just actions, but philosophies, I realized the true source of my anger was not the pretentious women or even their words, but the truth of their words. Mother was everything she shouldn't be, didn't need to be, in the abundant world we lived in. She could have simply enjoyed it with gratitude. She never did. That truth both grieved and strengthened.

"I would like Ginevra to become my personal maid."

My declaration shattered the silence as if I had hurled a rock through one of the windows.

My brother's laughter broke the silence.

I gave him a look that was as good as a slap.

"You're serious?" he sputtered.

"I am."

"You are not," my mother said, no, she declared.

"I truly am, Mother." I heard it; the disrespect emblazoned in my words. "You said yourself as we were leaving New York that it was time I had a maid of my own. Ginevra is the perfect choice. She knows all about fashion, is a wiz with her needle, and she's quiet and lovely and polite." Which was more than could be said for the catty, self-important Nettie, my mother's maid. Ginevra had told me all about her, her true self below stairs, how Nettie told all my mother's secrets, laughing about them with Mrs. O'Brennan and Mrs. Briggs. Ginevra would cherish my secrets as if they were her own, the very best feature for a lady's maid.

"It ish ridiculusss." Mother slurred her words. It was only teatime, but I knew, as did we all, she was half-rats already, as she was so very often, more often of late, earlier and earlier.

"It is not." I put my cup down, sat up straighter. "Mrs. Briggs herself acknowledges Ginevra's talent. She said so. She told Ginevra her work was better than Agnes's." The sloppy seamstress in New York.

"I will not have—" my mother began.

"Perhaps she is right for you, my Pearl."

My father spoke, spoke against my mother's wishes. I could have jumped up and thrown my arms around him. Could have, if such a thing was done in our family, in our gilded cages.

"Her father is one of the hardest workers I have ever known. His talent is beyond compare. Don't you agree, Clarence?"

My brother looked up, caught in a rabbit trap. His shoulders dropped, shrugged. "Actually, I do."

"Clarence!" my mother snapped. He had always taken her side, no matter the topic. Her face blanched beneath her fine powder.

"It's true, Mother," Clarence continued, slouching in his chair with the arrogant indifference that was a daily part of his wardrobe. "The violin he made me is quite something. And his teaching, well, it has actually made me want to learn—to play better."

My mother's mouth opened; nothing came out. A miracle.

"She has the right look for the job," Father continued, touching on Ginevra's beauty, a must for a lady's maid in a world where beauty is the greatest of all attributes. "And I know she is well educated, and well-read."

I bit my lip. He knew of Ginevra's education and literacy; knew I had given it to her. Our secret was safe in his keeping.

"Mr. Birch?" my father called out.

Birch stood just outside the door, always there, always listening. With but three steps, he stood in the Conservatory threshold.

"Please ask Mrs. Briggs to join us," my father requested of him.

"Right away, Sir." Birch bowed out of the room.

"You cannot allow thish, Orin," Mother whined at him, her head, grown heavy, slumped into the cup of one palm. "What will they say?"

The omnipotent "they;" the aristocratic, snobby "they." "They" were always there, always defining who and what we were. "They" were far too elusive, far too "them," for me to ever care what they thought.

"I *am* allowing it, Millicent." My father turned his full face to my mother. He looked at her as I imagined he must have looked on the battlefield.

"But Orin—"

"You called for me, Sir." Mrs. Briggs entered the room, dashing away my mother's tantrum, delaying it. Her dark storm clouds hovered over the horizon, drawing ever near.

"Ah, Mrs. Briggs, thank you for coming." My father greeted her respectfully. I wondered if he knew her true nature would he be as generous. "It's been decided my daughter is of the age where she needs a personal maid."

Mrs. Briggs nodded; she took the news in stride. "I'll make inquiries."

"No need." Father waved a hand. "It has also been decided that Ginevra will be promoted to the position."

"Ginevra!" The mask dropped; the true Mrs. Briggs revealed. "Ya cannot be—"

"It's been decided." My father stopped her; respect replaced with undeniable demand simply with the drop in his voice.

"But... but the girl knows nothing about being a lady's maid," Mrs. Briggs argued, though now she sputtered softly.

"Well then," I chirped like a bird gifted with a worm, "we shall have something in common, as I have never had one. We will learn together."

Father bestowed a pleased glance upon me.

"Have Nettie give her some speedy lessons," Father said. "From what I hear she is a bright girl, like her father no doubt, she will learn quickly."

"But... "

"That will be all, Mrs. Briggs, thank you," my father dismissed her swiftly but with his understated politeness ever at hand.

"Yes, sir." She left, but not without a backward glance at my mother, each face replicated the other's frustration.

"Orin, this is simply madness." As soon as the housekeeper was a foot out the door, my mother's storm came crashing in. On unsteady feet now, she stamped her foot, hands fisted by her side, shoulders pitching.

Who is the child now, I thought.

"She is from below stairs," she derided as if Ginevra came from the bowels of the earth.

Somehow, through lips pulled thin, a jaw clenched painfully, I corrected her.

"She is from Italy."

I did then what I should have done the rest of my life, to her and the way of life she championed to the point of cruelty. I turned my back on her.

GINEVRA

It was hard to remember a happier day, though I knew there were some, back before mama died. Their memories skirted my mind, tickled my dreams, sprinkled themselves throughout my days as salt is at a long meal.

This was the happiest day I could remember in this new world.

When Pearl told me what her plan had been, told me her father encouraged it, told me the truth of the change of my life, it was like a Christmas morn when I was still a child.

"You won't feel...strange?" Pearl asked me, eyes lowered as she twisted the ribbons that circled her small waist. "Well—serving me—will you? I want to give you some freedom, less drudgery, but I don't want our friendship to change."

Fondness turned to love then, as it would remain. I imagined why she would have such a concern, but it lived only in her imagination.

"I won't be serving you," I bubbled, smile so wide my face hurt, "I'll be helping you, as you have helped me."

Her gaze flicked up; it sparkled even as her shoulders slumped, as she expelled a breath so hard, she must have trapped it tightly.

Such feelings did not belong to Mrs. Briggs; I could practically see the smoke from the fumes of her fire when she confirmed the authorization of my new appointment from Mr. Worthington, when she showed me my new room—my private room.

It was more than a room. It was the key that unlocked the door to me, a door I had shut tightly, to all others save Pearl.

I could decorate it and arrange it in any way I wanted. I could read all night without any bitter words and huffs of frustration from someone else. As I took ownership of the room, I took ownership of a portion of my life lost to me since we walked through the grand doors of The Beeches.

Carrying the last armful of my possessions, a few more now than when I had arrived, I turned back to Greta staring with fire in her eyes at my back. I brushed her off as I did the heat off my back.

"Bye-bye." I trilled my fingers at her, speaking in that singsong tone of superiority she had used so often on me.

I barely had time to finish putting my clothes away when Nettie came for me.

"Come along wich ya' then." Such words said more than their true intent; they told me whose side she was on, not that I expected her to be any different.

I smirked away her disdainful displeasure. Though they may try, nothing she, Mrs. Briggs, or anyone could do to dump water on my flames of joy.

Nettie hurried me to the family side of the house. I walked tall and smart in my new uniform with the ruffled blouse at collar and cuffs, and a new skirt, not one worn by another before.

"Ya' will wake the young mistress every morn', bringin' her breakfast upon a tray. Also in the morning, you will treat her skin with the proper creams, as well as her hair. It is your job to see to her beauty, do ya' understand me? I amn't gonna' be telling ya' all tis agin." I nodded, followed her, her instruction, but not so much that I did not notice the change in her speech; she was Nettie from Ireland below stairs, the maid to the mistress above. Which one was real? "Pearl will need to change five or six times, depending on whether there's a ball or a banquet. Our women, even if they be young ones, must adhere strictly to the right dress for the right moment of the day."

Nettie talked fast and walked fast, but not too fast. I kept up, easily. Her lips thinned; her voice sliced. I nodded with a small smile. I would chide myself later for my enjoyment of her annoyance.

"Pearl will have a dress for morning calls, for receiving calls, for visiting, and for being visited. There are morning street dresses, at home morning dresses, riding dresses," she stopped to huff. "Now tere are those new walking suits," she was as displeased with the new fashion as she was me. "There are their evening dresses, those for home, for a dinner party, a ball, the opera..."

I stopped listening. I knew all about all these dresses, had been studying all about them throughout the long, cold, lonely winter. To help my dear Pearl into each and every one of them would please us both. I would get to wear them in spirit as I longed to do in life.

* * *

They all stopped talking as soon as I entered the servants' dining room. They may as well have put up signs, some would read angry, others disgust, many envy.

I held my head high as I took my seat beside my father.

"What is happening," he whispered to me in Italian between bites of his watery stew. "I hear them speak your name, over and over."

I leaned toward him. In our language, I told him, everything. The look he gave was not the one I expected. He would disapprove. He would tell me my grasp was further than my reach. He did none of those things.

My papa put down his spoon and sat back in his chair. He stared at me for a long time, or so it felt to me. He stared at me as if he didn't really know me, but as someone he would like to know.

He reached out his hand, took mine in it, and gave it a squeeze, a hard squeeze saying all he couldn't, all he didn't know how to say. My heart fluttered as I blinked back tears.

When Papa let go, I almost reached out to hold his hand again, longer, more. I didn't; I couldn't. I would hold the feel of my hand in his, in that moment, in that way, for the rest of my life.

We took up our spoons and ate our dinner.

The rest of the staff resumed talking, forced talk of unimportant topics. As they began to finish and scatter, to return to work or their evening off, I lingered. It was a meal to savor. Yes, the beef was a bit tough, the broth thin and a bit tasteless, but it was the finest meal I had had in this house, as I sat there in my new uniform, as I lived in the skin of one who would better herself. It was a comfortable fit.

My father gave my shoulder a quick pat as he left me. Most of my other fellow domestics passed me without a word, save for three.

"Good fer ya', gel," Mrs. Brown said, she didn't whisper, as her large form bumped my chair.

"Thank you," I said, thanking her for more than her words.

"Congratulations, Ginevra."

I turned, surprised.

Charlie, the second footman, stood in the doorway. His pleasure for me, clear on his freckled pale face beneath his slicked-back red hair, shone brightly with sincerity. I had denied his flirtations, both this year and last. Yet he stood there, happy for me as few were. He was a better man than I thought.

"Thank you, Charlie," I beamed. "Thank you very much."

He tipped his head and left. I smiled into my bowl.

"Don't be so pleased with yourself." Mrs. Briggs, the last to leave the room, was the last to speak to me. "You ah far too friendly with the young mistress already. Why do you think so few of the others like you?"

I let her talk. I kept eating. She would not sour the meal I ate upon with such relish.

"Don't be acting as if you ah too good for them. I'm warning you," she bristled and huffed off.

I may not be too good for them, or most of them, I thought, wishing I could say the words to Mrs. Briggs' face, *but I know I am far better than someone like you.*

* * *

We laughed loud and often—that first night as I helped her dress, helped her with her hair, getting ready for an intimate dinner party at the home of the Langdon's—laughter filled the room as surely as her expensive perfume.

"We must stop," I sputtered, nearly doubled over in laughter. "Your mother will anger at our fun."

"Oh, let her fuss," Pearl dismissed as I buttoned her long cuffs trimmed with just an edging of delicate lace. "I've never been happier, thanks to you."

I gave a tug on a strand of her long hair. She only laughed more.

We picked out her jewelry, just a ring and small earrings suitable for her age, and we completed her ensemble, my first creation.

She stood before the long pedestal mirror; her eyes moved up and down and back again. "Ginevra, you're a genius. I never would have thought to put the purple ribbon round my waist. It works perfectly with the dress."

It did. It set off the yellow silk and her creamy skin to perfection.

"It works because you are so lovely," I said, and she was, in part thanks to my work, but that I would keep as a gift to myself.

Pearl preened as I gathered the discarded clothes from the afternoon, the mess of hosiery and undergarments. As I whirled round. A glimpse caught me, froze me before the windows of Pearl's room. There, in the distance, the Newport Harbor glistened as if diamonds floated on the surface.

PEARL

"You can't see it from your room, can you?"

Ginevra spoke not a word. Her gaze remained upon the vista.

"Can you?"

Ginevra shook her head.

"My father didn't mean to do it, you know. He didn't mean for there to be no windows up there. The architect, well, he thought it brilliant," I rushed to defend my father. Someone had to. I always would. "And my father, well, my father is sometimes too far in his own thoughts...I don't think he realized."

"No to worry," Ginevra turned, the smile on her face one she put there, not one that came to her, a trace of her accent slipping through on the crest of emotion. "I can come here now, to see you and it."

"You know," I said, suddenly remembering, knowing the happiness it would bring her, "as my personal maid, you may have my dresses considered out of style and unwearable in society."

Ginevra's dark eyes gleamed. "Dresses? For me?"

"Oh yes." I ran to my wardrobe and pulled out a few garments worn last summer, or lighter ones worn through the winter season in New York. No more than a year old, they would be deemed out of style. A green and white striped dress with a high lace collar and short cuffs, a lovely yellow polka dot number with a box pleat skirt and an apron drape all trimmed in black silk. I pulled them out, one after the other, and threw them on my bed.

"They're all yours if you want them," I said. I turned.

Ginevra had not moved an inch, not made a peep.

"Do you want them?"

Ginevra didn't answer me, not with words. She ran to the bed and scooped them up in her arms as if they were a newborn babe. She held them close, an embrace, one she pulled me into. Simple words of gratitude fell short. I didn't need them.

"Don't let anyone take them from you, Ginevra." I knew the realization of what I had done, making her my maid, was not all good, there would be a price to pay, perhaps for both of us. She had overcome so many obstacles since we first met; I knew that in raising her up, I had raised more of them up as well. My teeth bit upon themselves; what kind of world was it where a young woman bettering herself would be looked down upon, by many, too many?

"Don't let them take any of this away from you."

* * *

Ginevra bustled about my room, putting away discarded dresses, unused hairpieces.

"Leave that, Ginevra," I impatiently instructed. "It is not your job, and we must go."

Her brows flew up her face so fast I thought they would fly right off.

"We?" she squeaked, a hand upon her chest.

"Of course, we, silly." I took her by the shoulders, patting the tips of her collar down, tucking in the back of her shirt. "You are my personal maid. You must accompany me should I have need of you."

She hadn't moved. "What do I do?"

"There will be a room, not far from the ballroom or the dining room or wherever the party is anchored." I shrugged. "And you will wait."

"Wait?" Her head cocked to the side. "Wait for what?"

I tapped my foot. I saw a discussion between Nettie and me in the near future. This was for her to have told.

I heaved a breath, expelling my frustration at Nettie before Ginevra thought it belonged to her.

"Me, Ginevra. You will wait for me. In case I need you to fix my dress should I spill on it, should a heel catch and rip it."

I had seen the maids often, crowding in a small room, all dressed in black, a murder of crows. I had rarely seen them do anything.

What I saw was Ginevra's creamy skin blenched, her fingers tied and knotted themselves. I took them in my hand; I freed them.

"It will be the most tedious time you've ever had. It is very rare that something happens." My words prodded; I saw a crow now as a dove.

"I'm sorry, Ginevra, you should have been told about this. I am sorry it will be so very boring for you."

Her stoic face cracked like the shell of an egg. Ginevra rushed to the mirror, pushing back any loose strands back into her bun. Satisfied, she returned to my side.

"Not boring," she preened, "I am going to a party."

We left my room, our laughing trailing behind.

We didn't get far. Mother waited on the stair landing.

Her hard eyes racked every inch of me, searching, hoping, for something to criticize. She found nothing to bite on. She bit herself with such ire, ate away whatever softness lay deep inside if there was any left.

"You must watch your behavior with your maid," she sniped, not speaking Ginevra's name as if Ginevra didn't have one or Mother didn't know it, as if Ginevra weren't but a few steps behind us. "They will call her a parvenu, the other servants will, mark my words. What they will call you, the servants, our friends, will be much worse. I will not have it."

"I really don't care what they call me, not below stairs or anywhere else," I assured her, echoes of her own nasty determination, locking my eyes firmly with hers. "Ginevra is my friend as well as my maid. If they cannot deal with it, it is their problem and yours, not mine."

With that, I walked away from my mother, frozen on the wide landing of the wide white marble stairs, Ginevra just a few steps behind. The late evening sun, streaming its tangerine rays through the high arched windows, fell into the cracks beginning to show on Mother's face. I knew I would paint them one day.

"Come along, Mother, we mustn't be late," I called back to her. I bit my lips together before my laugh could wiggle out of them.

GINEVRA

We looked so similar; we were faceless. Dressed alike, no one could tell one from the other. It was the way "they" preferred us to be, a necessity in their lives but not in possession of lives of our own.

It did little to spoil the newness of this experience for me. I had never watched them, them all together as they were now, this closely ever before. In the watching, "they" became simply "them."

From the small hidden room just off the cloakroom, I could see them nodding to each other in the same way, walking the same, talking the same. I never knew so many words could mean so little. They laughed the same, as practiced as any performance, save for Pearl's mother. She had an array of laughter; which one she bellowed through the room seemed to depend on the sex of the person igniting it. Each held different notes; few were not off-key.

It did not take me long to become, if not bored as Pearl had warned, at least unimpressed. I watched Pearl instead. Her added flair, that I gave her with my touches upon her clothes, that came from within her, radiated about her as if the sun shone forever upon her back. She smiled wider when she gave someone her real smile. She walked fluidly, not as if her back was flat to the wall.

I knew her eyes as well as I did my own. I knew that though they latched here and there, they did not find what she sought. I did not know what he looked like, but I knew who she looked for.

As Pearl made her way out onto the porch that wrapped itself about the house like a comforting blanket, my gaze followed her through the windows. As her path led her off the porch and onto the backyard, my link to her broke. I was a seamstress intent upon repair.

"Come back here," one of the faceless others hissed at me as I slipped to the threshold of our cubby, as I set one foot out of it.

"I thought my mistress waved me to her," I lied.

I did not go far, but two more steps, just enough to see through the ballroom instead of into it, to see the backyard through the back windows.

There she was, glowing in the marching dawn, still looking.

"Do you know who she looks for?"

I gasped, clamped my hand upon my mouth. The man's voice poked me sharp and quick like the needles I plied, a needle with a high dose of masculinity.

With my hand still upon my mouth, my gaze sidled away, finding a pristine white shirt and perfectly knotted tie.

I raised my gaze to find his, the color of a glittering jewel.

I moved my hand away, wiping the sweat upon my skirt.

Full lips twitched.

"You are her maid, are you not? Pearl Worthington's maid?"

He knew me for what I was and how I was, but his kindness remained.

"Yes. I am, yes." I finally managed, knotting my hands behind my back.

His chin ticked ever so slightly at my accent. That and nothing else.

"Well then, do you know who she is looking for?"

I did not know if this was 'the' Frederick. If I spoke his name to him, it would not do well for Pearl. If it was not, I would reveal her secret, those I kept as well as my own.

"I no kno..." I cleared my throat of its bad grammar with a cough. "I do not know."

He sniffed as he smiled. I did not fake my lack of knowledge well.

"Then perhaps I shall have to go and find out for myself," he said.

"As you wish, Sir." I gave a bob of my head. When I looked up, he stood beside me still.

The edges of his face rounded; he looked at me for me.

"Why is it the most beautiful girls have the most beautiful maids?"

Did I suddenly stop understanding English? Did he really just say I was beautiful?

I hoped he had. I hoped he was not Frederick.

With a nod of a dark-haired head and a jaunty smile, he left me.

PEARL

It wasn't a largely attended affair. There were only about one hundred of us at the modest mansion, Gravel Court, of George Tiffany and his wife, Isabella. It was one of those sedate, family affairs, the kind my mother detested, and I thoroughly enjoyed. Good, but not overly rich food accompanied by quiet, sincere conversation. Peaceful.

Yet I wanted more. Not the more my mother wanted, but a more that surprised me.

As I strolled about the Italianate villa, in and out again, along the porches festooned with merry guests, down the lush, rolling humps of lawn, this "new woman" searched for a man. I searched for Frederick, longing for his eyes to see me so splendidly attired, longing for the look in his eyes when he did. With each step I took, discontent darkened me as the setting sun did all of Newport.

"You look splendid, Miss Worthington."

I whirled at words snatched from my mind. I caught my face before surprise and more disenchantment ran off with it.

"Thank you, Mr...?" How dreadful I was for forgetting his name. He seemed to hover on the outskirts of everywhere these past few days.

Full lips turned up at one corner, the corners of his eyes crinkled. I had to raise my eyes to find his. When I did, I found the most distinctive brown eyes I had ever seen, warm and amber, like Father's brandy. "Butterworth. I am Herbert Butterworth, we met at—"

"At Crossways, yes, of course, I remember you, Mr. Butterworth," I reassured him and myself. Could one handsome face truly make all others invisible?

He bowed slightly as some gentlemen still did with enchanting chivalry. Slim but muscular, his clothes conformed elegantly to his broad shoulders, his slim waist.

"Thank you, Miss Worthington. It pleases me to hear you say so."

Who was I looking for a moment ago? I can't remember.

"Is this your first time summering in Newport?" How I detested those etiquette books my mother forced upon me; how grateful I was to have read them. They put words in my mouth when my brain could not find any.

"It is my first time in Newport, yes," Mr. Butterworth replied. We began to walk without either one suggesting it. Our stroll was a natural one among nature's beauty, stars began to twinkle in a sky still magenta with the echoes of the setting sun. Lanterns hung on trees and porticoes lit our way, as if we traversed from one star to another. "But I fear I shan't be summering. I'm only here for another week. A short visit, I'm afraid."

I did not know this man save for this passing acquaintance, but the ring of disappointment was a familiar one.

"Do you wish you could stay longer?" I asked.

He stopped walking, as did I. He turned to me; those eyes held me in their grasp.

"I do, Miss Worthington." His eyes never left mine. "I do indeed."

* * *

As Ginevra readied me for the next afternoon's coaching parade, we chatted about last evening; I chatted, she nodded and 'eh hemmed' as she contrived the upper part of my hair into a twisted curl on the right side of my head and perched my hat tilted to the left.

"So many of the girls praised my outfit," I told her truthfully, hoping to banish the darkness. "They adored all the little touches you added."

She grinned. "*Si*, sometimes it is little things that make us special."

Ginevra stopped brushing the rest of my hair, the long lengths that would fall to my waist in silky waves, smoothed by her ministrations. She came 'round to stand before me.

"Why you frown?" She stared hard at me, too hard, for she saw me as others didn't or couldn't. I knew I couldn't lie.

"Frederick," I said flatly.

"He was not there?"

My head shook, but only slightly. "No, he wasn't, but…"

Glowing amber eyes reflected in my mind, a reflection that softened the firm line of my lips.

One brow rose up Ginevra's face. "But...?"

"Well, there was a fine, that is," I floundered needlessly. From Ginevra, I could not run. "A Mr. Butterworth was there. He was rather...engaging," I hedged, foolishly.

"Hmm, engaging, was he?" Ginevra looked away, back to her tasks, though she saw right through me. "And who is this Mr. Butterworth?"

It was my turn to turn, to spin away from my vanity to the woman standing behind me.

"You know," I pondered, surprising myself, "I don't really know."

Her brow quirked again; one corner of her mouth matching it.

"Seems to me you do not need to know."

Before I could deny her words, she took my shoulders and twisted me, my back once more to her.

Ginevra returned to brushing my hair. She knew how it soothed me.

GINEVRA

As I had the summer before, I snuck down to watch them, though the need to sneak was no longer mine. As long as I had done my duty to Pearl and her bedroom, my time was my own, as long as I was always at the ready should she need me. Yet what I did I felt strange to do in the open; the need for invisibility, that still wore my name.

I stood just behind the stone pillar to the left of the gravel drive. In my dark uniform, I was unnoticeable behind the high scrolled iron gate, as notable as the flowerless box hedges growing beneath the carved tops of the beams of stone. I watched them, every day I watched them, cold in the shadows even on hot days.

The men sat tall; their silk stovepipe hats even taller. Leather-gloved hands held reins and whips. Boutonniered chests puffed up, chins stuck high. Their topcoats matched the vivid green of the trees lining the avenue, their yellow-stripped waistcoats as bright as daisies. This place, this world belonged to the women, but this strange parade was men's delight. The women sat behind them, dressed and laced in pale colors. Their large, fancy hats sat on their heads like mushroom caps, their stiff, upright necks the stems.

Some carriages were bigger than others. Phaetons, barouches, victorias, four-in-hands. Pearl taught me about them with as much detail as she did reading and writing.

"A 'whip,' " she told me, "was a coaching master. He will always observe the proper protocol while driving. They must know who they may pass and who they may not." She had rounded a downturned gaze upon me. "We are ranked you see, and if someone of a higher standing is behind us, we must give way. We must all know our place." Her words were so bitter they must have stung her tongue. She shook herself as if she shook off the cold of winter. "But some," she had giggled, "like the Belmonts and the Bennetts, well, their howling swells, are they not?"

"Howling swell?" What a frightening person they must be. "It is some kind of beast?"

Pearl rolled her eyes as she did a lot at my questions, but her smile held her patience. "A howling swell is more, much more. They deck out their coaches so much more elaborately, flowers everywhere, on the horses, on the carriages. They're so much showier. Mother always wants Father to fuss up our carriage."

"Does he?" I asked.

Pearl shook her head. "He couldn't be bothered, dear. If he had his way, we wouldn't coach at all." She had stared out the window. "I wish he had his way."

She never saw me in my hiding place. I was as unnoticeable as my simple dark uniform. At least she never showed she did. She wouldn't, for both our sakes.

I watched them, every day I watched them, my nose full of the fecund scent of the flowers all around me, my mind saw me on one of them, dressed in one of the frothy, delicate dresses I so longed to wear, pictured myself as one of them. I knew the truth, even then. My station had been improved, as had my clothes, but there were heights one such as me could never scale.

Pearl passed, but it brought me little joy. Her dress as fine as any, her small, tasseled parasol fluttered prettily until she would become old enough to wear a wide-brimmed hat. Her back was as straight as the stone pillar I stood behind. All was as it should be, save that the small smile she allowed to sit upon her face looked as if it hurt.

What she never told me was why. Why at the same time every day did all these rich folk put on their fancy clothes, get in their carriages, and parade up and down Bellevue Avenue? Their horses crunched out a rhythm, bells jangling. Their wheels clattered on cobblestones. Their horns tooted. They never actually went anywhere. They drove up and then down.

They nodded to each other as they passed, small movements, the same gesture. I did not understand. Their eyes did more work, scouring each other's clothes, each other's carriages, and who rode in them. The air changed, thickened, as it always seemed to when they gathered.

I looked for him in every carriage, though I did not know I did at the time. A whip or a howling swell; that was the question.

Often times the villagers climbed the hill leading from their small houses and shanties down by the water, and stood along the fences and high walls, watching, like me. To those in the carriages, they were nothing more than rails in a post, not worthy of a glance.

So many days I watched, I came, ever so slowly, to figure it out. Yes, it was to see and be seen by each other that brought them out, lining them up with such precision, leading them from one end of the avenue to the other and back again. But I knew, I came to know the real reason.

They needed to see each other done up and perched up to know who they pretended to be was really who they were, who they thought they were. These coach parades were daily reminders, their fairy tale was real life, or was their real life a fairy tale? Out in the air, on the road, no one could see the dirty clutter of their lives shut away behind the gates and mammoth doors of their "cottages."

The carriages rumbled past, like me, going nowhere.

PEARL

"It's going to be the party of the summer," Mother preened as she opened the few replies to my birthday celebrations at the breakfast table, all of us around her. Intimacy in this intimate setting was still as elusive as ever; if we reached out our hands, they would grasp only empty air. "I'm still so enraged that I had to do them myself. Damn that Miss de Baril."

"I really don't need a grand affair, Mother, just something with a few of my friends..." It was all I wanted; all it should be. The days of the huge balls, my coming out, were just around the corner. I held onto the days of a small group of giggling girls, of silly backyard games, and lovely little remembrance gifts for as long as I could, if I could. I could not.

"Well, of course, Pearl," Mother didn't deign to look up, at me, the party's guest of honor. "But there must be a few of my friends as well." Ah, the truth of the matter, for her. Her truth was bent, if with nothing more than how few of the ladies of Newport were really her friends.

"Ouch!" she cried, sucking a finger. "Another little paper-cut. Oh, how many I have suffered with these invitations. Damn that Miss de Baril."

Not a one of us spoke. It was a subject sure to charge up of my mother's inner beasts. None of us dared remind her that Nettie, not her, had addressed the hundreds of invitations, had seen to their distribution, not her. All Mother could fixate on was that *the* Miss de Baril hadn't done them. If my mother cut herself, it was on her own misplaced frustration.

Miss Maria de Baril had been one of the chosen, a member of an original Newport family who had lost their money and their social status. The wise young Maria had turned her years of being in the game—and her claimed Inca ancestry—to her benefit. Stout, dumpy, forever over-plumed with beads hanging from neck and wrists, her handwriting was the finest on the island. She had become *the* social secretary after creating masterpiece invitations for one of Mrs. Astor's great balls. Her fame—her skill—had become so *en vogue*, in such demand, that she became the chooser, deciding for herself for whom she would or would not complete work. My mother fell into the latter category. She could have been thrown off a cliff for all the screaming she had done about it when the letter of rejection arrived from Miss de Baril.

Our silence was not a hindrance to her ranting.

"She claimed she was far too otherwise occupied, but I know better." Mother threw down the envelope in her hand and turned to my father as if she would stab him with the jewel-encrusted opener still in her hand. "I am not fully accepted; we are not fully accepted."

So it went, another breakfast, another meal trapped in the cage of my mother's tantrums.

Her rant lasted nearly an hour. My father and I suffered in silence. Our appetites diminished as her shrill grew sharper. Only my brother fed her obsession, for he too seemed to be growing as obsessed. He played tennis and polo, belonged to all the right clubs. He was handsome as ever, there can be no doubt, perhaps more so as his face cut with the sharpness of manhood. Something had changed though, changed in him that changed the outer him.

To me, he had lost the cherub sweetness of his youth, innocence lost to cravings, though they would find him little satisfaction. He wanted only the prettiest girl, trifling with hearts as if they were the ball on the tennis court, bouncing them back and forth, to him and away. He who was once my hero on the mount had shrunk before my eyes.

"I've tried my best with Mrs. Astor and Mrs. Vanderbilt, and of course, with Mr. McAllister. They smile ever so prettily to my face and then never accept our invitations. We must do something. You must do something, Orin."

"Eh, what's that you say?" My father came back from his mental distance at the sound of his name.

"You must do something to get the Astors and the Vanderbilts to Pearl's party." She slapped her hand on the table. We all jumped.

"I know exactly what to do!" Her loud exclamation sent the birds from their perch on the statues just outside the open windows. "I need some money, Orin, perhaps a good deal of it."

Father looked at her without a word. Still in her silk dressing robe of pale yellow, hair loose and tumbling down her back, she was another woman—a different woman—until she opened her mouth. Intelligence burned in her pale eyes; if only she set it upon a worthy task would it find its true purpose. It never would. If she made such a demand, he would make her do so fully; he would not prod her along.

"We must pay *Town Topics* to cover the party. They will not give it any mention unless we do. And it *must* be mentioned. All those who declined the invitation must see just how fabulous it will be."

The society journal, *Town Topics*, was *the* social news source in Newport. The good, the bad, and the fictionalized became ever more so—so often exaggerated, distorted, and even extorted—if its writers covered it. No wonder they called them rags.

"Will its success not be gratifying enough?" my father asked. He would rather allow the horses to defecate on the rag than read it.

"Oh, Orin," Mother pleaded, ever so sweetly, leaning forward to allow him a view of the assets she brought to the marriage, "how can it be a success unless everyone knows about it?"

My father peered at my mother as if he looked at someone he did not know, or care to know. He squinted at her, perhaps looking for the woman he had married, though I don't think she was that woman anymore. Pain mottled his face. He turned his gaze to me. The darkness dispelled.

"For my Pearl, I will do it."

Like a switch thrown, Mother became herself, all sweet cajoling gone like the morning mist on a good wind off the land.

"Must you still call her that? She is almost a grown woman."

She had gone a step too far.

Father glared across the table at her as I imagined he would at a particularly difficult employee. He jabbed the air with a pointed finger.

"She is, and always will be, *my* Pearl." The finger thumped upon the table, an exclamation mark upon his words.

I looked quickly down at my plate, quickly shoveled a forkful of food in my mouth before it could reveal its smile.

"Speaking of my Pearl's birthday," my father continued with a strange note of amusement in his voice. I looked up. The hint of a smile played at lips hidden beneath his bushy mustache. "I know it's still a few days away but considering how fair the day is I think I should give you your present now."

"You have a present…for me?"

My fork clanged upon the dish; my eyes bulged as my voice squeaked. My father had never gotten me a gift, purchased something for me without the involvement or approval of my mother, ever. That in itself was the best gift he could give me.

"I have two gifts for you," he leaned toward me. How I longed to paint the jubilant mischief brushing across his face. It would be as rare a depiction as the Mona Lisa. He charmed me, utterly and completely. He rose from his chair and pulled the cord by the door. Unheard on the third floor, a bell chimed, a flag dropped. Within minutes, Geoffrey, his valet, stood at the door.

"That box, if you would, Mr. Tobin," my father requested. "And please alert Mr. Grayson to have the other item readied as well."

"Very good, Sir," Geoffrey backed out of the room with the smallest tilt of his head.

My mind whirled. What could my dear father have gotten me that came in a box *and* required the assistance of Mr. Grayson, the grounds superintendent? It couldn't be a horse; I had a fine one, had had many already in my life. Those he had given me as my right and for his enjoyment as well, for my mother never cared to ride with him. She hated what it did to her hair.

"Orin," my mother hissed, "what have you done?"

He looked at her, all pretense of patient condescension surrendered.

"I have done nothing but acquire my dear Pearl a special gift for her birthday. Ah." He forgot my mother and her narrow-eyed suspicion as

Geoffrey returned, a large box topped with a glorious pink and green ribbon in his hands.

My foot waggled beneath the table. How I longed to reach for it like the child I had been not long ago. I waited, allowing my father to make his presentation.

"This, my Pearl," he said, standing, taking the box, and delivering it to my lap, "is only part of the gift, but you must have this to enjoy the other properly."

I removed the ribbon slowly, wanting to keep it, rather than rip it as my mind prodded me. I lifted the top off...

"Oh, Father," I whispered, wonderstruck.

"Oh, dear Lord, Orin," my mother's voice hissed with venomous displeasure.

I stood, allowing the bottom of the box to drop, holding the outfit up by the shoulders and against me. Though I felt its fine fabric, its unique form pressed against me, I couldn't believe it. To see it for what it was, gave the rest away.

"Really, Father?!" the words burst from me. I threw myself in his arms.

As he wrapped his strong arms tenderly about me, he whispered in my ear, "Truly, my Pearl. I hope you never grow so old you forget to have fun." He held me away from him, staring deeply into my eyes, bore into them. "Don't let this life stop you from having fun."

I stared up at him. He had never spoken such words to me. It was always implied, though never said, his disapproval of the privileged life we had, of the freedom and imprisonment it caused. I thought it had to do with his father, with what had been done by the grandfather I had never met.

"I promise, Father," I said. Truer words I had never spoken.

"Well, go on then, go put it on and come outside when you're ready." Father smiled childlike.

I threw the clothes back in the box where its accessories still remained, pressed the whole bundle to me, and ran to the door.

"Ginevra!" I shrieked, knowing I would need her help donning the very strange clothing.

"How could you, Orin?" I heard Mother say as I left them behind. Opening that box was like opening Pandora's.

"Actually, very easily, Millicent," Father replied.

I laughed as I ran up the stairs.

* * *

With Ginevra's help, I donned the ever so fashionable, ever-so-scandalous clothing.

Ginevra took one look at the clothes, one look at me, and said, "You must remove your corset."

"I must?" I questioned, dubious, but so filled with hope it astounded even me. The corset upon me came off with all due and joyous haste. With her help, I wiggled into the newly designed corset, one with stretchy material down the sides.

"I can breathe!" I chirped, doing so deeply, feeling my ribs and their new ability to expand, and flouncing about with the freedom of an uncaged bird.

The prim button-down white shirt enhanced with a tie, short and not nearly as fancifully knotted as those men wore, but a tie, nonetheless, gave me a dashing flair. The jacket was of such a lightweight material...

"It is sailcloth," Ginevra said as she helped me into it. I strained my neck to look at her over my shoulder. The question formed, needing to be asked, but my longing for what lay ahead was a greater need.

It barely felt as if I wore a jacket. What a jacket it was. Bright with blue and white stripes, it had the tightness along the forearms and the large leg-o-muttons at the top, as did most of our clothing in those days, but it stopped... at my waist. There was nothing of the cumbersome knee or floor-length coats about it.

Yet the jacket was not shocking when compared to the bottom half.

"Bloomers!" Ginevra and I cried together. I saw how she looked at them...like a starving man looked at bread. It wasn't the first time I had seen that look. Strange how easily I recognized it.

"We shall get you pair," I said. Joy is never so great as when it is shared.

Ginevra waved a hand at me. "I will make myself a pair."

I stopped. This day was full of surprises. "You can do that? You can make clothing, not just repair it?"

"Oh, *si*, yes," Ginevra nodded as she turned the bloomers this way and that, studying them. "I can make many things, fine things."

I grabbed her by the hand, the clothes. What must be waiting for me outside, forgotten if only for a flash of time. "Make me a dress, Ginevra. Make me the finest gown for my birthday party."

Deep brown eyes scrutinized me as if it were a first glance. "Do you mean it? You, you would wear it?"

"Yes," I cried, swinging our arms and the clothes held aloft between them, "of course, I would, as long as it is nothing too outrageous. With your sense of style, I would imagine it will be quite different."

Her face bloomed, roses on her cheeks, hibiscus in her eyes. "Not quite different. Maybe a little." She giggled, as did I.

"Come, get these on you." She returned us to the moment, my moments she gladly gave me.

"These" were named for Amelia Bloomer, a grand lady who had been working for women's rights, another "suffragette." Ginevra and I still read about them voraciously in the paper and magazines, each time ticked us forward, like the second hand of a clock.

The bloomers hugged the waist as a skirt would, they had yards and yards of fabric around the upper portion of my thighs, until just below the knee, but there they were cut in two, like men's pants. Well, they were pants...women's pants! They cuffed tightly below the knee. Ginevra fluttered through the tissue paper in the box and pulled out the most darling short hose, patterned in diamonds of light and dark blue, as well as flat-soled shoes of thin leather with tassels at the end of their laces.

Ginevra finished primping me and stood back.

"*Magnifico*," she breathed. Then held up a hand. "Eh, how your mother would say…mahvelous."

We shrieked with laughter and fell against each other.

"Pearl!"

My father's voice from below.

"Come along now, my Pearl, the best is yet to come."

They must have heard our laughter, oh how my father must have loved it. I was certain of it, as certain as I was that my mother cringed at each peal.

With one last squeeze, I pulled Ginevra with me.

* * *

It stood at the bottom of the front steps, held up by the ever-tweeded Mr. Grayson.

"Oh, Father." I stood before it, mouth agape. It was the finest bicycle I had ever seen. It was the new sort, the safety bicycle it was called. Gone were the penny-farthings with the enormous front wheel and the small back one. These wheels were almost the same size, the back being just slightly larger. Nor was there a bar running from the padded seat to the handlebars. It had been dropped much lower, to just above the chain that connected the two wheels.

"It is so you can step through." My father showed me, with great delight in doing so. "The man at the shop told me it made the sport so much more ladylike. Is that not so, Millicent?"

My mother stood at the top step, arms entwined so tightly across her chest like a protective shield. Her creamy skin was blotched red as if every speck of blood in her body lay livid upon it. Ginevra, standing behind her, caught my gaze with a bulge of fear.

"Tell me you do not mean for her to ride that…thing…along the avenue, Orin."

My father laughed, spite-tinged laughter. "That's exactly what she will do."

"But what will they say?" Mother ran down the steps, her voice reaching a tone only dogs could hear.

I pulled away, but my father's hand on my back stopped me. I stopped listening as well, as much as I could, turning their acrimonious words into nothing but a hum in my head. His determination rendered her fury impotent. Their arguments were the background noise of my life. In that moment his subdued voice, while still restrained, echoed with a resilience I had never heard him use when speaking with her. Something had changed. I found I became more concerned with whatever that was than with how this argument would end. His victory—my victory—was a certainty, of that I had no doubt. The why frightened me.

"Enough, Millicent, enough," my father demanded, commanded. My mother's lips clamped together tightly until a line of white appeared around her mouth.

"Off we go, my Pearl. Come, I'll help you."

Help me he did. He showed me how to put one leg through, one foot on one pedal, and push off.

I yelped as the force of my legs drove the machine faster and faster. I jig-jagged as my arms chaotically joggled the handlebars. He ran beside me, grabbing one handlebar, steadying me. I found balance.

"You've got it, my Pearl, you've got it!" he cried, releasing his hold.

I did. Off I flew.

GINEVRA

I followed them down past the gates. I stood behind the stone statue that was her mother, behind her father whose pale chuckles sparkled with joy. Pearl wobbled for a bit, but soon she became this beautiful creature gliding down the street. Her long dark hair streamed behind her like a kite's ribbon.

We watched Pearl fly down the length of Bellevue Avenue, past the mansions and their haughty, haunting occupants. It was the perfect street for such a device, mostly flat and smoothly packed dirt, the cobbles ended just after the Casino farther north.

"Oh, this really is the worst, Orin," I heard her mother complain sharply. "Look at how she is being stared at."

Mr. Worthington never took his gaze off his daughter. "Must we always care what they see?"

"Of course we should," she bit at him. "However, will we move up if we don't?"

He turned to her then. I shuddered, grateful such a look was not pinned on me.

"You don't always care, Millicent, do you?"

I had no clue what he meant. I didn't want to. She offered him no answer; her silence was her answer. I saw it in the bitter twist upon Mr. Worthington's face.

Pearl came flying back to us, cheeks blooming as pink as the roses in every garden, her face alight with exertion and pleasure.

"Come, Ginevra, come with me," she called out.

I didn't move until Mr. Worthington looked back at me over his wide shoulder. "Go on, girl."

It was enough.

I brushed past Mrs. Worthington, shivering as I slipped by her coldness.

I stopped beside Pearl and her new contraption. "I do not know how. I no have the right clothes."

"Just sit on the seat," Pearl instructed me, "I'll do the rest."

Thoughts and worries fled in fright at what awaited me. I bunched my skirts about my legs, straddled the small seat, and put myself into her keeping. We wavered a bit as my extra weight sent Pearl off-kilter. Soon enough she adjusted, and soon enough we were off.

I became a bird flying through the sky, the wind washed over me like the freshest water, cleansing my face, my mind, my soul. I closed my eyes, surrendering to it.

"Look at them." Pearl laughed the words flying back to me on the same wind.

I opened my eyes and saw two women—statues captured—sculpted by disbelief and disgust. Mrs. Fish and Mrs. Vanderbilt stood on the steps of Marble House. A vast lawn away, their shock and revulsion blossomed as clearly as the deep blue hydrangea blooms just behind the iron fence.

I laughed along with Pearl. We cared for nothing but the freedom, the feeling of it.

We turned 'round in the wide corner where Bellevue Avenue became Ocean Drive and made our way back. Pearl waved to the women still frozen in distaste. I turned my head, hiding my unshrinking smirk.

I jumped off as we turned into the path to The Beeches. Pearl's parents still stood there waiting for us, together but apart.

"Enough, Pearl," her mother's command drenched us like a bucket of cold water. "You must return. And you," the frost in her voice chilled my bones, "you are to serve her. That's what you are paid for."

It was a sting, as she meant it to be, but not one sharp enough to spoil the moment. Side by side, Pearl and I walked the bicycle to the carriage house where Mrs. Worthington insisted it reside.

"Have you ever felt anything like it?"

We shared wonder as if we had dreamt the same dream.

"No, never," I agreed. I put my hand on one of hers that steered the device. "Thank you," I said, without saying for what. Her lips spread wide. I could see every one of her teeth. She knew.

PEARL

The morning of my birthday came with the birth of golden light.

Ginevra brought me breakfast in on a tray, though I rarely lounged, rarely simpered in my bed. It didn't matter that it was the fashion, it was a fashion that did not fit me well. She set the tray about me, opening the heavy draperies, and threw open the windows. As if the walls fell, my room now sat outside amidst the brilliant sun, hot breeze, and chirping birds.

Then, without a word, she left me.

"G...Ginevra?"

She should have stayed with me. It was part of her job, yes, but a treasured one, treasured by us both. We'd plan the day's outfits, all of them, and talk, our talk, not that of a mistress to a maid. She had left, left me on my birthday. It couldn't be. She wouldn't. She didn't.

Ginevra returned in a few moments, her hands full.

I became one of the birds, a crow for I crowed. I jumped up, nearly tumbling my breakfast tray and all its contents onto my bed. In Ginevra's hands was quite the loveliest evening dress I had ever seen.

"It's pink and green!" I blurted, slipping the tips of my fingers over the soft fabric, making it real with the touch.

Ginevra beamed, holding her creation as if it were an infant, and brought it to my wardrobe, hanging it against the outside of the doors. I fell back upon my bed, staring at it.

In so many ways, it was much as the evening dresses of the day were. The bodice was fitted tightly, the skirt, though still bustled, was narrow, straighter than was the fashion a few years ago. What she had done with ribbon and lace, green ribbon and pink lace, I had never seen. It was remarkable, remarkably gorgeous. The short, puffed sleeves made of pink chiffon were pleated at the top and cuffed just above the elbow, but the cuffs were made of braided green ribbon, a trimming I had never seen, and ended with just the hint of scalloped pink lace.

Along the bottom of the skirt and its slight train, ran another row of the twisted green trimming, as did the waist, though there were three rows of it. Those rows came together at the back and flowed freely over the small bustle, just past the end of the small train. The precision of her stitching was as fine, if not better, than anything from Worth. It was art—art I would wear.

From the ribbons encircling the waist, Ginevra had brought them upward vertically, striping the bodice. Where the bodice ended in a scoop neck, the ribbons continued, on their own, meant to lay against my skin. They gathered together, connected to a choker made of three rows of the pink lace. I had never seen anything like it, not on any woman or in any magazine.

"Ginevra!" I gave a whispered shout. "It is...you are...magnificent."

I jumped up and pulled her to me. Her cheeks plumped against my shoulder.

"You like it?" she asked with a need, uncertainty plaguing her pride.

"Like it?" I held her away from me. "I adore it. You are so...I didn't know you could..." words failed me. "When did you learn to design like this? How did you learn?"

Ginevra lowered her chin in that charming way she had, charming for its freedom from affectation. Peeking at me through lush lashes, she grinned.

"From reading."

Our laughter rang in my ears for all of that day and night. Almost all of it.

* * *

As was the fashion, I walked into the ballroom on the night of my birthday party a half-hour after the last guest arrived. Here, white stucco relief decorations were everywhere, on the doors, the paneling, and the cornice, moving on to form an elaborate ceiling frieze with a center medallion of winged cherubs. Light from the crystal chandelier, ormolu wall sconces, and Louis XV andirons glittered off the richly carved woodwork of cream and white, and the gilded mirror frames. It was, perhaps, the most stunning and tasteful room in our cottage.

When I stepped in, every eye turned, every flapping lip stilled. Gasps rose up like fog, especially loud from the gathering of women and the girls, at the sight of my ensemble, my hair.

Ginevra had tried to talk me out of it, warning me of tempting trouble. I would not be daunted. To wear a dress such as the one she made me insisted I wore my hair up, to reveal it and me as they should be. But, to wear one's hair up proclaimed females as women, no longer girls; a privilege that awaited those turning eighteen. It had become a marker along the path of women's lives. It was a sign, as bold as any written on a board, that a girl had reached marrying age. In my mind, I was a woman, one far wiser than my mother. Conventions and consequences be damned.

Self-pride is a road to ruin.

They gathered around me, crowded me, asking about the dress as if it hung on a mannequin—where did it come from, who made it—turning me around and around as they gawked and sputtered surprise and praise.

Only one woman made her distaste plain, though I imagined there were others of the older set who felt the same.

With her porcelain smile firmly set, Mother came and took me by the arm.

"Yes, yes, dear girls, she looks quite…extraordinary," she said to my friends, detaching me from within their protective circle, "but Pearl must make her way about, must greet all her guests. I know you understand."

She didn't care if they did. Her fingers pinched my arm; a bruise would be in full bloom by morning.

"That…is *not* the dress I bought you." Her frozen smile didn't thaw a bit. I thought she would draw blood with her icicle teeth. "Where is that dress and where did this…this…thing come from? And how dare you wear your hair up! You've humiliated me."

"Do you like it, Mother?" I pushed, safe in the milieu. "It was made especially for me."

"You will march yourself upstairs this minute," Mother hissed at me, mouth so close her spittle pinged my face. "You will change your dress and put down your hair."

A year ago, I would have done just that.

"This gown is perfect for me, and this hairstyle belongs to this gown. And like it, it will *not* be changed." She had taught me ruthlessness; she had only herself to blame for being my first victim.

"It's bizarre," she condemned me for condemning her, for that's how her eyes saw it. "It's—"

"Pearl, you glorious girl," Consuelo Vanderbilt, such the dearest of friends, scampered to us, taking my mother's smile for a real one. "That is the most amazing dress I have ever seen. Is it by Worth?"

"Hello, dear Consuelo." I tugged my arm, a small tug. My mother released me before anyone could see how tight her grasp was, and I hugged my friend. "No, it's not. It's actually by a new, up-and-coming designer, I'll tell you all about her. You'll excuse us, won't you, Mother?"

Mother's hot glare flicked between Alva Vanderbilt's daughter and me. She had no choice in her answer.

"But, of course, dear," my mother said, her voice came out of her nose with a discordant twang. "Be sure to pay your respects to Consuelo's mother. And Mrs. Astor, of course." She pointed in the corner where, wonder of wonder, the queen of Newport society sat enthroned, her courtiers around her. I was almost sorry to see her here, sorry my mother's tactics had worked. It would only encourage her to do more.

"I will, Mother, in just a minute. I promise." I meant it. To have Mrs. Astor in our home was a feat. It mattered a great deal, though I despised that it did, loathed that one woman could have such power over others. Yet there was a part of me—the small part of me who wanted Frederick to pay me more attention—that knew the value of having her here.

Consuelo and I chatted, strolling around the room, greeting other guests and friends, whirling on the social merry-go-round. Dizziness found me in the whirl of my thoughts on the carousel of my mind. How could I both revere and despise, long to run to and from, with the same need?

As we came back 'round, to the corner just to the left of the main door with its glittering gold grand piano, I squeezed Consuelo's arm.

"I must do my duty," I whispered to my fellow conspirator. I ticked my head in the direction of Mrs. Astor just beside the piano before the cold fireplace where she had taken up reign.

Consuelo hid her pale smile behind her gloved fingers. "Best of luck," she whispered and took herself off.

"Dear Mrs. Astor, how wonderful to have you here," I exclaimed softly, feigning the confidence that spoke the words, confidence that should have owned naturally. I felt an odd notion to curtsey. "And you as well, Mrs. Carey." That would be Mary Astor Carey, *the* Mrs. Astor's sister-in-law.

Caroline Schimmerhorn Astor, known simply as *The* Mrs. Astor. Her ever-present partner in censorship, Ward McAllister, forever blathered about the importance of beauty before brains to someone who wasn't. In my eyes, and others as well I think, Mrs. Astor was nowhere near beautiful. She had a large jaw and far too prominent a nose. She was short, and dare I say, dumpy. Yet the climbers forever compared her to Queen Victoria; she dressed and acted the part, embracing it completely.

According to Mrs. Astor's gospel, it took three generations of wealth, acquired not through work but through birth, to attain social acceptance. Her husband, William Backhouse Astor, Jr., was the grandson of the John Jacob Astor, he who had made his fortune investing in real estate, a pursuit deemed acceptable. She could trace her lineage back to New York Dutch aristocracy, a true "Knickerbocker," as they were called.

Husband was never very close to wife, not in spirit or location. He was far more dour than she; he possessed none of the refinement and ambition his wife demanded in others. He cared more for his horses, yachts, and—if rumors were to be believed—other women.

I didn't believe they were rumors; they were just more tales of another philandering married man in this cloistered community, tales rooted in fact as deeply as our beeches are rooted to the ground. Of all the things these people thought of themselves, the most harmful was that they were, or thought they were, above reproach.

With such credentials, she felt justified in dictating the rules of this society, a notion I could not accept. Who was anyone to judge another? Yet judge she did.

The ladies greeted me warmly and invited me to sit on an ottoman at their feet. Where else.

To my surprise, our conversation was lovely. I wondered whom exactly I conversed with, the true woman or the truth she allowed. She was, after all, the bastion of this elegantly macabre way of life I struggled to embrace.

I rose, excusing myself to see to other guests, the only correct excuse. I had done myself proud; I'd said all the right things at all the right times and in just the right manner. In the eyes of these women—upon whom so many fates depended—nothing but an approved impression gleamed. Staying too long in their company, as my mother did so often, could undo it all, untying slips of knots just tied. I had little care to be a knot along this particular rope, but it was the only one in my hands at the time.

"I will take my leave of you, ladies." I rose with perfect grace, imitating a manner studied for years, and with a small bow of my head, made my departure from them. Their salutations of their enjoyment of my company followed me like the train of my dress.

Nerves I had held at bay now rushed upon me. I could only keep my composure and my graceful gait into the next room, where—thankfully—punch, wine, and champagne waited. I took up a glass of the latter and leaned against the wall, just the other side of where the social autocrats sat.

I should have walked further away.

"What a lovely young woman," I heard Mrs. Astor say and I sighed relief into my glass.

"Indeed," agreed Mrs. Carey, "she is a fine tribute to her father."

"And what a surprise considering her mother, though I suppose it explains her appearance."

The wine in my mouth turned bitter. I should have walked away but couldn't.

"We really should take her up," Mrs. Astor proclaimed, their idiom of acceptance, that which every man, woman, and child strived for, the crowning achievement for anyone in our circle.

"Do you not think her too…too modern?"

Mrs. Astor huffed. I think it was a laugh. "Perhaps a little modern is not an entirely bad thing. It shows spunk. I like spunk."

"However can we take her up when we haven't the mother?" Mrs. Carey lowered her voice, yet not her displeasure.

"Taking up that girl will be quite easy," Mrs. Astor assured. "Taking up *that* woman will never happen, not as long as I breathe."

There it was, my mother's irony.

"I suppose it is not right to punish the daughter for the mother," Mrs. Carey insisted. "And the father is such a dear man. He has suffered enough, I think. Seeing his daughter done well will surely comfort him. Relieve him of the pain his wife causes him."

Of what pain did they speak? They could not know how my mother harangued my father, her coldness to him. Or was it that evident? Was it some other pain?

"Quite right," Mrs. Astor agreed. "For the father's sake, we will ignore the mother."

"She may take it as a sign of her own acceptance."

Mrs. Astor laughed outright. "I hardly think so, dear. Accepting the daughter will not find me anything but cordial to that awful woman."

"Nor I," Mrs. Carey concurred.

"It's settled then. Be sure to include Pearl on your guest lists, my dear. She will have to deal with her mother's disappointment, not us."

I could hear no more. Taking up another glass, of what I do not remember now, and did as I should have done. I moved quickly from the room, from the nearness of these sitting magistrates, and made my way to the farthest room I could find.

In the library, I sat at a bridge table that had just lost its fourth, but it was not this ever more popular game of cards that I pondered, but this tenuous game of society in which I existed. At seventeen, I was finally deemed old enough to learn and play the game taking society by storm, ousting whist from its lofty position as the favored card game where it had sat for centuries. These days it seemed no matter the occasion, someone would demand a game of bridge. I was never more grateful for the trivial pursuit as I was in that moment.

I felt so very grown up as they allowed me a seat at the table. The cards in my hand trembled; I held them tighter. I partnered with Herbert Butterworth, and we played against my brother and Frederick. I floated between two worlds, one dark and sultry, the other golden and dashing. I played more than one game in that moment.

Herbert, as he insisted I now call him, taught me a great deal that night, as if I hadn't learned too much already. Would I have played differently if I knew that night was the last night I would see Herbert that summer? Perhaps. But the path of life called "what if" was too fatiguing to traverse. I strayed from it as much as I could.

Within a few deals, a few tricks, I had the nuances of the game down pat. Within a short span of time, the glow of its novelty dimmed as quickly as a candle snuffed out for the night.

If this was the glory of adulthood, I would readily choose the normality of childhood, for in comparison, its peace and idleness were surely more enticing.

GINEVRA

From the hidden corners of The Beeches, I watched her sail into the room. My eyes closed as I heard the gasp of wonder over her gown, my sigh released my held breath. It was as if the clock had already struck midnight and it was already my birthday and not hers.

This small group of Pearl's friends gave her the gift of their company and their genuine well wishes. She whirled from one to the other, chatting and laughing, and beaming.

I watched her dance many a dance, most often with just two men. One I recognized as the charming man that had called me beautiful at Gravel Court. In my mind that was his name, The-Man-Who-Called-Me-Beautiful. When they danced, I watched him more than her. Before these men, her face changed, a similar change, one of blooming cheeks and sparkling smiles.

It was as it should have been, a night that belonged to Pearl and her alone, no matter how often her mother pushed herself into the center of the room, she could not achieve the center of attention. That belonged to her daughter. Mrs. Worthington's face showed pleasure and displeasure in equal amounts. I understood; it was an understanding that frightened me.

Yes, Pearl owned the night. It should have been a night of nothing but delights, but there it was again, the bitter stab of jealousy. This night it bore two names. I envied those young women, envied their freedom and their beauty, their dresses and their jewels. And I envied them Pearl. She should belong to me and no one else.

I walked away then, fairly certain the dress wouldn't need me. I knew she didn't. I could not watch any longer.

* * *

I lay in my bed listening. Even from two floors above, the sounds of laughter and music drifted up to me. I listened to the sounds of the crickets chirping in the warm night air. I listened to the clock tick its way onward until it tolled midnight.

It was my birthday.

My father had made no mention of it, no mention of plans or gifts. I didn't expect he would. My birthday was too full of shared remembrances of my mother, shared grief.

I knew the servants knew of my birthday as well. I knew they would do nothing at all, and they hadn't.

Listening to the tolls, I heard the quiet of my life. The tolling stopped long before the loud silence of my mind, long before sleep found me. It didn't find me for long.

* * *

"Ginevra!" The insistent hiss came from the door.

I opened eyes heavy with sleep...or did I dream.

"Ginevra, wake up!" It came again.

I bolted upright, looked around, found the sliver of light from the hall lamps slipping in my door.

It was there I found her. Pearl.

"What are you doing here?" I whispered, jumping from my bed, jumping to the door, grabbing her hand to pull her in, but she wouldn't allow it.

"Put on your robe," she commanded, pulling her head out the small space, checking the hall, up and down as I donned the garment. With it on, I went to her again. I saw the small sack she carried in one hand.

"What have you—"

This time she grabbed my hand, "Come on!" she giggled. I shushed her even as I followed her.

I should have known where she would take me.

* * *

We didn't climb the beeches that night. She was still in the dress I had made her, swearing to me that she never wanted to take it off. I was robed but barefoot.

Beneath the great canopy of the beeches, we sat. Pearl opened the sack and pulled out her treasures. A lone candle on a silver stick. She struck a match to it and the canopy beneath the beeches glowed from within.

I swallowed back a lump of tears as she pulled out a piece of cake, a piece of her birthday cake, but it was to me she sang, it was my birthday we celebrated.

We wrapped ourselves together in the beautifully embroidered and fringed shawl, the last of her treasures, the one that became my greatest treasure, her gift to me, and talked.

We didn't talk about her party, the fabulous clothes, the equally fabulous people. We chattered about our bicycle rides, about our dreams, and little else.

The greatest gift Pearl ever gave me was herself.

PEARL

The heat wave hit us the next morning, but it was frigid in the breakfast room.

Mother sat ramrod straight, as always, yet the kinks in the rod began to show. Veins pumped on her forehead. She snapped at her food rather than bite it delicately from the tip of her fork. I hung from an unraveling thread; it was just a matter of time before it snapped. Silent trepidation screamed from my father and Clarence. We held our breath. We didn't need to wait long. She shifted her pose in her chair ever so slightly.

"I've instructed Mr. Grayson to give Pearl's bicycle away," she said and sipped her coffee.

"Mother!"

"Millicent!"

Father and I chorused outrage.

Clarence quickly dabbed the corners of his mouth with his serviette and stood. "I must be off. I have court time with Henry." He was out of the room before his words.

I glared at his back, despising him for his cowardice. A big brother's place should be beside his younger sister—not during a card game or a party—but when the chair she sat upon tipped, daring to tip over.

I reached my hands across the table; hers were just out of reach.

"You can't do this, Mother," I pleaded without shame.

She glared at me, "And you can't do many things, but you do."

Mother stood and threw her napkin on the table, anger contained set loose.

"Did you really think you could defy me in so public a manner, humiliate me as you did last night, with no consequences?"

I gaped up at her open-mouthed. "But...but everyone complimented me."

"So they said to your face," Mother jabbed me with her words. "You have no idea what they said to each other, behind my back."

"Don't you mean...," *my* back, I started to say. The brightness of epiphany, wrought by the slip of her tongue, strangled me.

She knew. My mother knew how the community spoke of her. For her it was a mortal wound, I understood. But this anger—her anger—did not belong to me alone. Part belonged to 'them,' those she idolized. She would deny any ownership of the status she herself created.

"You throw away convention without a thought, without consulting me. Why should I not throw away your toy?"

I knew crow must become a part of the breakfast I must eat.

"You're right, Mother." My voice softened with contrition. It echoed in my head as desperation. "I should have shown you what I was wearing, how I planned to wear my hair. I, well, I thought to surprise you."

"That was no surprise. That was rebellion, against me."

"No, it wasn't." It was rebellion against so much more. She did not need to know it.

"You're right, Millicent." My father spoke. His words drained my blood. My head wobbled on my weakened neck. "But I think the punishment should fit the crime. This was a mere infraction. Besides, Pearl looked stunning last night. I'm quite sure that is all that is being said."

Relief sailed into sight, but it had not yet landed.

"This was no in-frac-tion." Each syllable of the last word contained even more bitterness.

"I think we shall refrain Pearl from riding the bicycle for two weeks. As long as her behavior during that time is suitable, it will be returned to her."

They glared at each other, two generals at the front lines. The ticking of the foyer clock matched my heart pumping in my ears.

Mother's top lip curled. I had never seen such a beautiful woman so ugly.

"Very well then. Have your way, you always do."

Father's face contorted with sarcastic laughter trapped within. I could not blame him. Mother held on to delusion as a drowning man does a life raft. In it, she saw their marriage as if it existed as Father would have it. It was a grand delusion indeed.

Mother stomped away from us. Not a backward glance as she left the room. She left us stewing in the heat of her anger.

Father spoke to me then, even as his gaze stayed upon Mother marching away, "I think that might be the last time I saved you, my Pearl. The last time I can."

I swallowed hard but could not swallow away the lump in my throat.

Father looked at me. For the first time, I knew the incredibly success-ful and ruthless businessman he was. I glimpsed the core of him, a man who would do whatever it took to break his own bonds, of rebuilding, of regaining respect. I saw how much he wished me to be like him.

"The rest is up to you."

I remember when I was a child, my mother's hair had been a lovely sort of light brown, dark blonde mix. The strands of each tone flowed together in her long hair, adding richness and depth to the elaborate coifs so popular in those days. From the moment she met Alva Van-derbilt, it was no longer enough. Like Mrs. Vanderbilt and Tessie Oel-richs too, my mother had to become a redhead. Her need to be one of them led to the most awful of grueling ordeals, every month, a two-day ordeal.

The closely guarded formula from Paris required several compli-cated and messy steps. They dyed the hair black first, then green, then finally the desired hue of red. No woman dared be seen in such a frightful state—and she looked frightful indeed—so those who chose the practice were prisoners of their own making, prisoners in their dressing rooms during the long unsightly process.

I confess those two days every month became a blessing for me. Mother could not be out and about, could not see where I went nor with whom I went. As much as her obsessive need to change herself to fit in revolted me, I took full advantage of this nasty habit.

Ginevra helped me don a walking outfit that morning. Though it was warm, storms threatened, the booming sort only the heat of sum-mer brought on. It was no day for the beach.

"Run upstairs and grab your bonnet," I told her, shooing her with my hands as she gave me her one brow raised, quizzical look. "Go on. Let's take a walk together, shall we?"

There was nothing untoward about a young lady taking a walk with her personal maid as her chaperone. There were no rules, those unwritten ones, against it. They would not know I walked with my friend, not my maid.

Ginevra hurried to do my bidding, hurried to enjoy such a trivial thing as a walk, a simple pleasure of life that had been denied her all last summer. It was only minutes until we were out on Bellevue Avenue, me with my parasol, her with her bonnet.

The moist warmth slowed our pace. The dust of the road tossed upward as the carriages past us had no strength to fight its oppression and fell back to the ground quickly, defeated.

"Have you been painting?" Ginevra asked once we were safely away from The Beeches, safely away from prying ears.

My lips spread without effort.

"I have, a great deal," I said. "In fact, I've done much to further my career as an artist."

"What? What have you—?"

"And you, Ginevra," I put her off, not yet, not just yet. "Have you been designing?"

"I have," she nodded, clasping her hands together, curiosity distracted but not entirely. "I have sketchbook with so many of them. I must keep it hidden, though. I think Mrs. Briggs looks in our rooms."

I stopped. My arm in hers, jerking her backward.

"That's deplorable. You are a hard worker in the employ of the Worthingtons. She has no right to invade your privacy in such a way." Outrage held me in its pinching grasp. I would do something about it, though I didn't know what or when.

Ginevra shrugged it away. "It is her way. I do not think she is alone. I have heard others, other staff from other cottages, say same happens to them."

Pain stabbed my jaw; my body told me of my anger. No wonder there was such dissatisfaction among staff, so many escaping from their posts to find employment in the mills and factories. Work in the mill might have been harder, but often hard work is an easy price for self-respect.

I threw off my rage as best I could and commenced our stroll. I did not want it to shadow our time together as the dark clouds rolling in attempted to do.

"Well, you must keep on," I insisted, "I look forward to wearing more of your wonderful creations."

"You do?" Her voice rose until the last note flew up skyward.

"I most certainly do. In fact, perhaps you could think about designing day dresses, something a bit more subdued, less frothy. I may have need of them."

It was Ginevra's turn to stop, her unspoken question clear, in the tilt of her head. We were knit too closely to keep a single strand of my truth from her. It was time. I told her of my future hopes, knowing she would breathe not a word of it to anyone.

"Oh, Pearl, how wonderful, for you it is the perfect thing," Ginevra cried, her enthusiasm overtaking her quiet nature. "But, but your mother—"

"Oh, Mother be damned," I bit the words out with a snap of my jaw. "I don't care a whit for what my mother may think." I stopped. The thought stopped me. I put a hand on Ginevra's arm. I held her gaze with mine. "I don't want to be like her, Ginevra. I don't want to be her."

I said it aloud. Relief cleansed me.

My sad demons, ones she saw clearly, darkened her gaze. She put her hand on mine. "And you never will be, Pearl. You are not made...like her."

There was little grace to her truth, there did not need to be. The astonishing truth served better.

We walked on, arm in arm.

"Lispenard Stewart lives there," I pointed across the avenue, to a lovely white colonial-style mansion, small for Bellevue, with a columned porch that wrapped around the entire front and north sides.

"Lis...pee...nard? That is a name?" Ginevra croaked on laughter. I joined her.

"It is, actually. And oh, what a rake he is."

"Really?"

Gossip. We told ourselves we were above it when, in truth, no one was. Everyone savored a taste of it now and again.

"He's near to forty but still not married. Some consider him the most eligible bachelor in Newport this season. He's very tall, very trim, and *very* flirtatious, a grafting machine. With every female, woman, or girl—"

A crack of thunder boomed, though only I heard it. The crackle of lightning bolted through me.

I had seen him work his magic on my own mother, not that it was rare for men to flirt with her. It seemed different with him, looked different.

"And that's Oakville Villa. It belongs to the Osgoods. After that is Lyndenhurst. Mr. Hodgson built it as we were building The Beeches. He was an officer in the Navy." I kept a running commentary about our neighbors and the splendid homes as we moved along at a leisurely pace.

Time passed and so did the street beneath our feet.

"Here's Marble House, the Vanderbilt house," I told her. "This is where Consuelo... Consuelo!"

Even as I spoke her name, my friend appeared, as if summoned by my words of her. She was just coming out her door. She waved to us, jumped back in, and came back out, parasol in hand. She called back into the house with a frown on her lips and creases on her brow. She came anyway, no matter what the words were.

With her sweetness, she embraced me. I returned it in kind.

"We're on a stroll, Consuelo, can you join us?" I asked.

"It would be my pleasure," she said. She had that aristocratic diction so common among our set, but hers was neither forced nor contrived. It danced off her tongue; one could close one's eyes and be soothed by it. In that shy way of hers, she turned her huge dark eyes, like stars with their thick fringe of curled lashes, to Ginevra.

"Oh, dear me, where are my manners," I said quickly. "Consuelo Vanderbilt, this is Ginevra Costa, I've spoken to you about her. Ginevra, please meet Consuelo."

Consuelo held a long, delicate hand out. Ginevra hesitated but took it.

"*Buon giorno,*" my clever Ginevra said. Somehow, somewhere along her journey from last year to this, from stranger to onlooker, she had already learned that among some, her Mediterranean background was an admired attribute, not a despised detriment. How proud I was of her, the way she held herself tall and straight, the way she let her own beauty show through her servant's uniform. Yet I could see the way she looked at Consuelo. I had, after all, seen so many other people look at my fabulous friend in just such a way for so many years.

Tall and willowy, she had what they called a piquant oval face atop a swanlike neck framed by thick, luxurious dark brown hair. Perfect, porcelain skin, long-legged, and full-lipped, her beauty was hard to miss, and yet it affected her not at all.

"You are Ginevra?" Consuelo asked with quiet excitement, her form of it. "You are the talented dress designer?"

Ginevra blushed, glimmered at Consuelo's words.

"No, Miss Vanderbilt—"

"Oh, please call me Consuelo, and, if I may, I will call you Ginevra?" Consuelo's manners were as impeccable as they were amiable.

"Consuelo," Ginevra dipped her head, "I am no...not a designer. I am merely a maid who can sew."

Consuelo shook her head. "Do not toy with me, Ginevra. I saw the dress you designed and made for our friend. It was a masterpiece. You had all the men fawning over her."

"The men weren't—" I tried to hide my pleasure behind modesty.

"They fanned, eh, no, fawned, over her beauty," Ginevra stood taller with possessive pride, "not my dress."

Consuelo twirled her parasol toward Ginevra. "Well, I won't argue over her beauty, but your dress most certainly framed it."

"No one fawned." I stamped my foot at being ignored, being praised. I had little experience with it.

"Oh dear, Pearl, you cannot fool us." Now they conspired together. "If I recall two men, in particular, did a great deal of fawning. Frederick was one, and who was that other?" Consuelo tapped fingers covered with thin lace upon her mouth. "The dashing fellow with the black hair and golden eyes."

Did I stumble or did Ginevra? I couldn't see it clearly. Not then.

"His name is Butterworth, Herbert Butterworth," I stated plainly, or thought I did.

"Oh yes, that must be him. Look at her blush, Ginevra?"

When I turned, I saw Ginevra as I had seen her the very first day she came to The Beeches, pale and fearing what lay ahead.

"Are you all—"

"I am fine, *sì*." Ginevra dropped her chin, pulled her bonnet lower down her face.

"Do you wish to return?"

She shook her head without taking her eyes away from the dirt street beneath our feet.

"Well, I have a wish," Consuelo saw nothing of what I did, "I long for you to make something for me."

Ginevra's head snapped up then, eyes owlish. She struggled with her enthusiasm before it walked ahead of her. Two years in Newport and already she knew the power that was the Vanderbilts. I could not imagine what such a request must have meant to her.

"*Grazie*, Consuelo, it would be an honor," she said. I did not hear the gusto I expected.

"Good, that's settled then." Consuelo hooked one arm about mine, the other about that of Ginevra. We continued our constitution.

"Speaking of dresses," I said. The conversation needed to be steered in a different direction, though for who I wasn't certain. "Mother has said Worth will be here soon, visiting us all, dressing us all, all alike." My note of displeasure was as clear as the robin calls all around us.

"I'd rather look like the rest. It makes it so much easier not to be seen."

If Consuelo could have thrown off the mantle of being a Vanderbilt, no matter how grand and bejeweled, I believe she would have. Her life had been one in constant control, not her own, but that of her governess and her mother.

The woman who called Consuelo her child commanded every room in which she was present. Alva Vanderbilt was a mighty force to reckon with as an acquaintance. I cringed, imagining myself as her daughter.

Consuelo served as an accessory to her mother's grandeur; she preferred it, learned how long ago. Her lesson was much like mine. I had learned from my mother as well, learned who I didn't want to be.

We chatted more as we walked, now a trio. Consuelo's undeniable inner grace kept Ginevra in the conversation whenever possible, no matter Ginevra's station or her changed mood. We rounded Bellevue onto Ocean Drive and stopped at the top of the bluffs overlooking Bailey's Beach.

The waves churned in, pounding the shore. The ocean was angry, angry at the clouds that made the water dark, that kept us from our daily frolicking, angry as if it missed us.

"I feel like the ocean," Consuelo said, or did she think it aloud. "It's crashing in on me, wave after wave of it, I fear."

"Whatever do you mean?" I asked. I had never heard her speak so despondently. Consuelo was intelligent and educated, as curious as I, as Ginevra. A serious girl, yes, but this gloominess was not her either. On the other side of me, Ginevra nodded, her own eyes upon crashing waves.

Consuelo shook her head and forced a smile. "Oh, don't listen to me, Pearl. It's just one of those days," she answered. It was no answer.

I would not pry. I could only hope she would share her worries with me if there were truly any. As I hoped Ginevra would.

GINEVRA

When my next afternoon off arrived, I remembered my walk with Pearl and Consuelo. It encouraged me to take a walk of my own, taking my new freedom as a lady's maid out for a walk. It was perfectly acceptable for me to do so alone as I wasn't one of the chosen and didn't have to conform to their strict rules.

I needed separation, space to think.

I had taken the lovely yellow striped dress Pearl had given me and reduced it down to something more in keeping with who I was. I had no wish to look like—or pretend to be—anything more. Would I *be* one of them if I could? There was more and more of me that thought I would, an itch I couldn't scratch. Yet I knew it as a young girl's silly dreaming, at least I hoped that's all it was.

At the bottom of Memorial Boulevard, I stopped before turning right.

The ocean lay in front of me, on its daily progress of forward and back. The sun glinted off the peaks of the waves, reflecting pure golden light at me. Golden, as were his eyes.

Moving fast, the world blurred around me. I let it.

It couldn't be true, I told myself. I had been telling myself the same thing for days. Pearl had only ever spoken of Frederick. She couldn't have feelings for the man who called me beautiful.

She must not, I commanded, but of whom?

"Pardon me, Miss," the gentle singsong voice of an Irishman brought me out of my tumbling thoughts, as he almost tumbled me to the ground.

"No need. My fault." It was. I could not stand like a block of stone on such a busy street. Driving my thoughts onto safer ground, I straightened my lovely new, old dress and continued.

I couldn't change, not a stitch, of the dull uniform I must wear whenever I was in service, which was every minute save two afternoons a week. On those days, I craved some of the style I longed to create, to plume myself in at least a few of the feathers forever worn by the grand birds of this community. I felt quite fashionable, quite pretty, as I headed north on Bellevue then down Memorial Boulevard to Thames Street—in my head I said it as Pearl, as the chosen, said it, with the English pronunciation—"temes"—running along the waterfront, lined on the other side by shop after shop.

Though paid each week, I spent little. I saved my money, for something special. I just wasn't sure what that something was yet. I did enjoy looking in all the windows, seeing all the trinkets and such the Townies sold to the summer elite. Many of them did very well. They had no problem gouging the snobs who lived up on the hill in their mansions, sometimes charging triple what they would to a neighbor, a fellow Townie.

In turn, though they bought from them, the families on Bellevue detested the Townies, only they called them 'footstools,' for it was on these people's backs they lived. Their fresh food came from Townie farms, their goods moved on Townie ships, their trinkets came from Townie shops. If they would not offer gratitude, it seemed right to me that they paid for it.

I was off to the Redwood Library, the oldest in Newport, a place of great esteem, a place an American founding father, Thomas Jefferson, had once visited. Renowned not only for its books but for its looks, designed to resemble a Roman Doric temple.

I hoped to find more magazines or books on fashion and design, more things to keep hidden from Mrs. Briggs, more things to keep me busy and hide others. What I found was an article about a mysterious place, one right in Newport, one just around the corner from where I sat.

It took me no more than three minutes to arrive at its base, though it was a bit of a climb as it stood atop a grassy hill where once a mansion sat, one owned by a man named Benedict Arnold; the article did not paint a pleasant picture of this man.

Struck dumb by its presence, I could think of nothing save the words I had read. The Old Stone Tower was, or so the article claimed, citing a study of the mortar by a Reverend Dr. Jackson, was of Viking origin. Supported by eight pillars, four of which faced the main points of a compass, the upper portion was round, well not really round as some parts were wider than others, and rose nearly thirty feet. Between the pillars were rounded arches one could walk through. Of course I did, and I was not alone; people in groups and pairs circled around me as I circled the tower.

Within its shade, I shivered, though the day was frightfully hot. I chided myself with a giggle; I carried myself away on words of temple and pagan and otherworldly worshippers. Unearthly or not, I could see why so many made it a point to walk by it to see it for themselves.

With goosebumps still upon my skin, I stepped out of the shade, taking my first steps back towards The Beeches. They stopped before they began.

He was there. And he was not alone. Two young, beautifully dressed women walked with him, one on each arm.

They could be Pearl and me.

The thought jumped into my head of its accord. I didn't know what it meant; not my thought or his presence with them. I would. One day.

PEARL

Leaving Ginevra this time was both easier and harder.

We had spent so much more time together this summer, not only under the beeches, but in my room, riding my bicycle once it was returned to me, and on our walks, which we had taken to doing more and more often. Her presence by my side seemed to unlock a room hidden within me, hidden even to myself. That summer I explored the room I had never entered. In that room, with her, I laughed truer and confessed more than I ever had.

I knew when I returned she would be there, as much in my life if not more. As I grew older, as she did, there would be more occasions for her to accompany me, more times we could spend together. I clung to those thoughts for they made the leaving easier... if only a little.

In silence, Ginevra packed my trunks, shrouded in the sadness I had placed about her shoulders. It would take me a long time to erase the look on her face when I told her she would be staying in Newport.

"Mother won't let me take you to New York," I explained as we sat upon our limb last night, our last night that summer under the beeches.

The wind had turned, coming out of the north rather than off the warm ocean. We huddled close, wrapped once more together in the shawl I had given her for her birthday, the shawl she wore even over her nightgown.

"She said, if I am to have a lady's maid in New York, it must be a New York maid," I did a passable imitation of my mother's annoying annoyed voice. It made Ginevra smile, but only a little. "I had to agree, or I wouldn't have any maid. At my age, it would be, well, it would embarrass me. I had to agree, you see that, don't you?"

Ginevra had looked at me then, taking her eyes off the stars hanging so close above us, so many more stars we could see as the beeches had already begun to weep away their leaves.

"Of course, yes, I understand."

I don't think she did. Perhaps she understood why I did what I did but not the actions of my mother. She was not alone.

Mother and I warred, and Ginevra was the battleground we fought over. Promoting Ginevra to my ladies' maid had been a battle I won. Mother's counterattack was her refusal to allow Ginevra to accompany me to New York. Knowing a truth and understanding it are two very different things. I couldn't understand a mother who intentionally wanted to hurt their child.

"I made her promise, though, that the New York maid would stay in New York. That here you, and only you, would ever be that to me."

Ginevra had smiled a real smile then. I breathed deeply of the chilly air and my relief.

"Do not worry yourself," Ginevra had said softly. "I will sketch and make many beautiful dresses for you while you are away. I will go to the library." With Mother and Mrs. Briggs away, she could be the Ginevra she truly was; there was solace to be found there and she knew it.

"That will be well then," I had said, but I needed to say more, I leaned down, resting my head on her shoulder. "You know you are more to me, more than a maid, or a seamstress, or even a designer. You are so very much more."

I had never known such a direct gaze as hers that was upon me in that moment.

"You are...," she had grinned again, "*famiglia mia.*"

I had understood her perfectly.

GINEVRA

Pearl's leaving didn't feel as bad this year. The ghostly shadows didn't haunt me as they did last year. I missed her more, more than ever. Yet, I accepted it; acceptance is a great ointment.

PEARL
1897

We weren't back in Newport but a few hours when I took Ginevra beneath the beeches. I had to tell her of the great Alva Vanderbilt, how she was—it was rumored—an adulteress.

"The Vanderbilts went on a cruise with a few friends, including OHP. Well, it seems—"

"OHP?" Ginevra asked on a thin breath. She was spellbound, astounded that the great bastion of proper behavior was nothing more than a loose woman.

"Oh, sorry." I was in such a rush to get it all out I didn't stop to think. Gossip will do that to you. "Oliver Hazard Perry Belmont, he owns Belcourt, up Bellevue, just a bit past Marble House. His first wife, Sarah Whiting, was already pregnant when they married, but they divorced the same year."

"No!"

"Oh, yes." We were deep into it now, safe within the beeches. "And there were rumors, for years now, about the amount of time Alva spent with OHP." Only here did I dare call them by their first names. "He's a very handsome man, outgoing like Alva. But of course, no one could prove it. We are all so incestuous here, aren't we?"

Ginevra agreed once I defined the word for her.

"It seems, as the story going around proclaims, that OHP joined the Vanderbilts on the *Alva* for a summer cruise to Europe." I leaned closer to her, voice a squeaky whisper, words coming fast. "One night, Willie took himself off to some resort. When he came back..."

Ginevra pinched my arm. I toyed with her, but she would have none of it.

"When he came back...he found them...together!"

Ginevra's eyes popped. "Together, together?"

"Oh, yes, together. In *that* way!"

"*O Dio mio,*" Ginevra breathed.

"Oh my God is right. It's really rather ironic." I mused. Ginevra nudge me to do my thinking aloud. "Well, they were never a good match, Willie and Alva. Everyone who's anyone knows he spent all that time on his yacht, named *Alva* no less, to get away from her. But he was rarely alone."

"With friends?" Ginevra panted, hungry for more.

"No, with women, lots of women."

Ginevra nodded slowly. "Ah, *si*, ironic." Then she shook her head. "I cannot believe that such a woman would, that *that* woman would..."

"She did. And now they're getting a divorce."

"A divorce!" Ginevra cried out, slapping a hand over her mouth. The birds squawked complaints as they flew out of the trees.

With her deeply rooted Catholic faith, such an action must have seemed even more scandalous. We sat in silence for a while, a good long while. If I could reach into her mind, I would see a reflection of my thoughts, ones of pretentiousness and hypocrisy.

For all that we disapproved of the force that was Alva Vanderbilt, she was a fixture in our lives, an impenetrable stone, no matter that we chafed at where such a stone sat. Her disgrace unnerved, made the immovable movable, chinked away at what we thought we could depend on.

In our quiet contemplation, we heard the voices draw close.

It happened now and again, when we were secreted beneath the beeches, when people—groundskeepers, my brother and his friends, my parents—would come out to the grounds, whether working or taking a stroll.

Usually, we would abandon our haven beneath the weeping beeches, for what good was it if others were near, their voices intruding, breaking the illusion of our existence in another time and place. We would sneak out from the far side of the commotion, our minds shifting away from our alternate reality, like waking from a dream with the disappointment of its untruth. Though there were times when we stayed when others were near, times we shouldn't have stayed.

The small octagonal teahouses marking the entrance to the sunken gardens sat upon marble stair daises punctuating the rise at the end of the vast verdant lawn. Like small little palaces, with their copper dome-shaped roofs and their gleaming white stone. Ginevra thought the wrought-iron balustrade ring on top with the eight urns set at all the corners, made it look like a crown.

I liked the doors. French doors, of course, my mother would have no other kind, with round over-doors set atop each of the four entrances. I loved the sight of their delicacy centered amidst the hard stone. Like me, in this "cottage" my mother had demanded, fragile within its sturdiness.

There were times when Ginevra and I snuck into them, when my mother entertained no one, no small tete-a-tetes. Those times were rare. We made our place in the vast foliage cave beneath the weeping beeches. Freedom and segregation, no matter how disparate, were ours there, as we wanted it to be.

On the warmest days, such as this one, the doors of the teahouses stood wide open on all four sides. Here my parents, though in truth rarely my father, had afternoon tea sheltered beneath these small cupolas, the women perched primly upon the scrolled iron chairs, the men flounced with an elegant flop, everyone grateful for the shade and the strong breeze the wide-open space of the yard conjured up. The wind swept through, clearing away the heat, taking with it any words sprinkled about haphazardly.

On the same breeze, the voices came to us, especially if the intruders—as we always called them—chose the one nearest to us, nearest to our world beneath the beeches, the one closest to the carriage house.

Far too often, Ginevra and I would stay perched like mute monkeys on one of the lower, horizontal branches and listened. Far too often, we heard things we shouldn't have.

If we had heard this conversation a few years ago, it would have had no power, its impact lost to our innocent ignorance. We were older now. Their words became brutal fists with our comprehension.

"I really don't know how long I can stand him. I can't bear looking at him." Mother's voice was a shrill complaint. It scattered frightened robins from a nearby maple.

She spoke of my father, I knew. Ginevra knew as well, she told me so with the drop turn of her head.

"You could leave him, my dear. Alva has paved the way."

Her words plunged a dagger into my heart.

I wasn't exactly sure who encouraged my mother to do such a heinous act. I wish I did so that I could hurt her in some way, as she hurt me. The ever so practiced, haughty diction could have belonged to any of the privileged women who made Newport their summer home. The way she pronounced "we" had all the arrogance of superiority so rife in this small world. Whoever she was, she was cut from the same cloth as my mother.

Mother sounded wounded and suffering. Not the sort she feigned with such practice so often, but real pain. "Yes, but unlike Alva, I would most probably lose everything, possibly even the children." She lowered her voice. Ginevra and I craned our ears.

Ginevra's hand took mine. I didn't know until she did, how much it shook.

"But you know there are ways, many ways, of finding happiness away from him." The other woman laughed then, salt on the wound she had opened in my heart. "I have seen the many sways who pay you so much attention. I'm sure any one of them would help relieve your...dissatisfaction."

Innocence does not equate to stupidity. I had a vague notion of what the woman encouraged.

"It is just like that article said," I whispered, unsure to whom I spoke, Ginevra or myself.

"What article?" she hissed back.

"Remember, the one by the 'woman' named Belle, who turned out to be a man. The one who wrote for *The New York Mirror*. Remember he wrote—"

"Don't." Ginevra squeezed hard on my hand in hers.

"I remember exactly what he wrote." Ginevra was no longer with me, or I was not with her. "*They bring money and gaiety to the town, but they have introduced a very serious evil. I mean an expensive lifestyle and a too great fondness for convivial entertainments. Older women pursued younger men. Younger women chased older men. Fortune hunters of all ages ran after anyone with money. And some highly unconventional women took up with each other and were spied kissing on the lips.*"

A tight-lipped grimace sat upon Ginevra's mouth. She remembered. How she disapproved of us.

Mother laughed then, a sound I had not often heard. I had no care to hear it—that laugh—ever again.

"Perhaps, my dear, perhaps you are right. Perhaps it is the thing to do." she snickered. "Perhaps I already have. And perhaps Orin already knows."

A gale-force wind overtook the sweet summer breeze drifting through the leaves; I gripped our branch lest it fell me to the ground.

Ginevra turned and gripped me, held me on the branch. Upon her sun-spackled face, lay true sympathy.

"What? What has she already done?" she whispered.

I had no answer for her, not a sure one, or the depth of the act.

"Things are changing," I said, it was all I could think to say.

"What…things?" she asked.

"The world," I said, believing it. How right I was and how sorry I would be for it.

* * *

As had become the fashion, Mother insisted we take a family photograph every year. Since Father built The Beeches, it became the backdrop for this picture. In truth, there could be none better.

We gathered together, the four of us. On the top step of the second terrace, Mother and Father stood close but not together, shoulders touching but nothing else, nothing that mattered. The imposing, almost frightening statue of *Le Furie di Atamente*—The Madness of Athamas—behind them, somehow appropriate. Clarence and I stood on a step below, I before my mother, he before my father. Father rested a hand on Clarence's shoulder; Mother did the same on mine. I shuddered at the touch.

"Smile brightly, everyone," Mother chirped, as she always did at such moments. My father never smiled for these pictures. I offered what I could, a grimace.

The photographer hunched over his machine, hiding himself with a heavy drape of dark fabric. The flash popped and smoked. The moment captured.

When I saw the finished product some days later, I thought it should be a painting. Photographs captured truth; paintings interpreted it. This photo captured little of our truth.

GINEVRA

Each morning's awakening seemed brighter than the one that came before. I hated Mrs. Worthington more every day. The reunion with Pearl that should have been nothing but one joyous day after the other was dark and cloudy, no matter how bright the sun shone.

Pearl took her breakfast in her room more and more, as much to be away from her mother as to be with me. If she heard her mother's voice, the clack of her mother's low-heeled, kid-leather calf boots, Pearl ran in the other direction. Should Mrs. Worthington be out of doors, in the garden or a teahouse, Pearl remained inside.

I watched Pearl changing before my eyes. At eighteen, we both had begun to look like the adult women we would soon be, but she looked older, older than she ever had. My helplessness toward her kept slumber away many nights. All I knew to do was to be with her whenever I could, as much as I could.

She rarely left her room those first few days after hearing what we heard as we hid beneath the beeches, and when she did, I was by her side, or as close as I could get.

Worse, so very much worse, Pearl didn't paint, hadn't since that day.

Now she seemed only to wish to read, to escape into someone else's words, someone else's life.

She sent me to her father's library for her, for a particular book.

"I'll get it," I told her, as if I spoke to a child, "but only if you promise we go to the beeches to read it. The day is very fine, and your mother is not at home. You need some air."

I shuffled back a step when Pearl agreed.

I had been pretending to be my stern grandmother, putting on a show, never imaging she would take my threat seriously.

As Pearl slowly ate, slowly roused herself from the half-awake state she barely existed in, I left her for the library.

I had to circle the room to find it; one book in a room filled with glorious books. As I did, I passed Mr. Worthington's desk. Two photographs lay on it. One already in its frame, the new one the Worthington's had just taken a few days ago, *that* day. The old one hung off the edge of the massive desk, naked without its frame, already forgotten. I almost walked away, but something in it—two somethings—caught my eye.

On the corner of the house, where visitor carriages entered, the corner where the Worthington's guests were dropped off, the gleaming wood of the family's crest could be seen in its place on the wall, the shield-like crest my father had made for Mr. Worthington. I smiled to think the photographer had captured, in a way, my father's image as well. It was his imprint on this family moment. He wasn't alone. I was there with him.

I could barely see myself. I had to squint my eyes and hold the thick, heavy paper close to my face. But there I was. I was the ghost behind the sheer inner curtains in Pearl's room. It seemed fitting.

I took Pearl's book from the shelf, taking it from the room to her. The picture I took for myself.

PEARL

I stood at my window and watched. She thought she was being so clever, so furtive, but she didn't know I had been watching her, as much as I could, every day since that day. I knew *this* day—*this* moment—would come. I needed Ginevra.

It took a while for Ginevra to arrive. It was past eight o'clock. I had dismissed her an hour ago, thinking I would read in bed and fall asleep. I felt so very tired these days.

In the quiet of the house, I heard the carriage wheels crunch on the gravel path, and I knew.

I didn't need to see my mother, dressed to the nines, to know it was she, though see her I did. She jumped in the carriage, snapping her hand at Mr. Morgan, to go, to hurry. I didn't need to think too long or too hard to fathom where she was going. I had a good notion.

"Pearl?" Ginevra knocked on my door but didn't wait for my call to enter. Fear thinned and riddled her voice. She had been looking at me with a gaze full of it for days.

"We have to go," I said without a greeting. I reached into my wardrobe and grabbed two long coats, one for each of us. It was a warm night, but the coats had wide collars; when turned up, they would hide much of our faces.

"Go?" Ginevra's head bobbled like that of a turkey. "Go…where?"

I stopped though I didn't want to, but she deserved to know.

"My mother has gone out. She told no one. But she was dressed…," I hesitated. How startling it was that Mother's couture had been the final clue.

"…she was dressed to impress, but there is no party, no dinner or ball for such finery."

Ginevra said nothing; I sighed, relieved.

"We are going to find her. I think I know where she is going."

Ginevra knew then too.

It was no secret that the men and women, both young and old, in this cloistered community—the rarified among the rare—defied the rules, both legal and moral. The newspapers were forever filled with the tawdry stories of our tawdry lives. When I was younger, when I knew no better, I thought they had all been made up; people's jealousy will do such things. How foolish I was. Illicit trysts were as much a part of the summer activities on Newport as was sailing and tennis.

Ginevra said nothing as I took her hand, pulled her through the family portion of the house and out of it, through the Conservatory. I hurried her to the carriage house, gave a hurried explanation to one of the groomsmen—I couldn't remember his name, I don't now—for why I needed a buggy.

"My dear friend is ill," I said climbing on the sidebars and onto the driver's seat, thrusting my head for Ginevra to sit beside me. I grabbed the tasseled snapper and the reins from his hand before he could gain a tighter hold on them. "Pull up the top, would you, good man?"

I used my father's pleasant authority. The young man did as I instructed. Ginevra and I were now faceless bodies, the folding canvas of the buggy covering our heads, sheltering us, at least on the back and the sides.

"Thank you. You needn't wait up. I'll tend to the horses when we return, though we may be gone all night. I wouldn't want to deprive any of you hard-working men of your sleep."

"But, Miss..."

I snapped the reins, the horses responded, and his words were lost in the sound of the wind rushing past my ears, the crunch of the wheels on the gravel.

Ginevra held on tightly, silently.

She said nothing until we came to Memorial Boulevard and took a right, not a left. Those who lived on Bellevue Avenue and Ocean Drive never turned toward that part of the island. Almost never.

"Where are we going?" Ginevra had to yell for me to hear her over the crashing of the waves, the sluicing of the wind.

Without looking at her, I said, "Hanging Rock."

GINEVRA

A few people—couples, loud groups of mafficking young men—walked along Memorial Boulevard. A few more passed us in carriages. More than a few stopped, staring at two young women alone in a carriage, driving themselves. It was a sight out of sorts.

Once we made our way past Easton's Beach, where the Townies and the staff went to swim—the poor people's beach—less and less stared at us, we were less oddly out of place.

Pearl scared me. Her driving was uneven, and she had a way with horses, I had watched her many times. Her face was not her own, but an ugly version of her, one twisted with hate and anger. I wanted to scream at her to stop, that she didn't need to see what we both knew we would see. She knew the truth of her mother, as I did, as her father did, as most of the cottagers did. To see it would make it too real, the pain of it too real.

I turned to her; the wind snatched my hair, slapping the side of my face. I opened my mouth and shut it just as quickly. If this was what Pearl needed to do, nothing would stop her. If I tried, I could lose her. It wasn't worth the risk.

She turned off Memorial onto Purgatory Road. When I saw the street sign posted on the corner of the stonewall of the fire station, I slapped a hand over my mouth, trapping in bitter laughter. Pearl whipped the carriage around recklessly as we turned again, as all the people and the buildings faded away, as we plunged onto a rutted forest road, the trees rising, writhing in the wind above and around us.

"Whoa, whoa, slow now," Pearl whispered to the tall brown stallion pulling us along. He shook his long head, his shaggy mane whipped and stilled. Pearl slowed us to a trot, and then a walk. The four-beat gait of the horse's feet matched that of my heart.

The woods swallowed us. Owls hooted at us, angry at the presence of more intruders.

In the thick gossip that was a dish served at every staff meal, I had heard of Hanging Rock, heard all the nasty things the nasty women of the house said about it. I always thought they spoke out of desire, what woman wouldn't long for, if even a little, the romance of a secret meeting in the woods.

A river ran through the trees, we heard its gurgle. A pond was not too far off; I could smell that odor particular to fresh water, a greener smell than the ocean. It was a beautiful place, even in the dark, or especially so.

According to Mrs. Briggs, Nettie, Greta, and the rest, this was where the cottagers came; here a husband from one cottage and a wife from another came to meet when their spouses were in residence, when no other place allowed them to be together.

"Pfft, pfft," Pearl made the strange sound with her lips and pulled back hard on the reins.

"Look, there," she pointed, whispering.

I peered round the edge of the canopy, over my right shoulder. A loud groan filled my head. I left it there.

There was one of the Worthington's finest carriages. Next to it, another, equally as fine. I followed Pearl's finger and saw Mr. Morgan, off his driver's perch, walking a good distance away from the two carriages. He walked in a circle, one arm across his chest, the other stroking his doorknocker mustache. It looked as if he'd been walking the circle going nowhere for a while. It looked as if he had walked this walk before.

Pearl slithered down from the seat.

"Where are you going?"

"Ssssh!" she hissed at me, a finger to her lips. The same finger pointed to a group of tightly clumped birch trees.

I wanted to scream out, loud enough for Mrs. Worthington to hear me, for Mrs. Worthington to stop doing what we both knew she did. Pearl waved at me to follow. I did. If she must see, she would not do it alone.

Lifting our skirts, stepping high but soft, twigs cracking, leaves crunching beneath our feet, we made it to the cover of the birch trees without notice. Pearl bent sideways, peered around the tree trunks, and gasped.

"What, what is it?" I tugged on her sleeve.

She turned to me. Bright in the darkness, her eyes blazed with a white-hot anger.

"Lispenard Stewart!" her whisper was a scream.

O Dio mio, I said again, in my head this time.

I remembered all the awful things she had said about the man. I think Pearl had hoped, as I had, that if her mother was stepping out on her father that it was for love. Unrequited love was a pitiable thing, a thing that broke hearts with its tender pain. This man knew nothing of love. What he and Mrs. Worthington did had nothing to do with love.

I knelt below Pearl so I could peek around the trees as well. I shouldn't have. I couldn't stop myself even if I tried.

They kissed and groped and fondled to their heart's content, touching each other only where a husband and wife should, touching each other as if Mr. Morgan was not just a clearing away. I heard Pearl's angry breath above me, felt the shaking of her legs against my back.

"We should go," I muttered.

Pearl didn't move.

The man with the ridiculous name was kissing her mother's throat under the ear. He moved his lips across to the front, moved his lips lower, and then lower still.

I heard Pearl hitch a sob, the revolt loud.

"*Basta!* Enough," I grumbled, stood, and grabbed her arm. I pulled her, had to pull hard, but I pulled her away. She had seen enough. She had seen too much.

We made it back to the buggy without discovery. Pearl turned the horse's head, turned us 'round, and the moonlight found her face drenched with tears. Somehow, she brought us safely out of the woods, back onto the hard-packed dirt of Purgatory Road. There she stopped. Her arms dropped, as did her head. Her shoulders shuddered. I wrapped her in my arms and held her until they stilled.

"These people," she spat, I knew in her mind she was no longer one of them. How could she be? "How great they perceive themselves to be. All their money, their mansions, their fineries. It is all a false life."

She looked at me, her face twisted with pain, looking at me for an answer I did not have.

"It is not what life should be."

I couldn't disagree with her. I had watched them for three years, the grand parties, and the new clothes, every year more stunning, more elaborate. I watched—helpless and disgusted—when I saw the perfectly good clothes thrown out because they were no longer "in fashion." I had stared, astonished, in the kitchens as the footmen brought down huge trays of uneaten food. The staff would help themselves to the leftovers, as I had done on more than one occasion. And yet there was still so much of it, it filled bin after trash bin, food tossed away when there were so many going without. It seemed that for all they had, they always wanted more. They tossed people away with the same ease as last season's clothes.

"Take us home, Pearl," I said in her ear for I held her still. "I must get you in bed."

Pearl nodded, raised her head, and raised the reins.

"Heehaw!"

Before we could move again, the howl burst behind us, the carriage sped past us.

"Is that…is he…," I stuttered, astounded.

Even as a servant, I had heard what a coachman James Gordon Bennett, Jr. was. Everyone had heard about the races he organized, raced in, and bet on heavily. But this…

"Hah!" Pearl barked, a guard-dog bark. "Yes, that's him, that's Bennet."

We saw him race away, in all his glory, all of him. He was completely naked.

Pearl started laughing, kept laughing as she drove us back to The Beeches, laughed still as I changed her, and put her to bed. There, the laughter turned to tears as sometimes laughter can.

PEARL

They called Newport the playground of America's rich. We had made it so. With palace dollhouses and circus balls. For a brief, shining moment, it was the grandest place on earth. But, if it was a playground, then we, all of us—the Astors, Vanderbilts, Stuveysants, Belmonts, and those whose names may not be so well remembered—we were its children.

Every childhood must end, too often with toys broken and hard lessons learned and more than a tinge of regret and longing for what was...what could have been.

* * *

I didn't ring for Ginevra the next morning. It was not really morning yet at all, but still dawn. My eyes felt heavy and swollen; the rest of me felt numb. I threw my combing coat on over my nightgown and wandered out of my room. Directionless in so many ways.

The house had just started to wake. I could hear vague noises from two floors below, the kitchen workers no doubt.

Here, on the family floors, the only sounds were the ticking of the clocks, as out of sync as my family. I floated, my feet not touching the ground, a translucent specter of myself. The sight of my mother broke my connection, images I could not erase from my mind no matter how hard I pushed.

I made my way down the wide, white stairs. At the bottom, I began to turn right, heading for the Conservatory, heading for the little solace the room brought me. A noise to my left stopped me. I turned to it, creeping down the hall toward my father's library.

I stopped just outside the door, peeking in as I had so many times before.

I saw him then, saw him standing, staring out the window.

I watched my father as he stood at the edge of the cliff. Everything about him reeked of his despair, his unbuttoned coat, unruly hair, wrinkled trousers. His shoulders drooped. I had never seen him like this. I looked at a man I did not know.

* * *

Ginevra dressed me that night, holding my limbs, twisting my body, as she would a rag doll. I readied for one of the fabulous parties given by the Wetmore family at Chateau-sur-Mer, one of the first, one of the finest, cottages of them all. Though I had been there a few years ago for a birthday party for William Wetmore, Senator Wetmore's youngest, I had attended as an "adult." Mr. Wetmore, a two-term governor of Rhode Island, and now a Senator, was one of the more gracious cottagers, and Chateau-sur-Mer embodied his demeanor. This evening's fete was to honor his daughter Edith's engagement. I had looked forward to the event for weeks. I wanted to be anywhere but there.

"Just do your best to get through night," Ginevra nattered at me, only a few of the words finding their way into my consciousness. "Find Consuelo and stay with her and all will be well."

Ginevra took my face in her hands, putting her face inches from mine. "You can do this, Pearl. Be yourself, not your mother's daughter. I will be a room away, always."

I put my hands on hers. Gratitude swept through me for her giving, loving heart. I nodded and slipped away, not a thought to what I wore or how I looked.

* * *

The castle by the sea was alive. A dazzling shoal of fish swam beneath the atrium-like central hall, swayed beneath the forty-five-foot glass ceiling. Those not in the stream watched from above, from the balcony encircling the entire hall. I was drowning.

We did as we always did. My mother shot off like an arrow loosed into her "group" of friends—a group including Lispenard Stewart. My brother swaggered off to a bevy of young men and flirtatious young women. My father turned away.

I stood alone. I floundered about, my greetings curt but mannered, looking for some hook to be caught on. I found Consuelo in a deep conversation with Edith, the Wetmore's oldest daughter, a lovely woman seven years my senior, aglow with new love.

"Are you saying that women... *women*," Consuelo emphasized the word as if she had never said it before, "women are playing tennis?"

"I saw them myself," Edith responded with a bright smile on her long, but not unbecoming face. Edith wore her fine blonde hair bigger, her brocade skirt narrower, her bustle smaller than was in fashion, but knowing her—in the acquaintance manner that I did—I wondered if she wasn't *making* fashion rather than following it. At this moment, though, her words held me spellbound.

"Where... where did you see such a thing?" I barged into the conversation like a steamship coming into port. So astounded, I forgot all my manners. Luckily, Consuelo didn't.

"Pearl!" she chirped, greeting me with a quick embrace. In the squeeze of her arms, I remembered protocol and made the proper greetings to the small group of women around Edith, including Mrs. John Jacob Astor IV, Ava Willing, a dark-haired beauty in her thirties.

Formalities attended to, I had to have the answer to my question. The words overheard, now planted in my mind, forced the others out. I turned to Edith. "You saw women playing tennis? Where?"

"Indeed, I did. Ava was with me. It was at the most prestigious tennis club in England. Wimbledon, it's called," Edith explained, Ava concurred.

Captivated, Consuelo and I couldn't ask enough questions: how well did they play, what did they wear, was it a true tournament? We talked for far longer than we should; we should have been socializing with others. There was something in the conversation, a bonding of like feminine minds, which could not break apart. It held me together.

Until I saw him.

I had only seen Frederick once since we returned to Newport, though I had seen him often in New York. He swaggered into the room, beside him, Herbert Butterworth. Herbert didn't swagger.

If I lied to myself, I would say that men didn't matter; only my education and my painting mattered. If I lied to myself. I didn't.

Other young women my age were either already betrothed, engaged, or at the least had a steady boyfriend. When I thought of all those varied layers of relationships, I thought only of two men—these two men.

Consuelo took me by the arm, "Excuse us, ladies," she said to the group around us, or at least I think that's what she said. "I want to show Pearl the lovely Tree of Life."

I vaguely remember her hold on me, her leading me through the crowd in that crooked sort of fashion people must walk through a room full of other people. Consuelo pulled me into the alcove below the stairs. There *was* a tree of life here; I had never seen it. The painting rose the full three stories of the back of the stairs, all the way to the ceiling where bright birds fluttered against a deep blue sky. I longed to join them.

"I called on you Tuesday," Consuelo whispered, but she never let go of me. She held onto my hand. "But your mother said you weren't accepting visitors."

I laughed. It tasted as bitter as it sounded. Did I ever tell Consuelo about Frederick and Herbert and my growing feelings for them both? I couldn't remember. It didn't matter. She would have seen.

In that moment, Consuelo looked at me as if she didn't know me. She didn't, not the true me, the me I was becoming.

"Is that what Mother said? Remarkable." I pushed away thoughts of my mother for they made my head spin, my stomach ache. "Tell me."

"I just heard about it myself, the very day I came to call," Consuelo spoke softly, tenderly, as if speaking to a wounded child. She did. "Apparently they met at some college event. Herbert is staying with the Havemeyers."

The ache in my stomach twisted.

"For the entire summer." Consuelo put on the finishing touch.

I raised my eyes, brows high and stuck upon my forehead. "All summer? Here? In Newport? Together?" Sentences were too complex to form at the time.

Consuelo simply nodded.

I laughed again, an ugly sound of reckoning in a summer full of it.

"Are you quite well, Pearl? Should I call your mother?"

"No!" I snapped, too quickly, too harshly. "I'm sorry, Consuelo," I said, immediately contrite at the hurt on this dear girl's—this sensitive girl's—face. "No, I'm not feeling my best."

"And such news as this can only make it worse."

I looked at her but didn't see her. I thought of my parents, of their marriage, of what marriage would mean to me among these people who were so grand and so awful all at the same time. Had I been saved from such a fate by being forced to make a decision I didn't know how or want to make? Or were such thoughts only those of my battered heart?

"Thank you, Consuelo. Thank you for telling me."

She embraced me again and we returned to the party. I stood by her side the whole night. Most of it.

* * *

I could have been a child in a playground, trapped on a titter-totter. I sat in the middle. On one end sat Frederick, on the other Herbert. All through that night, and long after, they took turns, up and down in my attention, in and out of my heart.

I didn't try to get off. If I did, I would have to walk to either one end or the other. It seemed easier, safer, to stay in the middle. I couldn't stay there forever.

GINEVRA

I watched Pearl watching the two men as they made their way into the ballroom.

Pearl and Consuelo disappeared from my view, and I flit this way and that to find them but couldn't. I took the moment. I watched only Herbert Butterworth, the man who called me beautiful. He followed Frederick around. Where Frederick was loud, he was soft. Where Frederick was flirtatious, he was only amiable. I knew which choice Pearl would make. I put my head against the doorjamb I hid behind, wondering how I would live with it.

As soon as Pearl and Consuelo returned to the room, Frederick cried out her name.

"Pearl! There you are." He left a conversation in its middle and strode to her, Herbert right beside him, no longer behind.

I couldn't hear their conversation from where I stood. They were too far away, and the musicians had struck up the first chords of the evening as servants laid out pastries, coffee, and tea. Both men looked to Pearl. Lips moved and I imagined the words they spoke.

Pearl shrugged a shoulder, a pretty grin across her face. I couldn't tell if it was real. She reached out a hand... and took the one Frederick held out to her. Together they walked to the refreshments. I dropped my head again and sighed. My prayers may have been silent, but they were mine.

"Hello again."

That voice found me. He had found me. It was not what I prayed for, yet it seemed an answer.

"*Buona notte*," I answered in Italian as I had with Consuelo last summer. It would be foolish to deny its effect on some people, the right people.

It was only a moment, but it stretched on and on. We looked at each other in silence.

"It is a pity you are not allowed to dance," Herbert finally said. "You do like to dance, don't you, Miss...?"

I forgot my name for a moment.

"C…Costa, Ginevra Costa," I gurgled, perhaps giggled a little. I despised myself for it.

Until he smiled.

"Well then," he held out his hand for me to shake. I took it. I would never feel the same again. "I am Herbert Butterworth."

I know.

"Pleased to meet you, Mr. Butterworth." Our hands remained entwined.

"Oh no, Herbert, if you wish."

I do.

"Then I am Ginevra," I replied. I released his hand; I had to, or he would have felt mine shaking.

He bowed his head, tossing back a gleaming swath of black hair as he rose up.

"Do you like to dance, Ginevra?"

What could I do? I was helpless.

"I do," I said truthfully.

Herbert tilted his head to the side as he looked down at me.

"Then it truly is a shame," he whispered this time, and, with another nod of his head, stepped away, away from the room where all the maids sat in the nowhere of waiting, away from me.

I escaped as far into the small room as I could. I could see no more.

* * *

I sat at the staff dinner table the next night, barely eating, barely saying a word to my father. All I could think about was Pearl. Pearl and her mother. Pearl and Frederick. And Herbert Butterworth.

It had been weeks since we learned her mother's truth, since we saw it. She hovered in a fog of confusion and brought me with her.

I barely stirred even as someone sat down next to me; no one had ever sat next to me before. The others—well some of the others—had come to be nice. Perhaps that wasn't the word. Perhaps they had come to accept me, at the least appreciate the work I did for Pearl. It was enough, I supposed.

"Zee food here, iz good, ya?"

She was a lovely young woman, broadly built and tall, her hands were rough and work-worn, but her smile was bright through thin lips, and her blue eyes sparkled.

"It is," I said, "very good."

We made our introductions. I introduced Anja, a new chambermaid, to my father, who delighted him with Italian words of greeting.

The three of us chatted for a while. Like a sweet dessert, it was a lovely treat to be treated with such kindness by another of the staff. Like us, Anja was new, and so something of an outsider. This closed group, as bigoted and prejudiced as those they served, opened easier to her German heritage.

Happy and kind, Anja endeared herself to me quickly. I might have a friend below stairs after all. Though such a friendship could never equal what I had with Pearl, no matter how many steps separated us.

The table talk turned to gossip as it so often did. Anja, new to the area, hung on every word, asking questions. As the others answered her, I heard the latest news, the terrible news of Pearl's dear Consuelo. Her name, her mother's name, was on everyone's tongue, more than their food. As the story unfolded, I understood. It was a tale of heartbreak.

I wanted to rush from the room immediately, rush to Pearl to tell her. Of course, I couldn't. The time would come when I could.

* * *

As our years together grew, I would often sneak downstairs at night when the house slept. Feeling like a specter in the Persian cotton nightdress Pearl had given me, I floated down to the rarefied air engulfed in the diaphanous material.

One time, her brother stepped out of his room, his door diagonally across from Pearl's own.

"Sis," he hissed at me, "what the dickens are you doing?"

I froze, hand on the crystal doorknob. With my dark hair, so like Pearl's, falling about my shoulders, robed in her nightdress, he could not tell the truth of the person in the musky light.

I shrugged my shoulders and made a sleepy sound of nonsense.

"Get back to bed," was all he said in reply.

I hurriedly did, ever so grateful for the striking resemblance to my dear friend.

Snuggled beneath her covers, we would giggle, wish, dream without sleep, gifting each other with the deepest parts of our souls.

Tonight would not be a night for laughter.

"Ginevra?" Pearl roused, squinting at me in the dark. "Is that you?"

I hurried to her bed and jumped in. I surrounded myself with the plush pillows that rose from it like little islands, a good place to hide should someone else come in.

"I, I have something to tell you," I said. She sat up.

"What is it? Why didn't you tell me when you readied me for bed?"

"I couldn't. Your mother and father were both awake, both in their rooms, they might have heard."

"You're scaring me, Ginevra." Pearl pulled me up to sit beside her. "Tell me right now."

I did.

"It is Consuelo. Her mother is forcing her to marry the Duke of Marlborough."

Pearl dropped her face into her hands. Her words muffled. "I knew it would come to this. They have been fighting about it for months."

I had been in Consuelo's company with Pearl and not a speck of this dirty linen had I seen on her pristine clothes, in her perfect manners. I pestered Pearl with my thick silence.

"Consuelo is in love. She is secretly engaged to Winthrop Rutherford."

It was my turn to cover my face. The strange lives of these people broke hearts as the chef did eggs, yet they clung to it.

"You have no idea, Ginevra, no idea just how malicious her mother is." Pearl squirmed out from the bed linens and faced me. "When we were children, she wasn't allowed to go to a school, not even the best private schools in New York. Alva insisted she was tutored at home by a governess, and later by two or three tutors at a time. Granted, she learned a great deal. I think she can speak at least three languages."

I nodded, taking her hand, squeezing as if to squeeze out more words from her. Her need to say them was in every huff of air she took.

"Alva has been a tyrant to her all her life. When Consuelo was young, Alva forced her to wear a steel rod against her spine, strapped to her waist and shoulders to ensure she learned proper posture."

I shuddered, "That is horrible! It is tor..." I struggled.

"Torture," Pearl finished for me. "It was, but that was not the worst of it. If Consuelo didn't like the clothes Alva picked out for her, if she found the courage to tell her mother so, she was severely reprimanded. 'I do the thinking, you do as you're told,' Alva would say to her. And then... then...," Pearl's lips trembled, her eyes grew moist.

"And then..."

"And then Alva would whip her, whip her with a riding crop."

The crop could have struck me, so sharp was the pain from her words, pain for Consuelo, pain for them all.

I envied these "cottagers" their life, their wealth, their beautiful homes, clothes, jewels. I wanted such a life for myself. Or did I? Hearing such things as this, made my wants as thin and elusive as passing summer clouds.

"As Consuelo grew to be so beautiful—"

"She is a true beauty," I agreed.

"Isn't she?" Pearl said, not a speck of envy spoiled her pride. "Well, her conniving mother knew that beauty would serve her well. Alva's been pushing members of royalty on her since she was as young as fourteen, fifteen. How better to become a true aristocrat rather than just a filthy rich American?"

"But Consuelo wanted none of it. She met Winthrop just this past winter. It was love at first sight, for both of them. They became secretly engaged, though I don't know why."

"What do you mean?" I whispered. It felt the only way to speak of such things; here with Pearl beneath the linens, we were mere specters in the dark of night.

"Well, Winthrop is from a very powerful family. He is directly descended from Peter Stuyvesant who was a governor. No, that's not right." Pearl closed her eyes, rubbed her forehead. "Director-General, that's it. He was the Director-General of New Netherland."

It was my turn to scrunch my face. "I never heard of this place."

"Oh, but you have. It's now called New York."

My eyes burst wide. "Why did not this man please Alva?"

Pearl shook her head. "Alva wanted a royal marriage for Consuelo and nothing less. And so, the staff is saying that Alva is forcing this marriage, Consuelo's marriage to the Duke?"

I nodded, my unbraided hair rustling on the pillows. "Yes, but they did not say how she is being forced. I did hear them say the Duke does not want the marriage either."

Pearl sat, steamily silent. The heat of her anger came off her in waves, as if she was a fireplace filled with wood in full flame. This anger—on Consuelo's behalf—overshadowed her own confusion and heartache.

"I will call on Consuelo tomorrow, first thing." She punctuated each word with a fist strike upon a pillow.

I slipped out of her bed and gently pushed her back down, covering her with the fine linens and tucking her in as my mother had once done to me. "Yes, tomorrow. For now, sleep."

I left her knowing she wouldn't.

PEARL

Ginevra and I didn't leave The Beeches, we hurried. As we approached Marble House, we slowed and stumbled. Though officially separated from her husband, Alva Vanderbilt had retained possession of their magnificent cottage. It had never looked like this before.

The staff scattered about in total disarray. Serious men, dressed in serious black, went in and out of the front door as we approached it. The Vanderbilt butler did not attend the portal, so we let ourselves in. More staff hurried around us, blind to our presence. In front of us rose the grand circular staircase with its fountain beneath.

"Come on," I hissed at Ginevra, pulling her by the hand when she hesitated.

Safe in an invisible cloak, we climbed the stairs and hurried down the hall to Consuelo's room. I knocked at the door.

"Please go away," Consuelo's weak response found us through the wood. We entered despite them.

"Consuelo, darling, it's me, Pearl." Darkness shrouded the room, curtains drawn tight, not a single lamp lit. Slivers of sunlight slipped in the folds of the drapes, dust danced in the beams. It looked so unreal, as dreamlike as the rest of the house.

"Oh Pearl," Consuelo cried softly, my name mangled on a sob. I rushed to her. Ginevra remained at the door. To guard us or out of respect? Either way, I was thankful.

I sat and pulled Consuelo to me. "What is happening? What is going on here?"

"Oh, Pearl," she whimpered again. Was that all she would or could say?

The words gushed out of her; a dam demolished. Her mother and Lady Paget—one of the 'Four Hundred' who had fallen on hard times, who now used her connections to make money as a marriage bro-ker—had pushed them together, Consuelo and the Duke. Her mother had cajoled, begged, and then demanded Consuelo marry him.

"I r...refused, over and over." Consuelo looked up at me with her big brown eyes, there was so much there to see, so much that broke my heart. "I had never spoken to Mother like that in my whole life."

Ginevra sniffed indignation. I agreed but said nothing.

"I told her that Winthrop and I would be married, even if we had to elope."

"Oh my. Good for you," I praised her for her courage, even knowing it would not have been well met.

"She locked me in, locked me in my own room." Consuelo slapped the bed upon which we sat.

I slapped my hand to my mouth.

"I wondered why I hadn't seen you these past few weeks. I thought you were away, that's what your mother has been telling people." At least those people who would listen. After her tryst with OHP, after word of the pending divorce came to light, the great Alva, became ostracized by many, but not all. "But your door is not locked now."

Consuelo shook her head. "No, my maid unlocked it, but only to tell me that my mother is ill, seriously ill."

Unkind words taunted my tongue; words of disbelief and manipulation, but I refused them. They would serve no purpose other than to feed Consuelo's discontent.

"How ill is she? How is she ill?"

"They say, the doctors say, she may have had a mild heart attack." Consuelo looked at me. Guilt turned her beautiful face into a gruesome mask.

I cast a look over my shoulder to Ginevra. I saw my skepticism upon her face.

"When they finally let me in, she really did look terrible..." I thought Alva always looked terrible, "...and when I sat by her, she said the stress of all this, with the Duke, was too much for her. She said it could kill her."

I had never longed to be one of the Great Triumvirate or Mrs. Astor than in that moment. If I were her peer, I would stomp into Alva's room and give her a good smack. How dare she manipulate this sweet girl like this? Especially after what she had done.

"What are you going to do?" I asked softly, refusing to heed my rebellious thoughts.

Consuelo shrugged; more tears came. She answered me as she dried them, "What else *can* I do? I will marry the Duke."

I could say nothing against her decision, no matter how against it I was. I would be her friend.

We stayed with her until she calmed...until she lay back on her silk-covered pillows and her eyes grew heavy.

Though my mother was no better than Alva was, she was no worse. Her attempts to control me as Alva controlled Consuelo were not as successful. I had my father to keep her from going too far. Though I wondered as Ginevra and I walked slowly home, gloomy in the bright morning, if Father wasn't around, would I be treated in the same manner? I knew my mother's ambition equaled and exceeded that of Alva Vanderbilt. What I didn't know was how far she would take it if she could. I knew only that my secrets, my painting, and my ambitions, could find me in a similar state. How far would I go to fight her?

My mother and her lascivious behavior, my struggle between Frederick and Herbert, the confusion and pain of both fell away. Consuelo and the world in which she struggled to survive took up all the space of my mind.

These men were the leaders of the country, the businessmen upon whose work the country worked and was fed. They had lifted the country out of its sorry state left behind after the War of Secession. These women were the bastions of good taste and deportment, at least on the surface of life. The homes they built were the finest in the country. They brought such beauty in their architecture and their art as few other places did. I knew they would stand the test of time, as did the chateaux and palaces they mimicked. They were a gift to all who would ever see them. Surely, these people deserved some respect for all they had accomplished; for all that they had given to Newport and their country. Were their true selves to be forgiven for it? Did what they achieve negate how they behaved? The question was a ghost that would never wisp out of the edges of my mind.

GINEVRA
1898

I waited for her beneath the beeches, thinking only of her arrival, not that of anyone else. When she returned and found I was not waiting for her in her room, Pearl would know exactly where I was. I didn't have to wait long.

Our embrace was warm and lingering. The time spent apart, forced on us, seemed longer every year though the days numbered the same. We were almost eighteen, just a few days away from it. Growing up meant growing more, dealing with more. There was no denying it as there was no seeing it coming.

We no longer climbed the tree that had held us so tenderly. We sat like the grown women we were on a blanket beneath the beeches, beneath the protective cavern that, like us, had grown and changed. It hid us now, more than ever.

Pearl laid back, her head on the blanket, and stared up into the sky. "I've finished school," she said. Where was her joy in saying it? She rolled over. "Well, I *might* be finished with school."

She teased me and she knew it. I heard it as clear as the larks singing above us. Her lopsided grin told me so. I poked her in the ribs, and she giggled as she used to when we were up in the tree.

But still Pearl said not a word.

"Tell me." I pulled her hair, hair that she now wore up every day, a mark of her change. "Tell me." I yanked harder.

Pearl did.

I gasped, I laughed, I hugged her. And I withdrew, enveloped in my maid's uniform, but only for a blink of time. She had spoken of it before, but only as one speaks of stars and dreams. Now she had done it. My joy for her was real and deep. She bathed in it.

"I'm not sure what Mother will say."

There it was, the note of sadness in her song of joy. I took her hand. A battle lay before her. It brought us to Consuelo and the battle she had lost.

Consuelo had married the Duke of Marlborough in November. Pearl had been there, as had everyone who was anyone in the lofty air of the upper east side of New York, all the "Fifth Avenoodles." I almost cried when Pearl told me Consuelo had cried, how so many thought they were tears of happiness.

"Speaking of men," Pearl rounded on me, giving me a yank of my hair, "have you met anyone while I was gone?"

The sun and its brightness went behind a wispy cloud, the same cloud passed across my face.

"No, no one really," I told her.

"But someone?"

"No, yes, but only…mostly simple men." I shook my head. I could not tell her.

Pearl took my chin in her hand. "And you are anything but a simple woman."

I smiled, then it slipped off my lips, away from me.

"I think I have seen too much… too much of your world. You have taught me so much of life. It is hard to settle for simple when you know there is more out there." I waved my hands about. Where were the English words for the Italian ones pounding in my head?

If I had met such simple men before—before Newport and before Pearl—I would have been more than happy to spend the rest of my life with him in his simple life. How can one be shown heaven then be told they must settle, once and forever, for purgatory?

I needed her to know, to see my feelings.

"It is a long des…deso-late, yes?"

Pearl nodded.

"A long deso-late road ahead for me, one with no end, no turns, no beautiful scenery. The sameness, it is…bleak. It will drive me mad."

Pearl hitched herself up on her legs. "I'm sorry if what I've done, teaching you, showing you, has brought you sadness."

I grabbed her fast and held onto her tightly. "Never say it again. I would not have it any different. I am so grateful."

"I will find someone for you," she said in my ear, then pushed me away, her face bright with the idea forming in her mind. "I swear I will. He may not be a rich man, not this kind of rich." She waved her hand at the house across the lawn, "But perhaps a well-to-do merchant, perhaps one who has traveled and seen something of the world. That is the sort of man you need. Leave it to me."

I laughed at her. "Have you become match-maker like Lady Paget?"

"Oh no." She pulled in her chin, face scrunching as if she had bitten into a lemon. "I'll be much better at it."

Together we laughed. Together we laid back down on the blanket.

"Have you been sketching?" she asked me after a time, when the birds grew used to our presence and swooped into our cave within the tree.

"Yes, some," I answered. In truth, I sketched all the time.

"Yet you haven't made anything for me since that beautiful dress."

Pearl sat up again. Her stare singed me with the heat of the sun.

"I want you to design a wardrobe full of clothes for me."

It was my turn to rise up. "And you would wear them?"

"Of course I would, silly, as long as they are not too outlandish."

"No, no," I assured her, "I want to stay…current. But I think I have ideas on how to make them better, eh, u-nick."

"Unique," she corrected me.

"Ah, *si*, unique."

"Good. I adore unique. I think they should be serious, clothing for a serious woman doing serious work."

I understood. She would not let go of her hopes. Neither would I. I nodded.

"Good," she said, "it's settled then."

Nothing was ever settled in this world of ours.

PEARL

I don't know why I chose that particular day to approach Mother. Being back in Newport, back with Ginevra, I was a different me, a better me. And I was a day away from turning eighteen, a day away from my "coming out."

Coming out. Such silly words. As if all young women existed in some impenetrable shadow until they turned eighteen. As if they weren't really people until then. Especially in those days, when more and more women felt as if they weren't real... and had begun to demand to be.

Mother had been in a tizzy about the affair for months and months. She sought out tizzy even when it did not find her. Living well didn't suffice, only living dramatically would.

It was my coming out, but I had little to do with her ebullience. Even the invitations, delivered by hand by our liveried coachman, didn't carry my name. Such invitations never did.

Mr. and Mrs. Worthington
At home
Friday evening, July 2
At nine o'clock

For all its vaguer, everyone seemed to know what it meant; it was a secret knowing of this insulated world. Mother had been jovial for weeks, full of ecstatic brightness I had only glimpsed here and there throughout my life, ever brighter as accepting responses came to our home. Surely her cheerfulness was welcoming, fertile ground.

Like many women of the age, my mother's bedroom served as her study as well as a private place to entertain a few ladies for tea. I found her at her desk, a magnificent piece of mahogany with trims of gold. I loved that desk, wished it for my own. Mother sat there, as I knew she would be, going over the last-minute details of the fete. Her corner room faced the back of the house. Its windows were a vista to nature's beauty that was our yard, our gardens, and the ocean in the distance.

Mother had arranged her desk to face in the opposite direction, to look upon the white and black marble fireplace with the stunning portrait of her. Painted by none other than Giovanni Boldini, an Italian painter renowned for his flowing style, he rendered a softness that made every woman he painted beautiful, whether they were or not.

"Pearl!" she greeted me with enthusiasm rarely tossed my way. "Come, look at the plans for the decorations."

For minutes uncounted, I indulged her. Not to feel excitement would be pretense. How could I not be excited by the addition of indoor trees upon which candles with pink globes would be festooned, the huge ribbons of green and pink that would be hung from the candelabras and draped to the four corners of the ballroom. It really was quite lovely. Amidst such glamor, I would be the guest of honor.

There are times when what the mouth and mind say denies the truth of the heart and soul. I wanted this moment that would be mine alone. Yet I still wanted more. The battle within raged on and I had no clue as to which side would win. Ginevra fought in a similar battle.

Mother seemed to have exhausted herself. She had barely taken a breath as she pointed out every little detail. She finally stopped to sip her tea. It was the moment.

I opened the letter clenched in my hand, the paper grew moist in my sweaty grip, a letter Mother hadn't noticed, though I'd made no secret of it.

"I have something to show you, Mother." My hands betrayed me, trembled as I unfolded the letter.

Mother snatched the paper from me, read it once, stared at me with a gaze narrowed and hard, blue eyes turned grey, and read it again. She dropped it on her desk. It had smothered the roaring flames of her enthusiasm. She was, once more, the mother I knew.

"Isn't it amazing?" I denied her face and all it said, I cared only of what the letter said.

It was an acceptance to Rhode Island School of Design in Providence, the capital city of Rhode Island, Newport's state. What began as a project for a group called The Centennial Women, a group devoted to raising money to exhibit works by women at the Centennial Exhibition in 1876, grew to such success, raising vast sums of money, that they set their sights in another direction.

It was Helen Adelia Rose Metcaffe, a Rhode Island native, who suggested the group put their funds into the formation of a college specifically to teach all facets of the arts. While not exclusively for women, the advancement of women artists was the school's primary focus. Mrs. Metcaffe had served as president until her death the year before. Then her daughter had then taken over the reins. It was one of the preeminent arts colleges in the whole country, and they had accepted me...me! I wanted to shout it from the rooftop.

"Who told you to apply?" Her dark stare found me as she rose and walked to the fireplace, stood beneath her portrait. Now two of her gave me a brittle look.

"No one *told* me to apply. I did have the encouragement and support of Mrs. Taligrin," I said, hoping the name of the headmistress of my New York school would carry some weight with my mother.

"She had no right to do so." My mother's beauty vanished beneath her anger. How horrified she would be to know how much older it made her look.

"Mother, very few women are accepted to Rhode Island School of Design, only those who exhibit a true talent. It is that fine a college, that prestigious. And I am to be one of them."

There came no praise, no gladness, nor pride. Only a warning.

"You waste your time with such matters. They will do you no good, no good at all."

The smooth curves of her face became hard edges as she gazed out the windows. She saw nothing of the beauty that surrounded us, only the "they" that lived around us.

"Look at the poor Jones girl," My mother took a step toward me, a finger pointed at my chest. I took a step back. "What was her name, Edna?"

"Edith, Mother, her name is Edith, Edith Wharton. And she is a very talented poet."

My mother snapped her fingers. It was a harsh crack. "Talented poet, indeed. And what has it gotten her? A first betrothal broke, after two years, no less. And why?"

Her pale skin, bleached with great care, flooded with blood. "Because her future mother-in-law found her too…intellectual."

The last word she spoke as if she called Edith a strumpet. She turned her back, turned to her portrait.

"You will not be attending. Tell them so."

"But Mother I—"

She spun on me like a whirlwind, her face a storm. "Tell them you will *not* be attending."

A boulder dropped upon my chest. I tried to breathe past its crushing weight but couldn't. Hope became an illusion. I took the letter. I retreated from her and the room.

I stiffened in the cold of the empty hall. The sounds of the servants on the back stairs came to me like mice in walls on a cold winter morning. For a few moments, I looked upon the message in my hands with contempt.

Not for long. Though the words swam beneath my watery gaze, they gave me what I needed most. Mother would not let me attend, but I had been accepted. I would most likely not attend, not next year at any rate. I held as tightly to that thought as I did the letter, that and the happiness Ginevra had shown for my accomplishment. She had been the champion of my cause, even knowing it may separate us for long periods of time, perhaps forever.

I went in search of my father, knowing the reception would be different. He would not go against my mother, not in this. It was too big a battle; it could end their never-ending war. It didn't matter. In this shallow world, I knew the joy of accomplishment for accomplishment's sake. He would celebrate it with me.

GINEVRA

We fluttered about her room like butterflies in a field of wildflowers, not knowing which blooms to choose, wanting to choose them all.

It was a rehearsal of sorts. Pearl had told me she wanted her hair styled in the new Gibson fashion, and I had spent days looking at the pen and ink drawings of Charles Dana Gibson. He claimed his drawings were a representation of thousands of American girls. He had, in fact, started trends—the wider, higher, more elaborate bouffant, the swan-hill corset with its straight busk inserted in the front to give women's body more of an 'S' shape when seen from the side.

Pearl had ordered herself just such a corset and we spent some time adjusting the gown I had made her to fit the new shape. The emphasis was changing. The fragile waif woman was fading away while the more curvaceous woman was finding her time. It was an omen, surely it must be.

I studied myself harshly in the mirror. I boasted nothing like the graceful thinness that these privileged women possessed. I knew they had much to credit their undergarments for the slim waist and barely perceptible hips. Did I not help Pearl don these very garments daily? Yet the glass before me made it clear, even with such assistance, my form would always be fuller, fleshier, built more for the physical labor it must do.

I looked down. The beautiful dress Pearl had so lovingly given to me that very morning—worn only in her room—stretched and wrinkled across my form as if it silently screamed for release from its torture on the rack of my body. It further denied me that which I so longed to be. Long and thin, not rounded and fleshy. It denied me one moment of gliding into a room, privilege in every slim and upright posture. I blamed my body for the lack of such an opportunity. It was a stupid distraction from the truth, but one easier to accept.

I envied Pearl in that moment... I hated myself for it.

I altered the dress to perfection. I began a trial attempt at the hair.

I sectioned it, twisted, and backcombed each section to create the illusion of more and fuller hair, rolled them back toward the main bun in the back center of her head, where I secured them with combs adorned with diamond chips. When all was in place, I picked out a few strands here and there, by the sides of her face, down the back of her long slim neck. The natural wave of Pearl's hair needed not a touch from the curling tong. The wisps of her bangs, parted in the middle made the perfect frame for her lovely face.

My work done, I turned her 'round to her vanity and its mirror.

Pearl blinked and blinked again. Her mouth opened then closed. It opened again and I worried. A useless worry.

Pearl turned and took my hand, "You have made me so very beautiful."

My shoulders dropped, releasing the tight pain that had been biting me as I worked.

I leaned down and pinched her lovely chin. "God made you so very beautiful. I only help him a bit."

Pearl jumped up, laughing, hugging me, and swinging me about until I laughed too. I almost laughed away the ghost of jealousy hovering in my shadow. Almost.

PEARL

I get to dance...I get to dance.

As protocol dictated, I stood beside my parents at the door to the ballroom, greeting each and every guest as they arrived, accepting their good wishes on my "adulthood." All I could think about was dancing.

So often in the last few years, I had attended such parties, mostly those of a more family-friendly occasion, thinking it cruel that *they* allowed *older girls* to attend, but did not allow them to dance. Oh, how I loved to dance. I had taught Ginevra every one of the popular dances of the time. Beneath the beeches, we would whirl and twirl as I taught her the waltz and the two-step. We laughed as we tripped and fell on each other, confused by who should lead and who should follow.

My dreams—my fantasies—were different from many of the other young women my age. Yet the desire, the longing, to be led about the dance floor, seemingly helpless, in the arms of a strong man, was a desire I could not deny. To feel his strong arms around my back as he looked into my eyes...

"Pearl, *dear,*" my mother's insistence pulled me out of my daydream. "Please greet our guest. He's a friend of Mr. and Mrs. Havemeyer. This is Herbert Butterworth. Mr. Butterworth, our daughter, Pearl."

Herbert and I shared a smile. I prayed he could not see the tremble of my lips.

"*Enchanté, mademoiselle.*" Tossing back a thick wave of almost black hair, he leaned over and kissed my hand. As he straightened, my eyes fed upon him. He wore his swallowtails and pristine white shirt and tie in a way I had never seen, though every man there dressed the same.

"I...I...it's a pleasure to see you again, Mr. Butterworth."

"You know each other?" Mother pushed in, tried to break a moment that belonged solely to Herbert and me.

"Please call me Herbert," he said graciously to me.

"What a lovely greeting, isn't it, Pearl," my mother fawned all over him. Even from the corner of my eye, I could see her gaze eating him up. *Not this one, Mother,* I thought, *please not this one.*

"*Certainement,*" I replied.

He smiled wide. His teeth were perfect, sparkling white behind full lips. "You speak French?" he asked me in that language.

I answered him in kind, never more thankful for my education, snidely grateful my mother spoke not a word of it. We spoke of his recent trip there and my own experience in Europe. The rest of the room fell away...

...until my mother poked my ribs with her sharp elbow.

"Ah, here is Mr. and Mrs. Havemeyer and their son Frederick now," she held out a hand to them, ignoring Herbert as he had ignored her, or because he had.

Oh, good Lord. My body grew warm and moist beneath my beautiful gown. Once more, I sat in the middle of the titter-totter.

Herbert took my hand again as if doing so would return my gaze to him from where it sat upon Frederick. Herbert leaned closer. "May I have the honor of your first dance?"

He asked for a great privilege. A debutante's first dance—and the partner she chose to dance it with—said much about them both. Mother had arranged for Willie Vanderbilt to partner me, and I had agreed. It seemed fitting, as we were childhood friends.

I knew all that but suddenly, didn't.

"Pearl, dear...," Mother began. She had heard. I didn't want to know what choice she would have me make. I made my own quickly.

With just a moment's hesitation, I answered him, "You may."

Herbert stepped away with a bow of his head to my parents, a quick glance back with those golden eyes of his. I didn't break his gaze, not even when my mother poked me again, not until she leaned toward me, raised a hand as if to pull up my long gloves, and pinched my arm.

"I said you look smashing, Pearl." Frederick stood before me. When did that happen? In his dark eyes, I could see myself—they were full of me. What a moment ago would have found me weak-kneed now made me squirm. What had I done?

"As do you, dear Frederick," I replied as he took my hand and, like Herbert, bowed over it. His golden-haired head reminded me of the gold in Herbert's eyes. "I... I'm so very pleased you've come tonight."

"I wouldn't have been anywhere else, I assure you." He spoke to me, yet his eyes skipped out to the room filling fast, a room of black and white and silk cravats, of silk and pearls and colors of a garden in full bloom. That skip... it was enough.

The faces swam before me after that, my smile was no longer forced. It seemed interminable until the small orchestra began its cacophonous warming up.

Then, he was there, standing before me with his long hand reaching out for mine. I took it gladly.

Herbert circled me around the room, my arm rested on his raised one, the opening move of the German cotillion. It was a natural first dance for a debutante. It paraded her around the circle of her guests.

I knew the sight we made together. I could see it in the bright blurry gazes as he whirled me before them.

I looked away from Frederick's tight mouth as if it wasn't there.

Herbert danced as if he was born to it. When it came time to face each other—when he needed to move me across the room, twirl me before him—he did so with all the mastery I had ever imagined.

It was my first dance. It was my first dance with Herbert, but not my last. I remember little else.

GINEVRA

I hid in the small upstairs pantry. From there, I could see through the open doors of the dining room and into the ballroom. I watched Pearl. She glowed beneath the praise of the many guests. She smiled with gratitude as so many women fawned over the beauty of her gown, of her hair. I felt my own glow.

Until he walked in. Until I saw her face when he did. To know someone truly is often to know them better than they do themselves. What I saw dimmed my glow, leaving nothing but spots of it in my eyes.

My gaze longed to linger on him, but my mind demanded I watch her.

When Frederick and his parents entered, when Pearl's skin paled, her eyes spinning, not knowing where to land, I watched my own battle stride across her face.

When Herbert took her hand, his other gesturing out toward the open space for dancing, I knew what he asked.

I closed my eyes and began to pray. It was not a thing to pray for.

I sighed as he took her to the dance floor, easily the most handsome young man there, though I didn't think he was as young as Pearl and me. He had a more mature look, a more lived look. I thought that perhaps he was in his mid-twenties. For all Pearl's beauty, for all that she was the center of attention, it was hard not to look at him, at his face. Together, they were heartbreakingly breathtaking.

Herbert knew the prize he had won. As he whirled her round, a tinge of arrogance spread over his superior smile, pinned his brows high upon his smooth forehead. My fingers prickled, my breathing came harshly, as if I breathed through a trap.

As one dance led to the next, as the many guests joined Pearl and her partner on the floor, I had to look away from them. My gaze fell and caught on Mr. and Mrs. Worthington.

To look at them, you would never know how little love existed between them, or that she gave herself to another. Their perfect smiles showed none of it. How very practiced these people were.

I watched a performance, as well-rehearsed as any musicale or opera. It was nothing but false gaiety. Would such a life truly make me happy? I was no longer sure. I didn't think I could be so many different people as each occasion called for it. I knew only how to be myself, though I was no longer sure who that was.

I was repulsed and yet filled with desire at their affluence, their monumental abundance of wealth, and everything it could afford them, which, of course, was everything. Envy and adoration vied for dominance in my mind, leaving a wasteland of confusion.

"Good evening, Ginevra."

He had snuck up on me, again. What a knack he had for it.

I dipped my head. "Good evening, Mr. B—"

Herbert held up a pointed finger and grinned.

I lowered my face and the grin on it. "Good evening, Herbert."

"Much better," Herbert cheered softly. He stood with his side toward the pantry door, the rest of him remained out in the party.

There we stood.

"Congratulations." The word burst from me without any help. One dark brow slanted crookedly upon his smooth face. "On first dance." I damned my continued failure to master English fully, tried again. "The first dance with the debutante. It is honor."

"*Grazie. Molto gentile da parte tua.*" Herbert replied.

Did he try to comfort me, speaking in my tongue, telling me I was kind?

My lips trembled in something resembling a fey grin.

Herbert shuffled a step closer. I heard his breathing. He gave me no choice but to look up.

"I might be a very lucky man," the golden eyes held my face in their warmth. "To know two such beautiful women, women who are always together." He licked his full lips then bit upon the bottom one. Did he have nothing else to say? It was a hope both for and against.

"Yes, many would say that makes me very lucky." Herbert swayed forward, rose up on the tips of his toes.

What did that mean? I drowned in an ocean of unknowing and in-experience, an ocean thick with desire if that was what it was called. I had never met it, not truly, ever before.

The room faded. It was just he and I. I forgot Pearl's name. The worst thing I had ever done.

"I hope you have a pleasant evening, Signorina Ginevra," Herbert said.

It was the first time I had ever been addressed so, how I would have been addressed all the time were we still back in Italy.

"*Grazie*," I managed, barely. A thief I could not name had stolen all other words from me.

He turned. I followed the left side of his body, the 'v' line from shoulder to waist. He turned back. His face said that he knew I still looked at him.

"I will see you again soon, I'm sure."

I stood in the wondering again—where his words put me—and watched him walk back, lost him in the swirl of people. Lost, as I was lost.

* * *

I no longer watched, could not, as I should have done. I should have been watching for any signal from Pearl that she had need of me. If I watched, I would have only watched him. I would have watched Pearl, and if her behavior was different with Herbert than it had been with Frederick. There had been others, but I knew it had come down to these two men. One I wanted for my own. I might as well have wanted to touch a star.

I laughed at myself, at my foolish desire, as I lay down to fitful sleep.

It took two days for the house to recover, for all the cleaning to be done, for the staff to return the house to its everyday condition.

I was on my way to Pearl's room to dress her for coaching when James, the first footman, stopped me on the stairs.

"Your father wishes to see you," he informed me, "in Mr. Worthington's library."

I stood like a statue, one with a jaggedly carved face.

"Go along with you," James said, retreating down the stairs.

I wasn't sure what I was most shocked by, my father's request to see me or where. I went rapidly.

I took one step in and the other stopped in mid-air. They were all there, the entire family. Annoyance splotched all over Mrs. Worthington's face, more emerged when she saw me in the door.

Mr. Worthington turned to follow her gaze.

"Ah, Ginevra, good," he said to me. Then to my father, "We are ready then, Felice, please show us."

His excitement was contagious. Pearl shared hers with me with a twinkle-eyed wink.

My father stepped over to something large, something covered in one of the fine linens used to cover the furniture through the long winters. He was a tall man who always seemed shorter, his head forever tucked down to his shoulders. Not today. He stood tall beside the mysterious item, the loveliest wisp of a smile on his lips. Without a word, he pulled off the linen.

I'm not sure which of us gasped the loudest, myself, Pearl, or—most surprisingly—Mrs. Worthington. Who would not be astonished by what we saw?

"Oh, I say," Mr. Worthington whispered with undeniable worship.

He stepped to the breakfront, as I now knew such pieces were called, and ran his hands over it with the same caressing touch that my father had touched the wood before he had formed this masterpiece.

The six-foot-tall breakfront boasted two glass panel doors; around each, the wood was carved in a row of perfect scallops. The crown was more elaborate: a lion's head rose up from the middle and crescent-shaped carvings curled away from it in either direction. But the eye could not travel far from the center, the beam between the glass. A man guarded at the top, a saint or a scholar with a flat-topped hat that curled at the ends and a book in his hands, each page finely carved and visible. The folds of his robe flowed with such realism, I could swear I saw it move. A precious dog curled at his feet. Downward the design continued, globes and shapes and more scrolls. My father's attention to detail, his perfection at it, astonished me. I had never seen anything like it. I had never felt so proud of him.

"Thank you, Mr. Costa. It is a beautiful piece. I shall be quite the envy of all my friends," Mrs. Worthington said, breaking the revered silence my father had spun on us. It was the highest praise this woman could give. The praise was short-lived. "You may leave us now. And you, girl."

My father didn't seem to notice the rudeness of her dismissal or the brevity of his triumph. I knew, for him, the creation was all the triumph he needed.

As we made our way below stairs, I held him with a hand on his shoulder. He turned.

"I am so very proud of you, Papa." The words gurgled in my tight throat, constricted with emotion. "Mama would be too."

He said nothing. He put his hand on mine. His mouth quivered but said not a word. He didn't know how to say such words.

Papa sat straight and tall in his chair that night as we ate dinner with the other servants. Words whirled around him as they always did, but he took no notice that none were directed at him, as few ever were.

When Mr. Birch rose, and we all followed, many left the table. The few that stayed behind, lingering over their coffee and private conversations, James and Charlie, the first and second footmen, took chairs beside my papa.

"Your work, Felice," Charlie said, pronouncing my father's name not only correctly but with respect, "that is a right fine piece of work. Well done, Sir."

"Too right," James agreed. "I had no idea you had it in you, old man."

It was a strangely formed compliment, but my father preened at their words, though I doubt either could tell.

"*Grazie,*" my father said, dipping his head, corrected himself. "Thank-a you. Thank you both."

How glad I was that I sat beside him that night. It was one of the finest moments we ever shared in all of our time in this country. We would share it together forever in my memory.

PEARL

A switch had flipped. I did not know where the switch was, but above it lay my name.

It reminded me of that moment when all the candles and sconces in the house were replaced by gas lamps. There was so much more to see. Such was my life. There was so much to do, that I could do, and I reveled in it.

Invitations now came directly to me. I was an entity in my own right, not simply the 'family' in *To Mr. and Mrs. Worthington and Family*, but now *Miss Worthington*. They came in droves. I attended every one. I'm not sure why I continued to say yes, not because I wanted to, but because I could. Not once did I stop and ask why I didn't want to. I should have.

Young men flocked around me like bees on the first blooms of spring, as if denied the company of a comely woman for the length of a harsh winter. If I was honest with myself, and I tried to be, though I often failed, I had to acknowledge that some of the attention stemmed from my father's burgeoning fortune. Something had happened over the winter, an expansion that brought our financial worth up to the exalted level of the Astors and Vanderbilts. It brought my worth up as well, my worth as a bride, as a commodity.

I hoped some of the attention was for my own worth. For the beauty that I was often complimented on, that I sometimes believed. For my grace and impeccable manners that had been drummed into me, that had been secured by the inheritance of my father's quiet grace. And most of all for my intelligence.

It came as a surprise. I filled the role of coquette as well as a fish could fly. The loud false laughing that was fodder for a man's ego, the fluttering of my lashes as I caught the eye of a handsome young man across the room. No, I was not superlative at such comportment.

But I was learned, I was educated and informed, and if a man spoke to me of more weighty matters, I did not fade into the background but plunged in, head first. I did, much to my mother's annoyance, and some of the men as well, especially if I dare contradict them and from a point of knowledge. They would excuse themselves from my company quickly, never to return to it. Their absence went easily unnoticed.

A few seemed delighted with my knowledge and my wit. Herbert Butterworth was one such man.

Herbert seemed forever to be no more than a few steps away. At dinners, he often sat next to me. At dances, he was an ever-ready partner. I remember the first day he came to call, when he and I sat in one of the teahouses. It was in that moment that I truly felt like an adult. It was also when I learned who the real Herbert Butterworth was. Or so I thought.

Herbert took my arm as we strolled across the lawn of The Beeches. We must have made for a lovely sight: him in his navy blazer trimmed in gold piping, me in a soft yellow afternoon dress of layers of chiffon trimmed in lace, a parasol to match. For a sharp, flashing second, I thought to take him into the beeches. The notion passed quickly. It was my place—Ginevra's and mine. I could never share it with anyone else, except perhaps someday with my children and hers.

"Your cottage is magnificent, Pearl." Herbert stopped us at the edge of the lawn and looked back on my summer home. Genuine appreciation shone in his exquisite eyes. He was staying at Sherwood House for the season, with the Havemeyer family. While Sherwood House was a lovely cottage, I knew, with shameful pride, it could not compete with the grandeur of The Beeches.

"That's very kind of you to say, Herbert. It is one of my father's greatest joys."

"Your father is a remarkable man," he replied, looking down at me with those eyes. It was the best thing he could have said. The best thing he didn't say was that he knew Frederick had been here and on more than one occasion. Did they both know the titter-totter they both sat on?

I lead Herbert to a teahouse, all four doors flung open. A silver tray with an etched crystal decanter filled with fresh lemon water and the same etched crystal glasses waited for us, appearing as if by magic. In truth, by the hands of staff who possessed some magic, that of being invisible.

We had never been this alone before. I squirmed, slouched back, flung myself up, back straight. My hands twirled my glass without bringing it to my mouth. Herbert sat—or should I say slumped—in his chair, arms behind his head as he swam deeply into my opulence.

"How...how were your years at Harvard?" I blustered. It seemed a natural question, for I knew he had recently finished his education there. My own hopes of college, forever lurking in my mind, made my curiosity genuine.

"Wonderful," he replied, smile wide and bright. He leaned toward me as he told me of his experiences there. He spoke mostly of the mischief so rampant on the campuses of young men at college. As much as I wanted to hear about his classes, the academic environment, Herbert made me laugh with his stories until my eyes ran with tears.

Herbert stood, picked up his linen napkin, and towered over me. Ever so slowly he leaned down and gently dabbed my wet cheeks. The spark of his touch flashed through the whole of my body. I could not take my eyes from his face so close to mine, from his lips.

Such a look was far too forward, far too intimate. I broke it off with a soft "thank you," and picked up my serviette.

"Tell me, what are your plans now?" I had to turn the conversation. I had to defend against the onslaught of this powerful attraction. It was the proper thing to do, and I hid behind the proprietary. It was too soon. I wasn't ready.

Herbert returned to his seat. He did so with a previously absent stiffness.

"I'm really not sure," Herbert answered. "Father wants me to go into business with him, but I have little interest in business."

"What *are* you interested in?"

His penetrating look—his amber gaze fixed upon my face—answered the question. I dropped my eyes, lifted my glass, anything to hide the flush heating my face.

Herbert laughed, whether at the question, or me, I still don't know. He laughed, and it was merry, and I relaxed again, a bit. He threw his arms open wide, threw back his head to look up at the pure blue sky.

"I'm interested in living."

It was an answer I didn't expect, wasn't sure I could understand.

"I want to travel, to see the world, to experience the world and all it has to offer," he explained his sentiment. "My father is stingy, but still there is enough for me to do so."

"What about a profession?" I badgered; it was not well done of me, but it was me. I had always envied men their freedom to do whatever they wanted. It seemed wasteful to squander it.

I had asked the same question of Frederick as if the answer was a secret password for entry into my heart. His answer had stupefied me, "We'll see what comes along."

These young men who had everything seemed to want for nothing, not even purpose.

Herbert's lips formed a frown that was also a grin. "Professions are over-rated. Living, and living well, now that's what truly matters."

I could not fault him, nor Frederick, or even my brother, for being a product of the society in which they were born, in which they were raised. So many of the young men his age, with family fortunes that were, ostensibly endless, seemed to have the same unfocused, offhand approach to life. Had they not been bred to it? These vibrant men with the best educations would put it to little use if they had their way. While I, I who had longed to study, to contribute, to be...something...was denied the chance. I did my best not to bristle. Perhaps he saw something of it.

"And of course, a family of my own." Herbert leaned on the table toward me, his full lips opened ever so slightly, his penetrating eyes fixed squarely on me. "A wife with the same verve for life, a wonderful mother for my children. Of course, I want these things too."

Things. The word rumbled around in my mind but didn't latch. I could think of little else save those lips and those eyes. Still, the thoughts were insistent, the question ever pestering me pestered... is that all that awaits me?

Herbert and I sat and talked for the rest of the afternoon. He returned to join the family for dinner. Something physical, an intangible feeling represented by a bodily reaction, happened to me whenever he was near. I could not deny it.

As I lay my head on my pillow that night, the pestering words repeated in my mind until they became a scream... is that all that awaits me?

* * *

I was grumpy and difficult the next morning as Ginevra readied me for the beach. I was rude to her, and she didn't deserve it. My unsettled feelings came out as complaints. Mother's insistence that I continue to wear the older style of beachwear only added heat to the oppressively hot day.

Ginevra and I did our dance, getting me into the ridiculous clothes in the simple wooden shacks that served as dressing rooms at Bailey's Beach. They were a quarter of the size of my closet.

"Oh, these clothes are simply ridiculous," I snapped as she helped me into my beach attire, a floor-length black—black, for the beach, on steaming hot day—dress. The whalebone collar was so high and tight I could barely breathe in air already so thick with steamy moisture. Thick black stockings covered my legs. Heelless leather slippers encased my feet. My corset strangled my waist to the prescribed eighteen inches. Then the hat. It was festooned with flowers and feathers and was far larger than any other of my many others.

"It is bit of monster, *si*?" Ginevra said as she pushed in the long steel pins, gouging my scalp though she didn't mean to, to hold it tight to my hair.

Either blind or a saint, Ginevra was unruffled by my ruffled feathers. She soothed and calmed, though I didn't deserve it. I knew what she thought of the ensemble from a fashion point of view. It was always there on her face, as if she bit into something distasteful, whenever she dressed me in this costume, which was far too often.

"Is it not bad enough that I can't feel the sun, but to have to swelter beneath this...thing?" I rolled my eyes, gave a stomp of one foot. I regressed at least ten years with my tantrum.

Ginevra's reply was to lower the veil to hide my face from the damaging sun and to squeeze my hands into the tight gloves. Finished she stepped back, not saying a word. I think she did so to keep me quiet as well.

I hugged her.

"I'm sorry, Ginevra." I shook my head even as I continued to hold her. "I don't know what's wrong with me today."

"No to worry," she said. Her English was so incredibly improved, yet there were a few sayings that were uniquely a combination of her mastery of her new language and a hint of the old, expressions inimitably her own. "Sitting by the ocean is good place to think. Think on it."

I never knew where her wisdom came from, only that I was grateful for it.

I released her and headed for the door.

"Pearl?" she called me back.

I turned to find her, a grin full of half-amused irony all over her lips, as she held out my large black parasol to me. I laughed; it felt good.

"Go to the beach, Ginevra," I told her. "I'll instruct Morgan to take you back to the house so you can change. I know it's not your afternoon off but I'm giving it to you. No one should work in this heat."

"Thank you," she chirped, pleasure as bright as the blistering sun on her face. "I would love a swim."

I bonked her gently on the head with my folded parasol. Her swimming costume, one she had made herself, would actually be refreshing.

With her giggling in my ears, I stepped onto Bailey's Beach.

* * *

The small cove of Bailey's Beach sat at the very end of Bellevue Avenue, where it became Ocean Drive. The Fish's Crossways overlooked it from its high perch above. The same Smith who had bought so much of the land where our cottages now stood, had bought this beach as well, with a partner named Joseph Bailey. Even then it was beautiful, but so very primitive, nothing more than a field leading to sand. Mr. Bailey, I had heard, regretted the purchase, believing all it would get him was enough driftwood to keep him warm for the winter. It was, back then, in the middle of nowhere.

The cottagers used to spend their afternoons at Easton's Beach, closer to the center of town, but that changed when the mill workers from Fall River began going there as well. It was just a few years ago that my set turned to this beach instead, having no desire whatsoever to associate with people who brought their mid-day meal in buckets. They created the Sprouting Rock Beach Association, named for the large boulder that punctuated one end of the deep crescent-shaped shoreline. Another association that took a drop of blood to join.

As I stepped out of the small cabana, I wondered if I would see Herbert or Frederick or both. I wondered if I wanted to.

I stomped onto the sand with all the dissatisfaction I felt. I couldn't understand why this beach, this crescent-shaped, small plot of land, with seaweed always at one end and rocks at the other, was the 'chosen' beach. There were eighty-one outside cabanas and the dressing rooms were rough and tumbled wood shacks. It was far from the finest on this beautiful island.

'They' had not only chosen it; they had made it exclusive, more exclusive than anywhere else in Newport. Newcomers and climbers might work their way into the Casino, the men into the Reading Room, and the families into the Clambake Club. But it could take years—decades—to be welcomed into the Sprouting Rock Beach Association. According to the newspapers and tabloids, if one could ever believe a word of them, it was the most difficult and the most sought-after private club to join in all of American 'society.'

I suppose its physical attributes were not its finest characteristic; that distinction belonged to its clientele.

I sat on a blanket I pulled close to the ebbing sea, away from the others who did not seem to value it, watching the tide pull it farther and farther away from me. I sat and brooded. I sweltered beneath the punishing sun as I punished myself with thoughts. I floated outside myself, chiding myself for my ingratitude. I had a privileged life, highly privileged, yet these days the parts that didn't fit had a far more ill fit. I closed my eyes as if I could block them out. In the few seconds my mind was still, I heard the cries and gasps.

I looked round. Almost everyone was on their feet, even the elderly matrons who rarely moved from their chairs beneath their wide umbrellas. They stared and pointed to a woman in the water. Elsie Clews.

She was one of us, her father being Henry Clews, a powerful financier from New York, a friend to my father. His wife, Lucy Worthington as she was, was Father's distant cousin. As I craned my eyes against the flashes of light sparking off the ocean waves, I finally saw what everyone else did. Elsie dared to swim without stockings.

More and more cries of outrage rose up from the sand like castles, bursting from those far too old to understand. Men of all ages, though the older ones did so surreptitiously, gazed on, admiration as clear as the water before them, through which they could see her legs whenever a wave caught the end of her skirt, undulating it up and down.

My shock wore off quickly. My admiration never would. I jumped up and plunged into the water, wading closer to her. The delight on her face shone like the sun above our parasols.

"How does it feel, Elsie?" I had to ask.

Others might have asked how she had dared such an act. I need not for I knew her. I knew her to be of a like mind with myself, with Ginevra, and with other women looking for better, wanting better, wanting more.

When she turned to me, I saw tears glistening in her eyes.

"Glorious. Simply glorious," she whispered along with the whoosh of small waves. "My skin is tingling. My toes are ruffling in the moist sand."

She looked down at her legs and feet with disbelief, as if they belonged to someone else.

"Glorious," she repeated.

I smiled with her even as I left her to it. I knew what I would do.

* * *

When I stood in the bathing house the next day, I chided myself for my reticence. Elsie had not hesitated. She walked, sans stockings, with her head high, led by a wide smile. I simpered in fear.

Ginevra helped me dress, as she had the day before, but I dismissed her quickly, once more giving her the day to herself, sending her back to The Beeches. She could see what I was about; she could not try to stop me. I quickly re-entered our dressing shack, and just as quickly removed my stockings.

Already the sensation was marvelous. The bathhouses were exclusive, but they could not block out the air. The cool breeze found my legs beneath the black skirt of my bathing costume. I closed my eyes, remembering the child I was, running about with bare legs, grass tickling my feet. The memory was what I needed.

I opened the door.

How glad I was for the glare of the sun on the beige sand, for in its glare I could see little of the stares that greeted me. Those I could see, I ignored.

I entered the water and gasped. Its cool fluidity was unlike anything I had ever felt. The water-soaked sand beneath my feet mushed between my toes as if I stepped in creamy butter. I closed my eyes and luxuriated in the sensations and in my defiance. There would be a price, a hefty one, but it was one I was more than willing to pay.

* * *

My father took me to the Casino the next day, along with Herbert Butterworth. It had been two days since Frederick had called upon me, the same two days since my moment with the ocean.

My father had had an ugly tangle with my mother about it, who still wanted to punish me for my, in her words, "deplorable behavior" at the beach. He had triumphed in the end, extending the invitation to Herbert. I think Herbert regretted it afterward. I know my father didn't.

Tennis week in Newport was one of the highlights of the social season. The year after the Casino opened in 1800, it hosted the first national tennis championship, the United States Lawn Tennis Tournament. Of course, back then only the bluebloods were allowed to play. Brahmin Richard Sears won that first year, and the seven to follow. I saw pictures of him in his blazer, knickers, wool socks, and canvas shoes. He looked quite dashing.

Looks played as much a part in the tournament as did the tennis. It was one of the greatest opportunities for us cottagers to deck ourselves out in our finest and go about in them, to see and be seen in them.

Where one sat was almost as important. Seats in the Grandstand were status symbols claimed by birthright. Most belonged to the Vanderbilts and the Astors, the Belmonts and the Goelets.

The former Mrs. Alva Vanderbilt, now Mrs. Oliver Hazard Perry Belmont, attended. Some still ostracized her for her divorce and her quick marriage to the man of her infidelity. Alva laughed merrily in the face of them. I would have as well. She had not only retained ownership of Marble House, but she now resided in OHP's Belcourt, a sixty-room mansion she was completely renovating to her specifications. Just as miraculously, her mortally threatening illness had disappeared when her daughter had married the duke. Oh yes, she laughed often and well. I listened to it all that day as my father's recently enlarged fortune made it possible for us to acquire seats in the Grandstand now as well, rather than along the sides where we used to sit.

Today's tennis would be different from any other. Today women would compete.

My mother refused to attend; sticking to the antiquated notion that physical exertion was bad for the feminine form. As Wimbledon had done, the Casino had ceded to the pressures of the growing force of the suffragists, many of whom, surprisingly, were among the cottagers, and had allotted this day—one day—to a small ladies' championship.

As the women took to the court, there were as many cheers as there were jeers.

"Well, you have to give it to them. They must have known the reception they would receive," Herbert said in a low voice, though I'm not sure why he spoke so quietly. "It certainly takes courage."

I thought they looked remarkable, still lady-like in their crisp white button-down shirts adorned simply with what looked almost like a man's casual tie, their simple but full-length skirts. They fastened their long hair back tightly and, on their heads, sat the simplest of white caps, like those my brother wore as a child, fitted tight on the head with a small, curved brim to shade their eyes from the sun.

The battle in the stands, for and against these women, raged on as they began to play. Once begun, many closed their mouths to open their eyes.

These women played with all the grace and athleticism of the men, running cross-court, forward and back, hitting with precision. It was the most astonishing sight I had ever seen. They fought for every point with the determination of a soldier.

My wide-eyed gaze found Ginevra at the fence, it returned to her again and again. Her mouth never closed; her jaw hung open as if it were no longer attached to her head.

"Well," said Herbert between rounds, "they may not hit as hard or as far as men, but they do pretty well."

I wanted to ask him how well he could play if he had to do so in a full skirt and corset. Of course, I didn't.

"Thank you, Father," I said instead, taking my father's arm. "Thank you for letting me see this."

He put his hand over mine and smiled his small smile.

GINEVRA

It was a short walk for me, the three-quarters of a mile from the Beeches to the Casino. It was a lovely walk along the tree-lined road as carriages rumbled past, the smell of the ocean never far away.

The entrance was much like some buildings in Italy, with its stretched arched gateway. The man who created the Casino, Bennett I think his name was, allowed staff and Townies in, but only on special days, days such as this. I had been there a few times before, attending to Pearl, the only other way a servant could attend.

We couldn't do anything but watch. A hollow gesture then, but one I enjoyed anyway. I liked to watch, even if I must do it while standing along the fence. The players in their crisp white clothes glowed in the sun. Their exertions revealed what the body could do. I had seen them bowling once. It reminded me a bit of *bocce*, the game my father loved to play back home, with its precision of the rolling of small, heavy balls.

I met a few of the townsfolk as we stood along the rails; heads perched above like birds whose eyes flicked here and there. They denounced these wealthy people and their exclusivity even as they stood for hours watching them. A few I spoke to reacted with their own snobbery when they heard my accent, fading though it was. It was good they could not hear the cynicism in my voice then. Yes, most strayed from me...the English, Irish, and Germans. We Italians were still on the low rung. Most stayed away, but not all. I made a few friends, long-time Townies, a group of girls as eager to see the women play as I.

I watched Pearl as well, to see how she fared. I tried to lie to myself, convince myself that I didn't long to be on the Grandstand with her, draped in fineries, with my arm in Herbert's. I was not very convincing. My dark eyes once more turned green. They rarely strayed from my study of Pearl and Herbert. If I stared long enough, would I see their truth? One I needed to know desperately.

With her father on one side and Herbert on the other, Pearl stood in reality as she felt in her mind. She smiled, here and there. Her smiles were so often forced lately. She did her best, as did I, making the most of my afternoon off.

When the women took the court, I traveled to another world, as much as I had when my father and I boarded that ship. Any thought of men, of loving them, faded like the first dreams of slumber. They were women like me, strong women, women with muscles and flesh who were proud of them. They conquered that court as any soldier had ever taken a battlefield.

My head twisted back and forth, up and down, following the ball from one side of the net to the other, from the court to Pearl in the stands. Our eyes met as often as the racquets met the ball. In her face, I saw all the wonder I felt.

We were no longer alone.

It changed us even more.

PEARL

Without instigation, not a word or a note, Ginevra and I found each other beneath the beeches after dinner that night. What we saw that day demanded it. We had to meet in private, where mother's ears or those she employed could not hear. To speak of the shared experience made it all the more real. Our words ignited the images set so deeply in our minds. Though a fence had stood between us, we had experienced it together.

"I am in awe of what they've done, what they do," I said, lying back on our blanket, my gaze following my mind into the vast sky and all its possibilities.

We had talked so long, talked of every move the women had made, the late setting summer sun had finally bowed to dusk, and stars began to twinkle in the twilight, the patches of it we could see through the lush beeches.

"And me," Ginevra sighed as she too laid down beside me. "Such courage."

Her words hung heavy in the thick humid air. They struck me as if a heavy branch had fallen on my stomach.

"Am I a coward?"

Ginevra sat up fast, propelled by my question.

"You have done nothing cowardly," she insisted, a deep furrow plowing the flesh between her brows.

I shook my head; twigs and leaves snapped and rustled beneath it. "I didn't speak up to Mother, I didn't fight her."

"But you applied to college." Ginevra's insistence sounded like anger. "And you were accepted. You did that."

Had I told her how grateful I was for her? I hoped I had. I hoped I'd shown her.

I sat up. "And you have made some magnificent clothes…are designing ever more beautiful ones."

Ginevra had shared her sacred sketchbook with me on more than one occasion. Each time her flair, her mastery of design of fashion became greater. My request, for serious clothes for a serious woman, she had taken to an exquisite place. Her long jackets incorporating a diminishing bustle on a narrowing skirt were fabulous. Her incorporation of feminine touches kept the men's clothing-inspired outfits unique and feminine, comfortable and serious.

She shrugged but with a pleased smile and that shy dip of her head. "Where we to go from here?"

"That's the question, isn't it?"

Our gaze held, locked upon each other, locked on confusion that wore the same clothes, the same strangeness of our existence. She longed for wealth, for the elegant life I led. I felt restrained by it; it had become a gilded cage.

"You should have been born to this life, not me." I looked at my darling companion, not trying in the least to divest myself of the longing for her simple life.

She merely shook her head at me, said simply, "No. We only want what we no have."

Her wisdom was her own. Though I had taught her many things over the course of our years together, such insightfulness into the human condition was not one of them.

We hovered in the stillness, the poignancy of the moment. Around us, the night and all its creatures took their place. Crickets complained of the heat; owls hooted at them for silence. In the encroaching mist, the ever-present scent of the ocean settled in.

"Deciding is upon me, Ginevra," I whispered with a close of my eyes. If the world did not hear it, it would not be true; if I did not see the world, it could not see me. "Do I marry? Who do I marry? Or…"

"Or?" Her hushed whisper nudged me.

I threw my arms up, beseeching the heavens. "Or…something else. But what else?"

"Fate provides, we decide." It was the loudest murmur I had ever heard.

I rolled onto my side, dropped my head into the palm of my hand. "Did you make that up?"

Ginevra snuffled. "No. I read somewhere. But it is true, no?"

"It is true." I studied her profile as she studied the canopy above us, now a silhouette against the gray twilight. "Sometimes it provides too much to decide and sometimes too little."

"Think of only one. Decide one, and then worry about the others." Ginevra didn't turn to me as she spoke. I dropped back on the blanket.

"One," I mused, rustling my fingers in the leaves that had fallen to the ground, thinning like brittle old paper. "I know I will probably marry. I do long for love and marriage and children especially. But who?"

"Who then?" Ginevra said stiffly, as rigidly as she lay upon the ground. Gone was the joy that had brought us there that night. Did she fear losing me?

"Frederick or Herbert. Herbert or Frederick." I said their names aloud. Deciding was truly upon me.

Ginevra sat up quickly, turned her body toward me. There was something in her face, in the small gap of her lips…something hung there, demons wrestled behind her eyes.

"What is it, Ginevra?" I took her hand. "There is nothing we cannot share."

I hoped to encourage; her face grimaced. She threw herself back down.

"No, it is…it nothing." Was it? "It is worse then, your deciding, yes?"

She could see me without any light. She always could. But did I see her?

* * *

Herbert dined with the family on our last night in Newport. I hadn't invited him. Perhaps Mother had. It was a congenial table, I think, for I forgot the flavor of the well-cooked veal and the tang of the wine on my tongue.

As Father stubbed out his cigar, Herbert paid his respects to my family.

I walked him to the door and out of it. I stood on the top step before the large doors, he on the one below. Our faces were level, his eyes bore into mine. I couldn't move, couldn't breathe. He lowered his face to mine, his lips to mine.

Their softness was everything their fullness promised. He moved them slowly, ever so slowly over mine. Who knew the touching of lips could tingle down my toes, could be the essence of human intimacy. Gently, his tongue opened my lips, gently touched the tip of my tongue with his.

I fell into his kiss. I tumbled and spun in a bottomless warmth and softness. I could fall like this forever.

GINEVRA

Our goodbyes were as tearful as ever, maybe even more so this year. That change, the threat of it that Pearl had spoken of once, threatened closer and closer. We could both feel it. We both worried over it. When she left, my worries would be my most constant companion.

I followed her carriage down the long drive and out the gate, watched it as it rumbled down Bellevue Avenue. I would see her, this Pearl, for as long as I could, for I didn't know which Pearl would return.

GINEVRA
1899

I barely knew her when she came back. Familiar features had taken on a haughty mask. I should have expected it. I think I did. The letters from her, far less than any year before, had dropped the seeds of it.

One letter, one piece of news was especially telling, above all the others. That letter I had carried in my pocket for most of the winter. That letter lay deciding at my door.

Pearl didn't rush to greet me. I saw her first when I followed Charlie who carried her luggage to her room, stuffed trunks for me to unpack. I stood in the doorway, watched her preen in her mirror. Only in the reflection did she see me.

"Ginevra, dahling," she said, spinning hesitantly from herself. If she knew she sounded like her mother she didn't seem to mind, as she would have in years gone by. Crossing the room, she did not embrace me. She kissed me on both cheeks with cold lips and held me out to look at me. It was a greeting so like her mother's, cold and dense in a cloud of perfume. In that moment, I thought I had lost her.

"Well, look at you. How…womanly you have become."

My body had changed, a buxom chest, wide hips, though my waist had stayed slim, even without a corset. But I hadn't, not the me inside.

I looked down, ashamed. A shame made worse by the changes in her. Taller than ever, she had not gained weight and her body had slimmed even more. Small breasts, straight hips, and her only curves were those made by her tight corset.

The Pearl inside had changed. She moved with such grace, such mature refinement. Pearl held her head straight and tall on her long slim neck, her nose high in the air where it had never been before.

"You look beautiful, Pearl," I said with all honesty, brushing away the concerns as we had brushed away the limbo of winter for the Worthington's return. "Betrothal suits you."

She didn't expect those words. I saw it in the way Pearl spun away from me.

"Thank you, Ginevra," she said, her words echoed hollowly.

Scratchy silence came between us. I filled it with the massive undertaking of unpacking. Pearl had brought back more dresses than ever. Would she no longer wear those I made for her? With them came more accessories and jewels than ever before. Of course, the ring was the greatest of all her newest items.

Pearl sat at her vanity all the while. I glanced at her here and there, as I whirled about the room. Her face looked sculpted out of stone.

I finished up, helped her change into a more comfortable afternoon dress, and made my way for the door.

"Ginevra?" She called me back. When I turned, I saw Pearl, my Pearl, standing before me again. I could have cried. She had changed, like so many things, but there was still something of the true Pearl remaining. "Tonight."

It was all she needed to say.

* * *

Below stairs, things were a frantic flurry. Even here, change was everywhere.

So many of the kitchen maids and chambermaids were new, driving Mrs. Briggs to distraction with their constant questions, with her overbearing demand for things to be done in just a certain way. So many of the previous maids had taken positions elsewhere, in factories and mills. There were more opportunities for them to do so than there had ever been.

I spent more time sketching and studying.

Greta was no longer with us, but Anja still was. I was pleased to see her even though she would only wink at me. For all the times we sat together at dinner, or on the odd servant's terrace on the stone roof, she kept our friendship casual when among the other servants. I didn't blame her, even for all the hurt it gave me. The new batch of servants was as filled with the English and the Irish as the last; Anja would not limit any new relationships with the newcomers by her relationship with an I-talian.

I had two friends, one from above stairs, one from below. To the world, both friendships didn't exist. I must be joyful for them, secretly in my heart. Better in secret than an empty heart altogether.

I helped in the laundry as Pearl took her nap. I would rather work, be useful, than retreat to my room, as Nettie would whenever Mrs. Worthington didn't require her services. Alone, in my room, my deciding grew too big; it left little space for me. My helping didn't seem to endear me to the staff much, perhaps a little. It made no difference to me; I didn't do it for them.

As the time for the staff dinner drew near, I thought to help in the kitchen and to get a drink of water, for the hot steaminess of the laundry always made me thirsty.

I opened the frosted glass door that separated the laundry from the cooking areas...and stopped, drew back a single step, far enough away not to intrude, close enough to see and listen.

My father stood in the doorway to the main kitchen, near the shelves filled with copper pots and pans of every size and shape. Beside him stood Mrs. O'Brennan, the assistant chef, taking pots down, putting others up. When she looked up, looked up at my father, I saw something that chilled my heart. She looked at him with familiarity and fondness.

I couldn't see my father's face, but I didn't have to. He spoke to her with such gentleness; he spoke to her in English. God grabbed my entire world and shook it until everything fell in different places, wrong places.

Many of his words were wrong. Mrs. O'Brennan only smiled and gently corrected him. When she didn't understand him, or him her, a look passed between them, a wordless communication. It troubled me more than their words, as much as the hint of smiles playing on my father's face.

Waves of emotion rolled on me—I rocked on them, heel-toe, heel-toe. I forgot my thirst, my step faltered as I turned away. I looked for something—anything—to quiet my mind.

PEARL

I waited for her beneath the beeches. For the first time, I worried she would not come to me. I knew my behavior toward her had been abominable. Ever since I had accepted Herbert's proposal, I had been trying to accept the life ahead of me, embrace it. Accept it I might, embrace it too, but it could never have affected how I treated her, how I spoke to her. It should never.

This way of life was like a pernicious illness; it infested every part of you. It was hard to turn from it once fully immersed in it, fully embraced by it. There was no medicine for some illnesses.

The winter had been a whirlwind. The instant I allowed Herbert to place the four-carat diamond on my finger, everything changed. We became "the" couple, the guests of honor at so many formal dinner parties, at cotillions and balls. From then on, I was freer from my mother than I had ever been in my life. The irony was, now that I was engaged, she wanted me by her side as she never had before, sought out my company and my companionship with far too much fervor. Did she merely want to step into my light, have some of it shine on her as well, or if, in the gesture, had I, at long last, earned her approval?

I cared little about the latter. I knew Mother's true colors and they would never change; they would never be a hue I found appealing. The freedom from her was something else altogether. It was what I longed for so often over the last few years. It was something I now reveled in. How can one not be changed when everything in one's life was changing? The trickier question, one that gnawed at me like a rat on spoiled cheese, was if I had accepted Herbert merely to be free of my mother?

"Hello, Pearl."

I jumped. I had been so entrenched in my thoughts I didn't hear the swoosh of the leaves as she pushed them aside to enter our cathedral, or the snap of the twigs beneath her feet as she approached. She was there, that was all that mattered.

I jumped up and ran to her. I gave her the embrace I should have given her as soon as I saw her. I felt her arms hesitate, had I lost her? When her arms, at last, rose up to encompass me, relief nearly broke my heart.

"I'm sorry," I said into her shoulder.

Ginevra said nothing. She held me tighter, pulled her head back to kiss my forehead, then held me some more. It was everything I needed.

I don't know how long we held onto each other. I know we were holding on to more than just our physical beings. We gripped our past with fisted hands; if we opened them, we'd both fly out, fireflies that had burst with light and escaped.

"When I am married you will be with me," I told her, still holding on to her, refusing to release the ties that bound us. "All the time, wherever I go. Mother won't be able to stop that any longer once I am a wife with my own home."

Ginevra's body became a stick in my arms. If she stood there, like that, long enough, she would grow roots.

I held her away from me but held her still. Her face was a canvas yet to see even a dot of paint. I splotched it with black, the darkness of fear, and a dingy blue of disbelief.

"Herbert has promised to take me to all the great museums around the world. And you will go with me." With the last words, I gave her a shake by the shoulders still in my hands. She finally spoke, though I wished she hadn't.

"Why him, Pearl?"

Now she was stone. So grey, I didn't see her lips move.

"Why H...him and not the other?"

GINEVRA

I thought I had lost her, lost her to the gayness, the surface frivolity that seeped down into them, like sparse summer rain on earth dried to dust. When she said those words, when she called me to our private place, I knew she was still in there. Still Pearl, but not.

I was still Ginevra, but not.

I had spent the winter studying, sketching, and sewing. I thought of her. And I thought of him. Especially after the letter came.

I remembered our last time beneath the beeches—mine and Pearl's—when we spoke of deciding. The news the letter brought, brought deciding to my door.

Should I tell her of Herbert's flirtations? Were they flirtations or just my dreams and hopes, my envious wanting, blurring my vision, making me see things that were not there? Or did he use his charms to win me over to ultimately win her? I didn't know. I didn't know how to know.

How much easier it would have been if she had chosen Frederick. The nattering in my mind would have been shut up. I could have simply let fate take me where it would. But she didn't, it didn't. The nattering grew louder, some of it slipped past my lips.

"Why H...him and not the other?"

PEARL

Ginevra turned to me. "Does he make you happy? Will this truly make you happy?"

How I wished she hadn't asked me these questions, not that question.

"He's a wonderful man," I said with truth. "He has been the very picture of respect and romance, more than any woman could want, could dream about. And he is so understanding of my love of art. He buys me books and books filled with beautiful images. Frederick cared nothing about art, only about those newfangled carriages, those engine ones."

Ginevra's silent stare accused me.

I tried to ignore it. She wouldn't let me.

"Is this truly what you want... will it make you happy?"

She questioned again, still waiting for an answer.

I left the question in the air, still so fresh and green with the early days of summer.

Together we lay back on our blanket to look at our stars.

"If you were a man, what would you do with your life?" Instead of answering her question, I asked one of her.

Ginevra laughed a little, a throaty laugh, a woman's laugh.

"I would have my own design house, as Worth does," Ginevra dreamed aloud. "I would sell my fashion, my clothes, all over the world."

"And every woman in the world would want to wear them."

She laughed again. "And you? What would you do if you were a man?"

I needed no time to think, to answer. "I would travel the world, go to all the great museums, but I would need no chaperone, no one to take me there. Most of all I would study art, learn its history, all its nuances. Perhaps I would have a gallery showing, in Paris of course, where I might be discovered as the next great talent."

"And you would," she whispered, fully in my dream world, walking there beside me. "Your eye, it sees the beauty and your hands recreate it."

We lay back with our dreams, our eyes closed, our hands clasped. In her grasp, I could feel the same need, the same longing I felt. We could not live in them forever. Life was about to happen. I would make sure it would happen with us together. I needed her to be sure. I lifted myself up and leaned over her.

I looked at her with all the intensity in my heart, all the love and all the loyalty. "Nothing will ever break us apart, keep us apart. I promise you."

Oh, how I wish I had kept that promise.

* * *

The newspapers proclaimed we were living in Gay Nineties. If so, it was Harry Lehr who brought us there.

Gone were the staid and somber manners as dictated by Ward McAllister, as gone as Mr. McAllister was himself. He had passed away two years before in the obscurity he caused by writing *Society as I Have Found It.* It was his last grasp for the same media attention the true "Four Hundred" garnered. It was a scathing work, denouncing the very people who had given him so much power and so much reign over the practices of their life. He hadn't named names, but the implied characters were too close not to recognize those he spoke of and those who knew them. Ginevra and I had laughed about his character, one he named Milly, a grasping climber who couldn't keep her skirts down.

Ousted from the very world he created, he died at his dinner table, completely alone.

Harry Lehr wore none of the chains of good manners, though he did often wear ladies' clothing, much to the consternation of most of the men. Tall and strong, a young and handsome blue-eyed blond, he came with no pedigree, worked as a wine salesman, yet his charismatic charm, his youthful, almost childish, vivaciousness was infectious.

From the moment Mrs. Evelyn Townsend Burden invited him to Fairlawn, her Newport cottage, he infiltrated himself into the good graces of the titular mistresses of our society, Mrs. Astor, Mrs. Belmont, and her triumvirate, none of them could get enough of him. They followed him into the world of the absurd, with monkeys as dinner guests and birthday parties for dogs. Tonight would be no exception.

Tessie Oelrichs and her sister, Virginia Fair, had, years ago, bought one of the most coveted plots of land on all of Newport. It perched above the Cliff Walk near the very tip of the peninsula. As heirs to a silver fortune, they had the means to do so. The cottage, Rosecliff, as it stood then, was far too sedate, could no longer compete with the grand mansions now surrounding it. Tessie set herself, and a vast amount of her inheritance to make it *the* cottage. That night, she would reveal it to us.

I arrived on Herbert's arm, a place where I had begun to feel more comfortable. His patience with my mother and her grand schemes for our wedding only strengthened my fondness for him.

"My word," he whispered, breathless, as we walked in, but, in truth, there were no words for what we saw.

The white terra cotta bricks that formed the exterior made the mansion look like something out of ancient Greece. To step inside was to step into a wonderland. The firm of Stanford and White modeled the cottage based on Louis XIV's Grand Trianon Palace at Versailles, but we never expected this...this was a palace in its own right.

Herbert and I walked about the H-shaped mansion as if we were tourists visiting a European palace of old. Through the arched entryway, painted ceilings rose twenty feet above our heads, before us a curving marble staircase rose in the shape of a heart. The opulence struck us dumb. The same could not be said for those in the ballroom. Conversation abounded, riotous laughter exploded, especially that of Harry Lehr. We followed it.

It was the largest ballroom in Newport, occupying the entire central area of the ground floor. It glimmered and shimmered, as did those who stood below its trompe-l'oel ceiling of painted clouds and its perfumed chandeliers. As I entered the fray, I couldn't help but think of Ginevra. Tonight, like so many that had come before, she accompanied me. Already I pictured us beneath the beeches glorifying the mansion, vilifying those who filled it that night.

For all our obscene opulence, you couldn't fault this clique of people, this minute elite segment of the populace, for their devotion to beauty and elegance, for their desire to not only acquire the best the world had to offer but to truly enjoy and experience it, to immerse themselves in it. These cottages—these palaces—were not false gods, but the true object of their adoration. They had the means to have the best life had to offer; they saw no reason not to.

Of all the sights astounding me that night, perhaps the greatest by far was the vision of Harry Lehr and Tessie Oelrichs flaying about on the dance floor to the sounds of Ragtime music, a highly syncopated, piano thumping sort of music, one I had never heard in the hallowed halls of Newport or New York before that night. Others, equally as exuberant, or perhaps equally as inebriated, crowded around. My mother, of course, danced openly in the arms of Lispenard Stewart. Those who watched laughed at their antics. I simply stared. Herbert laughed.

"Well, this looks like great fun," he said, surprising me. "Shall we give it a go?"

My nose crinkled on my face. I narrowed my eyes as if that would bring the man I knew into focus, that man would not, I thought, be so willing to participate in such distasteful goings-on.

When Reggie Vanderbilt grabbed his partner and hoisted her up on a table to dance on its top, Herbert slapped his leg with laughter. I could not. How strange it was that I, one who longed for change, couldn't embrace this one. Before me was the picture of hedonism and luridness for which the papers forever degraded us.

"Not for me, Herbert," I rebuffed the offer. As I did, a face in the crowd flashed into my gaze. "Oh look, Consuelo is here." I caught a glimpse of sanity in a sea of the insane.

Herbert unhooked my arm from his. "Go," he gave me a gentle push. "Go. I know how much she means to you."

How grateful I was for his understanding; I touched his cheek with it. "I won't be long. I promise."

"Take all the time you want," he replied. I took a step away. "But, I say, would you mind if I gave it a try?" he asked, pointing to the dance floor. "I'll find one of our friends who might partner with me."

It was forever done, partners dancing with each other's partners, but Herbert had never done so before. As his fiancé, his future wife, it would be something I needed to become accustomed to. I scratched away the itchiness his request brought out in me.

"Of course, dear," I conceded, turning away, making for Consuelo.

I could allow it; I didn't have to watch it. I threw myself into Consuelo's arms, forgetting, for a while, the depravity raging around us, forgetting about Herbert.

Like myself, my quiet friend found the night perplexing. They were half-mad, I think. We all were, but on what I'm not sure...the wealth, the ridiculously elegant affluence. Or perhaps just ourselves.

GINEVRA

If fairy tales were real, their reality took on the mythical at Rosecliff. It took the luxury of The Beeches and doubled it, tripled it. I could barely keep still in the maids' waiting room for the longing to walk about, to see more.

The butler's pantry where they kept us was a slim hallway away from the ballroom. Every loud guffaw, every thumping foot, every drumbeat of the wild music reached our ears. A few of the girls danced with each other in the small space. Nettie was there, silent and snobbish in her superiority. I tapped my foot along to the beat. I closed my eyes and imagined myself among them, as I had so often over the years, too often. In my mind, I wore a splendid gown, groomed to perfection, on Herbert's arm who whirled me about the dance floor as if I were his queen, as if I were the best of the best of them. The longing, the yearning...despised without escape.

The night wore on. I sneaked around the corner, sneaked a few peeks into the ballroom. Each time I found Pearl in conversations with her friends, not for her this glass-smashing ruckus. She needed no adjustments. Pearl looked as perfect as when she had left her room.

Here and there, I saw glimpses of Anja and James. Mr. Oelrichs had asked for the loan of their services; she didn't have enough servants of her own to cater to this many guests. Mrs. Worthington was only too happy to comply; she deluded herself that the asking made her a special friend of Mrs. Oelrichs. She would never give up her deluded dreams. They chose Anja for the young, attractive, hard worker she was. James was chosen, well, for being so incredibly attractive.

As he had grown from a young man into a man, or perhaps as I had grown into a woman, I found him more and more strikingly handsome. Charlie had continued to flirt with me, continued to try to charm me into strolling out with him. Charlie was no temptation. I could not say the same of James.

How well I remember those nights when Pearl taught me to dance beneath our beeches, moving to the chirp of the crickets, our shadows flickering in the light of our candles, warm winds lifting our hair, cooling the back of our necks with a touch that tingled. When I had closed my eyes, I imagined James' arms around me, not Pearl's. James' or Herbert's.

I turned away from the riotous party. Without purpose, I allowed myself a trip below stairs for some water, perhaps a bite to eat. I slipped down the first flight of stairs, turned onto the first landing...and stopped. As quick as I stopped, I hurried on, slipping past them as though I had seen nothing, though what I had seen I could never have unseen.

Harry Lehr sat on the top step to the next set of stairs, beside him, very close, another man, locked in Harry's embrace, their lips upon each other's.

There was no world where such men did not exist, nor women—for that matter—if rumors were to be believed. The innocent person I was, having lived as a child in my parents' home, the rest of my life in the confinement that was the life of a servant, I had never seen such things for myself. I would have lingered—watched—if I could, as one lingers before the bearded lady at a circus.

I hurried away unthinking, or thinking of what I had seen, seeing nothing else, not where I walked or who was there. That's when he found me.

"Ginevra!" The harsh whisper came from out of the dim light of a long corridor to my left, forming a 'T' with the one I walked through, leading to the kitchen.

I couldn't see who called. Murkiness blurred facial features, smudged them to the unrecognizable. I turned and walked toward it. It was my first mistake, but not the last.

As soon as I got close enough, he reached out to me, his hand a vice on my arm, pulling me against the wall.

"I knew this moment would come." Herbert stood before me, pressed me against the wall. His lips found mine.

I fell into his kiss, my first kiss, one that tasted of wine. I tumbled and spun in a bottomless warmth and softness. I could have fallen like that forever.

A part of me did, she saw me in his arms—my own hovered off my sides—saw me in this life, his life. In the moment, I forgot everything.

I forgot her.

Until I didn't.

What I saw was what I truly wanted to see, me in her life. Sitting beside her on a carriage in the parade, on the beach where surely the sand must be made of gold dust, or with a drink in our hands as we stood side by side at a fabulous party filled with the fabulous, with the Four Hundred.

My arms rose, so close to him, my palm brushed the smoothness of his silk evening jacket. My hands came up...

...and pushed upon his shoulders, pushed him away, but only a few inches.

Those eyes of his, already heavy with liquor, narrowed at me.

"What is it, Ginevra, why do you stop when you want so much to continue?"

"I can't. I won't." The words belonged to me as much as they did to him.

"Why, because of Pearl? It is perfect don't you see?" Herbert's lips, those that had just touched mine, spread in a crooked, lopsided grin. "I will have her intelligence, her brightness, and cool beauty as well as yours... your warm beauty and your fiery passion. All under the same roof. It will be so easy."

I shook my head so hard I heard the rattle of my tangled thoughts.

Herbert's fingers dug in the flesh of my upper arms like clamps.

"It is the way of us," he cajoled. It was the way of "them." "Pearl knows that, especially with that mother of hers." His chest puffed up as he snickered. "We are the captains of industry, rules don't belong to us, they belong to regular people. *We* are far from regular."

He was not the exception, but the rule, like all the other aristocrats that summered here. He fell fast and hard from the lofty perch I had placed him on.

"Y… you have not worked a day in your life," I spat the sour sting rising in my throat, burning my tongue. "You are the captain of nothing."

Darkness spread across Herbert's face; the snooty smile slithered out of his eyes like a snake going to ground. Were he not inebriated he would still not be able to shrug off the truth of his life. "She is but your mistress and you, her servant."

"No, oh no!" Whatever spell he had on me, he broke himself. "We are friends."

"Hah!" His guffaw was so thick with insult, I longed to slap my hands over his mouth, or perhaps just slap him. "*We* do not become friends with servants."

I had never heard prejudice in his voice before; now it was so loud it pained my ears.

"I will have you, Ginevra. I will have you both."

"I…" I opened my mouth to protest. I should have screamed. I didn't. It was my second mistake; one I would make again.

He plastered his lips against mine, crushing them, slathering my face with his spit, trying to pry my lips open with his tongue. The voice in my head screamed for help. That scream, a torment. No one heard it but me. How I hated for my first kisses to be this, nothing of the romantic gesture of my dreams, but a sickening violation.

I pushed at him, gaining only inches between us. I turned my head away to the light at the end of the hall, to the next hall where I needed to run. I would have run out of my skin if I could; I no longer wanted it. His hands, hard hands that moved all over me, had ruined it. Bile puddled in my mouth, gagging me. I couldn't get out from between him and the wall.

The light flickered. A shadow appeared. Then, a person. Anja!

I saw her silhouette in the light, her thin form rushing past with a large empty tray in her hands. I saw her step back quick; she'd seen something. It stopped her. I reached a hand out.

Herbert grabbed my head and turned it back, wrenching my neck as he crushed his mouth on mine once more. I tried to call out to Anja, to anyone, but it came out muffled. It sounded like a moan. He pulled back with a greasy grin on his face. Then he saw my hand. His gaze followed it.

"Hurry along, girl," he bellowed at her. She did.

In the diversion, I squirmed, almost finding release. I could not let him touch me more, could not let him kiss me, again.

"You will take your hands from me, Sir," I snarled beyond the quiver, one that had taken possession of my whole body.

"Or what?" His hands squeezed my buttocks. There would be bruises on every part of me.

I opened my mouth to nothing. Or what? A fine question, one for which I had no answer. I was but a shadow that could be replaced by any other. Nameless, faceless, powerless. That's what we were in this place, one of the most splendid on earth. Even as I began to drown, I found a buoy.

"I will tell Pearl...everything."

He sputtered laughter; spittle pinged my face.

"Then you are a fool. She'll never believe you."

I knew different. I knew the bond of our friendship, of our sisterhood. The knowledge gave me strength.

My hands, braced against the wall, came up quickly. Grabbing the back of his head by the hair, I yanked, even as my knee came up to blight his swollen genitalia.

As he howled, as Herbert bent double in pain, holding himself, I squirmed from out of the trapped corner. I ran, not to my father or Pearl's father or even Mrs. Briggs, as perhaps I ought to have done. I ran to Pearl.

PEARL

It was late into the night, well into the early morning of the next day before we took our leave from Rosecliff. I couldn't find Ginevra anywhere, though Herbert had assured me he had looked everywhere.

"She probably went back to The Beeches," he hurried me along. "I'm sure she knew you were all right before she did."

I believed him.

Ginevra wasn't in my room waiting to attend me, but her note was. The scratches on the paper were so maligned—barely legible—the words so intent, they frightened me. I ran to the beeches as they implored, still in my full evening attire.

"Ginevra?" I called as soon as the curtain of branches and leaves fell closed behind me. "Ginevra?" I said again; I saw her but didn't, not my Ginevra.

Rumbled and dirty smudged clothes covered her trembling body, her shirt half tucked in, half falling out of the tight waistband of her skirt. Strands of hair had escaped her bun; they floated around her as if she floated in water. Tear tracks slithered from her swollen eyes down her cheeks.

I dropped by her side, heedless of my gown—one of hers—so very frightened.

She looked up at me as if I were her savior or her mother, the whole of her expression pleading for salvation.

"What is it? What has happened?" I begged even as I held her close.

Ginevra told me, told me everything, every wretched word came out between more sobs. My mind went numb, stopped listening, started screaming, screaming against her words.

"How could you!" I jumped, snapping viciously.

Her head snapped sideways as if I had slapped her. I had.

"I thought you would pick Frederick. I did not think—"

"You've always wanted my life, you told me yourself." My body bumbled about our little clearing. I heard the crunching beneath my feet as if someone else stomped around. I felt my hands tearing apart the perfectly coiffed hair she had arranged for me, but I felt no pain...not from that. "You wanted my life and now you're trying to take it. You—"

"I said only I wanted life like yours, not yours." Ginevra was on her knees. "As soon as you made your choice, I no longer...it was him. He wants us both."

I heard and saw nothing of her, of my Ginevra, only someone who wanted to hurt me.

"Well you can't have it and you can't have him," I screamed as I ran from her, from the beeches, and across the lawn, tears of my own streaming out of my eyes, lost in the wind behind me. Yet even as I ran, thoughts, terrible thoughts of Herbert found their way in. I didn't believe her. I couldn't believe her. Yet, somewhere in the hurricane of my mind, a small voice warned me, *watch him.*

I threw my hands over my ears. I wanted to block out that voice, those words. I couldn't. I would heed my own warning.

GINEVRA

I picked myself up somehow. Somehow, I walked across the lawn and into the house on legs disjointed. I fell once, only to get up and start again.

I had to get to her. My heart tore apart into pieces of anger, regret, and sorrow. The anger bit me, deep inside. I should not have spoken to him, or smiled, or hoped, or dreamed.

Maybe I shouldn't have said anything to Pearl. Maybe I should have accepted my place as an object for these people to do with me as they wished.

The thought stopped me. I shook my head. I had to have said it, had to have told her.

In the house, I padded as quietly as I could to her room. I found her door closed. I reached for the handle. It wouldn't turn. Pearl had locked it, locked me out.

"Pearl, let me in," I whispered, knocking softly. "Let me help you undress. Let me talk to you."

"Go away!"

"Pearl, I—"

"Go away, damn you!"

I recoiled from the door as if she had thrown me out of it. I stood there, listening to the clocks and their arrhythmic ticking. I listened to her cry even as I cried.

As I lay my head down on my pillow, I don't know how long after, the tears were still flowing, but my thoughts cried out, refusing not to be listened to.

I couldn't let her marry such a man. I couldn't let her marry *that* man. I loved her too much. Even if it meant I would lose her, I wouldn't let it happen.

PEARL

The rest of the summer was cold without her, yet I could not release my anger. It was a tangled knot within me. She was still my maid; that incision I could not—would not—inflict upon us. But I could not say why; the why of it was far too elusive. It was there somewhere within me, but my grasp came away empty whenever I tried to reach for it.

It would have been so easy to let her go.

It could end the battle between Mother and me. I did not so much hate to lose as I loathed for her to win.

Ginevra would stay. I would stay with her, somehow. For now.

There were no meetings beneath the beeches. There were no long talks of our deepest feelings, our truest desires. They were never out of my mind. I couldn't abandon them for they were far too dear. I suffered in the purgatory between what we had been and what we had become.

I did that summer the one thing I set out to do, the one thing I told Ginevra I would do. I sent a letter to Rhode Island School of Design, not to decline their acceptance, but to ask for a deferment. With each word, I would forget. I would forget how she had wronged me, lied to me. As I wrote the letter, flashes of her smile, never more perfect than when she was proud of me, distorted the words I tried to pen.

The other thing I did, I did with no one knowing. I watched Herbert.

Another grand event was in the offing, hosted by Mrs. Fish and Harry Lehr in honor of a very special guest, the Czar of Russia. Bellevue buzzed for days about the presence of royalty, as if it made them royal too. Tiaras and glimmering jewels were in vast supply as we arrived at Crossways. How disappointed, how angry they were when the Czar turned out to be none other than Harry himself, dressed for the role, speaking with a hideous Russian accent. I saw it on their faces, the repressed frustration. I had no pity for them. Such is the price for worshipping false gods.

Herbert was as attentive as ever, getting me a drink, a bite to eat, checking on me if too much time passed while engaged with others. I didn't tell him about my letter. I knew he would understand, at least, I thought he would; he was a modern man after all. I would broach the subject to him after the wedding.

We spoke often of the growing suffrage movement, of women such as Harriot Eaton Stanton Blatch, who, with Susan B. Anthony, Elizabeth Cady Stanton, and others of similar courage, were publishing, in volumes, a *History of Women's Suffrage*. Herbert's comments were always ones of support. I knew he would support me in my intellectual endeavor, I was sure of it.

"Do you need another drink, dearest?" Once more, he appeared at my side just as I had taken the last sip of my drink as if he had been watching and waiting for the moment to serve me. In my mind, I cursed Ginevra again, for planting such plump seeds of doubt.

We danced the two-step, a whirling, exerting twirling of a dance. I could feel the moisture thick on my face when the song ended, as we all clapped enthusiastically at the orchestra's lovely rendition, at our own expertise.

"Please excuse me, Herbert, I must wash."

He kissed me on the forehead, no care for the beads of sweat on my brow. "Of course, my dear, of course."

In the brown marble and gold washroom, I dabbed myself dry, plied another layer of fine pale powder to my now dried face, smoothed a few errant strands back into my coif. I looked as I should, a woman of the age, what was it Twain had called it? Oh yes, the Gilded Age. And I was gilded.

I floated out, light as a feather on the warm breeze of my life. My worries seemed to have fallen away as Herbert and I had pranced upon the dance floor.

I left the small powder room, stepped lightly through the marbled corridor, and stopped.

Herbert danced with another. It was not that he danced that stopped me, but the way he danced.

I didn't know the young girl he partnered, but she looked younger than I. His bracing arm pressed firmly against the curve of her lower back, pressing her close to him, into him. She didn't fight him, didn't hold herself away as she should. Perhaps she was too busy looking up at him with adoring eyes. He looked down at her. There was no adoration there, only lust. I knew it as soon as I saw it.

I turned away, turned back into the powder room to wash my face again, to wash away the thoughts barging their way back into my mind. I convinced myself that my mind played tricks on my eyes, vision infested and diseased by Ginevra's confession.

I threw the thoughts away as I would anything poisonous and returned to my friends. The night no longer glittered; the stars no longer twinkled.

Herbert dropped me at my house. I almost asked him of the girl.

GINEVRA

I attended Pearl every day—five, six times a day. She allowed me to, in the way of "them," a stranger tending to their every need.

I had never known such aloneness, not even after mama died. This was different, for Pearl was still here, but she wasn't.

I tried to tell my father.

I went to his room with all intentions of doing so.

I wandered about his room, picking up his tools, putting them down. Picking up a new viola he was making, one that would have the most amazing back piece, he showed me the design. There would be an inlaid pattern of different types of wood, very small pieces, over a thousand of them.

"It is amazing, Papa," I said in English but switched to Italian. "Your talent grows the longer we are here."

Papa put down his work and stared at me. "Something trouble you?"

His English was much improved. I knew Mrs. O'Brennan had a hand in that. I was now only grateful to her for it.

The words—that night—it was all right there in my mind, on my tongue. Could he see them?

I couldn't get it out, couldn't tell my father of my shame. I had much to feel ashamed for, for I had dared to dream a dream that did not belong to me. Yet when I had tottered on the line between right and wrong, I had tilted as I should, as the daughter this man and my mother had raised me to be.

I was not the molester, yet I felt the dirt of it, no matter how often I washed. It was not only how a servant was made to feel, but women, all women. We were at the mercy of men, and they knew it. If we dared to defy them, we were wrong. How the world had come to be this way would forever remain a mystery to me.

Papa saw my struggle. He waited.

The haunting images of that night returned, floated into my mind as they so often did, silent and disturbing. They scared away sleep; they poisoned my food. I could not put those pictures in my father's mind.

I shrugged it off. "Nothing I cannot deal with," I lied.

Papa's head tilted; his gaze pierced. "You do what you have to do to survive in this world, Ginevra." He switched to Italian; his words flowed with his wisdom. "There will always be struggles. The strong overcome them."

Yes, they were wise words, true words. They didn't help at all.

I left him then and wandered about, running from the ghosts.

I would return to our place beneath the beeches as if it were a clock whose hands moved backward. Each twisted branch we walked on I walked on again, each feathery leaf a note of laughter, each broken twig the trust I had broken, each bird I frightened away Pearl.

I returned again and again. In truth, I waited for her. I waited in vain.

PEARL

The tennis tournament was upon us again and once more Herbert accompanied me. He was with me—with the family—almost every night. Almost.

As the players took the court, as their numbers dwindled down to the winner, socializing became the main sport of the day, and I a willing player. If I smiled enough, the smile would become real and hide the pain.

I grieved for Ginevra for all she had hurt me, grieved as if she had died. She had in a sense. But she had left a legacy, an endearing sense of consternation about Herbert.

From that night on, that gut-wrenching night, and the heightened awareness it brought me, I saw things differently. Or did I see things that weren't there? Which was the truth? The answer was as elusive as where the fog went after it rolled out each morning.

Through my new eyes, I saw Herbert's eyes watch my every move. I told myself it was proprietary protectiveness. I couldn't be sure. I tested it.

"Please excuse me, I'm off to the powder room," I whispered in his ear, straining up on tiptoes to do so.

He patted my hand, gave me a smile and a nod. I set off.

The facilities at the Casino were in the main building, the entrance under the archway. I entered the archway, but not the building. Instead, I hid in its shadows and watched Herbert.

Within minutes, he detached himself from the group of men he had been chatting with and made his way to a group of pretty young women. They were, in fact, women I knew myself, as did Herbert. There was relief there if I looked properly; he merely socialized with our friends. He was the flirtatious sort, but only flirtatious.

I could have seen him that way but didn't. Because of his face.

It had changed again, as it had on the dance floor that night. His eyes narrowed and softened, he licked his lips, and his cheeks flushed. He removed his hat and ran his hands through his thick hair.

What have I done?

* * *

Though I feigned tiredness, Herbert joined us for dinner the next evening. It was a quiet dinner with just the family and Herbert. There were no others to socialize with, no other women. It would be a peaceful dinner. At least, I thought it would be.

Mother entered the dining room last. She had chosen her moment of entrance with great care.

Sitting without a word, she acknowledged Herbert's gesture of pulling out her chair with a quiet nod.

I glanced at my father. His rough features twisted as did my thoughts. The answer came quickly.

Mother opened her hand, opened the letter she had folded up in it, and threw it on the table before me.

"I thought we were finished with this nonsense," she said, teeth snapping.

Without picking it up, I could see the distinctive crest of the scrolled lettering within a circle, *RISD*.

My hand flinched, ached to grab it, to read it, to see if they had agreed to a deferred acceptance. My hand moved a few inches and stopped.

"You opened my mail?" I snarled as she had to me.

Mother didn't deny it.

Instead, she glowered at me.

"I thought with all the changes in your life," her eyes flicked at Herbert, "that you had put this silly notion behind you."

"What is it?" Clarence grabbed the letter before I could stop him. Quickly he read it through. He was just as quick to laugh. "You, Pearl, *you're* going to college?"

I had never wanted to slap his dashing, pompous face more than I did in that moment.

I jumped up and around the table, snatching the letter from his clutches.

"I thought one of us should."

I tasted the flavor of nasty on my tongue. A small twinge of regret for having said it pinched me, a very small twinge, passing quickly.

Clarence had flunked out of Yale, though in truth I believe it was what he wanted all along. The real person hurt by it, by my words, was my father. His world overflowed with disappointment, no matter how he tried to pretend it didn't.

"What is this about, Pearl?" Herbert asked when I returned to my seat, a harsh whisper.

I shot my mother a stabbing look. I wanted to have this conversation with him, but at a time of my choosing, in a manner of my choosing. She had ruined that as she did everything else.

I told Herbert about my acceptance, about my mother's insistence that I decline.

"I thought that, well, I thought perhaps as your wife, as a woman of standing in my own right, that I could attend, with your approval, of course." The words rushed from me. I held my breath. I shrugged off the irksome irritation that I must ask for his approval at all.

"Well, that is quite an achievement, Pearl, to be accepted to college," he said amiably with a wide smile. His eyes narrowed ever so slightly, only I could see it. "I thought we were going to travel for a while and, of course, find a home of our own."

"Of course you would," Mother piped in, now she too smiled, a smile of triumph. "That's exactly what you should be doing."

"And, hopefully," Herbert put his arm around my shoulders. His touch was as tender as his voice, "Soon after we are married, we'll start our own family."

My mother clapped her hands together gleefully. My father stared at me. He saw my truth. I saw his dismay. There was nothing either one of us could do for the other. It was a high and thick wall surrounding us, built by those who delimited us.

Herbert continued to regale me with all the wonderful things we would do once we were man and wife. He tenderly talked me out of my plans. I thought I would have been surprised.

I wasn't.

GINEVRA

I packed her trunks as I always did. This year there was no talk of letters, no talk that began, "when I come back...when I see you next." I half expected her to fire me, to banish me from her sight as she had banished me from her heart.

Pearl sat like a stone as I swarmed around her, taking extra efforts to treat her belongings with great care. Without her seeing, I packed the suit dress I had designed and sewn for her during the long hours of the summer we spent apart. The one she loved so much. I didn't want her to see it until she arrived in New York. Without me there, her reaction would come freely, whatever it may be.

I followed Pearl and her trunks, in the arms of James and Charlie, out of the house and to the waiting carriage. I stood on the bottom step. Though she didn't look at me, I stared at her with a pleading gaze. I could have been one of the hobos with their tin cups that I sometimes passed as I walked along Thames Street, so deeply did my mind beg her to look at me, to say something to me.

Without a glance, she took James' hand, put one foot on the lowest carriage step...and stopped.

Pearl turned back. Her gaze fell on me, dropped on me. I saw something, something hopeful. Her lips parted, I waited for a word, any word. None came.

Just as quickly, her face darkened. It closed to me once more.

Pearl got in the carriage and shut the door...shut me out.

It would not be that last look that would warm me through the cold winter, but the one that came before, the one that had brought her a step back to me.

PEARL
July 1900

I was still engaged when we returned that summer, the plans for the wedding, one to rival any of our clique, were in its final stages. The date was set for the end of September, to take place here in Newport.

My sadness at not going to college remained like lint in my pocket.

The number of times I had surreptitiously watched Herbert being flirtatious mounted. But that's all I had ever seen, trifles. Powerful fripperies, if there were such things, effects as clear as the early summer sky.

My father had not raised me to be a fool. I knew in this stratified world, a flirtatious fiancé would more than likely become an adulterous husband. They thought it was their right, part of their birthright, as if their possession of wealth lifted them above the laws of morality. My opinions of such men came from my father, not my mother. Was it for the best? To be a bastion of decency often brought only loneliness and heartbreak in a world where the definition of decency changed as often as women changed their outfits.

It was *my* right to tolerate it or not. On that, I had still not made up my mind even as the date of our nuptials drew ever closer. I had never caught Herbert in an aggressive assault such as the one Ginevra had claimed he made upon her. I had not seen that one either. The opportunities for such disgraceful behavior were far too readily available. Confusion was the blood that pumped through my heart.

Herbert, college, my mother's life, my father's, *this* life. Which life? Ginevra and forgiveness. They were the ghosts that plagued me.

Selfishly, I needed my friend.

As Ginevra helped me unpack, I spoke to her. I had to.

"How…how was your winter?"

She spun as if struck, her lips quivered, her eyes filled with tears. Her body began to shake so much I thought she would fall. I ran to her, helped her to a chair. Ginevra hid her face, her tears, behind her hands. I moved them aside and knelt before her.

I talked to her. I did not talk of what had passed between us; I would not pick at a wound still open.

I talked of trivialities, nothing more than the social events through the winter. I didn't know any other way to start again.

Silence fell on us, we swam in it, our hands clasped, the connection reaching toward our hearts. I almost cried with the joy of it.

"I wrote to RISD, you know, last…last summer." It seemed wrong to speak of that time.

"You did?" Ginevra sat up, wiping her cheeks with her palms, her palms on her skirt. "What did you say?"

"I asked for a deferment."

She cocked her head to the side. "A de-fur-ment?"

She wouldn't know such a word. "Yes, it's when you ask them to hold your place—your acceptance—until you are ready."

"Did they give this?" Ginevra squeezed my hands so tightly my bones crushed against themselves.

Her jubilance was like jumping in the ocean at its warmest point in the summer. I felt terrible to turn it cold.

"They did, but Herb…my fiancé doesn't approve. He has grand plans for us to travel. Perhaps later." I said the words, but I didn't believe them any more than she did.

Ginevra stood and began to put my things away as if she could put away her palpable dejection, her worry. There weren't enough drawers and wardrobes for it all.

I asked her about her own dream, had she been drawing, designing. I told her about finding her gift, the lovely suit dress. I told her how often I had worn it through the autumn.

She dropped her head. I expected bad news.

"I have. A lot in fact."

It was my turn to squeeze her hands.

"Will you meet me beneath our tree tonight? Will you show me?"

She did not speak or could not. She took me into her embrace, and she nodded.

GINEVRA

We sat for hours beneath our beeches. The loneliness I had lived through last summer whooshed away with the wind as it sluiced through the tangled branches and the fluffy leaves.

Pearl studied my sketchbook as if it were the Worth catalog; commenting on what she loved and what she thought could be improved. She experienced my success, my growing talent, as if it were her own. In part, it was.

For a time, we were just…there—in our special place—together. In the united silence, we made our way through the bumpy ground that was rebuilding, not with words, but with being—tender, compassionate being. I would have stayed there the rest of my life if I could.

Pearl would still not admit that Herbert did what he did. I would still not say that he didn't. We put it aside, up on the high shelf of our lives that we would do our best to ignore, to let it gather dust and be forgotten.

I did not say sorry again. She did not speak of forgiveness. We were back together again. It was the best I could hope for; I should have hoped for more.

* * *

My world was clean and new again. Pearl was back in my life. For how long or how deeply, I didn't know. At that time, I didn't care. I saw only the beginnings of a path through prickly thorn bushes.

Pearl's words of encouragement, her complete faith in me and my designs, had given me such inspiration.

The night bell chimed for lights out. I swam too deeply in my inspiration to truly hear it. I left one candle burning as I made more sketches, as I changed the others as Pearl suggested; wonderful suggestions.

"*Whatt*…do you think you ah doing?"

Mrs. Briggs stood in my doorway. I hadn't heard her turn her key, open the door; there was no sound in my world of dresses.

"I...I am..." No matter what I said, it would make no difference. This woman's dissatisfaction with her own life ruled her completely.

"Give me that," she demanded. I clutched it to my chest and took a step backward. She stomped toward me and grabbed the book from my hands, her gnarled fingers turned page after page.

She laughed, at me, at them.

"You will learn to accept your place."

As quickly as she had come, she left. My treasured sketchbook in her hands.

* * *

Morning found me in silent mourning for my work and I could not hide it. Pearl reached out a hand, halting mine as I brushed her hair.

"Whatever is the matter, Ginevra?"

Her face was Pearl's face, my Pearl, though it had changed from a girl's to that of a woman. I told her.

"How dare she!" Pearl jumped from her chair. "Damn that woman."

Before I could stop her, she ran off. I followed. Down the back stairs and into the office Mrs. Briggs shared with Mr. Birch, barging in without a knock.

"You have something belonging to my maid." Pearl stood with hands on her hips, deep red splotches bursting and growing on her pale skin.

"Miss." Mrs. Briggs jumped out of her chair. "I beg your pardon. I wasn't expecting a visit from anyone above stairs."

I almost laughed. Even as Mrs. Briggs stood in the face—the fuming face—of one of her employers, she had to make her displeasure known. It was an unwritten rule, as powerful as the one that prohibited staff from certain parts of the family house, which demanded that Mr. Birch or Mrs. Briggs be informed before a family member came below stairs, as if they needed permission in their own home.

"This is no visit," Pearl snapped, unmoving. "Did you or did you not take something personal belonging to Ginevra?"

Mrs. Briggs' upper lip curled.

They stood toe to toe. Mrs. Briggs said not a word, not of denial or admittance. Clock hands stopped moving. Pearl didn't move, not even a flinch.

Mrs. Briggs moved first. She turned from Pearl, turned to her small desk, unlocked, and opened the top drawer. From there she removed my sketchbook, slapping it in Pearl's already outstretched hand.

We began to turn away. Pearl spun back.

"Never," she hissed, taking a step toward Mrs. Briggs, a sharp finger pointed at the housekeeper's face. "Never take something that belongs to Ginevra, or any of the staff, ever again. I don't care how long you have served this family, I will see you gone, my father will ensure it."

Mrs. Briggs said not a word. Her eyes narrowed to slits. Her lips formed a tight white line on her face.

"And if you punish Ginevra for this," Pearl held up the sketchbook, "or my retrieval of it, the same applies. Am I understood?"

Not a sound.

"I said, am I understood?" Pearl was a gladiator and I her ward. She commanded with mature authority, a magnificent force to behold. If she could only see herself, what might she do?

"I understand you perfectly," Mrs. Briggs finally replied.

Pearl smiled. It was a frightening sight. "Good," she said, hooking her arm in mine. "Come along, Ginevra."

I allowed my savior to lead me away in victory.

PEARL

Mother wouldn't accept my no to it. Once more, she planned a great fete for my birthday. It was the only one in the summer, the only one in the family that could be celebrated in Newport.

Between the engagement party—parties—that were held in our honor, I thought Herbert and I had been celebrated far too much already. I shied from the limelight as quickly and eagerly as my mother ran to it.

With Herbert on my arm, adorned in one of Ginevra's fabulous creations, I stepped hesitantly into the role of guest of honor that night and did my best to enjoy it.

Ginevra was never far away. I saw her peeking in time and time again. We weren't 'us' again, but we were on our way. Could my heart embrace complete forgiveness? Could my life embrace them both in my life?

I deserted these questions, lost them in the magic of the night.

There was magic of both sorts that night, the light... and the dark.

GINEVRA

Each time I slipped out to check on Pearl, she looked happier than the time before. Healing, as slow as it could be, had such power.

The night wore on. I peeked out once more. Pearl danced in the arms of that man. As he led her about, as he spun her around, he saw me. What was that saying? I had just read it in a new book taking the world by storm... *Dracula*, that was it, by a man named Bram Stoker. He coined an expression in that shivering work, and I shivered as I felt it... *if looks could kill.* Such was the look that man aimed at me.

I hurried away from it.

I hurried below stairs. I needed some water. I could barely swallow. I needed to be where there were more people. Such fear and rage did that man bring out in me. I fled toward safety.

I made my way to my father's room hoping he was still up. I found his room empty. I went in search of him, needing his quiet reassurance, but couldn't find him. I made to return upstairs.

That's when *he* found me.

"I don't know why you fight this, fight us," he whispered, it hissed like steam as he grabbed me by my upper arms, pushing me into the shoeshine room.

Herbert Butterworth shook me so hard. His face swam in my eyes. His words thumped in my ears.

"You told her, didn't you? Didn't you?" He shook me harder, pushing me deeper and deeper into the room. "But it did you no good, did it? She will still marry me."

He had pushed me into the darkest corner of the room, up against the stonewall and the metal table before it.

"I know you want me. I see you watching me. I know what I see is—"

"No, you're wrong." I pushed back. He laughed. "I watch Pearl, not you."

Herbert ran his fingers along the line of my jaw. I closed my eyes. "There's no need to lie to me, Ginevra."

His hand dropped to my leg. Groping fingers hitched up my skirts. The other fumbled at his pants.

Though his hands no longer held me, disbelief did. It shackled me.

He leaned against me; his naked flesh rubbed against mine.

"I *will* have you both. I deserve both of you."

They were the last words Herbert Butterworth would ever say.

GINEVRA
1900 Now

Every second is a blur. I stand by the body, the gun—still warm—in my hand. The voices creep towards me as I imagine old age does. There is a moment of escape, escape I could take. I don't. I don't know who had seen what, who had seen Pearl. For her, I stay where I am.

The first voice I hear is that of Mr. Worthington. He's first in the door, but barely. He stops as if struck, punched by the sight before him. His eyes dart from the body, to me, to the gun, to the body, to me.

"Ginevra…" he whispers my name. I'm not sure what I hear in it. Not condemnation. I think it's disbelief. I hang onto that. I know the best thing I can do is tell as much of the truth as I can. The tears I don't have to beckon come on their own.

"He tried…tried to r…rape—"

"Oh, my dear child." Mr. Worthington is by my side in an instant. His arms are around me. In this sympathy, I lose control, the grip I hold so tightly unravels. I collapse against him. Sobs rack my body. I can't embrace him with the gun still in my hand. I let it drop to the floor, metal hits wood with the sound of thunder. I grab onto him. My head spins, my legs tremble beyond stability. I crumble into the man I had respected since the moment I met him. I hide my face in shame. He leads me to a chair.

The other men, the other voices, reach us. Mr. Worthington stands between them and me—a shield.

He leans down to whisper in my ear, "We have to call the authorities, Ginevra."

I knew it as truth, but I'm living—floating—in a dream, a nightmare. I simply nod. I hear the gasps of the men at the door as if I'm at the end of a long tunnel and they stand at the other end.

"Birch, please send someone down to fetch the police, if you would. And ask Mr. Costa to join us." Mr. Worthington raises his hand, punctuates each word with it. "Just to join us, nothing more."

"R...right away, sir." The stalwart Mr. Birch has never sounded so flustered. He closes the door without instruction. A comfort.

The voices on the other side rumble against it, but it's too late, I think. They've all seen, the body, the gun, me. Mr. Birch bellows at them, "Stand back," with all the authority he owns. He owns a great deal of it.

Mr. Worthington crouches down before me. He takes my face by the chin, turning it one way, then the other. I know what he sees, why his face darkens with anger.

"We will make sure the police see this," he says.

I can't look up, but I must tell him. "There...there are other marks...in...other p...places." The tears still flow. My breath hitches between words.

"Oh, my dear," the sweet man lowers his head, drops it into the palm of his hand.

"We will...you will have to make sure they see those as well." He doesn't look up, perhaps he can't.

"I..."

I can't finish. The door opens and my father walks in. With a slowness—a stillness that creeps inside me like the cold wind as it blasts its way through winter—he studies the room, the body, me, the gun. His face is not so tender. I hope fear makes it so.

Papa walks to me. Now he sees my face. Now his changes. It churns with anger.

In Italian, he asks me, "What happened, Ginevra?" his voice quakes.

Mr. Worthington quietly steps away, steps to the door.

As I tell Papa in Italian, I tell him the lie, but even as I do, I wonder if and when I will tell him the truth.

"They've come, Ginevra," Mr. Worthington says, after opening the door to a faint knock. He stands beside us once more. "I will accompany you to the station," he says. "But you must not say very much, Ginevra. All I want you to say is that he attacked you and you defended yourself. When they ask for details, and they will, Ginevra, many, many times, I want you to pretend you don't understand English well. I want you only to say he attacked you and you defended yourself. Do you understand?"

I nod my head. I must act the part I have spent all these years fighting against, the unintelligent immigrant. I quickly whisper to my father all Mr. Worthington said.

"I go too," my father says, one of the few times I hear him speak English in front of Mr. Worthington.

"Of course, Mr. Costa, of course," Mr. Worthington assures him.

The police barge in as if the killing is happening in that moment, blackjacks in their hands. Mr. Worthington quickly says the words he told me to say.

I hear many words, many voices—the police, Mr. Worthington. I'm in the middle of a beehive. The buzzing in my head is a scream. Father asks me to translate but I can't. I can't understand myself. It is all too much.

The cold of the handcuffs is like a slap on my face. It snaps me back, but only for a moment. I realize what they are, what is happening. They take me by the arms. They stand me up. The world turns black.

* * *

I wake up in the cell. The gate isn't closed, isn't locked. My papa and Mr. Worthington are there. They rush to me as they see me wake.

Papa asks if I'm all right. I almost laugh. Instead, I nod my head, and with his hand, I sit up. Mr. Worthington reaches into the inner pocket of his swallowtail jacket. How odd it is to see him in it here. He pulls out a flask, removes the cap, and hands it to me with a quick look over his shoulder. My hands remain cuffed, so he puts it to my lips, tilts it back. I cough and sputter on the fire the liquid sets on my throat. I jut my chin out. I want more. He gives it to me.

Mr. Worthington squats before me, our eyes inches apart.

"I have insisted they take pictures, Ginevra, of your bruises, the marks...," he stumbles, looks up at my father.

"All, Ginevra," my father says. His bottom lip is trembling. The last time I saw his bottom lip tremble was the day we buried my mother. "You must expose, show, all of them."

I look at my father. He can't mean it. I look at Mr. Worthington who nods his head in silence.

"More," I say to him. He puts the flask to my lips, holds it there longer.

All those years I had wanted a photograph taken of me, as the Worthington's did every year. I will finally get my wish. I will suffer another violation to prove I was violated.

* * *

The steel bars clang to a close. I stand in the middle of the cell. My bug-eyed gaze flits from the small cot where I see fleas popping on it, to the damp stone of the other three walls, to the small slit of the barred window, set too high to see anything but sky.

I hold out my arms. They can almost reach from one side to the other. My arms shake as I put them back by my sides. How long will I be in this cell? Will the end of my days dwindle in such a place?

The memory returns. That moment I first stepped foot in my first room at The Beeches.

My legs crumble. My body falls on the infested mattress.

Ingratitude has its way in the end.

I wash as well as I can with the rag and bucket of water they give me. Yet as I put the scratchy wool prison gown once more on my body, I still smell the awful odors. Odors from others who had worn it, perhaps the last thing they wore.

All I think about in this moment are the beautiful dresses Pearl gave me through the years. I think about how wonderful I felt when I wore them. I wonder if I will live to wear them again.

PEARL

I wake. Sweat saturates me. As if his form escapes the prison of my mind, his face hovers before my eyes. I rub them hard, but he will not disperse. I stare at him. His face constantly changes, from the handsome one to the gruesome one, from the seducer to the defiler.

My body shakes with hate and fear. Some of the hate is for myself, for what I did and did not do, for what I believed and what I should have. I brought him into our lives. I didn't listen to her. I allowed myself to be carried off on a journey I knew, in the depths of my heart, was not for me.

I had bitten a piece of Mother's poison fruit and all its false promises, its false life.

I am the guilty one.

As I lie here, I begin to pray, not for me, or him... but for her. *Please, dear Lord, if this specter must haunt me for the rest of my life, I accept it, I welcome it. But please, please save her.*

* * *

"I'm sorry, Miss, I'm not sure I understand you."

Frank Morgan, our chauffeur stands between the carriage door and me, sweltering in a morning sun already set to blister. His aging face, though still handsome, twists and pinches at my choice of destination.

"You do understand me, Mr. Morgan, and you will take me there." I use the voice I had heard so many of the powerful women of Newport use. I channel Mrs. Astor and Mrs. Vanderbilt. "I am a woman of twenty-one years, and you work for me. You will take me where I tell you to."

I have never spoken like this, and though my voice quivers, I refuse denial of my demand.

Mr. Morgan, as ever in his long livery coat and breeches in forest green velvet, his tall top hat, looks up to the main house, looks to see if anyone—my mother—watches us. No one is.

"Very well, miss, to the jail it is." He steps aside, opens the carriage door, and helps me climb in, gently holding the edge of my long black skirt. It is the façade of mourning I must wear. The carriage shakes as he takes his place on the driver's bench. My hands shake as they grip the book I grasp so tightly in my hand. The book I bring to Ginevra.

It is a short journey along the full northern portion of Bellevue Avenue onto Spring Street and around the corner to Marlborough Street. The solid square building looks daunting, frightening, as it should for a jail. Bricks painted white does little to dispel the impression. It stands beside the First Methodist Episcopal Church of Newport. I wonder if those trapped within can see its tall bell tower, if looking at it brings any solace. I hope so.

With Mr. Morgan's help, I step out of the carriage, blinking in the brightness, climb cement stairs with shaking legs, and enter the building. Once more I blink, this time in the murkiness. The foyer is small. A well-locked door stands before me. Just to my right, a barred opening where a uniformed policeman sits on the other side. He looks at me, strangely, but says not a word.

"I am here to see Ginevra Costa," I say with as much surety as I can muster. It isn't much. Now, inside this building, the one housing those who are accused but cannot afford bail, are held till they are put to trial. Its presence of doom invades me. I will not turn back.

"This is no place for a lady like you to be, Miss." The guard rises and looks down his crooked nose at me, face striped by the shadows of the bars.

"It is Miss Worthington," I say, using the power of my name for one of the few times in my life. "She is my lady's maid. I have every right." As I speak, I pucker my lips as I had seen Mrs. Astor do on many an occasion. I discover puckered lips don't quiver as much.

"She murdered your fiancé," he says, bordering on impertinence.

"All the more reason." I'm growling now.

He angers me. How dare he speak to me in such a way?

"Now unlock that door and let me inside." I point, keeping my hand outstretched, waiting for his response. He stares at me, gauging me.

With an unenthusiastic nod, he does as he is told.

He brings me to a small room, three walls of more white brick. The other wall is made of bars and a gate. With obvious reluctance, he opens the gate and gestures in.

"Wait here, Miss," he says, it's a grumble.

Even as a visitor, to be so confined...I squirm, I itch to run. I almost cry thinking of her here day and night, for a week now. I hear the rattle of chains.

She's here. Ginevra stands outside the gate, her hands manacled together by metal cuffs. I bite my lip to stop the tears. I have never seen her so pale; her lovely olive complexion looks yellow. She's so thin, her lovely curves barely discernable. All those years she longed for the slim body so in vogue, she has attained, in the worst possible way. The worn, drab grey prison frock hangs on her like a sack.

The guard frees her hands from their restraints and lets her in, locking the door, locking us in. I rise, move to her, but stop.

"Some privacy, if you please," I say to the guard, still standing just outside the gate.

"Ten minutes, no more," he replies, and moves off, though I think he does not go very far.

I rush to her side, throw my arms about her. Ginevra drops her head on my shoulder.

"You should not be here," she mumbles, sobs, into me.

"There is nowhere else I should be."

GINEVRA

Pearl puts the book down on the scarred wood table between us. I almost laugh, almost.

I smile even as tears pinch the back of my throat. It was the old, tattered version of *Huckleberry Finn*, the book I the first book she used to teach me to read.

"Are you eating, Ginevra? Are they feeding you well?"

Pearl reaches across the table to take my hands. I try to pull away, ashamed of the marks the cuffs put on them, but she holds me firmly.

I nod. "There is plenty of food. I...I don't have much of an appetite."

"Well, you wouldn't, would you," she says.

"Why have you come?" I whisper. How I fear her presence will somehow give the truth away. It must stay hidden, buried as deep as I can bury it.

Pearl pounds me with her stare. "I've come to see my dearest friend. It is the right thing to do." Her eyes tell me her words are for the benefit of those who may be listening.

"How is my father?" I have to ask; unsure I want to hear the answer.

"As well as he can be, I think," she replies. I nod, knowing with my father how hard it is to tell.

"My father spends a great deal of time with him."

My breath hitches on a sob. Such news as this truly helps me. So different, yet so alike, I know my father will find comfort with Pearl's father. It is the best I can hope for him.

Pearl squeezes my hands, still in hers. "He's hired a lawyer for you, Ginevra, one of the best, from New York."

I shake my head. I can't help feeling it is the wrong thing to do. How many difficulties it will cause with the other families, the other important families. "Your mother must be fit to be tied."

Pearl smiles a little, shrugs her slim shoulders. If her mother is angry, Pearl is enjoying it.

"I don't think it will matter. I don't think it will help." Helplessness is all I know.

"It will. It must," she insists.

Her courage, her loyalty, is a never-ending stalwart surprise, a gift.

"I've also come to give you this book. I know how much it means to you." This meaning, this truth, is for me. I hold to it tightly.

With a quick glance to the hall outside our cage, she slips two fingers in the book, pulls out a folded piece of newsprint.

"Look," she whispers, lips barely moving, eyes flitting everywhere.

She opens the book, lays the article on the other side of it, blocks it with the cover, and taps the newsprint. The headline, large and bold, is easy to read. Repeating acts from days of old, we bend our heads over it:

MRS. CRANE OF GAINESVILLE, OHIO, SET FREE ON CHARGE OF MURDER IN SELF DEFENSE.

"They will not believe me as they believed her." I drop my back against the steel chair.

"Why ever not?" Pearl asks sharply, her eyes rove the paper as if the key to my freedom hides on it.

I tut at her hope. Or is it her guilt blinding her?

"I am, was, a servant—"

"A lady's maid." She cuts me off sharply.

"A servant still." I shake her off. "And he was the son of a rich and powerful man. It is my word against that of a privileged ghost. The ghost will win."

* * *

The lawyer and Mr. Worthington sit on the other side of the table from me this morning, waiting.

They wait for me to say something. I don't know what words to use.

In the long hours of confinement, I had rehearsed the story, fixing it here, changing it there, and practicing it so it would make sense without making too much sense.

Now they flee me. At the moment I must say them, they betray me.

"Could I have a drink of water?" I ask, wrangling for time for the studied words to return.

The lawyer, Mr. Fonsworth, beckons the guard. The guard goes grudgingly to fill my request. We wait; they stare at me. I stare at my hands. Glass in hand, cold water sliding down my tight throat, I look back at them.

"I want you to take your time, Ginevra," Mr. Fonsworth says. Old and gray and a bit hunched over, there is, however, something about him that is commanding, fortifying. "But you must give us all the details."

His emphasis on "all" tells me he knows some of the details will be difficult to speak. There is only truth in that.

I begin my tale.

* * *

They stare at me in silence. It is a prod upon my tongue.

"It...it was not like the first time, the first time Mr...he touched...me," my hesitation is not an act; my fear is true. "He—"

"Wait...what?" Mr. Worthington balks.

"This man accosted you before?" this from Mr. Fonsworth.

They look sideways at each other.

"What happened and did anyone see you?" Mr. Fonsworth asks.

I nod. I tell them of that time. I hang my head as all the pain that came after rush back into my memory. There is no need for lies in this tale.

PEARL

I hide around the corner of the jailhouse. As soon as I see my father and Mr. Fonsworth leave, as they get in my father's carriage and pull away, I rush in.

The guard is not pleased to see me, not pleased Ginevra has another visitor. I don't care. I stand with arms folded across my chest, asking him if I should call my father and the lawyer back. He lets me in to see her.

She looks worse than ever. Ginevra tells me she had to tell the "story," the whole story, to them. She tells me how hard it was. She didn't have to. I can see it in her red, swollen eyes, her ravaged face, her hands twisting in her lap.

Ginevra tells me the details of her "story" and the response. I too see where the weak point is. But it's not true.

I'm shaking my head. She's still talking but I'm no longer listening.

"I must say something."

Ginevra stood so fast her chair flew over. Her hands are on me before I look up. I hear the guard barreling toward us.

"Say nothing, nothing," she hisses at me. "It is done. I have made the story."

I'm shaking my head. The guard is almost on us.

"Promise me, Pearl," she raises my hands to her, kisses them, "for all that we once were, promise me."

In her eyes, I see all our moments, all her love. I make the promise.

* * *

As I walk home, not caring who may see me leaving the jailhouse, not caring about much save Ginevra, I take no notice of the others strolling about around me. Until I almost walk into them.

A highly ranked married couple. I make my apologies, which they accept with practiced casual grace. We take our leave. I turn and watch them walk away. They smile at each other, laugh with each other. I know they are both having affairs with others. I believe they know it too. Yet they chose to live the lie, chose to live as liars.

The thought stops me. Perhaps it is the choice I must make myself.

* * *

Yet another day I sit across the metal table from her. I come more and more often as the date of the trial draws closer and closer, drawn to her repeatedly. This time she is the strong one as if she came to console me.

I try to speak of silly things, of gossip, the kind we used to laugh at together. I talk of my mother's antics and how terrible she is behaving. It is a foolish attempt at foolish conversation. I find it hard to say what I need to say. At last, the words come.

"I'm so sorry, Ginevra." The tears flow, racking my body. I can do nothing to stop them even if I want to. "My dearest, dearest friend. I should have believed you. For that is what you are...the dearest and truest friend. I shouldn't have..." I cannot finish.

I reach my hand out blindly. She takes it.

"You were in love. Love blinds. I thought I was in love." She hangs her head; something runs up her spine and she shivers. "I saw it with my parents, how blind they were to each other's faults. It is the curse of love, *si*?"

"I love you," I lament, for it is true. I love her as I would love a sister, far more than I love my brother or my mother, and yet I abandoned her at the most crucial moment. I had become one of them, I see it clearly now. The riches, the lifestyle, all they said about us in the newspapers. I let the glittering wave of it carry me away on its golden tide. But the sea was not golden, it was only the reflection of the sun, and the clouds have come out, come to stay.

The guard comes. He tells me I have to leave.

"You are not alone, Ginevra. Please remember. Please know how sorry I am."

Ginevra smiles at me, eyes glisten. "I know, *mia cara amica*, I do know."

The guard shuts the bars between us. In this moment, I realize what I must do.

"I will get you out of here."

Ginevra's face falls. My words reveal too much for she knows me too well.

"Pearl, please do not do…"

I walk away before she finishes.

GINEVRA

Alone again in my cell, my eyes weep silent tears. If not for the bars around me, I could have been back in my room in the hidden floor of The Beeches, crying myself to sleep as I had so many nights. Except this time, they are tears of joy. Pearl's words touch the deepest part of me, the heart that still beats, if too quickly. Her loyalty, her expressions of love—no, not expressions—the truth of her love fills my frightened soul.

Whatever happens to me I will know I lived this life as a true friend, as a person loved. It will have to be enough.

Even as the warmth of dear Pearl's love blankets me, my mind catches on her last words, and I am full of fear.

PEARL

AUGUST 1900

For two months, I relive that night in my dreams. I know I will for the rest of my life.

For almost two months, Ginevra has sat in a cell. Finally, the trial is beginning.

Each day my father, Ginevra's father, and I take the Ferry to Providence. Each day Mother screams at us not to go, not to shame us. Each day we take a carriage to the Customs House on the corner of Weybosset Street. Each day we enter the mean-looking granite building with its metal domed roof to sit and listen, to worry and cringe as the State makes its case against Ginevra. Each day we sit on the hard benches directly behind Ginevra. My presence on her side brings more than one mean-spirited word our way.

The large room reeks of wood, sweat, and desperation. The tall windows sit high up the walls. They're open, but the breeze, what there is of it, doesn't reach us, does little to dispel the heat and gloom.

Anja is called to the stand. I grab the hands of the two men on either side of me. They don't know what I do, that Anja had seen the first assault Herbert had made on Ginevra. They look at me brimming with hopeful excitement as if I am a stranger. It doesn't matter, it is short-lived. The prosecution calls her. I don't realize what that means.

Mr. Tanner, the current Attorney General of Rhode Island, is trying the case himself, no doubt for the notoriety it brings him.

He stands at his table, a hunched back, gray-haired man well into his seventies, yet his eyes burn with intensity and intelligence.

"Miss Schneider, can you tell us what you saw on the evening of July the twenty-seventh of last year at...," he puts his glasses to his eyes, looks at the papers on the desk before him, "...at Rosecliff?"

"Vell, I saw a lot a things that night. It vas party, you know."

The people packing the gallery snicker. The twelve men of the jury do not. The judge bangs his gavel for silence. He gets it.

Mr. Tanner looks over the top of his glasses at Anja. "What did you see—specifically—when you went downstairs at one point?"

Anja squirms. She knows exactly what he wants her to talk about. Everything about her—the slump of her body, the clamped lips—says she doesn't want to. She must.

"It vas dark and I vas in a hurry." Anja tries to preface her tale. I think she does well.

Mr. Tanner is out of patience. "Did you see Miss Costa that night downstairs?"

Anja nods. "I did."

"Was she alone?"

Anja will not go where Tanner wants her to unless he pulls her by a leash.

"No."

"Who was she with?"

"Mr. Butterworth, as vhat vas."

"Did you see them kissing?"

"No."

"Did you see them in an embrace, holding each other?"

"Vell, I saw hem holding her, that iz for sure."

Mr. Tanner moves to the front of the table. He pushes, looks at the men in the jury box, then back to Anja.

"Did Miss Costa call out to you? Did...she...call...for...help?"

His staccato delivery delivers drama; each word pounds her.

Anja shifts in her seat as if she sits on pins. She looks to Ginevra; her eyes fill with tears.

"Your Honor?" Mr. Tanner prods.

"You must answer the question, Miss," the judge instructs Anja.

She shakes her head. "No, she...she didn't call to me, she did not calls out."

A gasp shutters through the courtroom. My hope is dashed.

"I'm done with this witness, Your Honor."

Mr. Fonsworth stands up so quickly Mr. Tanner is not in his seat yet.

"Miss Schieder, do you know the defendant well?"

Anja shrugs. The corners of her mouth twitch. They can go either up or down. "Pretty vell, not as vell as I should." It is her way of apology. I knew it, as did Ginevra, who gives Anja a small smile, as best she can.

"And have you ever known her to be a woman of low morals? A loose woman?"

"No!" Anja yells, slaps her hand on her mouth as she cowers at the judge. "Geenevra iz a lady, a true lady."

"Have you ever known her to dally with any of the men of Newport society?"

Anja is shaking her head before Mr. Fonsworth finishes his question. "No, never. She does not even have a boyfriend, even vith those who vould vant her to be."

Anja puts fisted hands upon the rail before her. They shake as she squeezes.

"Just one more question, Miss." This time it is Mr. Fonsworth who walks around to the front of his table. "On the night in question, you testified that Miss Costa did not call out to you…with words." Here he looks at the jury. "But did she make any gesture towards you?"

"Yes, yes," Anja slips to the edge of her seat. "Her hand, her arm, I saw it, reaching out."

"Reaching out as if for help?"

Mr. Tanner jumps up. "Objection, Your Honor, leading."

Anja doesn't wait for the judge's ruling.

"Yes, for help. She needed help."

The judge bangs his gavel. "Strike that," he yells, turns to the jury. "You will not take that answer into consideration."

What useless words. They heard it; how could they dismiss them from their minds?

"I'm finished with this witness," Mr. Fonsworth says as he retakes his seat.

Father leans down, whispers in my ear.

"It was a good cross-examination," he says, "the best he could do."

I nod. I pray. I know all we need is enough doubt.

Mr. Tanner calls the arresting officer to the stand, Officer Callaghan.

An Irishman, I think bitterly, knowing their feelings about Italians.

Officer Callaghan describes the scene, the gun, and the body at Ginevra's feet. It is damning, especially the last question and answer.

"Did Miss Costa tell you that anyone had seen Mr. Butterworth assaulting her, pushing her into the room?"

"No, Sir," the burly man answers. "I asked her the very same questions. She said no one saw them."

It isn't enough for Mr. Tanner.

"So, in a house—a mansion—filled with guests and servants, not a single person saw anything that took place between them?"

I almost stand up... almost yell out. Only the presence of my father beside me stops me.

"No, not a single soul," the policeman replies.

The men of the jury turn to Ginevra, look at her with hard eyes. I have never felt such frustration.

Mr. Fonsworth stands. "May I approach the witness, Your Honor?"

The judge nods. Mr. Fonsworth moves to the witness stand, the officer in it, with grainy photographs in his hand. I knew what they were, what they showed.

"Have you seen these pictures, Officer Callaghan?"

"I have. I was there when they took 'em."

"What do they show?"

Now the mutton shunter is not so quick to answer, but he must.

"They show the defendant."

He's being pedantic. Mr. Fonsworth will have none of it.

"What does it show about the defendant?"

"It shows her all bruised up."

"Like she had been struck, perhaps more than once?" Mr. Fonsworth asks as he walks to the jury, as he passes the pictures out for them to see. They are repelled. I see it clearly.

"Yes."

"How do you think she suffered these bruises?"

Officer Callaghan shrugs with a sneer. "I don't know. I didn't *see* her get 'em. Maybe she did it to herself. Or maybe she likes that kind o' thing."

"How dare you?" I cry out, my father holds me down. The courtroom erupts again.

Mr. Fonsworth returns to his chair, his body reeks of disgust.

The judge bangs the gavel. "Court is in recess until tomorrow morning at eight."

I cry the entire journey back to The Beeches.

GINEVRA

I sit primly, quietly, just as Mr. Fonsworth told me to do, showed me how to do. It is torture.

To hear me talked about so badly, each word is like the stab of a dagger. I want to jump up, I want to cry out, I want to turn around to my father and tell him not to listen. That he hears these things is the worst thing of all.

I keep my face as blank as I can; it is a great struggle. The other lawyer is finished, he tells the judge on the second day of the trial. It is our turn. It is my turn.

"Are you ready?" Mr. Fonsworth leans toward me, whispers to me.

My anger helps me. I nod repeatedly.

I take the stand. I swear on the Bible. I pray that my lies, that they are to protect another, will be forgiven.

Mr. Fonsworth is tender as he questions me, questions that give my side of the story, my experiences, the first time, and most especially the second.

"How was the second time different?"

"He...he was different. He was mean...angry."

I begin the story.

"I had been upstairs, in the pantry outside the breakfast room. It is done, you see, the maids stay close in case their mistress needs help with dresses and hair." My hands fly about. I know what they say. I drop them into my lap and squeeze. "He...Butterworth saw me, saw me peeking in the ballroom checking on Miss Pearl. Right away he stared at me, angry."

"Why? Why would he be angry at you?" Mr. Fonsworth asks.

"I...I had told Pearl, of the first time. She must have told him." I shrug, trying to shrug away those days from my life. I can't look at Pearl. I know the pain these words cause her.

"Ah, yes, I see. Continue."

"When he saw me, when I saw Pearl no longer need me, I left. I went downstairs for some water, to maybe see my papa. He must have followed me, but I didn't know, didn't hear. My father was not in his rooms. He didn't like it when the house was full of guests. I was on my way back upstairs when...when..." My throat closes. I cannot even will it open.

"It's all right, Ginevra," Mr. Fonsworth reaches out a hand and pats my fisted hands. "We are here to protect you."

His kindness is almost too much. I have to finish. I rush out the rest.

"He pushed me into the shoeshine room. It is the room next to the gunroom. He—"

"You're absolutely positive?" Mr. Fonsworth cuts me off to ask, to accentuate my answer. "Is the gun room immediately next to the shoeshine room?"

"It is. The Worthington's will tell you so."

I hadn't planned it, but the jury turned to look at Pearl and her father. They see their nods.

"Go on, Ginevra," Mr. Fonsworth prods me gently.

The room falls into silence. I fall into its abyss. Somehow it helps. I feel it is just Mr. Fonsworth and me.

"He grabbed me and...and touched me. He said many things, bad things, about me, about Pearl. He ripped my blouse open. The b...buttons flew, popped off. Now I get angry, for what he was doing, for what he has done to us. I start to push back. He grabbed me by the arms," I show them, crossing my arms so each hand can grab the top of the opposite arm, "and he shook me, shook me so hard, it was...I lost my breath. He yelled at me, told me I was nothing, yelled at me to just do what he wants. He threw me against hard stonewall, banging my head. The pain...it makes me angrier. I pushed back. I kicked him, very hard. He let go and I ran out the door."

I stop for a minute. I am breathing very fast. Tears drop on my lap. I wipe my face.

The worst is coming, the middle of the story that never happened.

He followed very fast, too fast, pushing me into the next room, the gun room. It was a mistake, yes. For both of us. I grabbed a gun and he laughed at me. Telling me I would not shoot him, that I was a coward. I...I held the gun to his face, tell him to get away from me.

"With his face to me, he backed out of the room. Out the door, he walked backward, in front of the door to the shoeshine room. I wanted him to go the other way, toward the kitchen. I—"

Mr. Fonsworth holds up a hand, "How far away is the kitchen from where you are?"

I lift one shoulder and close my eyes to think. "It is after the big laundry room that is after the gun room."

"And was anyone in the kitchen?"

"Yes, many, but they were very, very busy. Rushing in and out. Lots of cooking."

"Did you cry out to them? Did you cry for help?"

"I...yes...no, I didn't. But...but we were yelling so loud at each other. They didn't hear. They couldn't. I could hear banging of pots and pans and trays over our yelling. The house was filled with noise."

It is the weak part of my defense. They had told me so the first time I told them my story. I do my best to stress just how noisy it was.

"I yell at him to get away, to go, but he doesn't. Then...then..." I shake my head, "I don't know what happened, all went very fast. He grabbed my arm, my wrist, the one with the gun. He twisted me around, my arm and the gun are behind my back. Pushed me...he pushed me, back into shoeshine room. We moved so fast, almost running, we slammed into table, hard against my legs." I can't talk fast enough. I want to vomit it out. "My legs, the pain is like fire. He put his other hand on the back of my head and slammed it down on the table, marble table, bending me over. I get dizzy. He let my head go. I felt his hand fumbling...f...fumbling with his pants, pulling up my skirt. He squeezed...clawed my...my..." The pain, the humiliation of this mostly true moment rushes at me. I feel the gagging fear, the helplessness. I want to scream, to run, just as I did then.

"Your buttocks," Mr. Fonsworth helps me.

I nod. "It feels...it felt like he was tearing my skin. But my hand...my hand..." I reach it out as if the gun is there, "my hand is still holding the gun. When he squeezed me…I…I squeezed it!" I yell the last words, blasting them like the shot of a gun; they tumble away into a horrifying silence.

Mr. Worthington's eyes are moist. His are not the only ones.

Mr. Fonsworth looks at me. "I am so very sorry, my dear."

He believes me, as does Mr. Worthington and my father. So much of it is true that they can. I look at the jury.

O Dio mio let them believe me, for her.

We reach the end. My face is dripping with tears. The judge gives me his handkerchief. I nod my thanks, wipe my face, and my nose. I feel raw and naked. I am as violated with the telling as I was with the doing.

It is the other lawyer's turn. I twist and squeeze the judge's handkerchief in my lap. My nails dig into my own hands. I must keep my emotions there. I cannot let the jury see too much of my anger, the fury that burns my blood. Mr. Fonsworth advised me not to let it show. I can feel the heat pumping through me.

Mr. Tanner stands up. His first question is an arrow pointed straight at my heart.

"You testify that you told your mistress about the first incident with Mr. Butterworth. What was her response?"

I want to hang my head, shake it, turn away. I can do none of those things.

"She did not believe me."

I glance quickly at Pearl. Her body curls forward, tears wet her face as her father puts an arm around her shoulders. It is as painful for her to hear as it is for me to say.

"Isn't it true that you didn't want to be a maid?" Mr. Tanner looks down at the papers in front of him. "That you wanted to design clothing?"

Damn Mrs. Briggs.

"Yes. Who does not want for better?"

"Your Honor?" Mr. Tanner looks to the judge, who looks down at me.

"Just answer the questions, Miss, nothing more."

I nod.

"You wanted more than better, didn't you?" The old man with the mean face walks around to the front of his desk, takes a step toward me. "You wanted Miss Worthington's life, Miss Worthington's fiancé?"

"No!" I yell.

The judge bangs his gavel; Mr. Tanner doesn't stop.

"And everything that happened between you was consensual...you agreed to it, wanted it? That's why you didn't cry out when you saw Miss Schieder, why you never cried for help."

"No! No!" My voice, so loud, so harsh, carries over the banging.

Mr. Tanner is yelling now. "Herbert Butterworth wanted it to stop. He didn't want you any more...," he raises his voice even higher, "...and that's why you killed him, isn't it?"

"No!" I jump up as I scream. "I didn't want him, not ever. I shot only to stop him, to save myself, not to be r...raped. I would never have done that to Pearl."

The judge yells at me to sit down, to be quiet. I refuse.

"She is more than my mistress, my employer, she is my dearest friend!"

"Enough!" the judge screams now. The courtroom is shocked silent.

I look at the faces of the men in the jury. I don't know if they hear my words or only see my anger. There is no sympathy in their faces, their hard eyes.

"I'm done with this witness, Your Honor," Mr. Tanner says, walks to his chair, and sits down. He looks very pleased with himself.

"You are dismissed," the judge says.

I can barely walk from the chair. I almost fall as I step down. I can barely see through my tears. I stumble to my chair beside my lawyer. He says nothing but takes my hand. He doesn't look at me.

PEARL

We stand outside the courthouse waiting for a carriage to take us to the ferry. My father and Mr. Fonsworth whisper to each other. Their efforts to keep me from hearing are useless.

"I don't know if Ginevra's testimony helped her case or hurt it," Mr. Fonsworth murmurs.

"She seemed to give the right responses," Father says.

The lawyer nods, "But it was the way she said them. I told her to keep her emotions under control."

"And just how was she to do that?" I charge my way into their conversation, a soldier on a battlefield. "She was almost violated and that...man implied that she wanted it, that she killed Herbe...him in cold blood. Should she have been a meek and mild woman succumbing to whatever is said to her?" Outrage fuels my tongue.

My father rubs my arm, "No, my Pearl. But when a jury sees such emotion, such anger, it is easier to believe the things she's accused of."

"It makes no sense," I cringe.

"No, it doesn't, Miss Worthington, but it is the truth," Mr. Fonsworth tries to calm me. "What we need is someone to speak on her behalf."

"But there's no o—" Father begins.

"I will speak for her," I say, I declare.

"Pearl!" Father yelps. "You cannot—"

The carriage pulls up. I make for it. "Later, Father," I say, get in the carriage, and sit back. The discussion, here and now, is over.

GINEVRA

The cell in the Providence jail is even smaller than the one in Newport. Other women cry, scream, and beg for help. It wells up all around me. I try to cover my ears with the thin, stained pillow, but it doesn't work. I hear their pain as loud as I hear my own.

"You have a visitor," the guard says with pure displeasure.

I uncover my head. My father stands on the other side of the bars.

There is no visitor's room here. We speak through the bars. I run to them, to him, as much as I can. His hands cover mine as they grip my cage.

"Why have you come, Papa?" I ask him in Italian. I want no one to hear our words. "You shouldn't be here, shouldn't see me... like this."

Papa stares at me as if he's never seen me, as if he's seeing me for the first time. He struggles with words, struggles with emotions, as I have never witnessed.

"I came..." his voice cracked and caught, "...I came to say I am sorry."

I flinch in surprise. "You? You are sorry? For what, Papa?"

He hangs his head, even as he still holds my hands, hangs it so low it falls between his long arms.

"I was not the father I should have been." He looks up. A single tear trails slowly down his face. "I should have watched out for you more...better."

I realize he had just heard the story of what happened to me, the true parts...a father hearing how a man abused his daughter. It is a thing that should never happen to any father.

"Oh, Papa, it was not your fault," I say, I mean it. "Please do not blame yourself. There was nothing you could have done to stop it."

"I could have kept you home. We should have stayed in Italy."

I shake my head, a pendulum. "If we had, I wouldn't have lived in such luxury. I wouldn't have met Pearl, wouldn't have all she has given me."

Papa's head pops up. "What? What has she given you?"

I smile. I tell him of the years beneath the beeches, of the many nights of magic there. I tell him of my dream of being a designer, how many of Pearl's clothes are my creations, how she has let me believe I can be what I dream to be.

Papa is tearful again, but I can see it comes from my happiness, and his gratitude.

"Whatever happens, Papa, I will always love you. Always love you for bringing me here."

His arms reach through the bars, and he holds me as best he can. It's the best he ever has. It's all I need.

PEARL

Long past the time when I should have been asleep, long past the time the house has gone to sleep, I slip out of my room.

I check, but my father is not in his bed. I didn't expect him to be.

On the pads of my bare feet, I walk down the cold marble stairs to his library. He stands in the middle of the room, directionless, yet so elegant in his velvet smoking jacket, one that accentuates his broad shoulders—shoulders I have stood on the whole of my life. I will remember him looking like this.

"Can't sleep either, Father?" I disturb his reverie.

He turns, looks at me for a long time without saying a word.

"No," he finally says, walking toward me, "I can't sleep. I can't sleep because of you. Why must you take the stand? What can you say other than she is your friend, was a good worker? Why, my Pearl?"

Even now, as my actions disturb him so, I am still "his Pearl." The question I had been asking myself since we left the courthouse earlier is answered. My decision is made.

"I think you should sit down, Father."

He stares at me a moment and then sits in his high-backed, winged chair by the window.

I sit on the ottoman before him.

I tell him everything, not the story of Herbert that he's heard all along, but the real story.

As I tell him, his face turns red, purple. His hands clench into fists. Every muscle in his body becomes stiff and rigid. By the end, he is shaking. If Herbert were still alive, Father would kill him.

"We have to fix this."

"No," I shake my head, "*I* have to fix this."

GINEVRA

As soon as the judge takes his seat, Mr. Fonsworth stands up.

"Your Honor, I call Miss Pearl Worthington to the stand."

I spin in my chair. I want to jump from it to stop her. I don't know what she's going to say, and the fear sickens me.

The courtroom buzzes like bees in a nest disturbed.

Pearl stands and passes through the swinging gate on her way to the stand.

"Pearl, don't, please." The words fly from my mouth.

"Quiet, please." The judge bangs his gavel, his eyes on me. Pearl gives me a small smile over her shoulder as she continues forward. She's wearing the suit dress I designed and made for her. She takes the oath.

Mr. Fonsworth asks her all about me, about our relationship. Pearl, as calm as I've ever seen her, answers with brightness and command, no one can question the truth of her words, of us.

"Thank you, Miss Worthington," Mr. Fonsworth says. "You may step down."

Pearl doesn't move, instead, she says, "Don't you want to know what I saw that night?"

The court gasps as one, a wave barreling onto the beach.

Mr. Fonsworth is confused, and it shows. He didn't expect this from her. He recovers quickly.

"*Did* you see something that night?"

Where there was none for the near hour he questioned her, there are tears now. They are as real as she is.

"I saw Herbert, I saw him. I followed him following Ginevra below stairs." She stops. My stomach heaves into my throat.

"I saw him push her up against the wall, I saw him forcing kisses on her."

Quietly, Mr. Fonsworth prods her for more. "What was Miss Costa doing?"

"She...she was pushing him away, telling him to stop."

Pearl is reliving it. I can see it in her eyes. I can see her pain.

"What did you do then?"

I can't breathe. I pull on the high collar of my gray prison dress but still can't find any air.

Pearl hangs her head, covers her face with one of her hands.

"I walked away. I was so ashamed, so humiliated by his behavior. I was in shock. But only for a few minutes." She's sobbing now. As he did with me, the judge pulls out his handkerchief from beneath his robe and hands it to her.

"I started going upstairs, to get my father, to get Ginevra help. But...but halfway up the servants' stairs, I heard the gunshot. For a few moments, I was afraid to go and look, I didn't know who would be shot, who may be dead."

Pearl raises her head, looks squarely at the jury.

"I feared most that he had killed Ginevra. Before I could move again, my father and a great group of men, overtook me on the stairs, got to the room before me. I couldn't see. I heard Ginevra's voice and knew she was alive. I felt such relief."

Mr. Fonsworth knows the whole courtroom is spellbound. He asks his next questions very slowly.

"Do you believe Mr. Butterworth deserved to be dead?"

Mr. Tanner is on his feet. "Objection, Your Honor."

Before the judge can speak, Mr. Fonsworth does.

"Withdrawn." He looks at Pearl once more. "Do you believe Miss Costa killed Herbert Butterworth in self-defense?"

Pearl turns to me, bestows a tearful smile upon me. "Absolutely. I have no doubt of it whatsoever."

The room explodes. People are on their feet, yelling for Pearl, against Pearl and her words, for and against my innocence.

The judge is banging on the gavel so hard I think he's going to break it.

"Fonsworth, Tanner, to the bench," he yells above the ruckus.

They stand before him. He whispers, but not soft enough. Those of us closest, Pearl and me, can still hear him.

"Mr. Tanner," the judge directs his words to the Attorney General, "do you want the case to go to the jury, or do you wish to retract the charge? Between the pictures and Miss Worthington's testimony, a highly regarded witness, I'm not sure if you have a case. At least not one free of doubt."

Every gaze in the now silent courtroom watches as Mr. Tanner stares at the all-male jury. He can see how they are looking at me, at Pearl. Yes, they are all men, but they are all merchants and townies, they are the registered voters of Newport. The aristocrats are New York citizens and so not allowed to serve, though Pearl told me some had tried. He stares at them for a long time. It feels as long as I have lived in a prison cell. He turns back to the judge.

"Drop the charges, Your Honor."

I drop my head to the table. I can't control my sobbing. I feel a hand on my shoulder, look at it, know it as my father's, and grab on to it to keep me from fainting away.

Once more, the judge bangs his gavel.

"The charges against Miss Costa in the matter of the State of Rhode Island versus Miss Ginevra Costa have been dropped by Attorney General Tanner." The judge turns his pale blue eyes on me. For the first time, I feel he looks at me as a human being. "You are free to go, Miss Costa. This court, and all its officers, apologize to you for the hardship it has caused you and your family."

PEARL

As two pairs of fathers and daughters, we return to The Beeches together. For the entire journey home—the carriage ride, the ferry ride—I refuse to let go of Ginevra's hand, her father keeps the other for himself.

We don't talk much. What is there to say? What do people say in the wake of a hurricane? There is wreckage, but there is survival. One will haunt us for the rest of our lives. We can only hope the other, the survival, will someday overcome the haunting.

"I'm guessing you could do with a good meal, Ginevra?" My father breaks the taut silence. We all laugh, if only a little. "You will dine with the family tonight, you and your father."

For all my father has done for Ginevra, for Mr. Costa—the cost of the lawyer, the daily absence from his own business affairs—this is by far the most tender thing he can do for them. It is a great honor few servants ever experience.

I squeeze Ginevra's hand harder. She smiles softly at my father and gives a small, simple nod of her head.

We dock in Newport and enter another carriage, our carriage with Mr. Morgan on the reins. As we turn onto Bellevue Avenue, we see them.

People are rushing south, away from the town center, toward the cottages. Hundreds of them, clogging the avenue.

"What is going on here?" Father sits forward, sticks his head out the carriage window. It is the worst thing he can do.

They see him. The yelling starts as well as the cheers. As in the courtroom, the world seems divided by support for Ginevra and against her.

"Newspapers," Mr. Costa says. He understands first. I have no time to be amazed by his English. "They follow them."

As we come up to our cottage, we can barely make the turn into our drive, so many people stand before it. Among them, lots of men with notebooks, and many more with cameras. It is as Mr. Costa knew it to be.

Mr. Morgan drops us at the door, and we rush in, hoping to get away from the madness. Instead, we entered it.

"What have you done?" Mother's screech fills the marble foyer.

She is as I've never seen her, hair unpinned and unruly, sticking out in all directions, clumped where she's tangled it with hands fisted to white. Her morning dress is in remnants, blouse hanging out of her skirt in places, top buttons no longer in existence, skirt creased in bunches, twisted and gripped. She runs at me, grabs me, shakes me.

"You have ruined us, ruined us forever!"

I can't speak, can't breathe.

"Leave her alone!" my father yells, steps between us, pulls Mother off me by her shoulders.

"She has ruined us!" she still cries out, pelting my father's face with her spittle. "Why did she do it? Why did she say those things?"

"Because they are true," Father says calmly as if it will help. It doesn't.

Mother shakes him off, stumbles round in a vortex of confusion and anger. Her hands twist once more in the nest of her hair.

"She didn't have to say it, she didn't have to speak. The girl is nothing but a servant."

Mr. Costa flies up the five marble stairs from the door foyer to the grand one. He frightens me with his quickness, with his rage.

"She is my daughter. She is innocent girl."

He slaps my mother into silence by the force of his emotions. She staggers back from it.

We wait, the four of us, wait to see what she will do, what other horrid things she will say to us. I never expected it.

Suddenly calm, eerily calm, Mother steps to me, locks her eyes with mine. In a voice I don't recognize, she speaks to me, and only me.

"You are dead to me."

GINEVRA
SEPTEMBER 1900

For days, weeks, we hole up inside the house. We can't go out. The crowds won't leave. Every day there are more of them, more newspapermen and photographers. If they even glimpse someone in a window, anyone, the bulbs flash like summer heat lightning.

The staff complains constantly to Mrs. Worthington, who screams at them; to Mr. Worthington, who tries to convince them it will all die down, to give it time. But they can't do their jobs. Those who are married and live in the small houses just outside the wall can't get in. Delivery carriage drivers whip the people back in order to make their way past the gate.

Life—all our lives—are in limbo, neither coming nor going. Days stretch out endlessly before us. I hear the Worthington's fighting about leaving, about returning to New York. Mrs. Worthington screams for it. Mr. Worthington will not run away.

"I have never been, nor will I ever be, a coward," he tells her.

Days and nights blur, turn to weeks without notice.

Pearl and I can't even go to our trees, not in the daylight. The south wall is too low. They line up, three rows deep, just waiting for a glimpse of anyone.

We read together in her room. I help below stairs. My guilt for what they are all suffering makes me do it. Most are so much kinder to me now. I sniff at the irony. I must suffer violation, almost hung as a murderer, in order to gain their respect, their kindness. I no longer want it. Only Mrs. Briggs stays true to herself. She hates me more than ever. I don't care.

I creep up to my room, having spent hours in the kitchen, helping Chef Pasquale, helping the kitchen maids clean up until the room sparkles like new. I exhaust myself. It's the only way I can sleep.

I open the door to my room. Even without lighting a lamp, I see the piece of paper on my bed. I rush to it, grab it, read it.

Pack your things, say goodbye to your father, and meet me beneath the beeches. P

I stand there for a long time. I read it over and over. I know what it means but am unsure what it means to me. Words tumble in my head like the small rocks at the beach pulled forward and backward by the surf. At last, one word speaks louder to me, the loudest of all.

Freedom.

* * *

I enter Papa's room, my bulging bag in my hand.

He sits at his desk facing outward, toward the door, toward me, as if he is waiting for me, waiting for this moment.

I take a step in. Papa stands and takes a step toward me.

I drop my bag and rush into his open arms.

We stand there for the length of a life, for the embrace may have to last us that long.

"I will write to you, Papa, all the time," I sob against his still firm chest. He squeezes me tighter.

"I may not have shown it," he says in Italian, kissing the top of my head, kissing my cheek, more kisses than he has ever given me, "but you are the greatest joy of my life."

I can't leave him, I can't.

The words in my head torture me. He has no one without me. Or does he? For the first time, I am grateful for what I saw between him and Mrs. O'Brennan. I pray there is something real for him there. I can't bear the thought of him alone.

"You will bring me greater joy; I know you will." Papa steps back, but only a few inches, gazes deeply into my eyes, eyes that are so like his. "You will do great things, live a great life. There is no greater joy for any parent."

I pull him to me again; sob again, knowing I have to leave, have to rush away from this pain.

I do, somehow, I do.

I'm at the door. I look back. I have to.

Papa is smiling. I will remember him that way always.

I turn.

"Ginevra?"

He stops me. I turn back.

"Your mother would be so proud of you."

Somehow, I smile past my tears. I nod with wrenching gratitude.
It was the best thing he could have said to me.

PEARL

It is almost three months since I killed my fiancé. Most nights I wake in a sweat. The dreams are so real, the visions keep repeating that moment again and again.

I don't remember why I chose that night, that moment—of all the moments I watched him, wondered about him—to follow him. It was as if something compelled me to do so.

I snuck behind him, on tiptoes so my heels would not clatter, holding my skirt up and close so that it would not whoosh. I was so quiet I heard him—heard them—too easily. I followed their sounds, his repulsive anger, her mewling. Or did she moan? I snuck my head around the threshold of the shoeshine room.

They were plastered together. His hands, his lips, were on her. She touched him, my Herbert. He pulled at her skirt, at his pants. She didn't seem to fight. Dizziness, nausea overtook me. I swayed barely able to stand on my feet. My vision blurred through the lens of tears, tricking me for a moment. But only a moment.

"I will have you both."

I heard Herbert's words as if he stood at one end of a very long tunnel, and I at the other. I emerged from the mist.

From hating Ginevra, I could think only of saving her. I think I became someone else. I remember little of the minutes, the seconds after I saw them, saw him.

Somehow, I moved to the gunroom and put a pistol in my hands. Someone, some part of me, went back to the shoeshine room, back to the nightmare.

In the time it takes the eye to blink, to put finger to trigger, I raised the gun and began to squeeze. My hand swayed; I closed my eyes. I fired the gun without aim. Someone, a dark part of me, fired the gun without a moment's hesitation.

PEARL

With two heavy cases, one in each arm, I slip down the marble stairs. I don't look back to my room, to the pink and green loveliness that had watched me grow, heard me laugh and cry. It is only a place. they are only things. I will have my own.

The sleeping house watches me as I slip down the ground floor gallery, toward the Conservatory and its door to the terraces. I hear the gurgle of the fountains I love so much. I will miss the sound greatly. It gave me peace when there was little for me to find elsewhere.

"Do you have any money?"

The voice jumps out at me from the dark corner. I drop my bags with a yelp. I inch forward.

I see my father in the dim light of the moon streaming through the glass walls.

"How...how did you know?"

My father chuckles as he stands up, as he comes to stand before me.

"Because I know my Pearl. I know what she wants, what she dreams of, what she deserves."

I throw myself into his arms as I had throughout my life. I pray silently that this is not the last time I will feel his strength around me.

Father puts his lips to my forehead, leaves them there as the clocks tick, as the fountain runs. I close my eyes to the feel of it.

I don't know how many minutes later—is it really only minutes—when Father pulls back, reaches into his pocket, and pulls out a pouch. He takes my hand and places in it my palm. I can feel a thick roll of bills, I can only imagine of what sort.

"Go, my Pearl," he says, once more in our embrace. "Go show the world what my Pearl can do."

They were the best words I could hear. They give me the strength to release him, to release this life and head for the new.

"I will, father, I promise you."

I pick my bags up again and head for the door. He stops me with his words.

"No matter where you go, no matter what you do, you will always be my Pearl...always and forever."

I turn back to him. I see his tears match my own.

"I will be, Father...always and forever."

GINEVRA

"Pearl!" I hiss as she finally enters our place beneath the beeches. Though I hadn't been waiting long, it felt too long.

She drops her bags, throws herself in my arms.

"Are you ready?" she asks.

"Yes...no...yes...ready for what?"

Pearl pulls back. I can see her shining face in the patches of moonlight the beeches allow to reach us.

"Are you ready to live?"

I laugh. I can't help it. I have followed this glorious woman for the majority of my life. I would follow her anywhere.

"*Si*, yes, I am. I am ready to live. But how? Doing what?"

Pearl struts a circle around me, twigs snap beneath her feet, leaves flutter, disturbed by the short train of her dress. They lift up into the breeze, fly away free.

"I am going to college, to the Rhode Island School of Design." she smiles mischievously. "And so are you."

"Me?" I gape at her. "Me? In a college? Where?"

Pearl runs to me. Grabs me again.

"Why, to the very same college. They teach art, Ginevra, all forms of art. Sketching, drawing, painting...and fashion!"

"No!" I can't believe her words, for the first time in our lives.

"Yes!" she cries.

"But...but how will we pay for it...how will we live?"

Pearl pulls out a pouch and hands it to me. I can feel the thick wad of money in it.

"We have this from my father," she tells me, even as she's reaching into her reticule. She pulls out another pouch. This one jangles. "And we have this from my mother."

She puts that one in my other hand. I bounce it on my palm; the tinkling of jewels matches the twinkling of the stars. I look up at her. At the same time, laughter blurts from us.

Together we look up, look around. I know, like me, she is remember-ing all our times here. I know she is thinking the same as me... all our dreams, those we talked of for hours here, are just a few steps away.

"You saved me, Ginevra," she whispered as I would in church.

Even in the dark, her confusion is clear to see. "No, Pearl, you saved me."

I kick the ground. I know how I had saved her. What she had done for me was different.

I turn. We stand face to face.

"No, Ginevra, you saved me from becoming my father."

I gasp with understanding. Pearl was never going to be like her mother. She would have lived a life of looking the other way, waiting home alone at night and wondering, of knowing the truth and all its pain, with little to do about it. As her father did, as he may continue to do.

We pick up our bags and take them.

PEARL

"To the ferry, if you please, Mr. Morgan," I say to our driver. He looks anything but pleased. He will do as I say. "We'll get the train in Fall River," I whisper to Ginevra. I want none of the servants to know. My mother can't find out.

We climb into the carriage. It begins to turn away.

Together we look back as we pull away from The Beeches, my summer home, the only home Ginevra has known for the last six years.

We stare at it. That's when we see; that's when we hear.

My father stands in the Conservatory still, as still as the statues surrounding him. Even in the dimness, we can see his eyes never leave the carriage. I know they won't until he can't see it, see us, at all.

On the warm night breeze, we hear the sound. The mournful, beautiful sound of a violin.

GINEVRA

We are two young women, dressed much alike in the simple clothes of a shopgirl. We look like the sisters we have become.

Sitting across from each other, I snicker as Pearl rubs her fingertips together, an automatic reaction to the grubbiness of seats in lower class, not the private car she has always been accustomed to.

Her nose crinkles.

I laugh. I can't help it. "It will be dirtier and smellier out there, out in my world."

Her gaze catches mine and holds. I know I smile. I feel it all over my face. I see her own smile born on her lips grow in her eyes.

Pearl slumps down, wiggles her way deeper into the shabby chair. "Sounds wonderful."

Our laughter is lost in the whistle of the train as it pulls away from the station.

THE BEGINNING

Dear reader,

We hope you enjoyed reading *Gilded Summers*. Please take a moment to leave a review, even if it's a short one. Your opinion is important to us.

Discover more books by Donna Russo Morin at
https://www.nextchapter.pub/authors/author-donna-russo-morin

Want to know when one of our books is free or discounted? Join the newsletter at http://eepurl.com/bqqB3H

Best regards,
Donna Russo Morin and the Next Chapter Team

The story continues in:
Gilded Dreams by Donna Russo Morin

To read the first chapter for free, please head to:
https://www.nextchapter.pub/books/gilded-dreams

Author's Note and Acknowledgements

It has been a life-long pleasure to live in the shade of these magnificent mansions, to mark and celebrate some of the major moments of my life in glorious Newport, Rhode Island, and to play with my children—now grown men—beneath the beeches.

The Beeches as rendered here is, in fact, The Elms, the summer 'cottage' of Mr. and Mrs. Edward Julius Berwind of Philadelphia and New York. Designed by Horace Trumbauer under the direction of the Berwinds to model it after the French Chateau d'Asnieres outside Paris, The Elms construction was completed in 1901 for a cost of $1.4 million dollars. Its interior and exterior have been depicted with detailed accuracy under the auspices of The Beeches. However, the Berwinds, for all that history has recorded them, are nothing like the inhabitants of The Beeches.

The interesting lifestyles, including those concerning love, marriage, and the suffrage movement have also been depicting in accordance with historical records. And while there have been famous murders committed among the rich and mighty in this community, none took place in this era, among these specific people.

Loving Newport as I do, I have been a member of the Newport Preservation Society for many years, attending some of the most informative, inspiring, and enjoyable events in these glorious mansions.

I am indebted to the Society for all their support and collaboration on this book, as well as to the Newport Historical Society.

As I have with every book I've ever written, many of the characteristics of many of the characters are based on family, friends, and myself. This book is no different. Felice Costa is based on my paternal grandfather, Michele Galiano Russo. My grandfather was, in fact, a violin/viola player and maker who came to this country, just as Felice did. One of his violas is on exhibit at the Smithsonian Institute. Though he passed from this realm to the next when I was only eight years old, I have heard many lovely tales of this tall, quiet man. Among them is that he often played in Newport and for the very rich. There is a breakfront exactly matching the description of the one in this book residing within my grandfather's descendants. We have been able to trace it as having once resided in Newport; exactly how it came to be in our family is still a mystery.

To my grandparents, I applaud you for the courage to make the hazardous journey, to create lives in a new land, and to make my birthplace a land where dreams belong to those who believe and work hard, as they taught me to do. I will be forever grateful.

And to Grandpa...I hope you played for me.

It has been a life-long pleasure to live in the shade of these magnificent mansions, to mark and celebrate some of the major moments of my life in glorious Newport, Rhode Island, and to play with my children—now grown men—beneath the beeches.

The Beeches as rendered here is, in fact, The Elms, the summer 'cottage' of Mr. and Mrs. Edward Julius Berwind of Philadelphia and New York. Designed by Horace Trumbauer under the direction of the Berwinds to model it after the French Chateau d'Asnieres outside Paris, The Elms construction was completed in 1901 for a cost of 1.4 million dollars. Its interior and exterior have been depicted with detailed accuracy under the auspices of The Beeches. However, the Berwinds, for all that history has recorded them, are nothing like the inhabitants of The Beeches.

The interesting lifestyles, including those concerning love, marriage, and the suffrage movement have also been depicting in accordance with historical records. And while there have been famous murders committed among the rich and mighty in this community, none took place in this era, among these specific people.

Loving Newport as I do, I have been a member of the Newport Preservation Society for many years, attending some of the most informative, inspiring, and enjoyable events in these glorious mansions. I am indebted to the Society for all their support and collaboration on this book, as well as to the Newport Historical Society.

As I have with every book I've ever written, many of the characteristics of many of the characters are based on family, friends, and myself. This book is no different. Felice Costa is based on my paternal grandfather, Michele Galiano Russo. My grandfather was, in fact, a violin/viola player and maker who came to this country, just as Felice did. One of his violas is on exhibit at the Smithsonian Institute. Though he passed from this realm to the next when I was only eight years old, I have heard many lovely tales of this tall, quiet man. Among them is that he often played in Newport and for the very rich. There is a breakfront exactly matching the description of the one in this book residing with my grandfather's descendants. We have been able to trace it as having once resided in Newport; exactly how it came to be in our family is still a mystery.

To my grandparents, I applaud you for the courage to make the hazardous journey, to create lives in a new land, and to make my birthplace a land where dreams belong to those who believe and work hard, as they taught me to do. I will be forever grateful.

And to Grandpa...I hope you played for me.

About the Author

Donna Russo Morin is the internationally bestselling author of ten multi-award-winning historical novels including **GILDED DREAMS: the Journey to Suffrage,** the sequel to **GILDED SUMMERS.**

Her other award-winning works include **PORTRAIT OF A CONSPIRACY: Da Vinci's Disciples Book One** (a finalist in *Foreword Reviews BEST BOOK OF THE YEAR,* hailed by Barnes and Noble as one of *'5 novels that get Leonardo da Vinci Right'*), **THE COMPETITION: Da Vinci's Disciples Book Two** (EDITOR'S CHOICE, Historical Novel Society Review), and **THE FLAMES OF FLORENCE,** releasing as #1 in European History on Amazon.

Her other titles include **THE KING'S AGENT,** recipient of a starred review in *Publishers Weekly,* **THE COURTIER OF VERSAILLES** (originally released as **The Courtier's Secret**), **THE GLASSMAKER'S DAUGHTER** (originally released as **The Secret of the Glass**), **and TO SERVE A KING.** She has also authored, **BIRTH: ONCE UPON A TIME BOOK ONE**, a medieval fantasy and the first in a trilogy.

A twenty-five-year professional editor/story consultant, her work spans more than forty manuscripts. She holds two degrees from the University of Rhode Island and a Certificate of completion from the National Writer's School. Donna teaches writing courses at her state's most prestigious adult learning center, online for Writer's Digest University, and has presented at national and academic conferences for more than twenty years. Her appearances include multiple HNS conferences, Writer's Digest Annual Conference, RT Booklovers Convention, the Ireland Writers Tour, and many more.

In addition to her writing, Donna has worked as a model and an actor with appearances in Showtime's *Brotherhood* and Martin Scorsese's *The Departed*.

Donna is expanding her writing talents and has begun writing for the screen including the adaption of her **Da Vinci's Disciples Trilogy**. The pilot has thus far won four awards.

Her sons—Devon, an opera singer; and Dylan, a chef—are still, and always will be, her greatest works.

www.donnarussomorin.com

Made in the USA
Las Vegas, NV
04 September 2023

77060426R00198